THE
AMBIVALENT FORCE
Perspectives on the Police

THE AMBIVALENT FORCE

Perspectives on the Police

SECOND EDITION

ARTHUR NIEDERHOFFER

Professor of Sociology and Anthropology
John Jay College of Criminal Justice
The City University of New York

ABRAHAM S. BLUMBERG

Director, Administration of Justice
Professor of Sociology
University of Missouri, Kansas City

THE DRYDEN PRESS
HINSDALE, ILLINOIS

If law is not made more than a policeman's nightstick,
American society will be destroyed.

—JUSTICE ARTHUR GOLDBERG

Library of Congress Cataloging in Publication Data

Niederhoffer, Arthur, comp.
　　The ambivalent force.

　　1.　Police—United States—Addresses, essays,
lectures.　I.　Blumberg, Abraham S.　II.　Title.
HV8138.N48　1976　　　363.2'0973　　　　75-26614
ISBN 0-03-014226-1

Copyright © 1976 by The Dryden Press, a division of Holt, Rinehart and Winston.
Previous copyrights © 1973 by Rinehart Press; © 1970 by Ginn and Company.

PRINTED IN THE UNITED STATES OF AMERICA

6 7 8 9　　081　　10 9 8 7 6 5 4 3 2 1

Contents

Preface

The unrelenting forces of social change have placed the police at the center stage of history. Widespread disruption of existing social arrangements will be an inevitable feature of the historical agenda in the decade ahead, and we may be sure that it will be the police who will be at the storm center of each episode of crisis or catastrophe that is bound to occur with grim regularity.

In the ghetto, on the campus, at demonstrations, or wherever social protest is most threatening, the spotlight is on the police. Society is asking the police not only to protect it, but also to preserve it. The people of America turn to them as saviors, and demand an end to lawlessness and violence. In spite of this ostensible acceptance, there is still distrust and resentment. Ambivalence about the police is revealed by a report to the National Commission on the Causes and Prevention of Violence that is quite alarming in its import:

> . . . that a reader might well conclude that the men in blue are more of a threat to American democracy than the individuals and organizations whose stated purpose is to overthrow the system of government.[1]

It is obvious that too much of the thinking about the police tends to polarize around the simplistic approaches of the flattering police buff or the excoriating critic.

Though deeply involved in every phase of the pervasive urban revolution, the police have failed to realize the dimensions of their own transmutation. It is time for an evaluation and a redefinition of purpose, function, identity, and philosophy. Police academy

[1]*New York Times*, June 15, 1969.

training and police science programs at more than 700 colleges may be defeating their own legitimate goals by serving up substantially the same material that has been no more than adequate for the last twenty years. It is no longer enough to pass on the conventional wisdom of the force that reflects the past glory of the system. The time-honored shibboleths will not bridge the gap into the present. To respond to this need, our objective is to bring together in one volume the sort of materials that police seldom see because so much of their training tends to be either technical or legalistic in nature.

We have sought as a realistic goal to bring together the variegated approaches of the academic behavioral scientist, the journalist, the psychiatrist, the lawyer, the policeman, the historian, and the administrator in their assessments of some major features of the police occupation and role.

In Chapter 1, "The Social, Historical, and Comparative Setting," we have attempted to fill what seems to be a void in all serious discussions of the social context in which the police function. Strikingly revealed are amazing historical similarities in the relative permanence and continuity of the problems of the police as they confront the violent and disruptive episodes of every epoch. In this section we also have made some suggestions and predictions with regard to the future roles of the police.

Following the agonizing reappraisals of our society and its institutions occasioned by the aftermath of Vietnam and Watergate, many of our most cherished hopes and beliefs were demolished. It is in this spirit that Chapter 2, "Police Role and Career," examines some of the truths, as well as the myths and the masks of the police role utilizing racial, ethnic, and class variables as the focus of analysis.

In Chapter 3, "Police Organization and Control," we deal with the organizational and institutional constraints of the police system with careful attention to the bureaucratic qualities that determine the life styles, career lines, and policy decisions of police organizations. It will be readily apparent from this group of readings that the police share many of the dilemmas and unresolved conflicts of professionalization common to other occupations. In this revised edition, however, we have introduced an important element of police organization which is rarely discussed in the literature: an analysis of the detective branch in relation to other units of the police system.

The police world view is examined in Chapter 4, "Police Values and Culture," and the sources of their carefully nurtured values, including loyalty, authoritarianism, and defensiveness, are explored. Of interest to them will be the fact that other professional groups (e.g., medical students, bankers, and politicians) undergo rather similar estrangement as they become more experienced and sophisticated in their work situation. In addition, we have introduced a new set of articles dealing with the theme of police corruption, a constant issue which has more recently surfaced as a major cause for concern in many communities.

Chapter 5, "Police Discretion," opens up one of the gray areas of police work. The art of being a police officer involves a prudent exercise of virtually unlimited and uncontrolled discretion in the performance of duty. The selections present some of the social, organizational, psychological, and ideological variables that operate in this unstructured field. Supreme Court decisions can barely penetrate this area, which is shrouded by a blue curtain of secrecy. We believe the new

material introduced in this section does much to clarify old problems and develops new tools and insights for understanding police discretion.

The next chapter, "Police and Society," emphasizes the most sensitive aspect of modern police work-relations with the ghetto and other urban communities. The sad fact emerges that the great bulk of police time is devoted to service for people in trouble, but the level of hostility toward police is as great as ever.

In Chapter 7, "Police and the Legal System," a sense of the range of legal issues that touch upon the police is presented. Of special interest for police in the future is the important discussion of the issues in connection with "stop and frisk," a thorny problem that will certainly be with us as long as people choose to live in crowded cities. We have attempted to present materials that would apprise police practitioners and theorists of some of the possible directions in which the legal system appears to be going, and the manner in which these trends affect police practice.

Chapter 8, "Critiques of the Police," comprises a sober and balanced view of the police by serious and responsible individuals who find much that they would like to see changed in our police institutions. Many of the controversies over the police are seen in a new perspective connected with broader ideological positions ranging along the political continuum. However, on the whole, our emphasis is on maintaining a sense of balance and avoiding doctrinaire positions that are not supported by data or experience.

It is our feeling that the final chapter, "The Future of Law Enforcement," which is a completely new addition to this work, constitutes one of the most important statements by a group of outstanding authorities, embodying their perceptions of the directions of law enforcement in the crucial decades to follow. The range of material is comprehensive in terms of the level of enforcement agency involved, as well as the geographic distribution of the commentators. As a consequence, the views presented are, we hope, national and diverse in their scope rather than parochial.

If this work may be said to have an overarching theme, it is a stress on the uncertainties, ambiguities, and ambivalences of the police role in society in the past and the present, all of which will probably persist in the foreseeable future.

We wish to acknowledge the support and cooperation of our many friends and colleagues and in particular to express our gratitude to Mrs. Ann Bonet and Mrs. Florence Grossman who did so much to help us bring the revised edition to fruition. In addition, we owe a special debt to Elaine Niederhoffer for her significant editorial contributions.

ARTHUR NIEDERHOFFER
ABRAHAM S. BLUMBERG

CONTRIBUTING AUTHORS TO THE SECOND EDITION

It should be noted that at least 14 of the contributing authors served as law enforcement officers, ranging in rank from patrolman to chief, and were affiliated with major police departments across the country.

Richard Ayres
Attorney
Washington, D.C.

George Berkley
Professor of Political Science
Northeastern University

Abraham S. Blumberg
Professor of Sociology and Law
City University of New York

William M. Bowsky
Professor of History
University of California at Davis

James Breslin
Journalist and Novelist

David Burnham
Reporter
New York Times

Jacob Chwast
Consulting Psychologist

John P. Clark
Research Associate
Department of Sociology
University of Minnesota

Elaine Cumming
Professor of Sociology
University of Victoria

John Darnton
Reporter
New York Times

David Durk
Lieutenant, New York City Police Department
United Nations Consultant

Peter Feuille
Associate Professor of Management
University of Oregon

James Flora
Professional Artist

James C. Fox
Professor of Sociology
University of Minnesota

John F. Galliher
Associate Professor of Sociology
University of Missouri

A. C. Germann
Professor of Criminal Justice
University of California at Long Beach

Nathan Goldman
Sociologist

Donald F. Goodman
Associate Professor of Sociology
City University of New York

Harlan Hahn
Professor of Political Science and Urban Science
University of California at Riverside

Pete Hamill
Journalist and Novelist

Hervey A. Juris
Professor of Industrial Relations and Urban Affairs
Northwestern University

Yale Kamisar
Professor of Law
University of Michigan

Clarence M. Kelley
Director, Federal Bureau of Investigation

George L. Kirkham
Associate Professor of Criminology
Florida State University

Bernard Locke
Professor of Psychology
City University of New York

Peter Manning
Associate Professor of Sociology
Michigan State University

Jack Mark
Professor of Criminal Justice
Rutgers University

William J. Mathias
Director, Graduate School of Criminal Justice
University of South Carolina

Joseph D. McNamara
Chief of Police
Kansas City, Missouri

Theresa M. Melchionne
Assistant Professor of Police Science
City University of New York

Walter B. Miller
Research Associate
Center for Criminal Justice
Harvard Law School

Arthur Niederhoffer
Professor of Sociology
City University of New York

Leo Pfeffer
Professor of Political Science
Long Island University

Harriet Pollack
Professor of Government
City University of New York

Albert Reiss, Jr.
Professor of Sociology
Yale University

Thomas A. Reppetto
Professor of Criminal Justice
City University of New York

Clifton Rhead
Professor of Psychiatry
University of Illinois College of Medicine

Lawrence W. Sherman
Research Associate
Yale University

Jerome H. Skolnick, Director
Center for Law and Society
University of California at Berkeley

Alexander B. Smith
Professor of Sociology
City University of New York

John J. Sullivan
Professor of Law
City University of New York

Richard E. Sykes
Professor of Sociology
University of Minnesota

Martin Symonds
Associate Professor of Psychiatry
New York University School of Medicine

Harry Trosman
Department of Psychology
University of Chicago

Gordon Tullock
University Distinguished Professor
    at Virginia Polytechnic Institute

Leslie Waller
Novelist

Ruth G. Weintraub
Professor of Political Science
Hunter College

William A. Westley
Professor of Sociology
McGill University

Roy Wilkins
Executive Director, NAACP
    and Journalist

James Q. Wilson
Professor of Political Science
Harvard University

1 | The Social, Historical, and Comparative Setting

For all its seeming variety, law enforcement remains a slowly evolving creature of the past, rather than a new institution born in recent decades and fashioned by the exigencies of the present. Our objective in this section is to place the past and the present of law enforcement in a historical context. The concern with law enforcement problems depicted in the Magna Carta and illustrated so well in the medieval commune in Siena could be translated into the headlines of today. The lesson of history teaches us that for almost seven centuries the problems of law enforcement have been:

1. Abuse of power
2. Corruption
3. The quality of personnel and recruitment of suitable candidates
4. Deployment of personnel
5. Police relations with the public
6. Fear of violence and crime
7. The role of women in crime
8. The role of police in quelling riots and civil disturbances
9. The question of control of the police
10. The optimal size of the police force
11. Police training
12. The problems raised in connection with the granting of pardons and amnesties
13. The question of effectiveness of law enforcement vis-à-vis offenders who were politically and economically powerful
14. The problem of overcriminalization

Each of the foregoing remains a current issue. Even such a seemingly novel approach to police performance as granting additional compensation for more effective crime control has been employed in the medieval period in Europe.

The general duties of the police, their methods of patrol, the submission of law enforcement to judicial control, and the early involvement of police organizations in politics are all matters which have persisted and survived all the intervening political and social cataclysms. Indeed, it would seem that police institutions possess qualities which resist the impact of historical and social change. While the police are often seen as parochial, the reality is that the police culture transcends international boundaries and intergenerational differences.

The probability is that a police officer of one hundred years ago, or one from a nation remote in distance and culture, could with a very short period of orientation take his post in any one of our major urban centers and do a fairly acceptable job. The implications of this statement may generate a good deal of resistance. But it is important that police officers reflect on the historical issues and perspectives that have indelibly stamped their profession. They will then realize that their problems, roles, and duties are transhistorical in that they deal with fundamentals of society and of human survival.

1

The approach, therefore, has been historical, international, comparative, conceptual, and theoretical. This section traces the manifold threads of law enforcement from the ancient to the modern world.

We feel that this is the best method of arriving at a real understanding of what the essential features of the police role and performance are in modern society.

The Police and the Social System: Reflections and Prospects

ABRAHAM S. BLUMBERG and ARTHUR NIEDERHOFFER

Every generation experiences a quotient of conflict ranging from mild social turbulence to violent conflicts that may ultimately tear a society apart. History is often merely a record of past improvisations which have been employed to control these events. Consequently, decision makers invariably invoke the judgments of history as the ultimate precedents sanctifying the validity and rectitude of courses of action already taken or being contemplated. The traditions of policing and the norms of police institutions are largely the product of such ad hoc, extemporaneous measures applied to cope with social disorders in such diverse social and political environments as Boston, New York, England, post-revolutionary France, or even Italy at the time of the Roman Empire. In the main, civil disorders and other threats to public safety have served as the catalyst from which modern police institutions have emerged. While pervasive social change has had a measurable impact on the role of the police in transforming them from a basically peacekeeping force to a more service-oriented institution, the police agenda for the future remains to be written, the constraints of history and precedent notwithstanding. It is our purpose in this paper to make an assessment of the place of the police in our system of criminal justice. We wish to explore the past and present, and to examine some of the portents for the future of the police, while remaining keenly aware that historical precedents are often employed as a rationalization of the present.

Criminologists with an interest in history are quick to recognize that ours is not the best of times nor the worst of times in comparison to other epochs in producing criminals, assorted villains, social deviants, grim deeds of violence, murder, and genocide. While the technology available for inflicting harm upon others has undergone a radical maximization, it is probably safer to walk the streets of an American city today than it was those of medieval Italy or the Manhattan of one hundred years ago.(1)

We owe an everlasting intellectual debt to Emile Durkheim for his insightful notion that crime is an inevitable feature of social structure—that "crime is normal because a society exempt from it is utterly impossible."(2) In contemplating the meaning and pervasiveness of crime and deviance in the human situation, his classic formulation provides us with a timeless sense of perspective that transcends the recurring hysteria epitomized in the current catch-all political slogans of "crime in the streets" and "law and order." It is abundantly clear that Durkheim's analysis is confirmed, *inter alia*, by compelling historical evidence, and it should therefore not surprise us that most (if not all) of us have violated legal norms on more than one occasion without being labeled or officially adjudicated as delinquents and criminals.(3)

No matter which version of the official crime statistics one accepts, it is quite evident that very few of us are brought to book—i.e., apprehended, processed in the official enforcement and court machinery, and adjudged as criminals and delinquents. A society that committed the energy, resources, and personnel necessary to root out and punish all "wrongdoers" would create enough mass paranoia, violent conflict, and savage repression so as to become a charnel house and pass into oblivion. On the other hand, every society tends to produce its quotient of crime and deviance along with an apparatus to sort out those malefactors deemed most suitable for processing—usually those persons and kinds of behavior readily vulnerable to a successful labelling and adjudication process.(4)

The selection of suitable candidates for the adjudication process is not some version of a roulette game but has fairly well defined limits that traditionally have been imposed by the stratification system. The clients of our enforcement, court, prison, parole, and other rehabilitation systems are drawn largely from the lower classes.

A variety of interesting and useful typologies of crime have been developed by criminologists, depending upon the particular methodological approach they find congenial to their objectives.(5) One of our purposes in outlining the following typology is to demonstrate that much crime that inflicts serious social harm is not susceptible to the time-honored modes of policing. This is so because the emphasis is on high-visibility offenses and favorable cost-benefit ratios in processing them.

Modern crime may be said to exist at seven broadly distinct levels of occurrence. The most profitable and involving the least amount of risk is *upperworld* crime—it is the least vulnerable to the official enforcement machinery and is only rarely represented in the Uniform Crime Reports of the F.B.I. *Upperworld* crime is carefully planned like a military campaign in the walnut-panelled executive suites of corporations with billions of dollars in assets, in state houses, and in country clubs. Quite often the criminal venture is simply thought of by the participants as being shrewd business strategy calculated to produce a profit or to perform a "service" for the consumer, the voter, or some other constituency, often at the latter's expense. Illustrations of *upperworld* crime include "The Great Electrical Conspiracy" involving General Electric and Westinghouse among others; the peculations of Billie Sol Estes and the activities of the corporate and federal officials without whose help he could not have succeeded in stealing millions; the activities of Bobby Baker; the frauds and larceny connected with the federal highway program; the corruption of public officials to avoid prosecution; and the cost overruns in military procurement, including the irresponsible production of military equipment which, if not useless, may be dangerous to the ultimate con-

sumer.(6) One of the interesting features of *upperworld* crime is that if the crime is not one of obvious violence, and the defendants are white gentlemen of good background, the punishment for their seriously antisocial misconduct is very mild indeed.

An important component of *upperworld* activities is "consumer crime." It includes the social and physical harm inflicted upon the consumers of such products as automobiles, over-priced or dangerous drugs, food additives that are carcinogenic, unfair credit, harmful pesticides, and auto warranties that do not warrant. It includes damage to property and injuries to the person caused by industrial and vehicle pollution, and color television radiation. And it includes the built-in larceny of appliances requiring expensive repairs and designed to fail, of household improvement rackets, and of the many accidents and deaths caused by faulty heating devices, stoves, power mowers, and washing machines that are said to cause injury to 300,000 people annually.

The *Wall Street Journal* and *Consumer Reports* are often better sources of records of upperworld criminal activity than are official enforcement agencies such as the local police, the FBI, the Food and Drug Administration, or the Antitrust Division of the Department of Justice. These are ineffectual in dealing with the social harm ultimately inflicted by upperworld activities; prosecution of violators at this level is a relatively unusual occurrence.(7)

Related to upperworld crime, especially at the level of the political machine, is *organized* crime. The local political machines which ordinarily control local police and court officials afford the protection organized crime requires for its functioning. Its activities cut across state lines and national boundaries and range from legitimate enterprises such as labor unions to activities which cater to appetites and pursuits forbidden by penal codes—gambling, usury, drugs, pornography, and prostitution. Quite frankly, very little except surmise and conjecture is known about organized crime and organized criminals except that they are seldom grist for the mill of the conventional police, prosecution and court processes. At the moment, local enforcement agencies probably have more resources and undercover agents operating in pursuit of drug users than they have invested in studying the area of organized crime.

One of the major objectives of organized criminals is similar to that of their counterpart in upperworld crime—monopoly control of a particular activity. The myths surrounding the "Mafia" or

"Cosa Nostra" have become convenient symbols(8) which do not represent the real nature of organized crime in America. Rather than being the almost exclusive domain of Italian ethnics, it is in reality much more variegated, cutting across racial and ethnic lines. Indeed, one might more advantageously research organized crime in terms of an ethnic succession theory, or as a ladder of mobility of disprivileged working class and underclass ethnics. It is noteworthy that where organized crime is not trafficking in forbidden goods and services, it seeks out marginal and relatively undesirable activities in the world of legitimate goods and services which afford hazardous investment in ventures involving low-profit potential at best, unless the enterprises involved can be subjected to "monopoly" control of distribution and price. In this perspective one may better understand the social and economic implications of the propensity of organized criminals to become involved in labor racketeering and to infiltrate activities such as meat processing and distribution, detergent manufacturing, baking, fuel oil delivery, garbage collection, window washing, garment trucking and contracting, vending machine operations and linen supply.

Of late there has been a trend in literature to dichotomize organized criminals as either devoted family men trying to make their way in a difficult world of relentless competition,(9) or as ruthless bullies who sell diseased meat and who murder supermarket managers if they refuse to stock the inferior product owned by an organized-crime-controlled firm.(10) The net effect of such novels and films as *The Godfather* is that of a recruiting poster which keeps the myths alive and attracts new personnel to organized criminal activity.(11)

There is great difficulty, however, in distinguishing a significant number of conventional business practices from those we ordinarily attribute to organized crime, which admittedly uses extreme methods at times in resolving conflicts arising in the course of business competition. As a practical matter, it is difficult to distinguish between the ethics of usury and the legal "small-loan" business. Indeed, what are the differences, if any, between some of the major aspects of legal commercial factoring and illegal loansharking? The nexus of organized crime to upperworld crime and its relationships to local political machines and the political process need a good deal of further study—and action—beginning at the precinct level.

The third, fourth, and fifth levels of crime are respectively: *violent personal* crime, *public order* crime and *commonplace* crime. There is obviously some degree of overlap in all of these in that there are points of congruence in the severity of societal reaction to the offenses that may be involved, the degree of susceptibility of a particular offense to the official enforcement machinery, and the nature of the social harm that ensues as a result of the behavior.

Violent personal crime refers to the most feared offenses such as homicide, assault, and rape, that occur on the part of persons who ordinarily may not have a criminal history and most often do not think of themselves as "criminals," although society via its penal laws is quite severe in its disapproval of such behavior. But the criminal offense which incurs the greatest degree of public reaction and is virtually equated with "crime in the streets" is robbery. On a national level the number of robberies from 1960 to 1969 rose 177 percent. Recent research would tend to indicate that the factor of youth in connection with robbery is somewhat exaggerated because of the greater vulnerability of the young to arrest. However, of greater significance is the finding that blacks, with their feelings of relative deprivation and their rising expectations, as well as those of similar underclass groups, have grown impatient with barriers to their social mobility and will not hesitate to use violent means such as robbery, employing "techniques of neutralization" by way of defense.(12) However, so far as violence itself is concerned as a means to the achievement of goals, it is deeply rooted in American culture, especially in the southeastern region of the United States. Historical evidence indicates that southern expansionism, the institutionalization of the duel, a deep interest in military training and display, the lingering frontier nature of the South and its geographic distances, the functionality of frontier skills in the use and carrying of rifles, pistols, and knives, the need to redress insults to personal honor—all combined with low education and income— contributed to the development of cultural norms which have tended to justify violence. These underlying cultural and historical variables, it is suggested, account for the differences in homicide rates within the United States and those of comparable countries such as Canada and Australia.(13)

Of interest is the fact that in 1973 there were an estimated 19,510 murders committed in the United States. In 53 percent of these cases handguns were used. In the same year the FBI reports that there were 2,533 assaults on police officers in which firearms were used.(14) From 1964 through 1973, 858 police officers were killed in the course of their duties; in 96 percent of these attacks firearms were used. Of the 10 assassinations attempted or carried out on presidents or presidential candidates, all involved handguns except that of President Kennedy. (15)

Public order crime covers those categories of offenses which, as the name implies, are thought to offend the smooth functioning of what is thought to be the normative order of a society. Included here are the so-called "victimless crimes" of drug addiction, gambling, prostitution, drunkenness, abortion, and homosexuality, as well as such offenses as disorderly conduct and vagrancy. Offenses such as drunkenness, homosexuality, and vagrancy are sometimes referred to as "status offenses"; their very condition characterizes them as deviant or criminal.

The victimless crimes are so designated because there is technically no "victim." The principals have voluntarily and often eagerly exchanged forbidden goods and services, and seldom will any of the participants come forward to complain. Because of the consensual nature and relative secrecy of these "criminal" transactions, there is no complainant. As a consequence, these offenses tend to generate a good deal of illegal behavior and corruption on the part of the police as they endeavor to enforce the unenforceable. It is in the area of public order crime that the police tend to make a great many arrests while appearing to accomplish the least by way of solutions to problems. For example, one-third of all arrests in America are for some variation of the prosaic charge of "drunkenness" or "public intoxication," the usual variations being "intoxicated driver," "drunk in public place," "drunk and disorderly," or an old favorite, "drunk and resisting arrest." Violations at this level of criminal activity constitute the great bulk of crimes that are reported in the Uniform Crime Reports of the F.B.I. in any given year.

The fifth and least honorific level of crime is often the least remunerative, the least protected, and of the sort most readily available to persons of the lower middle and poorest classes because of their limited range of skills and circumscribed options for action; this can be called *commonplace* crime. Except for some confidence men and other professional career criminals whose activities may bring them into the world of organized and upperworld crime, crime at this level ranges from shoplifting to gang thefts. It

is usually the most visible sort of criminal activity and therefore the most vulnerable to the official instruments of law enforcement. Included in this category are vandalism, auto theft (there were 923,600 motor vehicles stolen in 1973, according to the FBI), burglary, check forgery, petty theft, and acts of fraud ranging from attempts to cheat or steal from public utilities, banks, large corporations, the government, universities, and other agencies of the "establishment."(16)

A sixth level of criminal activity is that of *political* crime. Technically, espionage, sedition, and treason are the only political crimes that are explicitly recognized in our penal statutes. Obviously, there are other offenses that have political overtones and implications, such as bombings, sabotage, flag desecrations, desertions, selective service violations, and assassinations. But in the main, political crime is best understood in terms of the underlying theme of Camus' novel, *The Stranger*, in which the author makes the point that criminals are often punished for the qualities they are thought to possess, rather than the deeds for which they have been condemned— witness Eugene V. Debs, Alger Hiss, Dr. Benjamin Spock, and the Berrigans.

In many instances the political criminal is not actually convicted for the substance of the real grievance harbored against him, but for a legalistic substitute; in the case of Alger Hiss, it was perjury. In a narrow sense all crimes may be seen as "political" in that the police, courts, and prisons are but administrative arms of a polity, its political apparatus, and its ideologies as embodied in the criminal laws. But true political crime is generally recognized by at least four characteristics:

1. The regime in power seeks to put down opposition to some aspects of its policies; it seeks to strike at those who have led that opposition and thereby to snuff it out.

2. The arrest or trial of a particular person or group of persons is used as an example or warning to others not to engage in similar behavior involving political opposition and to avoid seeking political goals which are in opposition to those of the regime in power.

3. Under the guise of prosecuting an individual or group of individuals for some substantive crime, the regime uses the criminal trial as a forum to discredit and stigmatize the holders of opposing

political views and seeks thereby to label them and their views as socially opprobrious.

4. The trial that ensues is inevitably an attempt to stage theatrically the public abasement of the defendant and/or his ideas, the primary objective being to anathematize his political position, rather than to simply convict him of a crime.(17)

Gresham Sykes has defined political crime as "those illegal acts that have as their objective the destruction of the society's system of power, changes of policy by means of violence, or the forceful removal of those exercising power in the system." (18)

The seventh category of criminal activity is *professional* crime, about which there is little information by way of systematic research. The traditional definition of a professional criminal is one who derives a substantial portion of his income from illegal activities. He is a "professional" in the sense that he develops a set of skills and has a major commitment to criminal activity as a way of life—as a career. His offenses are not casual but are carefully planned to the point of appropriate business arrangements, or "fixes" with enforcement authorities. The professional is in a sense a businessman exchanging information, techniques, and economic opportunities with a circle of associates who are engaged in similar activities.

In the last decade the professional criminal has apparently shifted to become a generalist rather than a specialist in one sort of crime. Further, certain types of professional crime, such as safecracking, have almost become obsolete. Technology and the computer have threatened other types such as check forgery. But because of his organizational ties, technical knowledge, and planning, the professional criminal remains relatively immune from the enforcement process when he commits such crimes as arson, hijacking, burglary, theft of securities, homicide, hustling, confidence games, credit card thefts, car thefts, stripping of autos, fencing stolen merchandise, and large-scale selling of drugs.(19)

We have been told that "the quality of a nation's civilization can be largely measured by the methods it uses in the enforcement of its criminal law."(20) If that is the case, then the system of criminal justice in this nation is symptomatic of the crisis facing America today. Our enforcement and court bureaucracies are organized and geared largely to detecting,

sorting out, and adjudicating the kinds of crimes and delinquencies most often and most visibly engaged in by the lower class and the socially marginal strata. (21) This situation produces some rather serious consequences both for the police and the other components of the criminal justice system in America and for those who are unfortunate enough to be caught up in it. One of the most obviously negative consequences of our system is that police organizations will tend to concentrate on public order and commonplace offenses that constitute the great bulk of crimes which are duly reported in the Uniform Crime Reports of the FBI in any given year. Not unlike any other bureaucracy, police organizations are anxious about their productivity and the budgetary grants which are related to it. Scarce resources must be carefully husbanded to get "the biggest bang for the buck." Public order and commonplace offenses serve as the requisite statistical data bolstering law enforcement budgets.

The word "bureaucracy" is not used as a word of opprobrium but is employed in its technical sense to mean the harnessing of people, skills, and resources in order to produce desired goods and services. Bureaucratization is a universal trend—we could not produce a Chevrolet or an aspirin without it. Some of its characteristics are: centralized control of the means of production; diffusion of responsibility and the division of work into specialties; the downgrading of the individual (the skills hired are of greater significance than the individual who possesses them); the cult of efficiency; submission to higher authority (a bureaucrat carries out his orders in conformance with the policies and work routines of his organization, although not always enthusiastically); and secrecy (bureaucracy is an administration of secret sessions to shield most areas of decision-making from outside view). Yet it is the very nature of these fundamental features of bureaucratization that weakens due process in our criminal courts and tends to compromise it in the enforcement process. Overcentralization produces means to an end that become ends in themselves—efficiency for the sake of efficiency or production for the sake of production. Routine treatment of clients that the bureaucracy is supposed to serve, buck passing, arrogance of court officialdom (prosecutors, judges, career civil servants) due to their relative insulation from the electorate, the secrecy of decision-making—these are some of the variables that contribute to the sordid conditions of our criminal process.

The universal dilemma of any police officer is best conceptualized in that which has been termed the "justice proposition": "Anger occurs in a man when his rewards are less than proportional to his investments."(22) The working police officer experiences frustration, tension, disappointment, and ultimately alienation because he perceives that the higher his degree of emotional investment in his work, the less satisfaction he accrues because of the rejections he experiences as a consequence of official behavior on the part of other elements in crime control and law enforcement systems. In time, his only defense against continuing disappointment in his role is to resent the judges, prosecutors, lawyers, and correctional officials who he concludes are negating his effectiveness and the integrity of his role. He develops a defensive strategy of low emotional investment in his work role in order to attenuate the anger, resentment and frustration that come with the meager rewards and satisfactions that he achieves.

In order for a working policeman to maintain a healthy equilibrium with respect to his occupational role, he must gain a realistic perspective of the nature of his function and role in the system of criminal justice as an ongoing process. Much of the tension in a police officer's life is due to the fact that a democratic society attempts to systematize two distinctive models of justice, the *due process model* and the *crime control model*, which are very often at odds with one another in terms of day-to-day operations and long-range goals.

An examination of the due process and crime control models reveals that the police officer is expected to perform effectively in terms of both models, thereby producing an unusual degree of strain and confusion in his work situation.

The due process model,(23) formulated by Herbert L. Packer, consists of the following elements and is prescribed in ideal terms as the official model for police behavior.

1. In terms of the due process model, the legal system exists as an obstacle course in order to protect the rights of accused persons. At the outset, therefore, such legal questions as jurisdiction, venue, statute of limitations, double jeopardy, and criminal responsibility must be examined and satisfied before an adjudication can be made.

2. Fact-finding and enforcement agents such as the police are seen as possessing a bias in their perceptions of a given case situation.

3. The criminal enforcement process is understood to be an adversary one in every phase of fact finding and guilt determination. In short, the enforcement process may be characterized as a struggle which focuses on the combative elements and emphasizes that truth emerges through the conflict that is produced by adversariness.

4. The emphasis is on quality controls. Each case is seen as a challenge in terms of producing a subjective product described as justice. Every case must be treated in terms of meeting minimum standards with respect to probable cause for arrest, notice of rights and of charges, a proper hearing, appropriate safeguards with respect to the assistance of counsel, constitutional privileges and immunities, a fair and speedy trial, absence of coercion, and rights to appeal.

5. Rejection of quantitative output as a measure of efficiency. The due process model rejects notions of efficiency as measured by quantity of cases disposed of as an end in itself. Instead, efficiency is measured in terms of quality to the degree that a particular case has met due process requirements.

6. The primacy of the individual. The due process approach views humanity as essentially perfectible. Human beings are rational creatures who are willing to give up a modicum of freedom to the state and to abide by social rules which are promulgated for the common good in order to achieve personal safety, security in the home, on the street, and in connection with possessions.

7. Limitations of power. Although individuals are willing to surrender some degree of personal action for the greater good of all (for example, by giving the state police power), the due process model requires that there be precise limitations placed on the powers of officialdom and others who govern them.

8. Power is an instrument that is potentially subject to abuse no matter how well intended the possessors and wielders of power may be.

9. Efficiency for efficiency's sake can be a form of tyranny in that it becomes a ritualized worship of the time table, the clock, the quota, and the great appeal of high output of product in return for relatively low input in terms of resources. Efficiency for efficiency's sake is ultimately destructive of the human values of personal liberty, safety, and security.

10. Presumption of innocence. The presumption of innocence attaches to an individual regardless of

what the factual or legal case may be at the outset. An individual may be guilty of some deed in fact, but nevertheless, in legal terms, must be considered "innocent."

11. The norm of equality. Every accused person regardless of his condition or station in life must receive all the quality inputs of the due process model. No distinctions can be drawn because of an individual's race, sex, or social class. The only inquiry that can be made that draws distinctions is that involving an individual's ultimate criminal responsibility due to immaturity or mental condition.

12. The due process model recognizes that there are serious limitations to the ultimate effectiveness of the use of the criminal sanction in attempting to regulate human behavior. Much of human behavior is much better regulated by other social agencies such as the family, peer groups, and professional colleagues.

The *crime control model* is the "work style" many enforcement organizations implement as the one which is most efficient and productive in day-to-day operations.

1. Repression of all criminal conduct is seen by the police and other enforcement personnel as of paramount value in society.

2. The failure to apprehend and convict wrongdoers is seen as leading to disorder and chaos in society. In terms of the crime control model, enforcement agents tend to see all human beings as essentially destructive, and but for the police and other keepers of the peace, mankind would descend to levels of savagery. The maintenance of public order and the safety of individual persons and property would be impossible without police measures to safeguard social stability.

3. The law-abiding individual is seen as a victim of predatory criminals who have received too much concern above that of their innocent victims.

4. Only an efficient enforcement process which focuses ultimate responsibility upon those who disrupt society can guarantee the freedom and safety of all.

5. As a consequence, the primary attention of our limited resources must be allocated to screening suspects, assessing culpability and guilt, and securing appropriate dispositions.

6. The high level of crime and other forms of antisocial behavior that are present in modern mass society can only be suppressed by the maximum utilization of the criminal process.

7. In keeping with this conception, a special stress must be placed on a high apprehension and conviction rate in order to deter potential offenders and to neutralize and incapacitate actual offenders.

8. Toward this end, speedy, unceremonious routines must be employed to move each case from prearrest investigation and arrest to postarrest investigation, preparation for trial, trial or entry of plea, and conviction, through disposition. Due process quality controls not only hamper police and other enforcement agents, but also release many offenders to commit further social harm. Certainty of apprehension and punishment are the only efficacious measures available to control crime and similar antisocial behavior.

9. In order to implement this objective, assembly-line techniques of efficiency, uniformity, and speed must be the performance ideal of the crime control model and its accompanying structure.

10. Further, there must be an early determination of guilt once a "suspect" becomes a "defendant."

11. As a practical matter, once a suspect becomes the focus of an investigation and moves toward becoming a defendant, police perceptions of this fact must inevitably produce a presumption of guilt, otherwise most working policemen would see their investigative efforts, which are to help formal agencies affix guilt, as meaningless gestures.

12. Finally, the emphasis must be on the very early stages of administrative fact finding. Both police and prosecution are seen as crucial, otherwise, the case will collapse at later stages after valuable resources have been expended in its prosecution.

Much of the confusion and many of the dilemmas that are faced by the police occur as a result of the attempt to create an intellectual synthesis and a practical fusion of elements of both models of the criminal process. However, the impact of attempting to do so is greatest upon the police, because they are the most visible actors in initiating the criminal process. Because of this visibility and because of misconceptions of their role in the criminal process, they often bear the brunt of much of the criticism from the public, from those in political power, and from other elements in the enforcement system. The basic contradiction may be expressed in the form of two conflicting conceptions of the police role: one, that the police mistakenly believe to be their function, and the other, which is justified in terms of the structural realities. The police officer's conception of his role vis-à-vis other groups is depicted below:

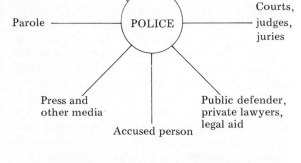

It should be noted from the foregoing formulation that the police officer conceives of himself as the fulcrum of the entire criminal justice system. It is because of this mistaken belief and his inability to assign an appropriate degree of significance in terms of power to other segments of the criminal process that tension, resentment, and ultimately disappointment in connection with his work situation are produced. It is one of the ironies of police work that although the powerful weapon of police discretion may initiate a prosecution, other actors and agencies may alter and reformulate a routine arrest, thereby imposing their authority and reality structure. What appears to the police officer to be his responsibility is now transformed into the focus of responsibility and task performance of other groups who will want to impose their perceptions and policies on the subject matter or case at hand. In summary, the police have very little control of other official agencies, organizational behavior, or the consequences of their official policies.

Depicted below is a second, more realistic, conceptualization of the police role vis-à-vis the criminal justice system.

From the foregoing, a more accurate assessment of the police situation in the criminal justice structure would be that of their role as an agency which among others, focuses upon the accused person in weighing such decisions as arrest, prosecution, bail, guilt or innocence, sentencing, probation, and parole. Thus, it may be seen that the police officer's sense of frustration is ultimately produced by the fact that he

is held to a due process standard by agencies that review his work, whereas the crime control model is the one that is demanded by his immediate superiors because of the cross-pressures of production norms and political demands. These cross-pressures lead the working police officer to mistakenly believe that he is not only a policeman, but simultaneously a judge, a jury, a prosecutor, as well as a probation and parole officer. His tacit assumption is that he has the burden of all of these in the crime control system. It is this unfortunate bias which is grounded in an erroneous conception of reality which places the police officer in an untenable position. Although he is unable to control the input in his work situation, he is nevertheless held responsible for any of the negative features of the end product of the criminal process. He thereby becomes a suitable target of displaced hostility on the part of the public he serves because of their chronic dissatisfaction with ever-increasing crime rates, which are often attributed to defects in policing and law enforcement.

The fundamental myth of our system of criminal justice is the assertion that ours is the "accusatorial" as opposed to the "inquisitorial" system. We point with pride to our rejection of methods of coercion, be they savage or subtle, in securing convictions. Instead, the burden is said to belong to the state to procure independent evidence to establish an individual's guilt. The rules envision a combative procedural system wherein prosecution and defense (who are admittedly possessed of unequal resources) will clash, and after the dust has settled, the data that determine guilt or innocence will emerge.

Unfortunately this model of criminal justice does not exist in fact. At each stage of the screening process a tacit but erroneous assumption is made. It is

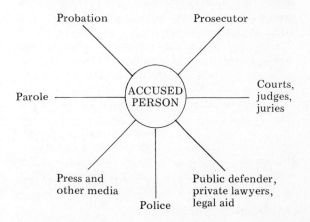

assumed that the accused ultimately will have his "day in court." Oversights, mistakes of judgment, and capricious behavior of enforcement officials will be reviewed carefully by the next higher authority. All the screening agencies in the system of criminal justice move a case along toward a trial that seldom occurs for ultimate resolution of the issues involved. (24) In most communities, only about 6 percent of criminal cases at the felony level ever go to trial—the rest are bargain plea cases. The conviction rate in these few trials may range from 70 percent to 90 percent.

Any systematic examination of the workings of the criminal justice system must begin with the police, who have become the most critical and perhaps even the most powerful subsystem in the enforcement and adjudication structure. Most of us do not fully comprehend the implications of the awesome power that the police possess in their exercise of discretion to arrest.(25) In a simple situation involving a defendant of modest means, arrest may cause a loss of job, a period of detention, the indignities of being fingerprinted and photographed, immeasurable psychic pain, at least several court appearances—and finally the expenditure of many hundreds of dollars for a bail bond(26) and a lawyer.(27) Arrest can be a powerful weapon—indeed, a form of summary punishment.

Of greater interest, however, is the fact that in practice the average police officer exercises greater judicial discretion over cases than does a judge on the court bench. In a recent Chicago study conducted in connection with a legal services program for youthful offenders, it was established that out of 500 possible arrest situations the police had arrested 100 persons and had finally presented a total of 40 for court action. The criteria employed in this decision-making process as to which cases were proper subjects for arrest and processing are known only to the police. The crux of the matter is that the police perform more important judicial functions in many cases than do judges;(28) and that critical variable is the source of the anxiety, resentment, confrontation, and violence that invariably occur between the police and other groups in our society.

The police—with limited formal training and minimal qualification requirements—are granted more latitude and discretion in dealing with the lives and welfare of people than any other professional group. In 1966 there were over 400,000 police officers in

the United States with a median level of 12.4 years of formal education. According to the research staff of the International Association of Chiefs of Police, the minimum training requirements for various occupations in the different American states, in terms of hours, are 11,000 for physicians, 5,000 for embalmers, 4,000 for barbers, 1,200 for beauticians—but less than 200 for police officers.(29)

Approximately a decade later, in 1975, the IACP reported that out of over 400,000 police officers in the nation, 54,838 were enrolled in college programs. (30) However, the median entrance salary of $8,789 for police officers as of 1974 reflected continued neglect of the police occupation in the public sector.

In the exercise of discretion the police officer is simply reflecting the social attitudes embodied in the biases of the larger middle-class white community as perceived daily through the lens of the police code.(31)

If one agrees with Durkheim that crime is normal, and with Ferri's Law of Criminal Saturation —that every society has a natural level of crime dependent on underlying social, historical, ecological, and demographic conditions,(32)—then one must realize that police are only one small variable in the total picture of crime prevention control. Subscribing to this belief, the sophisticated critic does not have much faith in minor technological improvements such as quicker response to a crime scene, simulation techniques, improvement of communication, computerization, and special squads and weapons. The truth is that these have more import as symbolic and psychological tokens of professionalism than as any meaningful evidence of commitment to the intellectual and ideological norms of conduct associated with the traditional professions. The new enforcement hardware tends to ease middle-class anxiety about violence and often helps to produce higher morale in a police force, but it accomplishes little in dealing with the underlying social context that has produced new levels of violence and crime.

Police discretion is one of the gray areas that cause a great deal of conflict.(33) It is impossible to eliminate completely the use of discretion by the police officer. No matter how well trained he is, no matter what guidelines he works under, no matter how close his supervision is, the majority of the police officer's decisions still will be characterized by a measure of subjectivity, idiosyncratic selection, and ideological interpretation in defining a given situation. Perhaps the best method of controlling and reducing the possibly harmful consequences of such discretion is the establishment of a system of external review. External review is preferable to internal review because a board composed of police officers would inevitably share the basic world view of the typical police officer who, understandably concerned with maintaining an organizational equilibrium that is often threatened by civilian complaints, may ignore or fail to see the larger social implications of his decisions. It is perhaps significant that the police and their line organizations have resisted outside review (34) while at the same time pressing their claims for professional status. They have been highly selective in their pursuit of professionalism: while they earnestly desire the privileges, perquisites, involvements, and status of the professional, in the area of civilian review they continue to cling tenaciously to bureaucratic secrecy and immunity.

Pressure to set statistical records in justification of police budgets has been overwhelming. This may be seen especially in narcotics cases, where police objectivity becomes problematic. Narcotics-related cases in the criminal courts of the larger cities constitute an important part of the caseload and are an interesting example of police craftsmanship. Police testimony in narcotics cases to establish probable cause where none existed has often sounded like a badly written script: "As I approached the defendant, he dropped an envelope to the pavement, which I retrieved. I asked him what was in the envelope and he indicated that it was heroin and that he had purchased it for his own use. I thereupon placed him under arrest." For a while, drug addicts in major cities all over the country were observed to be dropping glassine envelopes on the pavements as police officers approached. These sorts of arrest situations became stereotyped to the point wherein they were jocularly referred to as "dropsy" cases.

State legislatures, recognizing the fact that police felt handicapped by the standard of probable cause, passed the "stop-and-frisk" legislation, which wrote into law the much lower standard of "reasonable suspicion" as a basis for police stopping and interrogating persons on the street and frisking them for a possible weapon when an officer reasonably believes that he is in danger. Thus, police were given statutory comfort and support for that which they most likely were doing anyway when they were operating under the rule of probable cause.

It is noteworthy, however, that the president's Commission on Law Enforcement and Administration of Justice (popularly known as the Crime Commission) indicated in its report that the stop-and-frisk power is employed—to a decided extent—by the police against the inhabitants of urban slums, against racial minorities, and against the underprivileged. Police will make "field interrogations" of persons simply because they have clothing, hair styles, gaits, or mannerisms that square with preconceived police notions of what is suspicious. Often these persons are black.(35)

In June 1968 the United States Supreme Court, after lengthy deliberation upheld the stop-and-frisk practices of the police on the ground that the intrusion upon the person occasioned by the "stop" is justified if a police officer "reasonably" suspects a crime is in progress; and, if the police officer feels there is danger to himself or others, the "frisk" for a possible weapon is also justified.(36) This set of circumstances has been recently carried a step further in a Supreme Court decision upholding the procedure whereby even an anonymous complaint to the police can constitute reasonable suspicion for a "stop-and-frisk."(37) In a subsequent pair of cases involving traffic infractions, one involving an individual driving after his operator's license had been revoked (*U. S.* v. *Robinson*), the other involving a driver who did not have his operator's license in his possession (*Gustafson* v. *Florida*), the Court expanded police authority to conduct a search incident to a lawful arrest, even where the arrest involves a traffic infraction.(38) What is significant is that in both instances there was no assertion on the part of the officers that they were in any way fearful of the individuals arrested, nor did they think that the suspects might be armed with deadly or dangerous weapons. Upon being searched as an incident to the traffic arrest Robinson was found to possess capsules of heroin and Gustafson a quantity of marijuana. The effect of those rulings was to change the case law of those states (e.g., New York) which had held that a police officer could not search incident to a traffic infraction.

Thus a line of seemingly rational doctrine which began in *Terry* v. *Ohio* (wherein the defendant was armed with a pistol) has been escalated to justify an intrusion upon the person of individuals engaged in traffic offenses. In the ordinary course of events the typical traffic infraction or similar petty offense involves no physical instrumentalities, fruits of crime, or attempts to escape. An exploratory search in these instances, especially where there is not even the suspicion of possession of a weapon is often made as a means of finding contraband drugs on the person or in the vehicle involved. Here again, the hidden agenda of the pervasive impact of the drug laws distorts the values and priorities of law enforcement and wastefully expends scarce resources in the form of police, court, and correctional system manpower, despite the fact that our system is unable to handle the volume of cases the police are able to present for processing.

An extreme sensitivity to possible corruption is another source of constant strain in police departments and affects not only the use of personnel in the field but also their objectivity as fact-finding agencies. For example, one important activity may be characterized as "the watchers who watch the watchers"—a sizable group of police who are engaged in supervising the activities of other police officers, especially in the areas of vice and gambling The arrest of a bookmaker will arouse more enthusiasm and activity at headquarters than the arrest of a wanted rapist. It proves that the plainclothesman—and by extension the police force—is honest.(39)

There is in police departments an emphasis on "activity," "batting averages," "quotas," and "collars" as yardsticks to measure the worth of performance for purposes of promotion or assignment to less onerous duties. The refrain that one hears from many police officers is, "You've got to keep yourself covered. No one is going to back you; if you make a mistake, it's *your* ass that gets burned." And mistakes *are* made in the frantic and often feverish milieu in which police work is performed.

The police, prosecution, and criminal courts represent a closed community manifesting a defensive attitude toward "outsiders" and "critics." However, it is the police who are the most visible persons on the firing line; and they therefore tend to polarize all others into those who are "with us" and those who are "against us." Efforts to maintain organizational equilibrium and personal stability amid bureaucratic production, "efficiency" requirements, and stresses from without and within produce a high level of tension and anxiety. Many police officers feel they are caught in a double bind—that they will be criticized no matter what they do.(40)

The police officer in the ghetto is a symbol not only of law, but also of the entire system of law enforcement and criminal justice. As such, he be-

comes the tangible target for grievances against shortcomings throughout the system—against assembly-line justice in teeming lower courts, against wide disparities in sentences, against antiquated correctional facilities, against the basic inequities imposed by the system on the poor (to whom, for example, the option of bail means only jail). The police officer in the ghetto is a symbol of increasingly bitter social debate over law enforcement.

Politically, the police constitute a social lightning rod. Protests of all kinds that are directed at any of the varied institutional subsystems of American society invariably end up in a confrontation with the police even before they clash with the intended target of their grievances. In the process the anger and the fury of a protest movement are diverted, diluted, and sometimes even grounded out. The initial quotient of hostility is redirected at the police, who become the barrier that must be surmounted and subdued before a protest movement can address itself to the programs and priorities of its original agenda. It is in this role that the police serve their most important function in society—that of acting as a buffer in insulating and protecting existing political and social structures.(41)

On the other hand, it is naive to think of the police as simply a conservative force maintaining strict control in furtherance of the status quo. They perform a further, more subtle role in acting as a controlling radar calculated to keep a society within structural confines that tend to be somewhat narrower than its stated ideological commitments. Thus the police are the vehicle by which the limits, boundaries, and permissibility of social tolerance are tested. In this vein the limits of social tolerance with respect to such issues as sex mores, civil liberties, obscenity, political expression, and related matters are subjected to scrutiny and testing.

Another important police function symbolic in character is the police role in class relations. To the vast middle mass of America the police represent the somber reassurance that their tenuous status, security, and hard-won possessions will not be wrested from them. The middle classes welcome the police rushing into the breach wherever the turbulence of the have-nots precipitates disorder or threatens existing arrangements. However, it is the lower middle class and the police who have the greatest symbolic attraction and affection for one another. Both groups tend to perceive themselves as "in-betweens," being ground from the top by onerous taxes levied by an inept, impersonal government and from below by the heretofore disprivileged ethnics—newcomers who jostle them in the sensitive areas of schools, housing, and jobs. To the lower classes the police are a symbol of repression and control of their lives. Gambling, prostitution, and illegal drug and liquor distribution in lower-class areas are well known in their most minute details to the inhabitants but are often overlooked or unknown to the police. The lower-class person concludes that police presence is not to deter crime but to supervise and control the activities of the lower-class slum dweller.

It is a startling *déjà vu* experience for someone immersed in contemporary police problems to search early English history for the roots of our modern police system. The feeling grows as the record of the centuries is rolled back to the Magna Carta. Between the lines of the law can be found the same problems and complaints about the police: abuse of power, false arrest, oppression, apathy, and ignorance of and contempt for the law. For example, the Magna Carta of June 15, 1215, is replete with restrictions upon the police of those days, the sheriffs, bailiffs, and constables. It is a fair and reasonable assumption that since the following chapters were part of that epochal document, they were meant to correct abuses that were widespread.

> 28. No constable or other bailiff of ours shall take anyone's grain or other chattels without immediately paying for them in money. . . .
>
> 29. No constable shall require any knight to give money in place of his ward of a castle. . . .
>
> 30. No sheriff or bailiff of ours or any one else shall take horses or wagons of any free man for carrying purposes except on the permission of that free man. . . .
>
> 38. No bailiff for the future shall place any one to his law on his simple affirmation without credible witnesses brought for this purpose.

And the remedies of that ancient time were no different from those proposed today: recruit better police officers, stiffen the penalties for malfeasance, create a civilian review board as an external control upon the police. King John agreed that

> 45. We will not make justiciars, constables, sheriffs, or bailiffs except such as know the

law of the realm and are well inclined to observe it.

The barons opposing King John wanted more than mere promises and forced the king to consent to the supervision of a civilian review board of twenty-five barons with power to enforce compliance with the law. In fact, four of those barons acted as ombudsmen empowered to make preliminary investigations and complaints about transgressions by the King's police.

> 61. . . . if we or our justiciar, or our bailiffs, or any of our servants shall have done wrong in any way toward any one, or shall have transgressed any of the articles of peace or security: and the wrong shall have been shown to four barons of the aforesaid twenty-five barons, let those four barons come to us or to our justiciar, if we are out of the kingdom, laying before us the transgression, and let them ask that we cause that transgression to be corrected without delay.

In that century another important rule for police officers was promulgated in the Statute of Westminster, 3 Edward 1 (1275), to the effect that any sheriff who took a reward for doing his duty was committing the crime of extortion. He would be fined twice the amount he received and punished at the king's pleasure.

By the middle of the fourteenth century the situation had changed because of the spread of armed violence and rioting. The demand for law and order became paramount, and as a result the power of the police was increased. The counterpart of the "stop-and-frisk" law—the Statute of Northampton, 2 Edward 3 (1328)—gave the sheriffs legal power to arrest those who rode about armed by night or day. It became the duty of the sheriffs to arrest those who participated in assemblies or riots that disturbed the peace.(42) The beginning of the fifteenth century brought an intensification of the campaign for law and order. The Riot Act of 1411 not only made it mandatory for justices of the peace and sheriffs to arrest rioters, but also if they failed to do so, they were fined 100 pounds to be paid to the king.(43) With the riots came looting, and the response was the Forcible Entry Act of 1429 directing justices and sheriffs to arrest anyone taking part in insurrections, riots, routs, and assemblies in disturbance of the peace.(44) There was also a reminder for the sheriffs, under pain of prison and fine, to arrest those "malefactors" who "make forcible entries."

Behind the pages of history a powerful undercurrent of crime, violence, and public disorder was the force that directly and indirectly produced law and law enforcement. In general, an increase in disorder resulted in an increase in police power. A limit to this grant of power has been the traditional suspicion of the police in England and the United States. Sometimes the near-unanimous praise of Scotland Yard causes us to forget that this vaunted police force was born under a cloud, and only after seven years of political maneuvering by its sponsor, Robert Peel, was it able to overcome powerful resistance. The very word "police" aroused in the British people the repugnance and fear of a sinister spy system, and the idea of creating a large central police force was strongly opposed in the early decades of the nineteenth century by "men of good-will in all classes who genuinely believed, with the example of France before them, that police of any kind were synonymous with tyranny and the destruction of liberty."(45) Because of that distrust, the Metropolitan Police Force was disarmed. Only the naive believe that "bobbies" never carry weapons because England has always been so law-abiding.

Great Britain has established several levels of control over the police. The central responsibility for law enforcement and the state of law and order rests with the Home Secretary. He fulfills this by regulating police administration, ensuring compliance with important procedures such as the 1964 revision of the Judges' Rules, and giving final approval to the appointment of chief constables.(46) The secretary of state exercises control through substantial financial assistance to local police forces. In the boroughs and counties, watch committees supervise the police.(47)

A specious line of legal reasoning is advanced by those who want complete autonomy for the police. They rely upon the authority of cases like *Fisher* v. *Oldham Corporation*(48) in which Fisher, who had been falsely arrested by the police of Oldham, claimed damages from the town of Oldham on the theory that the defendants through their watch committee were the employers of the police and therefore responsible for their negligence. The court resurrected an old common-law doctrine and held that the defendants were not liable for the damages because the police are really servants of the Crown,

not of the local jurisdiction. In fact, some have advanced the argument that the police serve the "law" and therefore they are responsible only to the law.(49) By extension of the doctrine of municipal immunity from tort liability, it is concluded somehow that the police are not—and ought not to be—legally responsible to external control.

In the United States the majority of jurisdictions once held that municipalities were immune from tort liability arising from the acts of police officers.(50) As far back as 1897 Mr. Justice Holmes attacked the underlying legal concept (The King Can Do No Wrong) as a revolting survival because "the grounds upon which it was laid down have vanished long since, and the rule simply persists from blind imitations of the past."(51) Today the trend is in an opposite direction and the courts are imposing responsibility upon municipalities for the torts of their police officers.(52) If there is some question about the tort liability of municipalities, there is no doubt that the police officer himself is responsible for his torts committed in the performance of duty. In any case the police in the United States never built their hopes on this type of legal abstraction.

On the contrary, the police justify their fierce insistence upon autonomy—freedom from control by the mayor or by the community—with the down-to-earth slogan, "Police and Politics Don't Mix." This social myth has become a fundamental plank in an occupational ideology that was an inevitable outcome of the evolution of law enforcement in America. Among the 40,000 separate and overlapping police forces, those in our largest cities have become elaborate bureaucracies. Given the stress on competence, specialization, education, and technological improvement in bureaucracies, it was natural for elite police groups to think of themselves as professionals and then to form the vanguard of a movement to transform police work into a profession. The more professionalized they become, the more the police will resist control or review from the outside.

But are police and politics necessarily alien? The derivation of the two words shows that there is a close affinity. *Police* is derived from the Greek word *politeia*, meaning citizenship and connoting the control and regulation of a political unit such as a nation or a state. Similarly, *politics* comes from the Greek word *politikos*, meaning citizen; it is defined as the art or science dealing with the regulation and control of men living in society. More and more the two terms are becoming inseparable; since crime and "law and order" were issues in the presidential campaigns of 1968 and 1972, the police, in a sense, may be crucial to the political fate of America.

If political interference is a danger to police, how much more dangerous in a democracy is police interference in politics? The ominous political power of the police was revealed in the successful campaign of the New York City Police Department (represented by the Patrolmen's Benevolent Association) to defeat the Civilian Review Board in 1966 against the combined might of three of the most influential political figures in the nation: Mayor John Lindsay, Senator Jacob Javits and the late Senator Robert Kennedy.

Police officers may assert that they are only on duty eight hours a day and that they revert to their neutral civilian status at other times with the citizen's full right to participate in political activities. But there are some loopholes in this argument: the law clothes them with peace officer status at all times; they must carry their revolvers and shields constantly; and departmental rules control them rigidly even when they are "off duty." At any time, a police officer has special power and special status.

Possibly there was a time in the past when law enforcement was and should have been divorced from politics. As long as police duty meant the typical and traditional tasks—five to ten summonses a month, a few ambulance cases, several auto accidents, and an occasional arrest for disorderly conduct, auto theft, or even a serious felony—it might have been relevant to defend the theory that the police system would function best if the duly elected political leaders maintained a hands-off policy. This is no longer the case. In the urban arena the police are forced to relegate their conventional duties to a subordinate position. The concerned police officer now measures every action by asking himself, "Will this cause a riot?" When police departments must spend most of their effort in the prevention and control of riots, demonstrations, and protests, and when governments rise and fall according to the ability of the police to cope with this social dynamite, then one conclusion emerges: today, police work *is* politics. Mayors will exercise their right to control the municipal police force; it would be political suicide to evade this responsibility.

This is the message of the Riot Commission Report:(53)

Civil disorders are fundamental governmental problems not simply police matters. As the chief elected official, the mayor must take ultimate responsibility for all governmental action in times of disorder. To make this meaningful, he must have the corresponding authority and control. He must become fully involved in disorder planning and operations. He must understand the nature of the problems posed by a disorder, the strategy of response and the pattern of field operations.

In some cities, mayors have taken the view that disorders were entirely police matters. This represents a failure to accept a fundamental responsibility.

Residents of the ghetto responding to militant ideologies have begun to equate the police with an army of occupation—an army of a colonial power subjugating the black population. Our national armed forces are by law and custom subject to civilian control and review. As our local police forces take on the character (symbolic or actual) of an army, it becomes more vital that they too submit to some form of control, not only from the political structure above but from the community below. In a democracy a police department that is completely autonomous is dangerous, no matter how professional, how educated, and how dedicated it may be.

The one practical index of a police department's responsiveness to the community is the civilian complaint system. Where the police resist any external review by members of the community, the black community is likely to fear the police. It is significant that in the referendum on the review board in New York City, Manhattan was the only borough that was decisively in favor of the board, and this was largely a result of the Negro and Puerto Rican vote.(54) The police assert that no change is necessary in grievance mechanisms because a citizen has innumerable ways of registering a complaint against the police.(55)

The citizen may complain in person, by telephone, or in writing, identifying himself or remaining anonymous, to the police department. ... He may complain to the Police Commissioner, to the Mayor, to the City Manager, or to the City Attorney. He may complain to the County Board of Supervisors, to the Grand Jury, or to the Governor of the State. He may complain to a Federal Grand Jury, to the United States Attorney in his district, to the United States Attorney General, to the F.B.I., local office or at Washington, D.C., or to the President. Indeed the aggrieved citizen has many avenues of complaint open to him.

Given all the unanswered questions and thorny problems, it is amazing that the police in America can agree that there is one universal solution—professionalization. It has become a mystique of police philosophy, a Holy Grail. So much has been written on the positive contributions of professionalization that a totally unrealistic view of the matter has prevailed.(56) The concept of professionalism requires critical reexamination in order to achieve a more balanced perspective, in view of some of the negative implications that are present in the public thrust toward professionalization.

In the major police departments control of the system has continued within the orbit of a self-defined, self-perpetuating group. In many of the departments of the eastern United States they have been called the "Irish Mafia"; in others they represent a particular political force in a given city. Generally we can say of them, as we can of the governments of developed nations, that with continued power has come a reliance on tradition and a conservative ideology that resists any change as a threat to continued power. Concomitant with this resistance has been a general upgrading of the police occupation, mainly the result of two important trends, one internal, the other external. The first is the move toward professionalization that has come about through technological sophistication, specialization, and the formation of elite cadres whose well-educated members have pushed for recognition as professionals. The second trend is the growing importance of the police as a domestic army in America whose purpose is to control demonstrations, riots, and disorders. Out of this unique responsibility has developed a greater recognition of and higher status for the police system. Nevertheless the movement toward professionalism has been a mixed blessing.

1. Professionalization creates a struggle for power and polarizes a police force into two warring camps—the pros (professionals) and cons (conservatives). Whenever there is conflict at the top, it filters down; the men in the lower ranks are caught in a no-man's land and they are the ultimate victims of such intraorganizational conflict. In essence the internal struggle is characterized by an entrenched administrative oligarchy on the defensive against an innovative younger group seeking to capture the old regimes. The younger members often use the jargon, style, and ideological slogans of professionalism to accomplish their objectives; however, it remains to be seen, as they do assume power and leadership, whether their professionalism is one of substance or merely a careerist, politically motivated veneer.

2. Professionalism, by its stress on formal education, creates divisions and enmities among members of a police force in still other ways. Many police officers, especially the old-timers, are upset by the thought of going back to school. They resent the favoritism toward college men; they fear the competition of the educated; and they respond with cynicism or aggression because of their own frustration. On a more subtle level the academic influence creates malcontents. The latent effect of professionalism is that many are forced into academic environments far from the police orbit, where they become socialized in terms of the norms and ideologies of wholly different world views that are inconsistent with purely local concerns and narrow bureaucratic commitments. Professionalism and its concomitant colleagueship breed a cosmopolitanism destructive of authoritarian structures. The educated man is often a disenchanted man.

3. Professionalism creates turmoil in still another way. It cannot be grafted onto a traditional department. It requires radical changes in policy, techniques, and social relations. Old customs and values are threatened. The men become uneasy, and as the process speeds up, they become disgruntled and morale suffers.

4. Professionalism creates alienation. Necessarily exposed to the academic viewpoint, professionals lose their narrow organizational loyalty and become "cosmopolitans." Seeking the larger perspective, professionals sometimes tend to violate fundamental postulates of "tried-and-true" police tradition.

5. Professionalism creates many dilemmas for the police in the modern world. Professionalism increases the police demand for efficiency and objective standards in police work. In practice, this means that the professional police force is tougher and more impersonal than the nonprofessional can be in dealing with minority groups and youth.

6. Professionalism intensifies the demand for self-policing and autonomy. Despite this, the experience of our large cities proves that "civilianization," community control, and external review may be on their way, regardless of what the police may perceive as a threat to their integrity and professionalization.

7. Professionalism needs constant renewal by the recruitment of college educated individuals. However, the competition for a limited number of job slots may unfortunately pit ethnic groups, as well as male and female candidates, against each other. And all of these can assert some sort of legitimate claim for consideration.

8. Implicit in the principle of professionalism is the assertion that there be no political interference in police affairs. Professionalism, on the other hand, does stimulate police interference in political affairs —for example, the advertising and voting campaigns of the Patrolmen's Benevolent Association speaking as representatives of the New York City Police Department against the proposed Civilian Review Board in 1966.

9. Since professionalism can only be achieved or maintained as long as the police are held in high esteem by the public, there is a powerful tendency to cover up or to falsify reports and statistics of crime in order to maintain that prestige. Every bureaucracy is ultimately a self-serving instrument supportive of its own world views and the decisions it has already made or is about to make; the police are no exception.(57)

Police departments, like other large bureaucracies, have accepted the claims of psychological testing and psychiatric examination and screening. In one sense this is an improvement; it tends to replace the polygraph examination as a method of attracting and selecting candidates. The one important criticism of these selection methods is that police departments are searching desperately for the unique qualities that might predict the ideal, superior police officer who will have a trouble-free, simon-pure career. The major fallacy in this search is that a police force is most effective when it is composed of men who are quite different from one another as to temperament, intellect, life-style, ideology, motivating personality, fund of knowledge, skills, and expertise; in other words, it needs the college man, the ghetto resident, the soft-spoken intellectual, as well as the hard-nosed, rough-and-ready daredevil who enthusiastically welcomes dangerous assignments. Similarly, James Q.

Wilson has shown that of many possible types there are three major styles of police performance: the Service Role, the Watchman Role, and the Legalistic Role.(58) These styles require not only different personality types but different organizational roles, responses, intellectual requisites, and, ultimately, highly selective recruitment requirements of a more sophisticated kind than those presently employed.

The nature of the police career leaves the officer prey to cynicism and a Hobbesian view of the world. The great majority of the occupational experiences are concerned with people in trouble, in conflict, in violation of law. The main source of trouble is in the teeming inner city, where middle-class sensibilities are shocked by what is considered an alien, obscene, inferior way of life. People are seen at their most reprehensible and vulnerable moments. The officer feels that the police are the only experts holding this skewed segment of hard data. All arguments that stress human decency and perfectibility are rejected. Toward the department itself a strange ambivalence exists. In the back rooms of police precincts there are no more virulent critics of the police establishment than the police themselves. Although often an unwitting victim of a demanding bureaucracy, the officer develops fierce loyalties to the system and unites with other police against all outsiders who are critical of police activities. As retirement approaches, a process of gradual disengagement takes place, in which the officer makes tentative efforts at reestablishment in a social and emotional stance more compatible with civilian roles and world views.

There is at present a growing anxiety and a trend toward self-examination within the criminal justice system(59) involving a number of unanswered, perhaps unanswerable, questions such as: What is (or should be) the role of justice in America today? What is justice? How can the police improve their public image? What direction will police–minority-group relations take? Are restraint or the application of massive force proper strategies to use against confrontation demonstrations? Within the police system what can or should be done about the increasing antagonism between white and black members of the force? Is there a conflict of loyalty for the black police officer in situations involving black demonstrators? Is professionalization really an effective solution to the problems of the police? Is there a contradiction in policy when a department that wants to recruit college graduates is forced to seek minority group candidates with little formal education? What should be the policy toward the introduction of civilians into police work? Can the police maintain what they believe to be proper standards of efficiency in law enforcement and still abide by the limitations imposed by Supreme Court decisions? What guidelines should be established over the grey area of police discretion? What is the proper relation between the police and the other institutions of criminal justice? Should the police be law enforcers or peace keepers?

Regardless of the responses one might formulate with respect to the foregoing queries, there are a number of other issues and emerging phenomena which we discern as critical in the decade ahead:

1. Police unionization and an intensified orientation toward an industrial labor-management model of police organization appears to be an accomplished fact. The impact of this trend is as yet to be felt as a pervasive problem in undermining the traditional paramilitary police discipline. Job actions, strikes, and slowdowns may become more common forms of rank-and-file protest to achieve the usual trade union goals of wage benefits, job security, grievance and due process procedures, protection against layoffs, and the like. The wide import of police unionization is yet to be felt within police organizations and the communities they serve.

2. The role of policewomen remains a difficult one for many departments. The unease and resentment of their male colleagues and their wives will continue to create a climate of ambiguity for female recruits. Further, the on-the-job performance of policewomen remains to be evaluated since the evidence of performance remains fragmentary and incomplete.

3. Local police appear to be losing a good deal of control to federal and state agencies. Although there is a considerable amount of revulsion toward the notion of a national police force, there is an unmistakable drift in that direction, especially in terms of financial dependence and control of data systems.

4. A high rate of unemployment which could last into the 1980s poses a serious threat to our society. In the past the police have been employed to control picket lines in cases of labor disputes and to contain serious civil disturbances which were a product of labor protests, strikes, lockouts, and demonstrations by unemployed persons. As a con-

sequence of austerity budgets and other severe economic dislocations, the police will be called upon with greater regularity to furnish the "shock troops" to defuse the inevitable protests and disorders arising out of frustration and economic distress.

5. Municipal austerity will impose demands for greater productivity on the part of all civil servants, including the police. How will pressures for increased productivity affect police discretion; what shape will these pressures take; and how will they be applied?

6. As more police personnel possess college credentials and graduate degrees, police responses to their critics and defenses against their political superiors will become increasingly sophisticated. This aspect of police development will be interesting to watch, especially as the police develop men and women whose credentials, talents, and stature are the equivalent of those civil servants in some of the federal executive departments and the judiciary. It is of value to note that the British police system recruited its commissioners for over a century largely from the military, until they developed their own intellectual elite and professional leaders from within. The table on the following page depicts this progression.

7. The police will continue to be one of the major critics of the criminal justice system, as they are the major source of input to that system.

8. The intrusion of the police into the privacy of citizens for the goal of their protection and that of the community will be sharply defended as not being very different from what is already being done by a variety of social scientists.

9. Some of the major problems of the 1950s, such as gang delinquency, and the civil disorders of the 1960s will return as major police problems.

10. A more sympathetic Supreme Court may deflect the police from a service-oriented or legalistic role, back to an older, cruder style of policing.

11. The LEAA funding is tenuous and may dry up or be altered with an entirely new agenda for funding. This is certain to have an impact on the police, especially their community-relations programs.

12. The implications of the Kansas City patrol experiment appear to challenge some traditional beliefs as to the effectiveness of routine police patrol.(61) There will no doubt be a good deal of further research of this kind, because the Kansas City findings appeared to fly in the face of all police theory with regard to the utility radio car patrol.

Commissioners of Police of the Metropolis(60)

In office	Commissioner	Previous employment	In office	Commissioner	Previous employment
1829–50	Sir Charles Rowan	Army	1918–20	Sir Nevil Macready	Army
1829–68	Sir Richard Mayne	Law	1920–28	Sir William Horwood	Army
1850–55	Captain William Hay	Army	1928–31	Lord Byng	Army
1868–69	Col. D. W. P. Labalmondière (Acting)	Army	1931–35	Lord Trenchard	Royal Air Force
			1935–45	Sir Philip Game	Royal Air Force
1869–86	Sir Edmund Henderson	Army	1945–53	Sir Harold Scott	Civil Service
1886–88	Sir Charles Warren	Army	1953–59	Sir John Nott-Bower	Indian Police
1888–90	Mr. James Monro	Indian Police	1959–69	Sir Joseph Simpson	Police
1890–1903	Sir Edward Bradford	Army	1969–72	Sir John Waldron	Police
1903–18	Sir Edward Henry	Indian Police	1972–	Sir Robert Mark	Police

13. Of major concern to police organizations is the future direction of the new FBI. Critics and advocates alike are concerned with the future potential of the FBI because of its extraordinary influence and continuing residual prestige, despite Watergate and related misadventures of the agency.

14. In spite of the incredible volume of published data about the police, there remain many problems with regard to the validity of the data, especially with regard to personality, social class, police culture, and the like.

These questions only skim the surface. Every day brings new dilemmas; policy reverses itself from week to week. Under conditions of attack from without and anxiety and confusion within, the police are at the point of desperation. Law enforcement requires more than anything else a restatement and clarification of its mission. With that thought in mind, we have assembled a collection of meaningful and, we feel, interesting articles that:

1. Cover a wide spectrum of the police service, with emphasis upon the historical and comparative, to give perspective

2. With few exceptions meet the test of excellence in scholarship and substance that is demanded by learned journals and law reviews

3. Will prove helpful to police administrators and others who are interested in an analysis of the police system by respected scholars from various disciplines whose work may not be available in police circles

4. Can serve as a source book of descriptive and theoretical material, as well as a reservoir of stimulating and probably controversial ideas for police academies and police science programs at the college and graduate levels

5. Encourage the coming movement to raise police science from its current marginal status to parity with its sister disciplines in the academic world

It is our judgment that a police professionalism oriented toward technical expertise and proficiency, with an overlay of the argot of the academic world but without any real internalization of the traditional humanistic values of the ancient professions, is dangerous for the police practitioners and the society they are supposed to serve and protect. To date the police appear to be more interested in power than in the conventional norms and values of a profession. They applaud and vigorously seek the autonomy of the professional but are rather superficial and perfunctory in developing the kind of systematic knowledge base, academic involvement and research orientation, colleagueship, service ideal, critical self-analysis, and nonbureaucratic controls that are usually hallmarks of professionalism.

However, the latent consequences of sending young policemen into the academic world portend radical change in the traditional values of the police and ultimately in their impact on society.(62) The irony of all this is that what may have been an employment of the vehicle of professionalism to achieve and hold power could instead produce a disenchanted group of dissidents who displace their politically motivated superiors and work for real change in the police system instead of superficial adjustment.

Even if any of the assorted political, social, or military catastrophes that have been predicted for us should fail to occur, the police and their organizations are sure to be at the center of every storm in the decades ahead. The traditional route of "professionalization" alone will not be enough, either for the police or the society they are to serve, to assure a nonmilitary, nonpolitical police force oriented toward goals of due process without which no society that calls itself a democracy can survive. There are at least six steps that every police officer and police organization must implement in the decade ahead to insure a truly professional police force committed to due process while at the same time enjoying the perquisites and status other professional groups in society possess:

1. "Embourgeoisement"
2. Debureaucratization
3. Cosmopolitanization
4. Academization
5. Service ideal
6. Role redefinition

Many a police officer at the time of his recruitment is already possessed of well-defined perspectives characterized by simplistic views of the world. He tends to see the society he lives in through the lens of very limited experience, meager education, and in terms of his knowledge of people who are very much like himself. He has very little real knowledge or experience of contrasting life styles. If anything, he is likely to revere authority and mistrust the new, the strange, the different, the intellectual, or the "arty." His tolerance, if any, for sexual misconduct, atheism, extreme styles in clothing or hair, or radical political views is rather low. His handling of aggression by "directing it outwards"(63) is said to be one of the reasons he may be attracted to a police career.

Yet even if only part of what has been said in the behavioral science literature is true about these attributes of the working class,(64) from which most police officers are recruited, there is an urgent need to "middle class-ify" the force. There is no intention here to extol the alleged virtues of the middle class. Indeed, our purpose is to extract only the rational aspects of middle-class life, especially those involving intellectuality, restraint, tolerance, planning, and the development of skills, and apply them to the police role. That, in summary, is what is proposed by the process of *"embourgeoisement."*

Debureaucratization is admittedly a more difficult project—rather like growing roses without thorns.

Eliminating the negative, socially destructive features of bureaucracy while retaining its productive features would require the services of a divinely endowed virtuoso. For police organizations the most negative aspect of their bureaucratic structure is the protection afforded the inept, the incompetent, the mediocre, or the pathological individual. Bureaucracy tends to compromise the service ideal—the client is too often a secondary consideration. Bureaucracies often make demands in the service of the organization at the expense of service to the community. The very secrecy of bureaucracy and its admonition to "cover yourself" defeat the professional goals sought by police and other professions on the make.

For far too long the police as an occupational group have been out of the mainstream of society. This is due to more than the fact that the individual police officers find comfort in mutual support. The police simply have not been part of the other institutional communities; rather they have been a beleaguered group, functioning in an almost self-segregated enclave that tended to nourish the often resentful style characteristic of other marginal groups in a society. The process of *cosmopolitanization* is one that is inevitably tied to that of *academization:* the process of planting the police occupation in a firm academic base similar to librarianship, nursing, or social work. Police science courses are the mere beginning—an opening wedge into the academic community. Once in, there is so much in the liberal arts to absorb and enjoy. Without both the social and intellectual experience of academia, there is no possibility of the police developing a base in which to nourish, develop, and transmit any sort of professional body of theory, knowledge, and technical skills.

The *service ideal* is nothing more than dedication to the needs of one's clients or constituency. Whenever there is a conflict between personal goals and that of the client's interests, it is the client who must prevail. Too often bureaucracy defeats the needs of the client because it conceives of its own purposes as being paramount over those of its clients. Development of a service ideal is especially difficult since so much lip service is given to it while much of the time the client's needs are ignored.

It will perhaps be somewhat easier in the short run to effect *role redefinition* than any of the other processes. Much police work is of the social-worker, caretaker, counseling-service kind of activity.(65)

Thus, the police function must be reviewed and at least its crime prevention function narrowed to the kind of real crime control activities that would make the occupation more reasonable in its scope. At present these varied activities have reduced the law enforcement–crime control functions of the police to less than 20 percent of their total working time. When one is responsible for "everything," one is also vulnerable for the inevitable mistakes in carrying out the impossible. That is the heart of the police officer's lot.

REFERENCES

1. *See* William M. Bowsky, "The Medieval Commune and Internal Violence: Police Power and Public Safety in Siena, 1287–1355," *American Historical Review, 73*, 1 (October, 1967), pp. 1–17; Herbert Asbury, *The Gangs of New York* (New York: Knopf, 1928); James McCague, *The Second Rebellion: The Story of the New York City Draft Riots of 1863* (New York: Dial Press, 1968); Joseph Boskin, *Urban Racial Violence in the Twentieth Century* (Beverly Hills, Calif.: Glencoe Press, 1969); and Joel Samaha, *Law and Order in Historical Perspective* (New York: Academic Press, 1974).

2. Emile Durkheim, *The Rules of Sociological Method* (New York: Free Press, 1964), p. 67.

3. James S. Wallerstein and Clement J. Wyle, "Our Law-Abiding Lawbreakers," *Probation, 25* (March–April, 1947), pp. 107–112; Austin L. Porterfield, *Youth In Trouble* (Fort Worth: Leo Potishman Foundation, 1946); F. Ivan Nye, *Family Relationships and Delinquent Behavior* (New York: Wiley, 1958).

4. Kai T. Erikson, *Wayward Puritans* (New York: Wiley, 1966); Howard S. Becker, *Outsiders: Studies in the Sociology of Deviance* (New York: Free Press, 1963).

5. *See* Daniel Glaser, *Adult Crime and Social Policy* (Englewood Cliffs, N.J.: Prentice-Hall, Inc., 1972), pp. 27–66; Roger Hood and Richard Sparks, *Key Issues in Criminology* (New York: McGraw-Hill Book Co., 1970), pp. 110–140; Marshall B. Clinard and Richard Quinney, *Criminal Behavior Systems: A Typology* (New York: Holt, Rinehart and Winston, Inc., 1967); Don Gibbons, *Changing the Law Breaker* (Englewood Cliffs, N.J.: Prentice-Hall, Inc., 1965); James A. Inciardi, *Careers in Crime* (Chicago: Rand McNally College Publishing Co., 1975).

6. *See* Fred J. Cook *The Corrupted Land* (New York: Macmillan, 1966), for a detailed account of some of these examples of upperworld crime. Also Gustavus Myers, *History of the Great American Fortunes* (New York: Modern Library, 1936), and Matthew Josephson, *The Robber Barons* (New York: Harcourt, Brace & World, 1962), for further illustrations of upperworld crime to be found in the accumulation of some of America's most respected fortunes.

7. Mark Green et al., *The Closed Enterprise System* (New York: Grossman Publishers, 1972); also Morton Mintz and Jerry S. Cohen, *America, Inc.: Who Owns and Operates the United States* (New York: The Dial Press, 1971), pp. 285–330.

8. *See* Joseph L. Albini, *The American Mafia: Genesis of a Legend* (New York: Appleton-Century-Crofts, 1972); Dwight C. Smith, Jr., *The Mafia Mystique* (New York: Basic Books, Inc., 1975).

9. Gay Talese, *Honor Thy Father* (New York: World Publishing Co., 1971).

10. Nicholas Gage, *The Mafia is Not An Equal Opportunity Employer* (New York: McGraw-Hill, 1971).

11. Wilfred Sheed, "Everybody's Mafia," *The New York Review of Books* (July 20, 1972), pp. 23–27.

12. John E. Conklin, *Robbery and the Criminal Justice System* (Philadelphia: J.B. Lippincott Co., 1972), pp. 10–38.

13. Raymond D. Gastil, "Homicide and a Regional Culture of Violence," *American Sociological Review, 36*, 3 (June, 1971), pp. 412–427.

14. Federal Bureau of Investigation, U.S. Department of Justice, *Crime in the United States: Uniform Crime Reports, 1973* (Washington, D.C.: U.S. Government Printing Office, 1974), pp. 9, 172.

15. George D. Newton and Franklin E. Zimring in National Commission on the Causes and Prevention of Violence, *Firearms and Violence in American Life.* (Washington, D.C.: U.S. Government Printing Office, 1969), p. 41.

16. *See* Erwin O. Smigel and H. Laurence Ross, *Crimes Against Bureaucracy* (New York: Van Nostrand Reinhold Co., 1970).

17. *See* Stephen Schafer, *The Political Criminal* (New York: The Free Press, 1974).

18. Gresham Sykes, "The Future of Criminality," *American Behavioral Scientist, 15* (Jan–Feb., 1972), p. 413.

19. See Carl B. Klockars, *The Professional Fence* (New York: The Free Press, 1974).

20. Walter V. Schaefer, "Federalism and State Criminal Procedure," *Harvard Law Review, 70* (November 1956), p. 26.

21. L. P. Tiffany, D. M. McIntyre, Jr., D. L. Rotenberg, *Detection of Crime* (Boston: Little, Brown, 1967); Donald J. Newman, *Conviction* (Boston: Little, Brown, 1966).

22. George E. Homans, *Social Behavior: Its Elementary Forms* (New York: Harcourt, Brace & World, 1961).

23. Herbert L. Packer, *The Limits of the Criminal Sanction* (Stanford, Calif.: Stanford University Press, 1968).

24. Abraham S. Blumberg, *Criminal Justice* (New York: Franklin Watts, Inc. 1974); Jerome H. Skolnick, *Justice without Trial* (New York: John Wiley and Sons, 1975); Aaron V. Cicourel, *The Social Organization of Juvenile Justice* (New York: John Wiley and Sons, 1968).

25. Abraham S. Goldstein, "The State and the Accused: Balance of Advantage in Criminal Procedure," *Yale Law Journal, 69* (June 1960), pp. 1148—99.

26. *See* Ronald Goldfarb, *Ransom* (New York: Harper and Row, 1965), for an excellent analysis of the manner in which an archaic bail system tends to corrupt and often defeat the pursuit of justice.

27. Abraham S. Blumberg, "The Practice of Law as Confidence Game," *Law and Society Review, 1, 2* (June 1967), pp. 15—39.

28. Norval Morris, "Politics and Pragmatism in Crime Control," *Federal Probation* (June 1968), pp. 9—16; Arthur I. Stinchcombe, "Institutions of Privacy in the Determination of Police Administrative Practice," *American Journal of Sociology, 69, 2* (September 1963), pp. 150—60.

29. Seymour M. Lipset, "Why Cops Hate Liberals—and Vice Versa," *Atlantic, 223* (March 1969), p. 83.

30. *Law Enforcement and Criminal Justice: Education Directory 1975—1976.* (Gaithersburg, Md.: International Association of Chiefs of Police, 1975), p. 11.

31. Irving Piliavin and Scott Briar, "Police Encounters with Juveniles," *American Journal of Sociology, 69* (September 1964), pp. 206—214; Robert Conot, *Rivers of Blood, Years of Darkness* (New York: Bantam Books, 1967); Stanley Lieberson and Arnold R. Silverman, "Precipitants and Conditions of Race Riots," *American Sociological Review, 30, 6* (December 1965), pp. 887—98.

32. Enrico Ferri, *Criminal Sociology* (New York: Appleton, 1896), p. 53.

33. For detailed discussions of the impact and consequences of wide-ranging "police discretion," *see* Joseph Goldstein, "Police Discretion Not to Invoke the Criminal Process: Low Visibility Decisions in the Administration of Justice," *Yale Law Journal, 69* (March 1960), pp. 543—94; David H. Bayley and Harold Mendelsohn, *Minorities and the Police* (New York: Free Press, 1969); "The Cops," *The Nation,* (April 21, 1969) entire issue; William A. Westley, "Violence and the Police," *American Journal of Sociology, 59* (July 1953), pp. 34—41; Egon Bittner, "Police Discretion in Emergency Apprehension of Mentally Ill Persons," *Social Problems, 14* (Winter, 1967), pp. 278—92; Herman Goldstein, "Police Discretion: The Ideal Versus the Real," *Public Administration Review, 23* (September 1963), pp. 140—48; Richard C. Donnelly, "Police Authority and Practices," *Annals, 339* (January 1962), pp. 90—110. Ed Cray, *The Big Blue Line* (New York: Coward-McCann, 1967) is especially critical of police malpractice, as is Paul Chevigny, *Police Power: Police Abuses in New York City* (New York: Pantheon, 1969). Albert J. Reiss, Jr., *The Police and the Public* (New Haven: Yale University Press, 1971); Richard E. Sykes, James C. Fox and John P. Clark, *A Socio-Legal Theory of Police Discretion* (Washington, D.C.: National Institute of Mental Health, 1974).

34. Algernon D. Black, *The People and the Police* (New York: McGraw-Hill, 1968).

35. The President's Commission on Law Enforcement and Administration of Justice, *Task Force Report: The Police* (Washington, D.C.: U.S. Government Printing Office, 1967), pp. 183—85. Also C. A. Reich, "Police Questioning of Law Abiding Citizens," *Yale Law Journal, 75* (June 1966), p. 1161; Arnold S. Trebach, *The Rationing of Justice* (New Brunswick, N.J.: Rutgers University Press, 1964), pp. 4—6; Nicholas Alex, *Black in Blue* (New York: Appleton-Century-Crofts, 1969), a remarkable work on the role of the Negro policeman in law enforcement, and Robert Blauner, "Internal Colonialism and Ghetto Revolt," *Social Problems, 16, 4* (Spring, 1969), pp. 404—6.

36. *Terry* v. *Ohio* 392 U.S. 1 (June 10, 1968).

37. *Adams* v. *Williams* 407 U.S. 143 (1972).

38. *United States* v. *Robinson* 414 U.S. 218 (1973); *Gustafson* v. *Florida* 414 U.S. 260 (1973).

39. Arthur Niederhoffer, *Behind the Shield* (Garden City, N.Y.: Doubleday, 1967).

40. *Report of the National Advisory Commission on Civil Disorders* (New York: Bantam Books, 1968), p. 299.

41. William Turner, *The Police Establishment* (New York: G. P. Putnam, 1968).

42. *Statute of Northampton,* 17 Richard 2 (1393—1394).

43. *Riot Act of 1411,* 13 Henry 4 (1411).

44. *Forcible Entry Act*, 8 Henry 6 (1429).

45. Charles Reith, *A New Study of Police History* (London: Oliver and Boyd, 1956), p. 122.

46. Geoffrey Marshall, *Police and Government* (London: Methuen, 1965), p. 15.

47. Ibid.

48. 2 *Kings Bench* 364 (1930).

49. Geoffrey Marshall, *Police and Government* (London: Methuen, 1965), pp. 33–45.

50. Carol F. Dakin, "Municipal Immunity in Police Torts," *Cleveland Marshall Law Review, 14* (1965), p. 448.

51. Oliver W. Holmes, "The Path of the Law," *Harvard Law Review, 10* (1897), p. 469.

52. Herbert E. Greenstone, "Liability of Police Officers for Misuse of Their Weapons," *Cleveland-Marshall Law Review, 16* (1967), p. 399.

53. *Report of the National Advisory Commission on Civil Disorders* (Washington, D.C.: U.S. Government Printing Office, 1968), p. 178.

54. Algernon D. Black, *The People and the Police* (New York: McGraw-Hill, 1968), p. 211.

55. A. C. Germann, Frank D. Day, and Robert R. J. Gallati, *Introduction to Law Enforcement* (Springfield, Ill.: Thomas, 1962), p. 52.

56. Howard M. Vollmer and Donald L. Mills, eds., *Professionalization* (Englewood Cliffs, N.J.: Prentice-Hall, Inc., 1966).

57. *See* James C. Thompson, Jr., "How Could Vietnam Happen?" *Atlantic* (April 1968), pp. 47–53, for a military and diplomatic illustration of this problem.

58. James Q. Wilson, *Varieties of Police Behavior* (Cambridge: Harvard University Press, 1968).

59. Robert M. Cipes, *The Crime War* (New York: New American Library, 1968); Jonathan D. Casper, *American Criminal Justice* (Englewood Cliffs, N.J.: Prentice-Hall, Inc., 1972); David W. Neubauer, *Criminal Justice in Middle America* (Morristown, N.J.: General Learning Press, 1974); Jessica Mitford, *The Prison Business* (New York: Vintage Books, 1974); Jonathan Rubinstein, *City Police* (New York: Farrar, Straus and Giroux, 1973).

60. We are indebted to Philip John Stead for these data.

61. *The Kansas City Preventive Patrol Experiment* (Washington, D.C.: Police Foundation, 1974).

62. But *see* Richard N. Harris, *The Police Academy: An Inside View* (New York: John Wiley and Sons, 1973), for a critical view of police academy training.

63. Albert K. Cohen and Harold M. Hodges, "Lower-Blue-Collar-Class Characteristics," *Social Problems, 10*, 4 (Spring, 1963), pp. 303–34.

64. Seymour M. Lipset, *Political Man* (Garden City, N.Y.: Doubleday, 1960), pp. 97–130.

65. *See* Elaine Cumming, Ian M. Cumming, and Laura Edell, "Policeman as Philosopher, Guide and Friend," *Social Problems, 12* (Winter, 1965), pp. 276–86.

Task Force Report: *The Police*

THE PRESIDENT'S COMMISSION ON LAW ENFORCEMENT
AND ADMINISTRATION OF JUSTICE

The police—some 420,000 people working for approximately 40,000 separate agencies that spend more than $2½ billion a year—are the part of the criminal justice system that is in direct daily contact both with crime and with the public. The entire system—courts and corrections as well as the police—is charged with enforcing the law and maintaining order. What is distinctive about the responsibility of the police is that they are charged with performing these functions where all eyes are upon them and where the going is roughest, on the street. Since this is a time of increasing crime, increasing social unrest, and increasing public sensitivity to both, it is a time when police work is peculiarly important, complicated, conspicuous, and delicate.

Because the police have the responsibility for dealing with crime hour by hour, where, when and as

SOURCE: (Washington, D.C.: U.S. Government Printing Office, 1967), pp. 3–12.

it occurs, there is a tendency on the part of the public, and often of the police themselves, to think of crime control almost exclusively in terms of police work. One response to the recent increases in the volume of crime has been the charge that the police lack the competence or the will to keep crime within bounds. A far more common one has been the assertion that the police could keep crime within bounds if only the appellate courts, or civilian review boards, or corrupt politicians, or an uncooperative public allowed them to. "Take the handcuffs off our police" is a cry familiar to everyone.

The fact is, of course, that even under the most favorable circumstances the ability of the police to act against crime is limited. The police did not create and cannot resolve the social conditions that stimulate crime. They did not start and cannot stop the convulsive social changes that are taking place in America. They do not enact the laws that they are required to enforce, nor do they dispose of the criminals they arrest. The police are only one part of the criminal justice system; the criminal justice system is only one part of the government; and the government is only one part of society. Insofar as crime is a social phenomenon, crime prevention is the responsibility of every part of society. The criminal process is limited to case by case operations, one criminal or one crime at a time. Some "handcuffs" on the police are irremovable. It is with that plain fact in mind that this volume, whose purpose is to propose ways in which the police can increase their effectiveness, must be read.

The volume also should be read with an understanding of what the police actually do to combat crime. This is a subject that is often neglected, with the result that public expectations of the police and prescriptions for improving police work are unrealistic. The heart of the police effort against crime is patrol—moving on foot or by vehicle around an assigned area, stopping to check buildings, to survey possible incidents, to question suspicious persons, or simply to converse with residents who may provide intelligence as to occurrences in the neighborhood.

The object of patrol is to disperse policemen in a way that will eliminate or reduce the opportunity for misconduct and to increase the likelihood that a criminal will be apprehended while he is committing a crime or immediately thereafter. The strong likelihood of apprehension will presumably have a strong

deterrent effect on potential criminals. The fact of apprehension can lead to the rehabilitation of a criminal, or at least to his removal for a time from the opportunity to break the law.

When patrol fails to prevent a crime or apprehend a criminal, the police must resort to investigation. Some investigation is carried out by patrolmen, but the principal responsibility rests with detectives. Investigation aims at identifying offenders through questioning victims, suspects, witnesses and others, through confronting arrested suspects with victims or witnesses, through photographs, or, less frequently, through fingerprints or other laboratory analysis of evidence found at crime scenes.

When the number of square blocks—or in some cases square miles—of city each policeman must patrol is considered in conjunction with the many ways, times, and places that crimes occur, the severe limitations upon the effectiveness of patrol and investigation are placed in dramatic focus. Such consideration will also suggest why crime rates often appear to fluctuate with relatively little correlation to what the police do.

The rate of apprehension of offenders in property crimes is extremely low—approximately 22 percent of those reported. The police have greater success with violent crimes—approximately 59 percent of those reported. In large part this is because more victims of violent crimes know or can identify their assailants. The ability of a victim or witness to identify the criminal is the factor responsible for solving a large percentage of the crimes that are solved.

To say that the police have a limited ability to prevent crime is not to criticize the police. The police, more than anybody, are frustrated by the wide gap between the task they are expected to perform and the methods at their disposal to perform it.

Seen from the perspective of history, the anomalies of regarding the police as solely responsible for crime control become evident. In the preindustrial age, village societies were closely integrated. Everyone knew everyone else's affairs and character; the laws and rules of society were generally familiar and were identical with the moral and ethical precepts taught by parents, schoolmasters, and the church. If not by the clergy and the village elders, the peace was kept, more or less informally, by law magistrates (usually local squires) and constables. These in the beginning were merely the magistrates' agents, literally "citizens on duty"—the able-bodied men of the community serving in turn.(1) Not until the 19th century did policing even have a distinct name.(2) Until then it would have been largely impossible to distinguish between informal peacekeeping and the formal system of law enforcement and criminal justice. The real outlaws—murderers, highwaymen, and their ilk—were handled mostly by the military when normal procedures for crime control were unsuccessful.

The greatly increased complexities of society and its laws today only make more important the kind of unofficial peacekeeping that Jane Jacobs has called the "intricate, almost unconscious, network of voluntary controls and standards among the people themselves."(3) In communities and neighborhoods where the other instrumentalities of society whose success bears directly on controlling crime have failed—families, schools, job markets, and welfare agencies—the police must handle an enormously increased volume of offenses, both serious and petty.

It is when it attempts to solve problems that arise from the community's social and economic failures that policing is least effective and most frustrating. For, while charged with deterrence, the police can do little to prevent crime in the broader sense of removing its causes. On the whole, they must accept society as it is—a society in which parents fail to raise their children as law-abiding citizens, in which schools fail to educate them to assume adult roles, and in which the economy is not geared to provide them with jobs. The most eminent of modern police administrators, August Vollmer, once said: "I have spent my life enforcing the laws. It is a stupid procedure and has not, nor will it ever solve the problem unless it is supplemented by preventive measures."(4)

The difficulties and inherent limitations of law enforcement are seldom appreciated by the public when it considers what the police can do, and reacts to what they do. Americans are a people used to entrusting the solution of their social ills to specialists, and to expecting results from the institutions those specialists devise. They have entrusted the problems of crime to the police, forgetting that they still operate with many of the limitations of constables of years past, even though today's citizens are no longer villagers.

The adjustment of conceptions of what can be

expected of the police is particularly difficult for people who are themselves law-abiding and who live in a law-abiding community. For them the phenomenon of crime seems far simpler than in fact it is. The voluntary controls of society work well for them and, since they have no desire to violate the criminal law, their supposition is that crime must be a choice between right and wrong for all men, and that more effective policing alone can determine this choice. Thus public concern about crime is typically translated into demands for more law enforcement, and often into making the police scapegoats for a crime problem they did not create and do not have the resources to solve.

No one, of course, is more sensitive to demands for more law enforcement than the police themselves. They see the menace of crime most directly, and their lives are dominated by their professional task. In addition, they have encouraged and share the idea that they are inherently more capable of controlling crime than analysis has thus far shown them to be. In part, this conception derives from the efforts of modern police leaders to secure support and respect as professionals with a specialized ability capable of effective exercise apart from political control. And naturally enough the police, like men in all occupations, tend to view problems in terms of their own function and to have particular faith in their own skills to resolve them.

The police are fully aware of many of the restrictions that are placed upon them, and protest some of them. Their reaction is intensified by a general and often justified feeling that the very public that is responsible for these limits on effectiveness at the same time demands greater success in law enforcement. A leading police training text, for example, states:(5)

Many police executives are frustrated today, because of the heavy pressures brought to bear upon them and their agencies to eliminate crime and delinquency hazards and to successfully solve cases. . . . Instead of pressuring legislative representatives for changes in the law, many citizens pressure their chief of police. And much such pressure is without knowledge of the law and its limitations, its restrictive interpretations by the courts, and its scope.

In its more extreme forms this reaction has had serious consequences. It has intensified police sensitivity to criticism and to contacts or controls that imply criticism. It has evoked frequent suspicion and bitterness toward those sections of the public seen as responsible for police limitations: politicians, courts, civil libertarians. In combination this sensitivity, suspicion, and bitterness has become in itself a significant limitation on police effectiveness.

*   *   *

History of the Police

The face of America has changed since colonial days from a collection of predominantly rural and independent jurisdictions to an industrialized urban nation. Yet in several respects law enforcement has not kept pace with this change. As America has grown and policing has become correspondingly complex, the existing law enforcement system has not always been altered to meet the needs of a mechanized and metropolitan society.

Over the years, the proliferation of independent and, for the most part, local policing units has led to an overlapping of responsibilities and a duplication of effort, causing problems in police administration and in the coordination of efforts to apprehend criminals. America is a nation of small, decentralized police forces.

Other problems have plagued the police over the years. Forces have lacked an adequate number of sufficiently qualified personnel. Unattractive salaries and working conditions, and a general lack of public support have hindered police development. And the need for harmonious police-community relations has been a persistent problem, one which, unfortunately, has not been widely recognized until recently. Community relations problems are nothing new; they have existed since American cities were divided into subsocieties by virtue of different ensuing waves of immigrants from western, and later eastern, Europe, who started settling in urban centers before the turn of this century.

To understand better the prevailing problems that police agencies face today, it is helpful to examine their development in England as well as in the United States; for there are many weaknesses in the existing system that stem from practices developed in the rural colonies and from the colonial philosophy of law enforcement.

Early History of English Law Enforcement

France and other continental countries maintained professional police forces of a sort as early as the 17th century. But England, fearing the oppression these forces had brought about in many of the continental countries, did not begin to create police organizations until the 19th century. Moreover, England, in its early history, did not maintain a permanent army of paid soldiers that could enforce criminal laws when not engaged in guarding the country's borders against invaders. The cost of developing a force specifically for peace-keeping duties was believed to be too high for the royal purse. Private citizens could do the job cheaper, if given a few shillings reward for arrests. This simple law enforcement expedient, which had begun with Alfred the Great (870–901), can be recognized as the forerunner of American police agencies.

Primarily, the system encouraged mutual responsibility among local citizens' associations, which were pledged to maintain law and order;(6) it was called the "mutual pledge" system. Every man was responsible not only for his own actions but also for those of his neighbors. It was each citizen's duty to raise the "hue and cry" when a crime was committed, to collect his neighbors and to pursue a criminal who had fled from the district. If such a group failed to apprehend a lawbreaker, all were fined by the Crown.

The Crown placed this mutual responsibility for group police action upon 10-family groups. Each of these was known as a "tithing." From the tithing, there subsequently developed the "hundred" comprised of 10 tithings. From this developed the first real police officer—the constable. He was appointed by a local nobleman and placed in charge of the weapons and equipment of each hundred.

Soon, the "hundreds" were grouped to form a "shire," a geographical area equivalent to a county. A "Shire-reeve"—lineal antecedent of tens of thousands of sheriffs to come—thus came into being, appointed by the Crown to supervise each county. The constable's breadth of authority remained limited to his original "hundred." The shire-reeve was responsible to the local nobleman in ensuring that the citizens enforced the law effectively. From his original supervisory post, the sheriff soon branched out to take part in the pursuit and apprehension of lawbreakers.

It was during the reign of Edward I (1272–1307) that the first official police forces were created in the large towns of England. These were called the "watch and ward," and were responsible for protecting property against fire, guarding the gates, and arresting those who committed offenses between sunset and daybreak. At the same time the constable became the primary law enforcement officer in all towns throughout England.

In 1326, to supplement the "shire-reeve" mutual pledge system, Edward II created the office of justice of the peace. The justices, originally noblemen, were appointed by the Crown to assist the sheriff in policing the county. This led in time to their taking on local judicial functions, in line with the primary duty of keeping the peace in their separate jurisdictions.

The constable, who retained the responsibility of serving as a major official within the pledge system, meanwhile gained in importance. He became an assistant to the justice, responsible for supervising the night watchmen, inquiring into offenses, serving summonses, executing warrants, and taking charge of prisoners. It was here that the formal separation between judge and police officer developed.

As law enforcement increasingly became the responsibility of the central government in 14th century England, the justice, as the appointee of the King, exercised a greater degree of control over the locally appointed constables. By the end of the century the constable no longer functioned independently as an official of the pledge system. Rather, he was obliged to serve the justice. This essentially set the justice-constable patterns for the next 500 years. The "justice [remained] the superior, the constable the inferior, conservator of the peace"(7) until the second quarter of the 19th century.

Meanwhile, over these years, the local pledge system continued to decline. Community support languished, and with considerable reason.

What was everybody's business became nobody's duty, and the citizens who were bound by law to take their turn at police work gradually evaded personal police service by paying others to do the work for them. In theory constables were appointed annually, but in fact their work was done by deputies or substitutes who so acted year after year, being paid to do so by the constables. These early paid police officers did not rank high in popular estimation as indicated in contemporary references. They were usually ill-paid and ignorant men, often too old to be in any sense efficient.

But as the local pledge system was declining, innovations in policing were cropping up in the emerging cities of the 17th and 18th centuries. Those first law enforcement officers were increasingly assisted by a paid night-watch force. Although these nominally were responsible for guarding the cities against thieves and vandals, apparently they were not effective. Reportedly they did little more than roam the streets at night, periodically calling out the condition of the weather, the hour, and the fact that "all was well."

Industrialization in England

While England remained essentially a rural country, the dominance of the justice of the peace in law enforcement machinery aroused little formal opposition. But with the advent of the Industrial Revolution at the end of the 1700's families by the thousands began traveling to factory towns to find work. Inevitably, as the cities grew, established patterns of life changed and unprecedented social disorder resulted. Law enforcement became a much more complex enterprise.

Government and citizens alike responded to this need for better law enforcement. A number of fragmented civic associations, such as the Bow Street Horse and Foot Patrol, were formed to police the streets and highways leading out of London; and the Government passed statutes creating public offices, later to be known as police offices. Each of these housed three paid justices of the peace, who were authorized to employ six paid constables. These new posts thus helped to centralize law enforcement operations within a small area.

By the beginning of the 19th century nine police offices had been established within the metropolitan area of London, but there was little apparent effort to coordinate their independent law enforcement activities. This was reportedly due to the fact that each office refused to communicate with another for fear that the other might take credit for detecting and apprehending an offender.

In London especially, these weaknesses combined to make the police forces seemingly powerless to combat crime. Highwaymen on the road, thieves lurking in the cities, daily bank robberies, juvenile delinquency—all presented major law enforcement problems. However, out of this difficult situation emerged a unique remedy to discourage thieves from attacking citizens; in the early 1800's gaslights were introduced on the streets of London.

Many of the experiments in law enforcement before 1820 failed "because no scheme could reconcile the freedom of action of individuals with the security of person and property." In 1822, Sir Robert Peel, England's new Home Secretary, contended that, while better policing could not eliminate crime, the poor quality of police contributed to social disorder. Seven years later he introduced and guided through Parliament an "Act for Improving the Police In and Near the Metropolis." This led to the first organized British metropolitan police force. Structured along the lines of a military unit, the force of 1,000 was the first one to wear a definite uniform. The men were commanded by two magistrates, later called commissioners, who were given administrative but not judicial duties. Ultimately, the responsibility for equipping, paying, maintaining, and to a certain degree supervising the "bobbies," as they later became known, was vested in the Home Secretary. Because he was made accountable to the Parliament "for the exercise of his authority over the Metropolitan police, it could [thus] be said that the new force was under the ultimate control of a democratically elected Parliament."

Availability of competent manpower, then as today, became an immediate problem. It was difficult to recruit suitable men to serve in the "new police," for the salaries were poor and the commissioners selective. And there were other harassments. Parliament objected to appropriating Government funds to maintain a police force. The radicals were afraid of tyranny. The aristocracy, though willing to accept the protection of such a force, was disgruntled because the commissioners refused to abide by the traditional rules of patronage in making appointments.

Nevertheless, the London metropolitan police proved so effective in suppressing crime and apprehending criminals that within 5 years the provinces, which were experiencing increasing crime problems and violent riots, asked London for policing help.(8) Shortly after, Parliament enacted a series of police reform bills. Among them, one empowered justices of the peace in 1839 to establish police forces in the counties; and in 1856 another required every borough and county to have a police force.

As regular police forces developed, the justices of the peace voluntarily relinquished their law enforcement duties and confined themselves to deciding questions of law. Before this change occurred, the police had served as the agent of the powerful justices and had consequently used justices' authority to carry on investigation of those in custody. When the justices relinquished their law enforcement powers, the legislature gave no consideration as to what, if any, investigative responsibilities should be transferred to the police. As a result, the statutes for law enforcement officers that remain on the books today contain little recognition of the broad discretion that police continue to exercise.(9)

Law Enforcement in the American Colonies

American colonists in the 17th and 18th centuries naturally brought to America the law enforcement structure with which they were familiar in England. The transfer of the offices of constable and sheriff to rural American areas—which included most colonial territory—was accomplished with little change in structure of the offices. Drawing upon the pattern of the mutual pledge system, the constable was made responsible for law enforcement in towns, while the sheriff took charge of policing the counties. The Crown-appointed Governors bestowed these offices on large landowners who were loyal to the King. After the revolution, sheriffs and constables tended to be selected by popular elections, patronage then being on the wane.

In many colonial cities the colonists adopted the British constabulary-nightwatch system. As early as 1636 Boston had nightwatchmen, in addition to a military guard. New York and Philadelphia soon developed a similar nightwatch system. The New York nightwatchmen were known as the "Rattlewatch," because they carried rattles on their rounds to remind those who needed reminding of their watchful presence.

Urbanization in the United States

As American towns grew in size and population during the first half of the 19th century, the constable was unable to cope with the increasing disorder. As in England years before, lawlessness became more prevalent:(10)

> New York City was alleged to be the most crime-ridden city in the world, with Philadelphia, Baltimore and Cincinnati not far behind. . . . Gangs of youthful rowdies in the larger cities

... threatened to destroy the American reputation for respect for law. ... Before their boisterous demonstrations the crude police forces of the day were often helpless.

Again, as in England, many American cities began to develop organized metropolitan police forces of their own, Philadelphia was one of the first. In 1833 a wealthy philanthropist left a will that provided for the financing of a competent police force in Philadelphia. Stimulated by this contribution, the city government passed an ordinance providing for a 24-man police force to work by day and 120 nightwatchmen. The force was unfortunately shortlived, for the ordinance was repealed less than 2 years later.

In 1838, Boston created a day police force to supplement the nightwatch, and other cities soon followed its lead. Crime, cities were finding, was no respecter of daylight. There were certain inherent difficulties, however, in these early two-shift police systems. Keen rivalries existed between the day and night shifts, and separate administrations supervised each shift. Recognizing the evils of separate police forces, the New York Legislature passed a law in 1844 that authorized creating the first unified day and night police, thus abolishing its nightwatch system. Ten years later Boston consolidated its nightwatch with the day police.

Following the New York model, other cities developed their own unified police forces during the next decade. By the 1870's the Nation's largest cities had full-time police forces. And by the early 1900's there were few cities of consequence without such unified forces. These forces gradually came under the control of a chief or commissioner, often appointed by the mayor, sometimes with the consent of the city council and sometimes elected by the people.

These first formal police forces in American cities were faced with many of the problems that police continue to confront today. Police officers became the objects of disrespect. The need for larger staffs required the police to compromise personnel standards in order to fill the ranks. And police salaries were among the lowest in local government service, a factor which precluded attracting sufficient numbers of high standard candidates. It is small wonder that the police were not respected, were not notably successful, and were not known for their vitality and progressiveness. Moreover, the police mission in the mid-1800's precluded any brilliance:(11)

> The aim of the police departments was merely to keep a city superficially clean and to keep everything quiet that [was] likely to arouse public [ire].

Many of the problems that troubled these first organized metropolitan police forces can perhaps be traced to a single root—political control. As one authority has explained:(12)

> Rotation in office enjoyed so much popular favor that police posts of both high and low degree were constantly changing hands, with political fixers determining the price and conditions of each change ... The whole police question simply churned about in the public mind and eventually became identified with the corruption and degradation of the city politics and local governments of the period.

In an attempt to alleviate these problems, responsible leaders created police administrative boards to replace the control exercised over police affairs by mayors or city councils. These boards were given the responsibility of appointing police administrators and managing police affairs. Unfortunately, this attempt to cure political meddling was unsuccessful, perhaps because the judges, lawyers, and local businessmen who comprised the administrative boards were inexpert in dealing with the broad problems of the police.

Another attempt was made at police reform during the close of the 19th century. Noting that poor policing tended to occur mainly in urban areas, the State legislatures, which were dominated by rural legislators, required that police administrators be appointed by authority of the State. Thus State control became an alternative to local control of law enforcement. This move brought little success, for many problems had not been anticipated:(13)

> For one thing, the theory of state control ... was not uniformly applied. It was primarily directed at the larger cities, by legislatures seeking to [perpetuate] rural domination in public affairs.

In spite of increased state control, the large city continued to pay for its police service, and police costs rose. One reason was that police boards were not even indirectly responsible to the local taxpaying public which they served. In cases where the State and city governments were not allied politically, friction increased. It increased further when the State-appointed administrator instituted policy out of harmony with the views of the majority of the city population. It was not until the first decades of the 20th century that cities regained control of police forces in all but a few cases.(14)

After these sincere attempts at reform during the last half of the 19th century, police forces grew in size and expanded in function. However, there was very little analysis of the changes in society that made expansion necessary nor of the effect such changes would work upon the role of the police. Civil service proved helpful, spreading to local police agencies and alleviating some of the more serious problems of political interference. The concept of merit employment, which some reformers had been proposing, was embraced by some forces.

One of the most notable police advancements of the 1900's was the advent of police training schools, even though on a somewhat modest basis. In the early 1900's, the new policeman learned chiefly in the school of experience:(15)

> . . . Thus, for the most part the average American city depends almost entirely for the training of its police recruits upon such casual instruction as older officials may be able and willing to give.

In numerous areas, however, it was not until the 1940's and notably in the 1950's that police departments established and, in many cases, greatly expanded their recruit training programs.

State and Federal Law Enforcement Agencies

Although a State police force, known as the "Texas Rangers," was organized in 1835 to supplement Texas' military forces, modern State police organizations did not emerge until the turn of the century. In 1905, the Governor of Pennsylvania, in the absence of an effective sheriff-constable system, created the first State force. Its initial purpose was to cope with a public dispute between labor and management. Soon such continuing factors as the inadequacy of local policing by constables and sheriffs and the inability or unwillingness of city

police forces to pursue lawbreakers beyond their jurisdictional limits convinced State legislatures of the need for Statewide police forces.

The majority of State departments were established shortly after World War I to deal with the increasing problem of auto traffic and the accompanying wave of car thefts. Today all States except Hawaii have some form of State law enforcement body. While some State agencies are restricted to the functions of enforcing traffic laws and protecting life and property on the highways, others have been given general policing authority in criminal matters throughout the State.

The role of the Federal Government in law enforcement has developed in a sporadic and highly specialized manner. Federal law enforcement actually started in 1789, when the Revenue Cutter Service was established to help prevent smuggling. In 1836, Congress authorized the Postmaster General to pay salaries to agents who would investigate infringements involving postal matters. Among the more important law enforcement responsibilities later recognized by Congress were internal revenue investigation and narcotics control. Congress authorized a force of 25 detectives in 1868 and increased the number in 1915. In 1924, J. Edgar Hoover organized the Federal Bureau of Investigation in the Justice Department.

With the expansion of interstate movement of people and goods, and Federal involvement in all aspects of life, the responsibilities of Federal agencies have increased significantly within the last few years. These Federal agencies are responsible to departments of the National Government. The Treasury Department's Secret Service is, for example, charged with the protection of the President and with investigating counterfeiting and forgery of Federal documents. Civilian departmental agencies, with the sole exception of the FBI, function under civil service regulations.(16)

The manpower and jurisdiction of the FBI have increased greatly since its establishment. Some of the statutes that have been responsible for this expansion are the National Stolen Property Act, the Federal Kidnapping Act, the Hobbs Act (extortion), the Fugitive Felon Act, the White-Slave Act, the National Bank Robbery Act, Federal interstate gambling laws, and the Dyer Act. The last brings within the FBI's jurisdiction automobiles stolen and taken across the border of a State. Recent passage of strong Federal legislation has enhanced the FBI's role in the enforcement of civil rights.

Modernization

Serious study of police reform in America began in 1919. The problems exposed then and those faced by police agencies today are similar in many respects. For example, in 1931 the Wickersham Commission noted that the average police chief's term of office was too short, and that his responsibility to political officials made his position insecure. The Commission also felt that there was a lack of competent, efficient, and honest patrolmen. It said that no intensive effort was being made to educate, train, and discipline prospective officers, or to eliminate those shown to be incompetent. The Wickersham Commission found that with perhaps two exceptions, police forces in cities above 300,000 population had neither an adequate communications system nor the equipment necessary to enforce the law effectively. It said that the police task was made much more difficult by the excessively rapid growth of our cities in the past half century, and by the tendency of different ethnic groups to retain their language and customs in large cities. Finally, the Commission said, there were too many duties cast upon each officer and patrolman.(17) The Missouri Crime Commission reported that in a typical American city the police were expected to be familiar with and enforce 30,000 Federal, State, or local enactments.(18)

Despite the complexity of these problems, many hopeful improvements have occurred in the past few decades. Some cities, counties, and States have taken great strides in streamlining their operations through reorganization and increased use of technology and the use of modern techniques to detect and apprehend criminal offenders. Others are on the threshold of modernization. But many departments remain static. And it is these that obviously constitute a burden on the machinery of justice and are detrimental to the process of achieving a truly professional public service.

Profile of the Police

To understand many of the analyses and recommendations in this volume, it is helpful to have as background information a profile of law enforcement organization, manpower, and expenditures in the United States today. The statistical data, which are summarized in Table 1, are explained in this section. Much of the same information will be expanded in later chapters as different aspects of policing are discussed in greater depth.

Number of Police Agencies, Distribution, and Lines of Responsibility

There are today in the United States 40,000 separate agencies responsible for enforcing laws on the Federal, State, and local levels of government. But law enforcement agencies are not evenly distributed among these three levels, for the function is primarily a concern of local government. There are only 50 law enforcement agencies on the Federal level of government and 200 departments on the State level. The remaining 39,750 agencies are dispersed throughout the many counties, cities, towns, and villages that form our local governments.

If we look at a breakdown of the numbers of local agencies, it is again apparent that distribution tends toward the local unit, for only 3,050 agencies are located in counties and 3,700 in cities. The great majority of police forces—33,000—are distributed throughout boroughs, towns, and villages.

Because the concept of local autonomy in enforcing laws has prevailed throughout our history and because the many local policing agencies have held firmly to their traditional jurisdictional authority, responsibility for maintaining public order is today extremely decentralized. This decentralization is further accentuated by the fact that a police officer's responsibility for enforcing law is usually confined to a single jurisdiction.

The problems caused by decentralization are many, particularly where a number of police agencies exist within a radius of a few miles. Jurisdictional barriers are often erected between these agencies; maintaining adequate communication is difficult, and obtaining assistance from several adjacent agencies when needed becomes a complex operation.

The problems of decentralization have been overcome in part either by creating county, State, and Federal agencies or by increasing the responsibility of existing ones. These agencies have tended in many areas of the country to supplement and coordinate the work of local police agencies.

Table 1.   A Profile of Federal, State, and Local Law Enforcement Agencies

	Agencies	Full-time personnel				Dollars spent					Percent average annual increase, 1955–65
	Number in 1965	Number in 1955	Number in 1965	Percent of total in 1965	Percent average annual increase, 1955–65	Total in millions, 1955	Total in millions, 1965	Per capita expenditure, 1955	Per capita expenditure, 1965	Percent of dollars, 1965	
Federal	50	22,000	23,000	6.2	0.5	129	220	$0.78	$1.26	8.5	7.7
State	200	22,000	40,000	10.8	8.2	139	315	.84	1.79	12.2	12.7
Local	39,750	229,000	308,000	83.0	3.4	1,091	2,051	6.60	11.25	79.3	8.8
Total	40,000	273,000	371,000	100.0	3.6	1,359	2,586	8.22	14.30	100.0	9.0
Percent increase		35.9					90.3		72.7		

SOURCE: Memorandum from Michael S. March, Assistant Chief of Education, Manpower and Science Division, U.S. Bureau of the Budget, May 11, 1966.

The 50 Federal law enforcement agencies have directed their efforts mainly to enforcing national laws dealing with interstate violations or with such specific Federal violations as theft of Federal property, postal violations, and counterfeiting U.S. currency, or with enforcing such Federal statutes as those that control the import and sale of narcotics. The duties and activities of these agencies have been defined by Congress through a series of statutes passed over a number of years. It is because of America's strong tradition of local autonomy that the Federal Government has not become extensively involved in local law enforcement.

The States have the primary constitutional responsibility for maintaining order within their boundaries, and all of the States have exercised this authority by enacting broad criminal codes. But because local police departments have traditionally maintained law and order within their jurisdictions and because thousands of violations occur daily in all parts of States, the responsibility for preventing crime has been delegated by States to the local governments in which the violations occur.

Through legislation each State has defined the scope of police responsibility among its many agencies—the State police; county sheriffs; and city, township, borough, and village police. The States have not only divided the responsibility for enforcing law among these various agencies, but they have also determined the extent to which each agency may exercise its power. In addition, State legislatures have passed statutes setting the bounds of civil and criminal liability for police officers who overstep their authority.

On the State level of government the State police are the major law enforcement agents. Their primary responsibility is to enforce some State laws, to patrol highways, and to regulate traffic. They also provide services as needed to local police such as maintaining a State system of criminal identification, conducting police training programs or providing a State communications system. Some States, in addition, have created specialized agencies to enforce particular regulations, such as conservation or alcoholic beverage control laws.

At the county level of government, the sheriff is the primary law enforcement officer. He is an elected official, whose term usually spans from two to four years and whose jurisdictional responsibility primarily covers unincorporated portions of each county. His functions include keeping the peace, executing civil and criminal process, patrolling the area, maintaining the county jail, preserving order in county courts, and enforcing court orders. The sheriff as a rule performs only restricted law enforcement functions in incorporated areas within a county, and then usually only when the city requests his participation in such activities as patrol or investigation.

In suburban townships and municipalities, police officers are vested with broad law enforcement authority and perform functions similar to those of city police. In rural areas, where most of the 18,000 townships of America are located, police officers usually confine their activities to a limited range of ministerial and traffic duties. In the absence of a local police agency, the local unit of government relies upon the services of the sheriff or State police for law enforcement assistance. These duties may include patrol, investigation, or enforcement of traffic regulations.

Two additional types of police agencies operate on the local level of government. One is the police special service district, created to protect residents or industry in unincorporated portions of urban areas. But few of the Nation's 19,000 special service districts actually provide police service. Most have been created to provide fire protection, street lighting, drainage, and sewage treatment.(19) The second type is the force whose mission is highly specialized. Such forces may be established to protect parks, housing developments, ports, toll roads, and subways. But neither these forces nor police in special service districts have had significant impact on American police administration.

Personnel

There were 420,000 full- and part-time law enforcement officers and civilians employed by police agencies in 1966. The majority of these persons— 371,000—were full-time employees, and 11 percent, or approximately 46,000, were civilians. In 1965 there was an overall ratio of 1.7 police officers to every 1,000 persons.(20) (Tables 2 and 3 show police manpower and population ratios.) The total number of police employees at the local level of government has been increasing at an average annual rate of 3.5 percent over the past 8 years.(21)

Twenty-three thousand of the full-time officers serve at the Federal level of government, and 40,000

at the State level. The remaining 308,000 officers—or 83 percent of the total—are divided among the many county and local police agencies.

Table 2. *Full-Time Local Police Manpower per 1,000 Population*

	Police officers and civilians	Police officers only	Range in different geographical divisions
Cities over 250,000	2.6	2.3	1.5 to 4.1
Cities of—			
100,000 to 250,000	1.7	1.5	1.3 to 2.5
50,000 to 100,000	1.5	1.4	1.2 to 1.9
25,000 to 50,000	1.5	1.3	1.1 to 1.7
10,000 to 25,000	1.4	1.3	1.2 to 1.7
Cities under 10,000	1.4	1.3	1.2 to 1.9
Total	1.9	1.7	1.1 to 4.1

SOURCE: Federal Bureau of Investigation, U.S. Department of Justice, *Uniform Crime Reports, 1965* (Washington, D.C.: U.S. Government Printing Office, 1966), pp. 148–151. These data include civilian employees.

Of the 308,000 police officers serving on the county and local level of government, about 197,500 enforcement officers are distributed among the 39,695 agencies with jurisdictions in county or local areas. These include 3,645 cities of under 250,000 population; 3,050 counties; and 33,000 townships, boroughs, villages, and special districts. The remaining 110,500 police personnel are divided among the 55 agencies enforcing law in the 55 cities of the United States of a population over 250,000.(22)

Table 3. *Full-Time Local Police Manpower by Character of Jurisdiction*

	Population served	Number of agencies reporting	Number of police employees	Average number of employees per 1,000 population
City police	109,633,000	3,613	212,883	1.9
Suburban police[a]	40,251,000	1,770	55,040	1.4
County sheriffs	32,357,000	1,154	32,159	1.0

[a] Agencies and population represented in suburban area are also included in other city groups.

SOURCE: Federal Bureau of Investigation, U.S. Department of Justice, *Uniform Crime Reports, 1965* (Washington, D.C.: U.S. Government Printing Office, 1966), p. 149.

The number of personnel in local police agencies also varies to a considerable degree among locales. On the county level of government the 3,050 sheriff's offices range from a one-man force in Putnam County, Ga., to a 5,515-man force in Los Angeles County, Calif. The average number of police officers serving on the county level is small; only about 200 counties of the 3,050 in the United States have a sheriff's staff of more than 50 officers.(23)

In the local police forces below the county level of government the size of a force may vary from the 1- to 5-man force in the many boroughs and towns of the United States to the mammoth 28,671-member New York City police force.

Even within the radius of a major city, police forces have extraordinary range in size. Chicago, for example, has a total force of 11,745 civilians and officers. Within Cook and DuPage Counties, which encompass much of metropolitan Chicago, there are only 2,187 full-time officers enforcing the law among the 119 municipalities (other than Chicago) located there. One community in Cook County controls crime with only 1 full-time officer, assisted by a part-time complement of 26 people.(24)

Availability of Manpower

Due to the great difficulties of attracting capable personnel, almost all large police departments in the United States are substantially below their authorized strength. In 1965 a survey of about 300 police departments—including nearly all of the large city departments—showed that 65.5 percent of the forces polled were below authorized strength. The average force was 5 percent below its quota; the average large-city force was 10 percent below standard capacity.(25)

The difficulties in filling quotas are increased by a low rate of eligibility among police applicants. In 1961 a survey indicated that the acceptance rate dropped from 29.9 percent in 1956 to 22.3 percent in 1961. (See Table 4.) An even further rate reduction is suggested by recent experiences in two large metropolitan areas. In 1965, Washington, D.C., was able to hire less than 10 percent of people applying.(26) Los Angeles reported that only 2.8 percent of police applicants were accepted, and 4.9 percent of applicants for the county sheriff's police were hired.(27)

Manpower problems are also caused by turnover in personnel. Each year an average of 5 percent of a police department's force leaves the police service. In the next 10 years, as the mass of police officers recruited just after World War II reaches retirement age, many departments will face severe recruiting needs. For example, 41 percent of the existing Los Angeles Police Department(28) and 10 percent of the 83-man force in Joliet, Ill., will be eligible to retire in 1967.(29)

The present need for manpower and the anticipated rate of turnover both indicate that over 50,000 new police officers will be required in 1967 alone.

Table 4. *Applicant Success Rates—Regional Replies—1956, 1961*

Region	1956			1961		
	Applicants	Eligible	A.S.R., percent	Applicants	Eligible	A.S.R., percent
New England	2,934	992	33.8	2,107	700	33.2
Middle Atlantic	22,094	7,707	34.8	19,967	5,863	29.4
East North Central	7,111	1,211	17.0	5,939	879	14.8
West North Central	1,538	522	33.9	2,641	577	21.8
South Atlantic	5,518	1,580	28.6	4,851	1,125	23.2
East South Central	973	427	43.9	1,014	480	47.3
West South Central	1,881	689	36.6	3,066	764	24.9
Mountain	1,077	344	31.9	3,016	622	20.6
Pacific	7,887	1,795	22.8	13,018	1,420	10.9
Total	51,013	15,267	29.9	55,619	12,430	22.3

SOURCE: George W. O'Connor, *Survey of Selection Methods* (Washington, D.C.: International Association of Chiefs of Police, 1962), table 33.

Characteristics of Personnel

In 1960 the census showed that the median age of male local law enforcement personnel was as follows:(30)

	Years of age
Police and detectives	37.6
Marshals and constables	50.5
Sheriffs and bailiffs	45.4

A cross section of the age distribution of male and female police officers and detectives is seen in Table 5.

The median educational level of police officers has risen slightly in this decade. Figures released by the U.S. Department of Health, Education, and Welfare set the median at 12.4 years of education in 1966, a slight rise from the 12.2 level reported by the Bureau of the Census in 1960. A recent national survey of 6,300 police officers indicated that approximately 24 percent of patrolmen and 31 percent of top-level department administrators had attended college.(31)

Police personnel are predominately Caucasian. The 1960 census showed that only 3.5 percent of law enforcement employees throughout the Nation were non-Caucasian. A study by the Civil Rights Commission in 1962 revealed that only one-fifth of 1 percent of State police officers were Negro. Of the 36 Negroes serving as State police officers in the Nation, 24 were employed in Illinois.(32) The same Civil Rights Commission survey polled 271 sheriffs' offices and found that in 1962 there was a Negro-white employment ratio of 1 to 20 on the county level of government.

Some cities have recently recruited a substantial number of Negro officers. In Washington, D.C., for example, Negro employment in the past few years has increased from 14 to 19 percent of the police force, and in Chicago it has increased from 9 to 20 percent of the force.(33) And a notable event occurred in the South in January, 1967, when Lucius D. Amerson was sworn in as sheriff of Macon County, Ala. Amerson became the first Negro sheriff in a Southern jurisdiction since Reconstruction.

Employment Requirements

More than 70 percent of the Nation's police departments have set the high school diploma level as an educational requirement for employment. About one-fourth of the agencies require no more than some degree of elementary education.(34) Most large cities and counties maintain a high school education or its equivalent as a minimum standard, and at least 22 departments have raised their standard to require college credit. But 21 of these are located in California.

Physical requirements for police employment are rigid. The minimum standards usually require that a recruit be between the ages of 21 and 35, have nearly perfect vision, weigh between 150 and 250 pounds, and be at least 5 feet 8 or 9 inches tall. Many departments only recruit people who have lived within the police jurisdiction for a given period of time before employment. The requirement for pre-service residency may vary from 6 months to 5 years. In 1965 more than two-thirds of local law enforcement officers throughout the United States were born in the State in which they were employed.

Almost all local police departments require that an applicant take written intelligence tests. But these tests are in no way standard, and many are ineffective for purposes of measuring educational achievement or personal capability for service. In 1961 a survey showed that only about 15 percent of the local

Table 5. Employed Public Police and Detective Personnel, by Age and Sex, 1960

Age range	15–17	18–19	20–24	25–29	30–34	35–44	45–54	55–59	60–64	65–69	70–74	75+	Total
Number of employees:													
Male	41	163	12,381	36,733	46,117	71,389	38,633	10,518	6,805	2,840	1,130	728	227,478
Female	0	40	364	695	881	2,077	1,179	221	60	19	20	0	5,556
Total	41	203	12,745	37,428	46,998	73,466	39,812	10,739	6,865	2,859	1,150	728	233,034

Source: U.S. Department of Commerce, Bureau of the Census, *U.S. Census of Population: 1960. Subject Reports. Occupational Characteristics*, Final Report PC(2)–7A (Washington, D.C.: U.S. Government Printing Office, 1963), pp. 79, 89.

agencies screened their candidates for emotional fitness as a routine procedure. The National League of Cities, which sampled police departments in 1965, indicated that only 27 percent of the agencies responding conducted some kind of psychiatric evaluation of applicants.

Police Compensation

In the past 30 years, police salaries have risen, and the number of hours worked in a week have been reduced. The 40-hour week is now standard in the majority of agencies. In small communities median salaries for patrolmen have risen from a figure of approximately $1,600 in 1937 to $4,600 in 1966. Maximum salaries rose from a 1938 figure of $1,800 to a 1966 figure of $5,500. In larger cities during these same years median beginning salaries for patrolmen, which had been $1,900, rose to $5,300. At the same time median maximum salaries rose from $2,400 to about $6,600. Compensation for chief administrators on a nationwide scale in 1938 ranged from $1,980 to $12,500 per annum.(35) In 1965 it had risen to a range of $3,600 to $35,000.

The above compensation figures do not include retirement, health, and other benefits accrued by public police employees.

Police Training

Classroom training for recruits is a relatively new concept in American policing. During the early years of this century, experience on the job was the most prevalent method for learning police skills. In the last few years, however, there has been a marked trend toward formal training programs for recruits. Of the 1,352 cities responding to a 1965 survey, 84 percent of city police forces reported formal, in-service training for police officers.

In 1965, a survey of law enforcement agencies showed that 4,000 agencies had appointed over 16,000 new police officers between July 1964 and June 1965.(36) The extent of the recruit training programs provided by these agencies is reflected in Table 6. A 1966 survey indicated that 97 percent of the 269 agencies responding had formal training programs that ranged from 1 to 12 weeks.

While almost 100 percent of the police departments in cities over 250,000 in population conduct their own recruit training programs, many of the smaller departments either have limited training programs or none at all. Some departments which do not have their own training programs use the training facilities of other local, State, and Federal agencies.

Expenditures for Law Enforcement

As Table 1 shows, law enforcement services cost the Nation slightly in excess of $2.5 billion in 1965. Approximately $2 billion of this sum was allocated to local law enforcement agencies. The remainder was divided between State agencies, which received $315 million, and Federal agencies, which obtained $220 million.

The bulk of money for law enforcement is spent on salaries. At the local level a police department may spend between 85 and 90 percent of its budget for this purpose.

Like other services, the cost of policing has increased in the past few years. For example, since 1955, numbers of police personnel have increased about 36 percent and expenditures have soared 90 percent. The cost increase is primarily linked to the expense of salaries and equipment. If the present average increase in expenditures of almost 10 percent per year continues, law enforcement costs will total almost $5.5 billion by 1975—more than double the 1965 figure.

Clearly, law enforcement is competing for tax dollars with a large number of other social services provided by all levels of government, for police agencies over the past 65 years have received a declining percentage of increasing total government expenditures. In 1902, for example, police agencies were allotted 4.9 percent of total governmental fiscal outlay. In 1962 this figure had declined to 3.5 percent.(37) The percentage of governmental allotments to law enforcement continues to decline even though the cost of enforcing the law has risen from $8.22 per capita in 1955 to $13.52 per capita in 1964.

The costs of policing are highest in large urban areas. As depicted in Table 7, the per capita policing costs in a city of over 1 million people are almost twice the cost of police activity in cities of between 200,000 and 300,000 population. Furthermore, the relative cost rate in the largest cities is more than triple that of cities having fewer than a 50,000 resident population.

The trend toward greater per capita expenditure in large urban areas is not a phenomenon unique to law enforcement. It demonstrates that the complex

Table 6.   *Percent of Departments Providing Recruit Training by Program Length, 1965*

Population group	Weeks of training									
	Less than 1	1	2	3	4	5	6	7	8	More than 8
Over 1,000,000	100.0	100.0	100.0	100.0	100.0	100.0	100.0	100.0	80.0	60.0
500,000 to 1,000,000	100.0	100.0	80.0	80.0	80.0	80.0	70.0	70.0	70.0	60.0
250,000 to 500,000	100.0	88.0	84.0	84.0	84.0	80.0	68.0	52.0	52.0	40.0
100,000 to 250,000	100.9	97.7	85.3	77.5	67.4	58.4	46.0	34.8	24.7	14.6
50,000 to 100,000	100.0	91.0	76.1	64.0	53.4	43.9	29.2	12.6	10.5	4.7
25,000 to 50,000	100.0	81.6	69.5	53.5	42.9	34.1	23.8	9.7	6.2	4.5
10,000 to 25,000	100.0	74.2	61.5	48.3	38.6	29.3	21.0	7.6	6.0	2.9
5,000 to 10,000	100.0	63.3	49.4	33.9	26.1	21.3	15.3	5.7	3.8	1.6
Under 5,000	100.0	48.6	39.0	25.3	18.0	14.7	9.6	2.3	1.5	1.0
Percent of agencies	100.0	68.3	56.0	42.0	33.4	27.7	19.0	8.1	6.0	3.5
Percent of total officers	100.0	87.6	76.6	69.0	63.1	57.9	49.5	41.0	34.7	25.9
Number of total officers	16,169	14,178	12,399	11,162	10,203	9,362	8,011	6,632	5,619	4,199

Source: International Association of Chiefs of Police, "Police Training," report submitted to the President's Commission on Law Enforcement and Administration of Justice, Washington, D.C., 1966.

way of life found in large, populated cities today costs more than the relatively simple life of small towns. As expenditures for education, public welfare, and public housing increase, so do police budgets. A comparison between governmental expenditures in urban and nonurban areas is presented in Table 8.

Special Urban Problems

The relative urban-rural crime rate has been the subject of much statistical study in recent years. As crime rates have increased throughout the United States, the rate in cities has continued to be substantially higher than in less populous areas. For example, the FBI's "Uniform Crime Reports, 1965" indicates that the rate for robbery in urban areas was 88.6 per hundred thousand population, as compared to a rate of 9.9 in rural areas. The urban rate of aggravated

assault was 127.7 per hundred thousand population as compared to a rural rate of 58.3—more than double. Similarly, the urban rate for burglary was 732.7 per hundred thousand population as compared to a rural rate of 308.4. And the urban rate for larceny of $50 and over was 492.0 per hundred thousand population, while the rural rate was 176.2.

In addition to the greater incidence of serious crime, urban police face rising rates for other types of crimes. The increase of petty crimes, for example, is much more severe in cities than in nonurban areas. The problem of drunkenness has caused a major drain on police time in large cities, while in the small town the problem is likely to be handled quickly and informally in the relatively few cases where it comes to police attention. Major metropolitan areas also face increasing incidents of juvenile delinquency, fed by social conditions in the city. Finally, the complex

Table 7.   *General Services and Police Expenditures Per Capita by City Population, 1963–64*

	City population						
	50,000 and less	50,000 to 100,000	100,000 to 200,000	200,000 to 300,000	300,000 to 400,000	500,000 to 1,000,000	1,000,000 and over
City per capita expenditure on:							
General services	73.23	119.11	137.93	135.12	133.97	178.74	248.12
Police	8.74	12.19	12.78	13.92	14.82	19.21	27.31

Source: U.S. Department of Commerce, Bureau of the Census, Government Finances in 1963–64, table 4, p. 22.

Table 8. *Per Capita Local Government Expenditure Patterns Within and Outside Metropolitan Areas in the United States, 1962*

	Within SMSA's [a]	Outside SMSA's	United States
Total	267.05	199.68	242.96
Education	97.29	95.29	96.57
Highways	18.46	22.85	20.03
Public welfare	16.13	9.78	13.86
Police protection	12.59	5.28	9.98
Fire protection	7.79	2.91	6.05
Sewerage	8.44	3.93	6.85
Housing and urban renewal	8.69	1.61	6.16
Parks and recreation	6.43	1.77	4.77

[a] Standard Metropolitan Statistical Areas.

SOURCE: Advisory Commission on Intergovernmental Relations, "Metropolitan Social and Economic Disparities: Implications for Intergovernmental Relations in Central Cities and Suburbs," "Report" A–25, January, 1965, p. 51.

Table 9. *Mean Per Capita Expenditure of Cities on Police Services, 1951*

City type	Number of cities	Mean per capita expenditure
Major resort city	5	$11.36
Core city of major metropolitan area	77	7.33
Industrial suburb	68	7.17
High-income residential suburb	34	6.39
Low-income residential suburb	68	5.72
Core city of minor metropolitan area	106	5.56
Independent city	137	4.95
Mean for 462 cities		6.04

SOURCE: Ruth L. Mace, *Municipal Cost-Revenue Research in the United States* (Durham, N.C.: Institute of Government, University of North Carolina, 1961), p. 164, computed from data in U.S. Department of Commerce, Washington Bureau of the Census, "Compendium of City Government Finances in 1951," pp. 44–61.

city problem of daily traffic snarls requires police regulation and control different in degree from that required in small towns.

The changing makeup of urban population is another factor in explaining the increasing cost of police services today. Table 9 shows the per capita expenditures for policing in different types of urban areas.

Each large urban sprawl has one major section that serves as the commercial hub. Generally, the number of residents in this hub is relatively few in comparison to the surrounding area. During the day the middle and upper classes travel to the central area for business purposes, sometimes increasing the population enormously. Although Detroit's resident population, for example, had decreased 9.7 percent between 1950 and 1960, its weekday population had approximately doubled. The Detroit police force was, therefore, required to add 133 personnel, an increase of 2.8 percent, to serve a city whose population was decreasing.(38) Similar considerations apply to resort cities whose populations increase severalfold during the seasonal influx of tourists.

REFERENCES

1. Michael Banton, *The Police in the Community* (London: Tavistock, 1964), p. 5.
2. Charles Reith, *The Blind Eye of History* (London: Faber and Faber, 1952), p. 9.
3. Jane Jacobs, *The Death and Life of Great American Cities* (New York: Random House, 1961), p. 32.
4. August Vollmer, "Community Coordination," in V. A. Leonard, *Police Organization and Management* (2nd ed.; Brooklyn: Foundation Press, 1964), p. 246.
5. A. C. Germann, Frank D. Day, and Robert R. J. Gallati, *Introduction to Law Enforcement* (Springfield, Ill.: Thomas, 1966), p. 32.

6. J. Daniel Devlin, *Police Procedure, Administration and Organization* (London: Butterworth, 1966), p. 3.
7. Royal Commission on the Police, *Final Report* (London: Her Majesty's Stationery Office, 1962), p. 12.
8. Christopher Hibbert, *The Roots of Evil* (London: Weidenfield and Nicolson, 1963), pp. 125–128.
9. Edward J. Barrett, Jr., "Police Practices and the Law—From Arrest to Release or Charge," *California Law Review*, 50 (March, 1962), pp. 17–18.
10. Arthur Charles Cole, *The Irrepressible Conflict, 1859–1865*, Vol. VIII of Arthur M. Schlesinger, Sr., and Dixon Ryan Fox, eds., *A History of*

American Life in 12 Volumes (New York: Macmillan, 1934), pp. 154–155.

11. Arthur M. Schlesinger, Sr., *The Rise of the City, 1878–1898*, Vol. X of Arthur M. Schlesinger, Sr., and Dixon Ryan Fox, eds., *A History of American Life in 12 Volumes* (New York: Macmillan, 1934), p. 115.

12. Bruce Smith, Sr., *Police Systems in the United States* (2nd rev. ed.; New York: Harper, 1960), pp. 105–106.

13. Ibid., p. 186.

14. Ibid., pp. 186–187. State control of urban police continues to exist in certain cities in Missouri, Maryland, Massachusetts, Maine, and New Hampshire.

15. Elmer D. Graper, *American Police Administration* (New York: Macmillan, 1921), pp. 109–110.

16. John Coatman, *Police* (London: Oxford University Press, 1959), p. 50.

17. National Commission on Law Observance and Enforcement, *Report on the Police* (Washington, D.C.: U.S. Government Printing Office, 1931), pp. 5–7.

18. Preston William Slossom, *The Great Crusade and After, 1914–1929*, Volume XII of Arthur M. Schlesinger, Sr., and Dixon Ryan Fox, eds., *A History of American Life in 12 Volumes* (New York: Macmillan, 1931), p. 102.

19. *Modernizing Local Government* (New York: Committee for Economic Development, 1966), p. 32.

20. Federal Bureau of Investigation, U.S. Department of Justice, *Uniform Crime Reports, 1965* (Washington, D.C.: U. S. Government Printing Office, 1966), p. 32.

21. Memorandum from Michael S. March, Assistant Chief of Education, Manpower and Science Division, U.S. Bureau of the Budget, May 11, 1966, table 4.

22. *The Municipal Year Book, 1966* (Chicago: International City Managers' Association, 1966), pp. 444–45.

23. Conversation with Ferris E. Lucas, Executive Director, National Sheriffs' Association, Washington, D.C., Oct. 31, 1966.

24. Information received from the Illinois Police Association, Elmwood Park, Ill.

25. Raymond L. Bancroft, *Municipal Law Enforcement, 1966* (Washington, D.C.: Nation's Cities, 1966), p. 16.

26. President's Commission on Crime in the District of Columbia, *Report* (Washington, D.C.: U.S. Government Printing Office, 1966), p. 17.

27. American Trial Lawyers Association, *Crime and Its Causes in Los Angeles* (Lancaster, Pa.: Golden West, 1966), pp. 7–8.

28. *Wall Street Journal*, April 5, 1966.

29. *Herald-News*, Joliet, Ill., July 15, 1966.

30. U.S. Department of Commerce, Bureau of the Census, *U.S. Census of Population: 1960. Subject Reports. Occupational Characteristics, Final Report* PC(2)–7A (Washington, D.C.: U.S. Government Printing Office, 1963), p. 79.

31. Institute for Community Development and Services, Michigan State University, "Police Training in the Detroit Metropolitan Region: Recommendations for a Regional Approach" (draft submitted to the Metropolitan Fund, Inc., Detroit: 1966), p. 70.

32. U.S. Commission on Civil Rights, "Administration of Justice, 1963" (staff report, draft submitted 1963), pp. 13–16.

33. Ibid.

34. George W. O'Connor, *Survey of Selection Methods* (Washington, D.C.: International Association of Chiefs of Police, 1962), table 15.

35. *The Municipal Year Book 1939* (Chicago: International City Managers' Association, 1939), p. 424.

36. International Association of Chiefs of Police, "Police Training," report submitted to the President's Commission on Law Enforcement and Administration of Justice, Washington, D.C., 1966.

37. U.S. Department of Commerce. Bureau of the Census of Governments: 1962, Vol. VI, No. 4 "Historical Statistics on Government Finances and Employment" (Washington, D.C.: U.S. Government Printing Office, 1964), table 1.

38. Samuel G. Chapman, *Police Manpower and Population Changes in Michigan Communities of 10,000 or More Population, 1950–60* (East Lansing, Michigan: Institute for Community Development and Services, Michigan State University, 1961), pp. 8–9.

The Medieval Commune and Internal Violence:

Police Power and Public Safety in Siena , 1287-1355

WILLIAM M. BOWSKY

Rarely does the medievalist treat a theme of such contemporary interest as that of this paper. We need only recall how recently a major candidate for national office made the problem of crime in America's cities a significant public issue, or recollect the riots in Detroit and elsewhere. Yet even medieval historians have paid little direct attention to the specific problem of internal violence, particularly in Italy.

This article is a case study—an examination of police power and public safety in the heart of a Tuscan city-state from the late thirteenth through the mid-fourteenth century, when an oligarchy called the Nine ruled the Sienese commune. What follow are suggestions and tentative findings concerning Sienese urban police power that arose during preparation of a forthcoming general study of Siena under the Nine.

In order to bring the issue into the clearest focus, the concentration will be upon the mother city of Siena itself, to the exclusion of the *contado* or state bordering the city and governed by it. Nor can this be an examination of justice in the broadest sense, including criminal law, courts, and their jurisdiction and procedure. Rather it is an examination of the problem of the protection of the community from lawbreakers: their detection, apprehension, and detention—strictly police functions.

Basic questions must be posed, even though there is not always sufficient documentation to provide the most satisfactory answers. How did communal authorities conceive of the problem of police power? To what extent and degree did it concern them? How did the government deal with the problem? With what results? And what might such an examination contribute to our knowledge of other facets of life,

SOURCE: *American Historical Review*, 73 (October, 1967), pp. 1–17. Footnotes have been omitted.

values, or problems in a late medieval or early Renaissance commune?

The commune was in fact vitally concerned with the seizure, punishment, and removal from circulation of lawbreakers. Its prisons were foul, dank, and crowded. This is not surprising as the commune "farmed" the custody of its prisons to Sienese citizens or companies, who, in turn, in the manner of tax farmers, sought to recoup their expenses and to extract a profit from the prisoners. The result was no overgenerosity in the treatment of prisoners, who were regularly chained to the walls to prevent attempts at escape.

The government took considerable interest in the prisons. In 1330 new communally owned institutions were completed beneath the great Communal Palace, and prisoners were transferred to them from jails that the commune had rented in a private palace—jails in which over sixty prisoners had died during only the preceding two years.

Communal prison regulations of 1298, still unpublished, illuminate the attitudes of the governing classes toward crime and the bases for the distinctions made in the treatment of prisoners. The regulations provided for the division of the jails into three principal sections. The first consisted of two rooms, one of which served for the detention of those convicted of the so-called "enormous crimes," among them homicide, treason, arson, kidnaping, rape, poisoning, mutilation, torture, highway robbery, perjury, wounding and drawing blood, and breaking into a home for the purpose of theft. Another room held those convicted of lesser crimes. The second major section also had two rooms: one for convicted debtors and the other for women, regardless of the offense. Confined in the third section were those not yet sentenced but undergoing investigation or trial, with one significant exception: nobles and *boni homines* under investigation for any crime that did not entail the death penalty could live in a special house of detention, or, if they provided the highest communal magistrate (the podesta) with surety for good conduct, they could even leave the house of detention.

Thus, while the commune made what we would consider a wise distinction between accused and convicted, it made two additional distinctions: one relegating women to a separate category, and another providing special, lenient treatment for the commune's most powerful, wealthy, and politically important elements, both noble and popular, so long as they were the well-to-do citizens of good reputation generally understood by their fellow Sienese to be comprehended within the term *boni homines.*

Well might the government concern itself with public safety, for this was an age characterized by rapid resort to violence despite the centuries-old teachings of the Church. Inadequate documentation prevents an accurate estimate of the numbers of persons seized and confined, but an incomplete register shows over seventeen thousand persons from the city and *contado* fined for criminal acts from mid-1270 to mid-1296, while in a brief three weeks in 1298 only one judge for a single third of the city heard seventeen criminal cases. Almost every six months from two to fifty or more prisoners were released as religious offerings. And records do not give us the number of those who eluded capture.

No single class of society possessed a monopoly on violence. To expand upon the numerous episodes involving members of powerful noble families would belabor the obvious. Published chronicles alone are replete with tales of their murders, assaults, and minor battles. And wool manufacturer and wool-worker, shopkeeper, and manual laborer all are among those seized and sentenced. It might, however, be particularly timely to add in fairness that the students who frequented the Sienese *Studio* or university were quite law abiding, particularly as compared with their counterparts, at the University of Bologna and elsewhere.

The clergy were not exempt from the proclivity to resort to violence. Episcopal provisions of 1297 envisioned clerics committing every imaginable sort of crime from sedition and sodomy to brawling and breaking bones. And despite its generally good relations with the Sienese church, the commune adamantly enforced its own police jurisdiction against criminous clerics, even when this meant lengthy and expensive litigation and threats of excommunication.

The fairer sex produced its share of mayhem and bloodshed and for good measure seems to have been well equipped with sharp tongues, for whose use many were seized and punished. Not without interest is a sentence of 1342 against a woman who had struck a man on the forehead with a lantern and drawn blood. Her fine was increased because of her contumacy, but halved "because a woman against a man," doubled again "because at night," and doubled once more "because she struck him in his house." Like other townsmen, the medieval Sienese was no stranger to the idea that a man's home is his castle.

Crime and violence were not only common, but involved every sort of activity from the so-called "enormous crimes" to drunken brawling. The commune had to contend, moreover, with violence that erupted as a result of special situations it was not always able to prevent, particularly food riots. These occurred during the famines and food shortages that plagued Tuscany on several occasions during the first half of the fourteenth century. One such riot in 1329 cost the commune over L. 667 to reimburse only for stolen grain.

Such nonviolent crimes as bearing unauthorized weapons, breaking curfew, gambling, and frequenting taverns required law enforcement. Some offenses such as blasphemy and sodomy entailed what today seem to be disproportionately severe penalties, penalties that at times were executed. Thus in 1336 a blasphemer who failed to pay a weighty fine within ten days of being sentenced had his tongue cut out. The medieval Sienese was most horrified of and angered by sodomy, fearing the unleashing of divine wrath against the community that permitted it. The sodomite, or procurer for a sodomite, who did not pay three hundred lire within a month of sentencing was, reads a statute, "to be hanged by his virile members in the principal market place, and there remain hanging . . . for an entire day."

Communal authorities especially feared those acts of violence that could develop from a private fracas into a threat to the regime itself. Most troublesome were certain games that appealed so greatly to the Sienese that despite numerous prohibitions they were frequently played in the Campo, beneath the windows of the Communal Palace wherein resided the Nine and the podesta. Such games often began as simple fist fights, but progressed to the hurling of stones, the use of staves, spears, and knives, and rapidly degenerated into pitched battles. Yet they were so popular that on at least one occasion (1291) the City Council felt itself compelled to grant permission for "a game or battle of *elmora* in the Campo."

The heated and confused combat could easily turn the games into an attack upon the palace itself, whenever the participants felt sufficiently aggrieved against the regime or when groups conspiring the government's overthrow engineered the shift from game to open rebellion. Thus in early February 1325 various conspirators (including powerful Tolomei nobles) plotted to turn a game of *pugna* into open rebellion. The Sienese government was indeed well served by two hundred gold florins that it paid at the end of that month "to a secret accuser who revealed to the war captain the treason, conspiracy, and plot that had been arranged against the office of the Lords Nine . . . " as recorded in a register of communal expenditures.

Police were also directly involved in efforts to quell such outright rebellion and insurrection as that of early October 1311 to which its plotters had perhaps been emboldened by Henry of Luxembourg's victorious conclusion of the siege of Brescia, and hence the prospect that an imperial army swelled with Ghibelline exiles and warriors would soon pass temptingly close to Guelph Siena as the Emperor-elect journeyed southward to Rome and the imperial coronation.

Prior to the regime's final collapse the only major rebellion that placed it in mortal danger was that of October 26, 1318. In a pitched battle in the Campo that took many lives, at least 269 mercenary infantry, 81 mercenary cavalry, and over 20 crossbowmen defended the government. Beside them, 84 of the 100 *birri*, or police, of the Nine and commune valiantly battled and later received generous rewards for their efforts.

The manifold needs for law enforcement were as obvious to the medieval Sienese as they are to the modern historian, and the commune resorted to varied methods in efforts to provide such protection and to curb violence. Like other cities, Siena was subject to a strict curfew, and only such authorized persons as night guards, visiting physicians, and garbage collectors could appear on the streets at night without special permits. Others found outside their houses after the sound of the so-called "Third Bell" had rung two hours after sunset were subject to a fine of 20s., one such fine being collected from that lively

Sienese poet and correspondent of Dante, Cecco Angiolieri.

Another method of enforcement, already referred to, was reliance upon secret accusers who denounced to communal authorities those who they knew had violated specific laws. In return, an accuser's name was kept secret (much to the historian's annoyance), and he received one-fifth, one-fourth, or even one-half of the fine depending upon the offense, while the City Council granted even larger sums to those disclosing treason plots.

The principal instrument of law enforcement, however, was the police. What then of the police force, or rather, forces?

Most police duties were entrusted to hired foreign policemen. Their sheer number in proportion to the size of the urban population strikes the historian. By the mid-1330's there was a foreign policeman for each 145 inhabitants of Siena, men, women, and children, lay and cleric, if the reader accepts my recent population estimates. (Reliance upon previous estimates would yield a ratio of about 1 policeman per 73 Sienese.)

For the sake of illustration and contrast only, we may note that in the midwestern city of Lincoln, Nebraska, with a population of about 135,000, there is 1 policeman per 1,000 inhabitants. New York City (not without its crime problem) has a ratio of approximately 1 to 285. These obviously are modern cities, with methods of communication and control unknown in the thirteenth and fourteenth centuries, but the contrast remains striking.

More useful might be a comparison with a medieval Tuscan commune, but this problem has yet to engage the serious attention of historians. A ratio of 1 to 800 suggested for Florence during the first half of the fourteenth century is based on scanty research. More important, it fails to reveal what may have been the significance of this disparity between Florentine and Sienese police forces. Was there, for example, less need for police protection in the Arno city, were its organization and legislation more effective than that of Siena, or did the Sienese devote greater attention than their Florentine contemporaries to the problem of lawlessness and internal violence?

We should not speak of *the* police force. Even in the late thirteenth century the principal foreign magistrates in Siena, the podesta and the captain of the people, each had a group of police in the entourage or "family" that accompanied him into office and was paid by him from his own salary. Another police force served "the Nine and the Commune." Two new police forces were created during the following century: the police who formed a part of the "family" of the war captain—a new official whose office was regularized in the 1320's—and, in 1334, the *Quattrini*, particularly charged with the daytime custody of the city. This brought to five the number of foreign police forces.

The government was aware then of the need for police protection. It was also aware of inadequacies in the police system, and that system became the object of a mass of regular legislation. The regime experimented continuously with the size, organization, distribution, tours of duty, and jurisdictions of its police units.

The smallest force was that of the captain of the people: generally no more than 20 men in the late thirteenth century, 10 during the fourteenth. Its size reflects accurately that magistrate's decreasing authority in all areas of activity. The podesta's police ranged from a high of 60 to a low of 20 men, and the number was set at 40 by statutes of the late 1330's. The war captain's police, originally 50, were set at 100 by the same statutes, again a good measure of that official's increasing importance. There was considerable experimentation with the force of the Nine and commune, but usually it was 90 or 100. The *Quattrini* too were the object of experimentation: increased from 60 to 100 within months of their creation, 150 two years later, and then 100 from 1338 until the abandonment of the force.

The jurisdictions of these forces ordinarily overlapped and were the object of constant legislative attention. To select only a few measures at random, provisions of 1299, 1300, and 1306 assigned night watch particularly to the police of the podesta and of the captain of the people, while entrusting the podesta alone with supervision of the day watch. An act of 1308 charged the podesta with both day and night watch, and for this purpose granted him the disposition of some of the police of the captain of the people and many of those of the Nine and commune in addition to his own.

Provisions of 1334 for the custody of the city at night allocated a separate third of the area to the podesta, war captain, and captain of the people, but the first two could also investigate conditions in each of the remaining sections. The war captain and the captain of the people each received the same authority as the podesta to have the city searched for persons bearing prohibited arms and to hear, define, and terminate their cases. The *Quattrini* too sought all types of delinquents. Another act of 1334 ordered all foreign officials, their families, and all mercenaries to pursue and seize malefactors and deliver them to the podesta—except that the war captain's men were to deliver their prisoners to him.

Despite variations in size, composition, and jurisdiction, the foreign police forces had much in common, beginning with the overlapping jurisdiction itself. At the request of communal officials all forces were subject to official review in order to determine whether all were present, properly armed, and if any unauthorized substitutions had been made in personnel. Violators were fined. In addition to receiving regular salaries, foreign police, capturing and delivering a prisoner who was either already wanted or was later convicted received a cash reward. But, while effective service was rewarded, policing was to be a full-time task. A provision for the *Quattrini*, for example, forbade them from engaging in any trade or manual labor in the city under the penalty of a fine of twenty-five lire, almost five months' salary. And like foreign magistrates the police could not fraternize with the local populace. The nature of police duty was the same for all forces: separated into groups of two or more men they patrolled assigned portions of the city. Common characteristics marked the hiring of these forces. The policemen were not hired separately; rather the commune contracted for six-month terms with their captains or with the foreign official in whose entourage they were included.

Nor did the police have any special police training prior to entering Sienese service or while in that service. They were, in fact, nothing but foot soldiers or infantry hired for police duty, and in many documents they are referred to interchangeably as *birri*—police—or as *fanti* or *pedites*—infantrymen. Indeed it seems that the same type of men, at times even the same men, who served Siena as police at other times served Siena and other communes as mercenary infantry, even under the same captains. This phenomenon might be investigated by future historians of the origins and development of the *Compagnie di Ventura*, the Free or Mercenary Companies, and of the *condottieri* who attained such notoriety during the high Renaissance.

The government also took a strong and continuing interest in the type of men hired for police duty: all were hired (through their captains) by the commune's highest signory, the same signory that selected the podesta, captain of the people, and war captain. For the signory wanted more than skilled fighting men as police; police had to have the correct political persuasions. Statutes declared, for example, that the captains of the police of the Nine and commune were to be Guelph counts or barons, friends of the Church, and, especially, friends of the Sienese commune. They could not come from the Sienese state or from the cities of the podesta or captain of the people who would be in office at the same time, a wise precaution against the concentration of power in the hands of a single foreign official. This concern for the political leanings of the police is readily understandable when we recall how crimes of violence could become a political menace, and that police forces composed of trained infantry functioned indiscriminately in both areas.

The same lack of distinction between military and police functions and the same emphasis upon political coloration are evident when we examine the few police activities performed by the inhabitants of Siena.

The commune called upon members of the companies of the city for night watch, companies that had resulted from a fusion of military companies and companies of the society of the people, analogous to the situation in Pisa. Under the Nine the companies not only served in Siena's armies, but assisted in quelling fighting that involved the city's powerful noble families and in quashing major riots and rebellion. Their members swore to uphold the existing regime.

These companies supplied a pool of 600 men a month for night watch, with about 120 actually serving during any month. After 1324 the commune remunerated the men of the companies for these services. During the next decade this night watch was made directly responsible to the war captain (not, we may note, to the companies' traditional leader, the captain of the people).

Two members of each company selected by the Nine for a six-month term performed other police functions. Called *paciarii* or peace officials, they reported to high communal officials infractions of private peace agreements and acts of oppression and injuries that occurred among the members of their companies. The remaining police function performed by Sienese was assigned for six-month terms to representatives of the *contrade* or *lire*, the city's administrative and tax districts. Each district had one official or *sindaco* salaried by the commune whose task it was to report to the podesta crimes and law violations that occurred within his district, under the penalty of heavy fines for the neglect of duty. (And it is self-evident that the areas allotted to the military companies with their *paciarii* overlapped and duplicated the *lire* with their *sindaci*.)

We have seen something of how the communal authorities conceived of and dealt with the problems of internal violence, police power, and public safety. But how effective were their measures? It should be noted at once that the state was cognizant of some of the limitations upon its ability to secure and maintain internal peace and order. There are numerous indications of this awareness.

Like Florence, its more powerful northern neighbor, Siena still recognized the legality of the vendetta. Lacking the strength to eliminate the vendetta, the government concentrated upon limiting its application and narrowing the circle of persons who could practice it and against whom it could be waged. A timorous attempt of May 1306 to isolate the actual offender by forcing his relatives to renounce the possibility of protecting him with a vendetta against possible avengers served only to demonstrate the commune's weakness: the measure was not retroactive, and it exempted those most likely to become involved—the culprit's father, sons, and blood brothers.

More serious was the continued recognition in public law of the so-called "instrument of peace" (*instrumentum pacis*)—a notarized document secured by an offender from an injured person (or his heirs), granting that offender peace and thus eliminating the possibility of a legal vendetta. An instrument of peace was necessary before one convicted of a crime of violence could be freed at a religious festival or take advantage of special or general amnesties or compositions. So important was this document that the state dropped all criminal action if a defendant could produce such a peace document even during the course of a trial. Here, in effect, a public crime was reduced to the status of a private concern. (Nor was it a major advance in public law when in 1350, in order to prevent the state from being deprived of its fine by collusion between offender and offended, it was ordered that henceforth even those producing peace instruments would not be given peace by the commune until they paid 5 percent of the fine for the crime of which they had been accused.) While one may wish to interpret this attachment to the peace instrument as a desire to reinforce the commune's decisions with private agreement, it seems rather to be a confession of the state's inability to confer complete protection upon those who committed acts of violence.

The general amnesties, compositions, and commutations of sentences were themselves more than a device for filling communal coffers or for fulfilling some idea of justice; they were also an indication of the commune's recognition of its inability to capture and confine all lawbreakers. Many benefiting from such acts had never been captured. I have been able to discover no less than ten general amnesties and compositions enacted from 1302 to 1354, and they benefited well over five thousand persons from the city and *contado*, perhaps even double that number. Other individuals gained the same advantages as a result of private bills passed by the City Council.

The effectiveness of law enforcement against some of the greatest offenders, members of powerful, wealthy, and numerous noble *consorterie* or family federations seems particularly imperfect when we find that some nobles who benefited from general amnesty legislation were freed of four or more death sentences, each imposed for a different offense. Most impressive is the case of Messer Deo di Messer Guccio Guelfo Tolomei, acknowledged leader of the Tolomei *consorteria.* A leader of the rebellion of October 26, 1318, he had fled the city, captured the *contado* castle of Menzano in 1320, yielding it only when the war captain threatened to execute four innocent Tolomei, and in 1322 and 1323 played as much the role of the leader of a Free Company as that of a Sienese rebel as he ravaged the Sienese Valdichiana and Valdorcia with a large company that included Aretines and mercenaries in Florentine pay. He nonetheless benefited from a general act of 1339 and purchased the cancellation of five separate death sentences at the bargain rate of a thousand gold florins, for the price was the same regardless of the number of death sentences canceled. While such cases are rare, their very existence is significant.

On several occasions, when many members of some of the greatest noble *consorterie* engaged in acts of violence, rather than rely upon normal police legislation, Siena, like other communes, resorted to persuading them to conclude private truces. Those truces then received official government sanction, and violators were threatened with the severest penalties. The Nine forced the conclusion of such truces several times during the prolonged enmity between the Tolomei and the Salimbeni, and at least once during a Malavolti-Piccolomini dispute.

Following the precedent established by earlier regimes, the Nine licensed the possession of arms in the city through the sale of arms permits, though it limited these to the less dangerous weapons. Nonetheless they could not prevent men from appearing in public prepared for violence, and at any time well over a hundred men possessed such permits. While the government tried to restrict the area of the city where one could appear so armed, and this during the daytime only, it is alarming that, by the mid-1330's, eligibility for such permits had been extended even to foreigners. And we need scarcely emphasize that the existence of this system of arms permits was not justified by such reasoning as that which underlies our own Bill of Rights; it was rather an admission by the Sienese government of its inability to provide absolute protection for all of its subjects, and to prevent them completely from exercising their more violent proclivities.

But while the commune could not completely control all of its subjects' violent tendencies, it could and did resist attempted intrusions into its jurisdiction. Thus in 1307 and 1311 it engaged in major disputes with the inquisitor in Tuscany, the Franciscan Phillip of Lucca, who claimed the right to issue arms permits to persons not in his regular retinue, even to private Sienese citizens.

The recognized imperfections of the Sienese police system should not, however, be viewed against a backdrop of absolute perfection—a standard not attained by any human society. Nor should we forget that the communal prisons were always well tenanted; that even members of the greatest noble families such as the Piccolomini, and of families represented on the Nine, ended with the hangman and at the executioner's block; and that the commune did, in fact, destroy houses and palaces of convicted criminals of the highest station, including Tolomei.

The onslaught of the Black Death in 1348 seems

to mark a watershed. The plague struck Siena with exceptional severity, and the disorder and confusion that it left in its wake combined with a lack of available police to make the problem of police protection even more difficult and to strain the commune's every ability.

Already in the years immediately preceding the plague, marauding Free Companies had attacked the Sienese state. In 1342 the "Great Company" of Werner von Urslingen, self-styled "Enemy of God, of Piety, and of Mercy," visited it and could even embarrass the government by waylaying a war captain and his judge but a few miles from the city walls as they came to take office, robbing them of cash, lawbooks, armor, and silver vases worth at least five hundred gold florins. But such problems were dwarfed by the burning, murder, rapine, and extortion of the famous Fra Moriale during the summer of 1354. And before Siena bought him off with over thirteen thousand gold florins it even suffered the humiliation of paying him damages for horses killed by Sienese who had resisted him!

It comes as no surprise that the city itself was not immune from the increased violence of the postplague years. In 1350 the City Council lamented that there was a great increase in the number of crimes of violence, including bloodshed, brawling, and homicide, being committed within the city, and that criminals now acted with "ever-growing impunity" as it was simple for them to flee the city and evade capture. The commune's continued inability to cope with the deteriorating situation led it in 1352 to create a new "official for the custody of the city," complete with notary and family, to share the podesta's powers for guarding the city. A Ser Nuto of Città di Castello held the new office for a two-month term, but, as he accomplished little or nothing, the experiment was quickly abandoned.

During 1313 and 1314 the commune had imposed a truce on all citizens having mortal hatreds or enmities, allegedly because the commune was threatened with foreign invasion. The same reason was alleged for a similar measure in 1351, but, although it was extended to 1353 and its implementation assigned to the powerful war captain, it had little or no effect. And would the government have waited thirty-seven years to repeat such a device if it had originally been successful? There had certainly been sufficient threats of foreign invasion upon which to

draw for justification: the advent of the Emperor Louis the Bavarian and the incursions of Pisa, to name but two. The truce of 1351 seems at least as much a measure of desperation as of inspiration.

Public safety was further jeopardized in these dangerous postplague years by the abandonment of the force of *Quattrini* and by the reduction of the police of the Nine and commune from one hundred to eighty men—men retained, however, at increased wages owing to the lack of reliable, trained mercenary infantry for hire.

The atmosphere of increased violence, and the commune's decreased facilities for coping with it, was but one factor that contributed to the success of the rebellion that finally overthrew the regime of the Nine in 1355, but it should not be overlooked.

Throughout the history of the Nine, police power and public safety were major concerns to the highest communal authorities. Aware of the dangers of uncontrolled internal violence, they evolved a vast and complex body of police legislation and continually sought new approaches and solutions with admirable inventiveness and persistence. Even while admitting some of the commune's limitations they staunchly defended its right of sole police jurisdiction.

Before the plague the problem of crime control and police protection was generally kept within manageable limits, with a few striking, but temporary, exceptions. But during the postplague years immediately preceding the fall of the Nine the situation got increasingly out of hand.

Part of the difficulty was the tendency of all elements of society to resort to violence upon what we would consider insufficient provocation, and the persistence of the belief that personal vendetta was superior to recourse to public authority for the redress of private grievances of personal insult or injury. These factors alone necessitated a numerous police force.

But was not the problem of maintaining public safety increased by the existence of several police forces having overlapping and conflicting jurisdictions? These could lead to neglect of duty or to bitter distrust, suspicion, and rivalry in the competition for the rewards of successful captures. Perhaps, too, the failure to distinguish between violence wreaked by one citizen upon another and attacks upon the regime in power, between ordinary police functions and the need to defend the government militarily against violent overthrow, hindered further sophistication of police work.

Granted these complexities and the lack of modern means of communication and specialized police training, the system long functioned well. Its study offers insights into the nature and role of internal violence, and, in part, its relation to other aspects of life. Together with numerous analyses for other cities, it should provide material for a much-needed study of internal violence in the medieval and early Renaissance city-state.

Europe and America: *How the Police Work*

GEORGE BERKLEY

When it comes to police work, the democracies of Western Europe still strike any American observer as foreign countries. The gap between the Old World and the New is illustrated by their different approaches to the use of deadly force. In the United States, a policeman carries as standard equipment, a .38 special revolver and an 18-inch wooden truncheon. Some augment this with "sap" gloves (gloves loaded with lead), extra-heavy magnum revolvers, and, for riot-duty, yard-long wooden clubs. In Great Britain and Norway, policemen are not issued guns and carry them only on very rare occasions. Elsewhere in Scandinavia, policemen are issued guns but often leave them in their lockers when on daytime assignments. In virtually no European democracy do they carry guns when off-duty.

The standard firearm used in European police forces is the equivalent of our .32 automatic. It is not only much lighter than the .38 specials worn by our police, but is even less powerful than the .32 regulars carried by policewomen in New York City. Police truncheons in Europe are usually made of hard rubber; they break no bones and leave no scars. Sap gloves, magnum revolvers, elongated wooden billy clubs are very rare.

SOURCE: *The New Republic*, August 2, 1969. Reprinted by permission of *The New Republic*. © 1969 Harrison-Blaine of New Jersey, Inc.

The European policeman is not only more lightly armed than his American counterpart but is more restricted in his right to use what he has. In most European countries, a policeman can not fire a gun for any purpose other than to protect life, his own or some one else's. Even if attacked, he is often not to shoot unless the attack endangers his life. French police regulations, for example, state that "resistance to an attack which does not expose anyone to a serious danger, but only to an act of violence or assault, does not in itself justify the use of a gun."

A German policeman *does* have the right, under certain circumstances, to fire at a fleeing felon. He must, however, aim at the arms or legs. Every two months, he is tested to determine whether he can shoot this well. He fires at an escaping criminal on a movie screen, and if he hits him in the back or head he flunks the test. The American policeman not only has the right but, in some cases, even the obligation to shoot fleeing felons. In some jurisdictions, he is forbidden to fire warning shots first. The cardboard silhouette figures used on police firing ranges in this country place the bull's-eye on the main body area.

As a result of these differences in their "armaments" policy, European and American police forces show contrasting ratios in civilian deaths to police deaths. According to the President's Crime Commission, the number of civilians killed by the police in this country is more than three times the number of policemen who lose their lives while on the job. In most European countries, many more policemen die in the line of duty than do civilians as a result of police activity. In Sweden, four policemen have been killed by civilians during the past four years. The Swedish police meanwhile, have been responsible for only two civilian deaths during the past 13 years.

In all the upheavals that have rocked European countries lately, only one civilian has died as a consequence of police action—in Berlin in 1967, and the policeman responsible was promptly arrested, brought to trial. When 10,000 protesters rioted outside the U.S. Embassy in London in March 1967, the police sustained 117 casualties compared to 44 for the demonstrators. Actually, the police were the more lightly armed, since they had only their truncheons while the demonstrators had poles and fireworks. In a student riot in Berlin on November 4, the ratio of injured policemen to rioters was on the order of four to one.

While European policemen tend to be less aggressive than their American colleagues in the use of force, they are often more enterprising in other ways. The German police have perhaps shown the most initiative here. They put on puppet shows for young children, conduct traffic kindergartens for slightly older children, give bicycle courses for still older ones. Most of these programs are carried on at police stations. To serve adults, the German police operate crime prevention clinics, aid distressed motorists and give bus tours to elderly citizens, pointing out traffic hazards. Some have even given annual parties to traffic offenders they have fined "to show them that the police aren't mad at them!" Swedish police also run traffic kindergartens, instruct older children in legal responsibility and even hold family auto rallies. Swedish patrol cars are equipped with extra spark plugs, gasoline, etc., to help motorists in trouble. Swedish policemen also sponsor and lead over 20 hobby clubs for young people. In Denmark, in addition to carrying out similar activities, the police operate a "re-socialization center" for homeless men. Even the French police have begun taking steps in this direction. In addition to running traffic kindergartens, the Sûreté now operates some 40 summer vacation camps for young people, all staffed completely by policemen.

Such programs are not unknown in America: the first positive youth program in the history of police work was New York City's Police Athletic League. However, we look upon such efforts as public relations gestures, peripheral to the police function. Policemen assigned to such tasks are usually those men who are considered, and who consider themselves, to be outsiders within the department. In many cases, policemen themselves don't run the programs. New York's Police Athletic League itself is now largely a non-police organization with its own civilian staff.

German and Scandinavian police departments call their juvenile delinquency squads youth protection squads, and they refer to juvenile delinquents as "endangered youth." Policemen assigned to this function work closely with social workers, often going on joint patrol. The hobby clubs run by policemen in Scandinavia are generally designed for young people who show a penchant for getting into trouble. In Germany, the police sometimes take juvenile delinquents out for trips in police boats or for rides on police horses.

Most European policemen have discarded the practice of swooping down on a suspect in a predawn raid. When the Swedish police went to arrest the Russian espionage agent, Sven Wennerstrom, in 1963, they waited until he was crossing a bridge on his way to work. Two police cars then drove up and blocked the bridge at both ends. The officer in charge got out, introduced himself and shook hands with the Soviet spy before placing him under arrest. German police customarily wait for the breakfast hour before knocking on the suspect's door with an arrest warrant. When Dortmund police went to arrest five suspected communist agents last summer, they arrived at such a respectable hour that all but one of the suspects had left for work.

Even the police killer is often accorded a modicum of humane treatment. In September 1966, police in Gothenburg, Sweden, received a tip that Clark Olafsson, a thug who a few weeks previously had shot and killed a policeman, was seated on a ledge outside the city. Olafsson was known to be armed. Instead of going after him with guns blazing, the police sent out two unarmed members of the force to bring him in. The two athletic constables disguised themselves as track runners and ran several laps around the unsuspecting murderer before seizing him. In the ensuing tussle, Olafsson managed to produce his gun and fire it twice, slightly wounding one of his captors. But Olafsson himself did not have a scratch on him when he was brought into police headquarters.

In keeping with this behavior pattern, Europeans have shown much less resistance to the growing emphasis on civil liberties, a trend which has swept many of their judicial systems as it has our own. Germany revised its penal code three years ago, requiring the police to inform all suspects of their right to remain silent or to have a lawyer. There was no loud outcry, as the equivalent U.S. Supreme Court decision evoked from the American police.

France revised its penal code in 1962, setting much stricter limitations on the power of the police to detain and interrogate suspects. It produced remarkably little grumbling. Sweden has long had rules governing the rights of suspects, and the Swedish police officials I met seemed proud, rather than resentful, of them. The British, meanwhile, have operated uncomplainingly for over half a century under the famed Judges' Rules, which stipulate that a policeman must caution a person charged with a crime of his right to remain silent and that he must not question anyone taken into custody.

Although corruption has always been a nagging problem for many, if not most, American police departments, it is insignificant in Europe. Even in France, where hostility to the police is endemic, imputations that the police take bribes almost never arise. Not only do German policemen give traffic tickets to each other, but a Hamburg patrolman once made his wife pay a fine for beating their carpet outdoors. A Cologne policeman who found himself late for a court appearance in 1966 parked illegally and gave himself a parking ticket. (This didn't keep him from receiving a reprimand from his superiors.)

This picture of European policemen is subject to qualifications. Abuses have occurred and doubtless will again. Nevertheless, European policemen do tend to view their role differently. Why?

For one thing, European police departments place much more emphasis on education. Police recruits receive three to four years of training in Germany, two years and nine months in Italy, one full year in Sweden, six months in France and thirteen weeks in Great Britain. While the British lag behind most other European countries in this respect, their recruit education period still compares favorably with that of the United States. California, which has the highest police education standards in America, requires only 370 hours of education for municipal policemen. New York State requires only eight weeks.

The curricula of most continental police schools devote considerable time to nontechnical subjects, including legal instruction plus a good deal of political science, applied psychology, and similar studies. Some 20 to 25 percent of the German recruit's first-year training and 15 percent of his second year is devoted to the social sciences. He is taught to avoid all prejudices and generalizations about classes or types of people, to be mindful of the frustrations of motorists and act accordingly, and to keep his sense of humor.

Government, psychology and "social medicine" (which includes alcoholism and the problems of handicapped people), make up ten percent of the Swedish police recruit's classroom instruction. The text used for the course in government stresses minority rights and warns of the dangers of a police state. In 1964, French police schools inaugurated a 30-hour course in which the recruit is told he should make more use of his pen, his knowledge and his "human qualities," than of his physical force and weapons. It is pointed out that his duties are "first those of a citizen, secondly those of a civil servant and thirdly those of a policeman."

When it comes to grooming men for positions as officers or detectives, this discrepancy between police education in Europe and here markedly increases. In the U.S., the passing of a simple written examination, usually consisting of multiple-choice or true-false questions, is nearly always sufficient for advancement to command positions. Promotion to the detective force may come simply on the recommendation of a superior officer or a political connection. In Europe, such steps up the career ladder almost invariably require additional schooling, usually lasting from six months to a year. In Sweden, officers-in-training are taken on tours of psychiatric hospitals, alcoholism centers, prisons and other institutions.

Sweden earmarks some 300 of its top positions for lawyers who are recruited directly into the upper ranks. France recruits half of its lieutenant candidates from among civilians with a baccalaureate degree and half of its inspector candidates from law school graduates. German police forces are allowed to recruit 10 percent of their detective forces from the legal profession; applicants to the regular police who possess the *arbitur*—roughly equivalent to two years of higher education in this country—are allowed to apply for officer training three years earlier than can their less educated colleagues. England last year launched a new program under which a university graduate can advance from patrolman to officer at a fast pace.

European police forces also make more extensive use of women. They hold nearly five percent of all constabulary positions on the London police force. Some German states have set aside 10 percent of their detective positions for women. Scandinavian countries sometimes use policewomen for regular patrol work.

The recruitment of women and better educated men gives the police force a broader base and makes it more representative of the population. So does the use of civilians, who make up over 20 percent of the total departmental personnel roster in England and Sweden. Civilians do not just oversee but actually run most European police departments. Most of the top executive posts in Sweden, including the positions of police chief in the larger cities, are held by lawyers. A former judge directs the entire police operation, while a former teacher of French heads the main police academy in Stockholm. In Germany, not only are all police commissioners civilians, but so are most of their division heads, including the heads of the criminal police or detective forces. German police commissioners, as well as many of their division heads, usually hold doctorates in law. Half of the executive-level posts in the newly unified French police are held by civilians; the overall director of the national police is a former chief of staff at the Ministry of Education.

England has a more decentralized system than do the continental countries, and most police chiefs come up from the ranks. However, the commissioner of the largest and most important police force, the Metropolitan Police of Greater London, is more often a civilian than not. At least half of his division heads are nonpolicemen, including the assistant commissioner in charge of the famed Criminal Investigation Division. The Home Secretary in the British Government, meanwhile, issues rules and regulations covering the whole police force and can veto the appointment of, as well as require the removal of, any local police chief.

It was once customary in the United States at least in the larger cities, to appoint a civilian as the police commissioner. Today, these positions are usually given to professional policemen. When Mayor Lindsay tried to exert authority over the New York City police in 1966, his efforts were met with fierce resistance and were branded as "interference" by "outsiders."

The fact that civil servants tend to run European police departments tends to make these departments much more bureaucratic than ours. But interestingly enough, this may also produce democratic patterns of police behavior. Stripped of its negative connotations, bureaucracy implies, in essence, a system built on formal and standardized rules and procedures. The bureaucratic policeman is thus more likely to be impartial, less likely to be arbitrary in discharging his duties. The Berlin policeman I saw bending over an ill-clad drunk lying in the street and asking him in formal, polite German, "Where do you live, please?" illustrates my point. The same rules and manner apply to everyone.

With a civilian-controlled and bureaucratically oriented administrative structure, many European police systems are permitting their employees to share in decision-making. Nearly one out of every ten Swedish policemen sits on a joint-management board charged with working in some problem area. German policemen elect representatives to employee councils, which handle internal complaints and frequently have some say in the management of the force. Rank-and-file French policemen choose from their ranks nearly half the members of all police disciplinary and promotion boards. British police have representatives on the Police Council of Great Britain, which advises and negotiates with the Home Secretary. The result is greater understanding and acceptance of such key values as accommodation, patience, and consultation. More important, such participation affords the policeman an outlet for his grievances. If nothing else, administrative devices such as these serve as a safety valve for a group which is always under pressure.

Trade unionism also tends to further these ends and most policemen in Western Europe are members of a union. The police unions provide additional opportunities for ventilating grievances and for taking part in such democratic processes as electing officers and approving decisions. The union provides a two-way communications link between the police and society. The union's spokesmen and publications offer the public better access to the policeman's point of view. At the same time, these spokesmen and publications are channels for receiving and transmitting to its members ideas from the nonpolice world. To the extent that the union brings the police closer to the trade union movement generally, it may also help offset right-wing tendencies, which seem so natural to the protectors of law, order and property.

Another practice permitted in some continental countries may do even more to keep the police in the political mainstream. They are permitted in Scandinavia and Germany to take part directly in political activity and are even allowed to run for office. Denmark customarily has four or five policemen sitting in its parliament, German state legislatures are sprinkled with policemen-lawmakers, and a small town in southern Sweden has actually elected all four of its policemen to its town council. Since policemen are essentially lower- and middle-echelon civil servants, they tend to run for office as members of working-class parties.

If policemen in some European countries take an active part in legislative work, legislative bodies also take an active interest in police work. (In contrast, our city councils, state legislatures and, when it comes to the FBI, even Congress are loath to interfere.) Here are some examples of zealous legislative oversight:

A Scottish patrolman knocked down and gave a nosebleed to a persistently pesky teen-age boy who refused to let him alone. The incident produced such an outcry in Parliament that Prime Minister Macmillan (this was in '59), had to set up a high-level tribunal to assess charges of police brutality.

In the summer of 1966, the Swedish parliament was outraged when policemen were seen taking pictures of some anti-American demonstrators. Police Director Persson hastened to assure the irate lawmakers that the picture-taking was done by the criminal police and not the security police, and was done only to have evidence in the event any laws were broken. (In a previous demonstration, the participants had burned an American flag, and it is against Swedish law to mutilate the flag of a country recognized by the government.)

A German customs officer shot and killed a fleeing smuggler in 1964. The state legislature of North Rhineland-Westfalen staged a two-day debate on the question of firearms use by policemen.

A Paris policeman shot and killed a motorist who was resisting arrest. The emasculated French parliament resounded with cries for more stringent controls over the police. (The Paris police union expressed regrets over the incident and asked that policemen be given increased education to prevent such an occurrence from happening again.)

In addition to legislative bodies, there are other agencies exercising control over the police. Sweden's ombudsman keeps a close eye on the cops and does not wait for a complaint before taking action. In Germany, all detectives are officially classified as assistants to the public prosecutors of their respective states. Thus, they are directly supervised by the judicial branch. The French have a *juge d'instruction* or examining magistrate who oversees the entire conduct of a criminal investigation. In England, judges make up one-third of the watch committees (the other two-thirds are elected by the people) which have local supervision of the police.

The most important control mechanism, however, is the police themselves. Here, too, European countries seem far ahead of the United States. Drunkenness on the job in most European countries will bring a suspension of many months. Drunken driving, to say nothing of corruption or brutality, will bring prosecution in court and usually a jail sentence. A policeman's conduct off the job is supposed to be exemplary. An off-duty constable in England who threw a clod of earth at a cat that was tearing up his newly planted seedlings received an official reprimand.

Although in Sweden, most complaints from the public go to the ombudsman, the Stockholm police have a civilian lawyer who checks out all complaints that come to the police themselves. German police departments set up special booths at public events, asking visitors to make such complaints. The number of complaints against policemen in such cities as London and Berlin far exceeds the number filed against policemen in New York City. And a much higher ratio of complaints in these cities is sustained, nearly 20 percent in West Berlin.

The police do not create a political culture; they reflect it. They behave in a way the society they serve expects them to behave. Thus, if European systems operate in a manner more consistent with democratic norms and values than do ours, it should tell us something about American democracy, and what it tells us should give us cause for some concern if not alarm.

A Profile of Urban Police

HARLAN HAHN

Introduction

As Americans become increasingly concerned about the critical role performed by the police in enforcing the rules that regulate life in an urbanized nation, a growing interest also is developing in the characteristics and behavior of police personnel. The ability of policemen to fulfill responsibilities of upholding the highest standards of society and of imposing its most severe penalties on human behavior frequently may be dependent upon the personal values, traits, and activities of the individual law enforcement officers. Hence, the examination of those factors along with such matters as police recruitment and socialization forms an important prerequisite to the investigation of police practices. Without a clear understanding of the general attributes of law enforcement personnel and the way in which they affect the performance of law enforcement duties, it is difficult to appreciate the broad implications of police actions in the maintenance of social order.

I. The Police Recruit

A. Socioeconomic Origins

The socioeconomic origins from which officers are recruited may account for many of the more salient characteristics of the police. By a variety of indicators, studies have revealed that most men entering police ranks emerge from working and lower middle-class backgrounds. Two separate surveys of the graduates of the New York City Police Academy, for example, found that nearly eighty per cent of the fathers of policemen were employed as laborers or service workers.(1) In addition, questions about the

SOURCE: *Law and Contemporary Problems*, 36 (Autumn 1971), pp. 449–466.

highest prior position attained by police recruits indicated that most of them had not advanced beyond the status of clerical or sales worker.(2) Despite the relatively low pay and unfavorable working conditions connected with police duty, joining the force usually constitutes an advancement over the occupation held by the patrolman's father as well as over most other jobs with which the recruit himself has been associated. Thus, for many recruits, the prospect of becoming a policeman represents an opportunity for upward social movement and improved economic position.

Although many departments have required examinations that eliminate sizeable majorities of all applicants, an unusually large proportion of policemen have fathers or other relatives who worked in the same occupation. Studies in Chicago, New York, and elsewhere indicate that one-third or more of the police officers in the departments surveyed had relatives who were employed in police work or related fields.(3) A preference for police work often is passed from one generation to the next within a family. Familial influence on the decision to join the force may be partially responsible for the predominance of some ethnic groups, particularly the Irish, in many departments. An investigation of Chicago police sergeants found that two-thirds of the Irish officers had police relatives and three-fourths of those were members of the immediate family.(4) The handing down from father to son of police work as an occupation, contributes to the perpetuation of a common body of police values and traditions.

One of the most serious consequences of the relatively restricted forms of police recruitment is the difficulty of securing black policemen. For many years in most urban departments, the proportion of black policemen has been substantially below the actual percentage of minority residents in the city; and relatively few black officers have been promoted to high police ranks. Although part of this underrepresentation may have been related to the general problem of inferior training and other cultural handicaps faced by most black people, the continuing absence of black men in police forces as employment opportunities for minorities expand in other occupations creates a strong suspicion that there were efforts in many cities to prevent them from becoming policemen. Police work, like other occupations that have been influenced by generational succession and rigid patterns of recruitment, appears to have developed institutional norms and expectations that carefully regulate the types of persons who are allowed to join or succeed in the profession.

In addition to attracting predominantly white, lower middle-class recruits, law enforcement agencies draw few men with advanced educational backgrounds. Although approximately seventy per cent of the police departments in the nation have imposed the educational requirement of a high school degree or its equivalent, fewer than thirty percent of all policemen have ever attended college.(5) The average policemen—and top police administrators—probably have earned high school diplomas, but they seldom have been exposed to college educations. To the extent that higher education has become an indicator of status in middle-class America, police jobs have failed to match the rising standards of other occupations. As a result of their educational plateau, policemen probably consider themselves at a disadvantage in dealing with better educated and more respected members of the community.

B. Job Prestige

Somewhat ironically, citizens display a considerable reluctance to grant esteem to the men who are entrusted with enforcing the rules and norms of society. In 1947, a national survey of the prestige of ninety occupations found that policemen were ranked in the fifty-fifth position.(6) Apparently, public regard for the police has not enjoyed steady improvement. A replication of that study in 1963 revealed that policemen had gained only eight positions and still ranked below the middle of the range of occupations.(7) A pilot study of college students suggests that policemen of the higher ranks may be rated more favorably than the more visible patrolmen,(8) but popular respect for the men who have the responsibility of law enforcement has never been a marked feature of American culture. In many communities, police salaries fail to match prevailing wages for semi-skilled laborers. In general, the public

is unwilling to allocate respect and resources commensurate with the policeman's awesome power to regulate social conduct. Although the allure of such symbols of authority as the badge and uniform may be a persuasive inducement for many recruits, social status and deferential treatment by the public are not major motivating factors in decisions to join the force.

The popular perception of the prestige level of police work apparently is shared by policemen themselves. A survey of the New Orleans department found that most officers considered their job better than that of a furniture mover, auto mechanic, or bus driver, but not as good as that of a high school teacher, druggist, or business executive.(9) The working class backgrounds and limited educational achievements of most police officers probably have prevented them from aspiring to more lucrative or prestigious white collar jobs. The New Orleans survey reported that most police officers considered themselves to be moderately dependable and extroverted, but the following proportions of men ranked themselves as low on other characteristics: ambitious, thirty-two percent; intellectual, forty-eight percent; and sophisticated, eighty-one percent. Only nine per cent regarded themselves as highly ambitious, four per cent ranked themselves as highly intellectual, and no one rated himself as highly sophisticated.(10) This lack of self-esteem probably has an effect on the performance of police work. In deciding to join the police force, many men have abandoned plans of attaining lofty individual or economic goals. Confirmation of this finding was obtained from another survey of policemen in a large West Coast department which asked respondents to select the qualities that best described their present feelings, their probable attitudes in ten years, and their personal goals. In all three categories, the most highly valued characteristic was "good health and relative freedom from worry"; but "social prestige" and being "financially well-to-do" ranked at the bottom of the list.(11) It is evident from the personal profiles of practicing policemen that police work does not attract people with a commitment to strong personal ambitions or broad social objectives.

C. Job Security

The relative security offered by public employment is a major attraction of police work. A survey of policemen in Boston, Washington, and Chicago disclosed that job security and interest were the explanations most frequently mentioned for the decision to become a police officer. Most men did not refer to specific qualities of the work or to prestige and respect as the main reasons for entering the occupation.(12) In responding to questions about aspects of their position that they liked most, the largest proportion cited job security and retirement benefits.(13) Officers who had considered leaving the force mentioned salary and economic considerations as motives for changing jobs, but nearly half said that financial security and retirement benefits were the principal reasons they remained in the department.(14) Although economic considerations may play a major role in both preventing and encouraging police resignations, the survey revealed that most policemen have relatively modest financial goals. The largest group of officers endorsed $6500 to $7500 annually as an acceptable starting wage.(15)

The tendency of most policemen to emphasize job security and to attach major importance to relatively small salaries raises some serious questions about their motivation and the satisfaction that they derive from their jobs. A survey of New York patrolmen revealed that a majority agreed with the statement that any "recruit who thinks he is going to get much personal satisfaction just from performing police duties is due for a rude awakening." Nearly three-fourths of the men who had two years of experience also believed that it would be difficult to prevent policemen from resigning "if it weren't for the salary and other benefits connected with the job."(16) Apparently, most police officers find little enjoyment in those aspects of their work that involve serving others. Despite the critical nature of their duties of applying social controls to human conduct, policemen continue to regard their jobs largely as a means of securing economic rewards.

II. Police Socialization

A. The Basis of Police Solidarity

After policemen join the force, they normally are exposed to a brief period of training before being assigned to patrol duty. Most of the time spent by recruits in police academies or similar institutions is consumed by instruction in practical matters such as routine procedures for patrolling and handling suspects, physical conditioning, and the use of firearms. Only a limited number of hours, if any, is devoted to

courses in human relations or similar subjects that affect police encounters with the public.

Despite the highly pragmatic nature of police training, many rookies and their more experienced colleagues have developed the belief that the average patrolman must be "reeducated" before he reaches the streets. A survey in New York City indicated that a majority of the experienced police officers felt that academy training "cannot overcome the contradictions between theory and practice" and most police recruits believed that they would have to learn everything over again when they were assigned to precincts.(17) This disdain for academy training reflects not only a reluctance to think abstractly about their law enforcement experiences but also some significant features of the working relationships between police officers.

One of the most striking and unusual aspects of the police vocation is the high degree of solidarity displayed by most officers. United by the shared objective of fighting crime and by a common attitude toward the public, policemen display a degree of cohesion unmatched by most other occupational groups. A survey of New York City patrolmen, for example, found that more than two-thirds of all officers agreed with the statement that the "police department is really a large brotherhood in which each patrolman does his best to help all other patrolmen."(18) This sense of fraternal loyalty and support encourages cooperation in the performance of police duties, and also influences many other aspects of law enforcement activities. When rookie patrolmen emerge from academy training, they are exposed to the values and traditions of police work perpetuated by experienced officers. Most recruits find it difficult to violate bonds of departmental camaraderie by rejecting the advice offered by senior colleagues. Despite the efforts of many academy instructors and superior officers to promote new law enforcement practices, solidarity in police ranks has made established procedures highly resistant to change.

Police cohesion not only is characterized by mutually reinforcing attitudes about work and about organizational goals, but it also is reflected in activities during off-duty hours. Since many civilians are uncomfortable about including police officers among their close acquaintances, there is a tendency of policemen and their families to restrict their social contacts to other members of the force.(19) A study of police sergeants in Chicago reported that one-fourth said that "they spend off-duty time with other officers as often as once or twice a week."(20) When the members of a large West Coast department were asked to name their three closest friends thirty-five per cent of them were other policemen. The natural tendency to develop personal loyalties among fellow workers is promoted and accentuated by strong organizational ties in the ranks of police forces. Eighty-six per cent of the officers in the West Coast department had attended at least one police banquet during the past year and fifty-four per cent had participated in three or more such activities in the same period.(21) Social and fraternal groups within police departments, often organized by ethnic distinctions, are numerous and highly active in large cities. In addition, organizations such as the Fraternal Order of the Police and the Patrolmen's Benevolent Association have been formed in many departments to promote and protect the common interest of policemen.

The influence of fellow policemen can also have an impact on the development of an individual officer's ethical standards. In the normal performance of their duties, officers are brought into a close and continuing association with criminals and other elements of the population which have rejected society's moral code. As a result, policemen are exposed to more sources of temptation than most occupational groups. Although no accurate estimates can be provided concerning the amount of corruption that exists in police forces throughout the country, periodic scandals in major cities indicate that at least some policemen use their positions to obtain personal gains or favors. The unique experiences of policemen are likely to affect their ethical values. For example, the survey of New Orleans police officers revealed that two-thirds or more of them considered such acts as politicians taking graft, bribery to avoid a ticket, and cheating on an examination for promotion to be highly immoral; but forty-six per cent saw nothing seriously wrong with discrimination against minority people and fifty-seven per cent had no serious objection to overestimating damages for an insurance report.(22) In a study of patrols in Boston, Chicago, and Washington, sixteen and one-half per cent of the policemen were observed in misconduct that amounted to a felony or a misdemeanor, and an additional ten and one-half per cent admitted that they had engaged in similar practices.(23) According to a former Denver police officer who was involved in a major scandal in that city, police corruption often results from the solidarity of the police and their animosity toward the public. These factors produce the sentiment that "nobody likes us, so the hell with them." For example, before the amount of theft is determined in the investigation of a burglary, new officers have been encouraged by cynical references to public standards to pocket any remaining items—an additional loss which would be almost impossible to detect. After such promptings by fellow officers, "the young cop feels the pressure to belong so strongly that he reaches over and picks up something, cigars perhaps. Then he's 'in,' and the others can do what they wish."(24) Although many people find it difficult to understand how officers of the law can engage in lawless behavior, policemen are exposed to strong temptation and often provocation in the course of their work.

B. Effect on Internal Administration

The strong personal cohesion and organized activity that exist among policemen have a major impact on the operation and administration of police departments. A quasi-military structure of police organizations seldom is realized in everyday practice. Since police officers have developed unified and mutually supportive means of reacting to common problems, their superiors often encounter difficulty in attempting to gain firm control of the department. The effects of police solidarity are particularly evident in attitudes toward departmental rules and regulations. A survey of New York patrolmen revealed, for example, that most officers viewed the *Rules and Procedures*, the officially prescribed policies of the New York City Police Department, as "a guide for patrolmen and not something to be followed to the letter." More than eighty per cent felt that it would be "impossible to always follow the *Rules and Procedures* to the letter and still do an efficient job in police work."(25) Another survey concluded that three-fourths of all police officers in New York were "resigned to the necessity of violating rules in order to perform an active tour."(26) Prevailing attitudes toward departmental regulations greatly complicate the administrator's task of limiting the discretion of the cop on the beat. Since many patrolmen accept the guidance of fellow officers rather than the rules promulgated by their superiors, the cohesion of police forces is a major obstacle to the imposition of effective restrictions on police conduct.

In addition, some evidence indicates that the expectations of policemen cause supervisors to protect officers who have been charged with the violation of department rules. Most police administrators have advanced to higher positions from within the department, and they seldom are able to divest themselves of the fraternal loyalties that form an important part of police work in the ranks. The survey of New York patrolmen disclosed that from one-half to two-thirds agreed with the statement: "Most supervisors are careful to fit the *Rules and Procedures* to the situation rather than insisting the *Rules and Procedures* have to be followed regardless of the situation."(27) More than eighty per cent felt that patrolmen were "officially entitled to all the help" they needed from supervisors, and a comparable proportion believed that supervisors were "expected to give help without any reservations to patrolmen who need help."(28) From the perspective of police officers, superiors are not expected to enforce departmental rules to the detriment of patrolmen; but they are viewed as obligated to protect their subordinates from the restrictions imposed by political authorities and by the public.

When policemen are disciplined, the source of the complaint usually is attributable to an external influence. A survey in New York found that more than three-fourths of the patrolmen and fifty-six percent of the superior officers thought that an "average departmental complaint is a result of the pressure on superiors from higher authority to give out complaints."(29) Disciplinary action against policemen usually is ascribed to vaguely defined sources and not to immediate supervisors or other superiors in the department.

As a result of their dependence on superior officers for protection from unjustified criticism as well as their belief that most complaints arise from external pressures, policemen often display signs of severe anxiety at the threat of disciplinary action. Most police officers, for example, believe that the mere issuance of a charge against them would inevitably produce a guilty verdict. More than half of the patrolmen in New York and forty-one per cent of their superior officers thought that any officer summoned to appear before a disciplinary hearing would "probably be found guilty even when he has a good defense."(30) The basis of this fatalism is reflected in many aspects of police behavior. Law enforcement officers usually perceive themselves as being in conflict with political and community influences, and they protect themselves from the hostile forces by developing a form of solidarity that encompasses all members of the forces. The filing of a

complaint against an individual policeman may seem to destroy those safeguards. Deprived of the support of his supervisors and fellow officers, the policeman accused of misconduct feels himself at the mercy of alien elements. Consequently, even the most temperate criticisms of police conduct frequently are met with unexpected resistance and defensiveness. The perceived loss of departmental protection in disciplinary procedures leaves a residue of bitterness among many policemen. A survey of New York patrolmen who had served at least two years of duty revealed that sixty-three per cent believed that "the department's handling of civilian complaints" was unfair.(31) This sense of unwelcome martyrdom, particularly as a result of grievances that originate outside the department, is exacerbated by the importance of the threat of insecurity in a profession that places a premium on job security.

Despite the high degree of unity exhibited at nearly all levels in most police departments, there is some evidence that top administrators can have an important impact on the morale or performance of law enforcement organizations. Police officers display more concern for internal authority relations than employees of other municipal agencies,(32) and they are particularly apt to personalize authority in departmental superiors.(33) In some cases, these characteristics have produced a temporary responsiveness to departmental authority. One study of Chicago police sergeants conducted in 1960, when the department was embroiled in a major scandal, and in 1965, after a new "reform" superintendent, O. W. Wilson, had assumed control, found a substantial increase in favorable attitudes about how the department was being run.(34) In large measure, the new superintendent produced this change by promoting younger officers and by introducing "professional" law enforcement practices. However, since this type of transformation usually requires centralized authority, it often has been resisted by subordinates within the department. The professionalization of police departments, therefore, acts to undermine the professional stature of individual police officers by limiting their personal discretion in handling the problem of "clients" in the community.(35) While these reform efforts by police administrators probably have a temporary effect on the morale or activities of law enforcement officers, the eventual impact of this trend may be growing opposition and reduction in professional obligations.

The effects of the introduction of professional

norms and practices were evident in the attitudes of the Chicago sergeants. Before the "reform" administration came to power, perceptions of their relations with the public were much more significant than assessments of internal administration in shaping departmental morale. After the new superintendent had initiated his program of professionalization, however, perceptions of citizen respect had a strong impact on the morale of officers who thought that the department was being run well; but citizen attitudes had only a limited effect on the morale of policemen who remained dissatisfied with departmental management.(36) The increasingly positive evaluation of the police force was not accompanied by a growing feeling of public respect or by an increasing reliance on community support as a basis for forming judgments about the department. Most police sergeants maintained the conflicting views that the department had improved but that cooperation with the public had not reflected corresponding gains. Unlike other professional groups which have developed an expanded range of responsibilities and personal relationships with the public, the particular brand of professionalism that has arisen in police departments emphasizes the centralization of authority and a weakening of their relations with the community.

III. Police and the Community

A. *Alienation*

As police departments become increasingly professionalized, they tend to become self-contained rather than reliant upon the assistance of the public. The growing specialization of police functions, for example, reduces the importance of information obtained or contacts established by officers during their tour of duty on the streets. One of the principal means by which the police maintain their separation from the community is through a vigorous emphasis on secrecy. In part to protect themselves from public criticism, many departments rigidly enforce a policy of refusing to discuss police business with civilians.(37) By their defensiveness and alienation, departments may insulate themselves from both public disapproval and support.

1. *The Profile of an Introverted Force.* The increasing gap between the public and the police also is reflected in the characteristics of law enforcement officers. The modern city policeman who lives out-

side the area that he patrols, whose acquaintances are largely restricted to other members of the force, and who surveys his beat from a squad car, usually develops few contacts with residents of the neighborhood to which he is assigned. This estrangement is particularly critical in crime-ridden and potentially volatile urban ghettos. Several studies indicate that only a small proportion of policemen become familiar with the ghettos that they patrol. Not only do patrolmen fail to gain extensive information about the neighborhood, but most confine their contacts to relatively unrepresentative segments of the population. A survey of the policemen who patrol the ghettos of eleven major cities revealed that most were acquainted with store owners and merchants in the areas. More patrolmen were familiar with the organizers of unlawful enterprises such as crime syndicates, numbers rackets, and drug operations than with "important teenage and youth leaders," even though adolescents and young people were viewed as the principal antagonists of the police.(38) The limited relationships developed by the police in ghetto areas do not provide them with an understanding of the mood or the problems of the neighborhoods.

Some evidence has demonstrated that black policemen are able to establish better rapport with ghetto residents than their white counterparts. While less than one-sixth of the white policemen who patrol the ghettos of these eleven cities reported any involvement in the neighborhood, thirty-seven per cent of the black policemen either lived in the area or regularly attended local meetings, and fifty-six per cent of the black patrolmen had relatives living on their beats.(39) Another survey in Boston, Chicago, and Washington found that forty-one per cent of the black policemen, but only twenty-six per cent of the white officers, stated that they liked their assignments because they knew the people well.(40) In addition, eighty-nine per cent of the black patrolmen and only forty-eight per cent of the whites claimed that it was easy to get to know people on their beats.(41) Although the lack of public support was the most common complaint about police work in ghetto neighborhoods, most policemen—white as well as black—stated that they would not prefer to be transferred to another assignment.(42) The largest proportion of black policemen cited their familiarity with local residents as the aspect of their assignment which they liked most. However, a plurality of white policemen said that they liked their patrols primarily because they were "active."(43)

An accurate indication of the relationship between the public and the police was reflected when policemen in Boston, Chicago, and Washington were asked if they ever heard criticism about police practices from people on their beats. Seventy-eight per cent of the black policemen, as opposed to forty-six per cent of their white counterparts, reported receiving such complaints.(44) Thus, the findings suggest that the insulation of the police might be largely restricted to white officers and that the policing of ghetto areas by black patrolmen may offer an important means of improving communications between law enforcement agencies and the community. In responding to complaints from local residents about the police department, however, the usual sharp differences between all policemen and the outside community seemed to reassert themselves. The survey revealed that nearly all police officers—white as well as black—"feel obligated to defend the department when it is criticized."(45) Although black policemen seemed to enjoy a peculiarly close rapport with ghetto residents, almost all members of the force responded to strong public criticism with the usual feelings of suspicion and animosity toward the public that have pervaded police departments for years.

2. *Conservatism.* In addition to the loyalty and defensiveness that prevail among police officers and separate them from the community, restrictions on their political and social affiliations tend to shield the police from involvement in public issues that may be of crucial importance to the society. As civil servants, policemen are often restrained by local regulations from active participation in local controversies. In many areas, this policy apparently is based on an uncritical acceptance of Justice Oliver Wendell Holmes' famous dictum in a Massachusetts State Supreme Court case which upheld the right of a municipality to fire a police officer for discussing political issues by asserting that the man "may have a constitutional right to talk politics, but he has no constitutional right to be a policeman."(46) Furthermore, the police always have displayed a strong antipathy toward political intervention or pressures that might affect their law enforcement activities. As a result, policemen not only tend to reject the guidance and leadership of political officials and community leaders but they also fail to gain extensive exposure to political issues and processes. This lack of political experience is a contributing factor in the markedly conservative and anti-civil libertarian beliefs

among policemen. One researcher concluded after a careful investigation of a large West Coast department that "a Goldwater type of conservatism was the dominant political and emotional persuasion of police."(47) A survey of New Orleans policemen found that forty-two per cent would prohibit a Communist from being employed as a retail clerk and fifty-three per cent would remove any novel written by a Communist from the public library, regardless of the content of the book.(48) In addition, the strong conservative bias of most policemen often has been translated into departmental policies.

B. *Psychological Forces Shaping Police Behavior*

1. *Desire for Power.* The opportunity to wield authority over the lives and conduct of other men undoubtedly has been a major attraction for many police recruits. In some departments, efforts have been made to screen or eliminate recruits who display an excessive interest in gaining a superordinate position over other persons. Between 1953 and 1956, for example, eleven per cent of the applicants for jobs in the Los Angeles Police Department were rejected because they failed to meet minimum psychiatric standards.(49) Despite the attempts to remove persons who are unfit for police work, many men admitted to the force have been drawn to it primarily by the lure of the badge, the gun, and other symbols of authority rather than by the opportunities it affords for community service.

2. *On-the-Job Associations.* Personal backgrounds manifest themselves in the manner and language used by police officers in approaching the public. The unavoidable association between policemen and criminal or underworld persons has injected a larger number of slang terms and epithets in the police vocabulary than in that of other occupational groups. Also, police officers use this jargon with the public as well as among themselves. In a survey of persons arrested by the New Orleans police in 1962, twenty-six per cent of the respondents reported that the policemen used obscenities in making the arrest. (50) The socioeconomic sources of this language, which is more common in working-class than in middle-class styles of life, are reflected in the fact that the vocabulary of the police officer varied by the race, sex, and occupational level of the person arrested. One-third of the white arrestees mentioned that the policemen had used "tough talk" in making

the arrests, while a similar proportion of black arrestees cited racial slurs and epithets. Moreover, white-collar arrestees were more than twice as likely as laborers to report that the policemen had been courteous and had not used vulgar language.(51) The language used by police officers in making arrests not only reveals a strong pattern of deference character-ized by reluctance to use terms among higher status citizens which they would use with their social peers, but it also evidences an emphasis on masculinity.

The stress by policemen on both virility and conventional behavior has bred in them a particular distaste for sexual deviance. A survey of New York officers found that homosexuals were rated second to cop-fighters as those most disliked by policemen; they outranked other despised elements such as drug addicts, annoying drunks, and known criminals.(52) Another survey in New Orleans found that most policemen considered homosexuality more serious than bribing or assaulting a police officer but less serious than burglary, the sale of narcotics, or miscegnation.(53) The occupation of police officer probably provides many men with a means of asserting their masculinity—an ethos characteristic of the working class from which most of them have been recruited.

3. *Tension in the Nature of the Task.* Many observers have suggested that another factor which is instrumental in shaping the approach of police officers toward the public is their constant exposure to danger. They theorize that the perceptual threat of unexpected physical injury or even death accounts for much of police defensiveness and suspicion. However, a survey of policemen in Boston, Chicago, and Washington revealed that only two per cent cited danger as one of the undesirable features of their work, but thirty-seven per cent stated that their wives or families were concerned about this aspect of their job.(54) Police departments may tend to recruit persons who display unusually little concern about their personal safety, or perhaps policemen have become relatively immune to the anxiety caused by the threat of danger. In any event, the perceptions of policemen themselves suggest that fear for personal safety is less influential in molding attitudes than is commonly supposed.

Police perceptions of the public are shaped in part by the nature of the tasks that they have been required to perform. Merely by definition most contacts between policemen and members of the public involve aberrant personal conduct; otherwise the police would not have been called to the scene. Police officers usually confront people in rare mo-ments of crisis. A study of police-citizen interactions in three major cities revealed that a large proportion of hostile police actions were directed at persons who were emotionally agitated or drunk.(55) Continual exposure to distressed or abnormal people may be the basis for such a reaction.

In the investigation of major crimes the police may be placed in an unusual dilemma. Initially, their prospects for apprehending a suspect may depend upon the reports and cooperation of witnesses or victims. Yet a police officer has been taught by instinct and experience to assume a posture of suspicion and to maintain his distance toward all persons. A victim or witness may furnish the informa-tion needed to capture the offender. Yet he also may be deeply implicated in the crime, or in an emotional outburst, he may pose an even more dangerous threat to the officer than the suspect. Consequently, the attitudes of policemen toward the public have been characterized by ambivalence and tension.

Since the violators of important social norms are the principal objects of police attention, the hostility aroused by these criminals may be transferred by policemen to the public in general. Murderers, rapists, and thieves are hardly the kind of people likely to generate sympathy or admiration; the emphasis placed on their capture causes many policemen to adopt cynical attitudes toward everyone. In light of police concentration on the fight against crime and their lack of contact with the public in less traumatic circumstances, it is not surprising that the police have acquired a distorted and negative image of the people whom they serve. As William H. Parker, once Chief of the Los Angeles Police Department and a leading police spokesman, reflected, "I look back over almost . . . thirty-five years of dealing with the worst that humanity has to offer. I meet the failures of humanity daily, and I meet them in the worst possible context . . . I think I have to conclude that this civilization will destroy itself, as others have before it."(56) This pessimism about the future of society and the progress of mankind is a natural product of numerous encounters with the criminal public, but it has an unfavorable effect on the performance of many police duties. Conditioned by the belief that men are fundamentally immoral or depraved, policemen may find it difficult to grant people the respect that is necessary to establish a relationship of mutual trust and cooperation with the public.

IV. Police Discretion and Behavior

A. *Encounters with the Public*

The principal police response to disturbing and distasteful tasks is to adopt a posture of cautious suspicion. In fact, suspicion probably has become the trademark of the police officer in his relations with other people. An article in a leading law enforcement magazine advised policemen to investigate and question persons in twenty common circumstances such as situations in which people were either casual, nervous, or evasive when approached by an officer. (57) A literal interpretation of that list would bring almost all members of the public under police surveillance. The responsibilities of the police mission require officers to place great emphasis on conventional public conduct, and the uncertainties of their work cause them to regard even a slight departure from what they regard as normal behavior as a matter of potentially grave concern.

Yet the police do not stop all persons who appear suspicious or unusual; the reason for this is their discretionary authority. The use of the wide latitude granted police officers, coupled with their general suspicion and defensiveness, has created some major problems regarding the law enforcement practices that affect the public. In many encounters, police officers take actions primarily to preserve and protect their authority rather than to secure compliance with the law or to promote respect for law enforcement. While the discretion allowed policemen may be necessary to provide flexibility sufficient to deal effectively with individual problems and circumstances, it may be abused. Public fear that police discretion might be administered in an arbitrary or overly restrictive manner is aroused by the generally cynical attitude of the police toward the public.

Police encounters with the public are instigated basically in three ways. Most contacts between policemen and private citizens are so-called "dispatched mobilizations" launched by the initiative of citizens seeking police assistance by telephone or by personal visits to a station. Occasionally police officers on the beat or in patrol cars are summoned directly by citizens in "field complaints or mobilizations." On the other hand, when policemen take the initiative the incident is termed an "on-view mobiliza-

tion." Significantly, policemen enjoy the greatest freedom of action in "on-view" situations which seldom are monitored by police supervisors or witnessed by complainants and bystanders. The absence of citizen requests for aid and the ability of people to undermine police authority in "on-view" incidents has made them most likely to produce conflict.(58)

Most contacts between policemen and suspects or persons who were arrested have occurred in on-view mobilizations. A study in Washington, Boston, and Chicago revealed that although the largest number of police-citizen interactions were produced by citizen complaints, one out of every three transactions with suspects or offenders resulted from the initiative of police officers.(59) Policemen tend to exercise their legal powers largely in isolated circumstances of their own choosing where they are least susceptible to the scrutiny of police administrators.

B. *Discretion and Internal Control*

The structure and organization of urban police departments exhibit important characteristics that distinguish them from other social or political institutions. Unlike most groups, in which the range of available actions is constricted as status decreases and subordinates work primarily to fulfill the directives of upper echelon executives, police departments have developed the relatively unique feature of allowing discretion to increase "as one moves *down* the hierarchy."(60)

Police solidarity also has had a major impact on attempts to limit police discretion. In one New York study, less than one-third of the police officers agreed with statements that "each patrolman is not given enough latitude by his supervisors to handle the police problems in his area" and that they "often fail to take necessary police action due to a feeling that supervisors will disapprove of their actions." On the other hand, most of them felt that "supervisors almost never instruct a patrolman to reverse his plans when he has planned to make an arrest or to issue a summons."(61) Department supervisors are relatively ineffective agents for curbing the vast discretion of the average patrolman. The bonds of occupational loyalty and friendship that prevail in law enforcement agencies, as well as the natural propensity of all officers to stress and perceive antagonism between the department and the outside community, probably impede the ability of supervisors to discipline the activities of their subordinates.

The alternatives for controlling discretion provided the heads of police departments are limited somewhat by political and legal pressures; but the more important limitation results from the inability of leaders to effectuate internal controls. Except in a few areas such as traffic regulation, where ticket quotas and the technological resources of data processing equipment provide methods of comprehensive surveillance, police chiefs encounter imposing obstacles in their efforts to alter or even gain needed information about the activities of their forces. Thus, the usual processes of formulating organizational standards are greatly complicated in police departments. In many communities, police administrators have responded to this difficulty by failing to adopt explicit policies regarding critical law enforcement practices, but inaction has the principal effect of expanding the discretion of the cop on the beat. By neglecting the policy-making aspects of police work, law enforcement agencies exacerbate rather than overcome the problems created by the broad latitude available to officers at the lowest levels of police organization.

Even the limited number of specific guidelines provided by statutes and legal codes are liberally interpreted by police forces, and there is little effort to communicate their meaning to rank-and-file policemen. The growing complexity of legal regulations makes it almost impossible for any person without extensive training to become familiar with all forms of conduct that have been declared criminal. In addition, many of the offenses that produce a large proportion of all arrests are so vaguely written as to provide policemen with virtually unlimited opportunities for selective enforcement of the laws. However, the discretion granted the police by loosely drafted and inadequately understood legislation does not necessarily promote repressive or stringent law enforcement. In fact, the normal tendency of the police is to underenforce the law. The investigation of police-citizen encounters in three cities found that a majority of persons who made confessions of illegal behavior were not taken into custody.(62) The hesitancy of police officers to invoke the power of arrest apparently increases with length of service. A survey of 220 policemen showed that, while only six to thirteen per cent of newly appointed recruits believed that arrests were made because "the officer could not avoid it without getting into trouble," twenty-one to twenty-four per cent of the patrolmen who had served for more than two years and eighteen per cent of the superior officers chose this reason. (63) However, a "good arrest," or the apprehension

of a serious crime, is highly valued by most policemen; they seldom arouse intense criticism by producing an excessively large volume of arrests or by adopting harsh enforcement policies. Police decisions often are based upon popular concepts of morality rather than legalistic rules and upon a reluctance to impose seemingly unfair hardships upon others. Many policemen have developed an approach that views man as a corrupt being but that nonetheless attempts to maintain an understanding tolerance of his weaknesses.

Rules governing the exercise of authority often are reinterpreted by police officers to provide them with increased latitude and status. Perhaps the ultimate means of demonstrating police power is the use of physical force or violence. In a classic study, Westley found that the reason most frequently mentioned by policemen for the use of force was "disrespect for the police"; this reason was cited by thirty-seven percent of the officers interviewed as opposed to twenty-three per cent who viewed violence as appropriate only when it was impossible to avoid, nineteen per cent who would employ force to obtain information, ten per cent who would use it to make an arrest or when they knew a suspect was guilty.(64) Although "disrespect for the police" never has been recognized by the law as a legitimate justification for the use of force or violence, many policemen adopt the attitude that force can be applied to gain deference, to impose punishment, and for other reasons that exceed the bounds of legality. The instruments of force, symbolized by the gun and the nightstick provided by the state, frequently are used by police officers to enhance their own authority. Since policemen wield a great deal of discretion in low-visibility situations, it is difficult to impose effective control over the exercise of power. In addition, the cohesion developed by police forces regarding rights that are regarded as necessary to the performance of their duties has intensified the problem of limiting police authority.

Conclusion

Although generalizations about the police are fraught with numerous hazards as well as countless exceptions, the personality profile of the average policeman drawn from many studies suggests that he may possess several attributes that differentiate him from both the general public and other occupational groups. Not only do policemen reflect more conservative and defensive sentiments than other segments of the population, but they also seem to approach human nature with cynicism, suspicion, aggressiveness, and pessimism. The identification of some of those characteristics is probably based as much on popular stereotypes as on careful research, but close observers of police behavior frequently comment on the unusual personality attributes that seem to prevail among policemen. Even among the general public the mention of policemen may bring to mind memories of high school classmates, more renowned for their roughness or athletic prowess than for their intellectual acumen or sensitivity, who have joined the police force. There are difficult and important empirical problems in the identification of the personality attributes of policemen and in the determination of causal patterns among such characteristics. Perhaps the police force is an especially attractive source of employment to persons possessing particular attributes, or perhaps the nature of police work is primarily responsible for producing these characteristics. The resolution of this dilemma clearly has important implications for the evaluation of police conduct.

For many policemen growing indications of disapproval or resentment merely reinforce their basic perceptions of public animosity. Conditioned by their regular contacts with criminal segments of the population, the police have developed relatively low expectations regarding human behavior; given the nature of their work, many of them have not been disappointed. Furthermore, the unique solidarity that exists among police officers tends to make their judgment about the public both a self-fulfilling and a self-sustaining prophecy. Suspicion and distrust are perpetuated not only by the personal experiences of policemen but also by the attitudes and beliefs that prevail in most police departments.

Police perceptions of antagonism and estrangement from the public probably are primarily responsible for many other aspects of their conduct. The attributes that many observers identify as major features of police forces likely have developed as a result of their origins, experience, and response to the views of the community. Major difficulties are encountered in attempts to reduce or eliminate the undesirable aspects of police interaction with the public. Therefore, the outcome of efforts to improve the quality of law enforcement personnel and to regulate the exercise of police discretion may exert a crucial impact on the delicate relationship between law and society.

REFERENCES

1. A. Niederhoffer, *Behind the Shield* 36–37 (1967); McNamara, "Uncertainties in Police Work: The Relevance of Police Recruits' Backgrounds and Training," *The Police: Six Sociological Essays* 192 (D. Bordua ed. 1967).

2. McNamara, *supra* note 1, at 193–94.

3. McNamara, *supra* note 1, at 193; Spencer & Jewell, "Police Leadership: A Research Study," *The Police Chief*, Mar., 1963, at 40.

4. Wilson, "Generational and Ethnic Differences Among Career Police Officers," 69 *Am. J. Soc.* 522 (1964).

5. *The President's Commission on Law Enforcement and Administration of Justice, Task Force Report: The Police* 10, 126–27 (1967).

6. Hatt & North, "Prestige Ratings of Occupations," *Man, Work, and Society* 277 (S. Nosow & W. Form eds. 1962).

7. Hodge, Siegel, & Rossi, "Occupational Prestige in the United States, 1925–1963," 70 *Am. J. Soc.* 286 (1964).

8. Niederhoffer, *supra* note 1, at 21–23.

9. J. Fichter & B. Jordan, *Police Handling of Arrestees* 23 (1964).

10. Fichter & Jordan, *supra* note 9, at 15.

11. J. Skolnick, *Justice Without Trial* 269–70 (1967).

12. Reiss, "Career Orientations, Job Satisfaction, and the Assessment of Law Enforcement Problems by Police Officers," *Two Studies in Crime and Law Enforcement in Major Metropolitan Areas* 18–19 (undated).

13. *Id.* at 27–29.

14. *Id.* at 36–38.

15. *Id.* at 44–46.

16. McNamara, *supra* note 1, at 242–43.

17. Niederhoffer, *supra* note 1, at 211–13.

18. McNamara, *supra* note 1, at 246.

19. M. Banton, *The Policeman in the Community* 188–219 (1964).

20. Wilson, "Police Morale, Reform, and Citizen Respect: The Chicago Case," *The Police: Six Sociological Essays* 157 (D. Bordua, ed. 1967).

21. Skolnick, *supra* note 11, at 52.

22. *Id.* at 36.

23. *New York Times*, July 5, 1968, at 1.

24. Stern, "What Makes a Policeman Go Wrong?" 53 *J. Crim. L.C. & P.S.* 97, 100 (1962).

25. McNamara, *supra* note 1, at 240–41.

26. Niederhoffer, *supra* note 1, at 217–18.

27. McNamara, *supra* note 1, at 241–42.

28. *Id.* at 232–33.

29. Niederhoffer, *supra* note 1, at 207.

30. Niederhoffer, *supra* note 1, at 178, 214–16.

31. McNamara, *supra* note 1, at 235–36.

32. Peabody, "Authority Relations in Three Organizations," *Pub. Ad. Rev.*, June, 1963, vol. 23, at 87.

33. Peabody, "Perceptions of Organizational Authority: A Comparative Analysis," 6 *Ad. Sci. Q.* 461 (1962).

34. Wilson, *supra* note 20, at 139–49.

35. Bordua & Reiss, "Law Enforcement," *The Uses of Sociology* 275 (P. Lazarsfeld, W. Sewell, & H. Wilensky eds. 1967).

36. Wilson, *supra* note 20, at 151–55.

37. Westley, "Secrecy and the Police," 34 *Social Forces* 254 (1956).

38. Groves, "Police in the Ghetto," *Supplemental Studies for the National Advisory Commission on Civil Disorders* 103, 112–113 (1968).

39. *Id.*

40. Reiss, *supra* note 12, at 60–61.

41. *Id.* at 64–67.

42. *Id.* at 58–59; Groves, *supra* note 38, at 104.

43. *Id.* at 59–60.

44. *Id.* at 76–78.

45. *Id.* at 78.

46. McAuliffe v. New Bedford, 115 Mass. 216, 220; 29 N.E. 517 (1829).

47. Skolnick, *supra* note 16, at 61.

48. Fichter & Jordan, *supra* note 9 at 15.

49. Rankin, "Psychiatric Screening of Police Recruits," 20 *Pub. Personnel Rev.* 191 (1959).

50. Fichter & Jordan, *supra* note 9, at 30.

51. *Id.* at 28, 31.

52. Niederhoffer, *supra* note 1, at 122–23.

53. Fichter & Jordan, *supra* note 9, at 24.

54. Reiss, *supra* note 12, at 38–39.

55. Black & Reiss, "Patterns of Behavior in Police and Citizen Transactions," *Two Studies in Crime and Law Enforcement in Major Metropolitan Areas* 29–51 undated.

56. Interview by Donald McDonald with William H. Parker, in Santa Barbara, Center for the Study of Democratic Institutions, 1962, p. 25.

57. Adams, "Field Interrogation," *Police*, March–April, 1963, at 28.

58. Black & Reiss, *supra* note 55, at 4–13.

59. *Id.* at 74–80.

60. J. Wilson, *Varieties of Police Behavior* 7 (1968).

61. McNamara, *supra* note 1, at 210–11.

62, Black & Reiss, *supra* note 55, at 111–12.

63. Niederhoffer, *supra* note 1, at 200.

64. Westley, "Violence and the Police," 59 *Am. J. Soc.* 34 (1953).

2 | Police Role and Career

This section illustrates the central theme of this book which focuses on the ambivalence of the police, and parenthetically, the concomitant conflict on the part of academics, scholars and researchers who are equally confused and inconsistent in assessing the police role in society. If the police are not sure whether their principal function is to prevent crime or serve the public, the researchers are no more consistent in their conclusions. At one extreme is a group of experts who declare that the police personality is authoritarian or unduly suspicious so that the officer perceives his clientele as potential "symbolic assailants." On the other hand Symonds' research would appear to underscore findings that stress the essential mental health and altruism of police personnel.

In truth the ambivalence of the police is built into the very structure of law enforcement by the variety of duties imposed upon police practitioners by the law, custom, and ethical requirements of the society they live in. To illustrate, the police officer may be the enforcer with a gun shooting to kill, or a savior who risks his own life willingly in the hope of saving someone who needs help. He knows that in every important incident his action will draw vituperation as well as applause.

Legal codes, departmental regulations, and municipal ordinances governing police conduct generally can be arranged into five categories:

1. Protection of life and property
2. Preservation of the peace
3. Detection of crime and arrest of offenders
4. Enforcement of laws
5. Crime prevention

As an officer moves through each of these levels during the course of a working tour, the conflicting demands imposed by these distinct roles create the anxiety, conflict, and frustration which characterize the ambivalence of the police in today's world. Few other occupations create as much stress, nor do they have as much potential for serious repercussions. Indeed, behavioral scientists tell us that laboratory experiments embodying such conflicts, demands, and stresses often produce symptoms of neurosis and other dysfunctions in their subjects. The police officer faces these hazards without the cushioning of malpractice insurance to rescue him when matters go awry.

Police systems and organizations spontaneously generate special purpose units such as tactical patrol forces, crime prevention units, vice squads, and police-community relations units; each of these generates an empire and a power base within a department. In the competition for aggrandizement and for a larger share of the always-limited resources, the entire agency often becomes a battleground where there is a shifting balance of power. This situation is the structural and systemic equivalent to personal social-psychological ambivalence. Each reinforces the other. The net effect is that a police officer's personal uncertainties and role conflicts are symbiotically compounded by the organizational dilemmas.

Perhaps it is the dynamic nature of the subject matter, or the ephemeral style of the police environment, which causes confusion for academic researchers so that they too are uncertain as to the appropriateness of their concepts, data, findings, and conclusions with respect to the police. The difficulties inherent in police research are further exacerbated by the turbulent character of the modern academic environment in terms of distribution of grant money, promotions, and the political implications of one's findings. Finally, there is always the hidden agenda of ideological considerations.

Explanations of Police Behavior:

A Critical Review and Analysis

JOHN F. GALLIHER

In recent years many social scientists have attempted to explain why police behave the way they do in performing their duties. What follows is a review of some dominant themes running through the myriad of articles and books which have appeared on this subject in the last few years. This survey does not purport to offer an exhaustive coverage of all relevant literature but is intentionally selective to highlight some observable patterns. After this review, some observations will be made regarding the theoretical and empirical weaknesses in this research, and an analysis of some reasons for these deficiencies will be discussed. Finally, some suggestions will be made for profitable new directions for future research on police behavior.

Psychological Perspective

Several sociologists have focused upon the personality of the individual police officer as important in determining how he performs his role. Skolnick (1966:42–70) suggests that policemen have a "working personality" by which he means a set of cognitive tendencies which influence their work. By virtue of enforcing the law, the police become very supportive of the status quo. Skolnick argues that to believe in their task and appear consistent to themselves, police become extremely politically conservative. Moreover, because of their job, police officers are highly sensitive to signs of danger.

A young man may suggest the threat of violence to the policeman by his manner of walking or "strutting," the insolence in the demeanor being registered by the policeman as a possible preamble to later attack (Skolnick, 1966:46).

This helps explain police willingness to act against some citizens which might otherwise be interpreted merely as harassment.

Niederhoffer (1967:103–151, especially 118–119) speculates that police officers are transformed into authoritarian personalities by virtue of the police role. He (Niederhoffer, 1967:90–102) also suggests that they develop a cynicism toward the public which is a consequence of performing their job. Because their job throws them into contact with so many dishonest people, officers begin to see everyone as corrupt. Niederhoffer (1967:95) quotes a detective as follows: "I am convinced that we are turning into a nation of thieves. I have sadly concluded that nine out of ten persons are dishonest."

McNamara (1967:211–212) administered F scales to police recruits and found an increase in authoritarianism before and after recruit police training and a further increase after one year on the job. Police with two years of experience were found to be even more authoritarian than any of the other groups. This supports the notion that police apparently become more authoritarian as a result of their experience as police officers. McNamara (1967:212) suggests that this increased authoritarianism is likely to lead to disagreement with the courts' emphasis upon individual rights.

It should be noted that the significance of McNamara's research is somewhat blunted by Bayley and Mendelsohn's (1969:17–18) finding that police are, in fact, *less* authoritarian than other citizens. Also, Niederhoffer (1967:150) observes that in McNamara's research the mean score on the F scale was slightly less than that found by the developers of the instrument when testing civilians of a similar social class. Moreover, even if police are made more authoritarian by their occupational role, this says nothing about the structural determinants of this influence. Why is it that the environment is struc-

SOURCE: *The Sociological Quarterly*, *12* (Summer 1971), pp. 308–18.

tured to give officers experiences that increase their authoritarianism?

Demands of the Immediate Situation

Recently a number of articles have emphasized the great amount of discretion police are free to use in deciding to make an arrest. It has been found that police rely heavily on the characteristics of the immediate situation in making these decisions.

For example, Bittner (1967) found that police on skid row make their decision to arrest an individual mainly on the basis of the perceived risk of the person creating a disorder rather than on the basis of degree of guilt. Black (1970) and Black and Reiss (1970) found that a major component in this decision to arrest is the preference of the complainant. Some studies have also found that the deference displayed by the suspect has a bearing on the use of discretion by the officer (Westley, 1953; Piliavin and Briar, 1964). Regarding the choice of a disposition, Piliavin and Briar (1964:210) suggest that, "in the opinion of juvenile patrolmen themselves the demeanor of apprehended juveniles was a major determinant of their decisions for 50-60 percent of the juvenile cases they processed."

However, police use of discretion as well as suspects' behavior are not random occurrences. All occur within a social structural context. Unfortunately, some sociologists are mainly concerned with the demands of the immediate situation and neglect the broader social structure within which this interaction occurs. A relevant question in this connection, which is seldom asked, is, why does it seem that Black Americans more frequently than other citizens are loath to show respect for the police?

Role Conflict

Some studies of police behavior locate explanations in a social psychological, role conflict model. The basic idea is that officers perceive conflicting expectations from others regarding how they should carry out their job. Skolnick (1966:1–22) discusses the policeman's "dilemma" of enforcing the law while at the same time maintaining order. The police believe they are expected to do both, but order maintenance may at times require the officer to work outside the law ignoring a suspect's constitutional rights. Wilson (1963:199) suggests that this conflict between achieving order or catching a suspect is especially intense when a "crusade" is launched by a department to solve an important case. The rules of law require respect for civil liberties but during times of crisis, police feel compelled to forget this and to consider only the efficiency of means in catching the criminal.

Wilson (1963:198–199) observes another source of conflicting expectations. In a heterogeneous society one part of the public may want different kinds of enforcement from the police than do other parts. For example, urban liberals and Blacks feel differently about police use of force than other citizens.

Preiss and Ehrlich (1966:94–121) also report on police officers' perceptions of conflicting expectations of the various audience groups in which they are involved. One example of this role conflict which they report is discrepancies perceived between officers' wives' views and their supervisors' views regarding the appropriate limitations in the demands of their job (Preiss and Ehrlich, 1966:99–101). That is, officers perceive their wives as believing the obligations to the job should end after eight hours, while their supervisors see their obligations as continuing 24 hours a day.

The implication in all of this literature is that because of these role conflicts officers may be forced to make certain compromises, accommodations, and choices. Unfortunately, no theoretical models are offered to help predict the specific choices made. Perhaps this is true because of insufficient attention to structural bases of the role conflict.

Subcultural Approach

Other studies have sought to explain police behavior by using what is essentially a subcultural approach. The argument is that police officers are a unique group. Somewhat like delinquent boys, they are subjected to special strains and make collective rather than individual adjustments to these problems.

In an early police study, Westley (1953) found evidence of a police subculture as reflected in a code justifying the use of violence to coerce respect.

> The most significant finding is that at least 37 percent of the men believed that it was legitimate to use violence to coerce respect. This suggests that policemen use the resource of violence to persuade their audience (the public) to respect their occupational status. In terms of the police-

man's definition of the situation, the individual who lacks respect for the police, the "wise guy" who talks back, or any individual who acts or talks in a disrespectful way, deserves brutality (Westley, 1953:39).

Westley also found that this code forbids police from informing against fellow officers. Typically, officers indicated that they would adhere to this rule of secrecy which functions to protect the police against attacks from the community (Westley, 1956).

However, policemen cannot and do not employ sanctions against their colleagues for using violence, and individual men who personally condemn the use of violence and avoid it whenever possible refuse openly to condemn acts of violence by other men on the force (Westley, 1953:40).[1]

More recent research by Stoddard (1968), Savitz (1970), and Reiss (1968) supports the notion of a code of secrecy.

Skolnick (1966:53–58) suggests that the dangerousness of the police mission as well as the requirement that officers use authority against civilians contributes to solidarity. The reasoning is that the more hostility the police receive from the public the more isolated they become and consequently the more dependent they become upon each other.[2]

Although these studies have used socio-cultural variables in their analyses of police behavior, they have erred in defining the environment of the police as a given, as constant across all communities. One problem with such an approach is that it is impossible to use it to explain variations in police attitudes and behavior found in different communities. If we can observe differences in law enforcement practices in various communities, then it seems reasonable to expect differences in the nature of the subculture and related structural strains.

Departmental Characteristics Approach

The problem of explaining differences in policing styles has received some attention from those focusing on departmental characteristics as independent determinants of police behavior and attitudes. The

argument is that police behavior is a result of the particular situation found in each department.[3]

Wilson (1968a:9–30) compares the handling of juveniles in an efficient, highly-trained professional department and in a nonprofessional department. He found that the former was much more likely to process juvenile law violators officially than the latter. The nonprofessional department relied much more heavily on informal alternatives such as issuing warnings.

In *Varieties of Police Behavior*, Wilson (1968b) isolates three types of law enforcement style displayed by various departments. One style of law enforcement emphasizes service to the community, another strict enforcement of all laws, and one is mainly oriented to maintenance of order. Most important for this discussion is that Wilson pictures police departments as having some independence, as not being directly controlled by the community. One reflection of this independence is that it is not always possible to predict the style of law enforcement given the characteristics of the community (Wilson, 1968b:227–277).

Gardiner (1969:72) explains much of the difference in traffic law enforcement in two communities by the differences in the desires of the chiefs of the two departments. One problem with this type of analysis is that it implicitly assumes that the recruitment of chiefs into a department is random or at least not significantly affected by the social structure.

Neither Gardiner nor Wilson claim that the law enforcement style is completely independent of the community, but they are, nonetheless, unable to develop a conceptual model to handle these social structural relationships.

Socio-Cultural Approach

A few attempts have been made to describe how societies or communities seem to determine the characteristics of local police.

In comparing European police with those in the United States, Berkley (1969) found the latter much more prone to violence. This he claims is a direct reflection of American values.

If the American police are prone to use violent and repressive tactics, American society offers

---

[1] Westley's internal footnotes have been omitted.
[2] A similar point is made in Fogelson (1968) and Westley (1956:254–255).

[3] I am indebted to Patrick Donovan for suggesting this type of explanation.

them the means and the climate to do so. No other democratic nation compares to the United States in the acceptance and even glorification of violence as a way to solve problems (Berkley, 1969:197).

Banton (1964:86–126) explains many of the differences he found in comparing British and American police officers by virtue of the greater social integration in Great Britain. Since Britain is a more homogeneous society with citizens holding more consistent values, it is predictable that British police would be exposed to less violence. This allows the police to operate differently. There is less reason to smother all internal strains within a department and less reason for solidarity (Banton, 1964:118–119).

Stinchcombe (1963) compares urban and rural differences in the structural conditions which affect policing. In cities, large numbers of people are concentrated into relatively small amounts of public space. This makes police control of public places more economical. Moreover, it is in the cities that informal controls are weakest and where patrol is most necessary. Therefore, Stinchcombe says this makes sense of the fact that police in the cities can and do frequently act on their own initiative in making arrests. In rural areas it is both less economical and less necessary to patrol public places and, therefore, the rural police initiate fewer of their arrests and rely more on citizen complaints to attract their attention to a problem (Stinchcombe, 1963:152).

Although the approaches in this section take greater account of social structural influences than any of those preceding, on the whole they still offer an incomplete conceptual framework. *The fundamental problem in all the social science explanations of police behavior is that they take no systematic account of the influence of class conflict on law enforcement.*

Conceptual Models and Empirical Evidence

We have just seen that if the psychological characteristics of officers are studied, the implication is that this is important in understanding police behavior. By studying the demands of the immediate situation which officers face or their role conflicts, it is also sometimes assumed that we can better understand their method of operation. Others point to a police subculture or the department leadership to explain officers' behavior. Only those studies that emphasize the social structural environment of policing have the potential of directing attention to social class as a determinant of law enforcement style. All others, of necessity, would miss the importance of class conflict since they direct attention away from the social structure toward a low-level description of the action in immediate law enforcement situations.

Much of police behavior seems most easily explained if one considers that whenever there is a conflict of interests between the dominant classes in a society and less powerful groups, the police protect the interests of the former and regulate the behavior of the latter. The police role attracts authoritarian individuals and increases their authoritarianism once on the job. Perhaps this happens because of the demands made upon the police to suppress economic and racial minorities. Such tasks are most attractive to the authoritarian personality and undoubtedly any of an officer's initial doubts about such activities are lessened by an increasingly authoritarian orientation. The literature indicating that police are free to use discretion in making arrests also shows that this discretion is used to the disadvantage of minority groups (Skolnick, 1966:85; Goldman, 1963; Wald, 1967:139–151; Wilson, 1968a). Wilson's (1963:198–199) observations regarding the differing demands of Blacks and urban liberals compared to other citizens as a source of role conflict for the police can be interpreted in class conflict terms. Officers can be seen as experiencing role conflict in part because of different and conflicting demands from various social classes in the community. There is some evidence that police subcultures develop in a department both to legitimize and keep secret suppression of economic and racial minorities (Reiss, 1968; Westley, 1970). Department leadership and methods of operation can be interpreted as a response to the demands of powerful interest groups (Walker, 1968; especially 13–14). Simple descriptions of police personalities or specific situations faced by the police take no account of class interests and class conflict.

Mills (1943) observes that concern with specific situations among social scientists leads to such a low level of abstraction that the data can't be brought together within a theoretical framework. Moreover, he contends that this low level of abstraction does not permit an examination of the normative structures and how they are related to the distribution of power. This is exactly what seems to have happened in studies of the police. Social scientists have been busy collecting disparate "facts" about policing and have either been unable or unwilling to develop related conceptual frameworks which take account of the social structure, including a consideration of social class. Newman (1966:181–182) claims that sociological treatment of the criminal justice system including the police is lacking in a theoretical framework and, as a consequence, is empirically naive. This reflects Merton's (1968:139–155) well-known argument that without an integrated theoretical framework even intelligent fact-gathering is impossible.

An important test of any conceptual model is the degree to which it is congruent with and clarifies the bulk of relevant empirical data. Kitsuse and Cicourel (1963:136–137) maintain that since official rates of deviant behavior are compiled by specific organizations, these rates reflect organizational methods of operation. Using this reasoning, one readily available pool of information regarding police behavior is arrest data.

It is well established that in most areas of the United States the majority of those people arrested are poor and/or Black. As indicated earlier, some observers of arrest practices who emphasize that police can exercise great discretion show that in those cases where this discretion can be most easily exercised, the bulk of those arrested are poor and Black (Skolnick, 1966:85; Goldman, 1963; Wald, 1967:139–151; Wilson, 1968a). There is also an awareness of other discriminatory treatment given to economic and racial minorities by the police such as verbal and physical harassment (Reiss, 1968; Schwartz, 1967:446–447).

Curiously, these patterns found in arrest practices and other police treatment of minorities haven't influenced the theoretical models used in explaining police behavior. If they were used, social class and class conflict would necessarily be incorporated into explanations of police behavior. Cook (1967:120) observes that "there is no recognition that the processes of law enforcement serve the interests of dominant groups in the society and either ignore or oppose the interests of those in lower social strata." Perhaps the reason for this is that social scientists have been misusing arrest data. They have been using it as a basis upon which to generate theories of criminal behavior and have been neglecting its uses as a reflection of police behavior.

Here and there some cursory recognition of class does appear. Quite early in *Behind the Shield*, Niederhoffer (1967) introduces the notion of class and its effects on law enforcement. He quotes Joseph Lohman, the late Dean of the School of Criminology of the University of California at Berkeley, who was himself a police officer at one time. "The police function [is] to support and enforce the interests of the dominant political, social, and economic interests of the town, and only incidentally to enforce the law" (Niederhoffer, 1967:12). But if Niederhoffer mentions class quickly, he drops it even more quickly in favor of "the principle of equilibrium" meaning that police are mainly concerned with protecting themselves from all criticism from whatever source (Niederhoffer, 1967:13–15).

Wilson (1963:213) suggests in passing that a professional police force which applies the law equally to all citizens is impossible in a highly stratified community. Elsewhere in the same paper he says:

> Property owners, for example, may want maximum protection of their property and of their privacy; slum dwellers, however, may not like the amount of police activity necessary to attain the property owners' ends. Negroes and urban liberals may unite in seeking to end "police brutality"; lower-middle-class homeowners whose neighborhoods are "threatened" with Negro invasion may want the police to deal harshly with Negroes or to look the other way while the homeowners themselves deal harshly with them (Wilson, 1963:198–199).

Even though class is introduced, Wilson either cannot or will not follow through with any analysis. All he can bring himself to say is that this presents the police with an inconsistency.

In his Ph.D. dissertation, which was only recently published in full, Westley (1970) shows that police indicated they respond differently to different social classes. One policeman is quoted as saying that "in the better districts the purpose is to make friends out of the people and get them to like you. If you react rough to them, naturally they will hate you" (Westley, 1970:98). On the other hand, it seems just as obvious to the police that they can only elicit respect and obedience from slum dwellers by resorting to force (Westley, 1970:99). Westley (1970:96–99) suggests that part of the difference in the police perception of the affluent and poor is due to the differences in their political power—police are afraid to brutalize the wealthy because of their political influence. Moreover, the poor are seen as more disposed to law violation and conflict with the police because of their great economic need. Just as it appears that Westley is on the verge of a thorough structural analysis of police behavior, he tells the reader that police attitudes and behavior have subcultural roots, and surprisingly, he ignores the effects of class conflict upon this subculture.

Dirty Work at Home and Abroad

The fact that social scientists have not recognized the nature of police work is perhaps in some ways similar to the German citizens' unfamiliarity with the operation of the S.S. Hughes (1962) describes the apparent ignorance of Germans regarding the systematic extermination of the Jews. He contends that the S.S. was used by the German people to solve their Jewish problem. Most Germans felt that a Jewish problem did exist, but once the S.S. was created it not only took care of the problem but allowed most German citizens to remain uninvolved in the solution. Since the S.S. was sworn to secrecy, German citizens could claim ignorance of what this group was doing. One of Hughes' major assumptions is that the public doesn't accurately perceive the morally outrageous nature of dirty work and that this obfuscation is indeed a function of dirty work.

Some immediate similarities appear between the S.S. role in wartime Germany and the police role in the United States. Many Americans would doubtlessly agree that we have a Negro problem. The police, like the S.S., are highly secretive (Westley, 1956; Reiss, 1968; Savitz, 1970; Stoddard, 1968) which keeps their morally questionable acts shielded from most Americans. This functions to control poor and Black Americans in any way necessary while other citizens can continue to believe this is a free democratic society and yet have their property protected at the same time. In fact, the dirty work of policing American slums is so well hidden from the middle classes that even middle class sociologists fail to understand its meaning and function, the function being the maintenance of a highly economically-stratified and racist society.

The police are not a part of the dominant classes of American society, usually being recruited from the lower class or lower middle class (Preiss and Ehrlich,

1966:12; Niederhoffer, 1967:36—38; McNamara, 1967:193; Bayley and Mendelsohn, 1969:6). It is predictable, however, that largely lower class individuals would perform the police tasks since the delicate sensibilities of middle class and upper class gentlemen probably would not allow them to shoot a looter or harass Black youngsters, but they are not bothered by hiring someone else to do the job.

Social scientists studying the police have typically assumed that the individual police officer or department is independent to implement social policy much as they see fit. This assumption is reflected in much of the literature reviewed here which stresses the importance of police personalities, discretion, subculture, or police chiefs as determinants of law enforcement style.[4] It is incredible that social scientists would believe that a highly-stratified society would allow lower class or marginally middle class people such as the police to control major social policy.

If social scientists are unable to understand the place of law enforcement in class conflict, then it should not be surprising that other well-educated political liberals, radical students, and many Black Americans would see the police as a main source of trouble. Their criticism lends public credence to the social science research which implies that the police are somehow individually or collectively responsible for the way in which laws are enforced. To the degree that police are seen as independent, they will be held responsible to the same degree, or course, for the manner in which they operate.

Conclusion

It is sometimes suggested that if police were better organized, this would help them do a better job and would reduce police-community tensions (Wilson, 1968b; Berkley, 1969). Also, the suggestion is sometimes made that better-trained police would solve many of the problems they encounter (Berkley, 1969:87; Skolnick, 1969:290—291; Task Force Report: The Police, 1967:36—37). However, as Terris (1967:63—64) has shown, some cities with very well-trained police still have major police-minority problems. One interpretation for this is that as long as police are used for the purpose of containing eco-

[4] An especially clear illustration of this emphasis on the independence of the police is in Skolnick's *The Politics of Protest* (1969).

nomic and racial minorities, police-minority conflicts will not subside. If police are better educated and better organized, they will just become more efficient oppressors.

Since there are obvious differences in law enforcement styles across communities and countries, students of police behavior can profit by directing their research toward an analysis of what effect the presence of large numbers of economic and racial minorities has upon the style of law enforcement in a given jurisdiction. The question involves the relationship between the scope of class conflict and the behavior of the police. The answer to this question would include a description of the exact nature of the structural linkage between the community and local police departments and the kind of theoretical model(s) which would allow us to predict these linkages.

If it is assumed "that the processes of law enforcement serve the interests of dominant groups in the society and either ignore or oppose the interests of those in lower social strata" (Cook, 1967:120), one might make certain predictions for police behavior. Taking such a perspective one might predict, for example, that in heterogeneous communities with large numbers of economic and racial minorities police would behave in an oppressive fashion toward minorities because of the threat these people symbolize to the rest of the community. Following this reasoning this type of police behavior seems less likely to occur in more homogeneous communities.

The argument developed here is not meant to imply that consideration of class conflict is a *sufficient* condition for further understanding of police behavior but only that it is a *necessary* condition. It's not that class conflict alone can help us better understand police behavior but only that it is one element that must be considered.

REFERENCES

Banton, Michael. 1964 The Policeman in the Community. New York: Basic Books.

Bayley, David H. and Harold Mendelsohn. 1969 Minorities and the Police. New York: The Free Press.

Berkley, George E. 1969 The Democratic Policeman. Boston: Beacon Press.

Bittner, E. 1967 "The police on skid-row: a study of peace keeping." American Sociological Review 32 (October):699–715.

Black, D. J. 1970 "Production of crime rates." American Sociological Review 35 (August):733–748.

Black, D. J. and A. J. Reiss 1970 "Police control of juveniles." American Sociological Review 35 (February):63–77.

Cook, W. 1967 "Policemen in society: which side are they on?" Berkeley Journal of Sociology 12 (Summer):117–129.

Fogelson, R. M. 1968 "From resentment to confrontation: the police, the Negroes, and the outbreak of the nineteen-sixties riots." Political Science Quarterly 83 (June):217–247.

Gardiner, John A. 1969 Traffic and the Police, Variations in Law-Enforcement Policy. Cambridge: Harvard University Press.

Goldman, Nathan. 1963 The Differential Selection of Juvenile Offenders for Court Appearance. New York: National Research and Information Center, National Council on Crime and Delinquency.

Hughes, E. C. 1962 "Good people and dirty work." Social Problems 10 (Summer):3–11.

Kitsuse, J. I. and A. V. Cicourel. 1963 "A note on the uses of official statistics." Social Problems 11 (Fall):131–139.

McNamara, John H. 1967 "Uncertainties in police work: the relevance of police recruits' backgrounds and training." Pp. 163–252 in David J. Bordua (ed.), The Police. New York: John Wiley & Sons.

Merton, Robert K. 1968 "The bearing of sociological theory on empirical research." Pp. 139–155 in Robert K. Merton, Social Theory and Social Structure. New York: The Free Press.

Mills, C. W. 1943 "The professional ideology of social pathologists." American Journal of Sociology 59 (September):165–180.

Newman, Donald J. 1966 "Sociologists and the administration of criminal justice." Pp. 177–187 in Arthur B. Shostak (ed.), Sociology in Action. Homewood, Ill.: Dorsey Press.

Niederhoffer, Arthur 1967 Behind the Shield, The Police in Urban Society. Garden City, N.Y.: Doubleday & Company.

Piliavin, I. and S. Briar. 1964 "Police encounters with juveniles." American Journal of Sociology 70 (September): 206–214.

Preiss, Jack J. and Howard J. Ehrlich. 1966 An Examination of Role Theory, The Case of the State Police. Lincoln: University of Nebraska Press.

Reiss, A. J., Jr. 1968 "Police brutality—answers to key questions." Trans-action 5 (July-August):10–19.

Savitz, L. 1970 "The dimensions of police

loyalty." American Behavioral Scientist (May-June, July-August):693–704.

Schwartz, H. 1967 "Stop and frisk (a case study in judicial control of the police)." Criminal Law, Criminology and Police Science 58 (December): 433–464.

Skolnick, Jerome H. 1969 The Politics of Protest. New York: Simon and Schuster. 1966 Justice Without Trial. New York: John Wiley and Sons.

Stinchcombe, A. L. 1963 "Institutions of privacy in the determination of police administrative practice." American Journal of Sociology 69 (September):150–160.

Stoddard, E. R. 1968 "The informal 'code' of police deviancy: a group approach to 'blue-coat crime.'" Criminal Law, Criminology and Police Science 59 (June):201–213.

Task Force Report: The Police 1967 Washington, D.C.: U.S. Government Printing Office (Number 237–588).

Terris, B. J. 1967 "The role of the police." The Annals 374 (November):58–69.

Walker, Daniel. 1968 Rights in Conflict. New York: Bantam Books.

Wald, Patrica M. 1967 "Poverty and criminal justice." Pp. 139–151 in Task Force Report: The Courts. Washington, D.C.: U.S. Government Printing Office (Number 239–114).

Westley, William A. 1970 Violence and the Police: A Sociological Study of Law, Custom, and Morality. Cambridge: MIT Press. 1956 "Secrecy and the police." Social Forces 34 (March):254–257. 1953 "Violence and the police." American Journal of Sociology 59 (July):34–41.

Wilson, James Q. 1968a "The police and the delinquent in two cities." Pp. 9–30 in Stanton Wheeler (ed.), Controlling Delinquents. New York: Johy Wiley & Sons. 1968b Varieties of Police Behavior, Cambridge: Harvard University Press. 1963 "The police and their problems: a theory." Public Policy, A Yearbook of the Graduate School of Public Administration, Harvard University 12, 189–216.

Policemen and Policework:

A Psychodynamic Understanding

MARTIN SYMONDS

Policemen and policework form an important area of public service that openly and dramatically involves many aspects of our daily lives. In recent years, the police are being called upon, more and more, by the community to perform many complex services. No longer is the citizenry content to have the police perform the simplistic functions of the watchman or the guardian of the peace.

Yet the community tends to react to the police as if they were a distinct and separate body almost alien to the community. This response tends to confuse the majority of young men who become

SOURCE: *The American Journal of Psychoanalysis,* 32 (1972), pp. 163–69.

policemen. They consider their function as helping the public, and therefore they become upset and confused when they find themselves as part of a group that is feared, disliked, hated, or even assaulted in the performance of these services. Some individuals feel that these hostile attitudes are only seen in the ghetto. However, these negative feelings about policemen are openly expressed by individuals from all economic groups. The experience of meeting with indifference to outright hostility of the public towards the policeman eventually results in feelings of isolation and alienation of the police from the general community that they serve. This isolation and alienation reinforce the tendency of the police to close ranks and they then develop all the feelings and some of the responses that minority groups have when they are or feel isolated from the majority. However, there is one notable difference. The police are a minority group with physical power—a gun and a club—and they have been empowered by the community to use this delegated power in preserving law and order for a community they feel has isolated them.

The isolation of the police from the community is further widened by a trait that all police departments share in common, viz. a policy of official silence concerning their behavior. The police traditionally believe that public scrutiny of police behavior is biased and fault-finding and that only the police are truthful and fair. They must recognize that any organization of public service intimately involved with the welfare of its citizens that adopts the policy of paternalism and silence will increase the resentment and even the hostility of the individuals dependent on such services.

This paper is being presented in an attempt to increase the communication between the police and the public concerning police behavior. It is hoped that a dynamic understanding of policemen and their work will reduce the growing isolation that exists. In these troubled times, more than ever, there is an urgent need for the public to have confidence and trust in these essential services and for the public to experience the police as theirs and not "them or those."

Papers on police work are relatively few and almost none from official sources. The official policy of silence hampers effective communication. Insiders don't talk and outsiders don't know. Therefore, most of the published work is unofficial and anecdotal. It is usually written by former members of the police force whose subjective reporting is dependent on their former relationship with the police. There are also articles written by reporters who gather their material unofficially from former and present members of the force. These articles tend to be anecdotal and sensational. This may be partly due to the reporters' bias but it may be that the police department's official policy of defensive silence hampers any attempt at honest reporting. There are some notable exceptions to the subjective approach to police work. James Q. Wilson's *Varieties of Police Behavior*(1) and Arthur Niederhoffer's *Behind the Shield*(2) are two books that are serious objective studies concerning police behavior.

This paper is unofficial and is based on experiences and from material gathered through thirty years of contact with policemen and policework, part of that time serving as a policeman, and for the past ten years, as a psychiatric consultant to the medical unit of the New York City Police Department.

To fully understand policemen and police be-

havior, it is necessary to have some understanding of both the nature of police work as well as the nature of the police department.

The essential feature of police work is that it is work done under stress and it is the stress of rapidly changing conditions. The public expects from the policeman that good judgment be used under these conditions of stress, and yet police behavior that is performed under acute stress is usually re-examined under peacetime conditions. We should keep in mind the remarks of Lord Wavell, a field marshal of the British Army, who stated in one of his lectures, "Stupidity in (army) generals shouldn't excite or surprise one since they were selected from an extremely small class of human beings who were tough enough to be generals at all. The essential quality was not that they should be extremely clever or sensitive but that they should continue to function even if not particularly well in situations in which a more sensitive and less stable organism would have stopped functioning altogether."(3)

Another aspect of police work has to do with its purpose. The community has empowered a group of its citizens, the police, (it is of interest to note that the word *police* is derived from a Greek word meaning citizen) to preserve the peace of the community, to protect the life and property of all its citizens, to detect and arrest all offenders of the laws of the community, and in addition, to become a service-oriented group for selected emergencies involving the community. This latter function of service may occupy up to 80 percent of police work. When one looks over this list of police functions it would seem that all of them are helpful and beneficial to the general public, and yet it seems contradictory that the community often responds in a hostile manner to what ordinarily would be considered helpful efforts on their behalf.

An insight toward resolving the above contradiction came about while teaching a course on adolescent problems to professionals working with this age group. The topic of firemen came up and someone asked a question that had puzzled me: "Why do people, expecially from the ghetto, throw rocks and bottles at firemen who are there to help them?" The response from the class, all of whom were middle-class professional workers, was surprising. Those of the class who had a direct experience with firemen expressed negative and some bitter feelings towards them. "They ruined my car . . . they stole my father's watch." They talked about the fireman's destructiveness and aggression. Those who had no experience with firemen talked in terms of helpfulness and were shocked and upset at the attitudes of the other group. What I realized from the discussion is that firemen who work under stress were seen as aggressively helpful to the people they served. And that some individuals recalled only the aggressive aspects of the fireman's helpful behavior.

In the service-oriented functions of police work, the same phenomenon of aggressive helpfulness exists. Most individuals have defensive aggressive response to perceived aggression and overlook the helpful aspects of the policeman's behavior. A policeman in response to the question "What is your reaction to name callers?" said, "About the only time name calling really angers me is when it comes from someone I am really trying to help, like in an aided case or family dispute." Here the policeman only saw the helpful aspects of his behavior, but the individuals involved did not. A 13-year-old verbalized an insight into this aspect of aggressive helping when she stated, "Real help is when I ask for it; otherwise it is interference."

It is very likely negative attitudes of the public concerning service-oriented functions arise when the public experiences the help that policemen offer as unwanted, unasked and interfering. Newman and Steinberg in their paper, "Consultations With Police On Human Relations,"(4) quote a dramatic statistic of Morton Bard in "Family Intervention Police Teams as a Community Mental Health Resource" read at the 76th Annual Convention of the American Psychological Association in San Francisco, California, on August 30, 1968:

> 22 percent of police deaths and 40 percent of police injuries sustained nationwide are incurred as a result of calls to intervene in family disputes.

Another aspect of police work that contributes to negative feelings of the public is in the area of crime detection. A high percentage of police work in this area is involved in crimes already committed. They are called "crimes in the past." Larcenies and burglaries in the past, robberies, assaults, and rapes in the past form the bulk of police contact with the public in this area. In these crimes the victim has already suffered loss and sometimes has been brutally or tragically injured. Police professionalism of remaining neutral and objective in their investigations is experienced by the victim and his family to be unsympathetic, indifferent, and cruel.

In an article in The New Yorker, John Bainbridge(5) quotes the British constable, "There is a C.I.D. chap who sometimes stops on the street and buys a bunch of flowers for a woman whose place has been robbed. It only costs a few bob and it makes her feel better."

Somehow this British detective has recognized that the victim suffered more than just the loss of her valuables. In all victims there are always irrational feelings of self-recrimination and guilt concerning their own contributions to the crime. It would be helpful if the police could recognize this and empathize with the victims, thereby reducing the acute symptoms of guilt. The Karen Horney Clinic is now considering a program to help victims of crimes with the psychological problems that have disabled them.

As the various aspects of police work are reviewed, one is made aware of a common psychological trait throughout. In all of the functions defined as police work, such as preservation of the peace, protection of life and property, enforcement of all laws, and detection and arrest of all offenders—despite the fact that all these functions are desirable and in the public interest, all are acts of aggression. In addition, when we appreciate that service-oriented functions, which at times can comprise 80 percent of the total work load, can also be felt as aggressive acts even though the intent and the result of the police was to be helpful, we can say that most aspects of police work embody aggressive behavior on the part of the policeman.

Aggression is an interpersonal act which is reluctantly expressed by most individuals. It is rarely a spontaneous act. Most people can not express these "against feelings toward people" without feeling tension or anxiety. However, there are a number of individuals for whom aggressive feelings are a way of life. Dr. Karen Horney(6) described this individual well.

> The aggressive type takes it for granted that everyone is hostile and refuses to admit they are not. To him life is a struggle of all against all.

Even for this group, aggression is a defensive response to a world which is perceived as hostile. An example of this defensive feeling was expressed by the late George Jackson in his book Soledad Brother, (7)

> Over these ten years I've never left my cell in the morning looking for trouble, never once have I

initiated any violence. In each case where it was alleged it was a defense attack, in response to some aggression verbal or physical. Perhaps a psychiatrist, a western psychiatrist that is, could make a case against me for anticipating attacks but I wasn't born this way. Perhaps this same psychiatrist would diagnose from my over-reactions that I'm not a very nice person. But again I refer you to the fact I was born innocent and trusting. The instinct to survive and all that it springs from developed as it is today out of necessity.

Though all aspects of police work are aggressive in nature or experienced by the public as aggressive, most policemen do not have what Horney called an aggressive personality. The distinction is that the aggressive personality develops under the concept that the world is a jungle and to be aggressive is necessary for survival. Never for one moment does he consider his behavior as helpful to others or in the service of others. The police, on the other hand, with the expressed motivation of being helpful, find themselves continually taken by surprise at people's reactions to their behavior. It is commonly expressed by, "I'm only trying to help you." "Why are you giving me a hard time?" A previous paper of mine on "Emotional Hazards of Policework"(8) described how the screening process determined the police personality. It pointed out that the successful candidate for a policeman tended to be a conforming youth who was mainly drawn from the working class. Most conforming individuals, especially middle class youths, are uncomfortable with aggressive feelings and many of them are unable to express these feelings directly. Yet the policeman who is basically a conforming person seems to have no difficulty in expressing his aggressive feelings in the performance of his work. This seeming contradiction, i.e., the curious amalgam of conforming and aggressive behavior, is particularly present in upward-striving working class youths. They differ from most conforming individuals in that they are fully aware of their aggressive feelings and express these feelings as easily as the aggressive personality but these feelings are directed differently. In the aggressive personality there is indiscriminate expression of feelings in all directions—towards superiors, equals, and subordinates. The conforming individual, who is a policeman, is selective. He can express his direct feelings of aggression freely to subordinates, somewhat to equals

but never directly to superiors. This behavior is reminiscent of what the French call the "bicyclist personality"—one who bows his head above and kicks below. Winston Churchill, in describing a similar personality pattern, said, "They are either at your throat or at your feet."

We want to make this point about conformity and aggression very clear. When it was stated that conforming people have difficulty in expressing or acknowledging aggressive feelings we mean the direct expression of these feelings. They have many ways of indirectly expressing aggressive feelings. It is done through opposition, psychological deafness and dumbness, pseudoineptness, forgetting, proscrastination, passive resistance, etc. These indirect ways are quite effective and usually succeed in provoking and annoying everyone to whom these indirect feelings are directed. In general, conforming individuals are indirect with all groups. Policemen form a special group because of their background that can freely express direct aggressive feelings to everyone but authority. Example: If a fellow patrolman asks the clerical patrolman for a minor favor, he generally will be refused indirectly. "Upstairs is upset"; "Downtown won't like it"; "The heat's on"; "The Commissioner is on a rampage"; and there is a final deterrent that causes even the highest-ranking officials to pause: "They dropped a letter on you."

A clue to the understanding of the dynamics of this curious amalgam of conforming and aggressive behavior can be gotten by studying the school monitor. A teacher selects a child who is usually a conforming, obedient child to be her surrogate concerning discipline when she is out of the room. This child, in his desire to keep the approval and conditional love of the teacher, will carry out her commands, both direct and implied, about law and order. In his eagerness to please the teacher he may become officious, tyrannical, even aggressive in the performance of his duties. As long as the teacher commends him, he will perform eagerly and willingly the surrogate functions of her discipline and authority. That he becomes alienated from his peer group seems less important than the losing of adult approval. He appears to be more vulnerable to authorities' disapproval than to peer rejection.

In young children it seems peer rejection of the class monitor was not too severe since all the other children wanted to please the teacher as well, and to reject the monitor would be too anxiety-provoking.

Perhaps the teacher would find out and "get him." But in adolescence, those who seek the comparable roles of class monitor are individuals who feel they don't belong to their peers anyway and make strenuous efforts for adult approval. They generally are insecure, anxious, conforming youngsters with a strong desire called "recognition hunger," and they imitate all the traits of the authority to feed their hunger for approval.

"Recognition hunger" and its corollary "the need to be liked" is present in all of us. It is probably the driving force that motivates individuals into the helping professions such as medicine, the ministry, and social work, as well as the service-oriented functions of public service, such as firefighting and police work.

Yet if these driving forces for recognition and being liked are too excessive, it will cause a problem for those individuals who perform such helping functions. The doctor who continually expresses his thoughts about "ungrateful patients" or "they don't appreciate what I do for them" demonstrates an unresolved problem of "recognition hunger." Such a physician was exemplified in Gerald Green's book, *The Last Angry Man.* (9) Excessive "recognition hunger" in people in authority creates problems in those individuals who are dependent on them.

Since recognition hunger or its euphemistic equivalent "the need to be liked" is very strong in conforming individuals, whenever they act aggressively in the performance of their duty they require approval from their superiors. The conforming person idealizes his superiors. He invests them with all kinds of superstrengths. They must be superindividuals who cannot be questioned, perfectionistic and demanding, and above all, strong. Softness is equated with weakness and is despised. At this point it would be helpful if I distinguish between conforming and compliant behavior. It isn't the same. Conforming behavior is identifying with the aggressor and acting like him. Compliancy is submitting to the aggressor in which the compliant individual feels weak. That's why conforming individuals cannot stand tenderness or softness. To obey a soft-spoken boss means to feel compliant, which the conforming individual despises in himself.

That is the reason the police force, despite all kinds of superficial grumblings, welcomes a tough police commissioner. The commissioner becomes the ideal leader and he can commit all kinds of acts of power with impunity. He can demote, transfer, and increase hours. He can impose all kinds of hardships; indeed he can probably dismiss half the force and the rest will follow his orders. The only unforgiveable and unpardonable sin that a commissioner could commit is to "listen to civilians," for this would be considered a sign of weakness.

We may be talking about the past. During the last five years a shift in attitudes of authority may make some of the foregoing statements out of date. The behavior of the younger men seems to reflect profound changes in the attitudes toward authority. Attitudes toward authority are culturally determined. There are many variables such as family climate, religious background, and economic class attitudes. Generally there are three basic attitudes toward authority:

1. Reverence or awe. In this attitude authority is accepted without question. It is usually developed in homes which are quite strict, with strong religious backgrounds and where the father is the unquestioned boss. This was the traditional police attitude toward authority.

2. Challenge of authority. Here authority is still respected but questioned, and intellectual proof is required of the justifications of the decisions. In this approach the concept of fair or unfair arises. This attitude is usually developed in so-called permissive homes of the middle class, where children are encouraged to question. This attitude has been a recent trend for the past ten years.

3. Defiance of authority. Here authority is ignored, sometimes abused, and only physical force or fear, not respect, can make the individual who has this attitude submit. Usually this attitude is developed where growing up in a disorganized home life with a relatively nonexistent father. In many of these individuals there is a preoccupation with maintaining self-respect, proving one's masculinity by not taking anyone's crap, "not being taken in" ("I won't kiss anyone's ass"). It accounts for the surliness of individuals in service-oriented jobs. They see "thank you" as submissive words. They invest neurotic pride in their jobs. This attitude is fairly new in police and fortunately is unusual. This attitude provides fertile soil for the excessive use of force in the performance of police duty.

During the past 30 years of contact with the police, the prevailing pattern seen towards authority was reverence or awe. In the past five years we have seen increasing evidence of challenge and defiance of authority. How widespread it is, we don't know. One is less worried about the attitudes of challenge than about defiance. The attitude of reverence for authority also has its problems for the department. It demands that superiors be supermen and always on a pedestal. It is an attitude that can render an individual policeman prone to [two] of the industrial hazards of police work, namely, disillusionment and cynicism. A disillusioned and cynical policeman is an individual unusually vulnerable to corruption.

When the present police commissioner of New York City announced the principle of accountability of superiors for the behavior of his men, he touched on the crucial elements in the psychodynamics of policemen and their work. As a matter of fact we should not only underscore his policy, but implement it by stating that any change that could take place in police attitudes and their behavior can only come through the commissioner himself. It is in the nature of the police department that every rank other than the commissioner has "rubber-band" authority, i.e., any order given can be countermanded or rescinded by a higher rank. It is also in the nature of the police department that the commissioner's attitude is reflected downward. He must be unusually sensitive to the dynamics of the young man who is a policeman. If the commissioner shows ambivalence or hesitancy, the morale of his command drops. If he attacks the behavior of his men who are trying to follow his orders, he reduces morale. He must issue orders and indicate policy, establish principles of law and order that they can follow. He must support their honest attempts to carry out his orders. He must interpret and clarify his orders if they are ambiguous, otherwise he may excite the passive-resistant traits that are dormant in conforming individuals. Towards these ends the commissioner must educate his men to the concepts embodied in this paper that most police work, no matter how helpful it may be, is aggressive and people do protest aggressive behaviors. The awareness that police behavior has a psychological impact must be included in the professional training of a policeman.

The police, as part of their professional training, must become aware that present-day turmoil has also produced positive effects. Slogans of groups such as "Black is beautiful" or "Never again" are reflections of a growing sense of self and an emancipation from childhood docility or resignation to "aggressive mothering" or benevolent paternalism. It is in the psychologic nature of police work that the ordinary citizen will have negative feelings to policemen, despite the fact that the citizenry has selected the police to protect them. The policeman becomes the symbol of *superego* functioning, "thou shall nots" or "shoulds." All individuals, despite their intelligence, have irrational, negative feelings to anyone who limits them or frustrates them. What one hopes from an enlightened public is not that they love the police, but respect them.

REFERENCES

1. James Q. Wilson, *Varieties of Police Behavior* (Cambridge: Harvard University Press, 1968).

2. Arthur Niederhoffer, *Behind the Shield* (Garden City: Doubleday and Co., 1967).

3. James M. Tanner, *Stress and Psychiatric Disorder* (Oxford: Blackwell Scientific Publications, 1960), p. 4.

4. Lawrence E. Newman and J. Leonard Steinberg, "Consultations with Police on Human Relations," *American Journal of Psychiatry, 126* (April 1970), p. 1421.

5. John Bainbridge, "Profiles," *New Yorker,* August 14, 1971, p. 48.

6. Karen Horney, *Our Inner Conflicts* (New York: W. W. Norton, 1945), p. 63.

7. George Jackson, *Soledad Brother* (New York: Coward-McCann, 1970), p. 300.

8. Martin Symonds, "Emotional Hazards of Police Work," *American Journal of Psychoanalysis. 30* (1970), pp. 155–60.

9. Gerald Green, *The Last Angry Man* (New York: Scribners, 1956).

The Psychological Assessment of Police Candidates

CLIFTON RHEAD, ARNOLD ABRAMS, HARRY TROSMAN, AND PHILIP MARGOLIS

The problem of psychological assessment of an individual for suitability for a particular task can be at the same time one of the most vexing, stimulating, and gratifying topics to which the psychiatrist can turn his attention. As his role has expanded during the past several decades to include extension of his skills and knowledge into questions of social and community consequence, so there has been concomitant need for reformulation of concepts of individual psychopathology as it pertains to the total functional capacity of the ego.

Thus it seems in order to present this report of our experiences with the assessment of police candidates and officers in the hope of more exact delineation of the limitations as well as of the usefulness of such a program, examining in the process some of the variables that affect the success of the undertaking.

For an 18-month period from 1961 to 1963 the authors served at the request of the Chicago Civil Service Commission on a psychiatric advisory board, the purpose of which was to examine candidates for the Chicago Police Department for psychological suitability for careers in law enforcement. Beginning at the same time and continuing to the present, two of us have served in a similar capacity to the department itself, conducting examinations with men already members of the department. It is with the former experience that this report is primarily concerned; although reference will be made to experiences learned from the latter, time and space do not permit a more detailed examination other than to draw upon it for some of the formulations.

Ethical and moral issues

It seems appropriate to comment upon several ethical and moral issues which have been raised

SOURCE: *American Journal of Psychiatry*, *124*, 11 (May 1968), pp. 1575–80. Copyright © 1968, the American Psychiatric Association.

regarding the role of the psychiatrist or psychologist in candidate assessment. Those issues center about the questions of whether the kind of examination we have undertaken to conduct constitutes a legitimate use of the unique skills of the examiner, and, if he enters into the sphere of selection, whether he may ultimately do more harm than good to the individual, to society, and to himself.(1)

Implicit in those statements are the thorny questions of the applicants' rights to privacy: Do the examinations as conducted constitute an essential infringement of the individuals' basic rights? We do not feel that it is possible to side-step that question by answering, as has been suggested, that a true physician-patient relationship does not exist between examiner and applicant.(2) The modified associative interview, probing as it does in psychically sensitive areas, is uniquely suited to the mobilization of latent transference reactions and inappropriate responses of the sort regularly noted in the psychotherapeutic relationship. Whether it is wished by either party, the applicant begins, at some point in the interview, to respond as if he had independently come for help. Having structured a situation which elicits such responses, the physician is morally and ethically bound to treat it appropriately.

However, committed as we are to the concept that psychiatry is properly a medical specialty, we believe that psychological evaluation is no less an infringement of the rights of the individual than is evaluation of physical defects which might interfere with the proper performance of the police officer's duties, provided that the proper safeguards are established to prevent the individual's subjection to potential humiliation or public exposure. That topic has been carefully explored by Halleck and Miller.(3)

Germane to this issue is a consideration of the particular role played by the police officer in our society. Succinctly stated, we do not believe it to be an infringement of rights to refuse to place in the hands of a potentially paranoid person or an impulse-ridden character a lethal weapon or authority unrestricted in moments of stress except by the imposition of his own judgment. If one ponders the question of individual freedom, one may question whether the practitioner truly fulfills his dual obligations to society and to the individual by allowing (tacitly, by refusing to utilize his skills when solicited) a passive, inhibited man to place himself in a position in which a neurotically determined inability to mobilize aggression may result in his own death or that of the citizens he ostensibly protects. Is it proper to place a gun in the hands of a person whose personality organization is such that impulse control is poor, and hostile-aggressive feelings and/or sadistic fantasies are likely to be acted upon with a minimum of mediating ego controls? Such questions are neither hypothetical nor academic but are matters of concern for the public health and welfare.

Finally, it should be pointed out that the detection of mental illness, which is after all a legitimate psychiatric function, is also an integral part of the assessment process. Thus, to the question: Does the psychiatrist have more to offer in this area than would be gained if the selection were left to the judgment of experienced police officials, our answer, at least as it pertains to detection is an unqualified "yes." While the experienced official may be alert to eccentricities of behavior or to grossly aberrant thought or action in the applicant, the diagnosis of overt or latent mental illness, particularly in those individuals in whom such illness assumes a more subtle and less flamboyant form, lies properly within the domain of the psychiatrist. Further, those officials themselves are far from satisfied with the results obtained by more traditional methods. The Chicago Police Department has independently undertaken pilot studies to determine, at both the command level and the level of the recruit and the patrolman, whether it is possible to develop procedures for identifying "men with similar traits ... who may manifest bad behavior in the future or who may not remain in the Department long enough to justify the expense of employment."(4)

Assessment in the Literature

The greater part of the literature on problems of assessment stems from the experience of the military. However, such experiences are pertinent, with certain modifications, to groups of a quasi-military nature such as the police force. Glass,(5) Brill and Beebe,(6) and Egan,(7) all raised doubts regarding the efficacy of assessment programs in the military insofar as the ability to predict later efficiency was concerned. In a somewhat related vein Matarazzo,(8) studying suc-

cessful and unsuccessful police officers, concluded that future success could not be predicted on the basis of projective tests alone. Christy and Rasmussen,(9) on the other hand, in an excellent discussion of the Navy's human reliability program, felt that assessment and prediction would meet with greater success if evaluation were aimed at the determination of the *significance* of psychopathology rather than at its detection alone. The latter conclusion will be discussed by us in greater detail shortly, since it appears that certain traits ordinarily considered to be "pathological" are essential ingredients of the personality structure of the "normal" police officer.

Further, as Christy and Rasmussen also emphasized, detection of illness becomes more important (and hence, reliability of the assessment function increases) when psychiatric standards are lowered. Under such circumstances the reliability of the assessment function is in part an inverse function of the psychiatric standard for acceptance. Specifically, during the period our board functioned the Chicago Police Department was undergoing rapid expansion, standards were broadened to admit candidate populations which heretofore had been excluded by more rigid physical and educational criteria, and accordingly the diagnosis of incapacitating mental illness, neurotic or psychotic, (including chronic brain syndrome) was possible in 20.7 percent of the persons interviewed by us (9.6 percent of the total applicant population).

Procedure

Each applicant for the Chicago Police Department is required to pass the civil service examination for appointment as patrolman. In addition he must pass a physical examination and be subjected to a thorough background investigation of his moral habits, character, and past history. At the time of the tenure of the advisory board, successful applicants were given the Minnesota Multiphasic Personality Inventory and a variation of the Draw-A-Person test. Applicants with a combination of an extreme MMPI profile and marked disturbance in the projection of body imagery were recalled for individual testing, and the Rorschach, TAT, Wechsler-Bellevue, and such other tests as were indicated were administered. From that group the psychologist selected applicants with questionable results, who were then asked to appear before the advisory board, composed of at least two psychiatrists and the psychologist.

The Interview

The interviewers brought to the interview situation an orientation characteristic of a clinical setting. An atmosphere of seriousness, objectivity, and neutrality present throughout the procedure encouraged the applicant to present himself with frankness and to tolerate a diagnostic inquiry. Characteristically, the applicant was initially guarded; as the interview progressed, a greater degree of relaxation and openness developed. The candidate often became more spontaneous and engaged more readily in the interpersonal aspects of the relationship, a development thought to be related to the consistent, nonevaluative, inquiring attitudes of the interviewers.

A further factor in the elicitation of pertinent material was the interviewers' abilities to handle affectively laden material effectively. The candidate was able to examine charged issues when he felt the situation to be affectively and ideationally tolerant and stable.

The utilization of multiple interviewers evoked notable shifts and responses in both parties to the transaction: if an applicant found one interviewer harsh and critical, he might turn with greater freedom to a second. He might choose to respond to the silent interviewer rather than to the questioning one; he might experience varying forms of parental transference; he might respond to one interviewer as to someone against whom he must defend himself and to another as to one to whom he could relate more freely. Such a differential shift in the candidate was believed to be desirable, since it was interpreted as indicating a more discriminative sensitivity to object relationships and a greater capacity to relate reciprocally.

The interviewers frequently made use of projective questions during the course of the interview. Commonly the candidate was asked to describe a difficulty he had experienced and his method of handling it. Although his response frequently represented a displacement from his current life or from his response to the interview situation, it also afforded insights into the nature of the life situations which presented stresses. At the same time the applicant was afforded an opportunity to present his concept of integration or resolution of stress. The diphasic nature of such an inquiry was desirable because it did not prejudice the candidate in terms of negative components of his personality and at the same time indicated to him the interest of the interviewers in constructive solutions and attributes indicating ego capacities.

Psychological Profile

When the profiles obtained from the MMPI for more than a thousand candidates were tabulated and analyzed, significant differences from the norm were noted—differences which also occur regularly in the study of men considered successful officers. The group profile of the candidates significantly exceeded the average on the Pd and Ma scales, scales correlated with a willingness to take chances and with a propensity for acting-out. There was also a sharp, though somewhat less pronounced, departure from the average on the Pa, or paranoid, scale. The former occurred in a significant manner in 70 percent of the cases, while the latter was even more pervasive and was present in roughly 80 percent of those tested.

The picture which unfolds, then, is one of an individual who is more suspicious than the average person, one who is ready to take risks and is prone to act on his impulses. The MMPI alone, however, does not differentiate the "normal" from the "pathological" candidate. What appears excessive in the "normal" population may well be in the service of the ego in a cross-section of candidates and police officers.

The projective drawings served further both to delineate the pathological from the normal and to reveal a commonality of features to an extent unique to the population studied. A significant number of candidates drew figures in which great, and at times excessive, emphasis on virility and aggression were noted. For example, there were several hundred drawings in which muscle groups were exaggerated. Rather than with an open hand, the male was frequently depicted with a clenched fist. In over 300 instances an object resembling a club was in the hands of the figures. Although the fact that these men were candidates for the police force may have influenced the kind of image they projected on the psychological test, one is reminded of Freud's thought that a dream consciously conjured up by a patient has as much significance as one actually dreamed.

In instances where actual distortion of body image existed with extreme MMPI scores, the candidate was recalled for further individual testing, as already noted. That testing helped to differentiate those in whom the willingness to take chances, the propensity to act out, and the emphasis on virility were traits that could be utilized by the ego and those in whom the same traits were manifestations of chronic pathology. It was noted that a number of persons selected by means of psychological screening for further assessment demonstrated: 1) a willingness to take chances, and 2) an overemphasis on virility features in body imagery, two of the three salient selective features. The absence of the third feature, namely a propensity for acting-out, was frequently correlated with personalities whose abilities to mobilize and utilize aggressive energies in an effective manner were minimal.

Thus, it was believed that the psychological testing tended to provide a composite picture of a successful police candidate that was consistent in general with the type of activities police engage in.

Discussion

In their earliest meetings the members of the board came individually to the conclusion that the best interests of the police department would be served if their function was not limited to the detection of psychological illness but was extended to include an attempt at evaluating whether the candidates were psychologically suited to the stresses imposed on them by police work. Attempts were then made to establish criteria, which, as it developed, followed generally the variables cited by Cristy and Rasmussen.(10)

In addition to the function of screening a population drawn from remarkably similar backgrounds, it became necessary for the board members to acquaint themselves as thoroughly as possible with the demands of the police officer's job and to establish criteria for the type of personality best suited to it. From prior associations with law enforcement organizations, from talks, formal and informal, with Civil Service Commission personnel, and from contact with police officers and officials, what might be thought of as a composite, ideal police officer was drawn—an officer possessing traits desirable in a personality which must cope with the multiple demands upon the ego (internal as well as external) with which it is daily confronted.

A matter for particular concern for us was the applicant's ability to utilize aggressive energies in effective and adaptive channels. The police officer finds himself in occupational situations necessitating reality-adapted *action* patterns. Thus, the capacity to regulate and control aggression in terms of appropriate goals was given a high weight in the selection

process. We tended to be concerned about those applicants who manifested primitive, uncontrolled aggression leading to disorganized behavior in socially maladaptive patterns.

Similarly, it was believed that gross inhibition of aggression and avoidance or flight techniques such as passivity or alcoholism were likely to indicate a lack of mobility and capacity for appropriate motoric expression. The appearance of paranoid trends and suspiciousness was carefully evaluated in order to determine how much free play existed between such attitudes and their utilization by ego functions such as thought and judgment. Gross evidence of paranoid ideation is, of course, indicative of severe pathology; mild suspiciousness and freedom from suggestion, on the other hand, may be useful occupational traits; they appear regularly in the personality profiles of successful officers.

Conclusions

We have come to the conclusion that success or failure in a law enforcement career is not determined by unconscious conflict or by the nature of the ego defenses alone, but instead is strongly influenced by the degree to which the adaptive ego has remained undistorted in response to those conflicts. There appears to be in those persons who choose police work for a career a greater degree of paranoid ideation, a greater emphasis upon virility, and a greater tendency to act out than in the nonpolice population, and the egos of successful police officers utilize those traits in the service of normal day-to-day relationships. There remains in the "normal" officer sufficient autonomous ego function to allow for the expression of the conflict in a nonpathological manner; our concern has been for those in whom tendentious or litigious traits might be anticipated to interfere with the performance of police duties, or with those who would use the uniform and the position of authority to act out forbidden aggressive, sadistic, or sexual impulses.

In reviewing the work of the board over an 18-month period, we find that 30 percent of the applicants were recommended for rejection. Of those, 20 percent showed evidence of grossly incapacitating illness. Although we recognize that our report lacks the solidity of a carefully controlled study, it seems to us valid to conclude that an assessment program which makes use of both projective techniques and the associative interview we have described is superior to using either one alone. We also feel that to be of significance for assessment of success or failure, projective techniques must be supplemented by an interview in which the variable criteria are clearly defined.

REFERENCES

1. I. N. Hassenfeld, "Police Testing," *American Journal of Psychiatry, 122* (1966), p. 954.

2. E. F. Kal, "Police Testing," *American Journal of Psychiatry, 122* (1966), pp. 1064–65.

3. S. L. Halleck and M. H. Miller, "The Psychiatric Interview: Questionable Social Precedents of Some Current Practices," *American Journal of Psychiatry, 120* (1963), pp. 164–69.

4. G. Spencer, "A Study of Police Recruits in Chicago," unpublished paper, 1963.

5. A. J. Glass et al., "Psychiatric Prediction and Military Effectiveness," *U.S. Armed Forces Medical Journal, 7* (1956), pp. 1427–43.

6. N. Q. Brill and G. W. Beebe, "Some Applications of a Follow-Up Study to Psychiatric Standards for Mobilization," *American Journal of Psychiatry, 109* (1952), pp. 401–10.

7. J. R. Egan, L. Jackson, and R. H. Eanes, "A Study of Neuropsychiatric Rejectees," *Journal of the American Medical Association, 145* (1951), pp. 466–69.

8. J. D. Matarazzo et al., "Characteristics of Successful Policemen and Firemen Applicants," *Journal of Applied Psychology, 48* (1964), pp. 123–33.

9. R. L. Christy and J. E. Rasmussen, "Human Reliability Implications of the U.S. Navy's Experience in Screening and Selection Procedures," *American Journal of Psychiatry, 120* (1963), pp. 540–47.

10. Ibid.

A Sketch of the Policeman's Working Personality

JEROME H. SKOLNICK

A recurrent theme of the sociology of occupations is the effect of a man's work on his outlook on the world.(1) Doctors, janitors, lawyers, and industrial workers develop distinctive ways of perceiving and responding to their environment. Here we shall concentrate on analyzing certain outstanding elements in the police milieu, danger, authority, and efficiency, as they combine to generate distinctive cognitive and behavioral responses in police: a "working personality." Such an analysis does not suggest that all police are alike in "working personality," but that there are distinctive cognitive tendencies in police as an occupational grouping. Some of these may be found in other occupations sharing similar problems. So far as exposure to danger is concerned, the policeman may be likened to the soldier. His problems as an authority bear a certain similarity to those of the schoolteacher, and the pressures he feels to prove himself efficient are not unlike those felt by the industrial worker. The combination of these elements, however, is unique to the policeman. Thus, the police, as a result of combined features of their social situation, tend to develop ways of looking at the world distinctive to themselves, cognitive lenses through which to see situations and events. The strength of the lenses may be weaker or stronger depending on certain conditions, but they are ground on a similar axis.

Analysis of the policeman's cognitive propensities is necessary to understand the practical dilemma faced by police required to maintain order under a democratic rule of law. We have discussed earlier how essential a conception of order is to the resolution of this dilemma. It was suggested that the paramilitary

SOURCE: *Justice Without Trial: Law Enforcement in a Democratic Society* (New York: Wiley, 1966).

character of police organization naturally leads to a high evaluation of similarity, routine, and predictability. Our intention is to emphasize features of the policeman's environment interacting with the paramilitary police organization to generate a "working personality." Such an intervening concept should aid in explaining how the social environment of police affects their capacity to respond to the rule of law.

We also stated earlier that emphasis would be placed on the division of labor in the police department, that "operational law enforcement" could not be understood outside these special work assignments. It is therefore important to explain how the hypothesis emphasizing the generalizability of the policeman's "working personality" is compatible with the idea that police division of labor is an important analytic dimension for understanding "operational law enforcement." Compatibility is evident when one considers the different levels of analysis at which the hypotheses are being developed. Janowitz states, for example, that the military profession is more than an occupation; it is a "style of life" because the occupational claims over one's daily existence extend well beyond official duties. He is quick to point out that any professional performing a crucial "life and death" task, such as medicine, the ministry, or the police, develops such claims.(2) A conception like "working personality" of police should be understood to suggest an analytic breadth similar to that of "style of life." That is, just as the professional behavior of military officers with similar "styles of life" may differ drastically depending upon whether they command an infantry battalion or participate in the work of an intelligence unit, so too does the professional behavior of police officers with similar "working personalities" vary with their assignments.

The policeman's "working personality" is most highly developed in his constabulary role of the man on the beat. For analytical purposes that role is sometimes regarded as an enforcement specialty, but in this general discussion of policemen as they comport themselves while working, the uniformed "cop" is seen as the foundation for the policeman's working personality. There is a sound organizational basis for making this assumption. The police, unlike the military, draw no caste distinction in socialization, even though their order of ranked titles approximates the military's. Thus, one cannot join a local police department as, for instance, a lieutenant, as a West Point graduate joins the army: Every officer of rank must serve an apprenticeship as a patrolman.

This feature of police organization means that the constabulary role is the primary one for all police officers, and that whatever the special requirements of roles in enforcement specialties, they are carried out with a common background of constabulary experience.

The process by which this "personality" is developed may be summarized: the policeman's role contains two principal variables, danger and authority, which should be interpreted in the light of a "constant" pressure to appear efficient.[1] The element of danger seems to make the policeman especially attentive to signs indicating a potential for violence and lawbreaking. As a result, the policeman is generally a "suspicious" person. Furthermore, the character of the policeman's work makes him less desirable as a friend, since norms of friendship implicate others in his work. Accordingly, the element of danger isolates the policeman socially from that segment of the citizenry which he regards as symbolically dangerous and also from the conventional citizenry with whom he identifies.

The element of authority reinforces the element of danger in isolating the policeman. Typically, the policeman is required to enforce laws representing puritanical morality, such as those prohibiting drunkenness, and also laws regulating the flow of public activity, such as traffic laws. In these situations the policeman directs the citizenry, whose typical response denies recognition of his authority, and stresses his obligation to respond to danger. The kind of man who responds well to danger, however, does not normally subscribe to codes of puritanical morality. As a result, the policeman is unusually liable to the charge of hypocrisy. That the whole civilian world is an audience for the policeman further promotes police isolation and, in consequence, solidarity. Finally, danger undermines the judicious use of authority. Where danger, as in Britain, is relatively less, the judicious application of authority is facilitated. Hence British police may appear to be somewhat more attached to the rule of law, when, in fact, they may appear so because they face less danger, and

[1] By no means does such an analysis suggest there are no individual or group differences among police. On the contrary, most of this study emphasizes differences, endeavoring to relate these to occupational specialties in police departments. This chapter, however, explores similarities rather than differences, attempting to account for the policeman's general disposition to perceive and to behave in certain ways.

they are as a rule better skilled than American police in creating the appearance of conformity to procedural regulations.

The Symbolic Assailant and Police Culture

In attempting to understand the policeman's view of the world, it is useful to raise a more general question: What are the conditions under which police, as authorities, may be threatened? (3) To answer this, we must look to the situation of the policeman in the community. One attribute of many characterizing the policeman's role stands out: the policeman is required to respond to assaults against persons and property. When a radio call reports an armed robbery and gives a description of the man involved, every policeman, regardless of assignment, is responsible for the criminal's apprehension. The *raison d'être* of the policeman and the criminal law, the underlying collectively held moral sentiments which justify penal sanctions, arises ultimately and most clearly from the threat of violence and the possibility of danger to the community. Police who "lobby" for severe narcotics laws, for instance, justify their position on grounds that the addict is a harbinger of danger since, it is maintained, he requires one hundred dollars a day to support his habit, and he must steal to get it. Even though the addict is not typically a violent criminal, criminal penalties for addiction are supported on grounds that he may become one.

The policeman, because his work requires him to be occupied continually with potential violence, develops a perceptual shorthand to identify certain kinds of people as symbolic assailants, that is, as persons who use gesture, language, and attire that the policeman has come to recognize as a prelude to violence. This does not mean that violence by the symbolic assailant is necessarily predictable. On the contrary, the policeman responds to the vague indication of danger suggested by appearance. Like the animals of the experimental psychologist, the policeman finds the threat of random damage more compelling than a predetermined and inevitable punishment.

Something of the flavor of the policeman's attitude toward the symbolic assailant comes across in a recent article by a police expert. In discussing the problem of selecting subjects for field interrogation, the author writes:

A. Be suspicious. This is a healthy police attitude, but it should be controlled and not too obvious.
B. Look for the unusual.
   1. Persons who do not "belong" where they are observed.
   2. Automobiles which do not "look right."
   3. Businesses opened at odd hours, or not according to routine or custom.
C. Subjects who should be subjected to field interrogations.
   1. Suspicious persons known to the officer from previous arrests, field interrogations, and observations.
   2. Emaciated appearing alcoholics and narcotics users who invariably turn to crime to pay for cost of habit.
   3. Person who fits description of wanted suspect as described by radio, teletype, daily bulletins.
   4. Any person observed in the immediate vicinity of a crime very recently committed or reported as "in progress."
   5. Known trouble-makers near large gatherings.
   6. Persons who attempt to avoid or evade the officer.
   7. Exaggerated unconcern over contact with the officer.
   8. Visibly "rattled" when near the policeman.
   9. Unescorted women or young girls in public places, particularly at night in such places as cafes, bars, bus and train depots, or street corners.
   10. "Lovers" in an industrial area (make good lookouts).
   11. Persons who loiter about places where children play.
   12. Solicitors or peddlers in a residential neighborhood.
   13. Loiterers around public rest rooms.
   14. Lone male sitting in car adjacent to schoolground with newspaper or book in his lap.
   15. Lone male sitting in car near shopping center who pays unusual amount of attention to women, sometimes continuously manipulating rear view mirror to avoid direct eye contact.
   16. Hitchhikers.
   17. Person wearing coat on hot days.
   18. Car with mismatched hub caps, or dirty car with clean license plate (or vice versa).

19. Uniformed "deliverymen" with no merchandise or truck.
20. Many others. How about your own personal experiences?(4)

Nor, to qualify for the status of symbolic assailant, need an individual ever have used violence. A man backing out of a jewelry store with a gun in one hand and jewelry in the other would qualify even if the gun were a toy and he had never in his life fired a real pistol. To the policeman in the situation, the man's personal history is momentarily immaterial. There is only one relevant sign: a gun signifying danger. Similarly, a young man may suggest the threat of violence to the policeman by his manner of walking or "strutting," the insolence in the demeanor being registered by the policeman as a possible preamble to later attack.(5) Signs vary from area to area, but a youth dressed in a black leather jacket and motorcycle boots is sure to draw at least a suspicious glance from a policeman.

Policemen themselves do not necessarily emphasize the peril associated with their work when questioned directly, and may even have well-developed strategies of denial. The element of danger is so integral to the policeman's work that explicit recognition might induce emotional barriers to work performance. Thus, one patrol officer observed that more police have been killed and injured in automobile accidents in the past ten years than from gunfire. Although his assertion is true, he neglected to mention that the police are the only peacetime occupational group with a systematic record of death and injury from gunfire and other weaponry. Along these lines, it is interesting that of the two hundred and twenty-four working Westville policemen (not including the sixteen juvenile policemen) responding to a question about which assignment they would like most to have in the police department,[2] 50 per cent selected the job of detective, an assignment combining elements of apparent danger and initiative. The next category was adult street work, that is, patrol and traffic (37 per cent). Eight per cent selected the

juvenile squad,[3] and only 4 per cent selected administrative work. Not a single policeman chose the job of jail guard. Although these findings do not control for such factors as prestige, they suggest that confining and routine jobs are rated low on the hierarchy of police preferences, even though such jobs are least dangerous. Thus, the policeman may well, as a personality, enjoy the possibility of danger, especially its associated excitement, even though he may at the same time be fearful of it. Such "inconsistency" is easily understood. Freud has by now made it an axiom of personality theory that logical and emotional consistency are by no means the same phenomenon.

However complex the motives aroused by the element of danger, its consequences for sustaining police culture are unambiguous. This element requires him, like the combat soldier, the European Jew, the South African (white or black), to live in a world straining toward duality, and suggesting danger when "they" are perceived. Consequently, it is in the nature of the policeman's situation that his conception of order emphasize regularity and predictability. It is, therefore, a conception shaped by persistent *suspicion*. The English "copper," often portrayed as a courteous, easygoing, rather jolly sort of chap, on the one hand, or as a devil-may-care adventurer, on the other, is differently described by Colin MacInnes:(6)

> The true copper's dominant characteristic, if the truth be known, is neither those daring nor vicious qualities that are sometimes attributed to him by friend or enemy, but an ingrained conservatism, and almost desperate love of the conventional. It is untidiness, disorder, the unusual, that a copper disapproves of most of all: far more, even than of crime which is merely a professional matter. Hence his profound dislike of people loitering in streets, dressing extravagantly, speaking with exotic accents, being strange, weak, eccentric, or simply any rare minority—of their doing, in fact, anything that cannot be safely predicted.

[2] A questionnaire was given to all policemen in operating divisions of the police force: patrol, traffic, vice control, and all detectives. The questionnaire was administered at police line-ups over a period of three days, mainly by the author but also by some of the police personnel themselves. Before the questionnaire was administered, it was circulated to and approved by the policemen's welfare association.

[3] Indeed, the journalist Paul Jacobs, who has ridden with the Westville juvenile police as part of his own work on poverty, observed in a personal communication that juvenile police appear curiously drawn to seek out dangerous situations, as if juvenile work without danger is degrading.

Policemen are indeed specificially *trained* to be suspicious, to perceive events or changes in the physical surroundings that indicate the occurrence or probability of disorder. A former student who worked as a patrolman in a suburban New York police department describes this aspect of the policeman's assessment of the unusual:(7)

> The time spent cruising one's sector or walking one's beat is not wasted time, though it can become quite routine. During this time, the most important thing for the officer to do is notice the *normal.* He must come to know the people in his area, their habits, their automobiles and their friends. He must learn what time the various shops close, how much money is kept on hand on different nights, what lights are usually left on, which houses are vacant . . . only then can he decide what persons or cars under what circumstances warrant the appellation "suspicious."

The individual policeman's "suspiciousness" does not hang on whether he has personally undergone an experience that could objectively be described as hazardous. Personal experience of this sort is not the key to the psychological importance of exceptionality. Each, as he routinely carries out his work, will experience situations that threaten to become dangerous. Like the American Jew who contributes to "defense" organizations such as the Anti-Defamation League in response to Nazi brutalities he has never experienced personally, the policeman identifies with his fellow cop who has been beaten, perhaps fatally, by a gang of young thugs.

Social Isolation

The patrolman in Westville, and probably in most communities, has come to identify the black man with danger. James Baldwin vividly expresses the isolation of the ghetto policeman:(8)

> . . . The only way to police a ghetto is to be oppressive. None of the Police Commissioner's men, even with the best will in the world, have any way of understanding the lives led by the people they swagger about in twos and threes controlling. Their very presence is an insult, and it would be, even if they spent their entire day feeding gumdrops to children. They represent the force of the white world, and that world's criminal profit and ease, to keep the black man corraled up here, in his place. The badge, the gun

in the holster, and the swinging club make vivid what will happen should his rebellion become overt. . . .

> It is hard, on the other hand, to blame the policeman, blank, good-natured, thoughtless, and insuperably innocent, for being such a perfect representative of the people he serves. He, too, believes in good intentions and is astounded and offended when they are not taken for the deed. He has never, himself, done anything for which to be hated—which of us has? and yet he is facing, daily and nightly, people who would gladly see him dead, and he knows it. There is no way for him not to know it; there are few things under heaven more unnerving than the silent, accumulating contempt and hatred of a people. He moves through Harlem, therefore, like an occupying soldier in a bitterly hostile country; which is precisely what, and where he is, and is the reason he walks in twos and threes.

While Baldwin's observations on police-Negro relations cannot be disputed seriously, there is greater social distance between police and "civilians" in general regardless of their color than Baldwin considers. Thus, Colin MacInnes has his English hero, Mr. Justice, explaining:(9)

> . . . The story is all coppers are just civilians like anyone else, living among them not in barracks like on the Continent, but you and I know that's just a legend for mugs. We *are* cut off: we're *not* like everyone else. Some civilians fear us and play up to us, some dislike us and keep out of our way, but no one—well, very few indeed—accepts us as just ordinary like them. In one sense, dear, we're just like hostile troops occupying an enemy country. And say what you like, at times that makes us lonely.

MacInnes's observation suggests that by not introducing a white control group, Baldwin has failed to see that the policeman may not get on well with anybody regardless (to use the hackneyed phrase) of race, creed, or national origin. Policemen whom one knows well often express their sense of isolation from the public as a whole, not just from those who fail to share their color. Westville police were asked, for example, to rank the most serious problems police have. The category most frequently selected was not racial problems, but some form of public relations: lack of respect for the police, lack of cooperation in enforcement of law, lack of understanding of the requirements of police work.[4] One respondent answered:

> As a policeman my most serious problem is impressing on the general public just how difficult and necessary police service is to all. There seems to be an attitude of "law is important, but it applies to my neighbor—not to me."

Of the two hundred and eighty-two Westville policemen who rated the prestige police work receives from others, 70 per cent ranked it as only fair or poor, while less than 2 per cent ranked it as "excellent" and another 29 per cent as "good." Similarly, in Britain, two-thirds of a sample of policemen interviewed by a Royal Commission stated difficulties in making friends outside the force; of those interviewed 58 per cent thought members of the public to be reserved, suspicious, and constrained in conversation; and 12 per cent attributed such difficulties to the requirement that policemen be selective in associations and behave circumspectly.(10)

A Westville policeman related the following incident:

> Several months after I joined the force, my wife and I used to be socially active with a crowd of young people, mostly married, who gave a lot of parties where there was drinking and dancing, and we enjoyed it. I've never forgotten, though, an incident that happened on one Fourth of July party. Everybody had been drinking, there was a lot of talking, people were feeling boisterous, and some kid there—he must have been twenty or twenty-two—threw a firecracker that hit my wife

[4] Respondents were asked, "Anybody who knows anything about police work knows that police face a number of problems. Would you please state—in order—what you consider to be the two most serious problems police have." On the basis of a number of answers, the writer and J. Richard Woodworth devised a set of categories. Then Woodworth classified each response into one of the categories (see table at right). When a response did not seem clear, he consulted with the writer. No attempt was made independently to check Woodworth's classification because the results are used impressionistically, and do not test a hypothesis. It may be, for instance, that "relations with public" is sometimes used to indicate racial problems, and vice versa. "Racial problems" include only those answers having specific reference to race. The categories and results were as follows:

in the leg and burned her. I didn't know exactly what to do—punch the guy in the nose, bawl him out, just forget it. Anyway, I couldn't let it pass, so I walked over to him and told him he ought to be careful. He began to rise up at me, and when he did, somebody yelled, "Better watch out, he's a cop." I saw everybody standing there, and I could feel they were all against me and for the kid, even though he had thrown the firecracker at my wife. I went over to the host and said it was probably better if my wife and I left because a fight would put a damper on the party. Actually, I'd hoped he would ask the kid to leave, since the kid had thrown the firecracker. But he didn't so we left. After that incident, my wife and I stopped going around with that crowd, and decided that if we were going to go to parties where there was to be drinking and boisterousness, we weren't going to be the only police people there.

Another reported that he seeks to overcome his feelings of isolation by concealing his police identity: (11)

> I try not to bring my work home with me, and that includes my social life. I like the men I work with, but I think it's better that my family doesn't become a police family. I try to put my police work into the background, and try not to let people know I'm a policeman. Once you do, you can't have normal relations with them.

Although the policeman serves a people who are, as Baldwin says, the established society, the white society, these people do not make him feel accepted. As a result, he develops resources within his own world to combat social rejection.

Westville Police Ranking of Number One Problem Faced by Police

	Number	Per Cent
Relations with public	74	26
Racial problems and demonstrations	66	23
Juvenile delinquents and delinquency	23	8
Unpleasant police tasks	23	8
Lack of cooperation from authorities (D.A., legislature, courts)	20	7
Internal departmental problems	17	6
Irregular life of policeman	5	2
No answer or other answer	56	20
	284	100

Police Solidarity

All occupational groups share a measure of inclusiveness and identification. People are brought together simply by doing the same work and having similar career and salary problems. As several writers have noted, however, police show an unusually high degree of occupational solidarity.(12) It is true that the police have a common employer and wear a uniform at work, but so do doctors, milkmen, and bus drivers. Yet it is doubtful that these workers have so close knit an occupation or so similar an outlook on the world as do police. Set apart from the conventional world, the policeman experiences an exceptionally strong tendency to find his social identity within his occupational milieu.

Compare the police with another skilled craft. In a study of the International Typographical Union, the authors asked printers the first names and jobs of their three closest friends. Of the 1,236 friends named by the 412 men in their sample, 35 per cent were printers.(13) Similarly, among the Westville police, of 700 friends listed by 250 respondents, 35 per cent were policemen. The policemen, however, were far more active than printers in occupational social activities. Of the printers, more than half (54 per cent) had never participated in any union clubs, benefit societies, teams, or organizations composed mostly of printers, or attended any printers' social affairs in the past 5 years. Of the Westville police, only 16 per cent had failed to attend a single police banquet or dinner in the past year (as contrasted with the printers' 5 *years*); and of the 234 men answering this question, 54 per cent had attended 3 or more such affairs *during the past year*.

Closest Friends of Printers and Police, by Occupation

	Printers N = 1236 (%)	Police N = 700 (%)
Same occupation	35	35
Professionals, business executives, and independent business owners	21	30
White-collar or sales employees	20	12
Manual workers	25	22

These findings are striking in light of the interpretation made of the data on printers. Lipset, Trow, and Coleman do not, as a result of their findings, see printers as an unintegrated occupational group. On the contrary, they ascribe the democratic character of the union in good part to the active social and political participation of the membership. The point is not to question their interpretation, since it is doubtlessly correct when printers are held up against other manual workers. However, when seen in comparison to police, printers appear a minimally participating group; put positively, police emerge as an exceptionally socially active occupational group.

Police Solidarity and Danger

There is still a question, however, as to the process through which danger and authority influence police solidarity. The effect of danger on police solidarity is revealed when we examine a chief complaint of police: lack of public support and public apathy. The complaint may have several referents including police pay, police prestige, and support from the legislature. But the repeatedly voiced broader meaning of the complaint is resentment at being taken for granted. The policeman does not believe that his status as civil servant should relieve the public of responsibility for law enforcement. He feels, however, that payment out of public coffers somehow obscures his humanity and, therefore, his need for help.[5] As one put it:

> Jerry, a cop, can get into a fight with three or four tough kids, and there will be citizens passing by, and maybe they'll look, but they'll never lend a hand. It's their country too, but you'd never know it the way some of them act. They forget that we're made of flesh and blood too. They don't care what happens to the cop so long as they don't get a little dirty.

Although the policeman sees himself as a specialist in dealing with violence, he does not want to fight alone. He does not believe that this specialization relieves the general public of citizenship duties. Indeed, if possible, he would prefer to be the foreman rather than the workingman in the battle against criminals.

The general public, of course, does withdraw from the workaday world of the policeman. The policeman's responsibility for controlling dangerous

---

[5] On this issue there was no variation. The statement "the policeman feels" means that there was no instance of a negative opinion expressed by the police studied.

and sometimes violent persons alienates the average citizen perhaps as much as does his authority over the average citizen. If the policeman's job is to insure that public order is maintained, the citizen's inclination is to shrink from the dangers of maintaining it. The citizen prefers to see the policeman as an automaton, because once the policeman's humanity is recognized, the citizen necessarily becomes implicated in the policeman's work, which is, after all, sometimes dirty and dangerous. What the policeman typically fails to realize is the extent he becomes tainted by the character of the work he performs. The danger of their work not only draws policemen together as a group but separates them from the rest of the population. Banton, for instance, comments:(14)

> . . . patrolmen may support their fellows over what they regard as minor infractions in order to demonstrate to them that they will be loyal in situations that make the greatest demands upon their fidelity. . . .
>
> In the American departments I visited it seemed as if the supervisors shared many of the patrolmen's sentiments about solidarity. They too wanted their colleagues to back them up in an emergency, and they shared similar frustrations with the public.

Thus, the element of danger contains seeds of isolation which may grow in two directions. In one, a stereotyping perceptual shorthand is formed through which the police come to see certain signs as symbols of potential violence. The police probably differ in this respect from the general middle-class white population only in degree. This difference, however, may take on enormous significance in practice. Thus, the policeman works at identifying and possibly apprehending the symbolic assailant; the ordinary citizen does not. As a result, the ordinary citizen does not assume the responsibility to implicate himself in the policeman's required response to danger. The element of danger in the policeman's role alienates him not only from populations with a potential for crime but also from the conventionally respectable (white) citizenry, in short, from that segment of the population from which friends would ordinarily be drawn. As Janowitz has noted in a paragraph suggesting similarities between the police and the military, " . . . any profession which is continually preoccupied with the threat of danger requires a strong sense of solidarity if it is to operate effectively. Detailed regulation of the military style of life is expected to enhance group cohesion, professional loyalty, and maintain the martial spirit."(15)

Social Isolation and Authority

The element of authority also helps to account for the policeman's social isolation. Policemen themselves are aware of their isolation from the community, and are apt to weight authority heavily as a causal factor. When considering how authority influences rejection, the policeman typically singles out his responsibility for enforcement of traffic violations(16) Resentment, even hostility, is generated in those receiving citations, in part because such contact is often the only one citizens have with police, and in part because municipal administrations and courts have been known to utilize police authority primarily to meet budgetary requirements, rather than those of public order. Thus, when a municipality engages in "speed trapping" by changing limits so quickly that drivers cannot realistically slow down to the prescribed speed or, while keeping the limits reasonable, charging high fines primarily to generate revenue, the policeman carries the brunt of public resentment.

That the policeman dislikes writing traffic tickets is suggested by the quota system police departments typically employ. In Westville, each traffic policeman has what is euphemistically described as a working "norm." A motorcyclist is supposed to write two tickets an hour for moving violations. It is doubtful that "norms" are needed because policemen are lazy. Rather, employment of quotas most likely springs from the reluctance of policemen to expose themselves to what they know to be public hostility. As a result, as one traffic policeman said:

> You learn to sniff out the places where you can catch violators when you're running behind. Of course, the department gets to know that you hang around one place, and they sometimes try to repair the situation there. But a lot of the time it would be too expensive to fix up the engineering fault, so we keep making our norm.

When meeting "production" pressures, the policeman inadvertently gives a false impression of patrolling ability to the average citizen. The traffic cyclist waits in hiding for moving violators near a tricky intersection, and is reasonably sure that such violations will occur with regularity. The violator believes he has observed a policeman displaying exceptional detection capacities and may have two thoughts, each apt to generate hostility toward the policeman: "I have been trapped," or "They can catch me; why can't they catch crooks as easily?" The answer, of course, lies in the different behavior patterns of motorists and "crooks." The latter do not act with either the frequency or predictability of motorists at poorly engineered intersections.

While traffic patrol plays a major role in separating the policeman from the respectable community, other of his tasks also have this consequence. Traffic patrol is only the most obvious illustration of the policeman's general responsibility for maintaining public order, which also includes keeping order at public accidents, sporting events, and political rallies. These activities share one feature: the policeman is called upon to *direct* ordinary citizens, and therefore to restrain their freedom of action. Resenting the restraint, the average citizen in such a situation typically thinks something along the lines of "He is supposed to catch crooks; why is he bothering me?" Thus, the citizen stresses the "dangerous" portion of the policeman's role while belittling his authority.

Closely related to the policeman's authority-based problems as *director* of the citizenry are difficulties associated with his injunction to *regulate public morality*. For instance, the policeman is obliged to investigate "lovers' lanes," and to enforce laws pertaining to gambling, prostitution, and drunkenness. His responsibility in these matters allows him much administrative discretion since he may not actually enforce the law by making an arrest, but instead merely interfere with continuation of the objectionable activity.(17) Thus, he may put the drunk in a taxi, tell the lovers to remove themselves from the back seat, and advise a man soliciting a prostitute to leave the area.

Such admonitions are in the interest of maintaining the proprieties of public order. At the same time, the policeman invites the hostility of the citizen so directed in two respects: he is likely to encourage the sort of response mentioned earlier (that is, an antagonistic reformulation of the policeman's role) and the policeman is apt to cause resentment because of the suspicion that policemen do not themselves strictly conform to the moral norms they are enforcing. Thus, the policeman, faced with enforcing a law against fornication, drunkenness, or gambling, is easily liable to a charge of hypocrisy. Even when the policeman is called on to enforce the laws relating to overt homosexuality, a form of sexual activity for which police are not especially noted, he may encounter the charge of hypocrisy on grounds that he does not adhere strictly to prescribed heterosexual codes. The policeman's difficulty in this respect is shared by all authorities responsible for maintenance of disciplined activity, including industrial foremen, political leaders, elementary schoolteachers, and college professors. All are expected to conform rigidly to the entire range of norms they espouse.(18) The policeman, however, as a result of the unique combination of the elements of danger and authority, experiences a special predicament. It is difficult to develop qualities enabling him to stand up to danger, and to conform to standards of puritanical morality. The element of danger demands that the policeman be able to carry out efforts that are in their nature overtly masculine. Police work, like soldiering, requires an exceptional caliber of physical fitness, agility, toughness, and the like. The man who ranks high on these masculine characteristics is, again like the soldier, not usually disposed to be puritanical about sex, drinking, and gambling.

On the basis of observations, policemen do not subscribe to moralistic standards for conduct. For example, the morals squad of the police department, when questioned, was unanimously against the statutory rape age limit, on grounds that as late teen-agers they themselves might not have refused an attractive offer from a seventeen-year-old girl.(19) Neither, from observations, are policemen by any means total abstainers from the use of alcoholic beverages. The policeman who is arresting a drunk has probably been drunk himself; he knows it and the drunk knows it.

More than that, a portion of the social isolation of the policeman can be attributed to the discrepancy between moral regulation and the norms and behavior of policemen in these areas. We have presented data indicating that police engage in a comparatively active occupational social life. One interpretation might attribute this attendance to a basic interest in such affairs; another might explain the policeman's occupational social activity as a measure of restraint in publicly violating norms he enforces. The interest in attending police affairs may grow as much out of security in "letting oneself go" in the presence of police, and a corresponding feeling of insecurity with civilians, as an authentic preference for police social affairs. Much alcohol is usually, consumed at police banquets with all the melancholy and boisterousness accompanying such occasions. As Horace Cayton reports on his experience as a policeman:(20)

> Deputy sheriffs and policemen don't know much about organized recreation; all they usually do when celebrating is get drunk and pound each other on the back, exchanging loud insults which under ordinary circumstances would result in a fight.

To some degree the reason for the behavior exhibited on these occasions is the company, since the policeman would feel uncomfortable exhibiting insobriety before civilians. The policeman may be likened to other authorities who prefer to violate moralistic norms away from onlookers for whom they are routinely supposed to appear as normative models. College professors, for instance, also get drunk on occasion, but prefer to do so where students are not present. Unfortunately for the policeman, such settings are harder for him to come by than they are for the college professor. The whole civilian world watches the policeman. As a result, he tends to be limited to the company of other policemen for whom his police identity is not a stimulus to carping normative criticism.

Correlates of Social Isolation

The element of authority, like the element of danger, is thus seen to contribute to the solidarity of policemen. To the extent that policemen share the experience of receiving hostility from the public, they are also drawn together and become dependent upon one another. Trends in the degree to which police may exercise authority are also important considerations in understanding the dynamics of the relation between authority and solidarity. It is not simply a question of how much absolute authority police are given, but how much authority they have relative to what they had, or think they had, before. If, as Westley concludes, police violence is frequently a response to a challenge to the policeman's authority, so too may a perceived reduction in authority result in greater solidarity. Whitaker comments on the British police as follows:(21)

> As they feel their authority decline, internal solidarity has become increasingly important to

the police. Despite the individual responsibility of each police officer to pursue justice, there is sometimes a tendency to close ranks and to form a square when they themselves are concerned.

These inclinations may have positive consequences for the effectiveness of police work, since notions of professional courtesy or colleagueship seem unusually high among police.[6] When the nature of the policing enterprise requires much joint activity, as in robbery and narcotics enforcement, the impression is received that cooperation is high and genuine. Policemen do not appear to cooperate with one another merely because such is the policy of the chief, but because they sincerely attach a high value to teamwork. For instance, there is a norm among detectives that two who work together will protect each other when a dangerous situation arises. During one investigation, a detective stepped out of a car to question a suspect who became belligerent. The second detective, who had remained overly long in the back seat of the police car, apologized indirectly to his partner by explaining how wrong it had been of him to permit his partner to encounter a suspect alone on the street. He later repeated this explanation privately, in genuine consternation at having committed the breach (and possibly at having been culpable in the presence of an observer). Strong feelings of empathy and cooperation, indeed almost of "clannishness," a term several policemen themselves used to describe the attitude of police toward one another, may be seen in the daily activities of police. Analytically, these feelings can be traced to the elements of danger and shared experiences of hostility in the policeman's role.

Finally, to round out the sketch, policemen are notably conservative, emotionally and politically. If the element of danger in the policeman's role tends to make the policeman suspicious, and therefore emotionally attached to the status quo, a similar consequence may be attributed to the element of authority. The fact that a man is engaged in enforcing a set of rules implies that he also becomes implicated in *affirming* them. Labor disputes provide the common-

[6] It would be difficult to compare this factor across occupations, since the indicators could hardly be controlled. Nevertheless, I felt that the sense of responsibility to policemen in other departments was on the whole quite strong.

est example of conditions inclining the policeman to support the status quo. In these situations, the police are necessarily pushed on the side of the defense of property. Their responsibilities thus lead them to see the striking and sometimes angry workers as their enemy and, therefore, to be cool, if not antagonistic, toward the whole conception of labor militancy.[7] If a policeman did not believe in the system of laws he was responsible for enforcing, he would have to go on living in a state of conflicting cognitions, a condition which a number of social psychologists agree is painful.[8]

REFERENCES

1. For previous contributions in this area, *see* the following: Ely Chinoy, *Automobile Workers and the American Dream* (Garden City, N.Y.: Doubleday, 1955); Charles R. Walker and Robert H. Guest, *The Man on the Assembly Line* (Cambridge: Harvard University Press, 1952); Everett C. Hughes, "Work and the Self," in his *Men and Their Work* (Glencoe, Ill.: The Free Press of Glencoe, 1958), pp. 42–55; Harold L. Wilensky, *Intellectuals in Labor Unions: Organizational Pressures on Professional Roles* (Glencoe, Ill.: The Free Press of Glencoe, 1956); Harold L. Wilensky, "Varieties of Work Experience," in Henry Borow, ed., *Man in a World at Work* (Boston: Houghton Mifflin, 1964), pp. 125–54; Louis Kriesberg, "The Retail Furrier: Concepts of Security and Success," *American Journal of Sociology, 57* (March 1952), pp. 478–85; Waldo Burchard, "Role Conflicts of Military Chaplains," *American Sociological Review, 19* (October 1954), pp. 528–35; Howard S. Becker and Blanche Geer, "The Fate of Idealism in Medical School," *American Sociological Review, 23* (1958), pp. 50–56; and Howard S. Becker and Anslem L. Strauss, "Careers, Personality, and Adult Socialization," *American Journal of Sociology, 62* (November 1956), pp. 253–63.

2. Morris Janowitz, *The Professional Soldier: A Social and Political Portrait* (New York: Free Press, 1964), p. 175.

3. William Westley was the first to raise such questions about the police when he inquired into the conditions under which police are violent. Whatever merit this analysis has, it owes much to his prior insights, as all subsequent sociological studies of the police must. *See* his "Violence and the Police," *American Journal of Sociology, 59* (July 1953), 34–41; also his unpublished Ph.D. dissertation *The Police: A Sociological Study of Law, Custom, and Morality* (University of Chicago, Department of Sociology, 1951).

4. From Thomas F. Adams, "Field Interrogation," *Police* (March–April, 1963), p. 28.

5. *See* Irving Piliavin and Scott Briar, "Police Encounters with Juveniles," *American Journal of Sociology, 70* (September 1964), pp. 206–214.

6. Colin MacInnes, *Mr. Love and Justice* (London: New English Library, 1962), p. 74.

7. Peter J. Connell, "Handling of Complaints by Police," (Unpublished paper for course in Criminal Procedure, Yale Law School, Fall, 1961).

8. James Baldwin, *Nobody Knows My Name* (New York: Dell, 1962), pp. 65–67.

9. Colin MacInnes, *Mr. Love and Justice* (London: New English Library, 1962), p. 20.

10. Royal Commission on the Police, 1962, Appendix IV to *Minutes of Evidence*, cited in Michael Banton, *The Policeman in the Community* (London: Tavistock, 1964), p. 198.

11. Similarly, Banton found Scottish police officers attempting to conceal their occupation when on holiday. He quotes one as saying: "If someone asks my wife, 'What does your husband do?' I've told her to say, 'He's a clerk,' and that's the way it went because she found that being a policeman's wife— well, it wasn't quite a stigma, she didn't feel cut off, but that a sort of invisible wall was up for conversation purposes when a policeman was there." Ibid.

[7] In light of this, the most carefully drawn lesson plan in the "professionalized" Westville police department, according to the officer in charge of training, is the one dealing with the policeman's demeanor in labor disputes. A comparable concern is now being evidenced in teaching policemen appropriate demeanor in civil rights demonstrations. *See*, e.g., Juby E. Towler, *The Police Role in Racial Conflicts* (Springfield, Ill.: Thomas, 1964).

[8] Indeed, one school of social psychology asserts that there is a basic "drive," a fundamental tendency of human nature, to reduce the degree of discrepancy between conflicting cognitions. For the policeman, this tenet implies that he would have to do something to reduce the discrepancy between his beliefs and his behavior. He would have to modify his behavior, his beliefs, or introduce some outside factor to justify the discrepancy. . . . *See* Leon Festinger, *A Theory of Cognitive Dissonance* (Evanston, Illinois: Row, Peterson, 1957).

12. In addition to Banton, William Westley and James Q. Wilson have noted this characteristic of police. *See* William Westley, "Violence and the Police," *American Journal of Sociology*, *59* (July 1953), p. 294; Wilson, "The Police and Their Problems: A Theory," *Public Policy*, *12* (1963), 189–216.

13. S. M. Lipset, Martin H. Trow, and James S. Coleman, *Union Democracy* (New York: Anchor Books, 1962), p. 123.

14. Michael Banton, *The Policeman in the Community* (London: Tavistock, 1964), p. 114.

15. Morris Janowitz, *The Professional Soldier: A Social and Political Portrait* (New York: The Free Press, 1964).

16. O. W. Wilson, for example, mentions this factor as a primary source of antagonism toward police. *See* his "Police Authority in a Free Society," *Journal of Criminal Law, Criminology and Police Science*, *54* (June 1964), 175–77. In the current study, in addition to the police themselves, other people interviewed, such as attorneys in the system, also attribute the isolation of police to their authority. Similarly, Arthur L. Stinchcombe, in an as yet unpublished manuscript, "The Control of Citizen Resentment in Police Work," provides a stimulating analysis, to which I am indebted, of the ways police authority generates resentment.

17. *See* Wayne R. La Fave, "The Police and Nonenforcement of the Law," *Wisconsin Law Review* (1962), pp. 104–137, 179–239.

18. For a theoretical discussion of the problems of leadership, *see* George Homans, *The Human Group* (New York: Harcourt, Brace, 1950), especially the chapter on "The Job of the Leader," pp. 415–440.

19. The work of the Westville morals squad is analyzed in detail in an unpublished master's thesis by J. Richard Woodworth. *The Administration of Statutory Rape Complaints: A Sociological Study* (Berkeley: University of California, 1964).

20. Horace R. Cayton, *Long Old Road* (New York: Trident Press, 1965), p. 154.

21. Ben Whitaker, *The Police* (Middlesex, England: Penguin Books, 1964), p. 137.

Movie Cops—Romantic vs. Real

JAMES Q. WILSON

Two opposed views of the police are embodied in the recent motion picture portrayals of two fictional New York City detectives—Dan Madigan and Joe Leland. Madigan, from the movie of the same name, is drawn from the pages of Richard Dougherty's *roman a clef* about the New York City Police Department, *The Commissioner*; Leland is—well, Leland is the hero of *The Detective* which in turn is a vehicle for Frank Sinatra, and that may be all one need know about it.

Both detectives are involved in a homicide, but neither plot is a murder mystery—the facts of the crime, and especially who did it, are less important than the character of the officers assigned to deal with it. In short, these are not "detective stories," they are *police* stories. A detective story, in the classic sense, depends on the willing suspension of disbelief—everyone knows, or is supposed to know, that murders rarely occur on rich English country estates and if they do, they are never solved by a brilliant amateur sleuth who happens to be a weekend guest and who can somehow arrange for a final dénouement to be staged in the downstairs salon. A police story, by contrast, is supposed to be realistic—we know that in life things don't happen *quite* the way they do in the book or movie, but we are prepared to believe that things could very well happen this way, and that in any case life on the police force is probably pretty much as it is portrayed. A police story is a social commentary, a piece of reportage; a detective story is a puzzle.

In fact, of course, neither Madigan nor Leland are representative police officers. Most policemen are patrolmen, not detectives; most never handle a homicide and some never see one; indeed, most patrolmen are rarely involved in a major crime of any

SOURCE: *New York*, August 19, 1968, pp. 39–41. Copyright © 1969 New York Magazine Co.

sort. Patrolmen—that is to say, typical police officers —spend their time providing assistance, rendering (or failing to render) services, keeping the peace, and settling quarrels. Occasionally—and worse, unexpectedly—violence erupts. There is no glamor and little excitement, but a good deal of tension and uncertainty, about the job. A police story or police movie that gave an accurate account of police life would be about patrolmen dealing with confused, irritable, or unhappy lovers, parents, and kids. But such material is rather formless, even pointless, and motion picture directors who are not frankly experimental would probably find it hopeless. To provide a story line and hold an audience, police stories usually rely on an understructure similar to that of detective stories—the reportage is woven around a puzzle.

Once these limits on the genre are recognized and accepted, the police styles represented by Madigan and Leland become interesting. Neither style is drawn true to life, and Leland especially has little connection with any detective who ever lived. But Madigan is closer to the truth in countless details as well as in emphasis and manner, at least closer to the truth about what might be called the "Eastern Cop," which is a breed apart from the "Western Cop."

The Western Cop, suitably idealized, is Sgt. Joe Friday of *Dragnet*. Laconic, skilled, technically proficient and legally knowledgeable, he is the thoroughly professional member of the most professionalized police department in the country—Los Angeles. Occasionally he erupts in resentment at indifferent citizens, restrictive court decisions, "do-gooders," and hypocrites; occasionally we are allowed to suspect that Joe Friday would like, for just a few hours, to act and live like Madigan—kick down some doors, slap around some "bums," and accept the offers of free meals, drinks, and clothes. But there is never more than a suspicion; Friday plays it by the book, and the book covers everything. Besides, the computers and test-tubes back at headquarters make resorting to rough stuff unnecessary and the inspectors and disciplinary boards make it foolhardy.

Madigan would admire Friday's skill and courage but deplore his strait-laced methods and style. Dan Madigan lives beyond his means—a cop earns a lousy salary, and so Madigan takes things "on the arm." But he is only on the arm, never on the pad—that is, he takes "police discounts" and free meals and free hotel suites but he does not take money from gamblers or the hustlers. Madigan has heard about the Supreme Court decisions but doesn't believe in them; if they were not so irrelevant to what he does, he would spend more time being angered by them. He drinks a little too much, has a wife who doesn't understand why he has to spend so much time on police work (and her bitchiness makes him drink even more), and he is profoundly humiliated when a man he has gone to arrest takes his gun away from him and escapes. When another police officer is killed with that gun, Madigan is stunned. The man who took the gun and shot the cop is not an especially complex person—he is a professional killer, unmistakably vicious, perhaps pathologically so. To find him is all-important but also exhausting and unpleasant. Madigan squeezes informants, bullies secretaries who try to protect informants, enlists (and thus endangers) other citizens, kicks in doors, and is always ready to shoot. In the end, Madigan dies. We are not told whether his breed dies with him or whether, if that is the case, we should mourn or celebrate its passing.

Joe Leland is neither Friday nor Madigan; he is an idealized version of what police officers would be like if they didn't have to be police officers. He is supposed to be the Third Way, the "good cop" who is neither a professionalized automaton nor an Eastern gangbuster. He combines the virtues of both with the vices of neither. He is studious, even (in a primitive way) intellectual; but he is not stuffy like Joe Friday. He is a New York City boy, but one who takes courses at Columbia (not City College: *Columbia*). Like Dan Madigan, he is not puritanical—he likes attractive women and enjoys the things money can buy. But the extra money it takes to supply that kind of enjoyment he acquires by marrying it; no police discounts. Unlike Madigan, he does not use any rough stuff (though the lure of a promotion leads him to exert some intense psychological pressure on a suspect). Nobody would accuse Joe Leland of being a sissy—the grisly opening scenes, with the calculated use of shock words, establish Leland as a man who can take it. But later, when the police are rousting a nest of homosexuals, Leland becomes kind, understanding; not only does he stop another officer from pushing the suspects around, he takes the officer behind a patrol car and hits *him*.

But the crucial scenes, viewing the movie as a police story, are those which establish the attitudes of Madigan and Leland to the central-city slums. For Madigan, they are simply a fact; they exist. The people he meets in them are, for the most part, bookies, prostitutes, thieves, and murderers. There are innocent people there, to be sure, and occasionally one has to take special care to avoid hurting them when chasing the crooks, but primarily they are a silent backdrop. Information exists in the city, but one must use every artifice to develop it—derelict informers, easily intimidated clerks, shady businessmen who are vulnerable to subtle threats, young punks who hate cops and need a glimpse of terror. Nobody volunteers anything unless there is something in it for him.

Leland's case, by contrast, keeps him out of the slum. A rich man is killed in a luxurious apartment; the vital information is obtained in the elegant offices of a fashionable psychiatrist, a beautiful woman is interviewed in an elegant beach cottage. The only unsavory person is a man who is clearly psychotic and he is caught, not in the slum, but at a beach hotel. Leland may not experience the slum, it may not affect his work, but he has views about it. He refers to it as the "ghetto." It is primarily the result of the depredation of slum landlords and thieving or indifferent politicians; it suffers for want of decent housing and schools; it is a "garbage can" created by outside society and the police job is to sit on the lid.

Madigan dies; Leland crusades. Uncovering political corruption, Leland throws over his police career ("you could go all the way to the top," his captain tells him) to expose the scandal. There is an unspoken promise in the eyes of the beautiful girl in the beach cottage that she will sustain him in adversity.

Leland combines a simple personal morality with a complex and compassionate view of large social issues. He is unimpeachably honest; he is not on the arm and he beats another detective who is on the pad. He will not condone brutality or even psychological harassment (and he feels guilty that he once practiced the latter). He speaks approvingly of a girl who utters anti-cop statements, not in spite of her views, but because of them. He dislikes "phony intellectuals" but he does not despise their concerns; when they are "arty," he puts them down, but when they defend the needs of the lower classes, he agrees. His wife is a nymphomaniac; when he learns this, he abandons her immediately and irrevocably. But when he encounters a homosexual, he looks for explanations and he forgives.

Madigan, on the other hand, has a complex private morality and a simple public one. He is

married, but he sees other women; on the other hand, he does not sleep with other women unless suitably provoked by his wife. He takes money from some kinds of people and not from others; he terrifies an innocent secretary and afterwards dislikes himself for being "reduced to scaring old ladies." Even the police commissioner for whom Madigan works, and whose aggressive honesty leads him to distrust Madigan's methods, has a mistress and is disturbed by his inability to reconcile his behavior with the rigid code he seeks to impose on the department. Madigan sees the world at large, on the other hand, as divided into "good guys" and "bums." His job is to protect the former from the latter. It cannot always be done politely.

Leland is, for people who dislike the callousness of Madigan and the insensitivity of Joe Friday, the happy compromise. He is a man with a strong private moral code but without those political sentiments—"backlash" sentiments—normally found among such men. He does not project his private standards on the larger world—or more accurately, he does, but in a way that leads to constructive action (helping the ghetto by ending political corruption). Leland is depicted as a good cop—the "best detective on the force"—and a man liked by his superiors and admired by his partners. But this popularity is not purchased at the price of easy conformity to their lax standards; he lectures them about proper conduct (even the Negro detective gets a stern rebuke) and hits them when they fail to act in accordance with the letter of the law.

Many who would like to change the police (or, since we are not talking about police generally, the detective) often hope they can, by some combination of salary, training, reorganization, or legal mandate, create a force of bittersweet Joe Lelands. It will not happen. There may be a few Lelands, but they leave the police force as soon as they have a good alternative—they become consultants, advisors, federal officials, or even academics. It is not money, or organization, or training that defines the policeman's job; it is the job that defines the policeman. The nature of that job does not change, especially in the big city. The kinds of men who can handle it are relatively few, and no kind has all the virtues and none of the vices. Indeed, in considerable measure there are only two kinds of men, and thus two choices—Dan Madigan or Joe Friday.

Color Line a Key Police Problem

JOHN DARNTON

In the garage of a Chicago station house, a black patrolman removed his gunbelt, stared into the eyes of a white officer and said: "I'm going to beat your brains out."

According to three other black officers who moved in to break up the fight, it began when the white policeman hauled a black youth from a paddy wagon and clubbed him to the ground.

The white officer denied that he beat the prisoner. "But I'm not going to tell you what did happen," he said.

The recent incident is not an isolated one. In a number of major cities across the country—from New York to San Francisco—there is a rising hostility between black and white policemen.

In some cities, the conflict takes the form of a fistfight in the locker room; a racial slur scrawled on the precinct wall; a refusal to ride in the same patrol car with a colleague of a different color.

In other cities—San Francisco, Detroit, Chicago and Washington—there have been racial disputes in which officers are said to have drawn their service revolvers on each other.

"We've just been lucky that there hasn't been a real shootout," a black officer in San Francisco said.

"It's bad out here, man, real bad," said a black policeman walking his beat in Detroit's 10th Precinct. "And if something isn't done soon by somebody, you'll see a lot more black officers pulling their guns on white officers."

In many departments, undercurrents of racism have not grown into open animosity. But in others, the antagonism has come to the surface over the last two years, spreading and polarizing the men into two racial camps.

The reasons include the following:

1. The appearance of a new type of black officer, younger, more assertive than his Negro predecessor
2. The increasing numbers of black policemen, many of them recruited from the slums
3. The proliferation of new organizations of black policemen
4. Charges of discrimination against the blacks within the departments
5. In some areas, a trend among white policemen toward right-wing, antiblack conservatism
6. The divisive effects of "outside" events such as civil disorders and "law and order" political campaigns

The new breed of black policemen is a striking change from the old-time "colored cop," who became vilified by the black community as an "Uncle Tom."

"I don't know," said one older officer in Hartford recently. "These younger fellows are really talking out."

"We're black men first," said a 26-year-old San Francisco patrolman, Palmer Jackson. "We're black men first, and then we are police officers."

His statement is being supported from Watts to Harlem.

The new black policemen are usually in their early 20's. They are usually patrolmen, with fewer than three years on the force. Black pride is a magnet for many of them. They wear Afro haircuts under their police caps and Dashikis off duty. They greet one another as "brother."

Some of them live in the slum communities in which they are assigned to patrol. They identify with the communities and they talk—bitterly—about what they describe as the inequities of law enforcement there and the brutality of white officers toward blacks.

Badges the Same Size

"The black cop just isn't going to stand around and see that kind of stuff happen and do nothing," one policeman said.

"We were hired as the white man's assistant in

dealing with blacks," remarked Renault Robinson, head of the Afro-American Patrolmen's League of Chicago. "Now we've measured our badges with his and found out they are the same size."

"I'm tired of hearing where black children are beaten by white cops; where black women are insulted by white cops. We're going to knock 'em up, knock 'em down, break 'em in, and treat them just as they treat us," said Patrolman Leonard Weir, president of New York's Society of Afro-American Policemen.

If a new black policeman is an enigma to many older Negro officers, he is an anathema to many white officers.

A white officer in Chicago explained his feelings this way:

"I rode in the same car with one [a militant black policeman] once. He didn't say a word to me for four hours. Then all of a sudden he spouted off about 'racist institutions downtown.' I can't listen to that kind of talk."

"I wasn't prejudiced before," the officer continued. "Now I hate niggers."

A study in 1966 for the National Crime Commission, based on data from Boston, Chicago and Washington, found that 79 per cent of white policemen in black precincts were prejudiced. Forty-five per cent were classified as "extreme anti-Negro."

Negative Attitudes Cited

The same study found that 28 per cent of the black officers in these areas expressed negative attitudes toward blacks.

"In none of those three cities did we find the black militant officers. They have been emerging since then," said Dr. Albert J. Reiss Jr., a sociologist at the University of Michigan, who conducted the study.

Within the last two years, almost every major department in the country has seen at least one dispute that developed when a black officer objected to the treatment of prisoners at the hands of the whites.

In San Francisco, black policemen accused white policemen of using undue force in dealing with student demonstrators and threatened to arrest the white officers for brutality.

Also in San Francisco, a black officer rushed two whites, and, according to some versions, reached for his gun. He said the whites were beating a handcuffed black prisoner in a cell.

In York, Pa., one of the six blacks on the force resigned during recent disturbances. He objected to use of police dogs against blacks and a "senseless use of firepower."

And in Atlanta, a black patrolman held a news conference to state that he had witnessed three black prisoners being beaten by five white officers inside the station house.

Police officials in high echelons refused for the most part to acknowledge a racial division among the men under their command. But to many blacks—especially to those involved in organizing black policemen—there was no mistaking the seriousness of the situation.

Mr. Robinson, the president of the Chicago Afro-American Patrolmen's League, has more than 30 rules violations pending against him, including one for maligning a fellow officer after Mr. Robinson criticized an off-duty policeman for shooting a 16-year-old boy in the back.

Two weeks ago, Mr. Robinson was arrested on four driving charges and held briefly in jail. When he returned to his station house, he was told that a note was in his mailbox. "They had written 'nigger' all over it and stuffed it full of garbage," he said.

There have been other instances of name-calling. Racial slurs led to a fistfight in a police line in San Francisco and to the suspension of a black trainee who drew a revolver on an instructor in Washington.

In Boston, a policeman in a patrol car calling the communications center to report a fight between "two black men" was interrupted by an anonymous message from another car: "You mean two niggers, don't you?"

Often the feelings between blacks and whites come to a head over what has become in some places a delicate matter—riding in the same patrol car.

A San Francisco patrolman who angered whites by reading the Black Panther party newspaper in the station house gave this as a reason: "When the sergeant tells one of those guys that he has to ride with one of us, you see them. They start yelling and complaining and everything. They do it right out loud and nobody says a damn thing."

In many cases, the gulf has widened as blacks have withdrawn from traditional police organizations to form their own. Virtually every major city now has a black policeman's organization.

"We don't meet as policemen. We meet as members of the black community," explained Mr. Weir of the Society of Afro-American Policemen. Mr. Weir's group, founded in 1965, now has chapters in Newark, Philadelphia, Chicago and Detroit. Its headquarters is in New York.

The society's younger, more militant officers are currently challenging the leadership of the Council of Police Societies, which was formed in 1960 and now has 22 chapters.

But Mr. Weir still scoffs at black policemen in general, even those who join black organizations. "They're all mouth and no action," he said. "I don't want to hear the talk. I want to hear the thunder. I want to see the lightning."

Unlike previous ethnic organizations in police departments, the blacks are bound by strong complaints, which they tend to take outside regular channels in an attempt to gain support and establish rapport with the black community.

Two weeks ago in Chicago, the Afro-American Patrolmen's League held a news conference in Police Headquarters to announce that members would not be used as "strike-breakers" against black pickets at construction sites. Last week, the Coalition for United Community Action, a group seeking to put more blacks in the building trades, returned the gesture by holding a rally in support of the league, which says it is "under harassment" from the department.

The pledge of the Officers for Justice in San Francisco says in part: "We will no longer permit ourselves to be relegated to the role of brutal pawns in a chess game affecting the communities in which we serve. We are husbands, fathers, brothers, neighbors and members of the black community. Donning the blue uniform has not changed this."

The major concern of the black groups, and the one most responsible for stirring them to action, is their contention of almost continual brutality of the white policemen in the black slums.

"I have witnessed brutality and unnecessary roughness by white officers many times," said Capt. James Francis Jr. of the New York Police Department. "Every black cop has seen it."

A question that has divided many black groups is: Should black areas be patrolled only by black policemen?

In Hartford, 22 black policemen began a five-day sick-call protest because they felt they were being discriminated against by assignments to black areas. In Boston, during disturbances in Roxbury, black officers turned down a suggestion of the Police Commissioner that they all be assigned to the slums.

But in New York, the blacks and Puerto Ricans graduating from the Police Academy last week had only one complaint—they felt they were being assigned outside their communities.

In large part, the increasing membership in the black groups—and increasing friction with the whites —is attributable to the increasing influx of black policemen.

The National Advisory Commission on Civil Disorders found that blacks were under-represented, usually substantially, in every department for which statistics were available. Out of 80,621 sworn personnel in 28 major cities, only 7,046 were nonwhite.

Since the report was published in 1968, however, the numbers of blacks on the forces have significantly risen in several cities: In Washington, from 21 per cent to 30 per cent; in Detroit, from 5 per cent to 9 per cent, and in St. Louis, from 10 per cent to 15 per cent.

In New York, where black policemen remained at the level of 5 per cent for years, the figure has lately increased to 7 per cent. The department explains the disproportion in terms of the difficulty in recruiting blacks, but many Negroes on the force believe they are intentionally being kept at a minimum.

"With such a low ratio, the department never had blacks coming on in droves and therefore avoided the problems of other cities," one officer commented. "But as the ratio goes up, if it does, and younger black men join the force, they'll be different men altogether from what we were."

Many of the new black recruits are veterans who came in through two Defense Department programs that allow servicemen to be released from duty in the United States three months earlier for police training.

And many of them come from the slums. Why do they want to become policemen? "Where else can a young black without a college education find a job that pays $11,000 a year?" remarked the head of the Chicago Afro-American Patrolmen's League.

Because they come from the slums, a number of

the black recruits have a poor formal education and a record that sometimes includes a brush with the law. This has given rise to the theme of maintaining high standards in recruitment and performance, which is being sounded with increasing frequency by a number of established policemen's organizations.

Deeper Than Prejudice

Some observers see a rising conservatism among white officers that is more complex than simple racial prejudice. They argue that groups such as the Irish, who have a reverence for a kind of Puritanism on the force, are, in reality, reacting to an unarticulated fear that the police department is somehow losing its integrity.

"You should see the stuff they [Negroes] get away with," one white said. "Sleeping on the job. Being out of your district. Those are major violations. If it was a white guy, he'd be taken to a brick wall and be shot."

On the other side, a number of blacks see the recruiting program as inadequate. They feel that the hiring examinations are sometimes "white-oriented," that blacks are subjected to closer scrutiny during probation and that, in some areas, the whites use oral exams or rating systems to deny promotions to blacks who show sympathy to their own communities.

Black-white police relations are further strained during certain types of political campaigns. In Los Angeles, tension rose during the mayoralty campaign between Samuel W. Yorty and Thomas Bradley. In Philadelphia, it happened when the head of the National Fraternal Order of Police, John J. Harrington, publicly endorsed George C. Wallace for President.

In San Francisco, passion is currently running high over a coming election on a city charter change that would elevate the Negro community relations head from a patrolman to the rank of director.

The animosity has been displayed to the greatest degree during a time of civil disorder.

A white officer in Newark said: "I'm sorry, but after you've seen what I've seen—Negroes looting, burning, yelling—they just seem to be a bunch of animals."

A black in the same department said: "A lot of black officers I know stopped during the riots, stopped and asked: 'Could that be happening to me? Could I be over there?'"

"I was maybe what you'd call an Uncle Tom when I came on the force a few years ago," said a black policeman in Detroit. "But I saw things in that riot in '67 that caused me to see what a lot of these people [blacks] were feeling and saying.

"Then I understood a little more when they called me a 'traitor' and a 'white man's nigger.' It still hurts when I hear it—and I still do, believe me—but I can kinda see why they feel that way."

Sometimes the division between white and black officers seems as deep as the division between white and black cultures.

On a warm afternoon in San Francisco, a black policeman in civilian clothes stood in a doorway on Third Street in Hunters Point. He was engrossed in the scene before him. There were black faces all around.

One tall youth threw a dollar bill on the sidewalk. "Shoot it," he charged to the rhythmic snap of his fingers. "Shoot it." But he quickly pinned the bill down with a worn, pointy-toed shoe.

"Say brother, gimme some," he said. "Gimme some now, brother. What you say? You better turn me loose. Sister! Say there sister! Guess the sister's in a hurry."

The black policeman motioned toward the black youth. "That's what the white cop can never understand," he said. "The black cop sees that cat out there in yellow pants and he knows that's part of him. He sees beauty in blackness."

The Jewish Patrolman

ARTHUR NIEDERHOFFER

The Great Depression was mainly responsible for the entry of a number of Jews into the classically Irish police force.(1) In those days Jews faced prejudice. The prevailing attitudes toward them were of thinly disguised contempt, and disbelief that they would make good cops. Jewish policemen were forced to prove themselves worthy.

One Jewish patrolman finally convinced the opposition. He won so many awards for his police work that his nickname became "Medals." But his finest hour came when the other policemen, and his personal friends outside the force, started calling him "Reilly." There were not many Jewish "Reillys" at the beginning.

Jewish policemen faced more than prejudice. A high percentage of these newcomers were college men. They naturally became the target for the anti-intellectualism that policemen shared with many other Americans. A Jewish policeman with a college degree soon realized that for him the police world was out of joint. His handling of police situations often seemed feasible by college standards, but frequently was impractical according to the standards of traditional police practice. With middle-class antecedents, and his Jewish heritage, he almost inevitably attempted to solve problems verbally rather than by force.

There are several recurrent, unpleasant situations that confront the Jewish policeman. Often the non-Jewish policeman tries to be friendly by hailing him with *"Mach a leben?"* To the non-Jew this remark is equivalent to saying, "How are things?" To the Jew it not only is bad grammar, but also covertly insinuates that Jews are mainly interested in making money. It is also difficult for the Jewish policeman to deal with an anti-Semitic civilian. The problem is complicated by the fact that anti-Semites are reputedly sensitive to Jewishness and able to recognize a Jew quickly but are fooled by the police uniform which they associate with the Irish, or at least non-Jewish policemen. Repeatedly an anti-Semite will sidle up to the Jewish policeman and "out of a clear sky" start blaming the evils of the world on the Jews. Only a little less irritating to his pride as a policeman is the reaction of the Jewish occupants of a car that he has stopped for a traffic violation. The officer will hear them say in Yiddish, "Give him a few dollars to forget the ticket, and let's get out of here."

Today relative deprivation describes the state of Jewish patrolmen. A generation ago Jewish policemen, compared with members of different faiths or ethnic groups, had real grievances, they were discriminated against and treated as inferiors. Deprivation was not at all relative but absolute. Except in isolated instances this is no longer true. If the Jewish policeman experiences frustration today, it is probably due to his commitment to the traditional Jewish *Weltanschauung* from which he is not completely emancipated. This tradition is typified by the advice their leaders gave Jewish immigrants near the end of the nineteenth century:

> Select a goal and pursue it with all your might. No matter what happens to you, hold on. You will experience a bad time but sooner or later you will achieve your goal. . . . A bit of advice for you: Do not take a moment's rest. Run, do, work, and keep your own good in mind. . . . A final virtue is needed in America—called cheek. . . . Do not say, I cannot; I do not know.(2)

Jewish mothers-in-law have learned subtle techniques to disguise their disappointment at having gained a policeman son-in-law when they lost their daughter in marriage. For example, one mother-in-law bravely surmounted her loss of status by introducing her policeman son-in-law as a college graduate with two degrees. Others try to conceal the police blemish by describing the policeman relative as "in youth work" or, if he is lucky enough to be attached to the Police Academy, as "a teacher."

Jewish parents look forward to the wonderful day when they can proudly introduce their offspring with the ritual words, "My son, the doctor." It cannot give them the same degree of satisfaction to present, "My son, the cop." They suspect their friends of translating the words "My son, the cop" into an altogether different phrase "My cop-son." It is one of those ironical coincidences that in the Yiddish colloquial speech the term of mild contempt commonly used to signify "a person who will never amount to anything" is pronounced phonetically *"cop son."*

While contemporary Jews have no high regard for police work as an occupation, older Jewish people remember the old-country ghettos, and the respect they were forced to display to policemen. On the other hand, since several European nations barred Jews from the police force, émigré Jews are often secretly proud that in America a Jew can become an influential official with the power of life and death over others. This ambivalence is mirrored in the attitude of Jewish policemen who sometimes feel like failures, but are often inwardly proud that they have succeeded in an occupation that once had this particular significance for their forebears.

REFERENCES

1. Nathan Glazer and Daniel P. Moynihan, *Beyond the Melting Pot* (Cambridge, Mass.: The M.I.T. Press, 1963), p. 261.

2. Moses Rischin, *The Promised City: New York's Jews 1870—1914* (Cambridge: Harvard University Press, 1962), p. 75.

3 | Police Organization and Control

Police systems occupy a unique position in our democratic society. More than any other institutions and professions they have been subjected to strong control by civil authority. Furthermore, they have been dispersed and fragmented to insure their weakness. The benchmark of most professions is their autonomy and relative freedom from external controls. Striving to move toward professional status, the police can hardly hope to achieve this kind of independence. Instead, because of the political traditions of our nation, they meet a wall of resistance. And this may constitute the greatest barrier to genuine police professionalism.

The one exception where police have been able to maintain autonomy is in connection with the processing of certain complaints against the police. In our larger cities, when a civilian board for the review of citizens' complaints against the police has been established, police organizations have been uniformly successful in neutralizing the claims. This phenomenon is a testimonial to the ability of the police to orchestrate highly sophisticated techniques involving political and judicial strategies. The success of police resistance to this variety of external control may be the result of a coalition consisting of community power centers and the police, whose mutual interests appear to coincide with respect to the issues and threats that are symbolized by a civilian review board. The most sophisticated police leaders never lose sight of the fact that their power and organizational autonomy can only be asserted up to a point, at which time the external political forces and other community power centers are aroused.

Another type of police administrator, entranced by the glowing illusion of police professionalism, fails to perceive these limits. He works ardently for the autonomy and self-governance of his organization and is rudely disillusioned when he fails to attain his goals. Not only administrators, but also rank and file police officers who misinterpret the stress on education and technology as the fulfillment rather than the timorous first step on the road to professionalism equally share the misconceptions which lead to their frustration and disenchantment.

Police officers, who must deal with the challenges of the urban arena, cannot afford to be simplistic. The seemingly straightforward administrative problems such as recruitment, training, education, disposition of the force, problems of productivity, community relations, and cost-benefit issues are really much more complex; and all these administrative issues are fraught with potential political repercussions. The police administrator must be alert to the political dimensions that may require compromise or modification of a department's priorities and performance agenda.

If police leaders are insensitive to the external environment that we have described, then they may fail to comprehend the equally turbulent internal organizational milieu and its accompanying dynamics of struggles for power and the new directions of policing.

We recognize that it is extremely taxing to walk the rather narrow line required by the foregoing contingencies without becoming a cynic, a Machiavellian, or, at worst, a political hack. But that is the art of being a police administrator. Unless police officers and their superiors come to grips with this underlying reality which governs their organizations, they will not be able to advance toward the status and goals they seek.

The Researcher: *An Alien in the Police World*

PETER MANNING

INTRODUCTION

Since 1964 there has been a noticeable increase in the number of published studies of the police. Table 1 lists the major published and unpublished sociological studies of Anglo-American policing. The majority of them appeared after 1965, coinciding with public concern with crime and disorder in both Great Britain and this country.

It will be appreciated that the foci and methodologies of the studies listed in Table 1 are diverse, even though the substantive concern is the sociology of the police.[1] Thus, there are sociological studies of juvenile policing and of traffic, vice and detective work; there are also studies utilizing simulation, attitude surveys, historical methodologies, time-motion studies, organizational studies, and studies utilizing official crime and/or output/performance measures. In the following discussion, our concern will be with studies which relied primarily upon some form of systematic observation and fieldwork as the primary data-gathering technique. Although nearly all the studies listed in Table 1 involved some form of observation, substantially fewer employed it almost exclusively. These observational studies, as we shall call them, will provide the corpus of work examined here, and it should be noted that among them the majority are studies of routine police patrol.

Three review papers on access to police organizations are available (Manning 1972, Fox and Lundman 1974, and Lundman and Fox 1974). These papers, the author's own field experiences, and four other studies (Banton, Black and Reiss, Buckner and Skolnick) provide the bulk of information on problems of police fieldwork, the strategy and tactics of such research, and the functioning of police organizations. These studies are selected for special attention because they contain exceptionally thoughtful and self-revealing methodological appendices, as well as discursive reflections upon the significance and implications of the work. It is indeed unfortunate that more studies do not provide the reader with more penetrating considerations of the often intricate and fragile process of police fieldwork; all too often, entry problems, for example, are dismissed in a sentence or two. Exit problems are not discussed at all. As long as these matters are considered nonproblematic they will operate to pattern and alter the nature of the data derived in unknown and therefore uncontrolled ways.

SOURCE: This is an extensively revised and edited version of a chapter which originally appeared under the title, "Observing the Police: Deviants, Respectables and the Law" in Jack D. Douglas, ed., *Research on Deviance* (New York: Random House, 1972) pp. 213–68.

[1] Fox and Lundman claim an increased interest in the police among sociologists, noting that the "review of two major sociological journals, the *American Sociological Review* and the *American Journal of Sociology*, reveals that the rate of publication for the 25 years between 1940 and 1965 equals approximately one publication every two years. In the six years following 1965, however, the article and book review publication rate has exceeded three and one-half per year" (1974:52–53).

Table 1. *Selected Research Studies of Police: Published Works,*
Dissertations, Theses, and Works in Progress

Study	Method	Period of research	Research site
Published Works			
Alex, Nicholas. *Black in Blue*. New York: Appleton-Century-Crofts, 1969.	Interviews	1964–65	New York City
Banton, Michael. *The Policeman in the Community*. New York: Basic Books, 1964.	Interviews Observation* Questionnaire	1960–62	Scotland; 2 medium-sized U.S. cities
Bayley, David. *The Police and Political Development in India*. Princeton: Princeton University Press, 1969.	Interviews (students & public) Observations Records	1965–66	India
Bayley, David, and Harold Mendelsohn. *Minorities and the Police*. New York: Free Press, 1969.	Interviews (police & public)	1966	Denver
Bercal, T. "Calls for Police Assistance . . ." in Hahn, ed., *Police in Urban Society*. Beverly Hills, California: Sage, 1971; 267–77			
Bittner, Egon. "The Police on Skid-Row: A Study of Peace Keeping," *American Sociological Review, 32* (1967); 699–715.	Interviews Observations	1963–64	
_____ . "Police Discretion in Apprehending the Mentally Ill," *Social Problems, 14* (1967); 278–92.	Interviews Observations Psychiatric records	1963–64	
Black, Donald J., and A. J. Reiss. Many studies for President's Crime Commission Report, 1966–68.	Interviews Observation Questionnaire	Primarily summer 1966	"High crime" precincts: Washington Boston Chicago
Cain, M. *Society and the Policeman's Role*. London: Routledge and Kegan Paul, 1973.	Observation Interviews (officers, officers' wives)	1962–63	English rural county/urban center
Cicourel, Aaron. *The Social Organization of Juvenile Justice*. New York: Wiley, 1967.	Observation Police and probation reports	4 years	
Cumming, Elaine, Ian Cumming, and Laura Edell. "Policeman as Philosopher, Guide and Friend," *Social Problems, 12* (1965); 276–86.	Police Calls (incoming)* Interviews Observation	1961	
Daley, R. *Target Blue*. New York: Dell, 1974.	Observation (Deputy Commission, N.Y.P.D., 1 year)	1970–71	New York City
Drabek, T. E. "Lab Simulation of a Police Community System Under Stress." Columbus, Ohio: College of Ad. Science, Ohio State, 1969.			
Drabek, T. E. and J. Haas. "Laboratory Simulation of Organizational Stress," *American Sociological Review, 34* (April 1969): 223–38.	Observation Simulation	1968–69	

*Major data source

Table 1 (Continued)

Study	Method	Period of research	Research site
Drabek, T. E. and J. Chapman. "On Assessing Organizational Priorities: Concept and Method," *Sociological Quarterly, 14* (Summer 1973); 359–75.			
Gardiner, J. *Traffic and the Police.* Cambridge, Mass.: Harvard University Press, 1969.	Official statistics (traffic violations) Interviews (police chiefs, traffic officers, civic leaders) Questionnaires		National Mass. cities National
Harris, R. *The Police Academy: An Inside Observation View.* New York: Wiley, 1973.	Observation*	Feb.–April 1969	Rurban County, Mass.
La Fave, Wayne. *Arrest: The Decision to Take a Suspect into Custody.* Boston: Little, Brown, 1965.	Observation Court and police records	1956–57	
Manning, P. K. *Police Work.*	Observation* Interviews	1972–73	London, England
Niederhoffer, Arthur. *Behind the Shield.* Garden City, N.Y.: Anchor Books, 1967.	Questionnaire Observation	21 years	N.Y.P.D.
Piliavin, Irwin, and Scott Briar. "Police Encounters with Juveniles," *American Journal of Sociology, 70* (1964): 206–14. *See* also Piliavin article in Bordua, ed., cited below.	Observation	9 months	
Preiss, Jack, and Howard Ehrlich. *An Examination of Role Theory: The Case of the State Police.* Lincoln: University of Nebraska Press, 1966.	Observation Questionnaire* Interviews	1957–58	Michigan
Rubinstein, J. *City Police.* New York: Farrar, Strauss and Giroux, 1973.	Observation	1969–71	Philadelphia
Rubinstein, J., and J. Richard Woodworth. "Bureaucracy, Information and Social Control: A Study of a Morals Detail," in David J. Bordua, ed., *The Police: Six Sociological Essays.* New York: Wiley and Sons, 1967.	Observation Police records	1962–63	
Skolnick, Jerome H. *Justice Without Trial.* New York: Wiley and Sons, 1966.	Observation* Interviews Questionnaires	1962–63	"Westville" (Oakland, California)
Van Maanen, J. "Observations on the Making of Policemen," *Human Organization, 32* (Winter 1973); 407–18. (See dissertations.)			
Webster, John. *The Realities of Police Work.* Dubuque: W. C. Brown, 1972.	Police calls Time/motion data		"Baywood," California
Westley, William A. *The Police: A Study in Law, Custom and Morality.* Cambridge, Mass.: Massachusetts Institute of Technology Press, 1970.	Observation Interviews	1949	Gary, Indiana
Whittemore, L. H. *Cop!* New York: Fawcett/Crest, 1970.	Observation Interviews (patrolmen & detectives)	1967–68	New York Chicago San Francisco

*Major data source

Table 1 (Continued)

Study	Method	Period of research	Research site
Wilson, James Q. "Generational and Ethnic Differences Among Career Police Officers," *American Journal of Sociology, 69* (1964); 522–28.	Questionnaires	1960	Chicago
Wilson, James Q. "Police Morale, Reform, and Citizen Respect: The Chicago Case," in Bordua, ed., op. cit.	Questionnaires	1960–65	Chicago
_____ . *Varieties of Police Behavior: The Management of Law and Order in Eight Communities.* Cambridge, Mass.: Harvard University Press, 1968.	Observation (?) Interviews "Visitation"	1964, 1965 1966–67	Several Middle-sized U.S. cities

Dissertations (All Departments of Sociology unless otherwise indicated)

Bacon, Selden, "The Early Development of American Municipal Police." Yale University, 1939. Two volumes.	Historical study		
Black, Donald J. "Police Encounters and Social Organization: An Observational Study." University of Michigan, 1968.	Observation Police records	Summer 1966	Washington Boston Chicago
Brede, R. "The Policing of Juveniles in Chicago." University of Illinois (Urbana), 1971.	Observation Juvenile records	1970–71	Chicago
Buckner, H. Taylor. "The Police: The Culture of a Social Control Agency." University of California, Berkeley, 1967.	Observation	1966–67	Oakland, California, P.D.
Coates, R. B. "Dimensions of Police-Citizen Interactions: A Social Psychological Analysis." University of Maryland, 1971.			
Cross, S. "Social Relationships and the Rookie Policeman." University of Illinois (Urbana), 1972.	Observation Questionnaires		
Cummings, Marvin J. "The Frame-up." University of Colorado, 1967.	Observation		
Ford, Robert. "A Meeting With the Man: An Analysis of Police-Citizen Encounters in the Core City." University of Illinois (Urbana), 1972.			
Guernsey, E. W. "The State Trooper: A Study of an Occupational Self." Florida State University, 1965.			
Guthrie, Charles R. "Law Enforcement and the Juvenile: A Study of Police Interaction with Delinquents." University of Southern California, 1963.			
Harris, James. "Police Disposition: Decisions with Juveniles." University of Illinois, 1967.			
Lundman, Richard J. "Police-Citizen Encounters: A Symbolic Interactionist Analysis." University of Minnesota, 1972.	Interaction analysis Observation *See* Clark/ Sykes study, below.	1970–71	Three mid-western cities
Maniha, John K. "Mobility of Elites in A Bureaucratizing Organization: The St. Louis P.D., 1861–1961." University of Michigan, 1970.	Historical research		

Table 1 (Continued)

Study	Method	Period of research	Research site
McNamara, John H. "Role Learning for Police Recruits: Some Problems in the Process of Preparation for the Uncertainties of Police Work." University of California, Los Angeles, 1967. *See* also McNamara article in Bordua ed., op cit.	Questionnaires	1960–63	N.Y.P.D.
Pepinsky, H. "Police Decisions to Report Offenses." University of Pennsylvania, 1972.	Observation	1971–72	Minneapolis
Petersen, David. "Police Discretion and the Decision to Arrest." University of Kentucky, 1968.			
Pizzuto, C. L. "The Police Juvenile Unit: A Study of Role Consensus." Brandeis University, 1968.			
Sanders, W. "Detective Story: A Study of Criminal Investigations." University of California, Santa Barbara, 1974.	Field observation (detectives) Interviews Photos	1972–73	California county sheriff's office
Saunders, C. R. "High and the Mighty: The Middle-Class Drug User and the Legal System." Northwestern University, 1972.	Interviews (lawyers, students, narcotics agents) Observations	1967–70	Chicago
Smith, T. S. "Democratic Control and Professionalism in Police Work: The State Police Experience." University of Chicago, 1968.	Questionnaire* Observation Police records	1967	Maryland State Police
Tifft, L. "Comparative Police Suspension Systems: An Organizational Analysis." University of Illinois, 1970	Observation Interviews (police, citizens)	1968–70	Chicago
Trojanowicz, Robert. "A Comparison of the Behavior Styles of Policemen and Social Workers." Michigan State University, 1969.	Questionnaires	1968	Michigan
Van Maanen, J. "Pledging the Police: A Study of Selected Aspects of Recruit Socialization in a Large Urban Police Department." University of California, Irvine, 1972.	Observation Interviews	1970–71	"Union City"
Watson, N. "An Application of Social-Psychological Research to Police Work: Police Community Relations." American University, 1967.	Questionnaires Projective tests Interviews		
Wenninger, Eugene. "Bureaucratization and Career as Determinants of Participation in Police Occupational Groups." University of Illinois, 1966.	Questionnaires		
Wilde, Harold R. "The Process of Change in a Police Bureaucracy." Dept. of Government, Harvard University, 1972.	Historical data Observation Informal interviews		Detroit P.D.
Theses			
Comstock, D. "Boundary Spanning Processes in Complex Organizations." University of Denver, 1971.	Simulation (Drabek data)		

*Major data source

Table 1 (Continued)

Study	Method	Period of research	Research site
Daudistel, H. "Cop Talk: An Investigation of the Police Radio Code." University of California, Santa Barbara, 1971.			California county sheriff's office (cf. Sanders's study)
Dempsey, J. C. "Isolation of the Police Officer." Psychology Department, Colorado State University, 1967 (cited in Tifft).			
Works in Progress			
Bordua, David. University of Illinois, Urbana.	Observation Organizational analysis		Chicago
Carrier, John. "Women in Policing" (tentative title). London School of Economics and Political Science.	Interviews Historical research	1970–	London, England
Chatterton, Michael. Manchester University.	Observation	1971–	Manchester, England
Clark, J., and R. Sykes. University of Minnesota.	Observation (Interactional process analysis instrumentation)	1970–71 (15 months)	Three mid-western cities
Cummins, Marvin. University of Oregon.	Observation	1967–69	"Carolina City"
Ferdinand, T. Northern Illinois University.	Observation Questionnaires* Historical research		Several Illinois cities
Guenther, A. L. College of William and Mary.	Field observation (homicide detectives)	1974	Washington, D.C.
Levett, A. L. "Organization for Order: The Development of Police Organization in the 19th Century United States." University of Michigan, forthcoming. (Cited in Black, op. cit.).	Historical		
Manning, P. K. Michigan State University	Observation (narcotics agents) Interviews	1974–75	Washington, D.C. metropolitan area
Redlinger, L. J. University of Michigan.	Observation (narcotics agents) Interviews (agents, users, dealers)	1968–69, 1975–	San Antonio, Texas
Savitz, Leonard, Temple University.	Questionnaires		Philadelphia
Schiller, S. Chicago Crime Commission.	Observation (detectives)		Chicago
Shearing, C. University of Toronto.	Police calls (incoming) Police patrol	1971–72 1975–	Toronto, Canada
Sherman, L. W. Yale University, selected case studies of police corruption.		1974–	Selected U.S. cities
Walsh, James. Oberlin College.	Interviews*	1969–	Amsterdam London Dublin "4 American settings"

*Major data source

Table 1 (Continued)

Study	Method	Period of research	Research site
Ward, David. University of Minnesota.	Observation	1970–	Minneapolis
West, J. University of Bristol.	Observations Interviews	1972–	Bristol, England

NEGOTIATING ACCESS TO POLICE ORGANIZATIONS

The process of procuring entree into a going concern for the expressed purpose of engaging in social research is one of the most common problems of all social research, and, ironically, one the least understood and written about. Organizations, especially bureaucratically structured ones, are very sensitive to outside observation.[2] They maintain and monitor their social transactions with other organizations very carefully, and can demand reciprocity from the research person or project. Furthermore, tightly organized and bounded social systems such as police organizations maintain specific mechanisms for the control, sanctioning, and observation of intrusive elements within the organization. This tightly monitored system, characterized by coherence and specialization of role systems, allows organizations, unlike even loosely coordinated neighborhoods or social aggregates such as those represented in sample surveys, to sanction, terminate, constrain, and effectively control social research.

Insofar as the research project approaches the size, complexity, authority, and power of the group studied, there will be greater tension between the researcher and the researched. One could expect that problems of negotiating access, maintaining smooth communication, and managing the course of research increase as the project becomes more complex, that is, contains a greater number of persons, involves larger numbers of sites, requires a more complex division of research labor, or impinges on a larger number of the clients/functionaries within the group.

Police studies reflect this change in the pattern of relationships which obtain between researcher and

[2] Spencer lists five general reasons why public bureaucracies are sensitive to outside research: bureaucratic rigidity and the threat to personal careers, threat to the institutional authority, potential tarnishing of the subjectively constructed images and rhetorics of the organization, the threat to the legitimacy of the perspective of the research, and the problem of striking a satisfying research bargain (1973:92).

the researched. Although the focus of this review is upon observational studies, and these tend to be more craft-like than organizational, the differences encountered in negotiating access and maintaining it will be discussed if possible, given the limited number of discussions of these problems available, as regard to two types of research. An example of each of these two types of police study will be suggested.

Large-scale organizational studies, such as those reported in numerous publications by Black and Reiss, doubtless create more complex problems than does solo research. The prospect of a study as large and systematic as Reiss's may present a threat to the patrolmen observed and to the organization. Reiss investigated police-citizen transactions in eight "high-crime-rate areas" in Washington, Boston, and Chicago:

Twelve observers and a supervisor were assigned to each of the cities. Each observer was assigned to an eight-hour watch in a police district six days a week for six to seven weeks. Within each district the watches and beats were sampled and observers rotated across beats. Within this period of time, 92 Negro and 608 White officers were observed at least once. There was a total of 212 eight-hour observation periods of Negro officers and 1,137 observation periods of White officers. The police were mobilized in 5,360 situations; in 3,826 of them they had an encounter with one or more citizens. Some information was gathered on 11,244 citizens who participated in the encounters.

The observers recorded only a minimum of information during the eight-hour period, merely keeping a log of encounters. Following the period of observation, an observation booklet was completed for each encounter of two or more minutes duration. There were four types of booklets depending on whether the mobilization situation was a dispatch, a mobilization by a citizen in a field setting, a police mobilization in a field setting (on-view), or a citizen mobilization in a precinct station. The observer was asked to answer 48 questions about the encounter (if applicable) either by checking a response or writing a descriptive account. They completed

5,360 booklets during the period of the study. In addition, they responded to 23 questions about the observation period itself and the general behavior and attitudes of the officer as they learned it through observation and interviewing during the watch period. There are 1,349 such reports (Reiss 1968:355–56).

My own research on a Metropolitan London Police Department subdivision in the summer of 1973, to be discussed further below, is an example of the craft model or research using primarily observation, carried out by a single researcher, focused on interpersonal dynamics and meanings, and modeled in many ways after the classic Chicago pattern of "getting the seat of your pants dirty in real research."

The two types of police research, the craft and the organizational, have a number of social correlates significant for problems of access and management of research.[3] With the exception of research coordinated by Black and Reiss, Sykes and Clark, Bordua, and La Fave, the studies reviewed here fit the craft model. Unfortunately, few of the studies provide detailed information on the process of negotiating access to the host police organization(s). Those that do, imply, as seen above, an almost aleatory process of engendering and fostering permission and maintaining access. Let us discuss problems of access and of research management mindful of the qualitatively different problems associated with craft and organizational research.

Initial Access

Fox and Lundman (1974), in a perceptive summary of their experience in seeking and maintain-

[3] For example, of the observational studies considered here, only 23 percent (5) did *not* cite grant support, and all save one of those was a dissertation. The *source* of funding may have significant impact on the likelihood of obtaining access, but this issue is only discussed in reference to the Sykes/Clark research (as reported in Fox and Lundman and Lundman and Fox), a very large multiple-observer study carried out in three cities. Funding may in fact improve the chances of access; for example, LEAA, having disbursed nearly four billion dollars to state and municipal agencies in the criminal justice field, is able to provide assistance to researchers who require access to police departments. Studies by Bittner, Black and Reiss, Guenther, Manning, and Rubinstein were supported by LEAA or its predecessor, OLEA.

ing research access to police organizations (three successes and two failures), suggest that one can view the negotiating of entree as a process roughly divided into the entry stage, where previous informal roles are the most important determinant of success, and the maintenance stage, where intraorganizational relationships surface as the most significant source of stress and potential premature termination.[4]

Informal contacts permitting or facilitating access occurred through academic encounters (e.g., researchers met policemen in their classes); friends of friends (a friend introduced me to the person who became director of public safety in a nearby town where I gained research entree—we became teammates on a basketball team); previous work contacts (Rubinstein, for example, worked as a crime reporter in Philadelphia prior to beginning his research on the Philadelphia police); and family contacts (at least two researchers gained access to a department because their fathers were policemen). These generalizations seem to hold whether solo or organizational research models are employed. My London experience may be instructive since it exemplifies several types of contacts: informal and formal, academic or work contacts, and friendship.

> In the spring of 1971, Professor Michael Banton came to Michigan State to lecture (he was at that time on leave from Bristol teaching at Wayne State University in Detroit). I was asked to attend his lecture by a friend in the Department of Criminal Justice (I had advised his daughter and son as undergraduate majors in sociology). After the lecture, I was invited to a party at the friend's house and introduced to Professor Banton and to then Inspector Stephen O'Brien of the London Metropolitan Police (at that time visiting MSU's Department of Criminal Justice on a fellowship leave). The following night Professor Banton was to speak again and I was asked to a pre-speech dinner at the Faculty Club. While there, I sat next to Steve O'Brien and discussed

[4] Exceptions to the generalization that informal contacts are necessary for successful initial entree are: Buckner's study where he applied for and received a position in the police reserve where he worked as a policeman and carried out the research; and the studies of Harris, Guenther and Van Maanen, who achieved initial access through some combination of letters of inquiry, requests for interviews, and phone calls to police departments in the areas in which they lived.

my interest in police research and in coming to England. In the fall and winter of 1971 (nearly a year later), I began to arrange for a sabbatical in London. I wrote to O'Brien at Scotland Yard, asking if he could give me advice as to obtaining permission to do research on the Metropolitan Police. I also wrote to several other academics in this country and in Great Britain. Jack Douglas, who had first interested me in police matters, attended a conference on deviance in Edinburgh, Scotland, in June 1972 and phoned me to give me the names of persons in England to contact concerning police research. I wrote these people. In the spring I received notice that I would have a Visiting Fellowship at Goldsmiths' College in London and decided to press ahead on the police access problem. Steve O'Brien wrote back and suggested I write the Home Office for official permission, but closed with the suggestion that I call him if he could be of service. I wrote the Home Office. Just prior to leaving for London in August 1972 (a day or so before), I received a formal letter from the Home Office explaining that my request could not be met, that such requests should be accompanied by a statement of support from the sponsoring nation, and that it should be initially routed through the Foreign Office. I asked the dean of the College of Social Science at MSU to write such a letter as I left, but had little hope of success. Upon arrival in London, I began to ask around and to contact the people Jack had suggested. One of them was Maureen Cain, whose book on the police was to appear in a few months. I had dinner with Maureen early in September of 1972. She spoke highly of Peter Laurie, the British journalist who wrote *Scotland Yard* (a book I did not even know until I saw it in my neighborhood bookshop in Blackheath). I called Laurie, met him for a pint across from the Old Bailey; he said the person to see was Mike Chatterton ("The commissioner [of the Metropolitan Police] thinks the sun shines out of his asshole"). (I later became a good friend of Mike's, and he facilitated access to a police department during several brief research trips I made to northern England.) I felt overwhelmed, lonely, missed my collaborator in fieldwork who was always the spark in these low spots, and depressed. I let the research drift for nearly six months but finally telephoned Steve O'Brien, thinking I would be summarily referred back to the Home Office and encounter another dead end. I asked if I could see him at his convenience, and he asked me if I could be there in an hour and a half. I was. We talked for four hours, and it became abundantly clear to me that I really didn't know *what* aspects of policing I wanted to study. He suggested he knew an old friend (B. P.) who might be willing to let me study a subdivision where he (B. P.) was the chief superintendent. He asked if I could give him time to check with the training division of the Yard (where he was working) and call him the following Monday. I did and was asked to send a formal letter of request for access. It was approved, as was my subsequent trip to the Police College at Hendon. I was asked then to call (B. P.) "in a few days" after Steve had made informal inquiries. I got cold feet, waited nearly a week, and when I called, was asked what took me so long. I went to the subdivision two days later, hit it off well with the chief superintendent and the superintendent, and was introduced to a sergeant who gave me a briefing and set an itinerary for my research on the subdivision (it was to include days with the dog men, on traffic, with detectives, and more). Later I was asked to talk about the research with the commandant of the division and with the chief of C.I.D. (Criminal Investigation Division), and apparently I passed judgment. I began in earnest the next day and worked intensively in that month and in June, July, and August of 1973.

Skolnick's research also exemplifies the importance of informal contacts in access. It also, like my research, seems to have been shaped as much by drift as by rational planning. He began a research project in a public defender's office, and spent some two hundred hours there prior to shifting his research attention to the district attorney's office. Once there, he became interested in the work of the police and subsequently arranged through "contacts" in the prosecutor's office for an interview with the chief of police. The chief of the department (which Skolnick wrote "regarded itself as exemplary") "was willing to entertain the idea" (of a study) and assigned his aide, Lt. Doyle, to make introductions in the department:

The lieutenant was a genial man who had been on the force for almost twenty years, knew everybody, and was personally liked, as I later learned, throughout the department. We decided that the best place to begin the study was with the patrol division. . . . With the realization that law enforcement is not to be found in its most significant and interesting forms on the streets, I again consulted with Lieutenant Doyle (who was most helpful and considerate throughout the study). I felt that I ought to begin to study detective work, especially the work of the vice squad, but I also felt that I wanted to learn more about the policeman's use of legal authority in mundane and routine matters. . . . I decided to attempt to study that portion of it which seemed to me central to an understanding of the police as legal men, and perhaps also the most difficult to study: the working of the vice control squad (1966:31—34).

Skolnick apparently presented himself as a single researcher investigating a problem. His own legal interests and previous research contacts in the district attorney's and public defender's offices probably assisted the ingratiation process, as did his willingness to participate in a wide range of police activities, for example, shooting on the pistol range, driving vans in raids, listening in on phone calls, and signing as a witness to a confession.

Solo-craft researchers, since they are more concerned by definition with interpersonal dynamics and reactions of organizational members to them, write more about the informal negotiations that resulted in permission to do their studies. However, organizational-style research also builds on informal contacts. In the Black and Reiss (1966) studies, preceded by conversations and plans for a joint study by David Bordua and A. J. Reiss, Jr., an attempt was made to sample a range of police organizations according to a typology of the bases of legitimation (see Reiss and Bordua 1967). A *professional* department based on chief's tenure, administrative style, and so forth, as suggested by Wilson's description, was chosen (Chicago). A *traditional*, more "system-oriented" type of department was also to be chosen. Political changes in New York City at the time, involving the naming of Howard Leary as police commissioner, prevented the research from being done there, and Boston was chosen instead. These decisions were made from the "outside," as it were, and were based on Reiss's judgment of the possible problems of gaining access and of completing the study once an investment in organizing it had been made. Finally, a *transitional* department was to be chosen to represent the midpoint between the professional and traditional types of legitimation. A number of cities were considered: Seattle, Cincinnati, Washington, D.C., and Oakland, among others. Washington, D.C., was chosen. Contacts with the other departments (from previous research and consulting done by Reiss to [then-] OLEA) were critical in making the final

decision. The capacity of [then-] OLEA to insure access to the Washington, D.C., department was based on a number of complex interpersonal relationships (which are still active today). These relationships, involving Reiss himself, assured the success of entree and minimized the threat of collapse of the research as a result of public or line resistance to being observed.[5]

Secondary Access

Research in an organization creates new knowledge of the workings, politics, and limits of control of the levels of the organization over each other; and it soon becomes clear that the researcher (or the person in the organization who controls or deals with

[5] These interpersonal links can be alluded to. The once-commissioner of the N.Y.P.D., Patrick Murphy, was prior to that the director of public safety in Washington, D.C. On his staff in the D.C. department were two lawyers who later became top research administrators within LEAA. Their former boss at the D.C. prosecutor's office (prior to their work with the D.C. department and to coming to LEAA), was Donald Santarelli, the head of LEAA until September 1, 1974. Murphy now heads the Police Foundation, while one of his ex-deputy administrators at the N.Y.P.D. heads the police division research within LEAA (and serves under the two lawyers mentioned above). Both Murphy and another previous head of LEAA were at the time of the planned Reiss research associated with the D.C. police department. Chief Jerry V. Wilson, who approved Reiss's research, was second in command under Murphy. Wilson continues under LEAA funding to do research. The present chief of the D.C. department remains in close contact with two lawyers who were previously in the prosecutor's office and later in the legal department of the D.C. police; they continue their roles as the two most important research administrators in LEAA. A graduate student now working at Yale in police research formerly worked under Murphy at N.Y.P.D., and now holds a grant, with Reiss, from the LEAA police research division, now headed by Murphy's former deputy administrator. Reiss also holds a large grant from LEAA to evaluate the victimization studies. The present writer, now on a visiting fellowship at the National Institute (LEAA), obtained much of the above information while serving in this capacity, and the interview from which the above information on Reiss's police research was derived was made possible by fellowship funds for travel to New Haven in the early winter of 1975.

him), because of his information, has potential power over other members of the organization. Police studies demonstrate that police organizations are increasingly ribbed with conflict between blacks and whites, between staff and line, between younger and older policemen, and between the professionally and nonprofessionally oriented at any level (Walsh 1968). Research contributes to and may exacerbate these conflicts. Secrecy and ignorance play an important part in the power balances between organizational segments in a punishment-centered bureaucracy, and the research presence raises threats to this power equilibrium. The importance of the police norm of secrecy can hardly be exaggerated; for even after initial access, the problems in obtaining data remain. Westley wrote, "The time consumed in just getting to the data is enormous." He continues:

> The degree of rapport obtained had much to do with whether or not a question was pressed. This was of strategic importance because policemen are under explicit orders not to talk about police work with anyone outside the department; there is much in the nature of a secret society about the police; and past experience has indicated to policemen that to talk is to invite trouble from the press, the public, the administration and their colleagues. The result is that when they got the slightest suspicion that everything was not on an innocuous level they became exceedingly uncooperative and the rest of the men caught on in a hurry (Westley 1951:30–31).

The introduction of professionally oriented, educated, and thoughtful police administrators was a necessary condition for the recent growth of sociological research. They are the key to access (Lohman, a sociologist-police administrator, obtained for Westley access to Gary in the late forties). The majority of studies we now possess were done in departments that policemen view as "professional": Oakland, San Francisco, Chicago, New York City, and Atlanta. Bordua and Reiss discuss the research implications of police professionalization and the increasing centralization and bureaucratization of police operations:

> For the first time in American history the emergence of a self-consciously professional police elite coupled with increasing its (though far from complete) success in tightening internal control over departmental operations provides the demands for efficiency and productivity, but

also judicial demands for legality can be translated into operations. Developing professionalization of the police provides the necessary base for the application of sociology of law enforcement concerns. Perhaps even more appropriately put, it provides the base for carrying out the necessary sociological research which in the near future will be translatable into application (1967:287).

The paramilitary structure of the organization can be either an asset or a detriment to data gathering, particularly if the principal research tool is the standard questionnaire. It is usually an asset: as soon as administrative permission is granted, orders are issued to the officers to be interviewed or questioned to report and provide the data. The response rates under this condition tend to be very high. Since almost complete collection of data for a sample is obtained or access is categorically denied, one has "everything" or one has "nothing." The former was the case in a project where a student was able, through acquaintances of his father's, an ex-city patrolman, to obtain permission to survey a post and headquarters of a midwestern state police headquarters (Trojanowicz 1969). However, sponsorship by the professional segment also has *negative* potential in negotiating with lower participants, given initial access. In the Lundman and Fox research, initial access to one of their research sites was granted by the chief. He facilitated cooperation between the research team and the patrolmen by sending a memo explaining the research to each precinct, by organizing presentations by the researchers of their research equipment, techniques and aims, and by providing each of the observers with identification cards. In this case, difficulties were still encountered (interpreted by the authors as "errors" or attributed to bad memory although clearly one could see many of their persistent difficulties were intentional passive obstruction by patrolmen). The patrolmen may have speculated that the researchers were communicating information on their conduct or opinions to the administrators for use in discipline or promotion hearings, or for supervisory purposes. I was asked repeatedly if I was from A10 at the Yard (the internal investigation division), to which I laughed, saying I would be the first American ever trusted with the assignment. But I was also jokingly asked if I was reporting to "Old Ben" (the chief superintendent) and if I worked for the CIA. Since one must almost always have sponsorship from the top to engage in organizational research, lower participants' perceptions of the administrators will always shape their perceptions of the research and the researcher, as will the researcher's obligations (tacit and/or explicit) to those administrators (after all, to whom will any written final report go?). In one case cited by Fox and Lundman, the patrolmen voted on whether to accept the research (after it had been approved by the chief), and they rejected the proposal. Thus, the research was dependent in a formal sense on both the higher *and* the lower levels' approval.

It is more common that the relationships within the organization are based more on nonresearch roles than on formal approval or research organization-to-organization transactional relationships. But additional factors color the nature of the access process. The police are involved intimately with many aspects of the criminal justice system, and their actions are, in a sense, publicly reviewed by lawyers and the courts. Bordua and Reiss comment on this fact:

> Law enforcement is likewise intricately linked with a larger organizational system of criminal justice such that its output is an input into the criminal justice system where it is evaluated. Furthermore, it is directly linked to a municipal, county, or state organizational system that controls at least its budget, and also maintains a host of transactions with other municipal and community organizations in providing "police service." A police system thus engages in transactions not only with clients who are citizens demanding a service and with victims and their violators, but with a multiplicity of organizations where problems of service, its assessment, resource allocation, and jurisdiction are paramount (1967:291).

Buckner (1967:117–27) illustrates the extent to which the police are tied into reciprocal transactions with such community institutions as local businesses (especially restaurants), newspapers, sports arenas, and influential people. As a general proposition, police research is threatening to the police organization in an environment of exchange and negotiation, an organization that provides one of the few points of loyalty and solidarity for the policeman:

> In some cities in the Northern parts of the United States the police departments have been demoralized by political control, poor leadership,

and low rates of pay. The life of many districts seems competitive and raw; individuals pursue their own ends with little regard for public morality, and the policemen see the ugly underside of outwardly respectable households and businesses. Small wonder, then, that many American policemen are cynics. . . . Couple this experience with the policeman's feeling that in his social life he is a pariah, scorned by the citizens who are more respectable but no more honest, and need it surprise no one that the patrolman's loyalties to his department and his colleagues are often stronger than those to the wider society (Banton 1964:169–70).

All these aspects of police organizations—secrecy, threat, paramilitary organization, morale and self-esteem problems and internal schisms, and external relations—have created a research milieu in which the researcher often avoids telling the full aims of the research and asking many "sensitive" questions, avoids contact and interaction with certain persons, and constantly renegotiates roles. Nevertheless, uncontrollable external factors—a change in the chief or top administrators, a riot, or public outcry at police practice—can undermine, destroy, or terminate a project regardless of the planning, sensitivity, and caution of researchers.[6]

It is to the credit of sociologists that they have attempted to study very central issues in police action: brutality, response to citizens' calls, budgetary processes, citizens' complaints, and the enforcement of morality. The more one probes the questions of power and the allocation of resources, issues that threaten the organization as a whole, the greater the problems become of negotiating and maintaining access.[7]

[6] One police researcher told me he had developed a severe psychosomatic problem in the course of his study of a police department while trying to manage the complex grant monies and the various sponsors, federal and local, and avoid being ejected from the department for his research probing. This pattern of avoidance led him to avoid any involvement in one of the major demonstrations in the city, so as not to be caught in the middle of internal political forces in the department, particularly the scapegoating which followed the events. He has since been "thrown out."

[7] Albert J. Reiss, Jr., (personal communication) has suggested that the institutionalization of police research, for example, Kansas City's research program under Chief Joseph MacNamara, will have more

In summary, the more craftlike the research, the greater the likelihood of gaining and maintaining access to police organizations. The greater the number of researchers and organizations involved, the greater the access and management problems. A procedural focus, practically speaking, is to the advantage of the professionalizing segment of the organization and increases the probability of the research enjoying lasting legitimation. As will be seen, however, the research bargain may require termination by the researcher, and ethics and politics should always be at least as important as completing a study.

THE MANAGEMENT OF RESEARCH INSIDE POLICE ORGANIZATIONS

The tactical problems associated with police studies in one sense arise from attempts on the part of social researchers to understand the social reality of policing. The tactical problems encountered in these studies can be organized into three broad areas: the value confrontation which results from the interaction of social scientists and policemen; the typical problematic scenes characteristic of the occupation to which the researcher must respond by creating and maintaining a series of viable roles and identities; and the impact on the researcher of exposure to the dangerous aspects of police life and the ideology that surrounds it.

Buckner perceived the extent of his own tension when confronting these differences in personal style, values, and ideology:

. . . becoming a participant and going along with whatever is done, as I feel is necessary to truly experience what is going on, will provide the observer with a massive, and extremely difficult to counter, value confrontation. It is very hard to stick to some abstract value conception in the face of firsthand, disconfirming reality. The observer's personal values and the values of the group he is observing are thus in constant tension

until some resolution is reached; he finishes his study or he "goes native" accepting and supporting the values he is living and working with. Unless an observer is prepared to accept value relativism at an emotional level and to treat his own values as just another set of values "appropriate for some situations," long term participation in a group whose values diverge from his own will be an uncomfortable experience (1967:480).

Westley evokes his feelings in retrospect (in a preface added upon publication in 1970 to his dissertation originally written in 1951) of ambivalence toward the police. He describes himself as a young man "full of hope, strung tight with the experience [of the research] but passionately devoted to communicating an understanding of the police and how their world operated." He was also:

. . . afraid of the police after forcing himself to listen to their tune of violence in their lives, but full of the need to comprehend their humanity within this violence, to understand how the force of work and community gave this shape to their humanity. He found it hard to so share their point of view that he had rapport with their actions, and yet to ask them to bare details of self-incriminating conduct. There was a terrible tension in the flow of semiparticipant research, for to understand, he had to sympathize; but in attempting to sympathize he wanted to be liked. To be liked, he had to play by their rules and not ask too many questions. Thus, the work went in waves of carefully building up confidence and inevitably becoming involved in their regard, then asking questions, sharp probing questions, that soon caused rejection. This proved to be both personally painful, in the sense that thereafter he had to push himself on the men who he felt disliked and were afraid of him, and practically disastrous, since if the men refused to talk to him, the research would stop (Westley 1970:vii).

impact on police organizations than all the research done previously by social scientists. I agree. However, it is possible that the impetus to innovate in this way could only have come from social science research supported by the President's Crime Commission, the Kerner Report, the National Advisory Committee on Standards and Goals, and the events which precipitated their appearance.

Westley's remarks are important to recall because they are personally rooted in his own anxieties, and not phrased in cool and distant after-the-fact prose. More than a little practical decision making in the field is undergirded by such anxieties about one's own self and emotions. Further, the guilt that the middle-class field worker may feel during his involvement in the police world (perhaps because of an ambivalence to violence, authority, or to law enforcement) is precisely that which is sensed by police officers in their contacts—it results in a rather closely nuanced set of ambivalences and ambiguities which can often prevent full trust on either hand. (But is "full trust" necessary for fieldwork? Probably not.)

Other relationships also produce tension in the researcher. David Ward claims that it was difficult to have his wife call him "Professor Fuzz" when he came home after observing police patrol. The police researcher is often caught between the "liberal" values of his occupational group, his family, and his students—his most significant reference points—and the opinions and attitudes of the policemen he is observing.

The resolutions of such role dilemmas take interesting and instructive forms. One sociologist who has become a popular speaker at police training and educational conventions and at sociological seminars and meetings claims he has two speeches: one, an "anti-police" speech that he delivers to policemen, and the other, a "pro-police" speech that he delivers to his sociological colleagues.

This is one resolution of role conflict—the segregation of audiences and messages. In his research, using carefully selected observers from law, police administration, and the social sciences, Reiss found an instructive pattern of adjustment. Observation requires playing many roles, and it is simply a truism to state that these performances will in some ways reflect past socialization. Reiss explicates his strategy for selecting observers and training them to take the observer-plainclothes-detective role:

> The "fit" between observer role and plainclothesman posed problems both for officers and observers in police and citizen transactions. In our study, it was clear that as observers became sophisticated in the problems of the patrol officer, their potential for "going native" or having officers "thrust" the requirements of the role upon them increased. Indeed, situations occurred all too frequently that served to define and solidify the role of the observer as detective. . . .
>
> As in the study of interviewer effects, we discovered that prior socialization does have an effect on some kinds of data but by no means on all observations. Those with legal background reported more fully and seemingly more accurately on the legal matters, social scientists more readily judged the social class position of the

citizen, and so on. Generally, these are predictable differences. Yet, in the aggregate, these were not differences in kind but differences in the amount of error introduced into the observation (Reiss 1968:362).

Reiss describes his research, the only systematic attempt to assess differences in observers, observations, and the effects of the observational experience. All observers became more "pro-police," a second type of adjustment to role-conflict, but they did so in different ways:

> The social scientists, among the sociologists, had a beautiful sociological resolution of such role conflict as they experienced in becoming pro-police. Who are the police? They are the "poor men caught in the bad system," human beings like everyone else, some good, some bad, but on the whole really reasonable nice human beings. The job makes them what they are. Why? Well, in part because the environment they deal with makes it hard to be otherwise and more so because police departments make them that way. . . . Participant observation can be socialization with a sociological vengeance.
>
> Because of their association with sociologists as supervisors, some of the observers with training in the law also came to see the problem as poor men caught in a bad organizational system. More importantly, they began to see the law and the legal system not only as malfunctioning, but as lacking in relevance for the problems of police and citizens. . . those from the law responded as would-be reformers.
>
> The police officers changed least of all in their attitudes toward policing but, with one exception, developed a social science perspective. One of our police officers, from a major eastern city, expressed it clearly by saying that he saw all these things from a new perspective—these questions had never occurred to him. He became more objective and began to see things in broader outlines. . . .
>
> Interestingly, the graduates of police administration programs became more pro-police. They were less likely to take the textbook view of their more liberal professors and of top police administrators of the modern school, whom they now regarded as too far from the line. They no longer were part of the "empty holster" cadre. They knew (1968:364–65).

The marginality and value conflict between policemen and observers introduces a second theme, that of building viable roles. These value questions also bear on the role definition the researcher offers at the initiation of his research. It is fundamental to distinguish the initial role definitions, or roles sent and roles received. Roles sent and received by members of the host organization need not be stable over time, and as a general rule, are not. Some of the more interesting research chronicles trace the emergence and demise of role relationships of the researcher and the researched.[8]

The placement of the observer within the social system he is observing is an important aspect of role definition vis-à-vis segments of the organization, the data he obtains, and his own view of the world. Buckner felt he began to see the world as a "cop," and apparently this concerned him, although his reasons are not articulated (1967:471–72).

> I began to perceive the world from a police point of view, seeing vehicle code violations while driving, watching for accidents and setting out flares when in my private car, knowing certain sections of the city only for their geography of crime and violence, immediately going to a call box when I heard a burglar alarm or saw a traffic hazard while in civilian clothes, noticing suspicious people who seemed out of place, noticing prostitutes and pimps, and thinking of the solution to many problems in police terms.

Westley (1953) argues that the secretive nature of police organizations makes the role of outside observer very difficult to play. Buckner (1967), on the other hand, felt constrained by the limited view he was able to gather of the higher levels of the organization. Skolnick thought that "law enforcement is not to be found in its most significant and interesting forms on the streets" and focused his

attention on the enforcement of morals in the detective division (1966:33). The nagging doubt seemed to be that the organization could have been "seen" in another way. (And clearly since virtually every police study deals with lower participants' views, problems, and strategies, there is urgent need for studies of other segments of police departments— sergeants', lieutenants', and chiefs' decision making).

The notion of a fragile, processual, social order that is constantly being shaped, defined, and redefined as actors encounter and deal with the intersections of different definitions of social reality lies at the base of such a view of social research. In the stage of proffering and inviting, the system of relevances of the host group, in particular the fit between the life roles (age, sex, and nonoccupational identities) of researchers and researched becomes important. For example, the police culture is essentially a masculine culture with emphasis on virility, toughness, masculinity, and masculine interests such as sexual triumphs, sports, outdoor life, and so forth. (The overlap here with lower-class cultural themes is clear.) The researcher, if known and a male, will doubtless be called upon to pass certain "masculinity tests" in the proffering-and-inviting stage.[9]

David Bordua humorously recounted one of his experiences while doing observation. Bordua normally rode in the back of the patrol car and followed the patrolmen in to investigate a situation. On one occasion, while investigating a complaint, Bordua found himself leading the two policemen with whom he had been riding up a narrow, winding, and dark staircase. Although the order of march in leaving the car had seen the sociologist at the rear (where he

---

[8] See the articles in Richard N. Adams and Jack Preiss, eds., *Human Organization Research* (Homewood, Ill.: Dorsey Press, Basic Books, 1964); Gideon Sjoberg, ed., *Ethics, Politics, and Social Research* (Boston: Schenkman, 1967); and Arthur J. Vidich, Joseph Bensman, and Maurice R. Stein, eds., *Reflections on Community Studies* (New York: Wiley and Sons, 1964). Form, op. cit., suggests several role sets possible: social photographer or ethnographer, public relations expert, social engineer, teacher, scientist, and others. Given the paucity of information on the development and self-definition of police researchers, such a typology would be of little value.

[9] The only available work done by a woman is Maureen Cain's careful and detailed study (1973). Although she recounts sensitively the emergence of trust between researcher and researched (e.g., pp. 191, 199 ff.), she does not mention any sex-specific behavior which was directed toward her either as regards her as a person, or as an aspect of the research-observer role. It may be also that the English police are less concerned about physical proving of one's self (I was not asked to validate my masculinity in the course of my research). However, Cain provides a convincing example of the importance attached to masculinity and physical skill in fighting by P.C.'s struggling with a prisoner, "win or lose"; and being able to accept the outcome without complaint is an experience viewed as a necessary element in trust building (pp. 199–200).

definitely preferred to be), the policemen had arranged it so that Bordua was leading.

Similar testing of rookie policemen occurs. Bordua recounted an incident in a black bar in a lower-class area, where a tall, heavy-set black sergeant had arranged for a rookie to precede him on a "premises check" (a walk through a bar to establish that no gambling or illegal activities are going on and, not unimportantly, to establish the presence of the police in the area). As the rookie moved through a narrow aisle, a "drunk" lurched into his path. Every eye attended the scene, awaiting the outcome of this test. The rookie firmly grabbed the man's arm, moved him in front of himself, and sent him on to rest against the bar. As Bordua describes it, it was an act of skill and grace and established the young man as a potentially "good cop," able to handle himself in a spot without the use of violence or threats. These are risk-taking situations, and most middle-class people prefer to encounter such situations while water skiing or playing cards, where the level of risk is relatively low. They are part of police observation and an intimate part of police life.

This suggests that roles are offered and responded to constantly, and that situations always contain potentially definitive properties. Reiss found that his observers were continually being cast into the role of plainclothesman, as did Skolnick, who, for all practical purposes, became a detective.

> Under direct observation, detectives were cooperative. They soon gave permission to listen in to telephone calls, allowed me to join in conversations with informants, and to observe interrogations. In addition, they called me at home when an important development in a case was anticipated. Whenever we went out on a raid, I was a detective so far as any outsider could see. Although my appearance does not conform to the stereotype of the policeman, this proved to be an advantage since I could sometimes aid the police in carrying out some of their duties. For example, I could walk into a bar looking for a dangerous armed robber who was reportedly there without undergoing much danger myself, since I would not be recognized as a policeman. Similarly, I would drive a disguised truck up to a building, with a couple of policemen hidden in the rear, without the lookout recognizing me.
>
> At the same time, I looked enough like a policeman when among a group of detectives in a raid for suspects to take me for a detective. (It

twice happened that policemen from other local departments, who recognized that I was not a member of the Westville force, assumed I was a federal agent.)

> Even though I posed as a detective, however, I never carried a gun, although I did take pistol training on the police range. As a matter of achieving rapport with the police, I felt that such participation was required. Since I was not interested in getting standard answers to standard questions, I needed to be on the scene to observe their behavior and attitudes expressed on actual assignments (1966:35—36).

Skolnick apparently was able to select and modify his roles to fit his interests and those of the observed.

The researcher thus offers or proffers a role (the gloss "researcher" is far too inexact, since persons observed usually have little idea what specific identities that entails and thus it cannot be a very accurate summary of their imputations to the researcher [Brede 1972]). This role, offered for several quite complex reasons, may be dissembling. I admittedly did not *know* what precisely I wanted to observe— other than routine uniform patrol. Black and Reiss told police officers that the focus of their observer's attention was the conduct that citizens directed toward officers (and indeed it was, but of equal if not more importance was the conduct—and in fact misconduct—of the officers toward the citizen). Since all fieldwork has an emergent or crescive quality, such role alterations should not be surprising. However, "internal" or self-described role changes may not be attended to by the police at all, or variations in the perceptions of the research may change without the awareness of the researcher(s). Let us examine some cases where changes in the role of the researcher are well described.

The conditions for access may be such that some roles are precluded, or some are more than facilitated. Lundman and Fox (1974) described the demands made by the departments they studied: they included a "dress and conduct" agreement (students acting as observers in police cars should not look or act like "hippies"); a waiver of liability and an agreement that individual officers could refuse to be observed. This bargain (to be discussed below) constrains the roles possible to a quite narrow research—to a "subject" range (a dehumanizing label applied by Lundman and Fox to the officers they observed). Not surprisingly, the rather sharply etched "pure science" teacher-student role preferred by the researchers appeared to be rejected by the patrolmen. Rebuffed, the researchers began to play to mutual cynicism about science, social science, and social science research (as Westley implies above, it is very, very easy to slip into this self-demeaning role simply to keep the research alive). Once a more "personal" definition of the role relationship was preferred (or was it projected by the host patrolman?), that is, as a person "just doing a job," more stability in the relationships was observed.

However, it should be noted that large-scale social research by definition contains greater managerial and role relationship problems than does craft-style research. My adjustments to my role in London, ranging from dress to engaging in mildly devious conduct with my policemen friends (devious for them, not for me), were matters of taste rather than strategy. The large-scale project, on the other hand, requires a rational response to setbacks or the threat of premature termination. For example, Fox and Lundman describe the very complex set of procedures that they invoked whenever an observer was refused permission to observe a given patrolman. Two full pages of detailed instructions were provided. Inevitably, these attempts at rational readjustment of human relationships add a further exploitive/rational tone to the encounter, further distancing the person from the role, and the policeman from the observer. In a sense, each such attempt to rectify the research and to prevent its termination can be seen as having precisely the opposite impact. (It is fortunate, in my opinion, that the research survived such methodological overkill.)

It is important to keep in mind that any stability in a role relationship is in a sense "bought" through continual exchange and reciprocity between the observer and the observed. This is speaking both generally and specifically. The power relationship in fieldwork places the worker in a dependent position vis-à-vis his informants, and he must attempt to exchange valuables to retain interest, sympathy, and cooperation. One of these valuables is simple self-esteem, which flows from being interviewed or observed. The ways in which the observer justifies his use and invasion of the lives of his informants tend to take the form of "rhetorics of justification." Science and scientific work are a very useful rhetoric these days, as is the claim to present an objective account of the police problem to citizens. More concrete experiences also tie together police observers and

police officers. For example, several investigators have reported that the police asked them to assist in arrests, putting on handcuffs, monitoring radio messages, holding a suspect with a nightstick, or verifying descriptions of field encounters as an "objective observer."[10]

These are clearly moral decisions for the observer. This is a salient problem, given the uncertainty of police work and the great discretion allowed the patrolmen. According to Buckner, even recording information in the small field diary he carried raised the hackles of his partner:

> The sole feedback of a negative sort which I had was that one officer mentioned that some of the men were worried about me because I was over-educated and wrote down everything in my notebook, unlike many Reserve Officers. I handed him my notebook to let him see that all I wrote down were the details of each incident, which officers are required to do by department policy anyway. I told him to tell anybody who was worried that they could look at anything I wrote at any time they wanted. I had nothing to hide. This was literally true as I kept any private notes at home and did not carry them with me (1967:447−78, cf. Skolnick 1966:48).

A more important question than whether there is a reaction to the presence of the observer (the "reactivity effect") is whether there is an effect on the scene itself—is a "watched cop" the same as one operating only with a partner? Or put another way, what stabilizes a role relationship? None of the observers mention specifically any effect of their presence, nor do they speculate about the question—that is, ask what might have been. Skolnick, however,

[10] A special class of reciprocity is involved in the observation of police "errors." This is a general problem, as Hughes (1958) points out in the chapter "Mistakes at Work." It is made more difficult when the observer is also trained in the same occupation. Dorothy Douglas, an RN-sociologist, faced an extremely difficult moral problem whenever she observed "errors" in an emergency room (personal communication). John MacNamara (personal communication) also comments that the existence of secrets is always a part of the power structure of police organizations. People are likely to "save up" incidents, violations, and errors for strategic use against other parts of the organization or persons. (See below for further discussion.)

felt his presence was normalized by those he observed, once the observer-observed role relationship was stabilized:

> There is no certain control for this problem, but I believe the following assumptions are reasonable. First, the more time the observer spends with subjects, the more used to his presence they become. Second, participant-observation offers the subject less opportunity to dissimulate than he would have in answering a questionnaire, even if he were consciously telling the truth in response to standardized questions. Third, in many situations involving police, they are hardly free to alter behavior, as, for example, when a policeman kicks in a door on a narcotics raid.
>
> Finally, if an observer's presence does alter police behavior I believe it can be assumed that it does so only in one direction. I can see no reason why police would, for example, behave more harshly to a prisoner in the presence of an observer than in his absence. Nor can I imagine why police would attempt to deceive a prisoner in an interrogation to a greater degree than customary. Thus, a conservative interpretation of the materials that follow would hold that these are based upon observations of a top police department behaving at its best. However, I personally believe that while I was not exposed to the "worst," whatever that means, most of what I saw was necessarily typical of the ordinary behavior of patrolmen and detectives, necessarily, because over a long period of time, organizational controls are far more pertinent to policemen than the vague presence of an observer whom they have come to know, and who frequently exercises "drop-in" privileges.
>
> If a sociologist rides with police for a day or two he may be given what they call the "whitewash tour." As he becomes part of the scene, however, he comes to be seen less as an agent of control than as an accomplice (Skolnick 1966:36—37).

On the basis of the work reviewed for this article, one can assert that the process of role negotiation often leads to satisfactory research relationships, and that "reactivity" is sufficiently minimal to permit confidence in the data presented.[11]

[11] Anecdotal evidence suggests that police observers are privy to the most extreme police misconduct, e.g., physical beating, coerced cooperation (as shown in the film *Serpico*) and the like. However, like most of the events reported in the research reviewed

Danger is a part of a fair number of occupations, but only among a few does it occupy a significant part of the occupational "line" or public ideology. Being a policeman is one of these occupations. The police possess what might be called a "threat-danger-hero" notion of their everyday lives. The structure of rewards within police departments is very conducive to this ideology. Violent or dramatic public action—whether solving or preventing a crime, shooting a man, or aggressively patrolling traffic—is a source of promotion to the detective bureau, a way to "get out of the bag." In fact, much of police work is boring or involves frustrating, contentious hassles with citizens. The dangerous activities represent considerably less than 10 percent of police patrol time, and less than 1 percent of citizen-initiated complaints concern violent or dramatic crime (rape, murder, assault). (Black 1968: tables 2 and 18). The highly unpredictable, but potentially possible, dangerous scene is always a part of police patrol.

There are considerations of personal safety for both policemen and fieldworkers. Accompanying the police in the role of observer places one on the "right side of the law," reducing some dangers; but risks are nevertheless involved. Buckner once observed an incredible high-speed chase. It began with a car running a stop sign, which activated the police to give chase. The police pursued the stop sign violator through the city, breaking speed laws, ignoring stop signs, and ending with a crash that totaled the police car in which Buckner was riding. The chase was continued, it was later reported, by other police cars. The chased car was finally run off the road by police cars and smashed against a bridge abutment by one of them. The driver was charged, after a brief fight, with "two counts of reckless driving, two counts of assault and battery with an automobile, six counts of running a stop sign, and separate counts of trying to elude police, destroying public property, speeding, and drunken driving" (Buckner 1967:208—209). A police officer who read Buckner's thesis and made comments added:

> I thoroughly enjoy that kind of challenge. In a way, it is right out of the old West. During such

here (with the exception of the Black/Reiss research), the *frequency* of these events is unknown. Are they rarely observed by sociologists because they are not privy to them (or because policemen are on their best behavior when being observed), or are they in fact rare events?

an event you are pressed to your limit. The exhilaration is unmatched. Such events are thoroughly discussed among officers. Exceptional police "hot chase" drivers are known in the department as "wheelmen" (Buckner 1967:210).

Other sociologists have described similar chases in tones of mixed feelings of fear and excitement.

There are other, perhaps less common, kinds of dangerous situations that are encountered in a day's work; they are euphemistically called "civil disturbances." Riots may expose observers to danger from wild shots (most of them from police guns). Fights, crowds, and small collective outbursts also portend danger. Among the most dangerous of police activi-

ties from the perspective of injury or death are "domestic disputes," or family brawls, for these often involve knives, hand guns, rifles, and other handy missiles.

In summary, observing the police involves one in a secrecy-conscious, tightly organized bureaucracy peopled by men who see the world as dangerous, isolating, and untrustworthy and themselves as the last barrier between the citizen and social decay. Police research presents some special problems of value conflict, role management, and danger. The structure of the tactics to be used in this type of research is affected by problems of access, research style, sponsorship, location, and perspective on the action.

Standards Relating to the Urban Police Function
Adopted by the American Bar Association

Part I. General Principles

1.1 Complexity of Police Task

(a) Since police, as an agency of the criminal justice system, have a major responsibility for dealing with serious crime, efforts should continually be made to improve the capacity of police to discharge this responsibility effectively. It should also be recognized, however, that police effectiveness in dealing with crime is often largely dependent upon the effectiveness of other agencies both within and outside the criminal justice system. Those in the system must work together through liaison, cooperation, and constructive joint effort. This effort is vital to the effective operation of the police and the entire criminal justice system.

SOURCE: The American Bar Association's House of Delegates, meeting in Cleveland, Ohio, in early February, 1973, adopted without debate the Standards for the Urban Police Function. Published in *The Police Chief*, May 1973.

(b) To achieve optimum police effectiveness, the police should be recognized as having complex and multiple tasks to perform in addition to identifying and apprehending persons committing serious criminal offenses. Such other police tasks include protection of certain rights such as to speak and to assemble, participation either directly or in conjunction with other public and social agencies in the prevention of criminal and delinquent behavior, maintenance of order and control of pedestrian and vehicular traffic, resolution of conflict, and assistance to citizens in need of help such as the person who is mentally ill, the chronic alcoholic, or the drug addict.

(c) Recommendations made in these standards are based on the view that this diversity of responsibilities is likely to continue and, more importantly, that police authority and skills are needed to handle appropriately a wide variety of community problems.

1.2 Scope of Standards

To ensure that the police are responsive to all the special needs for police services in a democratic society, it is necessary to:

(i) identify clearly the principal objectives and responsibilities of police and establish priorities between the several and sometimes conflicting objectives;

(ii) provide for adequate methods and confer sufficient authority to discharge the responsibility given them;

(iii) provide adequate mechanisms and incentives to ensure that attention is given to the development of law enforcement policies to guide the exercise of administrative discretion by police;

(iv) ensure proper use of police authority;

(v) develop an appropriate professional role for and constraints upon individual police officers in policy-making and political activity;

(vi) provide police departments with human and other resources necessary for effective performance;

(vii) improve the criminal justice, juvenile justice, mental health, and public health systems of which the police are an important part;

(viii) gain the understanding and support of the community; and

(ix) provide adequate means for continually evaluating the effectiveness of police services.

1.3 Need for Experimentation

There is need for financial assistance from the federal government and from other sources to support experimental and evaluative programs designed to achieve the objectives set forth in these standards.

Part II. Police Objectives and Priorities

2.1 Factors Accounting for Responsibilities Given Police

The wide range of government tasks currently assigned to police has been given, to a great degree, without any coherent planning by state or local governments of what the overriding objectives or priorities of the police should be. Instead, what police do is determined largely on an ad hoc basis by a number of factors which influence their involvement in responding to various government or community needs. These factors include:

(i) broad legislative mandates to the police;

(ii) the authority of the police to use force lawfully;

(iii) the investigative ability of the police;

(iv) the twenty-four-hour availability of the police; and

(v) community pressures on the police.

2.2 Major Current Responsibilities of Police

In assessing appropriate objectives and priorities for police service, local communities should initially recognize that most police agencies are currently given responsibility, by design or default:

(i) to identify criminal offenders and criminal activity and, where appropriate, to apprehend offenders and participate in subsequent court proceedings;

(ii) to reduce the opportunities for the commission of some crimes through preventive patrol and other measures;

(iii) to aid individuals who are in danger of physical harm;

(iv) to protect constitutional guarantees;

(v) to facilitate the movement of people and vehicles;

(vi) to assist those who cannot care for themselves;

(vii) to resolve conflict;

(viii) to identify problems that are potentially serious law enforcement or governmental problems;

(ix) to create and maintain a feeling of security in the community;

(x) to promote and preserve civil order; and

(xi) to provide other services on an emergency basis.

2.3 Need for Local Objectives and Priorities

While the scope and objectives of the exercise of the government's police power are properly determined in the first instance by state and local legislative bodies within the limits fixed by the Constitution and by court decisions, it should be recognized there is considerable latitude remaining with local government to develop an overall direction for police services. Within these limits, each local jurisdiction should decide upon objectives and priorities. Decisions regarding police resources, police personnel needs, police organization, and relations with other government agencies should then be made in a way which will best achieve the objectives and priorities of the particular locality.

2.4 General Criteria for Objectives and Priorities

In formulating an overall direction for police services and in selecting appropriate objectives and priorities for the police, communities should be guided by certain principles that should be inherent in a democratic society:

(i) The highest duties of government, and therefore the police, are to safeguard freedom, to preserve life and property, to protect the constitutional rights of citizens and maintain respect for the rule of law by proper enforcement thereof, and, thereby, to preserve democratic processes;

(ii) Implicit within this duty, the police have the responsibility for maintaining that degree of public order which is consistent with freedom and which is essential if our urban and diverse society is to be maintained;

(iii) In implementing their varied responsibilities, police must provide maximum opportunity for achieving desired social change for freely-available, lawful, and orderly means; and

(iv) In order to maximize the use of the special authority and ability of the police, it is appropriate for government, in developing objectives and priorities for police services, to give emphasis to those social and behavioral problems which may require the use of force or the use of special investigative abilities which the police possess. Given the awesome authority of the police to use force and the priority that must be given to preserving life, however, government should firmly establish the principle that the police should be restricted to using the amount of force reasonably necessary in responding to any situation.

2.5 Role of Local Chief Executive

In general terms, the chief executive of a governmental subdivision should be recognized as having the ultimate responsibility for his police department and, in conjunction with his police administrator and the municipal legislative body, should formulate lawful policy relating to the nature of the police function, the objectives and priorities of the police in carrying out this function, and the relationship of these objectives and priorities to general municipal strategies. This will require that a chief executive, along with assuming new responsibilities for formulating overall directions for police services, must also:

(i) insulate the police department from inappropriate pressures including such pressures from his own office;

(ii) insulate the police department from pressures to deal with matters in an unlawful or unconstitutional manner; and

(iii) insulate the police administrator from inappropriate interference with the internal administration of his department.

Part III. Methods and Authority Available to the Police for Fulfilling the Tasks Given Them

3.1 Alternative Methods Used By Police.

The process of investigation, arrest, and prosecution, commonly viewed as an end in itself, should be recognized as but one of the methods used by police in performing their overall function, even though it is the most important method of dealing with serious criminal activity. Among other methods police use are, for example, the process of informal resolution of conflict, referral, and warning. The alternative methods used by police should be recognized as important and warranting improvement in number and effectiveness; and the police should be given the necessary authority to use them under circumstances in which it is desirable to do so.

3.2 Avoiding Overreliance upon the Criminal Law

The assumption that the use of an arrest and the criminal process is the primary or even the exclusive method available to police should be recognized as causing unnecessary distortion of both the criminal law and the system of criminal justice.

3.3 Need For Clarified, Properly Limited Authority To Use Methods Other Than the Criminal Justice System

There should be clarification of the authority of police to use methods other than arrest and prosecution to deal with the variety of behavioral and social problems which they confront. This should include careful consideration of the need for and problems created by providing police with recognized and properly-limited authority and protection while operating thereunder:

(i) to deal with interferences with the democratic process. Although it is assumed that police have a duty to protect free speech and the right of dissent, their authority to do so is unclear, particularly because of the questionable constitutionality of many statutes, such as the disorderly conduct statutes, upon which police have relied in the past;

(ii) to deal with self-destructive conduct such as that engaged in by persons who are helpless by reason of mental illness or persons who are incapacitated by alcohol or drugs. Such authority as exists is too often dependent upon criminal laws which commonly afford an inadequate basis to deal effectively and humanely with self-destructive behavior;

(iii) to engage in the resolution of conflict such as that which occurs so frequently between husband and wife or neighbor and neighbor in the highly-populated sections of the large city, without reliance upon criminal assault or disorderly conduct statutes;

(iv) to take appropriate action to prevent disorder such as by ordering crowds to disperse where there is adequate reason to believe that such action is required to prevent disorder and to deal properly and effectively with disorder when it occurs; and

(v) to require potential victims of crime to take preventive action such as by a legal requirement that building owners follow a burglary prevention program similar to common fire prevention programs.

3.4 Legislative Concern for Feasibility of Criminal Sanction

Within the field of criminal justice administration, legislatures should, prior to defining conduct as criminal, carefully consider whether adequate authority and resources exist for police to enforce the prohibition by methods which the community is willing to tolerate and support. Criminal codes should be reevaluated to determine whether there are adequate ways of enforcing the prohibition. If not, noncriminal solutions to all or a portion of the problem should be considered.

Part IV. Law Enforcement Policy-Making

4.1 Exercise of Discretion by Police

The nature of the responsibilities currently placed upon the police requires that the police exercise a great deal of discretion—a situation that has long existed, but is not always recognized.

4.2 Need for Structure and Control

Since individual police officers may make important decisions affecting police operations without direction, with limited accountability, and without any uniformity within a department, police discretion should be structured and controlled.

4.3 Administrative Rule-Making

Police discretion can best be structured and controlled through the process of administrative rule-making by police agencies. Police administrators should, therefore, give the highest priority to the formulation of administrative rules governing the exercise of discretion, particularly in the areas of selective enforcement, investigative techniques, and enforcement methods.

4.4 Contribution by Legislatures and Courts

To stimulate the development of appropriate administrative guidance and control over police discretion, legislatures and courts should actively encourage police administrative rule-making.

(a) Legislatures can meet this need by delegating administrative rule-making responsibility to the police by statute.

(b) Courts can stimulate administrative development in several ways including the following:

(i) Properly-developed and published police administrative policies should be sustained unless demonstrated to be unconstitutional, arbitrary, or otherwise outside the authority of the police;

(ii) To stimulate timely and adequate administrative policy-making, a determination by a court of a violation of an administrative policy should not be a basis for excluding evidence in a criminal case unless the violation of administrative policy is of constitutional dimensions or is otherwise so serious as to call for the exercise of the superintending authority of the court. A violation per se should not result in civil liability; and

(iii) Where it appears to the court that an individual officer has acted in violation of administrative policy or that an administrative policy is unconstitutional, arbitrary, or otherwise outside the authority of the police, the court should arrange for the police administrator to be informed of this fact, in order to facilitate fulfillment by the police administrator of his responsibility in such circumstances to reexamine the relevant policy or policies and to review methods of training, communication of policy, and supervision and control.

4.5 Method of Policy-Making

In its development of procedures to openly formulate, implement, and reevaluate police policy as necessary, each jurisdiction should be conscious of the need to effectively consult a representative cross-section of citizens in this process.

Part V. Control Over Police Authority

5.1 Need for Accountability

Since a principal function of police is the safeguarding of democratic processes, if police fail to conform their conduct to the requirements of law, they subvert the democratic process and frustrate the achievement of a principal police function. It is for this reason that high priority must be given for ensuring that the police are made fully accountable to their police administrator and to the public for their actions.

5.2 Need for Positive Approaches

Control over police practice should, insofar as possible, be positive, creating inducements to perform properly rather than concentrating solely upon penalizing improper police conduct. Among the ways this can be accomplished are:

(i) Education and training oriented to the development of professional pride in conforming to the requirements of law and maximizing the values of a democratic society;

(ii) Inducements to police officers in terms of status, compensation, and promotion, on the basis of criteria that are related as directly as possible to the police function and police goals;

(iii) Elimination of responsibilities where there is a community expectation that police will "do something," but adequate lawful authority is not provided. Either the needed authority should be given or the police should be relieved of the responsibility;

(iv) Systematic efforts by prosecutors and judges to encourage conforming police behavior through: (a) a more careful review of applications for warrants and (b) formulation of new procedures to simplify and otherwise provide easy access for judicial review of applications for warrants, thereby encouraging maximum use of the formal warrant process;

(v) Requirements that police develop administrative policies controlling police actions which, if reasonable, would be sustained and utilized by the courts; and

(vi) Effective involvement of the community in the development of police programs.

5.3 Sanctions

Current methods of review and control of police activities include the following sanctions:

(i) the exclusion of evidence obtained by unconstitutional means;

(ii) criminal and tort liability for knowingly engaging in unlawful conduct;

(iii) injunctive actions to terminate a pattern of unlawful conduct; and

(iv) local procedures for handling complaints against police officers, procedures which usually operate administratively within police departments.

Each of these should be continually reevaluated and changed when necessary to achieve both effective control over the exercise of police authority and the effective administration of criminal justice.

5.4 Need for Administrative Sanctions and Procedures

In order to strengthen administrative review and control, responsibility should formally be delegated to the police for developing comprehensive administrative policies and rules governing the duties and responsibilities of police officers together with procedures and sanctions for ensuring that these duties and responsibilities are met. Police administrative rules and procedures should establish effective investigative, hearing, and internal review procedures for alleged violations. Such procedures should include provisions for handling, monitoring, and reviewing citizen complaints in such a way as to ensure diligence, fairness, and public confidence. In developing such rules and procedures, recognition must be given to the need to conform procedures to administrative due process requirements, to develop means for ensuring impartial investigations, and to keep the public informed of all administrative actions as they are taken.

5.5 Municipal Tort Liability

In order to strengthen the effectiveness of the tort remedy for improper police activities, governmental immunity, where it still exists, should be eliminated, and legislation should be enacted providing that the governmental subdivisions shall be fully liable for the actions of police officers who are acting within the scope of their employment. Neither tort liability nor costs attendant to the defense of a tort action should be imposed upon a police officer for wrongful conduct that has been ordered by a superior or is affirmatively authorized by police rules or regulations unless the conduct is a violation of the criminal law. Instead, liability and incidental costs and expenses in such cases should be borne by the governmental subdivision.

Part VI. Police Unions and Political Activity

6.1 Collective Interest of Policemen and Limitations Thereon

(a) Policemen have a proper collective interest in many aspects of their job such as wages, length of work week, and pension and other fringe benefits. To implement this interest, the right of collective bargaining should be recognized. However, due to the critical nature of the police function within government, legislation should provide that there shall be no right to strike. Effective alternatives to the right to strike should be made available as methods by which policemen can pursue their collective interest; and model procedures governing this important matter should be developed.

(b) The right of police to engage in collective action, however, should be subject to the following limitations:

(i) The preservation of governmental control over law enforcement policy-making requires that law enforcement policy not be the subject of collective bargaining.

(ii) The need to preserve local control over law enforcement and over the resolution of law enforcement policy issues requires that law enforcement policy not be determined by a police union or other police employee organization.

(iii) The maintenance of police in a position of objectivity in engaging in conflict resolution requires that police not belong to a union which also has nonpolice members who may become party to a labor dispute.

(iv) The maintenance of proper control by the police administrator over his department requires that collective action not interfere with the administrator's ability effectively to implement the policies and objectives of the agency.

6.2 Police Officer Contribution to Police Policy

Policemen, as individuals and as a group, have a proper professional interest in and can make significant contributions to the formulation and continuing review of local law enforcement policies within individual communities. Methods should be devel-

oped by police administrators, therefore, to ensure effective participation in the policy-making process by all ranks including the patrolman who, because of his daily contact with operational problems and needs, has unique expertise to provide on law enforcement policy issues.

6.3 Political Activity by Policemen

Policemen share the individual right to engage in political and other protected first amendment activity. However, police should not use their authority or the indicia of office, such as the uniform, for this purpose because of their possible coercive effect nor should they engage in collective political activity which compromises their ability to view objectively conflicts with which they may be called upon to deal.

Part VII. Adequate Police Resources

7.1 Variety of Police Methods

Police should be provided with effective methods for carrying out the full range of governmental responsibilities delegated to them. Adequate development of such methods requires:

(i) a variety of skills in individual police officers;

(ii) arrangements for police officers to make referrals to the various private and public services and resources available in the community and the existence of sufficient resources to meet community needs, and

(iii) broad use of informal means of resolving conflict.

7.2 Important Function of Patrolmen

The nature of police operations makes the patrolman a more important figure than is implied by his rank in the organization. He exercises broad discretion in a wide array of situations, each of which is potentially of great importance, under conditions that allow for little supervision and review. Even with the controls recommended in these standards, in the interest of developing a police profession as well as in the interest of improving the quality of police operations generally, the patrolman himself should understand the important and complex needs of policing in a free society and have a commitment to meeting those needs.

7.3 Recruitment

In view of the broad diversity of the police role, experiments should be conducted which make use of different levels of entry for personnel and standards particularly relevant for the various levels. Such recruitment standards should be related directly to the requirements of various police tasks and should reflect a great degree of concern for such factors as judgmental ability, emotional stability, and sensitivity to the delicate and complicated nature of the police role in a democratic society.

7.4 Training

Training programs should be designed, both in their content and in their format, so that the knowledge that is conveyed and the skills that are developed relate directly to the knowledge and skills that are required of a police officer on the job.

7.5 Recruitment of College Graduates

College graduates should be encouraged to apply for employment with police agencies. Individuals aspiring to careers in police agencies and those currently employed as police officers should be encouraged to advance their education at the college level. Communities should support further educational achievement on the part of police personnel by adopting such devices as educational incentive pay plans and by gradually instituting requirements for the completion of specified periods of college work as a prerequisite for initial appointment and for promotion. To increase the number of qualified personnel, police departments should initiate or expand police cadet or student intern programs which subsidize the education and training of potential police candidates.

7.6 Police Education

Educational programs that are developed primarily for police officers should be designed to provide an officer with a broad knowledge of human behavior, social problems, and the democratic process.

7.7 Importance of Police Administrator

In addition to directing the day-to-day operations of his agency, the police administrator has the responsibility to exert leadership in seeking to improve the quality of police service and in seeking to solve community-wide problems of concern to the police. The position of police chief should be recognized as being among the most important and most demanding positions in the hierarchy of governmental officials.

7.8 Authority of Police Administrator

A police administrator should be held fully responsible for the operations of his department. He should, therefore, be given full control over the management of the department; and legislatures, civil service commissions, and employee associations should not restrict the flexibility that is required for effective management.

7.9 Qualifications for Police Administrator

In the screening of candidates to assume leadership roles in police agencies, special attention should be given to the sensitivity of the candidate to the peculiar needs of policing in a free society; to the degree to which the candidate is committed to meeting the challenge of achieving order with the restraints of the democratic process; to the capacity of the candidate to deal effectively with the complicated and important issues that police administrators must confront in the decision-making processes that affect police operations; and to the overall ability of the candidate to manage and direct the total resources of the agency. A community should employ the best qualified candidate without regard to his present location or departmental affiliation. Because of the fundamental importance of the objectives set forth in 10.1, the police administrator should be given the necessary support, job security, and procedural safeguards to allow him to achieve these objectives.

7.10 Police Department Organization

More flexible organizational arrangements should be substituted for the semimilitary, monolithic form of organization of the police agency. Police administrators should experiment with a variety of organizational schemes, including those calling for substantial decentralization of police operations, the development of varying degrees of expertise in police officers so that specialized skills can be brought to bear on selected problems, and the substantial use of various forms of civilian professional assistance at the staff level.

7.11 Research

A research capability should be developed within police agencies that will aid the police administrator in systematically formulating and evaluating police policies and procedures and that will equip the administrator to participate intelligently in the public discussion of important issues and problems involving the police.

7.12 Need for In-House Police Legal Advisor

Given the nature of the police function, police administrators should be provided with in-house police legal advisors who have the personal orientation and expertise necessary to equip them to play a major role in the planning and in the development and continual assessment of operating policies and training programs. The police legal advisor should be an attorney appointed by the police administrator or selected by him from an existing governmental unit.

7.13 Relationship of Legal Advisor to Police Administrator

In view of the important and sensitive nature of his role, a police legal advisor of the head of a police legal unit should report directly to the police administrator. The relationship of a police legal advisor to a police department should be analogous to that of house counsel to a corporation. The police legal advisor should provide independent legal advice based upon his full understanding of the police function and his legal expertise, and should anticipate as well as react to legal problems and needs.

7.14 Priority Tasks for Legal Advisor

Among the range of tasks that may be performed by police legal advisors, priority should be given to assisting police administrators in:

(i) formulating the types of administrative policies that are recommended in these standards;

(ii) developing law-related training programs pertinent to increased understanding of the nature of the police function, of departmental policies, of judicial trends and their rationale, and of the significant role of the police in preserving democratic processes;

(iii) formulating legislative programs and participating in the legislative process;

(iv) maintaining liaison with other criminal justice and municipal agencies on matters primarily relating to policy formulation and policy review, and assessing the effectiveness of various agencies in responding to common legal problems; and

(v) developing liaison with members of the local bar and encouraging their participation in responding to legal problems and needs of the police agency.

Part VIII. Police Performance in the Criminal Justice System

8.1 Relationship of the Criminal Justice and Other Systems to the Quality of Police Service

(a) To the extent that police interact with other governmental systems such as the criminal justice, juvenile justice, and public and mental health systems, police effectiveness should be recognized as often largely dependent upon the performance of other agencies within these systems.

(b) For these standards to be of value in the criminal justice system, other parts of the system must operate, as a minimum, in such a manner that: (i) criminal cases are speedily processed; (ii) prosecutors and judges carefully review applications for warrants and use simplified procedures and otherwise provide easy access for impartial review of applications for warrants; (iii) the lower trial courts, especially in the larger cities, are conducted in a dignified and orderly manner, considerate of and respectful toward all the participants; and (iv) sentencing alternatives and correctional programs are as diversified and effective as possible.

Part IX. Public Understanding and Support

9.1 Contribution of Legal Profession

Members of the legal profession should play an active role, individually and collectively, in developing local government policies relating to the police, in supporting needed changes in the form of police services, and in educating the total community on the importance and complexity of the police function.

Among other things, each local bar association should appoint a special committee with which the police administrator can confer as to appropriate means of achieving objectives proposed in these standards.

9.2 Responsibility of Educational Institutions

Educational institutions should undertake research and teaching programs which provide understanding of the complex social and behavioral problems which confront urban police.

9.3 The News Media

Public understanding of the police function is heavily dependent upon the coverage given by mass media to the newsworthy events in which the police are involved. Newspaper, radio, and television reporters assigned to reporting on police activities should have a sufficiently thorough understanding of the complexities of the police function to enable them to cover such events (as well as other matters that now go unreported) in a manner that promotes the public's understanding of the police role.

9.4 Openness By Police

Police should undertake to keep the community informed of the problems with which they must deal and the complexities that are involved in dealing with them effectively. Police agencies should cooperate with those who seek an understanding of police operations by affording opportunities for interested citizens to acquaint themselves with police operations and by providing access to the accumulation of knowledge and experience that the police possess.

Part X. Evaluation

10.1 Measure of Police Effectiveness

The effectiveness of the police should be measured generally in accordance with their ability to achieve the objectives and priorities selected for police service in individual communities. In addition, the effectiveness of police should be measured by their adherence to the principles set forth in section 2.4. This means that, among other things, police effectiveness should be measured in accordance with the extent to which they:

(i) safeguard freedom, preserve life and property, protect the constitutional rights of citizens and maintain respect for the rule of law by proper enforcement thereof, and, thereby, preserve democratic processes;

(ii) develop a reputation for fairness, civility, and integrity that wins the respect of all citizens, including minority or disadvantaged groups;

(iii) use only that amount of force reasonably necessary in responding to any given situation;

(iv) conform to rules of law and administrative rules and procedures, particularly those which specify proper standards of behavior in dealing with citizens;

(v) resolve individual and group conflict; and

(vi) refer those in need to community resources that have the capacity to provide needed assistance.

Traditional criteria such as the number of arrests that are made are inappropriate measures of the quality of performance of individual officers. Instead, police officers should be rewarded, in terms of status, compensation, and promotion, on the basis of criteria defined in this section which directly relate to the objectives, priorities, and essential principles of police service.

10.2 Responsibility of Society and Government Generally

The recommendations made in these standards require particular attention at the level of municipal government. Along with the recommendations relating specifically to police agencies, however, it should be recognized that police effectiveness is also dependent, in the long run, upon:

(i) the ability of government to maintain faith in democratic processes as the appropriate and effective means by which to achieve change and to redress individual grievances;

(ii) the willingness of society to devote resources to alleviating the despair of the culturally, socially, and economically deprived; and

(iii) the improvement of the criminal justice, juvenile justice, mental health, and public health systems as effective ways of dealing with a wide variety of social and behavioral problems, such as improvements in programs to provide assistance to citizens in need of help such as the person who is mentally ill, the chronic alcoholic, or the drug addict.

The Uneasy Milieu of the Detective

THOMAS A. REPPETTO

Introduction

The organization and administration of the detective or investigative function[1] has constituted a major problem area in American police administration over the past century and a half. If, as it has been pointed out, American police service, in general, comprises an amalgam of systems and a variety of behaviors,[2] the detective function is one of its most complex components. This article will examine some of the complexities, trace their origins and development, and identify certain basic patterns and trends in detective administration.

At the outset it should be noted that there are, in effect, two systems of detective organization—the local and the federal—which differ markedly in such aspects as personnel selection, career patterns, and jurisdictional scope. At the local level, detectives are selected from the ranks of the uniformed force. They then become members of a separate investigative section; however, they remain part of the regular police department. Theoretically (and actually in many departments) detectives are subject to rotation back to uniform duty. Alternatively, the federal system provides for the selection of detectives directly from civil life (usually from the college-educated) and sets them apart from the uniformed forces in semi- or wholly autonomous structures

where they spend their entire careers.[3] Local detective forces usually possess jurisdiction over a wide range of criminal activities but are limited territorially; federal agencies possess limited functional jurisdiction, but their scope of operation is national.

Since the national government employs nearly as many criminal investigators as local government,[4] the federal presence constitutes a significant influence on detective activities. This is in sharp contrast to the situation of uniformed patrol forces which comprise the bulk of local police services but are a negligible factor at the federal level. Thus, because of the existence of organizations like the FBI, certain law enforcement problems such as organized crime can be brought within the federal purview by relatively simple legislative or administrative action. Other problems, notably street crime, cannot because there is no federal law enforcement machinery to deal with them.

Historical Background

The present systems of detective administration are a product of the historical development of police departments. In eighteenth-century Britain and Amer-

---

[1] In this context detective work is defined primarily as criminal investigation. Policemen who simply patrol in plain clothes and juvenile or community relations officers whose work is largely of a social service nature would not be considered detectives.

[2] See, for example, Bruce Smith, American Police Systems (New York: Harper and Row, 1960); and James Q. Wilson, Varieties of Police Behavior (Cambridge: Harvard University Press, 1968).

[3] It should be noted that the local model parallels British police practice, while the federal model is similar to that found on the European continent. As might be expected, state government, or the intermediate level, follows a mixture of local and federal practice with patterns varying from state to state.

[4] In 1973 the 58 largest cities employed nearly 126,000 police officers. It has been estimated that only about 10 percent of urban police officers are assigned as detectives. (See President's Commission on Law Enforcement and Administration of Justice, Task Force Report: The Police (Washington, D.C.: Government Printing Office, 1967), p. 121. That would mean that there were about 12,600 detectives in these 58 cities. In the same year the FBI alone employed approximately 8,000 investigative personnel.

ica, the duty of patrolling the streets was carried out by watchmen who were charged with the maintenance of order and the prevention of crime in much the same way as the uniformed policemen of today; however, they did not engage in follow-up criminal investigation. If, for example, a citizen's home was burglarized, he would not call upon the watchman. Instead, he could appeal to a magistrate or justice of the peace who would assign constables to investigate the matter, arrest the offender, and recover the stolen property. Normally, the citizen complainant was required to pay a fee for this service.[5] Thus, watchmen and constables were quite different offices.

The watch system proved ineffective in the industrial era and came to be replaced by police departments of the type familiar to the present day. The first such force, created in London in 1829, was a uniformed body, and for a time the detective functions continued to be carried out by the magistrate/constable system. In 1842, however, a detective branch was created at Scotland Yard; thereafter the metropolitan police assumed responsibility for criminal investigation.[6] American cities underwent a similar progression.

Despite the merger of the two functions, the disparity between the duties of the uniformed patrolman and those of the detective continued to trouble police administrators. While the former position seemed to require the discipline and stolidity of a soldier, the latter required a higher degree of intelligence and initiative. In practice, few of the early policemen made successful detectives.[7] To remedy this situation, detectives were often recruited directly from civil life. While this method provided men of

greater skill than the uniformed force could offer, it frequently led to corruption, since many of the early detectives, particularly the Americans, were themselves former criminals.[8] By the 1870s a series of scandals[9] led to general adoption of the practice of appointing detectives from the uniformed force.[10]

The modern municipal police force, with the investigative branch as an integral component, has been so institutionalized at the local level that it has become the conventional wisdom presented in the standard police texts, where it is maintained that there is no essential difference between uniformed patrol and detective duties.[11] It is also posited that detective work should constitute an integral part of the duties of the regular police officer and that the rotation of individuals between the two roles is desirable.[12] Despite the prevalence of the textbook view, however, there seems no empirical evidence to support it; and of course, federal practice is entirely the opposite.

Historically, municipal police criminal investigation rarely reached even minimal standards of competence, particularly at the major case level, thus, the necessity to maintain relatively large national detective forces. Until the 1920s this need was filled by private detective agencies such as Pinkerton,

[5] The procedure described is illustrative of the practice in London circa 1800; see Anthony Babington, *A House in Bow Street, Crime and the Magistracy in London, 1740 to 1881* (London: MacDonald Ltd., 1969), pp. 186–93.

[6] A description of the origins of the detective branch of Scotland Yard is found in Belton Cobb, *The First Detectives* (London: Faber & Faber Ltd., 1957).

[7] Most of the early London policemen were ex-service men. Their unsuitability for detective work is a recurrent theme in Cobb, *op. cit.*, and is mentioned in T. A. Critchley, *A History of Police In England and Wales*, 2nd edition (Montclair, New Jersey: Patterson Smith, 1972), pp. 160–61.

[8] In the early nineteenth century it was commonly believed that "it takes a thief to catch a thief." An outstanding example of this thinking was the career of the master criminal, Eugene Vidocq, who served as chief of Paris detectives from 1809 to 1832. For an account of the malpractices of early American detectives, *see* Roger Lane, *Policing the City: Boston 1822 to 1885* (Cambridge: Harvard University Press, 1968), chapter 8.

[9] Even Scotland Yard was tarnished when in 1877 three out of four chief inspectors of the detective branch were found guilty of corruption, including men who had been brought in as direct entrants because of superior educational qualifications. Critchley, op. cit., p. 161.

[10] Although as late as 1920 cities as large as Pittsburgh, Kansas City, Louisville, Memphis, and Birmingham were still appointing detectives directly from civil life. *See* Raymond Fosdick, *American Police Systems* (New York: Macmillan, 1920), p. 328.

[11] George D. Eastman, ed., *Municipal Police Administration* (Washington, D.C.: International City Managers Association), 6th edition, 1969, p. 141.

[12] Ibid., pp. 142–43.

Burns, or the railroad police forces.[13] In the past half century, the private agencies have been replaced in this role by federal bureaus of "G-Men" and "T-Men."

The twentieth century, however, witnessed the rise of detectives to primacy in municipal police work, reversing the low status they originally held. In part this was a result of improved capabilities, such as fingerprinting and other criminalistic procedures, which produced more successful investigations. However, it is likely that the most significant factor was the development of the modern newspaper, which created a reading public eager for sensation. Murder and robbery, the daily fare of the detectives, made interesting reading, especially since an enterprising reporter could apply such adjectives as "dastardly" or "baffling" to even the most routine case. In contrast, the uniformed police officer's duties, mainly the maintenance of order and the resolution of minor interpersonal conflicts, were not newsworthy. Prior to World War II, crime stories were front-page news, and local detectives frequently became minor celebrities. By the 1920s the detective bureau was a unit to which ambitious men sought transfer and from which police chiefs emerged.[14]

[13] Many famous crimes, such as the murder of former Governor Steunenberg of Idaho in 1905 and the bombing of the Los Angeles Times in 1910 were related to organized labor activities and were therefore natural material for private detectives (the Pinkertons in the former case, the Burns agency in the latter). But even more conventional investigations were frequently turned over to private agencies. For example, it was the Pinkertons who in 1895 apprehended the famous mass murderer, H. H. Holmes (convicted of wiping out a Philadelphia family and suspected of the murder of numerous women in "Holmes Castle" in Chicago). In 1915 the Pinkerton and Burns agencies were engaged on opposite sides of the "crime of the decade"—the Mary Phagan rape-murder case in Atlanta, Georgia. (Not only did the case receive massive publicity, but the wave of anti-Semitism generated gave impetus to the founding of both the Anti-Defamation League and the modern Ku Klux Klan.)
[14] For example, in 1938 the Boston police commissioner, in a report to the governor, declared unequivocally that the detectives were the most important part of the force and requested the

Organizational Dilemmas

Within the local or municipal system there has been a continuing organizational dichotomy. This has been reflected in patrol-detective relationships and in the area-versus-functional task organization of the detective force. The conventional wisdom holds that the patrol division conducts the preliminary investigation and detectives the follow-up. In practice, it has been difficult to delineate the boundaries between the two activities.

The area-versus-functional debate has occasioned periodic reorganization of detective forces in many departments and as yet is neither resolved nor to a large extent understood. Depending on period and locale, detectives have been organized into special squads, such as homicide or robbery, and have been given city-wide scope; or in contrast they have been attached to a local precinct or station to work on a wide variety of cases. This has been characterized as the headquarters-specialist/precinct-generalist pattern.[15]

A common practice in many departments has been to maintain both kinds of units simultaneously. There is, however, considerable difference between the two. At the local or precinct level there is a need for personnel who are in intimate contact with the uniformed force and possess a close knowledge of the local area. This enables them to respond quickly to crime scenes, be briefed by patrol officers, and then draw on their local knowledge and contacts to clear the crime. For offenses such as street robbery and residential burglary, which frequently involve local

authority to promote them in rank without regard to civil service laws. *See 33rd Annual Report of the Police Commissioner for the City of Boston, Year Ending November 30, 1938*, 12 Mass., Public Document 49 (2938). In New York in the 1930s John Broderick, an ordinary detective, was better known than most high police officials even to the extent of his career being portrayed on the screen by a noted actor of the period. San Francisco in the 1950s chose a local (patrolman) detective celebrity to be the chief of police.
[15] An extensive comparison of specialist-versus-generalist detective organizations is contained in Richard H. Ward, "The Investigative Function: Criminal Investigation In The United States" (Ph.D. dissertation, University of California, Berkeley, 1971).

offenders (or offenders known to local people),[16] this arrangement possesses great utility. Thus, the precinct detective is in effect an arm of the patrol division, and like patrol officers, his principal asset is territorial knowledge. Clearly, it is a misnomer to refer to precinct detectives as generalists; rather they are territorial or area specialists. As the textbooks would suggest, the most useful preparation such detectives are likely to receive is service as a uniformed patrolman.

At the city-wide or major case level the situation is quite different. In order to solve crimes committed by skilled and mobile offenders such as master burglars, armed robbery gangs, and so forth, it is necessary to possess specialized expertise. That is, detectives are required to be acquainted with the offenders, tipsters, and fences who constitute the burglary or robbery "scene" or "network."[17] At this level, functional specialization is more vital than area or territorial knowledge. Even more importantly, in confrontations with professional criminals, organized racketeers, or in extremely complex cases, there is a need for detectives highly skilled in legal procedures, investigative techniques, and interrogation methods. Whether a sufficient number of individuals possessing these skills is likely to be found in the uniformed forces is questionable. Again the federal detective forces who largely concentrate on major crime have maintained a different organizational pattern, and their performance has generally outshone that of their municipal counterparts.

The Decline of Detectives

The 1960s has witnessed the development of a number of factors leading to a decline of the detective's primacy. First, it brought to the fore various problems which overshadowed the so-called "sensational" crimes. Civil disorder, juvenile delinquency, and the fear of "crime in the streets" have given new importance to the patrol force and to such specialized units as juvenile bureaus and community relations sections. Concurrent with these trends have been studies which clearly reject the image of the detective as a supersleuth.

Writers who have looked closely at the operations of detectives have found that the bulk of investigative work is clerical in nature. That is, the detective is charged with the task of preparing extensive reports on crime and arrests[18] but does not himself generate a great many arrests. This is supported by a study conducted in Los Angeles by a Presidential Task Force which determined that a relatively small number of cases was cleared through detective efforts as compared to the amount handled by the patrol division.[19] In a similar vein a Rand Institute study of index crime arrests in New York City concluded that arrests for property crimes were largely random events uninfluenced by the quantity or quality of detective efforts; and, further, that arrests for crimes against persons (murder, rape, or assault) were primarily attributable to information supplied to the police by victims rather than through any special investigative techniques.[20]

Two ancillary areas of criminal investigation have also received increased attention in the past decade. These are organized crime and internal security. As a result, many police departments and investigative agencies have expanded their intelligence units. Problems incumbent in intelligence work are numerous, so that in the present context it can only be noted that the growth of such activities adds to the skills required of the headquarters-specialist type of detective operation.[21] Nor in light of contemporary events

[16] For example, a St. Louis study noted that residential burglars were more likely to work near home than other types of offenders. *See* Sara Boggs, "Urban Crime Patterns," in Daniel Glaser, ed., *Crime in the City* (New York: Harper and Row, 1970), pp. 108–118.

[17] A discussion of criminal behavior in terms of a network is found in Neal E. Shover, "Burglary As An Occupation" (Ph.D. dissertation, University of Illinois, 1971.)

[18] Ward, op. cit., p. 97.

[19] President's Commission on Law Enforcement and Administration of Justice, *Task Force Report: Science And Technology* (Washington, D.C.: Government Printing Office, 1967), pp. 7–9.

[20] *See* Peter W. Greenwood, *An Analysis of the Apprehension Activities of the New York City Police Department* (New York: Rand Institute, 1970).

[21] The development of intelligence squads is not entirely new. Many police departments have used so-called "red" or "industrial" squads since the turn of the century. Likewise, special "blackhand" or "racket" details have a fairly long history. As early as 1909 the head of the New York City "Italian" squad was assassinated while investigating the Mafia in Sicily. What is perhaps new is the size and attention presently afforded such units. In this respect the Los Angeles police intelligence squad of the 1950s has been the prototype for the modern units.

is it necessary to mention the grave legal and political questions which arise from law enforcement intelligence activities.

Even such traditional areas as the investigation of common-law crimes have also been made more complex as a result of judicial decisions such as *Mapp*[22] (search and seizure), *Miranda*[23] (interrogation), and *Wade-Gilbert*[24] (identification). Simultaneously, the classic working technique of detectives—the case method—is in the process of being partially superseded by the strategic or systems approach whereby detectives consider whole crime categories rather than individual cases.[25]

Thus the detective craft has undergone critical analysis, has broadened its dimensions, and is being subjected to new and higher standards. In the light of these developments, there is an effort to create responsive organizational forms and techniques while still grappling with traditional problems. The following profile of the contemporary detective administrator provides some illustration of the nature of these problems, and the subsequent section will identify the major innovative trends in the organization of investigative services.

The Detective Administrator

The typical detective commander[26] is usually a career officer from the ranks of his own department. Often he has spent a number of years as a working detective, since it is widely held that knowledge of the craft is a requisite for his position.

A typical workday usually begins with the commander sorting through a pile of reports on new and old cases. Likely it is the former which will be read first since the news media or his superiors may quiz him on the latest murder or jewel heist. At one time a detective commander largely defined his role as that of chief investigator, by taking personal charge of the major cases. Indeed, it was almost obligatory for him to be photographed at the crime scene. Therefore, if he is of the old school, he may plunge directly into cases that strike his fancy, leaving the administration of his unit to an assistant or to divine providence.

Unlike patrol commanders, the detective chief cannot easily supervise his troops in the field, thus much of his time will be taken up in staff conferences with subordinates regarding personnel assignments and operational effectiveness. Normally the detective assignment is considered a desirable one in police departments. Whether this is due to the more interesting work, extra pay, greater freedom from supervisory constraints, or combinations thereof, there is usually a plethora of candidates. In departments where the selection of detectives is largely discretionary rather than governed by merit procedures, the chief will find himself constantly importuned by aspirants and their supporters. Given this situation, present detectives who exhibit laziness, insubordination or other flaws soon find themselves "back in the blue."

As regards operational effectiveness, in the more traditional departments, detective efficiency is predicated on solving the "hot" cases or making the "big busts"—with the decisions as to which are prime cases generally coming from external sources such as the news media or civic associations. Thus the latest trunk murder outranks several skid row stabbings, and the arrest of a bank robber is more loudly praised than is the apprehension of a score of juvenile burglars. In modern, so-called "professional" departments there is greater attention given to statistical summaries. While it has been argued that detective performance is the facet of police work most easily evaluated in managerial efficiency terms,[27] this is questionable. A Rand Institute study determined that crime clearance rates for detective units were highly manipulable, with the determining factor being the desires of individual squad commanders.[28]

In some departments the central problem of detective administration is integrity control, particularly in units where vice law enforcement is a major responsibility. Beyond outright corruption, the detective administrator must also confront a number of

[22] *Mapp* v. *Ohio*, 367 U.S. 643 (1961).

[23] *Miranda* v. *Arizona*, 384 U.S. 436 (1966).

[24] *U.S.* v. *Wade*, 388 U.S. 218 (1967); *Gilbert* v. *California*, 388 U.S. 263 (1967).

[25] *See* Greenberg, Yu, and Lang, *Enhancement of the Investigative Function*, Vol. 1, Stanford Research Institute (Springfield, Va.: NTIS, 1973), pp. 49–50.

[26] In this section the terms *commander* and *chief* will be used interchangeably and the discussion applies equally to the commanding officer of a squad of ten or to a bureau of one thousand.

[27] O. W. Wilson, *Police Administration*, 2nd edition (New York: McGraw-Hill, 1963), p. 290.

[28] Greenwood, op. cit., p. 18.

ethical questions. These relate to such matters as the use of informants and undercover operators, distinctions between controlled transactions and entrapment, and the extent to which detectives should join prosecutors and defense counsel in plea-bargaining negotiations.

A detective chief whose domain includes both criminal and vice investigations might find that his subordinates have differing priorities for enforcement according to their organizational specializations. The burglary detectives may be inclined to "pass" a junkie with a small amount of drugs if he can turn up stolen property, while the narcotics squad will forget a few nickel-and-dime burglaries in return for cooperation in apprehending a major peddler. Homicide investigators looking for information on a murder will view a busy prostitute as a source of information and leave her unmolested, while the vice squad will bust her.

The above examples are but a few of the many ambiguities present in detective administration. Clearly the ideal detective chief might well be a combination of IBM executive and professor of ethical jurisprudence. Since such persons are rare, and if existent, not likely to function well in the "real" world, most detective commanders rely on a combination of street sense born of police experience and good luck.

Current Trends in Investigative Services

At the local or precinct level, there has been an attempt to reintegrate the patrol and the detective functions. At the beginning of the 1960s the textbook wisdom of the professional or technical efficiency school of policing was to abolish precinct detectives in favor of specialized squads operating over larger areas.[29] However, even in instances where this has been done, "bootleg" or irregular detectives have emerged at the precinct level. This has taken the form of precinct anticrime units or tactical patrol squads undertaking officially forbidden follow-up investigations, thus demonstrating that practical necessity is more powerful than bureaucratic rules.

[29] O. W. Wilson, op. cit., pp. 291–92. This recommendation was implemented by its author when, shortly after assuming the post of Chicago police superintendant in 1960, he abolished district detective units.

In the past few years, the growth of neighborhood team policing[30] has promoted a trend to abolish or curtail formal detective roles and assign follow-up investigations to beat patrol officers. Justifications offered involve job enlargement for patrolmen and maximum personnel flexibility at the operating level. As noted, there is a clear need for follow-up capabilities at the patrol level. Whether this can be accomplished by regular uniformed officers will probably depend on the level of competence within a patrol force. Where the standard of officer quality is generally high, patrol officers are more likely to assume, and to achieve success with, broader responsibilities.

At the higher level there has been a movement toward regional squads or strike forces combining local, state, and even federal officers. Such units usually concentrate on major crimes and organized racketeering, and their area of operation transcends municipal boundaries. The regional concept in effect seeks to provide both a wider authority and a level of expertise beyond that of traditional municipal police departments. Whether these ad hoc arrangements can be institutionalized is not certain. The lines between local, state, and federal jurisdiction cannot be altered as easily as the boundaries between patrol and detective functions within a police department.

Conclusion

The problems of detective administration can be viewed in two dimensions. The first is the range of concerns common to police administration in general. These include such matters as integrity control, personnel supervision, and the measurement of individual and organizational effectiveness. The second relates to the peculiar demands of investigative tasks—a particularly vexing problem being the need for diverse modes of investigative service. At the neighborhood level, the principal problems are those relating to run-of-the-mill criminality, while at the metropolitan level the focus is on complex or wide-ranging criminal behavior. The imperatives of skill and organizational form manifest in each task vary significantly.

[30] The concepts of team policing are discussed in Peter B. Bloch and David Specht, *Neighborhood Team Policing* (Washington, D.C.: U.S. Department of Justice, 1973).

The history of detective administration has witnessed a progression from adjunct to premier role in police service, with the present status being one of decline and realignment. One current trend is to reintegrate detective tasks with patrol; another is to recast the local detective system in accord with the federal model. It is doubtful, however, whether the dimensions of detective work are fully encompassed by either of these trends, for detectives are more than

[31] A similar conclusion was reached in Greenberg, op. cit., pp. 14—15.

patrolmen and less than supersleuths. A third possible direction lies in the legitimation of the detective as an anticrime coordinator, based on the reality of his extensive quasi-clerical tasks. Thus the detective's function in relation to crime may be seen to parallel that of the architect toward the structural environment. As the latter is the interpreter, synthesizer, and designer of construction data, so, too, is the detective vis-à-vis crime data. Thus the detective in his most useful role may provide the authoritative estimate of the crime situation and the principal input to anticrime strategy.[31]

BIBLIOGRAPHY

Bloch, Peter B. and David Specht, *Neighborhood Team Policing*. Washington, D.C.: U.S. Department of Justice, 1973.

Greenberg, B., O. Yu, and K. Lang, *Enhancement of the Investigative Function*, Stanford Research Institute. Springfield, Va.: NTIS, 1973.

Greenwood, Peter W., *An Analysis of the Apprehensive Activities of the New York City Police Department*. New York: Rand Institute, 1970.

Lane, Roger, *"The Detectives," Policing the City: Boston 1822—1885*. Cambridge: Harvard University Press, 1968, Chapter 8.

Skolnick, Jerome, *Justice Without Trial*. New York: John Wiley & Sons, 1966.

Ward, Richard H., *The Investigative Function: Criminal Investigation in the United States*. Ph.D. dissertation, University of California, Berkeley, 1971; University Microfilms, Ann Arbor, Mich.

4 | Police Values and Culture

Police, who have already been socialized and shaped in one society, are required to adapt to a new world when they enter the police culture. When former stabilized values and the values of their new police world coincide, there is no conflict and consequently no problem. When the old style of life runs counter to the imperatives of their new culture, there is a need for resolution of the resultant conflict. The nature of the resolution will in large measure depend on such variables as the degree of commitment one has to the old or new, the age of entry for socialization into the new culture, the personality resistance or flexibility of the individual, and the strength of the value in the total hierarchy of values of the police culture.

The special structural qualities of the police culture include: the uniform, ceremonials, etiquette, power and authority, a unique set of duties, strong kinship and solidarity among policemen, a sense of isolation from the rest of the community and other occupations, and a perception of common hazards and dangers that are shared by all police officers. This combination endows the police organization with an irresistible psychological power, so that most officers internalize the traditional values of the police culture.

Many of these values have been identified by scholars. There is wide agreement that the basic traits of the police culture are:

1. Respect for power and authority.
2. Secrecy, especially in those matters where it may affect their colleagues and organization.
3. Loyalty to the organization even when it may mean compromises of all kinds.
4. A sense of minority group status and all that implies.

5. Political conservatism.
6. A broad cynicism which is rationalized in terms of knowing the real world and "what the score is."
7. Yet in spite of the cynicism there is an unquestioning belief in and loyalty to country, flag, family, and religion; an unswerving conviction that police do an exemplary job in combating crime, but are hamstrung by judges, courts, and corrections officials; an assumption that the trouble with America is lack of respect for the law, police, and constituted authority; and an associated doctrine that the cause of crime and related social problems is a widespread permissiveness.

As the police system changes, the values undergo transformation. With the unprecedented spurt in growth of the phenomenon of the college-educated police officer comes a questioning and reappraisal of police values. These individuals are more willing and better prepared to challenge the older police values which are seen as somewhat narrow in scope and not necessarily valid in many instances. Education, higher salaries, and fringe benefits have moved many police officers well into middle-class status. Their immersion in a new class position causes them to be receptive to a competing set of values that is at odds with a number of the traditional police values. Finally, the introduction in substantial numbers of minority groups, including women, to the police world has already had and will continue to have an impact on police culture. For those who wonder what the end result may be, we suggest it may be useful to follow this section with a reading of Chapter 9, "The Future of Law Enforcement."

Value Conflicts in Law Enforcement

JACOB CHWAST

███████████████████████████████

███████████████████████████████

Unless we are clear about our values, we are clear about nothing.

The social and personal values of the law enforcement officer[1] strongly condition the quality of service he delivers to different segments of the populace at large.

Looked upon broadly, the delivery of the basic police service—i.e., face-to-face police action—is the product of a multiplicity of overlapping processes which reinforce, contradict, or neutralize one another. Besides the external social processes in the community (including those which are legal) impinging upon police policy, decision-making, and eventual action, there are internal administrative and supervisory processes. Key determinants in the course the police pursue are the values underpinning these processes. Since these values serve, in essence, as goal-oriented guides for behavior, rendering them explicit removes them from the shadowland of unexamined assumptions and hypotheses not subjected to the searchlight of objective test and can clarify police objectives, methods, and results. Indeed, unless this elementary but difficult task is accomplished, the pervasive implicit value assumptions and directions underlying police work will continue their insidious reign.

Every police officer becomes aware of the distinction between the explicit and implicit values in his job—what is expected by the book and protocol, and what will be accepted and tolerated by his coworkers, superiors, and peers. If the net effect of these implicit values were good, we would be ahead of the game. Unfortunately, some values, like "picking up a buck," "beating time," "not knocking

your brains out," and "not hurting someone," are often quite destructive.

No one can quarrel with the existence of value systems and their different meanings for different individuals. One can, however, become concerned if an officer deals one way with a member of an underprivileged community and another way with one of the middle class because the latter is someone he can understand better, someone with whom he shares similar values. Of course, for these comparisons, there must be an equivalence of lawfulness or unlawfulness in the nature of the interpersonal contact between the officer and the other person. If so, then the outcome of the contact may hinge upon the presence or absence of a values conflict, a conflict uncontaminated by any contribution from the law itself as a system of values.[2] These difficulties between the police and the citizenry arise from a clash in the perception of what is valued—i.e., what is right or wrong, desirable or undesirable, good or bad. The clash in values occurs also at all levels within the police, vertically and horizontally.

Nature of Police Values

If this is the case, it would seem of cardinal importance to examine the nature of police values so as to comprehend better the specific ways in which they affect police work. This is especially imperative since, in dealing with the diverse peoples they encounter, the police might be projecting values which may be either totally or partially inappropriate or, at least, irrelevant to such encounters. Thus, if a police officer drives his knee forcefully into the groin of a sexual offender while imprecating, "You dirty degenerate," or rudely ignores a poor Negro woman's hesitant request for directions, or adverts to newly arrived foreign-born residents of low-income areas as "animals," the outcome of such encounters might

SOURCE: *Crime and Delinquency, 11* (April 1965), pp. 151–61.

[1] In speaking about law enforcement, I shall refer essentially to police officers.

[2] I would not wish to leave the impression that the law itself does not contain many conflicts with ponderous values impact, for indeed it does. I merely do not propose to deal with these at this time.

well be determined by factors not entirely germane thereto. They may instead reflect problems within the police—singular or plural. The basic concept underlying our law is that it applies with equal force to all, without fear or favor to any.

Police values, it need hardly be said, have many roots.(1) First, as is generally true for everyone, there are the fundamental values acquired during the early personal experiences of the police officer. Most important among these are the values he has assimilated from the significant adults in his life. These personal values differ somewhat for each person. Apropos of this, one can make many interesting conjectures about the value systems, home influences, and personality patterns of those entering police service. Many observers have used phrases such as dominance drive, sadomasochism, desire to control one's own antisocial tendencies, or to legitimatize criminal impulses, compensatory reactions for inferiority feelings, displaced aggression, and high F scores on the authoritarian scale. I would not care to dismiss these possibilities, but I cannot deny that in a number of instances I have been struck by the police officer's self-perception as a helping person. This view of himself, undoubtedly a rationalization to some extent, has even been held by the officer who has tended to behave in ways which have subverted the credo of integrity: seeing oneself as helpful seems to have nothing to do with honesty or its lack. Parenthetically, some research effort might be expended in this direction with special emphasis on relating this self-image to that of those gainfully employed in the ranks of the traditional helping professions: social work, psychology, and psychiatry. Indeed, this self-image fits into the debated view that the police officer is engaged in social service. Admittedly he may not qualify as a graduate social worker but he does perform a vital social function, one which cannot be ruled out by a narrow definition of police service. While the helping professions tend to aim for the release of growth potential, they may also have to control this release; while the police officer aims at the control of untoward activities disruptive to social well-being, he may also have to allow for some freedom from restraint to further this end.(2)

The second influence in police values is social in origin. In this category, one must first consider the contribution of influences outside the job: friends, relatives, school, church, recreational outlets, books, newspapers, etc.

Middle-Class Status

Since most police officers are members of the middle class, they share such common middle-class goals as looking toward the future and getting ahead, owning a home and a new car, being on time, and assuming responsibility. I'd even speculate that, in some respects, police are more middle-classy than the average, since many are recent entrants into that oft-admired, oft-castigated estate. Many of the police have been recruited from the lower socioeconomic class. At social functions of police groups, one is quite impressed by orthodoxy in dress, speech, and manners. This need to compensate for an earlier inferior status, which hardly needs further comment, creates other difficulties for them; values appropriate to their middle-class status can often come into conflict with their earlier or, possibly, current lower-class values and attitudes.

One must consider, in addition to these outside social influences, the social values inherent in the police apparatus. This apparatus is very powerful in effect. Here, we see formal or explicit value sources and informal or implicit value sources, which are, as often as not, antagonistic to each other.

Among the formal value sources, the influence of law and other explicit controlling instruments (such as manuals of procedure, guides for conduct, and official orders) are specifically paradigmatic for police performance. The controls often impose much more rigid experiences on police behavior than on other members of society and also expose the police to much more reprisal for error. Added to this vulnerability to criticism from their fellow men is the prominence of the police as the visible bearers of outer social authority.

As for antagonism between value sources, one may extol honesty and impartiality while another may exalt "bagging a prostitute" or some other offender who is considered fair game, so as to keep up a "batting average." One may promulgate the paranoid-like notion that "your greatest enemy is the public"; yet this runs counter to the realization that it is the public which you are serving and which, more materialistically, must be won over for a raise. This conflict results in peculiar mixtures of hostility, fear, and suspicion of the public, on one hand, and friendliness, candor, and cooperation, on the other. Another consequence of the conflict, in the public's view, is that sometimes the police are with them and sometimes they are not. Everything adds up to a picture of unreliability in police reactions.

Opportunity Structure

In applying the sociological concept of opportunity structure to delinquency, Cloward and Ohlin have exposed a side of the coin of which law enforcement is the obverse.(3)

In essence, they contend that when individuals cannot achieve success within a social system by legitimate means, they will do so by illegitimate means. Accordingly, the delinquent uses antisocial pathways to success—that is, to the fulfillment of basic needs and drives, including the social needs for recognition and approval. He does this because socialized pathways via academic laurels and status occupations are, in a real sense, foreclosed to him. To account for the direction of the antisocial expression, Cloward and Ohlin assert that this will be determined largely by the subculture in which the delinquent lives. They hold that if he resides in a conflict subculture, he will reflect this pattern of reaction by gaining "rep" through gang warfare or "bopping"; if he lives in a retreatist subculture, he will gain status by drugs; if he lives in a criminal subculture, he will gain it by nefarious activity. In some cases an evolutionary progression from "bopping" to "popping" occurs and may finally lead to outright criminality.

A parallel formula can be applied to the police, perhaps with greater fidelity in some ways because the social system of the police is even tighter. Few nonpolicemen can appreciate how much the police officer's life is governed by the job: on duty or off, in the city or out, with friends or foes. Since the police officer is primarily an agent of social control, his function has rubbed off on his life so that he, himself, is subject to rigid controls continuously throughout the course of his professional career.

In-Group Modes of Reaction

If the controls are not conspicuously external, the implicit in-group controls take over. In good part, the sequestration of the police as a viable subgroup is due to the conditions of their employment. Working around the clock, itself, is almost a decisive factor in determining who freetime friends and associates will be and also reinforces the adherence to police modes of thought, feelings, and action. Also, almost from the beginning, police officers are perniciously indoctrinated into the belief that "you can't really trust anybody but another cop." It's like being in a gang and not being able to trust a nonmember.

This also brings with it a cult of secrecy to which none but fellow officers may be admitted. Indeed, so selective does this become that subcults may develop whereby detectives share their secrets with only other detectives, sergeants theirs with only other sergeants, and so on. The guiding values of each of these subgroups may vary considerably, too. If the group is oriented to power, we may find an upper stratum elite which keeps itself distinctively apart from other members of the police organization. Within this group one often finds an unusual amount of rivalry which may become exhibited around questions of protocol. If the ranks are equivalent, jealousy can be so pronounced that even the usual amenities are dispensed with. I recall one case when two equally high ranking officers met at a staff meeting. The only acknowledgment that passed between them as each studiously avoided giving any suggestion of being impressed by the other was a mixture of rhinoceros-like snorts and grunts.

More recently, this power elite has been infiltrated by a new entrant with one or two scholastic degrees, who is shaking up the old order somewhat, at least to the point where some aging veterans have had to hurry to the colleges to take courses and keep pace. All of this is to the good, no doubt, but apart from this qualification the changeover is rather superficial. The locus of power still remains centralized in a power elite engaging in old practices; it is the same group with academic faces.

An unhappy short-term consequence of this phenomenon is the encouragement of lower-level personnel to higher educational attainment without adequate provision for use of their hard-wrested knowledge. Or almost as bad, if a place is made for them, it usually is one without commensurate rewards of compensation and status. In the long run, presumably, these men will rise, provided they don't become needlessly tarred and barred en route.

These eventualities are always immanent within an authoritarian structure which basically distrusts the intellectual who cannot accept a definition of relationships polarized around a dominance-submission axis. Intellectual operations with long-range implications are also distrusted in an organization which is ever impelled toward action and which is under almost constant declaration of a state of emergency. Despite sporadic efforts to the contrary, the police structure is essentially incapable of long-range planning.

Finally, this is also a structure with built-in xenophobia, and intellectuals or minority group members are usually perceived as outlanders. Many a fine officer I have known suffered acutely the consequences of this xenophobia during the benighted McCarthy period and afterward.

Unofficial Misalliance

If a subgroup of police officers is oriented to money, we may find the members contributing their "take" to a common pot from which each receives a share. The amount, of course, depends upon the participant's status in the hierarchy of the subsystem sustaining this unlawful enterprise, which is conducted with such dispatch and efficiency as to be the envy of the best examples of military action or lawful police work. No city has been exempted from such alliances. A particularly heinous twist in this pattern—the "take" being converted to "loot"—has happened recently in Denver, Chicago, and several other cities.

Trained in speed, power, self-discipline, criminal methods, and the use of weapons, the policeman-turned-criminal is a peculiarly dangerous adversary. Although desire for money and pleasure cannot be discounted as a factor for individual officers, the structural features herein delineated appear crucial in the formulation of such criminal combines. If a social system condones certain behaviors, based upon correlative dishonest values, such as the exploitation of bookies, policy-runners, prostitutes, and after-hours joints, the next step down the ladder is much easier. "Brass-button crime" flourishes when the soil has been prepared.

Much of the illegal activity within the police family is disposed of by informal means, but policemen may often be victims themselves. The civil liberties of police officers are unusually vulnerable to assault. In this respect, higher-ups can become extraordinarily insensitive, and indeed contributory.

Police Professionalization

This, quite naturally, raises important questions about the nature of police professionalization. In groping for a professional niche, the police might well abandon pontification and define their role with greater clarity.

In one instance, a police superior finally became aware of the need to create a positive public image of the police. Imbued with this idea, he tried to impart it in his lectures on community relations to subordinates. Invariably he would bark at the men sitting ill at ease before him: "Be courteous! Be helpful! Be democratic!" How did he fire their hearts and minds? And in what direction?

Obviously, no police superior can order the enactment of certain types of desired social behavior. He must approach this objective much more fundamentally and sincerely. If certain behaviors spring from correlative attitudes, the police administrator must try to deal basically with these attitudes using mature administrative, educational, and psychological knowledge. Of course, the changing of attitudes among subordinates is not uncomplicated; those of the superior must also be changed. A first step would be made, however, if the values matrix in which the attitudes are imbedded were better understood.

Although they have not been able to perform this delicate task, there has been less incapacity in police ranks to decry in stentorian tones criminal, immoral, or unethical actions among the citizenry or occasionally even among themselves in circumscribed areas. The real task and gain for the police in developing this understanding lies in building more effective police programs consonant with professional standards within the framework of a democratic society. In a way, "here lies the rub" because the most fundamental problem facing the police is the integration of what is an essentially authoritarian system into what is, hopefully, an essentially and overridingly democratic social, economic, and political system. It is a problem of maximizing autonomous functioning, implicit in professional status, within a social system which frowns upon individualization with the creative potential implicit therein.

How can Americans be secure in their freedom if those expected to preserve these freedoms are reared for practically all of their professional lives in an authoritarian atmosphere? Can unfree men preserve the liberties of free men? My own reaction to these compelling questions tends to be negative.

What is raised here is the ancient debate over ends and means. I find it hard to accept the idea that one can achieve democratic ends when the means or process whereby these are achieved is largely nondemocratic. Most troubling is the fact that much of this authoritarian paraphernalia is so unnecessary. Whether the system engenders sadism within some

men or whether sadism is already present in some
entering the police field, I do not know; probably
both obtain. I do know that the power inherent in
positions of authority within an encapsulated social
system like the police can corrupt foully and brutally.

From a realistic point of view, it might perhaps
be contended that American democracy is at the
crossroads in the relationship of its police to the rest
of its members. If one understands the fine interplay
between social controls and individual freedom of
expression, it is clear that the weight of the police can
tip the scale one way or the other. Of course, many
other social control instruments are significant factors, but the police seem most important.

Many in police circles will bring arguments to
bear against this position, but I still maintain that this
remains a basic problem, one which must be faced
and resolved. Furthermore, most police, even if they
don't see it in these terms, are keenly aware of the
confusion of goals and values in their job performance. Unfortunately, they don't know what to
do about the confusion besides providing more of the
same.

If the legitimate pathways to success within a
given social structure are blocked because of limited
opportunities, then illegitimate pathways will be
used. Now these illegitimate pathways may not
necessarily be illegal. They may simply be nonfunctional in getting ahead within that particular
opportunity structure. The limited opportunities
within a police department are a fact of life—despite
attractive advertisements to the contrary.

Alienation

Contributing most of all to the sense of limitation felt by many in police work is a basic feeling of
impotence in trying something new or different. This
feeling of impotence, by the way, is so pervasive that
police officers as a group tend to accept society as it
is and rarely become involved in effecting constructive change. True promotional opportunities are
available but they are insufficient; there is prolonged
waiting for tests, results, and appointments; salaries
barely keep pace with the cost of living. Worse still is
the feeling of alienation that the police experience,
despite routine cheerless reports of high morale. Even
putting the common query about police morale
shows a concern that it might not in fact be high. In
an authoritarian structure, perhaps, one must ask this
question to be reassured that things are not getting
out of hand; in a democratic structure, however, one

rarely asks the question because high morale is taken
for granted, like the freedom to speak and the right
to a respectful hearing which is not simultaneously an
investigation.

The feelings of alienation are extremely dangerous both to the police and to the individual
officer. If the officer feels estranged, disregarded
except upon command and unimportant when it
counts, the mask of distrust, cynicism, and ultimately, brutality may fit more easily. The mask
makes it much easier for him to cope with the inner
feelings of anxiety, frustration, despair, and loneliness
that become the "policeman's lot." It helps him to
get along, whatever one might think of the getting
along. Worn long enough, the mask fuses with the
face.

The brutalizing aspects of police work are un-
deniable, although some are fortunate enough to
escape them. Often the escape is possible when a
police officer finds a pathway for success which lies
outside those favored in the police structure. Here
also lies the element of integrity for the individual
police officer; certain choices can be made and he
may make the one with the lesser tangible return. I
know several police officers who would have received
lucrative assignments if they had but nodded their
heads. They declined because they believed that these
assignments would have forced them into compro-
mising positions from which they could not grace-
fully withdraw.

As for brutality, it is not a one-way street. The
social milieu outside the police framework has something to do with it. I have already mentioned the
value-molding effect of the press upon the police.
One must also remember the reinforcement of these
values by the judiciary, political powers, and other
important persons and symbols. I must also mention
again the influence of the middle class. It shapes in
good part the attitudes of its members, including the
police, toward life, limb, property, sex, work, education, and recreation. Middle-class attitudes stress
promptness, cleanliness, decorous speech and manners, and orderly habits. It is a future-oriented culture
in which the deferment of immediate pleasures for
eventual gains is highly valued. In lower socio-
economic groups, these values can be viewed quite
differently.

Lower-Class Values

In lower-class society, life is generally a scuffle, a
battle for survival; it rarely allows the luxury of a

vague dream of nice things to come. There is no particular importance attached to being on time, for instance, since its members have found that they always have to wait: for a job, at the social agency, at the clinic, in the court. Standards of cleanliness, personal hygiene, health, speech, manners, and habits appropriate for the success-bound are not necessarily perceived the same way.

The police officer, usually ill-equipped in understanding persons from different backgrounds or minority groups, finds himself on the firing line in the conflict between middle- and lower-class values. Already feeling lost in a big, depersonalized, authoritarian machine and thus alienated in his internal setting, he now has the added burden of feeling alienated in his external setting. This intensifies the distrust, suspicion, and underlying fear he already feels, and, when a crisis erupts—for instance, in making an arrest in a public place or breaking up a disorderly crowd—his reactions may be irrational and inappropriate to what the situation requires. In all of this, of course, the other persons involved may contribute more than their share. We should not allow ourselves to swing toward maudlin sentimentality; the poor and underprivileged have no monopoly on charm, courtesy, and kindliness. Indeed, the opposite is often the case, since persons from this group may feel that society, meaning basically the middle class, exploits and discriminates against them. As a consequence, their own resentment against the dominant middle-class world can become quite pronounced and the policeman represents a particularly conspicuous target. He not only is a visible and constant reminder of middle-class society and the yoke they presumably bear; he also enforces its values and, to some extent, its burdens. Under these circumstances, the police officer is also a victim in the conflict of values. He may be reminded forcibly of this when ashcans thrown from rooftops plop around him as he walks his beat.

Upper-Class Impact and Conservatism

One unusual feature further compounding value conflicts for the police is the contribution of the upper class to class value difference. The police guard royalty and chase street corner kids; they cater to the affluent and patrol the slums. They, thus, become quite vulnerable to the tastes and values of the wealthy managerial class of American society. This may affect their attitudes toward privilege, politics, property, and labor. Of late, labor has gained enough

respectability to dissipate an adverse stereotype and the "pinko" label. It has also learned how to establish better working relationships with the police.

Conservatism, in every form, fits tidily into the police scheme of things. The very nature of the police task with its emphasis on regulation and control is conservative. This conservatism affects attitudes toward politics, social custom, education, and the rearing of the young. From the very outset of a police officer's career, the pressure toward conformity is extremely intense. As one goes higher in rank, the pressure increases. Since conformity causes one to repress one's own impulses and freedom of expression, it results in considerable tension. The action-orientation of the usual police officer and the tension resulting from its inhibition becomes readily transmuted to anger. Some police cannot tolerate this emotion and may react quite violently, sometimes in ways which explode into headlines. For the rest, approved institutional targets for hostility—i.e., scapegoats—are available: roughing up uncooperative criminals, or abusing troublesome minority group members, or mercilessly issuing summonses on certain beats.

Although most police officers by far are fine men, certain officers will offer themselves up to do the dirty work in this scapegoating. And the dirty work can be illegal as well as legal. If it is in collections, the officer may become a "bagman." If it is in the exercise of force or pressure, he may act as a "hatchetman." Someone may be found in all ranks for all jobs.

Self-Hate

What the selective factor may be is not certain but it could be an expression of self-hate. It might be that those who volunteer for punitive service have little liking for themselves and, hence, none for others. I remember one officer who committed several acts of extortion and robbery, who previously had been considered a "good cop." He was always on the move and ever ready to take on unpleasant tasks and do the bidding of his superiors. At one point before he went beyond the pale, he mentioned that he couldn't keep on going and even talked of taking his own life. It might have been better if he had because he later took that of another man.

The reservoir of self-hate within the officer is probably also increased by the performance of a distasteful job, which in turn facilitates the next distasteful job. It is a vicious circle—one which could be rounded out by drinking in excess.

Police officers often complain about hating the job but they remain in it; there are the salary, pension, sick leave and vacation, security, a sick wife, a son in college, a daughter getting married, obligations, no other skills, no other background, no other job, no capacities or prospects, etc. It is a *job*, however, in the here and now and this creates another values dilemma. This dilemma may be less an issue for the small number of men in the upper ranks removed from the hue and cry; still, the inescapable fact is that most police officers perceive their work as a job. The demands implicit in doing a job, especially if one is friendly and sociable, and those implicit in discharging responsibilities accepted under an oath, can pull in two different directions. It is, in a way, the difference between getting along with others, on one hand, and acting as a punitive conscience, on the other. It is mighty difficult to warn, admonish, summons, arrest, or investigate someone with whom one is friendly.

This dilemma between compassion and duty has been portrayed countless times in literature and in the theater. It is a persistent one and will remain so as long as man has needs for affection as well as respect.

As for the alternative pathways to success mentioned above, the rather nonfunctional ones are found usually by officers who decide to withdraw from the "rat race." For some this withdrawal is an admission of defeat accompanied by isolation and self-absorption. For others, the withdrawal is not unhealthy. The individual who finds it hard to submerge himself in the larger police system may explore new avenues of growth and achieve self-fulfillment without yielding his values and principles. He may not achieve high rank vertically but he may achieve high status, often as perceived outside the department. One such opportunity for horizontal growth is in working with youth; another might be assignment to the police laboratory. I don't want to imply that these details cannot lead to higher rank; they may, but this usually means returning to the common pool, to "the rat race."

Quo Vadis?

This attempt to clarify the conflicting sets of values that have impact on law enforcement leaves much more to be explicated, for police work is completely swathed in values. It is of paramount importance that the police understand the nature of these values so that they might hew to the democratic line: they must know which values to enforce, which to learn more about, and which to respect and leave alone—even at the cost of so-called efficiency.

This discussion of the police apparatus does not add up to an oversimplified picture of a father figure. Nor should it add up to one of unbridled hostility. It does add up, I hope, to one of men often not self-critical in the right things and unduly so in the wrong ones. It is really an apparatus and therefore little concerned with individuals. Dismally, many police are proud of this demolition of the individual, of the interchangeability of human parts, of the automation of men. This was symbolized on the cover of a recent annual police report. It was completely covered with the faces of police officers: countless, anonymous, Orwellian faces. How much further can you push the loss of identity? How much further can you push alienation? I fear for the police as I fear for our joint existence. I will not agree, without the most agonizingly careful scrutiny, that our society requires that some people sacrifice their rights to individuality and freedom of expression in order that the rest of us may be protected in ours.

In a democracy, each one of us counts, even a policeman. I wish that police executives and the rest of us would take this fundamental credo to heart. A society consecrated to human values must not permit any of its parts, any of its apparatuses, to devalue any man. In the end, man is our greatest value.

REFERENCES

1. *See* Jacob Chwast, "Values Conflict in Treating the Delinquent," *Children* (May-June, 1959), pp. 95–100, for a related discussion.

2. Jacob Chwast, "The Significance of Control in the Treatment of the Antisocial Person," in H. A. Bloch, ed., *Crime in America* (New York: Philosophical Library, 1961), pp. 66–77; I. Weisman and J. Chwast, "Control and Values in Social Work Treatment," *Social Casework* (November 1960), pp. 451–56.

3. R. A. Cloward and L. E. Ohlin, *Delinquency and Opportunity* (Glencoe, Ill.: The Free Press of Glencoe, 1960).

The Policeman

JIMMY BRESLIN

There are a number of reasons why a young man in New York takes a job as a policeman, nearly all of which are the pension. The pension, half pay after 20 years, runs a policeman's life. It is the only thing he is afraid of losing and it is the only thing he wants out of the job. After 20 years, he retires and collects the half pay and works as a security man at a bank or a manufacturing plant somewhere. He starts this second job at between the ages of 40 and 45. He holds it until he can quit and collect Social Security.

At the end, he is a terribly bitter old man who wonders if he has wasted his life.

While he is a policeman, he has one outstanding quality. He will risk his life to save somebody else's. In all the debates about police, this is the one point on which there never is an argument. "Have you ever had a case of a fellow dogging it during trouble?" Michael Murphy, the Commissioner at the time, was asked one day. He was surprised the question was asked. "Not in my years," he said.

This is a point which should be remembered, and respected, by anybody thinking of calling a cop a name. Chicago, and the way police everywhere mindlessly applauded Chicago, still doesn't mean you can toss out the word bravery.

After this, you have just an ordinary working man who wears a uniform and has good habits and bad habits. Police on the job are capable of humor, kindness and common sense. After they finish working, they are invariably good company over a drink. Their record on graft is very bad and it does much to weaken their position in poor neighborhoods, where people are alert about what's going on around them.

The police have social standards which revolve around short haircuts, the Conservative Party and the pension. Since 1954, when Francis W. H. Adams, a former U. S. Attorney, was named Commissioner and immediately began improving the police job, the policemen of New York have become middle class.

Many of them live in the suburbs. Their only contact with poor neighborhoods comes from spending eight bitter hours working there. Their attitude toward Negroes and Puerto Ricans ranges from cold indifference to outright racist. When you do find a cop who is not like this, you find an exceptional human being. Mainly, however, the police reflect what nearly every other white person in New York always has felt about the racial problem. Historically, the New York public wanted the police to keep all Negroes where they were, and beat them if you want, and let's not hear any more about it. Now in a space of a couple of years, the big politicians and the influential people have decided they have consciences. Laws, and informed opinion, now demand freedom and equality for the Negro. And above all, stop beating them.

The policeman doesn't know where the hell he is. He rarely reads much. Brought up to believe in the flag and patriotism, he is suddenly assigned to a peace demonstration. Brought up and encouraged to despise Negroes, he is assigned to walk among them and somebody cuts an order saying he should understand them. Blind fury always is just under the surface of a blue uniform. The only way to get through a situation is with tight control. In New York, where there is a heritage of police supervision, 250,000 people marched in a peace parade and there were no incidents. Left alone in Chicago, the police rioted. The Mayor of Chicago has spent his time since extolling their actions. He guarantees the city more uncontrolled violence from its police.

In New York, a group of policemen once formed a thing called the Law Enforcement Group. One day some members of this outfit, with this blind fury inside them, showed up in court in Brooklyn wearing street clothes and George Wallace buttons and as-

SOURCE: *New York Post*, September 9, 1968.

saulted Negroes who were members of a small group known as the Black Panthers.

And two candidates for the Presidency of the United States came out in front of the nation and talked about cops as if they're really career foreign service officers of the State Department.

Anything a presidential candidate does or says or promises is not going to affect one minute of the tour of a patrolman in the 80th Precinct in Brooklyn. His worry is the sergeant, not the White House. So it seems to be a poor way to help a country, this business of reducing national issues and trying to put them all in the hands of some working guy making under $10,000 who has a wife and kids at home and still will put up his life for you and all he really wants is a pension.

The Contract

LESLIE WALLER

"I should think," Palmer said, "that you'd want to be fresh as a daisy for Big Vic Culhane."

Burns winced. "Don't call him that, please. I've been trying to lose that nickname for five years now."

"Negative public relations?"

"It's a lousy image. Sounds like a big city political boss or something."

"Well, he's big and he's Vic and he's a political boss."

"That's the trouble," Burns said. "He isn't."

"Come, now."

"Nobody is, any more," Burns assured him. "The breed died out during World War II."

"You aren't serious, are you?"

"Of course I am. Who have you got today to match a Tweed, a Hague, a Pendergast, a Croker? They don't make them that way any more."

"Not as blatantly," Palmer agreed. "But they still make them."

"Who? Jake Arvey in Chicago? Can you compare Jake's power to the kind Ed Kelly or Bill Thompson used to have? DeSapio in New York? His party's chopped right down the middle between the Tammany people and the ADA'ers. Which spells disaster for DeSapio."

SOURCE: *The Banker* (Garden City, N.Y.: Doubleday, 1963). Copyright © 1963 by Leslie Waller. Reprinted by permission of Doubleday & Company, Inc.

"Nevertheless," Palmer insisted, "when you want something done, you go to a man like that. He gets it done and he's the only one who can."

Burns shrugged and picked up his martini, "L'chiam," he said.

"Cheers." They sipped for a moment.

"I guess . . ." Burns paused and sipped again. "I guess it's about time we started your political education, Woody."

"Am I that ignorant?"

"Not as much as the average person, no. But that's not much of a compliment. The average person is an abysmal idiot who thinks politics is the way governments are run."

"And it isn't?"

"It isn't, no." Burns opened his pack of British cigarettes and took one out, staring at it thoughtfully for a moment. "It's a business. It's a way of making a living. It's a way to become somebody important and get paid handsomely for doing it."

"But, along the way, governments do get run, I should hope."

"That's a by-product of politics," Burns said. "The real business of politics is making a living."

"Pretty cynical."

"All right," Burns agreed. "I don't mind being cynical if it helps me see a thing straight." He shot his cuffs before lighting his cigarette, so that the flame of his lighter twinkled among the jeweled links.

"Like any other business," he went on then, blowing smoke into the air before him and patting it away, "the life blood of politics is the contract. Now, in politics, that word doesn't mean exactly what it means in other businesses. A contract . . ." He paused and squinted out into the dimly lighted room. "When I saw Vic for breakfast, I was carrying three contracts. A young guy from my old district up in the Bronx needed a job. That's one contract. A trotting track is opening upstate next month and they want Vic as a dais guest. That's the second. A friend of a friend is opening a store and needs a license fast. That's three."

"None of them sound too difficult."

"They're not. Now, watch this. Vic hands me two contracts in return. He wants to have a new building at one of the Catholic colleges named after his father. That's one. He also wants to know when a certain stock is going to be dumped so he can dump on time, too. That's the second. You follow?"

"Certainly."

"Stick with me. It gets a little tricky. Now, we've mentioned five contracts. Let's take any one of them. Let's say the stock thing. I now have this contract from Vic. I pick up a phone and ask my broker what he knows. He now has a contract from me. But maybe he can't deliver. My problem is I must deliver. So I make a lunch date with a vice-president in the company whose stock we're dealing with. That's the second phase of the same contract. In order to get the straight word from him, I have to offer something. What? I don't have the slightest idea. The lunch is for the sole purpose of finding out. Maybe he wants special plates on his car. Maybe he wants to be an honorary commissioner. Maybe he wants a season pass to one of the tracks. Maybe he needs a big redhead. Maybe he doesn't even know the answer to my first question, the one I haven't even asked yet. So I also call a market editor on one of the papers. He hears things. But to get information from him, I have to shell out information on something else. You follow this? One of Vic's contracts, just one, leads to at least three others."

"Sounds intricate as hell."

"Oh, this is nothing. Take one of the contracts I gave Vic. Let's say, the guy who wants the license."

"That shouldn't be too complicated for Culhane."

"No? Let's look at his alternatives. First of all, how hard should he try? I've told him it's a friend of a friend who needs the license, but I deliberately haven't told him how badly I need the contract. My reason for not telling him is simple. I happen to need it badly because the friend of mine is a client, a big one, and his friend who needs the license is a good-for-nothing cousin of his wife's who's a mill-

stone around his neck. If the cousin gets the license, he's off my client's neck and my client loves me. And his contract with my firm comes up for renewal next month. And he's a fifty-grand client. But if Vic knows how badly I need this license, it'll go down in his book as a major contract. He'll call it due someday by asking a major contract of me. And I'll have to deliver."

"I had no idea you—"

"Woody," Burns interrupted, "I haven't even started yet. This is all wind-up. Vic has to decide how hard he should try for the license, how much he's going to give away to get me what I ask. I'm a close friend, an old friend. We depend on each other. But my guess is he won't try as hard as he could. He'll try, because we're friends, but he won't try as hard as if I'd made it a major contract."

"Then you might not get the license."

"Possible. Not probable, but possible. I have to take that chance. Owing Vic a major contract is more to be avoided, at this point, than disappointing my client and his nitwit cousin."

"Why at this point?"

"I'll get to that later," Burns assured him. "Now. We assume that Vic decides to give it a good try, but not his best. He has the following ways of doing it. One, he calls his man at the board and asks what state the license is in now. The board guy tells him and Vic signs off, knowing that his man knows that Vic is interested in speeding along this particular application. So the board guy moves it up a little faster, not much, because Vic hasn't definitely given him that contract, but he does what he can. Two, Vic can call one of his State assemblymen or senators and ask him to put the pressure on the board. That way the assemblyman makes the contract with the board guy. He owes Vic his job as assemblyman, so he cancels part of his debt by building a fire under the board. Now, at some future date, nobody knows when, the assemblyman's contract with the board will have to be paid off. God Himself doesn't know what the board guy will ask for. But the assemblyman will either have to fill the contract on his own, or come running to Vic for help. Three, Vic can call one of the big distributing combines. These outfits live by trucking and being able to park in No Parking zones. They need police protection for their warehouses. They're vulnerable as hell without political help. At the same time, they have a great deal of power. They can make or break a store by the way they handle credit and deliveries. The board tries to keep the stores status quo. They don't like bankruptcies. It rocks the boat. They listen to the big distributors. If one of these outfits takes a personal interest in the license application, it moves up fast. Four, Vic can—"

"Hold up," Palmer cut in, "My head's beginning to swim."

"All right. But Vic has at least six ways of helping that license along without giving away too much leverage. If I'd made it a major contract, he'd have one other way, foolproof." Burns swallowed the remainder of his martini in one gulp. "That's about enough for your first lesson in politics."

"And you discussed five contracts this morning?"

"Five. By the time all of them have been fulfilled, there'll be a good fifteen more made as a result of the first five."

"A geometrical progression. Where does it end?"

"It never ends," Burns said. "Political contracts hop into bed and breed two or three for every one. I must handle ten a day. In a week's time, that's about sixty. Those sixty breed another, let's say, hundred and fifty. And those hundred and fifty breed at least three hundred. And those three hundred. . . . And, mind you, I'm just one guy. I'm a key guy," he added abruptly, "but I'm only one."

"Fantastic," Palmer said, sipping his martini. "Under the surface of this town, more things go on than the mind of man can possibly grasp."

"It's a live little village," Burns agreed. "I put in ten years in an even livelier town, Hollywood, but it was nothing to this." He looked up, snapped his fingers and nodded to a passing waiter. "What's good today, Henry?"

"The boiled beef is very good, Mr. Burns."

"All right. With horseradish sauce. Woody?"

"Lentil soup," Palmer said. "And, us, oh . . ."

"Roast-beef sandwich?" Burns suggested.

"Might not be bad."

"On rye, Henry," Burns told the waiter. "And two more martinis."

Palmer sat there and watched Burns play with his cuff links, smooth down his yellow hair, stub out his cigarette, glance at his watch and then make a quick survey of the room. Palmer decided that it wasn't important enough to resent the suggestion of a roast-beef sandwich and the ordering of two more drinks which would have to be consumed after the food had arrived. The important thing with Burns, he told himself now, was not to let anything unimportant he did bother you. If you got thrown by the trivial things about him that were irritating, you would end up hating him. And that would never do.

"Tell me," Palmer heard himself saying then, "do you believe that people pay for the enjoyable things of life?"

Burns turned to face him. His rather large eyes looked warily into Palmer's.

"Pay?" he asked. "I don't get you."

"Nothing. Just thinking out loud."

"Tell me."

Palmer made a meaningless gesture with his hand, angry at himself for having spoken so unguardedly. "It's nothing," he said again. "I just wondered about it, that's all. When you enjoy something in life, you usually pay for it later in some rather dire way. Just an observation."

"You still haven't answered my question, though."

"I don't know the answer," Burns responded. "I know what it's like in politics, though. For everything you get, you pay. It's all one big horse trade, Woody. You want something? You have to give the other fella what he wants."

Palmer took one of Burns's British cigarettes and lighted it quickly, before Burns could bring out his own lighter. "Which reminds me," Palmer said, inhaling smoke and finding it so mild that it might have been heated air. "Why don't you want to pin Vic Culhane down to any major contract at this time?"

"I'm saving him, pally."

"For what?"

"For you, sweetheart," Burns said. He sighed and pursed his lips in a most unhappy way. "Just for you."

Patterns of Police Corruption

Introduction

At the time of the Commission's investigation, police corruption was found to be an extensive, Department-wide phenomenon, indulged in to some degree by a sizable majority of those on the force and protected by a code of silence on the part of those who remained honest.*

Police Corruption: A Historical View

The Commission's findings were hardly new. As long ago as 1844, when the state legislature created the New York police force as the first municipal police department in the country, historians record an immediate problem with extortion and other corrupt activities engaged in by police officers.

Since that time, the New York Police Department has been the subject of numerous corruption scandals followed by investigations. In each case, the investigators turned up substantial evidence of corruption, which was greeted by public expressions of shock and outrage. While some reforms usually followed each of these periodic scandals, the basic pattern of corrupt behavior was never substantially affected and after the heat was off, it was largely back to business as usual.

In March, 1894, in response to allegations of police corruption made by commercial and reform organizations, a New York State Senate committee, financed by private organizations because of the state's refusal to provide funding, conducted an investigation of the New York Police Department.

SOURCE: *The Knapp Commission Report on Police Corruption* (N.Y.: George Braziller, 1973), pp. 61–69.

*The Commission's investigation ended on October 18, 1971, the day the first public hearings began. In discussions of the existence and extent of corruption, this report speaks as of that date—unless otherwise clearly indicated.

The committee, known as the Lexow Committee, found systematic police extortion of "disorderly houses," systematic payoffs by gambling operations to policemen throughout the City, and payoffs by organized confidence games. The committee also found that small grocery stores, builders, and "all classes of persons whose business is subject to the observation of the police, or who may be reported as violating ordinances, or who may require the aid of the police, all have to contribute in substantial sums to the vast amounts which flow into the station-houses . . ."

Seventeen years later, following the Times Square murder of a gambler who had reported police corruption to the newspapers, the Board of Aldermen (predecessor of the City Council) appointed a committee, headed by Henry Curran, to investigate the police. The committee found that corruption and inefficiency in the Department were in large part due to administrative methods which made intelligent direction and accountability impossible. The committee found systematic monthly police extortion of gambling and brothel operations, made possible by weak discipline and a failure of supervision within the Department. It found that the Department was hostile to civilian complaints, and that the police commissioner was not aware of the most important complaints. The aldermanic committee recommended, among other things, the establishment of an internal security squad, composed of men other than policemen, to secure evidence of police corruption.

A citizens' committee working at the same time reported that "corruption is so ingrained that the man of ordinary decent character entering the force and not possessed of extraordinary moral fiber may easily succumb." That committee recommended, among other things, separation of vice control from the constabulary forces of the police.

Some twenty years later, on January 25, 1932, Samuel Seabury, counsel to a committee appointed pursuant to a joint resolution adopted by the state legislature, reported the same condition of police corruption to committee chairman Samuel H. Hofstadter. The committee was granted special powers to grant immunity to witnesses and found that the

Police Department was deeply involved in extorting large sums from speakeasies, bootleggers, and gamblers.

On September 15, 1950, Harry Gross, the head of a mammoth New York City gambling syndicate, was arrested and subsequently agreed to cooperate with the district attorney. Having indicated his willingness to tell the district attorney and the grand jury about the police officers who protected his bookmaking operation, he was brought in for questioning. After giving his early background, he told of his first arrangements with members of the Police Department in the early 1940s. . . .

The intricate workings of the system need not be detailed. Payoffs were made to each squad which had responsibility for the suppression of gambling. In addition, hundreds of personal gifts of television sets, suits, furs, jewelry, theater tickets, and cars were given to members of the Department. The payoff system was most notable for its sheer magnitude: One million dollars was paid annually to the police for protection, in addition to numerous personal gifts. . . .

Studies of police corruption in other cities have likewise uncovered systematic police extortion of bookmakers, mutuel racehorse policy operators, brothels and prostitutes, and legitimate businesses.

It seems that the pressures upon policemen, the nature of the job, and the inevitable temptations are similar enough in any large municipal police department at any time to give rise to the kinds of problems found by this Commission and its predecessors.

Grass-Eaters and Meat-Eaters

Corrupt policemen have been informally described as being either "grass-eaters" or "meat-eaters." The overwhelming majority of those who do take payoffs are grass-eaters, who accept gratuities and solicit five- and ten- and twenty-dollar payments from contractors, tow-truck operators, gamblers, and the like, but do not aggressively pursue corruption payments. "Meat-eaters," probably only a small percentage of the force, spend a good deal of their working hours aggressively seeking out situations they can exploit for financial gain, including gambling, narcotics, and other serious offenses which can yield payments of thousands of dollars. Patrolman William Phillips was certainly an example of this latter category.

One strong impetus encouraging grass-eaters to continue to accept relatively petty graft is, ironically, their feeling of loyalty to their fellow officers. Accepting payoff money is one way for an officer to prove that he is one of the boys and that he can be trusted. In the climate which existed in the Department during the Commission's investigation, at least at the precinct level, these numerous but relatively small payoffs were a fact of life, and those officers who made a point of refusing them were not accepted closely into the fellowship of policemen. Corruption among grass-eaters obviously cannot be met by attempting to arrest them all and will probably diminish only if Commissioner Murphy is successful in his efforts to change the rank and file attitude toward corruption.

No change in attitude, however, is likely to affect a meat-eater, whose yearly income in graft amounts to many thousands of dollars and who may take payoffs of $5,000 or even $50,000 in one fell swoop (former Assistant Chief Inspector Sydney Cooper, who had been active in anti-corruption work for years, recently stated that the largest score of which he had heard—although he was unable to verify it—was a narcotics payoff involving $250,000). Such men are willing to take considerable risks as long as the potential profit remains so large. Probably the only way to deal with them will be to ferret them out individually and get them off the force, and, hopefully, into prisons.

Pads, Scores, and Gratuities

Corruption payments made to the police may be divided into "pad" payments and "scores," two police slang terms which make an important distinction.

The "pad" refers to regular weekly, biweekly, or monthly payments, usually picked up by a police bagman and divided among fellow officers. Those who make such payments as well as policemen who receive them are referred to as being "on the pad."

A "score" is a one-time payment that an officer might solicit from, for example, a motorist or a narcotics violator. The term is also used as a verb, as in "I scored him for $1,500."

A third category of payments to the police is that of gratuities, which the Commission feels cannot in the strictest sense be considered a matter of police corruption, but which has been included here because it is a related—and ethically borderline—practice, which is prohibited by Department regulations, and which often leads to corruption.

Operations on the pad are generally those which operate illegally in a fixed location day in and day out. Illegal gambling is probably the single largest source of pad payments. The most important legitimate enterprises on the pad at the time of the investigation were those like construction, licensed premises, and businesses employing large numbers of vehicles, all of which operate from fixed locations and are subject to summonses from the police for myriad violations.

Scores, on the other hand, are made whenever the opportunity arises—most often when an officer happens to spot someone engaging in an illegal activity like pushing narcotics, which doesn't involve a fixed location. Those whose activities are generally legal but who break the law occasionally, like motorists or tow-truck operators, are also subject to scores. By far the most lucrative source of scores is the City's multimillion-dollar narcotics business.

Factors Influencing Corruption

There are at least five major factors which influence how much or how little graft an officer receives, and also what his major sources are. The most important of these is, of course, the character of the officer in question, which will determine whether he bucks the system and refuses all corruption money; goes along with the system and accepts what comes his way; or outdoes the system, and aggressively seeks corruption-prone situations and exploits them to the extent that it seriously cuts into the time available for doing his job. His character will also determine what kind of graft he accepts. Some officers, who don't think twice about accepting money from gamblers, refuse to have anything at all to do with narcotics pushers. They make a distinction between what they call "clean money" and "dirty money."

The second factor is the branch of the Department to which an officer is assigned. A plainclothesman, for example, has more—and different—opportunities than a uniformed patrolman.

The third factor is the area to which an officer is assigned. At the time of the investigation certain precincts in Harlem, for instance, comprised what police officers called "the Gold Coast" because they contained so many payoff-prone activities, numbers and narcotics being the biggest. In contrast, the Twenty-Second Precinct, which is Central Park, has clearly limited payoff opportunities. As Patrolman Phillips remarked, "What can you do, shake down the squirrels?" The area also determines the major sources of corruption payments. For instance, in midtown Manhattan precincts businessmen and motorists were major sources; on the Upper East Side, bars and construction; in the ghetto precincts, narcotics, and numbers.

The fourth factor is the officer's assignment. For uniformed men, a seat in a sector car was considered fairly lucrative in most precincts, while assignment to stand guard duty outside City Hall obviously was not, and assignment to one sector of a precinct could mean lots of payoffs from construction sites while in another sector bar owners were the big givers.

The fifth factor is rank. For those who do receive payoffs, the amount generally ascends with the rank. A bar may give $5 to patrolmen, $10 to sergeants, and considerably more to a captain's bagman. Moreover, corrupt supervisors have the opportunity to cut into much of the graft normally collected by those under them.

Sources of Payoffs

Organized crime is the single biggest source of police corruption, through its control of the City's gambling, narcotics, loansharking, and illegal sex-related enterprises like homosexual afterhours bars and pornography, all of which the Department considers mob-run. These endeavors are so highly lucrative that large payments to the police are considered a good investment if they protect the business from undue police interference.

The next largest source is legitimate business seeking to ease its way through the maze of City ordinances and regulations. Major offenders are construction contractors and subcontractors, liquor licensees, and managers of businesses like trucking firms and parking lots, which are likely to park large numbers of vehicles illegally. If the police were completely honest, it is likely that members of these groups would seek to corrupt them, since most seem to feel that paying off the police is easier and cheaper than obeying the laws or paying fines and answering summonses when they do violate the laws. However, to the extent police resist corruption, business interests will be compelled to use their political muscle to bring about revision of the regulations to make them workable.

Two smaller sources of payments to the police are private citizens, like motorists caught breaking the

law, and small-time criminals like gypsy fortune tellers, purse-snatchers, and pickpockets who may attempt to buy their freedom from an arresting officer. . . .

The Impact of Bureaucracy on Attempts to Prevent Police Corruption

JOSEPH D. MCNAMARA

Police Corruption: The Historical Perspective

The first American police forces were established a relatively short time ago. Approximately 130 years ago, the first urban police force was started in New York City. Shortly thereafter, the City of Boston established a full-time "professional" police force, and other cities soon followed. Almost from the beginning, these urban experiments in policing had great trouble with corruption of those charged with enforcement. Political domination and partisanship interfered with the enforcement of law and, with few exceptions, the pattern continued until the mid-1950s when the first sustained police reform efforts began in the United States.

Corruption plagued Western towns as well as the older Eastern cities. Contrary to the accepted folklore about Old-West heroes, it was usually a simple matter to buy the sheriff in most western towns. For example, Lou Blonger arrived in Denver in 1880 when he was just a bit older than 20 and Denver was still a frontier town. He set up a saloon and dance hall, became involved in crime, and was soon involved in Denver's dusty underworld of that era. He paid off

the law from the very beginning. A direct line of communication between his office and that of the chief of police was set up. On Blonger's orders men were arrested and freed.

Police corruption in other areas is also well documented. In 1902, *McClure's* magazine commissioned Lincoln Steffens to investigate the conditions of municipal governments. As a result, he wrote six articles which became the classic, *The Shame of the Cities*. He found police corruption growing like a cancer in many cities. One full article was devoted to politics and police in Minneapolis. He wrote that in 1901 Alfred Elisha Ames, a physician, took office as mayor of Minneapolis. He laid plans, Steffens wrote, to turn the city over to outlaws. He made his brother chief of police, and named a former gambler chief of detectives. The three dismissed 107 men from the force as officers who could not be trusted to go along with corruption and charged the rest of the 225-man force a fee for the privilege of being retained. With the machinery built, Ames took over. Gambling, prostitution, pickpocketing and cardsharping were supervised by the detective division. Criminals negotiated with city officials for crime concessions—available for a fee—with monthly rent paid to the police.

In other United States cities such as Boston and New York, the development of powerful, corrupt political machines in the latter half of the nineteenth century obstructed efforts to develop police integrity. Police departments were weak and vulnerable to political pressures. Machine politicians found police forces to be among the most easily corrupted arms of

SOURCE: Paper presented before the American Psychological Association, New Orleans, Louisiana, August 30, 1974.

municipal government. Police departments became vehicles for political patronage; and direct involvement in crime by police, with some of the proceeds going to political bosses, was made a fine art. Also, police law enforcement was used on a partisan basis. Political allies were allowed to violate the law while opponents were arrested and harassed. The democratic process itself was subverted.

Political scientists analyzing the pervasive dishonesty in urban American government of this period have spotlighted factors they felt to be important in causing the corrupt conditions. They pointed out that the inherent American distrust of powerful government led to the development of a decentralized system with fragmented power. The concept of checks and balances was extended even to the local government, which meant that corrupt politicians who could cut through red tape were valuable to impatient entrepreneurs eager to get things done. Thus, there was a functional aspect to local government corruption inherent in the birth of a dynamic industrial society.

Robert K. Merton has pointed out that the corrupt political machine also possessed the latent function of providing necessary social mobility for immigrant groups. The existence of underlying class bias cannot be ignored in studying the history of municipal corruption. The early probers and reformers tended to be "nativists" while those they exposed were invariably "ethnics." Thus developed one of the common rationalizations to excuse police corruption. The ethnics often believed that the upper class was economically exploiting the working class and that police corruption was no worse than unethical business practices they felt were endemic to the upper class. The urban political machines, of course, exacerbated the class bias for their own benefit.

Since the machines usually encouraged and protected police corruption, it is no surprise that political independence for police became a key component of reform programs. However, more recent exposés of police corruption where political involvement was absent demonstrate that political independence is not a panacea.

Ironically, one characteristic of politically independent police organizations, namely, civil service personnel systems, are now identified by some police administrators as obstructions to reform efforts. These administrators charge that they are hindered by restrictive regulations in developing leadership which shapes a climate intolerant of corruption.

Although police domination by corrupt political machines is no longer the problem it once was, its historical importance cannot be minimized. Police tolerance for corruption is a political legacy. Reform is possible only when the old climate tolerant of corruption is destroyed.

The Police Bureaucracy

Suggestions for police reform have been essentially bureaucratic in nature. Perhaps one reason for the lack of complete success in police reform movements was the inability of the reformers to fully comprehend the complexities of organizational behavior. Fundamentally, the reformers believed that if an honest, politically independent police administrator were given the formal authority he would be able to purge corrupt officers from the ranks and achieve complete integrity within the organization.

Their solution is bureaucratically naive. President Truman summarized the problem succinctly when he said about his successor: "Poor Ike, he'll give an order and then be surprised when nothing happens." In other words, while legal authority is important to the administrator, it guarantees nothing. Unless the administrator is able to cope with the dynamic forces present in every organization, his achievements in preventing corruption will be marginal.

The first intellectual to study organizational behavior was Max Weber, the German theorist whose classic work on the characteristics of bureaucracy still influences students of large organizations. As early as the turn of the century, Weber foresaw the enormous impact of large organizations on individual freedom and life in both democracies and other systems of government. Weber identified key characteristics of bureaucracy which he held to be inherent in the efficient functioning of large organizations. As Weber saw it, such organizations were characterized by: a clear-cut division of labor, definitely placed responsibility for the performance of tasks, specialized experts, a hierarchical structure, formal rules, impersonal treatment of both employees and clients, recruitment of officials on the basis of ability and technical knowledge, and employee career status with protection from arbitrary dismissal. It is readily apparent that most police organizations fit Weber's paradigm.

On the face of it, the organizational characteristics identified by Weber would appear to support a corruption-free police system. Indeed, many of the reform suggestions closely parallel Weber's organizational components. For example, civil service personnel systems and political independence for the police are quite similar to recruitment based upon ability, and tenured career systems. And, a presidential task force report did, in fact, recommend definite responsibility for corruption control, specialized vice enforcement, a responsible hierarchical structure, formal rules, increased emphasis on ability and training, and other improvements quite similar to the "ideal typical" Weberian model.

It would have helped if the reform suggestions also reflected the more sophisticated views of organizational behavior provided by behavioral scientists who expanded upon Weber's work. Out of their studies came the concept of *dysfunction*. Simply stated, a dysfunction occurs when formal procedures set by large organizations produce behavior contrary to the achievement of organizational goals. Relating this concept, Weber's paradigm and police anti-corruption efforts yield a more complicated, but at the same time more valuable, view of police corruption problems.

The Crime Commission Recommendations

In 1964 the presidential campaign of the United States centered to some extent on "crime in the streets" as a key issue. Consequently, President Johnson appointed a prestigious crime commission which in 1965 through 1967 published the *President's Crime Commission Task Force Reports*, gathering together the best of expert opinion and practical experience in all of the areas of criminal justice.

One of the Commission's important reform suggestions was that all police organizations confront the problem of corruption by establishing an internal affairs unit. This would be the watchdog of the organization, a unit that polices the police in areas of corrupt practices.

And so, it was not unnatural that this important suggestion became the keystone in the approach to controlling police corruption. And yet a great deal of attention still focuses on police corruption. We find city after city having widely publicized problems of corruption with its police force. Arguments rage back and forth over the extent of the corruption. How

pervasive is it? Is it a few rotten apples or is it a norm? I suspect that these questions will continue for some time. But one danger that I think has come out of the many investigations and reform attempts is a mechanical approach to the problem of police corruption. One purpose of this seminar in which we are participating is to look deeper for fundamental causes. It is also important to develop a reform methodology which focuses on causes and avoids the pitfalls of excessive publicity and emotional dialogue on the extent and propriety of reform measures.

It is quite possible that the establishment of internal affairs units was actually dysfunctional in some police agencies in the United States. Attendant publicity was in some cases bitterly resented by rank and file officers as an attack on their integrity. Residual ill feeling toward management blocked the development of an anti-corruption climate.

In addition, the commonly shared danger and negative working conditions, such as unfair public criticism and hostility of minority groups, inherent in police work, together with the need for the police to cooperate and to perform as a team during moments of crisis and danger, contributed to the formation of a police subculture. As a result, internal affairs investigators have often been frustrated in their efforts to uncover corrupt officers by noncorrupt officers, whose personal values are contrary to those of the corrupt officers yet who are reluctant to participate in efforts to expose and prosecute corrupt officers because subculture norms condemn such activity.

Another danger in establishing internal affairs units is that such a division of labor may cause other personnel to shun their responsibilities to prevent corruption or to report it where prevention has failed. In addition, internal affairs units can easily fall into the dysfunctional practice of goal displacement, whereby the goal of preventing corruption can be displaced by one of producing a sufficient number of cases to avoid managerial criticism. Recent headlines reveal that the existence of an internal affairs unit is, like the other measures, no guarantee of reform. In fact, some past investigations indicated that internal affairs personnel, due to their assignment, collected more graft than other officers.

Another characteristic of large organizations identified by Weber is a hierarchical structure by which an organization's activities are controlled and directed. This, too, can be a negative factor in terms of corruption. Younger officers occupying lower positions in the organization may be personally desirous of being honest and having integrity. But they often may be forced into dishonest practices or to ignore corrupt practices because of the existence of this very hierarchical structure. This may occur when some of the people occupying higher positions are tolerant of corruption. The unfortunate truth is that, in many urban police agencies of the past, officers who opposed corrupt practices fell into disfavor with their superiors and were subjected arbitrarily and unfairly to discipline. Thus a force perpetuating corruption can flow from the very characteristic which Weber identified as being inherent in large organizations and which the crime commission saw as a reform measure.

Peer-Group Pressure

I think the idea that should be clear to us after this discussion of organizational dynamics is that we cannot look solely for mechanical formulas to prevent police corruption effectively, just as we cannot expect the police to be the primary factor in preventing citizens from committing crimes. Similarly, we should not expect the units which police the police to keep officers from dishonest practices such as corruption. Citizens, for the most part, refrain from committing crime because they have a personal value system which condemns this activity. They respond to peer-group pressure—the strongest influence of all. Therefore, the key to any police corruption control must be, quite simply, positive peer-group pressure.

Many of the committees investigating police corruption of the past described very vividly how officers were socialized into corrupt practices—in other words, how they responded to peer pressure to become corrupt. Therefore, the essence of the problem in controlling and preventing police corruption involves developing peer group attitudes that are intolerant of corruption. To be sure, the organization must still have an internal affairs unit and other organizational procedures which will combine with peer group pressure to reinforce the concept that corruption within the organization will not be tolerated. But the most important factor in the prevention of police corruption will be the rank-and-file attitude of police officers' condemning corruption as being wrong and contrary to their own code of behavior.

Having identified this essential factor in police corruption control, it is still difficult to describe how one establishes that climate. Investigations of police corruption have revealed too frequently that the heads of the agencies have been personally honest and opposed to corruption but, nevertheless, have been unable to establish an adequate anti-corruption climate within their department.

The Kansas City, Missouri, Experience

The Kansas City, Missouri, Police Department enjoys a national reputation for integrity and freedom from corruption. There are 1,300 police officers in the department and, we know, given the qualities of human nature and the law of averages, that from time to time there are bound to be individual cases of corruption within that large a group.

In my first year as the chief administrator of the department, I have been enormously impressed by not only the willingness but also the determination of the personnel to report possible corrupt actions by fellow officers. In several cases, patrolmen and detectives have provided information which led to the separation of other officers for corrupt practices. In a number of cases, officers on other investigations received information from informants or from citizens which indicated that police officers were engaging in corrupt practices. They promptly reported that information to the internal affairs unit, although they could easily have withheld the information without exposure. Although the information usually proved to be false, one has to be impressed by this behavior since investigations into some police agencies have revealed that one of the significant problems in rooting out and preventing police corruption is the reluctance of honest officers to report other officers.

The question arises: How does such a climate come into being? We must be honest and say that at one time Kansas City's Police Department was probably much like other departments which had corruption problems and, for that matter, still have corruption problems. Kansas City is, after all, the city which the Pendergast machine controlled for a number of years.

I have searched in vain during the last year for any unusual organizational structures, procedures, or programs which prevent corruption. In short, I can find no magical solutions for bringing about an anticorruption climate.

It was apparent that in 1961 when Clarence Kelley, now the director of the Federal Bureau of Investigation, was named chief, the department did have a corruption problem; several high-ranking officers were under indictment. There seemed to be some tolerance for corruption both within the department and among the citizenry. In addition, all the factors which contribute to corruption were present: police salaries were low; the prestige of the force, compared with present levels, was low; and the negative aspects of police work and frustrations of the police were very similar to those in other cities.

Yet, during his twelve years as chief, Director Kelley succeeded in creating a climate totally intolerant of corruption. Peer-group pressure discourages all but a minimum level of corruption, and there is no opposition to internal affairs investigations or disciplinary procedures related to corruption.

I asked Director Kelley how he did it, and in his reply he spoke of pride of leadership. Kelley was able to bring this pride into the area of departmental and personal integrity. He emphasized that it took time, that a constant effort was necessary to instill it and to reinforce it. He also noted the importance of a policy of periodic transfers from sensitive positions where there was greater danger of corruption. And, he mentioned that the department's performance during the 1968 civil disorders had provided the organization with a sense of unity because the police had been able to restore order quickly and with the confidence of the majority of the city's citizens. Further, he noted, pride fed itself. The department's national reputation for integrity was known to the officers.

It is also worth noting that the director felt that the city itself supported good government and professional law enforcement. It is a city free from machine politics. The department exists under a form of indirect state control in which the governor appoints four distinguished citizens as police commissioners. The mayor serves as an ex-officio member of the board of commissioners.

To some extent, the department is operationally independent of the city manager and the city council. On the other hand, there is a form of city control. The department's budget must be approved and its operational and capital funds supplied by the city government. Therefore, the responsiveness of the department to the community is great, although there is no direct control over police operations by the city manager and city council. The state government through the general assembly exercises marginal control through the ability to pass legislation amending the department's pay structure and career and pension plans. The governor appoints each commissioner for four-year terms at staggered intervals and in reality exercises no direct control at all. The complete policy responsibility rests with the five police commissioners who have the authority to hire and fire the police chief, as well as to adjust salary ranges internally. The police chief serves at the pleasure of the board without a contract.

Thus far, we have identified some of the factors which brought about something of a revolution in terms of a climate of integrity in the Kansas City, Missouri, Police Department. We cannot minimize the impact that the chief's positive leadership has on establishing a climate intolerant of corruption. I think it is worth noting that Clarence Kelley became chief after a twenty-year career in the Federal Bureau of Investigation, an agency which has long been noted for its freedom from corruption. And, in a sense, Kelley's achievement was that he succeeded in establishing the same intolerant climate for corruption in the Kansas City, Missouri, Police Department that exists in the Federal Bureau of Investigation.

Summary

I think we have identified a number of sound practices which accompany and reinforce the determination to prevent corruption. The presence of an objective internal affairs unit was also important in indicating the chief's determination to root out and to prevent corruption. The support of the community for a professional police agency and for programs to prevent any kind of police corruption was also important. And, awareness of the potential danger of corruption led to the formation of a wise policy of rotation of assignment in positions sensitive to corruption.

But the primary factor was the emphasis on pride, which created a climate of intolerance of corruption. The emphasis was on peer-group pressure to prevent corruption and not on an internal affairs unit which, if used unwisely, could easily have destroyed positive attitudes, led to anti-management feeling, and to the unfortunate practice which we know exists in many police agencies: the rank-and-file cover-up of corrupt practices.

In summary, there are no magic bureaucratic formulas for the prevention of corruption. If one has to identify the single most important factor, judging from the success of Clarence Kelley, it has to be stated that it is the enlightened leadership of the chief in establishing peer pressure against corruption.

Police Corruption:

A Commentary

JOHN J. SULLIVAN

_____

Corruption in the public service, and particularly in police agencies, is a matter of grave concern to all. Unfortunately, it seems that it has always been with us, and it is doubtful if we will ever reach the Utopian stage of no corruption.

We have been witnesses to high-ranking officials and judicial officers on both federal and local levels being involved in corrupt activities.

Our prison system has not been free from allegations of payoffs and transactions involving drugs and sex.

In 1961 the Denver Police Department was shaken by a scandal involving a burglary ring of police officers. Seattle, Washington, was involved in a scandal relating to payoffs to police from a vice ring. In 1974 the Philadelphia police were accused of engaging in criminal practices at all levels of the city police force. Sixty police officers have been indicted in Chicago and several Chicago commanders were relieved of their posts because they refused to take lie detector tests. In the first three months of 1975, allegations of corruption have been made against the police force of the New York City Transit Authority; detectives in the City of Mount Vernon in Westchester County, New York; and ten members of the Orange, New Jersey, Police Department as well as their commissioner of public safety.

_____

SOURCE: This paper was written expressly for inclusion in this book.

The various studies on police corruption cite many different reasons for the existence of this condition. David Burnham, correspondent for the New York Times, stated, "The evidence is overwhelming, the thin blue line often is crooked, and in many cities the pattern of corruption is strikingly similar. The corruption usually begins with businessmen making small and apparently harmless payments, referred to as 'clean graft' in New York and 'safe notes' in Philadelphia."(1)

The Knapp Commission says that organized crime is the single biggest source of police corruption through its control of gambling, narcotics, loansharking, and so forth. The next largest source, they claim, is legitimate business seeking to ease its way through local ordinances and regulations.(2)

Many zero in on the victimless crimes, such as gambling and prostitution. It is argued that these crimes do not reflect a true picture of society's moral standards.(3) There is a public demand for the services, and even though they are illegal, there are those who are willing to provide the service. Since the forbidden fruit is expensive and profitable, the people involved are willing to pay for protection. It is easy for a police officer to rationalize that since the service is in such demand, that the public doesn't care, and that the laws are unenforceable, he might as well share in the profits.

Another often-cited reason is that corruption is encouraged by arrest quotas. This in effect forces a police officer to perjure himself or to "flake" a defendant, that is, plant false evidence on him in order to "get on the sheet," or meet his quota.

In 1967, Irving Younger, a New York City civil court judge and former federal prosecutor, issued a blistering report in which he accused New York City plainclothes police officers of mass perjury in "drop-sies" cases. In this situation, a police officer would testify that as he approached a suspected bookmaker or policy writer, the suspect would drop the works to the ground, whereby the officer would then pick it up and seek to have it introduced into evidence as abandoned property. The judge cited countless affidavits that parroted the same fact pattern time and time again.(4)

It has also been said that in order for a conscientious policeman to perform his designated duties, he must often violate the very laws he is trying to enforce. In order to get the "bad guys" the police will justify illegal searches and seizures, flaking, perjury, and even, sometimes, excessive physical force. Some policemen thought that the restrictions imposed upon them by the Supreme Court in decisions such as *Mapp*, *Miranda*, and *Chimel* required them to think of new ways to play the game since the Court changed the rules. In some instances, department policy seemed to encourage such action.

In a monograph issued March 30, 1975, by the Police Foundation, Professor Herman Goldstein of Wisconsin University School of Law states, "Corruption is endemic to policing. The very nature of the police function is bound to subject officers to tempting offers."(5)

This is a disturbing proposition. If the statement is true, then it is not possible to ever eliminate corruption; it can just be controlled.

Forms of Corruption

Professor Ellwyn R. Stoddard of the Department of Sociology, University of Texas at El Paso, set forth the following definitions of several terms used to describe police deviancy, and which illustrate the wide spectrum of "blue-coat crime."(6) These practices are ranked so that those listed first would generally elicit the least fear of legal prosecution, while those listed last would invoke major legal sanctions for their perpetration.

Mooching Receiving free coffee, cigarettes, liquor, groceries, or other items either as a consequence of being in an underpaid, undercompensated profession or for the possible future acts of favoritism which might be received by the donor.

Chiseling Police demands for price discounts or free admission to entertainment whether connected to police duty or not.

Favoritism The use of license tabs, window stickers, or courtesy cards to gain immunity from traffic arrest or citation (sometimes extended to wives, families, and friends of recipient).

Prejudice Situations in which minority group members receive less than impartial, neutral, objective attention, especially those who are less likely to have enough "influence" in city hall to cause the arresting officer trouble.

Shopping The practice of picking up small items, such as candy bars, gum, or cigarettes, at a store where the door has been accidentally unlocked after business hours.

Extortion Demands made for advertisements in police magazines, or purchase of tickets to police functions, or "street courts," where minor traffic tickets can be avoided by the payment of cash bail to the arresting officer with no receipt required.

Bribery Payments of cash or "gifts" for past or future assistance to avoid prosecution. Such reciprocity might take the form of inability to make a positive identification of a criminal, or being in the wrong place at a given time when a crime is to occur, both of which might be excused as carelessness but not provable as to any deliberate miscarriage of justice. Differs from mooching in the higher value of the gifts and in the mutual understanding regarding services to be performed upon the acceptance of such gifts.

Shakedown The practice of appropriating expensive items for personal use and attributing it to criminal activity when investigating a break-in, a burglary, or an unlocked door. Differs from shopping in the value of the items and the ease by which former ownership of items can be determined if the officer is "caught" in the act of procurement.

Perjury The sanction of the "code" which demands that fellow officers lie to provide an alibi for fellow officers apprehended in unlawful activity covered by the code.

Premeditated theft Planned burglary, involving the use of tools, keys, etc., to gain forced entry, or a prearranged plan of unlawful acquisition of property which cannot be explained as a "spur-of-the-moment" theft. Differs from shakedown only in the previous arrangements surrounding the theft, not in the value of the items taken.

The definitions of "extortion," "shakedown," and "perjury" seem somewhat limited. Extortion generally means obtaining money or something of value by compulsion, force, or fear. A shakedown also involves receiving a payment either by bribery or extortion. Perjury involves false swearing or testimony.

Police administrators have become concerned in recent years about the increase in the number of cases involving "dirty money." Years ago, an officer "on the take" would distinguish between "clean money" and "dirty money." Clean money came from bookmakers, bars, tow truck operators, businessmen, etc. Dirty money involved drugs and prostitutes. Today, there seems to be little reluctance to take dirty money along with the clean.

Situations of this nature go a long way in undermining confidence in police organizations. The question is how many, if any, of these practices can a department tolerate before it loses the respect of the people and before its own members lose respect for each other.

Code of Secrecy

One of the difficult factors in trying to correct the issue of corruption in police departments is the so-called "code of secrecy" that allegedly exists. There is a fraternal spirit which binds members of the force. This spirit is apparently founded on the need of support and trust of each other based on the mutual fear and awareness of danger that the police officer faces. That this fraternal spirit exists no one who has been in police service can deny. It is argued that the spirit so closely binds members of the force that it also segregates them from the rest of society. Cops hang out with cops.

The code also serves as an obstacle to reform from within the police department as well as from without. This is evident in the attitude displayed against members of internal investigation units by other members of the department.

Professor Stoddard states that a recruit is often faced with the test of loyalty to his colleagues, and that he can be socialized into accepting illegal practices by mild, informal, negative sanctions, such as the withholding of group acceptance.(7)

It is difficult to answer the question of whether or not the character of a police officer is formed

before coming into the department or after. Can the need for peer acceptance cause a person of strong moral feelings to accept wrongful acts on the part of other officers and remain silent? Could such an officer be tempted to engage in minor transgressions, such as the free cup of coffee, the free meal, the ten dollars from the tow truck operator, etc., just to show he is one of the group? Unfortunately, the answer seems to be yes. Peer pressure is a compelling force and exclusion a cruel experience. It is difficult for any person to stand alone; and it is rare for one to rise above a situation and break the "code of silence" as Patrolman Frank Serpico did in New York City.(8)

However, recent incidents in New York City indicate that there may be a positive change in attitude occurring on the part of many police officers. In an interview reported in the *New York Post*, the head of the internal affairs division of the New York City Police Department indicated that a "new phenomenon" was being experienced by the Department: police officers were openly accusing other officers of misconduct or criminal activity. In the first three months of 1975, over 100 officers filed allegations ranging from graft to murder against fellow officers.(9) In another report, the New York City Police Department said it was encouraged by the fact that, in 1974, 30 percent of the corruption complaints were filed by fellow officers against their colleagues.(10)

Methods of Dealing with Corruption

After surviving scandal after scandal in the past two decades, police agencies are now starting to take another look at the methods they have used to curtail corruption within their ranks. It had been the common practice to investigate from within. While this must still be done, recognition is now being given to the need for the involvement of some outside agencies. Last year the Pennsylvania Crime Commission issued a lengthy report on police corruption in Philadelphia.(11) In addition, the Knapp Commission recommended that an office of special prosecutor be established to investigate corruption in the criminal justice system.(12) In 1972, Governor Rockefeller appointed Maurice Nadjari as a special deputy attorney general to supersede the district attorneys in the five counties of New York City with respect to investigating corruption in the criminal justice system. The special prosecutor has obtained indictments against police officers, judges, attorneys, and one district attorney.

Several innovative methods have been initiated within the New York City Police Department, some of them quite controversial. As a test of corruption, the department has planted "lost wallets," "weapons," and "narcotics" in an attempt to see if proper department procedures are carried out by those who come into custody of these articles. These tactics were objected to by the Patrolmen's Benevolent Association and individual officers. While they have not been used regularly, they did serve to show members of the department that there were still some officers who had corrupt tendencies. It also created an awareness that the administrators of the department were serious in their fight against corruption and would use innovative methods to combat it.

Amnesty or immunity from departmental prosecution is being offered to police officers who are caught taking bribes, etc. These officers are then expected to gather evidence against fellow officers in return for lenient treatment. This use of "turn-around cops" was noted by the Knapp Commission. The police department also makes use of "field associates," that is, officers not involved in any transgressions, but who are encouraged to inform on other police officers as a means of keeping the integrity of the department at a high level.

The use of the "turn around" and the "field associate" has caused quite a bit of discussion. Many officers consider it an unfair tactic, but in reality it is just as fair as the tactics used by the police themselves in dealing with criminals. The use of informers and undercover agents is a standard investigative tool. Immunity is commonly granted by district attorneys. There are dangers in such a program, and competing needs and values are involved—the need for honest police agencies and the values of due process, free speech, and privacy. Officers must be protected against overzealous and ambitious informers. Such a program must be carefully monitored by the police administrators involved.

It is difficult to measure the effectiveness of these tactics, but the results seen in New York City seem to indicate that there have been changes in attitude and behavior since these practices were introduced.

Whether the changes are being brought about by a new moral awareness or because of fear cannot be said at this time. However, fear of jail, fear of disgrace, fear of loss of pension, and fear that a partner may be an informer are all effective deterrents.

All of these measures are designed to break the "code of silence."

There are many other steps that may be recommended, ranging from the wearing of name tags to the imposition of jail sentences, but one that must be emphasized is the need for command responsibility.

In the battle against corruption, administrators must constantly stress the responsibility of superior officers to maintain an atmosphere within which corruption cannot flourish. They must be held strictly liable for the actions of the men under them, but they must also be supported by those above them.

It is incumbent upon the administration to be beyond reproach. It cannot be hypocritical, it cannot set quotas, it cannot alter statistics, it cannot make promotions on political grounds, and it must be fair in its administration of internal justice. It must have courage, for the solution to the problem of corruption must flow from the top downward.

REFERENCES

1. David Burnham, "City by City, Police Graft Follows the Pattern," *New York Times*, March 17, 1974, "Op Ed" page.

2. *The Knapp Commission Report on Police Corruption* (New York: George Braziller, 1973), p. 68.

3. Alexander Smith and Harriet Pollack, *Crime and Justice in a Mass Society*, (Holt: 1972), p. 124.

4. Irving Younger, "The Perjury Routine," *The Nation*, May 8, 1967, pp. 596–97.

5. H. Goldstein, *Police Corruption: A Perspective on Its Nature and Control* (Washington, D.C.; The Police Foundation, 1975), p. 52.

6. E. R. Stoddard, "The Informal 'Code' of Police Deviancy: A Group Approach to 'Blue-Coat' Crime," *Journal of Criminal Law, Criminology and Police Science*, 59 (1968).

7. Ibid.

8. For an interesting study of Frank Serpico, *See* Peter Maas, *Serpico* (New York: Viking Press, 1973).

9. *New York Post*, March 24, 1975, p. 3.

10. *New York Times*, April 29, 1975, p. 1.

11. *Report on Police Corruption and the Quality of Law Enforcement in Philadelphia*, The Pennsylvania Crime Commission, March 1974.

12. *The Knapp Commission Report*, p. 15.

Secrecy and the Police

WILLIAM A. WESTLEY

The stool pigeon, the squealer, the one who tells, is anathema to any social group. The label symbolizes the sanction against breaking secrecy which is found in many groups, ranging from the school class, through the production line, to the criminal gang. Secrecy maintains group identity, and supports solidarity since it gives something in common to those who belong and differentiates those who do not. A breach of secrecy is thus a threat to the group.

Secrecy would seem to be a phenomenon which is generic to social groups and therefore of special concern to the sociologist. Yet, except for occasional theoretical references(1) there is little research or writing which indicates its genesis, incidence, or function in modern society.

This paper concerns secrecy among the police. It reports part of a larger study of a municipal police department in a midwestern industrial city.(2) The report is based upon close observation of all phases of police work over a period of two years which included intensive interviews with approximately fifty percent of the men in the department and a large number of case histories.

This study of one police force has shown that the maintenance of secrecy is a fundamental rule. The generic characteristics of this rule were suggested by

August Vollmer twenty-five years ago. "Eradication of disgruntled agitators, incompetent policemen, police crooks and grafters takes much time since it is next to impossible to induce police officers to inform on each other. *It is an unwritten law in police departments that police officers must never testify against their brother officers.*"(3)

The Strength of Secrecy

In the course of the above study a special effort was made to confirm the existence of this norm and to determine its relative value and areas of applicability. Two questions were devised, any answer to which would reveal the policeman's orientation to secrecy.

The questions were as follows:

> You and your partner pick up a drunk who is breaking up a bar. While you are patting him down you discover that he has five hundred dollars on him. You take him back to the station in a car and your partner sits in the back with him to keep him quiet. When you check him in with the turnkey the money is gone. You realize that your partner has clipped him. What would you do?

When they had replied, the following question was asked:

> The drunk finds his money gone and prefers charges against you. In court your partner testifies that the drunk had no money on him when you discovered him. There are no other witnesses. How would you testify?

SOURCE: *Social Forces, 34* (1956).

Table 1. Number and Percent of Policemen
Willing to Report Other Policemen for Stealing

Response	Frequency	Percentage
Total	15	100
Yes	4	27
No	11	73

Table 2. Number and Percent of Policemen
Willing to Testify Against Other Policemen

Response	Frequency	Percentage
Total	13*	100
Yes	3	23
No	10	77

* Two men refused to answer this question.

These questions put the men in a dilemma because a refusal to answer *looked* incriminating, to refuse to report the partner and/or to testify against him *was* incriminating, and to agree to report or testify against the partner meant breaking secrecy.

The question was presented to 15 men in a series, and then dropped because of large-scale cancellations of interviews. Therefore the sample is very small, but not necessarily biased. Tables 1 and 2, above, present the results. Only one man stated that he would both report and testify against his partner. He was a rookie.

The results show that 73 percent of the men would not report their partners, and that 77 percent would *perjure* themselves rather than testify against their partners. While the limited size of the sample does not permit statistical generalization to the remainder of the force, other information strongly suggests that these results are representative.

To understand the full significance of these findings the reader must take into consideration the following facts: a) the support and enforcement of the law are the basic legal functions of the police, and they are fully conscious of this fact; b) policemen themselves maintain that biased testimony only leads to trouble in the long run, and c) the detection of perjury would result in the suspension of the man from the force, the loss of his pension time, make him liable to imprisonment, and probably ruin his career. If so, why do these men feel that they would

prefer to break the law, to perjure themselves, rather than break secrecy; *and* why did they tell this to an outside observer? To answer this question it is necessary to refer to the sanctions supporting secrecy, the functions of secrecy, and the manner in which new men are indoctrinated into the rule of secrecy.

Sanctions Supporting Secrecy

The men who were questioned were asked to explain their answers. Their replies delineate the sanctions supporting secrecy. This is illustrated by the following excerpts:

It would give you the name of a stool pigeon . . . and once you get that name you are an outcast from the police force. Nobody wants to say anything to you. Nobody talks to you. Nobody wants to be around you and you never get to know what's going on in the department.

If I did say that I saw the money, he would get the sack and, although everybody would think I was right, they would always remember that I had been down on my buddy. But, I would not say anything. I would always remember, though, that he had rolled the drunk, and one of my rules is that *if* we make a dollar we split fifty-fifty.

If I turned the man in everybody would be out to get me. They wouldn't talk to me. They would go out of their way to get me in trouble.

The other men would treat me with contempt. They would regard me as an unsafe officer.

The successful policeman needs the full support of his partners in order to act in tricky situations (many of which require illegal or semi-legal decisions), and in dangerous situations which every policeman meets from time to time. He needs access to the police grapevine because some of the most important orders are never put on paper, and he must be immediately familiar with day to day shifts in political orientation or the mood of the chief, if he is to keep in good standing. The person who breaks secrecy loses the confidence of his colleagues and in serious cases may be deprived of their support. He is always cut off from the grapevine. This represents an intolerable situation. Therefore, it is the most powerful sanction the police can devise.

The Functions of Secrecy

The functions of secrecy among the police are closely related to the manner in which the policeman is defined in the American community. Frequently, the people in the community have a low regard for the police and consider them corrupt, brutal, and incompetent.(4) Policemen are sensitive to this definition and in turn tend to regard the public as an enemy. To this extent the police, who are supposedly the pillars of the official morality, are in fact a conflict group. The manifest functions of secrecy are related to these conditions. Secrecy stands as a shield against the attacks of the outside world; against bad newspaper publicity which would lower the reputation of the police; against public criticism from which the police feel that they suffer too much; against the criminal who is eager to know the moves of the police; against the law which the police all too frequently abrogate. The activities of the police usually involve them in the illegal use of violence,(5) and often involve them in politics and corruption. They are constantly subject to investigations. Therefore they need secrecy.

Among the latent functions of the secrecy code one of the most important seems to be that it makes the individual policeman identify with other policemen, and distinguish himself from nonpolicemen. Thus, it functions as a social bond among the police, by giving them something in common (if only a sense of mutual incrimination). However, while secrecy fosters the sense of mutual identification, it does not produce a sense of trust. In fact, it seems clear that an unanticipated consequence of the emphasis on secrecy is that the police become intensely suspicious of each other. Thus, they are constantly testing each other to find out if the other is a stool pigeon. This is delineated in the following statement:

> It's a good idea to keep your mouth shut about what happens in the department. Not long ago I had a man test me out. When we were in a restaurant he told me a really terrific story about an incident in which a number of policemen were involved. Boy, it was really something. I could hardly wait to run over to tell my partner about it. But then I got to thinking and I decided to keep my mouth shut and later it turned out that he had told me the story just to see whether or not it came back to him.

Each man is careful to talk only about impersonal things and to stay out of dangerous areas of discussion, of which the most important are the affairs of other men in the department. Naturally, this varies with the garrulousness of the particular individual, but in general, policemen are close-mouthed and tend to be suspicious of each other. Thus, another policeman stated:

> It's more or less a rule that if you have any beefs, you keep them in your family. Don't start talking to people outside. If you are in the department for a while you eventually develop a survival of the fittest attitude. Everybody builds a barrier around himself . . . around his personal affairs. When you work with guys and they get to nosing around, they generally get to know too much about your personal life.

Indoctrination in the Need for Secrecy

The chief threat to the code of secrecy is the initiate, for he is yet largely a member of the outer world, with no emotional involvement with the group. Therefore, in the beginning care must be taken that he is not given premature access to secrets, and full acceptance occurs only when he is told the secrets. Among the police, the "rookie" is carefully observed and assessed, at the same time that he is constantly told about the need for secrecy. In fact, there is no area of police work where the code of secrecy is made more evident.

Fifty percent of the "rookies" (men in training) were asked what the experienced men had told them. *All* reported that *every* experienced man with whom they had been in contact had emphasized the need for secrecy with statements like: "Keep your mouth shut—never squeal on a fellow officer." They had this dinned into their ears by man after man, as they went the rounds of training, and the admonition was related to every conceivable kind of situation. They were all told to beware of stool pigeons who were regularly characterized in disparaging terms. This is what finally drove the lesson home. The rookies became aware of stool pigeons and learned to fear them. They became suspicious. The following statements by two rookies are illustrative:

> There are some guys you can't trust. They are just looking out for themselves. The men won't

tell you who they are. I don't want to work with a man who won't back you up.

There was one guy who did tell the names of some of these stoolies. I tried to find out, you know, because I don't like the idea of trial and error method, in a thing like that. But, when the guy gave me the names, I figured the reason he gave me the names is because he isn't much liked in the department and so was probably one of the stoolies himself. Most of the police won't tell you who the guys are. I think they don't want to because they are afraid you will reveal the source.

The experienced men, in turn, evaluated the rookies chiefly in terms of their discretion. Forty experienced officers (representing approximately thirty-five percent of the patrolmen) were asked what they considered to be the most desirable characteristic in the rookie. Forty-seven percent said that "he should keep his mouth shut" and another thirteen percent said that "he shouldn't be a stool pigeon."

Thus, the role was so important that it was made explicit to every new man by every experienced man; and the ability to keep secrets was considered essential to acceptance and a successful career.

Conclusion

It appears, then, that today in a midwestern city secrecy within the police group is an unwritten law, that Vollmer's statement of a generation ago might be expected to fit most city police departments today. The data suggest that the norm of secrecy emerges from common occupational needs, is collectively supported, and is considered of such importance that policemen will break the law to support it.

REFERENCES

1. The most prominent is that of Georg Simmel. *See: The Writing of Georg Simmel*, trans. by Kurt Wolff (Glencoe, Ill.: The Free Press of Glencoe, 1950), pp. 317–79.

2. William A. Westley, "The Police: A Sociological Study of Law, Custom, and Morality" (Ph.D. dissertation, Department of Sociology, University of Chicago, 1951).

3. U.S. National Committee on Law Observance and Enforcement, *Report on the Police* (Washington, D.C.: Government Printing Office, 1930), p. 48. The italics are mine.

4. William A. Westley, "The Police: A Sociological Study of Law, Custom, and Morality" (Ph.D. dissertation, Department of Sociology, University of Chicago, 1951), pp. 99–107.

5. *See* William A. Westley, "Violence and the Police," *American Journal of Sociology*, 59 (July 1953), pp. 34–41.

Police Who Go to College

BERNARD LOCKE AND ALEXANDER B. SMITH

Present day American life is characterized by mass demonstrations, minority group unrest, riots, and a rising crime rate. To contend with these

SOURCE: This article was written expressly for inclusion in this volume.

problems in some measure, the more efficient selection and better training of police has become a matter of vital concern to the entire nation. We need police who are not only intelligent, courageous, impartial, and honest, but who also have the personality qualities that permit them to function with sympathy, understanding, and flexibility in contending with group unrest, riots, and mass demonstrations. It is important to recruit the best police possible. Once we have recruited, it becomes just as important to train police in academies, give in-service instruction, and provide college training for those policemen already on the job.

Society tends to regard education as an almost magical mechanism for improving the individual and for uplifting the community. We support all education because it is "good." We accept higher education for the police for a variety of reasons: it gives policemen greater dignity; it improves their efficiency; it enhances their image; it is important for advancement in the field of law enforcement; it enables policemen to recognize and deal with social problems more expeditiously; it professionalizes the field of law enforcement, and so forth. Nevertheless, no empirical data have been collected to weigh the value of college education for police. The police training consultants who collaborated in the President's Commission on Law Enforcement and Administration of Justice in writing *The Challenge of Crime in a Free Society*, (1) stated that the complexity of police work is such that the quality of police service will improve significantly only when higher educational standards are required. Basic in the philosophy of any college established for policemen is the intention of developing knowledge and skills in its students so that they may be more effective as policemen and more effective as members of the larger society.

The John Jay College of Criminal Justice is the fifth of nine senior colleges that are part of the collegiate complex making up the City University of New York (CUNY). The older senior colleges, City College, Hunter College, Brooklyn College, and Queens College were established many years ago primarily to furnish traditional college education, tuition free, for the children of the New York City residents. Over the years these four colleges have exhibited enough flexibility, not only in taking care of the higher education needs of students preparing for law, teaching, medicine, etc., in the traditional manner, but also in establishing schools of general studies, vocational studies, and adult education.

In the early 1950's Brooklyn College started a police science program in its Division of Vocational Studies. A year later, with strong backing from the New York City Police Department, a similar program was launched at the Baruch School of the City College. Both of these programs offered courses in traditional police science: fingerprinting, traffic control, police administration, and interrogation. In addition, the usual college courses were made available, with a wider range of courses in the social

sciences—sociology, psychology, and political science. These course offerings were scheduled so that the police students could attend classes regardless of changes in their tours of duty.

These programs were not the first of their kind. In 1946, at the University of Southern California, a program for the training of policemen was established. After a slow beginning at other colleges and universities, the police science programs began to proliferate over the country, so that today there are more than seven hundred such college programs for police. These programs vary along a wide continuum of academic respectability. However, still unique is the John Jay College of Criminal Justice which opened its doors in September 1965. The John Jay College grants a four-year bachelor's degree and two-year associate degrees. Of colleges offering similar programs, it has the highest percentage of police students. In addition, the college offers master's degrees in four areas, and may ultimately have a doctoral program.

Originally, John Jay was known as the College of Police Science, but one year after it opened, the name was changed to the John Jay College of Criminal Justice at the request of the students, to indicate the college's broader concern with the entire process of criminal justice. Currently, over 40 per cent of the 10,000 undergraduate part-time students and a few of the 6,000 full-time students are policemen. Of the 1,000 graduate students, about 70 per cent are police.

The rewards for attending college for these New York City police are neither tangible nor immediate. While higher education may help prepare policemen for promotion examinations, there is no requirement that promotion to higher rank requires successful completion of any or all parts of a college education. While there are exceptions in the rest of the country, in New York City promotion to the higher ranks through captain is possible only through civil service promotion examinations. It is not necessary to go beyond the entrance requirement of a high school diploma, or its equivalent, to qualify for any advanced positions. College training does not enhance a promotional candidate's score.

The New York City Police Department is made up predominantly of descendants of Irish and German Catholic immigrants with Italian Americans making up a third large segment. Jewish and Negro police are small minorities. From an inspection of its student body enrollment, it appears that John Jay College is made up of students who reflect the same

proportions of ethnic, religious, and racial composition as is represented in the entire Police Department. From these facts, it may be concluded that the
social and cultural influences bearing on college and
non-college New York City policemen are quite
similar, and that the variable to be researched is the
personality factor.

There is strong opinion to support the proposition that almost everyone can benefit from higher
education to some extent, and that police, like all
other people, are better off with college training.
Nevertheless, not everyone who has the ability wants
to attend college, and the bases of the decision to
attend college should be considered and weighed.
While we realize that the cultural and social processes
are significant in encouraging people to attend colleges and universities, the matter of personality as a
factor in undertaking higher education has not been
sufficiently investigated. It should be kept in mind
that a field-theoretical position requires a consideration of both personal and situational determinants
of social behavior.

In the case of New York City police, the factor
that should be weighed is that most police who take
advantage of the availability of college attendance do
so without the hope of immediate on-the-job reward.
It therefore appears that there are personality differences between police who attend college and those
who do not attend. These differences are not only
basic to their election to go to college, but also may
affect their decision-making in crucial and sensitive
situations. A review of the literature fails to disclose
research exploring the factors bearing on the attendance of police in collegiate programs. The question
as to whether personality factors explain this attendance by policemen has not been examined.

The New York City Police Department and the
John Jay College of Criminal Justice offer an excellent setting in which to test a number of hypotheses
that personality factors are, in some way, responsible
for determining which policemen will attend college
under the circumstances. In speculating about these
personality factors, the aspect of personality that
makes it possible for policemen on all levels to use
authority and force constructively in these critical
times should be examined. It may be that the degree
of authoritarianism that determines the ability of the
policeman to function properly in these times is the
same facet of personality that encourages the policeman to attend college.

In order to test for authoritarianism two scales
were combined: a modification of the Dogmatism
scale following Rokeach(2) and a scale devised by
Piven.(3) The scales were similar in that they were
aimed at eliciting various aspects of authority; Rokeach was concerned with personal attitude toward
socialized authority; and Piven, who had investigated
attitudes of social workers, was concerned with
practitioner authoritative responses to clients. The
Rokeach scale was used rather than the one developed in *The Authoritarian Personality.*(4) The latter
had been criticized because its main measuring
instruments focused on Fascist authoritarianism. Ro-
keach(5) kept this criticism in mind in planning his
instrument, explaining:

> In other words, if our interest is in the scientific
> study of authoritarianism, we should proceed
> from right authoritarianism not to a re-focus on
> left authoritarianism but to the general prop-
> erties held in common by all forms of authori-
> tarianism. . . . What is needed is therefore a
> deliberate turning away from a concern with one
> or two kinds of authoritarianism that may
> happen to be predominant at a given time.
> Instead, we should pursue a more theoretical, a
> historical analysis of the properties held in
> common by all forms of authoritarianism regard-
> less of specific theological, philosophic, or sci-
> entific content.

Using the combined Rokeach and Piven scales,
research at the John Jay College throws light on the
attitude toward authoritarianism in several comparative situations.

College Police Versus
Non-College-Oriented Police

There is a common assumption in social psychology that certain personality types are attracted to
particular occupations. Highly neurotic individuals
are attracted to social work and psychiatry, homosexual males are attracted to nursing, and authoritarian personalities are attracted to correctional institutional work and police. In these times of social
unrest we need police whose personalities are such
that they are able to function effectively in critical
and explosive situations, particularly in leadership
situations. One of the important functions of higher
education is to develop leadership among the police.

This study demonstrates that police who are attracted to college are significantly less authoritarian than police who are not impelled to attend college. (See Table 1, below.) This implies that there are certain personality characteristics of police who attend college that make it likely that they will be able to function more effectively in accordance with the guidelines set down by the Supreme Court with respect to arrests, search, and seizure.

Table 1.   Responses of College (N = 104) and Non-College (N = 122) Police to Total Scale

	M	σ	σm	D	σ diff	t
College	−.11	1.81	.02			
				.42	.028	15.0*
Non-College	.31	1.81	.02			

* Significant at the .01 level of confidence.

SOURCE: A. B. Smith, B. Locke, and W. S. Walker, "Authoritarianism in College and Non-College Oriented Police," *Journal of Criminal Law, Criminology and Police Science*, 58, 1 (1967), pp. 128–132.

Table 2.   Responses of Police (N = 51) and Non-Police (N = 89) Groups to Total Scale

	M	σ	σm	D	σ diff	t
Police	−.23	1.75	.03			
				.19	.04	4.75*
Non-Police	−.04	1.77	.02			

* Significant at the .01 level of confidence.

SOURCE: A. B. Smith, B. Locke, and W. S. Walker, "Authoritarianism in Police College Students and Non-Police College Students," *Journal of Criminal Law, Criminology and Police Science*, 59, 3 (1968), pp. 440–43.

Newly Entered College Police
Versus Civilian College Freshmen

Our sample consisted of about 100 full time freshmen students (non-police) who had some direct or indirect interest in the process of criminal justice. These students were similar in religious and ethnic background, as well as scholastic background, to the entire student body of John Jay.

With the addition of non-police freshmen students, it became possible to investigate differences between them and college police, and thus answer the following question, namely, "Are there differences in authoritarianism between non-police freshmen and newly entered police college students?"

In comparing these two groups on the combined Rokeach and Piven scales, it was found that newly entered police college students were less authoritarian than the freshmen students who were not police officers. (See Table 2.)

Policemen Who Are College Graduates
Versus Non-College Police

The average age of the John Jay College graduate is about 40, and he has attended college over a period of ten years. Of these ten years he has gone to school for eight years, and has not attended college for two years in order to devote this time to preparing for promotion examinations. This college group averaged slightly more than eighteen years in the Police Department. Accordingly, in order to do a comparison, a control group was chosen with the same attributes of age and police service, but with no college attendance.

This study showed that as measured on the Rokeach scale (the Piven test showed no significance), the completion of a baccalaureate program resulted in a notable diminution of authoritarian attitudes in a police population as contrasted with a matched group of non-college police. (See Table 3).

In these days of social unrest, the role of the police officer has become crucial. Improper decisions by police have triggered riots (for example, Watts) and have exacerbated unrest.(7) The need for well-educated police officers to deal with these complicated problems is great, and the provision of an opportunity for a college education becomes a public obligation.

Table 3.   Responses of Police College Graduates (N = 39) and Non-College Police (N = 39) to Total Scale

	M	σ	σm	D	σ diff	t
Police College Graduates	−.45	.41	.07			
				.32	.099	3.33*
Non-College Police	−.13	.45	.07			

* Significant at the .01 level of confidence.

SOURCE: A. B. Smith, B. Locke, and A. Fenster, "Authoritarianism in Policemen Who are College Graduates and Non-College Police," *Journal of Criminal Law, Criminology and Police Science*, 1970, Vol. 61, No. 2, pp. 313–15.

REFERENCES

1. President's Commission on Law Enforcement and Administration of Justice, *The Challenge of Crime in a Free Society* (Washington, D.C.: U.S. Government Printing Office, 1967).

2. M. Rokeach, *The Open and Closed Mind* (New York: Basic Books, 1960).

3. H. Piven, "Professionalism and Organizational Structure" (D.S.W. dissertation, Columbia University School of Social Work, 1961).

4. T. W. Adorno et al., *The Authoritarian Personality* (New York: Harper, 1950).

5. M. Rokeach, *The Open and Closed Mind* (New York: Basic Books, 1960), p. 14.

6. *New York Times Magazine*, August 24, 1969, pp. 46–70.

7. S. Lieberson and A. R. Silverman, "The Precipitants and Underlying Conditions of Race Riots," *American Sociological Review, 30* (December 1965).

5 | Police Discretion

Probably no other area has received as much attention in professional journals, books, and newspapers as that of police discretion. Despite the attendant voluminous writing and discussion, police discretion remains the most confounded subject.

Practitioners of virtually every occupation and profession are charged to a greater or lesser degree with the responsibility for making decisions. Inherent in that responsibility is discretion, which is defined by the degree of freedom to make choices.

Police decision making differs markedly from other professions in two major areas:

1. In most other professions the limits of discretion are proportionate to the rank held in the professional hierarchy. Thus lower level workers and practitioners are usually circumscribed in the ambit of their power of discretion. And the power and possibilities of discretion are magnified with rank in the hierarchical structure. In the case of the police, however, the power of discretion which most affects individual members of the public is exercised by the lower-ranking field personnel, typically, the police officer on patrol. Usually it is the patrolman whose discretion is called into play in individual cases. In his discretion he may choose to use force, or to arrest, or to issue a summons, or instead, perhaps, to desist from engaging in any of the foregoing actions. Of course it would be a mistake to ignore the sweeping discretionary powers of the top administrators in any police organization. They make the "big" decisions with reference to tables of organization, budget, enforcement priorities, and overall departmental policy, as well as management of related housekeeping functions. Discretion is involved in all of these overarching issues.

2. The second critical difference is the time frame available for the making of crucial decisions. In most other professions, the practitioner often has the time and is indeed obliged to consult with his fellow professionals, to research an area in order to reconcile uncertainties, and to rule out inappropriate or dangerous courses of action. In medicine, for example, the medical student and the intern are roughly equivalent to the police officer working under stress, harried, functioning in a hostile environment, suffering from sleep deprivation, and making life-and-death decisions involving the fate of others. The important difference, however, is that the medical student and intern have available as immediate resources at the bedside of a patient the resident, chief resident, experienced nurses, their professors, and a variety of other clinical consultants, including their fellow students and interns. A sound teaching hospital prides itself on the fact that discretion and decision making are group efforts also monitored by senior colleagues who possess a vast reservoir of theoretical and clinical experience. In many instances clinical decisions are not only arrived at by team effort, but they can be modified or even reversed as necessitated by subsequent data. Further, medical practitioners have available to them, even in emergencies, the possibilities of obtaining hard data through the use of instruments, laboratory procedures, and a variety of diagnostic tests.

In the field of law, the student, the junior associate, or the senior partner can, even in a trial court situation, request an adjournment to consult, research, or to seek the resources of other practitioners in order to explore possible courses of action in a troublesome case. It is rare for even the most accomplished or renowned practitioner to try or argue an important case without the assistance of a team of experts. In addition, every legal transaction is preceded by intricate and often monumental preparation for trial or appeal.

The police officer is one of the few professionals who either works alone or with one partner who probably has no greater resources or experience than he. He must often make a decision in the most controversial cases without the benefit of precedent, extensive consultation, or research. He cannot pause for extended, sober reflection; nor can he ask for a delay in order to consult with a more experienced or supervisory administrator. His range of options are ambiguously defined by a melange of laws, customs, precedents, and departmental regulations. He has a limited technology available to him for a genuinely sophisticated diagnosis, as do practitioners of law or medicine. His client is not on an admitting table or seated in an office, but may often be a vague shadow in the darkness, dimly perceived in some kaleidoscopic scene problematic in its import. Often the officer must decide which is the transgressor needing restraint and which the victim needing succor. There is no detector to tell him whether the flash of metal he sees is a gun, a cigarette lighter, a knife, or a ball point pen. In some cases he may be able to ask questions, like a physician or lawyer. But the many conflicting claims made by the parties, the misleading statements by witnesses, and the demands of the situation requiring precipitous action, eliminate the possibilities of evaluating evidence and judicious weighing of alternatives. Keenly aware that there are no fail-safe devices to absolve him, the police officer is especially bothered by the finality and irreversibility of his most critical decisions. His course of action cannot be altered or even reversed. His actions are indelibly recorded and witnessed; and they become the subject of future review, litigation, and possible grounds for dismissal or even criminal prosecution.

Explanations which purport to illuminate the concept of police discretion have utilized lines of inquiry ranging from police personality, social class, race, and ideological factors, as well as situational determinants, such as the type of crime, the relative social standing of the complainants and offenders, and a host of other variables. On the one hand, police are accused of making too many arrests of minority, lower-class groups; on the other hand they are accused of not making enough arrests of more powerful groups. For some, police discretion is an evil which is to be eliminated, because of its potential for wrongdoing; yet others contend that the real art of police work is defined by the legal and structural limits of police discretion.

We believe it is impossible, as well as inadvisable, to contemplate the elimination of police discretion. The proper use of discretion, in most cases, can be taught as part of an overall training process. The excesses can be limited by adequate professional supervision. There will always be cases requiring the use of force where the police officer's discretion will be the basis for controversy. Police departments must accept this fact as a basic condition of their existence; and police officers must learn to live with this risk and the implications for being second-guessed.

Discretion to arrest or not to arrest is usually the central concern of the literature. There are some general guidelines that are connected with the police function and the officer's concept of his role. Generally, in serious cases involving a felony or certain misdemeanors, there will nearly always be an arrest. In trivial cases there will hardly ever be an arrest. Police discretion as it pertains to arrest is connected largely to a group of middle-level offenses, neither too serious nor too trivial. It is really this rather narrow range of cases which have produced the greatest controversies over police discretion. Even with young delinquents whose actions are not legally crimes, the policeman defines the act in terms of adult criteria. A forcible rape by a fifteen-year-old is interpreted as a serious adult felony, and the child is taken into custody; whereas a petty larceny by a fourteen-year-old is likely to be considered a minor offense, and the child would probably receive a warning.

When one understands the police culture in all its ramifications, one is less inclined to attribute arrest decisions to such variables as values, class differences, personality factors, ideological considerations, and racial or ethnic components, all of which appear prominently in the literature explaining police discretion. Community definitions as to what constitutes a case serious enough to call for an arrest govern a great deal of local police actions. These definitions are informal and tacit, rather than legally prescribed. In this area the policeman is in the same position as an anthropologist relying on cultural relativity to shape his judgment so that he may behave appropriately.

The other range of variables that we consider important are such things as the police officer's record of performance. Also, does he have to meet an arrest quota for that month? What time of day does an incident take place? Is it near the end of a shift or at the beginning of a tour? Will the policeman have to spend hours after his tour in processing an arrest? Will this interfere with a social or a family engagement? Does the department pay overtime for additional hours of work? Does the officer need the additional

compensation? Although rarely taken into account, these seemingly prosaic factors loom as controlling and compelling determinants of action.

In the section that follows we have selected articles which seem to us to be clearly representative of the various positions with regard to police discretion.

A Socio-Legal Theory of Police Discretion

RICHARD E. SYKES, JAMES C. FOX, AND JOHN P. CLARK

Introduction

The Problem

The literature on police delineates two distinct perspectives on the factors associated with the decision to take a suspect into custody. One approach has focused on the decision to arrest as limited by legal and judicial criteria with the conclusion that many of the serious problems of discretion are associated with the decision not to arrest (H. Goldstein 1963, 1967; J. Goldstein 1960; LaFave 1965a, b, c, 1962; Livermore 1970). The other has emphasized extralegal criteria (Black 1968, 1970; Black and Reiss 1970; Goldman 1963; Hartjen 1972; Peterson 1972; Piliavin and Briar 1964; President's Commission 1967; Westley 1953). This perspective is apt to emphasize problems of discretion associated with the decision to arrest.

The difference between these two perspectives is greater than is generally acknowledged in the literature. Those who emphasize decisions *not to arrest* suggest that more arrests should take place. Police

NOTE: This research was supported by the Center for Studies of Crime and Delinquency, National Institute of Mental Health, Grant No. R01 MH17917-02. Opinions expressed herein are the authors' and do not necessarily reflect those of the research sponsors or monitors.

should not have so much discretion to let suspects go. Those who emphasize decisions *to arrest* suggest that citizens are being apprehended for extralegal, personal reasons. Arrest is sometimes a conscious, sometimes an unconscious, exercise of harassment. The first group decries lax enforcement; the second group, unfair enforcement. Both groups see a violation of the rule of law since it is enforced differentially across the population.

The goals of the authors are:

1. To formulate a theory of police discretion which takes both these perspectives into account
2. To assess the weight officers give to factors emphasized in each perspective by analyzing data on situational dispositions of police-civilian encounters
3. To integrate both viewpoints into one *and* assess which viewpoint more accurately reflects actual police practice

Some Definitions

Discretion exists whenever an officer is free to choose from two or more task-relevant, alternative interpretations of the events reported, inferred, or observed in a police-civilian encounter. Alternatives include (1) definition of an event as one of official interest to police or not, (2) identification of a citizen as incumbent in a role of official interest to police or not, and (3) choice of actions towards events and citizens so defined and identified. "Official" implies the use of reports to recognize the commission of an offense, or special actions by means of which a citizen identified as a violator has imposed upon him a new status vis-à-vis the legal system. Such a status is usually assumed after initiatory arrest procedures.

The theory will be tested using data gathered by field observers who quantitatively coded the nature of a random sample of more than 3,000 police-citizen encounters, their outcomes, and more than a thousand hours of interaction between the participants. The intent of the research was to gather descriptive data on the nature of police activities as well as to collect data on the factors which influenced police decision-making. The data make it possible to compare the demeanor of officers and citizens across encounters, *statement by statement*, as well as by other cues, and to create profiles of such encounters. Such information permits study of the association of many variables with the decision whether or not to arrest.

A Theory of Decision Making

Role Attribution

In a police-citizen encounter the problem of the actors is to decide what position each is to occupy and what behavior the occupant of that position is expected to display. Role attribution and role-appropriate behavior are the result of the information exchanged by the participants in the encounter.[1] As a result a violator may be labelled. Subsequent behavior as policeman is contingent on this previous decision. When there is no predetermined agenda the most important variables seem to be those criteria by which actors decide to attribute identities and expectations to one another and then act in terms of such

[1] In his comments a reviewer makes some very pertinent suggestions which would expand information to include previous knowledge as well as information gathered during the encounter itself. Essentially we agree with this and later suggestions concerning the importance of other factors. However, our data indicate that over a *large* number of encounters, most of which occur in private places, relatively few involve people or places known to police either personally or by reputation. While such knowledge is apt to be decisive in individual cases, it does not account for much of the variance over a large number of cases.

attributions. The questions then are (1) in police-citizen interactions how do actors decide on identities, and (2) once identities are decided, what behavior follows?

We shall limit ourselves to answering those questions only insofar as officers' decisions about citizens are concerned. How do officers decide that someone is to be given the identity of violator? We conceptualized this problem of identity in terms of the decisions which the officers had to make. We proposed that officers identify the actors by a set of criteria henceforth termed *decision criteria*.

Decision Criteria

Integrating the legal and extralegal traditions of scholarship mentioned in the introduction yields four such criteria: (1) the law, (2) official or unofficial departmental policy, (3) the demeanor of the suspect toward the officer, and (4) the potential threat the suspect poses to the officer's safety. By these criteria officers decide whether or not to define a situation as one in which a violation has taken place and to identify individuals as violators. By comparing information to each criterion the officers can decide whether or not the criterion is satisfied.

Law

The state and municipal law establish various limits upon citizen behavior. If the behavior of citizens exceeds these limits and is known, that behavior may be defined as criminal by either the police or citizen public, and the legal criterion becomes salient. In most cases, police respond to citizen judgments (Black 1968:188–92, Clark 1965: 309–10, LaFave 1962:210–19, Reiss 1971:69–70). Once requested by a citizen, information is sought by the officer to determine the covariance of his and the

Basically, however, our problem is methodological. Previous literature on police addresses the importance of psychological and demographic variables. The model we propose pertains to a different set of variables and a different level of explanation. For this reason we view it as complementing rather than competing with other explanations. Not only this, but were we to include as many factors as probably influence decisions, there would be no analytic technique capable of handling either the number of dimensions or the limited size of our sample.

citizen's judgment. Except for motor vehicle offenses, which are primarily a function of departmental policy (Gardiner 1969), the uniformed patrolman directly witnesses and takes action on a violation in only a small percentage of cases (Reiss 1971:19–20, Wilson 1968:19). Information is sought from witnesses to determine whether or not an offense has occurred, and if it has occurred, whether it is a felony or a misdemeanor.

Policy

Police departments differ in the extent to which goal-relevant policy is official or unofficial. Official policy is that which is written and communicated by regularized means to department members (cf. Goldstein 1960, Parnas 1967). In the largest department included in this research, policy was often not explicit but might be inferred from official documents. The official policy was that offense reports were to be written for all complaints pertaining to crimes against persons or property, implying that other violations were not necessarily considered offenses, nor their perpetrators technically considered violators. Since policy often reflects administrative priority in the face of limited resources, such policy establishes a hierarchy among the multitude of goals. An officer's knowledge of policy may not involve so much a set of separate goals as a set of legally relative hierarchies. In a sense the organization predetermines the probabilities of certain identities being attributed within the broader mandate of law.

Respect

To a certain extent, law establishes rights and obligations of role incumbents. Historically an officer may use deadly force for self-protection or for apprehending a felon. With certain limitations the officer may seek legally relevant information, but the law is vague in regard to citizen behavior vis-à-vis an officer's role behavior. Verbal behavior which would be in clear contempt of court is often tolerated by a law officer (Reiss 1971:179–80). While the legal literature on police decisions gives only limited attention to the goal of maintaining respect for the uniform (cf. LaFave 1962:231–32) sociological literature emphasizes this factor considerably more (Bittner 1970, Piliavin and Briar 1964, Reiss 1971). Respect includes recognition or obedience to the legitimate exercise of authority by an officer. The brief and problematic nature of the officer's relation to the citizen makes this an area of concern from the officer's perspective. A citizen who does not display such respect may be labelled a violator.

Safety

An officer is vulnerable to attack by hostile, abnormal, or emotionally distraught persons. Personal strategies are often adopted for self-protection. Were safety not important, officers would not draw their weapons *before* many encounters, and therefore before any disrespect for their role has occurred. Indeed, police training literature emphasizes the need for caution, prudence, and superior force in the face of danger in order to maximize safety (Leonard and More 1971, Wileman 1970, 1971).

The officer makes decisions within legal and police constraints. If he decides to ignore these constraints he will do so either at serious risk to himself, or else by creatively using legal and policy criteria pretextually for violations that do not normally result in arrest. The possible combinations of legal and policy criteria are illustrated in figure 1. Generally it will be hypothesized that the more criteria are congruent with one another the more likely a particular outcome. For instance, the cell 1 cases, where a felony has been committed and policy encourages arrest, are very apt to end in arrest, while cell 6 cases are very unlikely to end in arrest. While it is possible for departmental policy not to require arrest for a felony, in the departments we studied this was not the case. It is also possible for arrest to occur by policy directive where no legal offense occurred, but such a policy if overt would make officers liable for false arrest. In the departments studied, as far as we are aware, no such policies existed at least insofar as the normal activities of uniformed police are concerned. In these data there is also no case in which the characteristics of cell 6 were satisfied and an arrest occurred.

Legal and policy criteria will henceforth be termed "formal constraints." They combine with respect and safety criteria as in figure 2. Six groups of goal criteria configurations were evident (figure 2). In groups 1 and 2 the officer had reason to believe felonies had taken place and that departmental policy directed that an arrest be made. In groups 3 and 4 misdemeanors have been committed. In groups 5 and 6 the officer's information led him to conclude that no legal violations had occurred.

Policy directive

Legal criterion	Arrest (+)*		Do not arrest (−)	
Felony (+)	1.	+ +	2.	+ −
Misdemeanor (±)	3.	± +	4.	± −
No violation (−)	5.	− +	6.	− −

*Where signs are the same, congruency exists.

FIGURE 1   Combinations of Legal and Policy Criteria

Possible cells

*Formal constraints

†Respect (+indicates disrespect)

‡‡Safety (+ indicates danger to the person of the officer)

FIGURE 2   Possible Configurations of Decision Criteria

Generally we would hypothesize that the greater the number of positive signs that exist, the more likely a citizen is to be identified as a violator; and the more negative signs, the less likely. If a felony has occurred we would expect that fact to outweigh all other criteria. Where there is no legal violation we would expect likelihood of arrest to increase as signs for other criteria are positive, but we would also expect that arrests would be pretextual.

Theoretically, a distinction must be made between arrest (official identification of a citizen as a violator) and enforcement of the law, since arrest is only one means of enforcement. An adequately broad perspective must encompass means other than those specifically prescribed by law or departmental policy, otherwise police behavior cannot be accounted for in most instances.

A flow chart of the series of decisions the officer must make (figure 3) delineates the process as follows: The officer, receiving information either directly or indirectly from evidence or testimony, compares this to decision criteria. If any information is relevant to criteria (i.e., a law has been broken, a policy is relevant, respect for the role is lacking, or his safety is threatened) the officer may take action, since by these criteria a violation may be defined or a violator identified. His action will be compared to criteria of means (criteria of behavior after a person is identified) at the same time that a citizen's reaction is judged. Thus, there is a continuous feedback cycle to both decision criteria and criteria of means.

For an outcome of arrest to occur, at least the legal criterion must be satisfied. If a minor violation, other criteria must be satisfied in addition. So-called "good pinches" occur when the legal violation is serious; or if not serious, the other criteria are satisfied as well. Generally, except for felony violations, we would predict that the more criteria satisfied, the more likely the arrest. These additional criteria are not necessary for arrest for most felony violations of the type with which uniformed patrolmen usually deal. Identification as a felon is sufficient for official labelling to take place.

Proceeding from this perspective we shall now examine its fit to the particular data collected in this study.

Data Collection

Observers gathered data while riding with police officers. These data were gathered by systematic observation of police-citizen encounters using an interaction coding system. Briefly, this coding schema permitted the observers to do the following:

1. To record the nature of the encounter, e.g., crime against person or property, a violation of private or public decorum, service needed;

2. To rate every encounter-relevant verbal interaction of police and citizens along several dimensions;

3. To code certain nonverbal behaviors as well as outcomes, and descriptions of citizen-actors involved.

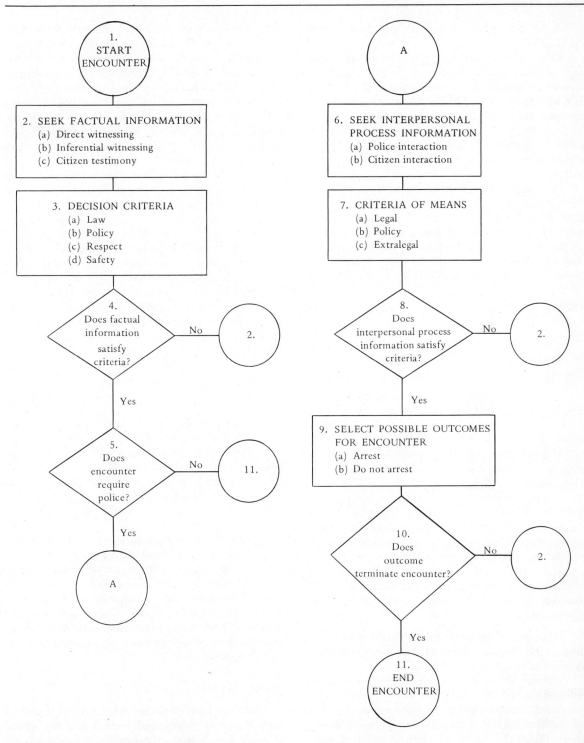

FIGURE 3 *Dynamics of Process of Law Enforcement*

A full description of the code may be found in Sykes 1972.

Five observers rode for more than a year in one city of about half a million and in two residential suburbs of about 25,000 population each. The full data base consisted of 3,323 police-citizen encounters observed during randomly sampled shifts of police departments in the three midwest communities. In about 15 percent of these encounters (N = 520) an alleged violator was present who was not a routine traffic offender.

Consistent with the above theory we will look at the effects of these factors in the decision to officially define a citizen as a violator. Arrest was the criterion for offical labelling as a violator. The "fit" of the factors to the criteria was decided by the observers. Interobserver reliability using Scott's coefficient ranged from 0.70 to 0.80 (Scott 1955).

Analysis

Legal Criteria

Most alleged violator-present police-citizen encounters fall into four of five legal categories:

1. From the officer's perspective, information indicates no apparent legal violation has occurred, or if it has, the violation was not witnessed by an officer.

2. From the officer's perspective, information indicates a misdemeanor has occurred which was witnessed by an officer.

3. From the officer's perspective, information indicates a felony has occurred or is occurring.

4. The officer is performing a ministerial function in making an arrest, e.g., serving a warrant or transporting a shoplifter arrested by someone else.

5. An additional but very small category consists of situations in which some action by the police is required, though not necessarily arrest; for example, threatened suicide.

Information includes not only that relayed through the communication net, but that information gathered after arrival at the scene.

The subject encounters, when ordered by legal criterion, reveal that 146 of 520, or more than one-fourth, involved either no technical violation or no violation for which the officers had the choice of arrest (Table 1). Many of these encounters were domestic disputes, arguments between neighbors, or calls about vaguely suspicious persons. In such cases the process of inquiry led to the conclusion that what was initially alleged by either officer or citizen as illegal behavior actually involved no violation. On the other hand, more than half involved situations where there was a violation of the law but no felony. Common in this category were loud parties, barking or unleashed dogs, unwanted guests, and many cases of public drunkenness.

If law enforcement were limited to arrest, and legal criteria were all that an officer used in his decision to place a suspect into custody, then it would be self-evident that the law is dramatically underenforced. In more than two-thirds of our cases (374) arrest could have been the outcome; but, in fact, arrest was the outcome in only slightly more than one-fourth of those cases (102 of 374) (Table 1). Since nonarrest decisions accounted for a much greater proportion of the cases than arrest decisions did, there must have been other factors than legal criteria which affected the decision to arrest. On the other hand, where a felony was involved, arrest almost always occurred.

Policy Criteria

The police departments studied had few official policy guidelines that were explicit other than the ones previously referred to. The former guidelines required offense reports in cases of possible crimes against property or persons. We might expect that officers would have treated these cases more seriously and thus arrest outcomes would have been more frequent.

It would appear from an examination of Table 2 that where minor technical offenses occurred, even in regard to property or persons, arrests were not made. In that regard, legal criteria and policy criteria together are inadequate to account for outcomes of arrest. On the other hand, where a felony had occurred or where the officers were serving a warrant or acting in a ministerial function, the legal criterion was adequate in itself.

Respect and Safety Criteria

Scholars have identified other extralegal criteria than those of safety and respect for the police officer's role, which influence the labelling of the

Table 1. *Arrest Outcomes and Apparent Technical Status of Violation after Receipt of Information by Officer (N-520)*

	Technical Status					
Outcome	1 No violation within authority of officer	2 Probable misdemeanor	3 Probable felony	4 Ministerial	5 Special cases	6 Totals
No arrest	146	241	3*	15†	13	418
Misdemeanor arrests	0	37	16	15	2	70
Felony arrests	0	4	23	5	0	32
Total	146	282	42	35	15	520
Percentage	28.0	54.2	8.1	6.7	2.9	99.9

*2 citizen arrests and 1 escape

†11 citizen arrests, 3 special cases involving transporting juveniles to a detention home, and 1 case in which a store owner who had arrested a juvenile for shoplifting was persuaded not to press charges after the juvenile was reprimanded by officers

violator. Briefly, these criteria include identification of the alleged violator as a minority group member, or as lower-class. Our data confirm that arrest is more likely for lower-class, nonwhite males. A subsequent article will deal with these data, but meantime, we have found that of the observed encounters, nearly half (Table 1) were either legal or policy relevant (146 involved no violations, 39 involved felony arrests, 20 involved arrests in ministerial capacity). Thus, these criteria accounted for the situational disposition of the violator. In the remaining violator-present encounters, legal or policy criteria were important in defining the behavior as illegal. Whether or not the offender was arrested, however, was undefined, since in only 12 percent (Table 2) of these encounters was arrest the outcome (41 of 282 misdemeanors).

This permits us to make an important distinction: there was a difference in our findings between interpersonal behavior between officers and citizens *incidental* to arrest, and interpersonal behavior which *led* to arrest. Where legal or policy

Table 2. *Arrests and Nonarrests by Type of Violation (N 359)‡*

	Status of Violation						
Type of violation	2 Probable misdemeanor		3 Probable felony		4 Warrant or transport		5 Totals
	A*	NA†	A	NA	A	NA	
Against property	5	29	12	0	7	0	53
Against person	2	6	1	1	4	0	14
Domestic dispute	3	11	3	0	1	1	19
Public decorum	29	174	10	0	2	0	215
Other	2	21	13	2	6	14	58
Total	41	241	39	3	20	15	359
Percentage	11.4	67.1	10.9	0.8	5.6	4.2	100.0

*Arrest

†No arrest or no arrest by the officers themselves

‡Does not include 146 cases in which no violation occurred and 15 special cases (see Table 1)

criteria were adequate or where the police were acting in a ministerial function, interaction itself, except as information relative to criterion, should not have been used to explain the decision to take a suspect into custody. Interaction incidental to felony arrest may have been polite or impolite, hostile or friendly, aggressive or not, and offenders may have been any class, color, and so forth, but in each case these factors did not ordinarily contribute to arrest outcomes. This modification has generally been ignored by previous scholars, but we found that it is important if police behavior is to be accounted for.

This distinction revealed that after officers had collected sufficient information, alleged violator-present encounters would fall into one of three categories:

1. Discretion without arrest option
2. Discretion with arrest option
3. Discretion limited to arrest

Table 3. *Mean Number of Impolite Statements per Discretion Category (N = 505)*

Discretion category	$\overline{X}$	S	S^2	N
Discretion without arrest	1.64	4.71	22.19	146
Discretion with arrest	2.30	5.96	35.54	282
(No arrest)	1.79	5.31	28.16	241
(Arrest)	5.29	8.37	70.01	41
Discretion limited to arrest	6.92	18.06	326.26	77

*Does not include 15 special cases (see Table 1)

In the first case, information available to officers indicated that no violation had occurred, that no legal criteria were relevant, and thus, arrest was extremely unlikely. In the second case, a violation had occurred and arrest was one option that officers may have exercised. In the third case, the violation was so serious that officers had almost no choice but to make an arrest and thus, legal or policy criteria accounted for arrest outcomes. Strictly speaking there was no arrest discretion in the last instance.

In the first and third cases interpersonal factors could not have accounted for arrest but may have affected strategies of officers. Since arrest was problematic in the second category, extralegal factors may have affected arrest because legal or policy criteria

already defined the behavior as illegal. At the same time, however, arrest on those criteria alone was unlikely.

Since so many violators of the law escaped arrest, *what conditions had to be present for a suspect to be arrested?* We will examine 282 encounters in which legal or policy criteria were relevant but did *not* themselves determine arrest (Table 4).

Table 4. *Arrest Rates by Level of Citizen Impoliteness (N = 282)*

Level of Impoliteness	Arrest rate (%)
1. None	9.7
2. Less than average	23.4
3. Greater than average	11.1
4. Much greater than average†	40.9

*Cases in which only a technical violation occurred (see Table 1)

†More than one standard deviation greater than the average level of impoliteness

Our data in this regard were utilized in several ways. First, we wished to determine if the frequency of impoliteness, or noncompliance, or the expression of anger, or the threat of violence, changed the chances that an alleged violator would be arrested. Secondly, we wished to determine if mutual or unilateral anger altered the probabilities of arrest.

In Table 4 the distribution of impolite statements by citizens in encounters is divided into four groups depending on the degree of displayed impoliteness. It is evident that in any given encounter, as the violator increased his level of impoliteness, his chances of being arrested increased dramatically. When this distribution is compared with nonarrest outcomes, the difference is statistically significant ($\chi^2 = 19.07$, d.f. = 3, $P > 0.001$).

A similar tendency was evident in regard to the effect of displays of anger on the officer's decision to take a suspect into custody (Table 5). Arrest rates were significantly higher when the citizen alone was angry or when both citizen and officer were angry than when neither was angry or the officer alone was angry.

When politeness was examined together with ordering and complying behavior, similar results were obtained (data not included here). Where no impo-

Table 5.   Arrest Percentages by Anger (N = 282)*

Anger	Arrest rate (%)
None displayed	8.6
Officer only	12.8
Citizen only	23.1
Mutual display	24.3

*Cases of probable misdemeanor, in which only a technical violation occurred (see Table 1)

liteness by either officer or citizen was displayed, the arrest rate was about 11.3 percent. If the officer initiated an impolite order or command, however, the arrest rate increased to slightly less than 15.8 percent. When the citizen initiated impoliteness or coupled that with noncompliance to the officer's legitimate authority, the rate of arrest increased to about 24.4 percent. And finally, if the impolite orders and impolite noncompliance were mutual, the rate rose dramatically to 40 percent regardless of who initiated the action.

Our evidence was very limited with regard to the probabilities of arrest when an officer's safety was threatened, if we did not consider impoliteness or anger as implicitly threatening. While citizen anger occurred in a third of all encounters observed, and officer or citizen anger occurred in nearly half the encounters, the incidence of violence or threatened violence was so low as to make conclusions difficult.

Our impression is that the actual commission of violence against an officer automatically led to arrest. The reverse was not necessarily true, since sometimes an officer may have attacked a citizen without arresting him and may have approached an encounter with his gun drawn as a precaution but with no further effect.

Conclusions

1. Careful documentation of police patrol activities has provided a basis for some empirically grounded criteria which police in three midwestern communities used in deciding whether or not to identify a citizen as a violator. The thrust of current police literature (and even the rhetoric of the police occupation itself) is that patrol officers have considerable arrest discretion. On the contrary, however, our studies indicate that in approximately half such cases, patrol officers in contact with alleged violators had little, if any, arrest discretion. Officers were not allowed to make an arrest because statutes and/or departmental policy did not encourage arrest; on the other hand, officers had no other option but to make an arrest because other authorities (e.g., the courts) or departmental policy so directed.

2. In any comprehensive explanation of a police officer's decision to arrest, one must first examine the real restraints which impinge upon the latitude of his decision making. One such significant restraint in our study was the requirement of law which often acted primarily as a suppressant of arrest relative to the demands of police by complainants. Another restraint was the finer distinctions made by the informal and formal policies of a particular police department. Patrol officers on rare occasions may have ignored such restraints, but direct observational data impressively attested to the impact of such restraints.

3. Outcomes of police-citizen contact could best be predicted by us by first employing legal or organizational policy models. These were, in effect, rules for defining the situation and identifying citizen roles, not extralegal models, such as those used for sociologically oriented research. Only after this large portion of nonarrest and arrest outcomes was removed did it seem advisable to utilize models which incorporated such variables as use of abusive language and failure to show respect for the uniform. Legal and organizational policy criteria generally had to be taken into account before extralegal variables had a chance to affect arrest decisions. But once these criteria were satisfied, the chances of arrest fell rather heavily on those who showed disrespect for the officer's role or threatened his safety.

4. One last general conclusion must be drawn from the data and the strong impression of our observations of police patrol activities. The overwhelming atmosphere of alleged violator-present police-citizen encounters was relatively calm, routine, and not particularly entangling for all parties concerned. In spite of the circumstances which generated the presence of police officers with their uniforms and weapons—the high incidence of drunkenness, the presence of adversaries, and the occasional presence of known past offenders—one must be impressed with the high degree of civility all parties accorded each other. This in no way is meant to diminish the role of uncivil behavior and its consequences, but is stated in order to accurately describe the observable character of most of the police-citizen encounters in our study.

Some Suggested Performance Criteria

Our data clearly show that a substantial proportion of encounters involve either discretion without arrest option or discretion limited to arrest. In both cases the so-called nonvisibility problem is less crucial, since in the first instance there is probably no legal violation, and in the second instance there is virtually always an arrest. The crucial cases are discretion with arrest-option cases. What criteria now seem to govern these cases?

We have distinguished enforcement from arrest. Enforcement is a broad category comprising techniques by means of which persons are brought into compliance with the law. In practice, arrest may be a means of enforcement or a means of punishment, two functionally different ends. If a person commits a crime of sufficient seriousness he will be arrested although he ceases and desists. In the case of a homicide an officer does not merely warn the suspect not to do it again or to stop murdering people. But in the case of a loud party, arrest normally follows the *refusal* of the suspect to hold a quiet party. However the law may read, in a great many cases, the arrest is not so much for having a loud party as for refusing to cease having a loud party. As our data show, noncompliance, especially impolite noncompliance, increases likelihood of arrest to 40 percent. No doubt this percentage would be higher if our data base distinguished degrees of seriousness of noncompliance.

We suggest that the law might more openly recognize the distinction between arrest as a means of enforcement and arrest as a punishment for an act by explicitly providing a formal "warning" and "compliance" stipulation. We suggest that most misdemeanors should be considered as instances where the officer's first duty is to enjoin the citizen to cease from his activity. He would issue a warning ticket and request that the citizen sign an indication of compliance. If the citizen were then to desist there would be no further legal hassle. Such a procedure would formalize present practice to a degree and make visible the great bulk of low-visibility decisions without overloading the jail house. It would also provide a record, should a citizen refuse to sign the compliance, to which both citizen and officer could refer. If, later in his shift, an officer were called back to the scene, he would have a record of a compliance and, given this record and a repetition of the original act, reason to arrest the citizen. If the citizen refused

to sign the original compliance, either because he felt he was innocent, or for other reasons, then the alternative of arrest would be clear to both himself and to the officer. Generally the compliance should be specific—that, for instance, the suspect agrees to leave the Triangle Bar, and not return there that evening, or that the suspect agrees to turn down his radio to a level acceptable to his neighbors. The warning-and-compliance procedure would be somewhat different from the issuing of tickets for misdemeanors now being tried in some departments.

A compliance would be somewhat like a "fix-it" ticket, but more immediate, since in most cases it would involve immediate compliance through ceasing an activity which is an annoyance to some other person(s) in the vicinity. Here we should note that all studies of uniformed police agree that more than three-quarters of police work is in response to citizen complaints, and that (unlike a speeder) unless the person complies the interpersonal annoyance is likely to continue and cause renewed complainant dissatisfaction. Compliances would be encounter-specific, not long-term contracts, and they would not become a matter of permanent record. They would be discarded and destroyed by officers at the end of some specific period of time, probably within the week.

The use of compliances would minimally formalize and make visible what is now practiced informally and invisibly. The amendment of many present laws pertaining to misdemeanors would formalize the warning function of the officer and make it mandatory, thus eliminating those inequities which result from an officer's directly arresting a person for an act in one case, while another officer negotiates or imposes some other outcome than arrest for the same act in another case.

The second factor which seems to influence discretion with arrest-option situations is the interpersonal respect which characterizes officer-civilian interaction during the encounter. When such respect is not displayed, arrest percentages increase dramatically. We have already commented on the lack of formal sanctions available to police in such situations and therefore their resort to informal punishment. We suggest that perhaps the law and the courts ought to take more notice of these relations. After proper warning, as with cases referred to above, officers should be able to ticket a citizen for certain specifically described acts of disrespect, notably for the use of gratuitous insult, especially that involving gutter language and insulting labels, or, alternately, such acts should be taken cognizance of by the prosecutor and/or the court should a case come to trial and ultimate conviction on some other ground.

The same rules should apply to police officers. It should be expected that they would exercise their authority with decent language, and that a citizen should have the same right to make a complaint against the officer as the officer does against him. One possible means of impartial evidence collection might be a requirement that officers carry small, portable recording devices in their shirt pockets which would record both their words to the civilians and the civilians' to them. The recordings would be erased within forty-eight hours unless a complaint by either a citizen or an officer was heard.

A third controversy relates to violence. The traditional right of an officer to use deadly force to apprehend a felon is now recognized by many to be an unwisely broad mandate, since the outcome may be equivalent to capital punishment for a theft. It is less widely recognized that violence is still used beyond the point of necessity and as an informal punishment by officers, mainly because of indifference or lack of control by their superiors. Generally, the law should make the use of violence against any person who is restrained, either physically or by handcuffs, grounds for immediate dismissal of an officer, as well as for civil and criminal action. An impartial officer of the court might be present at the jail when prisoners are brought in to determine whether either the prisoner or the officer is injured and to make a report in all such cases.

Fourth, police departments should develop new methods to control and to evaluate personnel. Our data indicate that a supervisor is present less than 5 percent of the time, and that he takes an active part in an encounter much less often than that. Generally, dispatchers can anticipate a situation which is likely to be "hot." Street sergeants should be present at the scene to control their men, especially in those situations where tempers fray and angry words are exchanged.

Additionally, departments should formally recognize that one characteristic of a good officer in cases of "discretion with arrest option" is that he is usually able to settle the situation short of arrest. Too many arrests for minor offenses suggests that the officer is ineffective in negotiating or imposing street solutions. Similarly, if an officer needs to use violence frequently this also indicates lack of interpersonal skill, for violence occurs in probably less than 2 or 3 percent of police-civilian encounters.

Perhaps one monitoring method would be for each officer to carry a book of precoded forms, one of which would be filled out for each call. On it the officer would indicate the original nature of the call; whether a legal violation appeared to have occurred over which he had power; whether alternatives to arrest were offered; whether any physical contact occurred between himself and any civilian during the encounter, and if so, the reason for it; what he assessed the nature of the human relations during the encounter to be; and what the final outcome of the encounter was. Such a card would simply require making checkmarks, but it would enable the department to maintain a continuous monitoring of officer activities, as well as require the officer to do some monitoring of his own activities and manner. Whenever aggressive physical contact occurred, a further explanation of the reason for and nature of the contact should be required. Each encounter report would be entered into the department's data system and would be utilized in personnel evaluations, as well as in evaluations of the nature of departmental activities and studies of the exercise of discretion.

Utilization of procedures similar to those recommended above would make low-visibility decisions more visible, but would permit the continuance of many of the informal practices which result in a much lower arrest rate than would occur with a slavish adherence to the letter of the law. Such procedures would further introduce control features into the patrol system, a system which presently suffers from lack of supervision.

REFERENCES

1. R. L. Ackoff and T. Emery, *On Purposeful Systems* (Chicago: Aldine-Atherton, 1972).

2. American Bar Association Project on Standards for Criminal Justice, *Standards Relating to the Urban Police Function* (Chicago: American Bar Association, 1973).

3. W. Ross Ashby, *An Introduction to Cybernetics* (London: Chapman and Hall, 1956).

4. E. Bittner, "The Police on Skid Row: A Study of Peace Keeping," *American Sociological Review, 32* (October 1967), pp. 699–715.

5. E. Bittner, *The Function of the Police in Modern Society* (Washington, D.C.: U.S. Government Printing Office, 1970).

6. D. J. Black, "Police Encounters and Social Organization: An Observational Study." (Ph.D. dissertation, University of Michigan, 1968).

7. D. J. Black, "Production of Crime Rates," *American Sociological Review, 35* (August 1970), pp. 733–48.

8. D. J. Black and A. J. Reiss, Jr., "Police Control of Juveniles," *American Sociological Review, 35* (February 1970), pp. 63–77.

9. Walter Buckley, *Sociology and Modern Systems Theory* (Englewood Cliffs, N.J.: Prentice-Hall, 1967).

10. J. P. Clark, "Isolation of the Police: A Comparison of the British and American Situations," *Journal of Criminal Law, Criminology and Police Science, 56* (September 1965), pp. 307–19.

11. E. Cumming, I. Cumming, and L. Edell, "Policeman as Philosopher, Guide and Friend," *Social Problems, 12* (Winter 1965), pp. 276–86.

12. John A. Gardiner, *Traffic and the Police: Variations in Law-Enforcement Police* (Cambridge, Mass.: Harvard University Press, 1969).

13. N. Goldman, *The Differential Selection of Juvenile Offenders for Court Appearance*, National Research and Information Center, National Council on Crime and Delinquency (New York: National Council on Crime and Delinquency, 1963).

14. H. Goldstein, "Administrative Problems in Controlling the Exercise of Police Authority," *Journal of Criminal Law, Criminology and Police Science, 58* (June 1967), pp. 160–72; J. Goldstein, "Police Discretion Not to Invoke the Criminal Process: Low Visibility Decisions in the Administration of Justice," *Yale Law Journal, 69* (March 1960), pp. 543–94.

15. Neal Gross, Ward S. Mason, and Alexander W. McEachern, *Explorations in Role Analysis* (New York: John Wiley & Sons, 1958).

16. C. A. Hartjen, "Police-Citizen Encounters: Social Order in Interpersonal Interaction," *Criminology* (May 1972), pp. 61–84.

17. W. R. LaFave, "The Police and Nonenforcement of the Law," parts 1 and 2, *Wisconsin Law Review* (January, March 1962), pp. 104–37 and 179–239; *Arrest: The Decision to Take a Suspect Into Custody* (Boston: Little, Brown, 1965); "Improving Police Performance Through the Exclusionary Rule," parts 1 and 2, *Missouri Law Review, 30* 3, 4 (1965), pp. 391–458 and 566–610.

18. W. R. LaFave and F. S. Remington, "Controlling the Police: The Judge's Role in Making and Reviewing Law Enforcement Decisions," *Michigan Law Review, 63* (1965), pp. 987–1012.

19. U. A. Leonard and H. W. More, *Police Organization and Management* (Mineola, N.Y.: Foundation Press, 1971).

20. E. W. Linse, Jr., *Due Process in Practice: A Study of Police Procedures in Minneapolis* (Minneapolis: University of Minnesota, 1965).

21. J. M. Livermore, "Policing," *Minnesota Law Review, 55* (1970), pp. 649–729.

22. R. J. Lundman, "Police and the Maintenance of Propriety" (Ph.D. dissertation, University of Minnesota, Minneapolis, 1972); "Domestic Police-Citizen Encounters" (mimeograph, University of Delaware, 1973).

23. James G. March and Herbert A. Simon, *Organizations* (New York: John Wiley & Sons, 1958).

24. R. I. Parnas, "The Police Response to the Domestic Disturbance," *Wisconsin Law Review* (Fall 1967), pp. 914–60.

25. I. Piliavin and S. Briar, "Police Encounters with Juveniles," *American Journal of Sociology, 70* (September 1964), pp. 206–14.

26. D. M. Peterson, "Police Disposition of the Petty Offender," *Sociology and Social Research, 56* (April 1972), pp. 320–30.

27. President's Commission on Law Enforcement and Administration of Justice, *Task Force Report: The Police* (Washington, D.C.: U.S. Government Printing Office, 1967).

28. A. J. Reiss, Jr., *The Police and the Public* (New Haven: Yale University Press, 1971).

29. R. E. Sykes, "Police III: A Code for the Study of Police-Citizen Interaction," *Observations, 3* (November 1972), pp. 20–40.

30. James D. Thompson, *Organization in Action* (New York: McGraw-Hill, 1967).

31. Stanley H. Udy, Jr., "Administrative Rationality, Social Setting and Organizational Development," *American Journal of Sociology, 68* (1962), pp. 299–308.

32. Ludwig von Bertalanffy, *General Systems Theory: Foundations, Development, Applications* (New York: George Braziller, 1968).

33. P. Watslawick, H. H. Beavin, and D. D. Jackson, *Pragmatics of Human Communication* (New York: Norton, 1967).

34. W. A. Westley, "Violence and the Police," *American Journal of Sociology, 59* (July 1953), pp. 34–41.

35. F. A. Wileman, ed., Guidelines for Discretion: *Five Models for Local Law Enforcement Agencies.*

36. F. A. Wileman and F. J. Crisafi, eds., *Guidelines for Discretion: Twelve Models for Local Law Enforcement Agencies.*

37. J. Q. Wilson, *Varieties of Police Behavior* (Cambridge, Mass.: Harvard University Press, 1968).

38. Thomas P. Wilson, "Normative and Interpretive Paradigms in Sociology," *Understanding Everyday Life*, Jack Douglas, ed. (Chicago: Aldine, 1970).

The Differential Selection of Juvenile Offenders for Court Appearance

NATHAN GOLDMAN

The following set of conclusions is drawn from data based on an analysis of the police records of the four communities, Steel City, Trade City, Mill Town and Manor Heights, and on a series of interviews with police in the city of Pittsburgh and in twenty-two minor municipalities around Pittsburgh. The problem of this research was to test the general hypothesis of the differential selection, by police, of juvenile offenders for court referral and to investigate this process of selection. These conclusions are presented with the reservation that, since they are based on four individual communities and a sample of policemen in a relatively circumscribed industrial and commercial area, generalizations to other communities may not be justified.

Conclusions

I. There is a wide variation in rates of arrest in different communities.
   A. Arrests per 1,000 population aged ten to seventeen ranged from 12.4 to 49.7, with an average rate of 32.6 per thousand.
   B. The gross variations in arrest rates may be accounted for principally by variations in arrests for minor offenses.
      1. In some communities · citizens are more apt to complain about minor of-

fenses such as trespassing, mischief, and disorderly conduct which are disregarded in other communities.

II. Not all children apprehended in law violation are recorded in the juvenile court.
   A. Among those apprehended by citizens, few are reported to the police.
   B. Among those apprehended by the police, not all are inscribed on police records.
      1. It is estimated that about half of the children who come to the attention of the police for law violation are taken to the police station.
   C. Among those officially registered on police records, only a small proportion, 35.4 percent, are referred to the juvenile court for official action.

III. There are wide variations in rates of court appearance of juveniles in various communities.
   A. Court appearances per 1,000 population aged ten to seventeen varied from community to community.
      1. Rates ranged from 4.1 to 17.1 with an average of 9.9 per thousand.
   B. The proportion of arrests referred to the juvenile court varied between communities.
      1. Rates ranged from 8.6 percent to 71.2 percent with an average of 35.4 percent.

IV. There is a differential handling by police of arrests, based on the seriousness of the offense.
   A. The proportion of arrests for serious of-

SOURCE: National Council on Crime and Delinquency, New York, 1963.

fenses varies from community to community.

1. Such offenses range from 6.1 percent to 37.1 percent of arrests with an average of 20.3 percent.

B. Arrests for serious offenses are more frequently referred to court than are arrests for minor offenses.

1. Between 71.4 percent and 100 percent with an average of 80.2 percent of serious offenses were reported to the court.

2. Between 2.3 percent and 71 percent with an average of 24.1 percent of arrests for minor offenses were referred to court.

C. Differences in the court referral rates are largely a result of the differential handling of minor offenses.

V. There are differentials in court referral rates of Negro and white children arrested for law violation.

A. Arrests of Negro children are more frequently referred to court than arrests of white children.

1. 33.6 percent of the arrests of white children and 64.8 percent of the arrests of Negro children were referred for juvenile court action.

2. Although arrests of Negro children were 5.7 percent of the total juvenile arrests, these cases constituted 10.5 percent of the total court referrals.

B. The rate of referral of Negro juvenile offenders to court varies from community to community.

1. 51.2 percent to 84.6 percent of the Negro children arrested in three communities were referred to court.

C. The differences in rates of referral of arrests of Negro children are largely a result of the more frequent referral of minor offenses of Negro children.

1. 79.3 percent of arrests of white children and 87.5 percent of arrests of Negro children for serious offenses were referred to court.

2. 22.6 percent of the arrests of white children and 53.2 percent of the arrests of Negro children for minor offenses were so referred.

VI. Conclusions regarding the differential disposition of arrests of boys and of girls are not justified because of the small number of female arrests.

A. It is suggested, however, that girls brought to the attention of the police are more liable to court referral than are boys.

1. Slightly more than half, 54.2 percent of the girls arrested, and 35.1 percent of the boys were referred to court. The differences between these rates, however, are *not statistically significant.*

B. There appears to be considerable variation in the court referral of girls in different communities.

1. These referral rates varied from zero to 75 percent.

VII. The rate of court referrals of arrested children increases with the age of the child.

A. Offenders below age ten are less frequently referred to court than are older children.

1. 20.9 percent of the children below age ten are referred to court.

B. Children between ages ten and fifteen were more frequently referred to court than were younger children and less frequently so referred than older children.

1. 30 percent of children aged ten to fifteen were referred to court after arrest by police.

C. Offenders between the ages of fifteen and eighteen were more frequently reported to court than were younger children.

1. 45.4 percent of these arrests were referred to court.

D. The increase in the rate of court referral with age is fairly consistent in different communities.

1. In one of the four communities studied there was a decrease in the rate of referral of offenders aged fifteen to eighteen. This appeared to be a special result of police attitude toward court "leniency."

VIII. There are distinguishable patterns of handling cases of juvenile offenders in different communities. These patterns are as follows:

A. A low arrest rate coupled with a high court referral rate. Very little differentiation in handling cases. Offense, sex, and race seem of little influence in disposition, with age the only discernible differentiating factor.

B. A high arrest rate, coupled with a high arrest rate for minor offenses. A very low court referral rate, based on seriousness of offense, sex, and age of the offender.

C. A moderately high arrest rate with a relatively moderately high court referral rate for all offenses. Differential reporting based on race and age.

D. A moderately high arrest rate with a low court referral rate. Referral varies with seriousness of the offense, sex, race, and age of the child.

IX. These patterns are a function of the relations between the police and the community.

A. In general, police will attempt to reflect what they consider to be the attitudes of the public toward delinquency.

1. The concern of the public with respect to minor offenses such as shoplifting, trespassing, mischief, disorderly conduct, etc., will determine the police arrests for such offenses.

2. The desires of the public with regard to official court handling of delinquency problems, as opposed to informal handling of offenses within the community will affect court referral rates.

B. Where there exists an objective, impersonal relation between the police and the public, court referral rates will be high and there will be little discrimination with respect to seriousness of offense, race, and sex of the offender.

C. Where there exists a personal face-to-face relation between the police and the public, there will be more discrimination with respect to court referral of an arrested juvenile.

1. Rates of court referral will be low. More cases will be carried on an unofficial level.

2. Disposition will be significantly determined by the seriousness of the offense. Minor offenses, even though they make up the bulk of the arrests, will be reported only rarely.

3. Sex and race of the offender will vary as factors in the referral process.

X. The differential selection of offenders for court by police is determined by the attitudes of the policeman toward the offender, his family, the offense, the juvenile court, his own role as a policeman, and the community attitudes toward delinquency.

A. *The policeman's attitudes toward the juvenile court.* This may be based on actual experience with the court or on ignorance of court policies. The policeman who feels the court unfair to the police or too lenient with offenders may fail to report cases to the court since, in his opinion, nothing will be gained by such official referral.

B. *The impact of special individual experiences in the court, or with different racial groups, or with parents of offenders, or with specific offenses, on an individual policeman.* This may condition his future reporting of certain types of offense or classes of offenders.

C. *Apprehension about criticism by the court.* Cases which the policeman might prefer, for various reasons, not to report for official action may be reported because of fear that the offense might subsequently come to the attention of the court and result in embarrassment to the police officer.

D. *Publicity given to certain offenses either in the neighborhood or elsewhere may cause the police to feel that these are too "hot" to handle unofficially and must be referred to the court.* In the discussion of police interviews it was indicated how this factor might operate to bring into court an offense of even a very insignificant nature.

E. *The necessity for maintaining respect for police authority in the community.* A juvenile who publicly causes damage to the dignity of the police, or who is defiant, refusing the "help" offered by the police, will be considered as needing court supervision, no matter how trivial the offense.

F. *Various practical problems of policing.* The fact that no witness fees are paid policemen in juvenile court was mentioned by a small number as affecting the policy of some police officers with respect to court referral of juveniles. The distance to the court and the detention home and the availability of police personnel for the trip were likewise indicated as occasionally affecting the decision of the policeman.

G. *Pressure by political groups or other special interest groups.* Such pressure may determine the line of action a policeman will follow in a given case. He considers it necessary to accede to such pressures in order to retain his job.

H. *The policeman's attitude toward specific offenses.* The reporting or nonreporting of a juvenile offender may depend on the policeman's own childhood experiences or on attitudes toward specific offenses developed during his police career.

I. *The police officer's impression of the family situation, the degree of family interest in and control of the offender, and the reaction of the parents to the problem of the child's offense.* A child coming from a home where supervision is judged to be lacking, or where the parents—especially the mother—are alcoholic, or one whose parents assume an aggressive or "uncooperative" attitude toward the police officer, is considered in need of supervision by the juvenile court.

J. *The attitude and personality of the boy.* An offender who is well mannered, neat in appearance, and "listens" to the policeman will be considered a good risk for unofficial adjustment in the community. Defiance of the police will usually result in immediate court referral. Athletes and altar boys will rarely be referred to court for their offenses. The minor offenses of feeble-minded or atypical children will usually be overlooked by the police. Maliciousness in a child is considered by the police to indicate need for official court supervision.

K. *The Negro child offender is considered less tractable and needing more authoritarian supervision than a white child.* He is generally considered inherently more criminal than a white offender. Exceptions to this general attitude were found in the upper-class residential area and also among white policemen in the crowded Negro slum area of Pittsburgh. The statistical data, except for the small mill town, do not corroborate these discriminatory attitudes expressed by the police.

L. *The degree of criminal sophistication shown in the offense.* The use of burglar tools, criminal jargon, a gun, or strong-arm methods, or signs of planning or premeditation, are generally taken by the police to indicate a need for immediate court referral.

M. *Juvenile offenders apprehended in a group will generally be treated on an all-or-none basis.* The group must be released or reported as a whole. Some police may attempt to single out individuals in the gang for court referral. Such action, however, exposes the policeman to the censure of the court for failing to report the others involved in the offense.

Discussion

It must be borne in mind that in this study the several variables were artificially isolated. In reality, no one of the factors which have been shown to operate in the determination of which offenders are officially reported to the court by the police can be found to exist alone. There is an interrelationship between the variables which cannot be expressed in statistical terms. Some of the factors discussed above among the conclusions may automatically exclude consideration of other factors. At times the task of the policeman may be akin to that of solving a problem containing a number of variables. At other times, *one* of the considerations mentioned above—such as political pressure—may force the decision of the police officer in a given direction.

The concept of juvenile delinquency is to some extent determined by the policeman in selectively reporting juvenile offenders to the court. As was indicated in the opening chapter of this paper, research in the field of juvenile delinquency has been based primarily on juveniles in a court, clinic, or in an institution. Institutionalized delinquents and offenders in a juvenile court had been, for the most part, apprehended and officially reported by the police.

The research has shown that the police base their reporting partly on the act of the offender, but also on the policeman's idiosyncratic interpretation of this act, and the degree of pressure applied by the community on the police. The collective pressures mentioned above, the attitudes of the community toward the offense, toward the offender and toward his family, affect the decision of the policeman in his reporting of juvenile offenses. In addition, the policeman's own private attitudes, his special experiences, his concern for status and prestige in the community may be important factors in determining which particular juvenile offender will be referred to the court. Once reported to the court, the child then becomes available for official scrutiny and study. The availability of a juvenile offender for official recording and for research studies on delinquency thus depends ultimately on the responsiveness of the police officer to a series of collective social pressures and personal attitudes. The policeman's interpretation of these pressures serves to select or determine the composition of the sample of those juvenile offenders who will become officially recognized from among all those known to him.

Selection of a sample of the population of offenders on the basis of collective pressures and private attitudes cannot help but result in a marked and unpredictable bias. It is on this biased sample that most of the juvenile delinquency research has been conducted. Generalizations based on such a sample can have only limited validity. For a more adequate understanding of the social and psychological processes involved in juvenile delinquent behavior it is necessary to observe juvenile offenders in the community in their earliest contacts with the police, before they have been selected by differential treatment. There can be no complete study of the etiological factors in juvenile delinquent conduct unless the unpredictable variable of the policeman is removed from the process. An adequate study of juvenile delinquency must begin at a point before the one at which the police officer begins to operate. To provide more valid generalizations, juvenile delinquency must be studied in the community where it occurs, where a relatively unselected sample of juvenile offenders may be observed.

The decision regarding the disposition of a given instance of juvenile law violation, by the policeman, may have some very significant effects on the future conduct of the child. The consequences of any act will significantly affect the behavior of the actor in similar situations in the future. The interaction, or exchange of gestures, between the policeman and the child apprehended in law violation may serve to increase or to decrease the probability of future excursions into delinquency. Thus the behavior of the police toward the child may be a significant determinant of the child's continued participation in delinquent conduct.

An important corollary of these observations is that the police must be provided training in the problems of handling children who come to their attention for law violation. They must be aided in understanding the possible effects of their attempts to "help" the apprehended violator by giving him "another chance," or the possible effects of discrimination with respect to the race of the child. Since he will be, by virtue of his job, in a position where he has to make decisions crucial to the child's welfare, and of great significance for the child's future conduct, it is important that he be supplied with the proper sensitivities and perceptions for making the best decisions for the child and for the community.

Police Violence:

A Changing Pattern

DAVID BURNHAM

Why does the policeman swing his nightstick? Does he often swing it unnecessarily? Are there ways to reduce the occasions when he resorts to force?

During the last few months, New Yorkers have become more aware of these questions as a result of violent confrontations between the police and peace demonstrators at the Whitehall Street induction center, hippies at Grand Central Terminal and students at Columbia University.

The use of violent force by the police, however, does not begin and end with the high drama of students occupying a university building or opponents of the war in Vietnam besieging an induction center. It is an integral part of the daily operation of any large police department.

To explore the sometimes violent world of the policeman, interviews were conducted with scores of city policemen, former policemen, sociologists, psychologists and specialists from such organizations as the International Association of Chiefs of Police and Brandeis University's Lemberg Center for the Study of Violence.

From talks with these authorities, many of whom are now involved in studies of violent police action, three broad conclusions emerge:

Apparently there is less police violence in New York today than there was in the "third degree" days of 20 or 30 years ago when such policemen as the late John J. Broderick won wide acclaim for beating up persons they decided were thugs and a gun fight was the quickest way to be promoted to detective.

The use of violent force by the police can be divided into four sometimes overlapping categories. First, the violent force the State Legislature has authorized the police to use while making an arrest. Second, the violent force that is tacitly authorized by

either public or police tradition to handle such offenders as the sex criminal or the "cop fighter." Third, the violence used by those policemen who enjoy hurting people. Fourth, the violence that erupts when policemen become afraid or are under great physical or mental stress.

To improve the control of violent force, many of these specialists believe major changes in the purpose, recruiting methods, training, organization and tactics of the police will have to be implemented.

A Problem Since 1931

Controlling violent force has been a central concern of enlightened police administrators since 1931, when the national crime commission of that day—headed by George W. Wickersham, a former United States Attorney General—sharply criticized police torture tactics then routinely used by many departments.

But police violence did not disappear with sharp words of the Wickersham Committee. In 1966, the second national crime commission, formally known as the President's Commission for Law Enforcement and Administration of Justice, sent observers to record police actions in Negro and white slums of Washington, Boston and Chicago. The observers accompanied 450 policemen on a total of 850 eight-hour tours of duty.

One out of 10 of these policemen, according to the Federal observers, used "improper" or "unnecessary" force. The incidents placed in this category included situations in which policemen beat a handcuffed man, another in which several policemen held a man while a patrolman beat him, and a third in which two policemen beat a confused mental patient they had pushed into a phone booth.

Major Cities Concerned

While the ratio of violent incidents to policemen found in the slums of three other cities cannot be applied directly to New York, it does suggest that police violence is a serious problem in all major cities.

SOURCE: *New York Times*, July 7, 1968, © 1968 by The New York Times Company. Reprinted by permission.

However, most authorities on the police have become wary of the phrase "police brutality" in this connection because they believe the term has become so supercharged with emotion. They feel the expression "violent force"—both authorized and non-authorized—is a more accurate way of discussing this aspect of police conduct.

Most authorities also agree, despite a lack of concrete evidence, that today's policemen resort to unnecessary violence less than they used to.

"It was not many years ago that every patrolman on the block used to take it upon himself to punish kids if they got out of line," recalled one police official. "And detectives used to regularly sweat out confessions. With the Supreme Court's increasing interest in crime and more vocal complaints from the poor, these old ways have just about disappeared."

Some Force Authorized

But as long as there have been police, some form of violent force has been authorized by law. Under the state's penal law, the police may use any force necessary short of death to complete an arrest.

In addition, policemen are authorized to use deadly force when in danger of serious physical injury, when pursuing a person who has committed such serious crimes as robbery, rape or arson, or when completing a felony arrest of a person who may be armed.

But authorities familiar with the operation of the New York Police Department—and other police agencies in the United States—know that the force authorized by law is only a part of the force actually used by the police.

One example of extralegal force, the second major category of police violence, is that used in the belief that its application has been tacitly approved by the public or by fellow policemen, according to most experts on police operations.

"Reaction of a Human Being"

"If you catch some terrible punk raping an old woman," said one experienced city patrolman, "you want to sock him and you may sock him. That isn't the reaction of a patrolman or detective, that is the reaction of a human being. The cops identify completely with the disgust most people feel about a real bad crime."

Until fairly recently, the patrolman continued, the New York police used violence in two other situations in which it believed the public wanted

violent force to be employed. "If there was a real bad murder, you would get the feeling that the public wanted the killer and they didn't care how we caught him," the patrolman said. "We also used to have the feeling that the public wanted us to keep pushing around homosexuals and other perverts."

William A. Westley, a sociologist now at McGill University in Montreal, found a somewhat similar pattern in the large unnamed city that he studied. In a report on "Violence and the Police," Dr. Westley quotes one rookie policeman:

" 'One of the older men advised me that if the courts didn't punish a man, we should. He told me about a sex crime and then said the policeman has the right to use the force necessary to make an arrest and that in that kind of crime you can use just a little more force.' "

Dr. Westley said he had found the "control of sexual conduct so difficult and the demand for it so incessant that the police come to sanction the illegal use of violence in obtaining that control."

But today in New York, many policemen agree, very few, if any, persons are actually beaten to get information, and the increasing public tolerance of deviant behavior has lessened the public pressure on the police to harass homosexuals.

One kind of unauthorized violence, however, still is regularly resorted to by the police, according to those authorities interviewed. That is the unwritten rule that a copfighter would be dealt with harshly, and often violently.

"All Hell Breaks Loose"

"An attack on a cop is viewed by the police as the most serious thing in the world," one city detective said. "When there is a 1013 call (The New York signal for a policeman in trouble) all hell breaks loose and patrol cars from all over the city respond.

"The rightful worry about our own safety leads to a belief that any kind of physical response—or sometimes even an angry word—is a cause for a crack across the head or a few punches. I've seen an old drunk being creamed for having taken a harmless swing."

William Brown, a former inspector in the New York Police Department who is now a professor of criminal justice at the State University of New York at Albany, agreed with the observations of the detective, although he did not condone the tradition.

Dr. Brown described the attitude of the average patrolman this way: "Anyone who wants to fight me is my potential killer." He added that the professional criminal was very aware of this police tradition and, once captured, usually was completely docile.

A Third Kind of Violence

The third kind of violence that most authorities believe occurs is that used by some policemen who enjoy inflicting pain.

In his study of the police, Dr. Westley said he had found a small number of men "who are clearly sadists, who frequently commit brutalities repugnant to the rest of the police."

The sociologist said, however, that it is difficult to weed out the sadists because of the general acceptance of violence and the extreme emphasis on secrecy by the police.

Dr. Nelson Watson, a psychologist on the staff of the International Association of Chiefs of Police, noted: "The very fact that police are the only group authorized by the state to use force tends to attract the occasional men who like to use it."

However, one New York patrolman voiced another view. "There are no sadists," he asserted, "just weak and stupid men who distort the hell out of the way the police normally operate."

Hans Toch, a social psychologist and professor of criminal justice at the State University of New York at Albany, agrees. "I doubt you'll find many real sadists in any police department. What you will find is a substantial minority of men whose reactions to certain standard situations tend to involve the use of force."

Dr. Toch has recently completed a study of assaults against policemen for the National Institute of Mental Health.

The fourth kind of violent force—that erupts during times of great stress—is the one most familiar to the public because it often occurs during demonstrations or riots that attract large numbers of newsmen and television cameramen.

Over the years, the New York Police Department has gained a national reputation for handling crowds and demonstrations with great deftness. During the looting and arson that broke out immediately after the assassination of Dr. Martin Luther King Jr., for example, the department won praise for acting with forceful restraint while actually arresting more persons than they did in Harlem and Bedford-Stuyvesant during the riots of 1964.

Contempt a Factor

However, a number of specialists said the personal contempt felt by many policemen for the values, goals and life styles of students, peace demonstrators and hippies had been an underlying factor in the outbursts of violence during the demonstrations at Columbia, Grand Central and Whitehall Street.

"You must remember that most policemen because of their training and background believe that civil disobedience is completely wrong," said Dr. Watson.

Former City Police Inspector William Brown added: "I think the student contempt of patriotism and materialism is, in some ways, much more difficult for the police to understand than the problems confronting a poor Negro living in Harlem."

"You must consider," said one college-educated patrolman, "that many cops have just bought houses in Farmingdale, L. I., that many are in the process of escaping from boyhoods in white slums and that this tends to make them super middle class.

"They really become outraged and confused when they hear some kid question the guts of those fighting in Vietnam or hear some Barnard girl shouting dirty words. Their idea of a woman is a nice, quiet young Catholic girl from Queens."

Dr. John P. Spiegel, a psychiatrist and director of the Lemberg Center for the Study of Violence, asserted recently:

"To the Irish, Italian or Polish police officer of working-class background, black-skinned activists and youthful protesters are the embodiment of everything that is alien, evil and destructive of the American social system. Militant youths and black militants are perceived not only as un-American, but also as nonhuman. Ruled out of the human race, they become nonpersons and therefore deserving of intense attack, as one would attack a rattlesnake."

One patrolman said another factor that could trigger violent police reaction is the physical and mental discomforts that demonstrations imposed on policemen. "It doesn't help your temper," he said, "when you are yanked out of your own precinct, away from your own commanders, herded around like cattle, made to stand around for hours and sometimes given vague conflicting orders. You tend to get mad at the demonstrators for causing you all these troubles."

In addition to the social fears and physical

discomforts gnawing at the composure of the individual patrolman, there is his fear of bodily injury.

"At some point when police are faced by a mob or crowd, fear erupts and the individual patrolman no longer seems to be able to discriminate and he strikes out at anyone near him," Dr. Spiegel said.

Physical Fear Cited

Physical fear, for example, may have been one reason why violence occurred at Columbia University on the afternoon of May 1.

A small detail had been ordered to clear a large number of students from the entrance to the campus at Amsterdam Avenue and 116th Street. Badly outnumbered, each patrolman immediately was surrounded by five or six angry, shouting demonstrators.

Suddenly, someone started swinging. One student jumped from a building onto the back of a policeman, seriously injuring him. A wastepaper basket and stick were thrown at the police. During the fight, the police pounced on five or six students, held them on the ground and severely beat them with their blackjacks. Only two students, however, were arrested.

Detective Disagrees

One detective disagreed with the suggestion that physical fear was an important factor in police violence, but he pointed to a different kind of fear.

"Most cops I know will walk into the mouth of a cannon. But they're terrified of words. Don't forget, most cops don't have any education, they're inarticulate.

"In a way, I think the police feel much more challenged by the words of the Columbia students than by any threat there may have actually been. The police feel superior to the Negro—they can laugh at him—but they don't feel superior to the students. This means they show a tolerance to the Negro that doesn't come so easily toward the students."

What steps can be taken to reduce the use of violent force by the police?

Many specialists believe the essential first step is for the police to recognize and accept the fact that they spend much more time helping law-abiding people than they do chasing criminals.

Noncrime Activities

For although policemen like to think of themselves as uniformed soldiers in an extremely dangerous war against crime, time studies done in a number of cities show that the average patrolman spends most of his time on such noncrime activities as calling ambulances, returning lost children and directing traffic.

In addition, despite some very real perils connected with police work, statistics indicate that crime fighting is not nearly as dangerous as either the public or the police believe. According to statistics from the city Personnel Department, for example, during the first nine months of 1966 firemen had three times more injuries and sanitation men had four times more injuries than policemen.

And in terms of number of days lost for each injury, the injuries suffered by the men of the Fire and Sanitation Departments appeared considerably more serious than those suffered by the police.

But despite the necessary business of keeping the peace and crime prevention, however, it is the violent aspect of police work that is most emphasized in the traditions of the department. Last month, for example, Mayor Lindsay presented the department's highest awards to 26 patrolmen and detectives for being the city's most outstanding policemen in 1967.

26 Men Honored

All 26 awards—three of them presented posthumously—went to men who had been in gun battles with armed criminals.

Despite the unquestioned heroism of these men, the department did not present a single award for other vital aspects of police work, such as preventing a riot or conducting an investigation that led to the nonviolent arrest of a notorious criminal.

"It is a fact that until very recently a patrolman who got in a gun battle was immediately rewarded with a promotion to detective," said one former city police official who now commands a department in another city. "And it is unfortunately a fact that the tradition of rewarding the man who winds up in violent confrontation is still a very real part of the New York Police Department and most other departments, too."

Morton Bard, a psychologist at City College who spent a short time as a New York policeman many years ago, believes the "widening gap between the present reality [of police work] and the outlook of the past is damaging and costly to both society in general and the beleaguered policeman in particular."

"Ill-equipped to understand and meet his realistic

service functions with the knowledge of the present, the policeman often resorts to inappropriate solutions more suited to the simple realities of the past," he said. "More often than not, repressive force indiscriminately and insensitively applied is regarded as the most effective means of coping with those functions that do not involve crime."

Dr. Bard, together with Dr. Bernard Berkowitz, a colleague at City College, is attempting to deal with this problem through their establishment of a Family Crisis Unit in the 30th Precinct, which covers the West Side of Manhattan between 141st and 165th Streets. This experiment was made possible by a grant of $94,736 by the office of Law Enforcement Assistance of the Department of Justice.

The Family Crisis Unit, which began its work a year ago, employs 18 patrolmen who have been given one month of intensive psychological training and specific orders to try to help resolve family fights that later might develop into serious crimes.

The potential contribution of this prevention effort can be understood when it is realized that in this country about one-third of all murders and one-tenth of all assaults are committed by one member of a family against another.

Unit Is Praised

Dr. Toch is enthusiastic about the Family Crisis Unit.

"The police have to head toward a tremendously increased—almost revolutionary—emphasis on positive, helpful ways of dealing with people," he said. "I am convinced that until such experiments as the Family Crisis Unit become operational that there can be no significant decrease in the amount of police violence."

Even without such a profound change, many authorities believe less pervasive steps could be taken to reduce police violence.

Some, for example, criticize the process by which the New York Police Department selects its men. Unlike many large departments, New York does not require a psychiatric or psychological interview for all applicants.

Instead, the city Police Department places heavy emphasis on a detailed background check in an effort to turn up any erratic behavior in the past as an indicator of possible trouble in the future.

Every applicant is given a general intelligence test and is interviewed by the department. One patrolman, however, indicated some doubts about the purpose and effectiveness of the departmental interview.

"The guy who talked to me," he said, "indicated he had been a motorcycle cop for the last 17 years and spent the entire talk trying to find out if I was an undercover agent from The Village Voice."

Though Dr. Toch and others questioned whether psychiatry had reached the point whereby a brief interview would significantly improve the screening process for New York policemen, others argued that any improvement would be welcome.

"Two Real Psychos"

"In my training company there were two real psychos who just shouldn't have been there," said a detective. "One guy was always playing with knives—he later stabbed someone—and another guy who took every word as a personal insult. Neither should have been cops."

The second part of the screening process—during which the precinct commanders are charged with critically examining the performance of probationary policemen before they become regulars—also was questioned.

"Once you make it through the Police Academy," said a former high police official, "you almost automatically become a cop. No real effort is made during this period to separate the bad apples."

Police records support this statement. In 1963, for example, 33 probationary patrolmen were dismissed. In 1964, 30 were dismissed. In 1965, 41. In 1966, 19. And in 1967, 14. The average number of new policemen joining the force during each of these years was more than 1,600.

Police training tactics and the direction given by top commanders also are considered extremely important factors in reducing police violence. One recent positive example, according to most specialists, was Police Commissioner Howard R. Leary's written order to his men in 1966 curtailing the use of pistols during riots and other demonstrations.

"No unnecessary discharge of firearm or unnecessary withdrawal of revolver from holster," the order said in part.

The result of this order is apparent from the statistics of the police action during the disturbances in Harlem and the Bedford-Stuyvesant section of Brooklyn in 1964 and the disturbances in the same areas this spring.

In 1964, the police fired more than 2,000 shots, most of them in the air. At least one person was killed and about 30 were wounded. This year, the police fired no shots and no one was reported killed or injured.

Police Cynicism

ARTHUR NIEDERHOFFER

In the police world, cynicism is discernible at all levels, in every branch of law enforcement. It has also characterized police in other times and places. During the French Revolution and then under Napoleon, Joseph Fouché, the minister of police, concluded that with a few exceptions the world was composed of scoundrels, hypocrites, and imbeciles.(1) Many years later, reviewing the American police scene in 1939, Read Bain found that policemen were committed to the belief that the citizen was always trying "to get away with something," and that all men would commit crimes except for the fear of the police.(2)

In an interview conducted by the Center for the Study of Democratic Institutions, the late Chief William Parker of the Los Angeles Police Department was asked, "Are you inclined to be pessimistic about the future of our society?"

I look back [he replied] over almost thirty-five years in the police service, thirty-five years of dealing with the worst that humanity has to offer. I meet the failures of humanity daily, and I meet them in the worst possible context. It is hard to keep an objective viewpoint. But it is also hard for me to believe that our society can continue to violate all the fundamental rules of human conduct and expect to survive. I think I have to conclude that this civilization will destroy itself, as others have before it. That leaves, then, only one question—when?(3)

A female store detective, with fifteen years of police experience to support her conclusions, states emphatically, "I am convinced that we are turning into a nation of thieves. I have sadly concluded that nine out of ten persons are dishonest."(4)

As noted before, it is possible to distinguish between two kinds of police cynicism. One is directed against life, the world, and people in general; the other is aimed at the police system itself.(5) The first is endemic to policemen of all ranks and persuasions—including the professionals. The second, common among patrolmen, is by definition excluded from the ideology of the professional policeman. The professional wants to transform and eventually control the system. This hope keeps him from cynicism.

Cynicism may be a by-product of *anomie* in the social structure; at the same time it may also prepare the way for personal *anomie* or anomia. Anxious over a personal failure, the individual policeman often disguises his feelings with a cynical attitude, and thus negates the value of the prize he did not attain. Frequently he includes in his cynicism all persons who still seek that prize or have succeeded in winning it, and, occasionally, deprecates the entire social system within which the failure occurred.

As the cynic becomes increasingly pessimistic and misanthropic, he finds it easier to reduce his commitment to the social system and its values. If the patrolman remains a "loner," his isolation may lead to psychological *anomie* and even to suicide (see Table 1).

For the period 1950–1965 the average number of suicides in the New York City Police Department was 5, and its rate per 100,000 was 22.7. In contrast, the general suicide rate in New York City, for the five-year period 1960–1964 was 11.5 per 100,000.(6) But this figure is derived from a population of 100,000 males and females in which the sex ratio (number of males per 100 females) was approximately 96.7. In addition, the suicide rate of males during that time was 1.7 times that of females.(7)

After the necessary adjustments are calculated, the suicide rate for males in the general New York City population is about 15 per 100,000. The average police rate of 22.7 is almost exactly fifty per cent more than this.

Anomie is not the inevitable outcome of police cynicism. Instead a policeman may be absorbed by the "delinquent" occupational subculture, dedicated to a philosophy of cynicism. This group may be deviant, but it is not anomic. It has a code of values and a clear, consistent ideology that function well in the police world. The members may be alienated from their former groups and goals, but they can be completely incorporated into this new reference group.

The third adaptation to cynicism is to overcome it, to regain commitment to the ideal of a decent and honorable career within the police force. Typically, there are two critical points in the advanced career of a policeman when he may discard cynicism. One crisis occurs when he considers retrospectively the many risks his career has involved. Fearing investigation, he may surrender his disaffection and resolve to do his job to the best of his ability. The second opportunity for reassessment comes when a man who is near retirement seeks another job and is often rebuffed. When this happens, a policeman's present situation understandably will seem more attractive to him.

Table 1.   Suicides in the New York City Police Department

Year	Number of Suicides	Size of Force Jan. 1 Each Year	Rate Per 100,000
1950	11	18,563	58
1951	3	19,016	16
1952	3	18,451	16
1953	6	18,762	31
1954	4	19,840	20
1955	8	20,080	37
1956	3	22,460	13
1957	4	23,193	17
1958	1	24,112	4
1959	8	23,636	34
1960	6	23,805	25
1961	5	23,515	20
1962	5	24,374	20
1963	3	24,827	11
1964	4	25,432	16
1965	7	25,897	26
Average per Year	5.0	Average Rate per 100,000	22.7

SOURCE: Annual Reports of the New York City Police Department 1950–1965.

In computing the rate per 100,000, the size of the force for the whole year was obtained by adding the number on the rolls of the department January 1 of that year to the number on the rolls January 1 of the succeeding year, and then dividing by two.

The process leading to cynicism and *anomie* may be viewed as a continuum stretching from commitment at one end to *anomie* at the other, with cynicism as the critical intervening stage. Since police professionals are committed to the highest ideals of police work, they belong at the commitment end; the cynics around the opposite pole. The following model illustrates the typical stages that succeed one another as the policeman moves from commitment to cynicism and *anomie*.

Return to commitment

1. Professionalism or commitment
2. Failure and/or frustration
3. Disenchantment
4. Cynicism → "Delinquent subculture"
5. Alienation
6. *Anomie*

Differences in the patterns of cynicism are apparently related to a policeman's age and experience. The following classification scheme indicates that there is a succession of typical stages in the growth of cynicism that runs parallel to the occupational career. (I am indebted to Professor Joseph Bram of New York University for his help with this typology.)

The preliminary stage, pseudo-cynicism, is recognizable among recruits at the training school. This attitude barely conceals the idealism and commitment beneath the surface.

The second stage, romantic cynicism, is reached in the first five years of the police career. The most idealistic young members of the force are precisely the ones who are most disillusioned by actual police work, and most vulnerable to this type of cynicism.

The third stage, aggressive cynicism, depends on the conjunction of individual cynicism and the subculture of cynicism. It corresponds to *ressentiment* because resentment and hostility become obvious in this period, most prevalent at the ten-year mark.

In the last few years of the police career, resigned cynicism replaces the former, more blatant type. This detachment may be passive and apathetic or express itself as a form of mellow if mild good will. It accepts and comes to terms with the flaws of the system.

Because these stages represent ideal types, there will probably be practical variations in style and degree. Cynicism as an orientation to life depends for proof of its existence upon inferences drawn from human behavior. I have included descriptive material that indicates the likelihood of a correlation between police work and cynicism.

A more acceptable method is what Kenneth Clark has termed that of the "involved observer."(8) Because I was a policeman for more than twenty years, and have read a large portion of the police literature, I am convinced that there is a great deal of cynicism among my former colleagues.

Even so, the scientific method is most persuasive. The sociologist tries to emulate the rigor of the physical scientist: he observes and describes, collecting data; he classifies and compares, moving from the empirical to the conceptual. Thus he constructs hypotheses that cannot usually be tested by scientifically controlled experiment. The compromise solution is to prepare a questionnaire, most likely to evoke forthright responses, submit it to a well-chosen sample, and then analyze the results to see whether the hypotheses are substantiated. In this fashion research may be lifted to theory. I have utilized all these methods, emphasizing the last, formulating and testing several hypotheses in my study of police cynicism. Although the study was completed toward the end of 1962, I believe that the tests of the following hypotheses are more than ever valid today.

1. For the first few years of a police career one's degree of cynicism will increase in proportion to his length of service, but it will tend to level off at some point between the fifth and tenth year of service. Generally, cynicism is learned as part of socialization into the police occupation, a process likely to take at least five years.

2. Newly appointed men will show less cynicism than more seasoned Police Academy recruits. In turn, the recruit group will be less cynical than the more experienced patrolmen: not only will the average degree of cynicism be lower, but there will be fewer cynics in the group.

3. Superior officers will be less cynical than patrolmen. According to my theory, cynicism is commonly a mode of adaptation to frustration. Cynicism should therefore vary positively according to the degree of failure and frustration. Men in the lower ranks have more reason to feel frustrated than do their superiors.

4. Among patrolmen, those with college educations will reveal a higher level of cynicism than other patrolmen because their expectations for promotion (still unfulfilled) were greater.

5. Patrolmen with preferred assignments (details) will be less cynical than other patrolmen.

6. Because foot patrolmen are of low status, they will be more cynical than patrolmen assigned to other duties.

7. Patrolmen who receive awards for meritorious duty will be less cynical. Patrolmen who are the subjects of departmental charges (complaints) will be more cynical.

8. Jewish patrolmen will be more cynical than non-Jewish patrolmen. Jewish tradition stresses that true success in life lies in becoming a professional man. A Jewish policeman who remains a patrolman is thus a double failure: he did not become a doctor or lawyer, and he has been unable to rise from the low rank of patrolman.

9. When members of the force have served for seventeen or eighteen years, and are approaching retirement, they will exhibit less cynicism. When policemen near retirement search for employment outside the police system, they find opportunities distinctly limited. As a result, their appreciation of, and commitment to the police occupation revives.

10. Members of the Vice Squad will be more cynical than members of the Youth Division. The specific work situation within the organization plays its part in shaping attitudes.

11. Middle-class patrolmen will be less cynical than working-class patrolmen. Their receptivity to professionalism should insulate against cynicism. The middle-class ethic is more sympathetic to the ideas of professionalism than is the ideology of the working class.

So far I have tried to establish the relationship between the police system and cynicism. Is the system the only or even the principal source of cynicism? Perhaps police candidates were cynical, or at least vulnerable to cynicism, before becoming policemen. Does this possibility weaken our theory? In one sense anyone brought up in America, by the time he reaches his twenties, has internalized, along with the admirable qualities of Americans, a host of materialistic and cynical patterns of thought. We need only think of the distrust of "do-gooders," the anti-intellectualism, the "I'm from Missouri. Show me!" stance, the proverbial wisdom that there is a bit of larceny in everyone. Thus, we are all mixtures of idealism and cynicism. Other things being equal, we can expect the cynicism to be outweighed by the more attractive qualities. The question then arises, "Why is the police system with all its concentrated effort incapable, in so many cases, of dissipating that cynicism or encouraging the potent idealism?"

Still the lingering doubt persists. Is it not likely that there is something unusual about an individual who chooses to become a policeman? If he is not clearly cynical, is he not typically authoritarian? And, then once more, is it not true that authoritarianism and cynicism are strongly connected?

REFERENCES

1. Louis Madelin, *Fouché* 1759–1820 (Paris: Plon-Nourrit et Cie., 1903), p. 394.

2. Read Bain, "The Policeman on the Beat," *Scientific Monthly, 48* (1939), p. 451.

3. *The Police: An Interview by Donald McDonald with William H. Parker, Chief of Police of Los Angeles* (Santa Barbara: Center for the Study of Democratic Institutions, 1962), p. 169. His view is that "The police departments have been demoralized by political control, poor leadership, and low rates of pay. The life of many districts seems competitive and raw; individuals pursue their own ends with little regard for public morality, and the policeman sees the ugly underside of outwardly respectable households and businesses. Small wonder then, that many American policemen are cynics."

4. Dorothy Crowe, "Thieves I Have Known," *Saturday Evening Post, 234* (February 4, 1961), pp. 21, 78.

5. An index of this attitude is the nearly universal desire to get out of uniform—the most visible sign of the police occupation. For this reason, there is not only a quest to become a detective, but also a refusal to wear the police uniform when off duty although a policeman has a right to do so. It is also revealed by the denigration of the police job. In a recently published study the author found that "For example, many of the Illinois police officers perceive their occupation to be a cause of ridicule to their children." John P. Clark, "Isolation of the Police: A Comparison of the British and American Situations," *Journal of Criminal Law, Criminology and Police Science, 56* (September, 1965), p. 313.

6. Personal communication from the Chief Medical Examiner's Office of New York City, September 20, 1965.

7. Ibid.

8. Kenneth Clark, *Dark Ghetto* (New York: Harper and Row, 1965), pp. xv–xviii.

6 | Police and Society

The police act as a barometer of the current state of a society, gauging the pressures and forces that are arrayed in the uneasy equilibrium which characterizes any social structure. It follows that the greater the stresses and points of conflict that appear in a given society, the greater the concomitant growth in and dependence upon the power of the police. When civil disorders and related disturbances become a real threat to existing institutional arrangements, more resources, greater funding, increased personnel, and significant augmentation of technology and authority are granted to police departments.

Inevitably, because of the real function of the police, social critics can label the police "the strategic arm of the ruling class." Claims for the validity of this observation are in large measure based on the obvious fact that the police are legally mandated to act as the defenders and protectors of existing political, economic, and property relationships. Historically, one of the least recognized, but perhaps the most vital role of the police in any large-scale society, is that of social lightning rod, or institutional scapegoat. Every attack upon an institution or a power center in society is deflected or defused by a phalanx of police who absorb the shock that originally motivated the attack. In this fashion a good deal of explosive anger and aggressive behavior is ventilated, shunted away, and displaced from the original objects of hostility.

Despite our own use of the generic phrase "police and society" we must warn students of law enforcement against excessive generalization, against the use of clichés such as "police and the community" or "police role in society," which are usually employed as "umbrella" concepts. Instead the student must focus on more explicit contexts such as the particular police officer, and a given beat, precinct, school, or any small segment of a community in which that officer has a significant impact. In other words, it is best to view the relationships between the police and society in microscopic rather than macroscopic terms. This is a more valid approximation of the true state of affairs.

Within one precinct the same corps of officers might be considered friendly servants within a three-block upper-middle-class area; a security force there to protect against burglaries and undesirable outsiders in a nearby residential area; or even the enemy, occupying still another zone of the same precinct.

Policeman as Philosopher, Guide and Friend

ELAINE CUMMING, IAN CUMMING, AND LAURA EDELL

SOURCE: *Social Problems, 12, 3* (1965), published by The Society for the Study of Social Problems.

This is the fourth report from a group of studies designed to throw some light upon the division of labor among the social agents whose central role is concerned with maintaining social integration by controlling various forms of deviant behavior.(1)

In earlier reports, we have adopted the convention of looking at social agents and agencies in terms of their relatively supportive or relatively controlling character. We have assumed that it is difficult for an agent to exercise both support and control at the same time and that any agent tends, therefore, to specialize in one or the other aspect of the integrative process.(2) Even when he is specialized, such an agent may be considered controlling when he is compared with some agents, and supportive when compared with others. Thus, the probation officer is more on the client's side, that is, supportive to him, than the policeman, but less so than the psychiatrist. Furthermore, the agent may be seen as supportive by the layman but experienced as controlling by the client, and *vice versa*. For example, the prisoner remanded by the court for psychiatric treatment may well experience his hospitalization as incarceration. Conversely, a chronic alcoholic may be grateful, in mid-winter, for a night in prison.

There is another aspect to this duality in the handling of deviance. While it is probably impossible to perform acts of support and control simultaneously, support without control is over-protection and invites passivity and dependency, while control without support is tyranny and invites rebellion. While the agent may specialize in one aspect of social control of deviance, the other must, nevertheless, be part of his repertoire.(3) Thus while physicians and clergymen are generally supportive of people in pain or trouble, such people are expected, in return, to perform appropriately the role of patient or parishioner. The support is overt, the control is latent. In general, the agent's training and professional ethics focus on the skills needed for the overt part of his role; the latent aspects are derived from and governed by general norms and values. Role conflict can be avoided in part by keeping the "contradictory" side of a role latent.

The policeman's role in an integrative system is, by definition and by law, explicitly concerned with control—keeping the law from being broken and apprehending those who break it—and only latently with support. For example, if you break the law, you can expect to be arrested, but if you go along quietly, you can, unless there is a special circumstance, expect to be treated reasonably.(4) In the course of controlling one member of society, moreover, the policeman often provides indirect support to another. For example, when he apprehends, and thus controls a wife-beating husband, he supports the wife, just as, in a reverse situation, the doctor controls the behavior of those attending a patient when he prescribes rest and

sympathy. Finally, besides latent support, the policeman often gives direct help to people in certain kinds of trouble. When he does this, the balance between support and control has shifted, and he is acting overtly as a supportive agent and only latently in his controlling role. He has, at the same time, changed from a professional to an amateur. This paper reports a study of the requests for help received by a city police department and the policeman's response to them, with special attention to what is assumed here to be the latent side of his role.

Methods of Study

Because there seems to be no systematic account of the day-to-day activities of policemen, two specific questions were posed: (1) What kinds of calls for help do policemen get, and (2) How do they answer them? Two kinds of data were collected. First, a total of 801 incoming telephone calls at the police complaint desk in a metropolitan police department were observed over a total of 82 hours. These hours were not evenly distributed around the 24 hours, for reasons connected with the field worker, not with the Police Department. As each complaint was received and disposed of, a description was dictated into a tape recorder. Fourteen selected prowl car calls were then observed. At the end of this phase of the study, the worker submitted field notes concerned with the general culture of the police station. Secondly, interviews were conducted with detectives concerning their special assignments. A formulation of the nature of the policeman's supporting role was then constructed from these data.

Results

The Complaint Desk. Figure 1 shows the hourly distribution of police calls. The daily peak activity is between the evening hours of seven and eight o'clock excepting for Thursday, Friday, and Saturday when it is between nine and ten. Because of the gaps in the data, there is a possibility that there is a peak at about noon in the first part of the week, but on both theoretical and common-sense grounds, it seems unlikely. The last part of the week also shows a greater volume of calls than the first. In general, the high rate of calls in the evening and on weekends suggests that problems arise when the social pulse is beating fast—when people are coming and going, regrouping, and, of course, engaging in informal rather than formal activities.

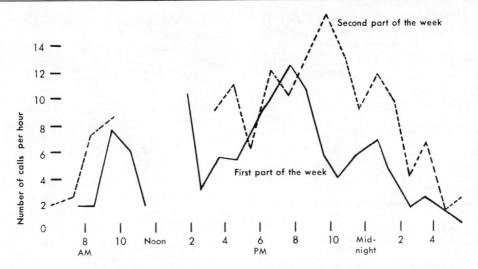

FIGURE 1   *Average Police Calls per Hour, First Part of the Week* (6 A.M. *Sunday–5* A.M. *Thursday*) *and Second Part of the Week* (6 A.M. *Thursday–5* A.M. *Sunday*)

In order to interpret these rhythms further, the 801 calls were classified according to their content, as Table 1 shows. One hundred forty-nine, or 18.6 percent of the calls, were excluded from analysis; 88 of these were call-backs on earlier complaints, 33 were requests for information only, and 28 were outside this police department's jurisdiction.[1] The remaining 652 calls were for service within the purview of these police. They are treated as independent, but the unit of analysis is the call, and not the caller, and results must be interpreted with this in mind.

The 652 calls included in the study were divided into two major groups: the first included calls for service in connection with things or possessions, while the second included calls for support or assistance with regard to problems of health, safety, or interpersonal relationships.[2]

The first (nearly one-third of the total of 801 calls) include traffic violations, reports of losses or thefts, calls about unlocked doors, fallen power wires, and so

on. These are part of the regular controlling function of the police and are not the main focus of this paper. The second major group (about one-half of all calls) is concerned with personal problems and therefore may reasonably be expected to include the need or desire for some form of support. These calls were subdivided into two types: (1) persistent problems occurring throughout the week; and (2) periodic problems occurring mainly on the weekend.

As Table 1 shows, the first type comprises 230 calls, of which about one-third are requests for health services, that is, ambulance escorts, investigation of accidents, suicide attempts, and so on; another third are children's problems, usually complaints about trespassing or destructive behavior; and the remainder are divided equally between incapacitated people, usually described over the phone as drunk or "psycho," and nuisances, usually noisy behavior.

Periodic problems comprise 167 calls of which more than a third are about disputes and quarrels of all kinds, both in families and among unrelated people. Almost half are concerned with violence or protection from potential violence[3] and the remainder are about missing persons or gangs of youths and hot-rodders.

---

[1] The latter two groups (61 calls) were excluded because there was no chance of a car being sent, and therefore they could not be compared with the remainder.

[2] It was surprisingly easy to classify the calls on these two major dimensions and coders had no trouble getting over 90 per cent agreement. Differences were reconciled in conferences.

[3] Most "protection" calls are for a "clothing escort," that is, for a policeman to accompany a person who has left his home, or been thrown out of it, into the house to get his clothing.

Table 1.   Classification of Calls to the Complaint Desk of a Metropolitan Police Department during 82 Selected Hours in June and July 1961

Type of call	Number of calls	Percent of total
Total	801	100.0
Calls included in analysis	652	81.4
1. Calls about "things"	255	31.8
2. Calls for support	397	49.6
Persistent personal problems	230	28.7
a. Health services	81	10.1
b. Children's problems	83	10.4
c. Incapacitated people	33	4.1
d. Nuisances	33	4.1
Periodic personal problems	167	20.9
a. Disputes	63	7.9
b. Violence	43	5.4
c. Protection	29	3.6
d. Missing persons	11	1.4
e. Youths' behavior	21	2.6
Calls excluded from analysis	149	18.6
Information only	33	4.1
Not police business	28	3.5
Feedback calls	88	11.0

Table 2 shows the distribution of the calls, by type, through the days of the week and the period of the day. It now appears that the heaping up of calls in the last part of the week is made up of two effects: first, routine police business and persistent interpersonal calls occur most frequently on Thursday, while periodic interpersonal problems heap up on Friday night. The meaning of this finding is not clear, but it may be that the tensions associated with the instrumental activity of the working week are increasing by Thursday and are then let go on Friday—payday—and on the weekend, when formal constraints are fewer. Because fewer of the other agents are available at these times, the policeman takes over many emergency health and welfare services, a kind of division of labor through time.

Almost three-quarters of all 652 calls were answered by dispatch of a patrolman in a squad car to the scene, while about eight percent received various kinds of advice or information, and about four-and-one-half percent were referred to another source of help. Of the 29 referrals, one was to a medical service, one to a social service, 19 to other legal services and the remaining eight to commercial concerns, such as the Telephone Company. Almost 15 percent of the calls were terminated—that is, service was withheld for reasons not determined, occasionally because no car was available.

In Table 3, we see that the probability of a car being sent out is inversely related to the rate at which calls are coming in. During the six time periods in which a total of 235 calls were received at a rate of fewer than eight calls per hour, 78 percent of them were responded to with cars. During the five time periods in which 417 calls were received at a rate of more than eight calls per hour, cars were sent only 68 percent of the time. This difference is highly significant ($\chi^2 = 7.54$, d.f. = 1), and suggests that cars are sent on a simple supply-and-demand basis. Furthermore, there is no difference among the three major categories with regard to the likelihood of a car being sent. Nevertheless, certain sub-categories of complaint are more likely to get service than others. As Table 4 shows, calls regarding violence (control), children and youths (support and control), and illness (support) are the most likely to be responded to with a car, although the likelihood of the law being broken—which defines the police mandate—is greater for some of these complaints than for others.

When the complainant reports a nuisance or a dispute, he has only one chance in two of getting more than advice—albeit philosophical advice. Thus, a man calls to say that he has had a fight with his girl and she hasn't come to see him, although he knows she is off duty from the hospital; the policeman says he can't make her come to his house—perhaps she doesn't want to—and goes on to advise the man that that's the way life is sometimes.

It is possible that some of the calls about violence are later stages of these unanswered dispute calls. For example, to one complaint, "My boy friend is mad at me and is going to beat me up," the answer was, "Call us again when he does."[4]

It is quite apparent that the policeman must often exercise, a kind of clinical judgement about these complaints, and that this judgement reflects his own values. The field notes suggest, for example, that policemen are sincerely, if sentimentally, concerned about children, and that negligent parents are likely to find the police at their most truculent. The following example is taken from the notes:

A call came from a very kindly-sounding Italian man at about 11 o'clock in the evening. He was reporting that he had found a little boy from next

[4] Police Chief Murphy describes this entry as "poor police practice."

Table 2.   Number of Calls to the Complaint Desk of a Metropolitan Police Department by Type of Problem,* Day of Week, Time of Day, and Hours of Observation during 82 Selected Hours in June and July 1961

Time of day, hours of observation, and type of call	Total	Sun.	Mon.	Tue.	Wed.	Thur.	Fri.	Sat.
All calls	652	50	69	55	76	95	54	253
(hours observed)	(82)	(8)	(14)	(9)	(9)	(9)	(6)	(27)
12:01 a.m.–5:00 a.m.	91	16	18					57
(hours observed)	(14)	(2)	(5)	(0)	(0)	(0)	(0)	(7)
Routine	28	4	8					16
Persistent	21	4	4					13
Periodic	42	8	6					28
5:01 a.m.–noon	52		9	19		17		7
(hours observed)	(13)	(0)	(4)	(3)	(0)	(3)	(0)	(3)
Routine	36		6	11		15		4
Persistent	10		2	4		2		2
Periodic	6		1	4		0		1
12:01 p.m.–6:00 p.m.	187	18		36	38	38	31	26
(hours observed)	(26)	(4)	(0)	(6)	(5)	(3)	(4)	(4)
Routine	88	9		12	18	18	16	15
Persistent	68	6		17	11	16	12	6
Periodic	31	3		7	9	4	3	5
6:01 p.m.–midnight	322	16	42		38	40	23	163
(hours observed)	(29)	(2)	(5)	(0)	(4)	(3)	(2)	(13)
Routine	103	4	13		17	15	2	52
Persistent	131	5	22		18	17	7	62
Periodic	88	7	7		3	8	14	49

* Departures from uniformity:

1. Periodic interpersonal calls occur more often than chance would indicate on Friday evening (χ^2 = 24.1, d.f. = 5, P < .01) and the early hours of Saturday (χ^2 = 8.4, d.f. = 2, P = .02).

2. Both routine police calls and persistent interpersonal calls occur more frequently than chance would indicate on Thursday, the former in the morning (χ^2 = 12.3, d.f. = 3, P < .01) and the latter in the afternoon (χ^2 = 13.1, d.f. = 5, P = 05.).

door wandering in the street . . . and he thought the police ought to know about the situation. A car was dispatched and reported that there was nobody home, and in fact, there were three smaller children in the house. . . . The captain dispatched a camera crew, child placement was notified and the children were immediately placed in a temporary placement home. A stake-out was set for the parents. Meanwhile the pictures had been developed and they showed four under-nourished, under-clothed little children lying in their own feces on a mattress on the floor. The refrigerator contained two cans of condensed milk and some rotten vegetables; the place was filthy and unheated. As the time went by, anger began to rise and when at about four o'clock in the morning the parents were brought in to the station everybody was in an ugly mood. . . . Had they been the least bit smart, glib, or said almost anything other than

"yes" or "no" while they were issued tickets, they would have gotten poked.

All-out support for the children is accompanied by the barest minimum of support to the parents in the form of approval for appropriately docile behavior.

The Squad Car. Certain calls are considered serious enough to warrant a captain following the squad car to the scene.[5] The following thumbnail summaries represent 14 calls made by the captains in a 23-hour period. Half of them were not considered

[5] The field worker could not go with the regular prowl car owing to a rule forbidding the officers to carry passengers. It is also possible that the captain did not want the field worker to see episodes that he did not himself monitor.

Table 3.   Per Cent of Calls to Which Cars Sent by Hours of the Day, Days of the Week and Type of Call, and
Number of Calls Received per Hour
(82 Selected Hours at the Complaint Desk of a Metropolitan Police Department, June and July 1961)

Time of day, type of call, and calls/hr.	Total		Sun.–Wed.*		Thursday		Fri–Sat.*	
	Calls	Per cent to which car sent	Calls	Per cent to which car sent	Calls	Per cent to which car sent	Calls	Per cent to which car sent
Total calls	652	72.1	250	72.8	95	71.6	307	70.0
(Total/hr.)	(8.0)		(6.3)		(10.6)		(9.3)	
12:01 a.m.–5:00 a.m.	91	80.2	34	85.3			57	77.2
(calls/hour)	(6.5)		(4.9)				(8.1)	
Routine	28	85.7	12	91.7			16	81.3
Persistent	21	71.4	8	87.5			13	61.5
Periodic	42	81.0	14	78.6			28	82.1
5:01 a.m.–noon	52	86.5	28	89.3	17	88.2	7	71.4
(calls/hour)	(4.0)		(4.0)		(5.7)		(2.3)	
Routine	36	88.9	17	94.1	15	86.7	4	75.0
Persistent	10	90.0	6	83.3	2	100.0	2	100.0
Periodic	6	66.7	5	80.0	0	—	1	—
12:01 p.m.–6:00 p.m.	187	73.8	92	70.7	38	71.0	57	80.7
(calls/hour)	(7.2)		(6.1)		(12.7)		(7.1)	
Routine	88	69.3	39	66.7	18	66.7	31	74.2
Persistent	68	80.9	34	76.5	16	75.0	18	94.4
Periodic	31	71.0	19	68.4	4	75.0	8	75.0
6:01 p.m.–midnight	322	66.5	96	65.6	40	65.0	186	67.2
(calls/hour)	(11.1)		(8.7)		(13.3)		(12.4)	
Routine	103	60.2	34	58.8	15	40.0	54	66.7
Persistent	131	72.5	45	73.3	17	76.4	69	71.0
Periodic	88	64.8	17	58.8	8	87.5	63	57.1

* Calls grouped because of similar distribution.

Table 4.   Disposition of 397 Calls to the Complaint Desk
of a Metropolitan Police Department Regarding Interpersonal Problems, by Sub-Category of Complaint
(82 Selected Hours in June and July 1961)

Type of call	Total calls	Per cent car sent
Total calls	397	76.8
Persistent problems	230	79.1
a. Health services	81	86.4
b. Children's problems	83	85.5
c. Incapacitated people	33	75.8
d. Nuisances	33	48.5
Periodic problems	167	73.7
a. Disputes	63	50.8
b. Violence	43	95.3
c. Protection	29	79.3
d. Missing persons	11	81.8
e. Youths' behavior	21	85.7

serious, but the field worker asked the captain to go to
the scene.

1. A man, reported by his ex-wife as dangerous
and perhaps mentally ill, is found asleep; his ex-wife
and her mother are in an agitated state. They report
that when the ex-wife came to the home the husband
shook his fist under her nose and said, "I have divorced
you, I want you out of this goddam house by
morning." The police officer woke up the man, who
once again threatened his ex-wife, and the officer then
told her that since it was his house and she was legally
divorced from him, she and her mother should "please
leave, and not cause any more trouble."

2. A car accident severely injures a woman and the
police supervise her removal to hospital.

3. A bartender asks for, and receives, help in
closing up so that there will be no problems—a routine

"preventive" police service usually given by the car on the beat.

4. A man has beaten up his female neighbor earlier in the day and she has called the police and preferred charges. At the time of this call, the man's wife had threatened this woman with a knife. All are drunk and are taken to the station for further investigation.

5. A call from a woman about neighborhood children bullying a small boy who wears glasses. The field notes read, "There was a lot of argument and a lot of screaming back and forth, nothing was particularly accomplished, the three policemen (captain and two officers from a squad car) stood around for awhile, questioned people, did a little shouting, got shouted at, then the whole thing sort of dissolved and was resolved in a manner that I don't understand."

6. A woman complains that her husband doesn't bring home enough of his money to feed the kids. She is advised to go to Children's Court.

7. Field notes read: "Husband destroying property at his house. He's drunk and he and his wife got in an argument over the children . . . the wife smashed the gift he had given her for Mother's Day. This set the incident off. He fought the officers, they handcuffed him, and is taken to the station—a psycho."

8. A slightly drunk man is an unwelcome visitor in his ex-wife's home. Police send him home in a cab.

9. An ex-patient from a mental hospital is missing from her relative's home. They will broadcast a missing persons call.

10. A drunk man claims he has been slugged, but cannot amplify so no action is taken. "This is a low IQ street," says the policeman.

11. A woman in her pajamas and covered with mud says her husband threw her out. He is at home drunk with the children. As he has a police record, two cars are dispatched, one with a tear-gas gun. The house is found in a shambles. The wife is taken to hospital, children to a shelter, and the husband is booked for investigation and possible psychiatric treatment.

12. Fight in a third floor apartment between a man and his wife. Policeman settles it in some undiscernible fashion.

13. A man has "gone out of his mind over a girl" and has gone berserk with a gun. The man is shipped to hospital and witnesses are taken in because the gun makes the affair a felony.

14. The call is "see if an ambulance is needed." A young Negro in a filthy crowded house appears to be in agony. Police examine him for knife wounds and being satisfied that he has not been stabbed, and that no further investigation is needed, send him to hospital in an ambulance.

There seem to be three types of cases here. In the first, the police act as guides or conveyors to the courts and hospitals, giving indirect support meanwhile. In the second, they appear to resolve problems by giving concrete information and guidance about what is and is not possible under the law. Here both indirect and overt support are given. In the third type, they appear to settle problems through some consensual method based on mutual understanding between the police and the people involved. Here support is fairly overt but control is, of course, latent because of the policeman's representation of law and order. Occasionally, the police give outright friendly support, as in the following incident from the field notes:

Sitting in the police station is an old man, a citizen wanderer who is on his way to Oregon, and has become dissatisfied with the Rescue Mission and walked out. He's going to spend the night out of the rain until the morning when he's going over to the Salvation Army.

It is, of course, not possible to say what proportion of the policeman's responses to citizens fall into these three types, nor indeed, to know what other types there may be, because of the method of selecting the squad car calls.

Detectives. Four detectives of the twenty in the department, selected only because they were on duty at the time of the field worker's visit, were asked to describe their ten most recent cases. It was felt that they might be assigned the more "professional" and hence controlling tasks. Two of them were specialists in theft and forgery and so their cases were, indeed, of this character. However, fifteen out of twenty cases described by the two general detectives fell into our two personal-problem categories, and were similar to the complaint calls except that they were being further investigated because of more serious breaches of the law.

Another detective, in charge of services to alcoholics, reported that in 1956 the police department sent him to Yale for training in the handling of alcoholics. He says, "As a police officer I saw people being arrested for drunk and re-arrested for drunk and I thought it was a pretty medieval way of going about trying to help a person with a basic problem and illness that the public was just kicking in the corner and that's how I wound up here." This officer handles about 900 alcoholics a year. Of these, he takes about 150 charged persons on suspended sentence from the court and tries to arrange for some agency to carry them—an outright supportive service.

Missing Persons. The sergeant in charge of this service estimates that he locates about 600 missing people from this area in a year, about half of them children. He further estimates that from three to five percent are mentally disturbed adults. This particular officer says that he sometimes counsels with children that he has traced after they have been returned home. At the same time, he complains to the interviewer that children don't respect police officers the way they did when he was young.

Detectives in charge of homicide and those on duty with the vice squad were not interviewed, so it is impossible to say what proportion of all detective work is supportive. These data suggest that it is similar to the patrolman's.

Police Culture. The field worker reports several impressions that are relevant to our interests. Although they cannot be demonstrated from these data, some of them are similar to findings from other studies. First, poor, uneducated people appear to use the police in the way that middle-class people use family doctors and clergymen—that is, as the first port of call in time of trouble. Second, the policeman must often enforce unpopular laws among these poor people at the same time that he sees these laws being flouted by those in positions of power.[6] Third, many policemen are themselves recruited from and sympathetic to the class of people from whom most of the "interpersonal" calls for assistance come.[7]

Fourth, the police have little knowledge of, and liaison with, social or even medical agencies, and seem to feel that these agencies' activities are irrelevant to the problems they, themselves, face.

Fifth, the police appear to have a concern not only for children but also for those they define as disturbed and ill. They are tolerant, for example, about many crank calls, and will, if a car is available, help a paranoid

---

[6] This seems to be most true of the vice squad and it was not covered here. Nevertheless, a lot of police station conversation was on this topic.

[7] This becomes less true, of course, as the police department becomes more professionalized, and is probably less true of this department now than it was in 1961 when these data were collected.

old lady search her house for the malignant intruder she feels sure is hiding there. Nevertheless, it is possible to see, both in episodes of prejudice against minorities, and in less dramatic ways, how their own values transcend the individual's rights. A field note says, for example, "A woman wants protection from her doctor who is trying to commit her to a mental institution; the officer replies, 'That's not police business, lady. The police cannot go against any doctor.' "[8]

Finally, many policemen are bitter about their low pay, the label "punitive" applied to them in a world that values "warmth," the conflicting demands of their jobs, and the ingratitude of the public. This bitterness is reflected, in this police force, in a catch phrase, "I hate citizens."[9]

Summary and Discussion

We return now to our starting questions: What calls are made on the police and how do they respond? More than one-half of the calls coming routinely to the police complaint desk, and perhaps to detectives, appear to involve calls for help and some form of support for personal or interpersonal problems. To about three-quarters of these appeals, a car is sent. When the policeman reaches the scene, the data suggest that he either guides the complainant to someone who can solve his problem or tries to solve it himself. To do this, he must often provide support, either by friendly sympathy, by feeding authoritative information into the troubled situation, or by helping consensual resolution to take place. We started with the assumption that these activities belonged to the latent aspect of his role, and he is certainly an amateur—these policemen have no training for this kind of service.

---

[8] This attitude is, of course, construed by some as a denial of the basic rights of the mentally ill person. *See,* in this regard, Thomas Szasz, *The Myth of Mental Illness* (New York: Harper, 1961). A trickle of manifestly disturbed people may be turned down for other reasons at the complaint desk. One agitated man complained that his back yard was full of snails; the officer replied, "What do you want me to do, come and shoot them?" Even so, the field worker reports that if the complaint officer had had a car available, he would probably have sent it out.

[9] It may be that the higher respect for policemen in England is related to the higher value on order and the lower value on warmth.

Why, then, are they called upon to exercise their amateur talents half of the time?

The reasons are probably complex. First, the policeman has to do much of what he does because he is on duty at times of the day when no other agent is available. Second, he deals with the problems of a group of people—the poor and the ignorant—that studies of our own and others have shown no other agent to be anxious to serve(5) and, third, he has knowledge of, and access to, very few other agents. In other words, he is part of an integrative system in which the labor is divided not so much on the basis of function as on the basis of the time of day and the nature of the target population. All citizens can count on emergency help from the police when there is sudden illness at night, but only a certain kind of citizen takes his marital troubles to them.

The policeman's supportive acts are not only the latent and hence amateur part of his role, they are also latent in not being recognized and legitimated by the other agents in the integrative system. These others, our own studies show, prefer to recognize the policeman's professional controlling function, which

they both need and often call upon.[10] Thus, it is as an agent of control that the policeman participates in a divided labor with social workers, doctors, clergymen, lawyers and teachers in maintaining social integration. The problems he faces appear to be a *failure of integration within the integrative system*, so that he cannot mobilize the other agents when he needs them.

Some modern advocates of "professionalization" of police work recognize that the policeman on the beat spends about half his time as an amateur social worker and they hope, instead of improving the referral process, to equip him with the skills of a professional. The policeman will then have a role containing both overtly supportive and overtly controlling elements. If our assumption that these are incompatible activities is correct, this development would lead to a division of labor within police work that would tend once more to segregate these elements. This, in turn, would result in a basic shift in the relationship of the police to the rest of the integrative system. All of this might remove the policeman's present reasons for hating citizens, but it would not guarantee that they would not be replaced with others.

REFERENCES

1. Earlier reports include: Elaine Cumming, "Phase Movement in the Support and Control of the Psychiatric Patient," *Journal of Health and Human Behavior*, 3 (Winter 1962), pp. 235–41; Isabel McCaffrey, Elaine Cumming and Claire Rudolph, "Mental Disorders in Socially Defined Populations," *American Journal of Public Health*, 53 (July 1963), pp. 1025–30; Elaine Cumming and Charles Harrington, "Clergyman as Counselor," *American Journal of Sociology*, 69 (November 1963), pp. 234–43.

2. This assumption is derived in part from studies of the division of labor in small groups—see, for example, Bales' "The Equilibrium Problem in Small Groups," in T. Parsons and R. F. Bales, *Working Papers in the Theory of Action* (Glencoe, Ill.: The Free Press of Glencoe, 1953)—and upon theories of role conflict—see, for example, W. J. Goode, "A Theory of Role Strain," *American Sociological Review*, 25 (August 1960), pp. 483–95. At another level of analysis, of course, we all control and support one another—by showing disapproval when our expectations are not met and by friendliness, responsiveness, understanding and sympathy when they are.

3. Certain highly skilled agents, such as psychoanalysts, may be able to phase their activities so that they are supportive in certain phases of the treatment

and controlling in others. It is doubtful if this is feasible in the ordinary run of events because of the ambiguity it would generate in social interaction; *see*, for example, Gregory Bateson, D. D. Jackson, J. Haley, and J. Weakland, "Toward a Theory of Schizophrenia," *Behavioral Science*, 1 (October 1956), pp. 251–64.

4. For an excellent discussion of the many problems inherent in the controlling function of the police, *see* Claude R. Sowle, ed., *Police Power and Individual Freedom* (Chicago: Aldine, 1962).

5. *See*, for a discussion of this problem in this community, Claire Rudolph and John Cumming, "Where are Psychiatric Services Most Needed?" *Social Work*, 7 (July 1962), pp. 15–20.

[10] There is reason to believe that most social workers, clergymen, and doctors have no conception of the amount of support policemen give during a day's work. There is also reason to believe that they do not want the burden of the "unmotivated" poor and ignorant, whom they believe to be increasing in number.

The Revolt of the White Lower Middle Class

PETE HAMILL

They call my people the White Lower Middle Class these days. It is an ugly, ice-cold phrase, the result, I suppose, of the missionary zeal of those sociologists who still think you can place human beings on charts. It most certainly does not sound like a description of people on the edge of open, sustained and possibly violent revolt. And yet, that is the case. All over New York City tonight, in places like Inwood, South Brooklyn, Corona, East Flatbush and Bay Ridge, men are standing around saloons talking darkly about their grievances, and even more darkly about possible remedies. Their grievances are real and deep; their remedies could blow this city apart.

The White Lower Middle Class? Say that magic phrase at a cocktail party on the Upper East Side of Manhattan and monstrous images arise from the American demonology. Here comes the murderous rabble: fat, well-fed, bigoted, ignorant, an army of beer-soaked Irishmen, violence-loving Italians, hate-filled Poles, Lithuanians and Hungarians (they are never referred to as Americans). They are the people who assault peace marchers, who start groups like the Society for the Prevention of Negroes Getting Everything, S.P.O.N.G.E., the people who hate John Lindsay and vote for George Wallace, presumably because they believe that Wallace will eventually march every black man in America to the gas chambers, sending Lindsay and the rest of the Liberal Establishment along with them. Sometimes these brutes are referred to as "the ethnics" or "the blue-collar types." But the bureaucratic, sociological phrase is White Lower Middle Class. Nobody calls it the Working Class anymore.

But basically, the people I'm speaking about *are* the working class. That is, they stand somewhere in the economy between the poor—most of whom are the aged, the sick and those unemployable women and children who live on welfare—and the semi-profes-

sionals and professionals who earn their way with talents or skills acquired through education. The working class earns its living with its hands or its backs; its members do not exist on welfare payments; they do not live in abject, swinish poverty, nor in safe, remote suburban comfort. They earn between $5,000 and $10,000 a year. And they can no longer make it in New York.

"I'm going out of my mind," an ironworker friend named Eddie Cush told me a few weeks ago. "I average about $8,500 a year, pretty good money. I work my ass off. But I can't make it. I come home at the end of the week, I start paying the bills, I give my wife some money for food. And there's nothing left. Maybe, if I work overtime, I get $15 or $20 to spend on myself. But most of the time, there's nothin'. They take $65 a week out of my pay. I have to come up with $90 a month rent. But every time I turn around, one of the kids needs shoes or a dress or something for school. And then I pick up a paper and read about a million people on welfare in New York or spades rioting in some college or some fat welfare bitch demanding—you know, not askin', *demanding*—a credit card at Korvette's . . . I *work* for a living and I can't get a credit card at Korvette's . . . You know, you see that, and you want to go out and strangle someone."

Cush was not drunk, and he was not talking loudly, or viciously, or with any bombast; but the tone was similar to the tone you can hear in conversations in bars like Farrell's all over this town; the tone was quiet bitterness.

"Look around," another guy told me, in a place called Mister Kelly's on Eighth Avenue and 13th Street in Brooklyn. "Look in the papers. Look on TV. What the hell does Lindsay care about me? He don't care whether my kid has shoes, whether my boy gets a new suit at Easter, whether I got any money in the bank. None of them politicians gives a good goddam. All they worry about is the niggers. And everything is for the niggers. The niggers get the schools. The niggers go to summer camp. The niggers get the new playgrounds. The niggers get nursery schools. And they get it all without workin'. I'm an ironworker, a connector; when I go to work in the mornin', I don't even know if I'm gonna make it back. My wife is scared to death, every mornin', all day. Up on the iron, if the wind blows hard or the steel gets icy or I make a wrong step, bango, forget it, I'm dead. Who feeds my wife and kid if I'm dead? Lindsay? The poverty program? You know the answer: nobody. But the niggers, they don't worry about it. They take the welfare and sit out on the stoop drinkin' cheap wine and throwin' the bottles on the street. They never gotta walk outta the house. They take the money outta my paycheck and they just turn it over to some lazy son of a bitch who won't work. I gotta carry him on *my* back. You know what I am? I'm a sucker. I really am. You shouldn't have to put up with this. And I'll tell ya somethin'. There's a lotta people who just ain't gonna put up with it much longer."

It is very difficult to explain to these people that more than 600,000 of those on welfare are women and children: that one reason the black family is in trouble is because outfits like the Iron Workers Union have practically excluded blacks through most of their history; that a hell of a lot more of their tax dollars go to Vietnam or the planning for future wars than to Harlem or Bed-Stuy; that the effort of the past four or five years was an effort forced by bloody events, and that they are paying taxes to relieve some forms of poverty because of more than 100 years of neglect on top of 300 years of slavery. The working-class white man has no more patience for explanations.

"If I hear that 400-years-of-slavery bit one more time," a man said to me in Farrell's one night, "I'll go outta my mind!"

One night in Farrell's, I showed the following passage by Eldridge Cleaver to some people. It is from the recently-published collection of Cleaver's journalism: "The very least of your responsibility now is to compensate me, however inadequately, for centuries of degradation and disenfranchisement by granting peacefully—before I take them forcefully—the same rights and opportunities for a decent life that you've taken for granted as an American birthright. This isn't a request but a *demand* . . . "

The response was peculiarly mixed. Some people said that the black man had already been given too much, and if he still couldn't make it, to hell with him. Some said they agreed with Cleaver, that the black man "got the shaft" for a long time, and whether we like it or not, we have to do something. But most of them reacted ferociously.

"Compensate him?" one man said. "Compensate him? Look, the English ruled Ireland for 700 years, that's hundreds of years longer than Negroes have been slaves. Why don't the British government compensate me? In Boston, they had signs like 'No Irish Need Apply' on the jobs, so why don't the American government compensate *me*?"

In any conversation with working-class whites, you are struck by how the information explosion has hit them. Television has made an enormous impact on them, and because of the nature of that medium—its preference for the politics of theatre, its seeming inability to ever explain what is happening behind the photographed image—much of their understanding of what happens is superficial. Most of them·have only a passing acquaintance with blacks, and very few have any black friends. So they see blacks in terms of militants with Afros and shades, or crushed people on welfare. Television never bothers reporting about the black man who gets up in the morning, eats a fast breakfast, says goodbye to his wife and children, and rushes out to work. That is not news. So the people who live in working-class white ghettos seldom meet blacks who are not threatening to burn down America or asking for help or receiving welfare or committing crime. And in the past five or six years, with urban rioting on everyone's minds, they have provided themselves (or been provided with) a confused, threatening stereotype of blacks that has made it almost impossible to suggest any sort of black-white working-class coalition.

"Why the hell should I work with spades," he says, "when they are threatening to burn down my house?"

The Puerto Ricans, by the way, seem well on the way to assimilation with the larger community. It has been a long time since anyone has written about "the Puerto Rican problem" (though Puerto Rican poverty remains worse than black poverty), and in white working-class areas you don't hear many people muttering about "spics" anymore.

"At least the Puerto Ricans are working," a carpenter named Jimmy Dolan told me one night, in a place called the Green Oak in Bay Ridge. "They open a grocery store, they work from six in the mornin' till midnight. The P.R.'s are willin' to work for their money. The colored guys just don't wanna work. They want the big Buicks and the fancy suits, but they jus' don't wanna do the work they have ta do ta pay for them."

The working-class white man sees injustice and politicking everywhere in this town now, with himself in the role of victim. He does not like John Lindsay, because he feels Lindsay is only concerned about the needs of blacks; he sees Lindsay walking the streets of the ghettos or opening a privately-financed housing project in East Harlem or delivering lectures about tolerance and brotherhood, and he wonders what it all means to *him*. Usually, the working-class white man is a veteran; he remembers coming back from the Korean War to discover that the GI Bill only gave him $110 a month out of which he had to pay his own tuition; so he did not go to college because he could not afford it. Then he reads about protesting blacks in the SEEK program at Queens College, learns that they are being paid up to $200 a month to go to school, with tuition free, and he starts going a little wild.

The working-class white man spends much of his time complaining almost desperately about the way he has become a victim. Taxes and the rising cost of living keep him broke, and he sees nothing in return for the taxes he pays. The Department of Sanitation comes to his street at three in the morning, and a day late, and slams garbage cans around like an invading regiment. His streets were the last to be cleaned in the big snowstorm, and they are now sliced up with trenches that could only be called potholes by the myopic. His neighborhood is a dumping ground for abandoned automobiles, which rust and rot for as long as six weeks before someone from the city finally takes them away. He works very hard, frequently on a dangerous job, and then discovers that he still can't pay his way; his wife takes a Thursday night job in a department store and he gets a weekend job, pumping gas or pushing a hack. For him, life in New York is not much of a life.

"The average working stiff is not asking for very much," says Congressman Hugh Carey, the Brooklyn Democrat whose district includes large numbers of working-class whites. "He wants a decent apartment, he wants a few beers on the weekend, he wants his kids to have decent clothes, he wants to go to a ballgame once in a while, and he would like to put a little money away so that his kids can have the education that he never could afford. That's not asking a hell of a lot. But he's not getting that. He thinks society has failed him and, in a way, if he is white, he is often more alienated than the black man. At least the black man has his own organizations, and can submerge himself in the struggle for justice and equality, or elevate himself, whatever the case might be. The black man has hope, because no matter what some of the militants say, his life is slowly getting better in a number of ways. The white man who makes $7,000 a year, who is 40, knows that he is never going to earn much more than that for the rest of his life, and he sees things getting worse, more hopeless. John Lindsay has made a number of bad moves as mayor of this town, but the alienation of the white lower middle class might have been the worst."

Carey is probably right. The middle class, that cadre of professionals, semi-professionals and businessmen who are the backbone of any living city, are the children of the white working class. If they are brought up believing that the city government does not care whether they live or die (or how they live or die), they will not stay here very long as adults. They will go to college, graduate, marry, get jobs and depart. Right now, thousands of them are leaving New York, because New York doesn't *work* for them. The public schools, when they are open, are desperate; the private schools cost too much (and if they can afford private school, they realize that their taxes are paying for the public schools whose poor quality prevent them from using them). The streets are filthy, the air is polluted, the parks are dangerous, prices are too high. They end up in California, or Rahway, or Islip.

Patriotism is very important to the working-class white man. Most of the time he is the son of an immigrant, and most immigrants sincerely believe that the Pledge of Allegiance, the Star-Spangled Banner, the American Flag are symbols of what it means to be Americans. They might not have become rich in America, but most of the time they were much better off than they were in the old country. On "I Am an American" Day they march in parades with a kind of religious fervor that can look absurd to the outsider (imagine marching through Copenhagen on "I Am a Dane" Day), but that can also be oddly touching. Walk through any working-class white neighborhood and you will see dozens of veterans' clubs, named after neighborhood men who were killed in World War Two or Korea. There are not really orgies of jingoism going on inside; most of the time the veterans' clubs serve as places in which to drink on Sunday morning before the bars open at 1 P.M., or as places in which to hold baptisms and wedding receptions. But they are places where an odd sort of know-nothingism is fostered. The war in Vietnam was almost never questioned until last year. It was an American war, with Americans dying in action, and it could not be questioned.

The reasons for this simplistic view of the world are complicated. But one reason is that the working-class white man fights in every American war. Because of poor educations, large numbers of blacks are rejected by the draft because they can't pass the mental examinations; the high numbers of black casualties are due to the disproportionate number of black career NCOs and the large number of blacks who go into airborne units because of higher pay. The working-class white man (and his brothers, sons and cousins) only get deferments if they are crippled; their educations, usually in parochial schools, are good enough to pass Army requirements, but not good enough to get them into the city college system (which, being free, is the only kind of college they could afford). It is the children of the rich and the middle class who get all those college deferments.

While he is in the service, the working-class white hates it; he bitches about the food, the brass, the living conditions; he tries to come back to New York at every opportunity, even if it means two 14-hour car rides on a weekend. But after he is out, and especially if he has seen combat, a romantic glaze covers the experience. He is a veteran, he is a man, he can drink with the men at the corner saloon. And as he goes into his 30s and 40s, he resents those who don't serve, or bitch about the service the way he used to bitch. He becomes quarrelsome. When he gets drunk, he tells you about Saipan. And he sees any form of antiwar protest as a denial of his own young manhood, and a form of spitting on the graves of the people he served with who died in his war.

The past lives on. When I visit my old neighborhood, we still talk about things we did when we were 18, fights we had, and who was "good with his hands" in the main events at the Caton Inn, and how great it was eating sandwiches from Mary's down near Oceantide in Coney Island. Or we talk about the Zale-Graziano fights, or what a great team the Dodgers were when Duke Snyder played center field and Roy Campanella was the catcher, and what a shame it was that Rex Barney never learned how to control the fast ball. Nostalgia was always a curse; I remember one night when I was 17, drinking beer from cardboard containers on a bench at the side of Prospect Park, and one of my friends said that it was a shame we were getting old, that there would never be another summer like the one we had the year before, when we were 16. It was absurd, of course, and yet it was true; the summer we were 17, guys we knew were already dying on the frozen ridges of Korea.

A large reason for the growing alienation of the white working class is their belief that they are not respected. It is an important thing for the son of an immigrant to be respected. When he is young, physical prowess is usually the most important thing; the guy who can fight or hit a ball or run with a football has more initial respect than the guy who gets good marks in school. But later, the man wants to be respected as a good provider, a reasonably good husband, a good drinker, a good credit risk (the worst thing you can do in a working-class saloon is borrow $20 and forget about it, or stiff the guy you borrowed it from).

It is no accident that the two New York City politicians who most represent the discontent of the white working class are Brooklyn Assemblyman Vito Battista and Councilman Matty Troy of Queens. Both are usually covered in the press as if they were refugees from a freak show. (I've been guilty of this sneering, patronizing attitude towards Battista and Troy myself at times.) Battista claims to be the spokesman for the small home owner and many small home owners believe in him; but a lot of the people who are listening to him now see him as the spokesman for the small home owner they would like to be. "I like that Battista," a guy told me a couple of weeks ago. "He talks our language. That Lindsay sounds like a college professor." Troy speaks for the man who can't get his streets cleaned, who has to take a train and a bus to get to his home, who is being taxed into suburban exile; he is also very big on patriotism, but he shocked his old auditors at the Democratic convention in Chicago last year when he supported the minority peace plank on Vietnam.

There is one further problem involved here. That is the failure of the literary/intellectual world to fully recognize the existence of the white working class, except to abhor them. With the exception of James T. Farrell, no major American novelist has dealt with the working-class white man, except in war novels. Our novelists write about bullfighters, migrant workers, screenwriters, psychiatrists, failing novelists, homosexuals, advertising men, gangsters, actors, politicians, drifters, hippies, spies and millionaires; I have yet to see a work of the imagination deal with the life of a wirelather, a carpenter, a subway conductor, an ironworker or a derrick operator. There hasn't even been much inquiry by the sociologists. *Beyond the Melting Pot*, by Nathan Glazer and Pat Moynihan, is the most useful book, but we have yet to see an Oscar Lewis-style book called, say, *The Children of Flaherty*. I suppose there are reasons for this neglect, caused by a century of intellectual sneering at bourgeois values, etc. But the result has been the inability of many intellectuals to imagine themselves in the plight of the American white working man. They don't understand his virtues (loyalty, endurance, courage, among others) and see him only through his faults (narrowness, bigotry, the worship of machismo, among others). The result is the stereotype. Black writers have finally begun to reveal what it means to be black in this country; I suppose it will take a working-class novelist to do the same for his people. It is certainly a rich, complex and unworked mine.

But for the moment, it is imperative for New York

politicians to begin to deal with the growing alienation and paranoia of the working-class white man. I really don't think they can wait much longer, because the present situation is working its way to the point of no return. The working-class white man feels trapped and, even worse, in a society that purports to be democratic, ignored. The tax burden is crushing him, and the quality of his life does not seem to justify his exertions. He cannot leave New York City because he can't afford it, and he is beginning to look for someone to blame. That someone is almost certainly going to be the black man.

This does not have to be the situation, of course. If the government were more responsive to the working-class white man, if the distribution of benefits were spread more widely, if the government's presence were felt more strongly in ways that benefit white communities, there would be a chance to turn this situation around. The working-class white man does not care if a black man gets a job in his union, as long as it does not mean the loss of his own job, or the small privileges and sense of self-respect that go with it. I mean it; I know these people, and know that they largely would not care what happens in the city, if what happens at least has the virtue of fairness. For now, they see a terrible unfairness in their lives, and an increasing lack of personal control over what happens to them. And the result is growing talk of revolt.

The revolt involves the use of guns. In East Flatbush, and Corona, and all those other places where the white working class lives, people are forming gun clubs and self-defense leagues and talking about what they will do if real race rioting breaks out. It is a tragic situation, because the poor blacks and the working-class whites should be natural allies. Instead, the black man has become the symbol of all the working-class white man's resentments.

"I never had a gun in my life before," a 34-year-old Queens bartender named James Giuliano told me a couple of weeks ago. "But I got me a shotgun, license and all. I hate to have the thing in the house, because of the kids. But the way things are goin', I might have to use it on someone. I really might. It's comin' to that. Believe me, it's comin' to that."

The working-class white man is actually in revolt against taxes, joyless work, the double standards and short memories of professional politicians, hypocrisy, and what he considers the debasement of the American dream. But George Wallace received 10 million votes last year, not all of them from rednecked racists. That should have been a warning, strong and clear. If the stereotyped black man is becoming the working-class white man's enemy, the eventual enemy might be the democratic process itself. Any politician who leaves that white man out of the political equation, does so at very large risk. The next round of race riots might not be between people and property, but between people and people. And that could be the end of us.

Universities and the Police:

Force and Freedom on the Campus

DONALD GOODMAN AND ARTHUR NIEDERHOFFER

In the beginning the student attacks the university. In the end he demands amnesty. He does so because his target, the bureaucratic multiversity remains underneath it all *alma mater*—protector as well as enemy: source of rights, privileges and immunities as well as oppressor.

Traditionally, in America, the relation of the university to its students has been *in loco parentis*. Has its heritage transformed the university into a sanctuary that confers immunities and exemptions, or at least protection from sanctions upon the academic community? Are the students wrong in expecting freedom from police interference? When the police penetrate the campus, are they comparable to an invading army?

SOURCE: *Yale Review of Law and Social Action, 1* (1970), published by The Yale Law School.

A limited right of sanctuary emerged in the medieval universities of Bologna, Paris, and Oxford, as a concession wrested from the civil authorities by the militant contingents of scholars from many lands, various classes, and divergent cultures. In Bologna, lacking civil rights and consigned to second class status, they banded together for protection in guilds and "nations." At last, victors in armed clashes with the townspeople, swift to resort to the threat of a strike or an economic boycott, they acquired substantial power within the university and over the city as well.(1)

With the growth of "student power" came a recognition of student prerogatives. The Privilege of Frederick I in 1158 clearly granted sanctuary status upon the studium at Bologna: it placed them "under the special protection of the Emperor [and provided that] in any legal proceedings against a scholar the defendant is to have the option of being cited before his own master or before the bishop."(2)

In France, the Church granted its primary charter to the University of Paris and accorded clerical status to all the students and masters, who thus obtained the right to be tried in the ecclesiastical courts(3) rather than in courts of civil jurisdiction.

After a series of bloody battles against the police and the citizens, the University of Paris obtained its form of sanctuary status in 1200, the year chosen by the University as the date of its founding.

> In that year, after certain students had been killed in a town and gown altercation, King Philip Augustus issued a formal privilege which punished his prévôt and recognized the exemption of the students and their servants from lay jurisdiction. . . .(4)

In England, the Universities of Oxford and Cambridge enjoyed special privileges almost from the time of their formation. Under a series of royal charters confirmed by the Act of 13 Elizabeth, c 29 (1571), Oxford was granted

> a large measure of exclusive jurisdiction now or formerly expressed in matters (1) ecclesiastical, (2) criminal, (3) civil, when a member of the University is concerned.(5)

The University had jurisdiction over its students and tried them in its own courts.(6) In the relation between town and gown, however, the apparent amity and respect barely cloaked a seething anger, and violence and rebellion constantly threatened.(7) Recurrent campus disorders in England ultimately led to the creation in 1825 of a university police force to patrol the cloistered precincts of Oxford and Cambridge.(8) By comparison, it was not until 1829, after years of bitter political struggle, that Sir Robert Peel secured passage of legislation establishing the Metropolitan Police Force, commonly known as Scotland Yard.

American universities have been greatly influenced by these medieval models, but they have never enjoyed the legal protection of sanctuary status. An American college student is actually at a disadvantage: the charters of incorporation or the statutes creating academic institutions usually give control of the government of the college to the president, administration, and faculty; and as long as that system of control is reasonable and appropriate the courts will not intervene to restrict it. At the same time, the State Penal Code applies with full force to the campus. The student is thus liable to double jeopardy, subject to the jurisdiction of two separate authorities.(9)

Of course, there are limits beyond which these sanctions cannot be applied, for a student does not give up his constitutional rights upon admission to the university. For example, the First Amendment right to freedom of speech and the Fourth Amendment right to protection from unreasonable searches and seizures remain intact.(10) And the student has a well recognized right to a form of due process of law in any quasi-criminal investigation conducted by the university (at least where the university is run by the state or has state affiliations).(11)

By themselves, these constitutional protections stop far short of according American students the sanctuary privileges of the medieval university. Until recently, nevertheless, the academic community felt secure in the knowledge that the external police power normally stopped at the gates to the campus. The reasons for this pattern of benign neglect are to be found in the ingrained reluctance of the chief instruments of law enforcement—the police—to encroach upon the domain of the university, and in the historical role that the university has forged for itself, a role requiring that its students be given certain prerogatives.

Police avoidance of the campus has a long tradition. A de facto treaty of nonaggression between police and the university is passed on by the older members of the force to the new generation of rookies as part of the conventional wisdom of the job. The normal scope of police jurisdiction is on the public streets from building line to building line. That is where the police officer operates with the most freedom, both personal and legal, and that is where his superior expects him to be. The campus seems a foreign territory, in fact, a forbidden land to a sergeant supervising a patrolman assigned to the street surrounding the campus. The patrolman, knowing this, feels uncomfortable in proportion as he moves onto the campus and away from the street. (Of course this does not apply to recent events where policemen are specifically assigned to locations on the campus to keep the peace.)

Further, the police crime prevention effort is directed toward major crimes such as robbery, burglary, and assault. In the world of police administration this is called "selective enforcement." Criminality on the campus, however, usually takes another direction; it is more likely to be victimless crime, in which there is no complainant, no obvious injury, and a smaller chance of obtaining a conviction. Therefore, as long as the police see crime prevention as their major function, the university is a dead end. An ambitious patrolman or detective needs a "good pinch" for his promotion. He is smart enough not to waste time looking for it on a college campus.

Neither do the more powerful members of the police bureaucracy relish confrontation with the university. One guiding principle of bureaucracies is that work is accomplished more efficiently when conflict with powerful enemies is avoided. The police certainly do not want to become involved in fierce, long-drawn-out battles against the universities. In too many cases, police action on the campus leads to political repercussions and angry debate over jurisdiction, constitutional rights and liberties, and accusations of police brutality. The police are well aware that the First Amendment applies with extraordinary force in the college community, and that its shadow will becloud any dispute over police performance.

In their role as citizens, too, the police are likely to view the campus as a *terra incognita*. It is wrong to assume that policemen are a strange, alien breed unlike the community from which they come and which they serve. They are the most typical Americans in America, and they share the average citizen's respect even awe, for the college—that realm of ideas, scholarship, and mysterious research. In their eyes there is a touch of the sacred in the groves of academe that ought not to be profaned.

In addition, many policemen have sons and daughters who attend college, and there is some reluctance to enter a situation where, behind the facade of a tough cop, an anxious father is thinking, "There but for the grace of God goes . . ."

Finally, most colleges maintain their own private campus police forces to avoid calling on the city police. The supervisors of these agencies are typically former law enforcement officers who have resigned or retired. They sustain close and friendly relations with the municipal police. The relation is one of comity: the city police hesitate to interfere; the campus police discourage such interference because it seems a reflection on their own ability to handle the cases that arise. In fact, the campus police tend to "cool it" and to downgrade the seriousness of a case in order that the city police will not feel compelled to intervene. This then, is another subtle pressure keeping the police away from the campus.

The other reason for the relative freedom allowed university students in this country is the role which the university has come to play in American society. In recent years, the university has been the major and almost the only, institution which can successfully conduct young people through the ritual passage from adolescence to respected adult status: "College is an initiation rite . . . for changing the semi-amorphous adolescent into a semi-identified adult."(12) Given the technological complexity of our society, every young person who hopes to achieve high status must submit to that long period of preparation which can only be completed at the university. Further, our society has a major interest in damming up the explosive force of ever-increasing numbers of young people behind college walls, in the hope that some will develop skills essential to the smooth functioning of the system, and that potential dissidents will be rendered docile or even transformed into supporters of the system. In any case, for the time that they are in college, the students' threat to the status quo can be diverted, postponed or blunted a little. The result has been an extension of adolescence at the upper as well as the lower age limits.

The university, then, has been the *rite de passage* for those who attend it. It has been the test, the ordeal, the initiation that "made a man of the student."(13)

The youth attending college was protected because society recognized the university as the insulated arena within which the difficult transition to adult status should be made, and within wide limits almost all tentative experiments at proving manhood were benignly tolerated. Only this attitude of tolerance permitted conspicuous indulgence in sex, drinking, fighting, wild auto racing, hazing, malicious mischief, panty raids, and finally drugs. (The upper-middle-class college fraternity and its lower-class counterpart, the gang, shared a marked similarity to each other and also to the puberty rite ceremony of primitive society.) Although college was the approved place for a young man to test himself and to challenge society, it was assumed that at the end of his college career he would be prepared to accept his role in the establishment without serious questioning or misgivings.

The universities, like all other institutions in our country, have weathered repeated assaults from without. They were unprepared to cope with an attack from within by their own "progeny," and as a result their vulnerability has been exposed. On the one hand the university is condemned as elitist because it excludes the lower classes and minority groups; on the other hand, open enrollment that would correct this alleged discrimination is to a large segment of the community the swan song of the traditional university. At the same time, the initiates are beginning to take seriously the myths invented by society to justify this period of exclusion from the "real world." They have been conditioned to believe that college will make them mature, guide them along the path to virtue, prepare them to step into positions of power, and demonstrate to them how to make the world a better place. The students demand that these promises be kept, and they demand control over their destiny. It does not matter what outrage, what ideology, what spirit motivates them. They are tired of waiting. They are on the march. Inevitably, this leads to confrontation with the university, and then the establishment.

This change in the students' concerns destroys the traditional rationale for insulating them from the consequences of their actions. In effect, they are refusing to be indulged; their "trespasses" reflect not mere youthful exuberance but genuine social and political outrage. Even more important, the role of today's student has caused the police to overcome their traditional reluctance to invade the campus when disorder occurs. This latter development, more than any other, signals the end of the *de facto* sanctuary nature of the university.

Consider the action of police in the "busts" at Berkeley and Columbia in 1968 and 1969. What can explain the magnitude of the police reaction to those disturbances?

One theory often set forth is the conflict of generations. While this may apply to the confrontation between students and the administration, it does not convey a true picture of relations between students and the police. If 30 is the cutoff age separating young from old, then thousands of policemen are below that age and belong to the younger generation. In fact, many

policemen are younger than the graduate students on the opposite side. Moreover, many policemen are attending college and are students themselves. Some older police officers may feel bitter toward college students with draft deferments because their own sons were taken by the armed forces for service in Vietnam, but this is hardly a case that fits the conflict of generations theory.

A more compelling explanation attributes police hostility toward students to class conflict. In this view the police are identified as working class or at best lower-middle-class people who envy and resent the upper-middle-class college students.(14) Upon closer examination, however, this theory proves untenable. The latent function of the police is the protection of the upper-middle-class world. On the psychological level, police internalize many of the upper-middle-class values, and on the behavioral level they are subservient to those whose interests they protect. Furthermore, class divisions have existed for a long time. Why should they suddenly take effect now, but not in the past? Far from being antagonistic to college students, the police before the time of the Berkeley uprising were most considerate of them. During the "panty raid" fad several years ago, hundreds of male students invaded the sacred territory of the girls' dormitories, swarmed up fire escapes, broke down doors, tore open drawers, stole panties and bras, and committed other less figurative crimes as well. These activities could hardly be labeled "good clean fun." Clearly the crimes of burglary, larceny, malicious mischief, and assault were spelled out if the police wanted to make arrests. What was the police response to the invasion and occupation of these college buildings? Almost joining in the spirit of revelry, the police usually took just enough action to cool the situation by turning hoses on the "boys" to dampen their enthusiasm. Rarely did the thought of arrest cross the minds of either the police or the demonstrators.

The annual rites of spring vacation provide another opportunity to test the power of the class conflict theory. Thousands of collegians mass at a relatively few popular beaches. There is drinking, dancing, sex and probably drugs. Certainly this situation should arouse the latent resentment of the police if class or generational conflict is the key. Generally however, the police, in spite of their supposedly rigid lower-class ethic, enter good-humoredly into the carnival spirit. Considering the many offenses, there are surprisingly few arrests made.

One other variation on the theme of celebration

also seems to nullify the class conflict theory. In the fall of 1968, after Ohio State defeated Michigan for the Big Ten football championship, 6000 celebrants took to the streets, smashed windows, knocked over telephone booths, and according to reports, were "joyfully escorted" along their way by the police.(15)

In addition, class divisions that may have existed between police and students are breaking down. With open enrollment spreading, colleges are becoming conglomerate mixtures of all classes.(16) Among the police, class mobility is rapidly increasing; a revolution has taken place, and its spirit is professionalization. Suddenly the police are inundating the colleges, not as policemen but as dedicated students working for their degrees. Inevitably, the values of the academic world are narrowing the differences between the perspectives of students and police. This is especially true of the higher ranks in large urban departments, and since they wield the power, they will act as a brake upon the possibility of a mass ideological attack upon the campus.

It is true that the influence of class has indirectly encouraged the police to assume a greater role on the campus. Powerful middle-class pressure groups who once threw their weight behind the sanctuary concept because they did not want their children arrested for youthful peccadillos have changed their views as colleges have gained the reputation of being centers for drug parties and sexual promiscuity. Frightened by this alien life of drugs, hippies, and sexual freedom, parents have come to identify with the values represented by the police, and to welcome the presence of the police on the campus as an antidote to the apparent permissiveness and lack of supervision.

Retaliation to personal insults is also, obviously, a powerful motivator of action. When a policeman is called a "pig," a "Nazi," a "motherfucker," or other choice epithets, or is physically attacked, he responds viscerally in spite of his training. And often unfortunately, he may exact a heavy retribution for such abuse.

Whatever the significance of class, generational, or personal conflicts, however, the major explanation for police reaction to student disorders is directly related to the shift in student concerns from traditional forms of self-expression to political confrontation. Like the new breed of students, the new breed of policemen have themselves developed a political ideology. Over the past decade, police have conquered their sense of isolation and provincialism. Instead of walking his lonely post, the modern policeman takes his position in special squads carefully trained to deal with meetings, sit-ins, and protests in favor of civil rights, against the war in Vietnam, for desegregation, against the schools and the universities. Constantly in the spotlight of the mass media, police have begun to realize their importance and power. Working shoulder to shoulder with masses of other policemen to control political demonstrations, they have become politicized themselves, and have become aware of their common interests across the nation. Such solidarity has convinced them that now, more than ever before, the police are that last thin blue line preventing chaos in America.

For men who believe this deeply, it is only a small step to conceive of themselves as a domestic army. Their answer to the accusation that they are an army of occupation in the ghetto, or an invading army on the campus, is that they are an army in a war against crime. To the charge that they are prejudiced against minority groups or college students, the police counter, "We are against criminals. They are the enemy."

> The police speak of the criminal sometimes as an animal, sometimes simply as "the enemy." He is seen as a "rat" or a "vermin"—whatever his position in the animal kingdom, he is something to be exterminated. As an enemy he becomes the target in the "war on crime," and the public pronouncements of law enforcement officials leave no doubt that it is a Holy War.(17)

Buttressed by the image of themselves as an internal army, police particularly resent college students who protest the draft and the war itself, and are even more virulent toward students who align with black power leaders, who are already viewed as "the enemy." Since the college students are America's future leaders, they are the direct beneficiaries of the police effort to maintain society in its present form. For them to turn against the police who serve them is, according to police logic, a shocking betrayal. When student activities were merely boisterous, police tolerated them with equanimity. But now that the students are making common cause with groups that the police hold in contempt, the university's privileged status has been undermined, and police are prepared to keep the college under strict surveillance if necessary.(18)

The ambivalence of the police toward the campus amounts to an institutionalized approach—avoidance conflict, magnified by the faculty, and the student body. In the past members of the academic community have been adamant in their attitude that policemen, as policemen, are unwelcome intruders, and have been successful in imposing that view of the situation upon the police themselves. Archibald Cox, chairman of the commission that investigated the Columbia University disturbances of 1968, expressed this position very clearly:

> There is a strong tradition, not only at Columbia but in most American universities, that Municipal or State police do not belong on the academic campus. The tradition is recognized by the New York Police Department whose top officials advised us that they would not send policemen onto the campus except at the request of the highest University officials.(19)

There are signs, however, that this firm line of resistance is giving way. Unable to devise effective strategies for dealing with campus disorders, university administrators have been unwilling to dismiss the option of calling in the police. As Theodore Hesburgh, president of Notre Dame University, expressed it:

> No one wants the forces of law on this or any other campus, but if some necessitate it, as a last and dismal alternative to anarchy and mob violence tyranny, let them shoulder the blame . . .(20)

Other authorities have been willing to discard totally the notion that the university should offer special protection for its students. Morris B. Abram, former president of Brandeis University, who successfully faced and conquered student protest, has asserted that

> Educators [have] had a distorted notion that the university is a sanctuary. The university is part of society and subject to the laws of society. The reluctance to use outside force to remove disrupters because they were middle-class was morally wrong and legally indefensible. The American university cannot be a democratic institution if it is to be an educational institution.(21)

Nor are administrators really adopting a more lenient stance when under the guise of avoiding hard-core police action they resort to the remedy of injunction against students. These injunctions are prepared by university legal staffs, and judges routinely sign them without notice or hearing of any kind for the defendants. Realistically, this is a more severe course of action than direct recourse to the police. It has been called a form of judicial overkill. One legal critic has stated:

> Just as the use of the injunction against labor raised social problems as well as legal ones, so it does when leveled against students. Public opinion plays an important part in the outcome of student protest activities. The issuance of an injunction broadens and deepens a conflict: it brands as lawless in the public mind not merely the conduct of a few individual leaders or activists who are the nominal defendants but the entire protest movement, however justified, and no matter what its target.(22)

What trends will emerge from this confrontation? The clamor for law and order will increase. Acutely aware of the barometer of public opinion, the police will probably formulate a policy of more stringent prevention and control of disturbances both on and off the campus. Even more sensitive to the mood of the electorate, political leaders will promote freer use of the police to quell such disorder, and university administrators will be increasingly pressured to allow such interference.

The ebbing of student protest can hardly be attributed to this thread of more repressive measures, but there is a definite change of direction away from the campus. Enthusiasm has been blunted and solidarity has cracked. Internecine struggles are splitting off cults and sects from the main body of the movement. Such loss of momentum characteristically converts revolutionary energy into forms of ritualism that strikingly resemble religious rites of purification and revitalization. Thus, each new campus incident brings an automatic and predictable repetition of slogans, chants, and non-negotiable demands. Faced with increasing hostility from without, and decreasing impetus from within, student militants disenchanted by hollow victories that seem to have changed nothing, are likely to drop out of the college world. They will pursue the quest elsewhere—for catharsis of the soul in the psychedelic world of drugs or in the utopian commune; for rectification of society in the cults of violence; and for purification of the total environment in associations that are still amorphous.

This somber transformation must never obscure the need to protect and nurture the students' right to dissent. It is the singular obligation of the university to encourage new, unorthodox, or radical ideas to the point where they can survive on their own. Unpopular causes are integral parts of this matrix. For the university and for society as a whole to flourish, the protection of diversity and dissent is mandatory, even at the price of disorder.

Yet the traditional bases for such protection are no longer viable. The student's new conception of himself destroys, by definition, his claim to immunity, especially as he sallies forth beyond the confines of the campus; and the attitudes of police and university administrators which made that immunity a social and psychological reality have altered drastically as they adjusted to the new developments. It is time, then, for a reappraisal of the need, rights, and privileges of both the student and the university. Until now, the university's role in fostering the new and radical has received only accidental protection. Such protection must now become deliberate; the university must struggle to achieve a new sanctuary status. It must also learn to regard the student movement not as an alien sport but as the culmination of a proud tradition of inquiry and dissent. And the movement itself must continue to live up to that tradition, for insofar as it fails to do so, it can no longer claim to function as the conscience of society.

REFERENCES

1. Hastings Rashdall, *The Universities of Europe in the Middle Ages, 1* (London: Oxford University Press, 1958), pp. 142–69.

2. Ibid., p. 144.

3. And later in the University's own academic courts. Ibid., pp. 290 and 417.

4. Charles Haskins, *The Rise of Universities* (Ithaca: Cornell University Press, 1966), p. 15.

5. *Encyclopedia of the Laws of England, 3*, p. 439.

6. William Blackstone, *Commentaries on the Laws of England, 4* (Boston: Beacon Press, 1962), pp. 325–26.

7. In 1411, for example, the proctor at Oxford University led a group of Oxford students armed with bows and arrows against the Archbishop, who had been sent to impose censorship on the University. The immediate result was the closing down of the University. The proctor's name was John Birch. (cf. Rashdall, op. cit., 3, pp. 131–35.)

8. "An Act for the better Preservation of the Peace and good Order in the Universities of England," 6 George IV, c. 97 (1825).

9. William W. Van Alstyne, "Student Activism, the Law and the Courts," in Julian Foster and Durward Long, *Protest: Student Activism in America* (New York: William Morrow & Co., Inc., 1970), pp. 540–41.

10. Admittedly, the peculiar nature of the college-student relation imposes a special interpretation of the law. For example, the Fourth Amendment prohibits unreasonable searches and seizures of persons, houses, papers, and effects. The dormitory room is the student's house. It is also the university's responsibility to see that its regulations are obeyed, that the safety of the student body is not threatened, and that enough order is maintained so that the academic intellectual enterprise may flourish (*Goldberg* v. *Regents of University of California* 248 Cal. App. 2d 867, 57 Cal. Rptr. 463 [1967]). Some cases have recognized these dual claims and have decided that the police entered a student's room legally when they were authorized to do so by the administration where there was reasonable cause to believe that important university regulations were being violated (*People* v. *Kelly*, 195 Cal. App. 2d 72 [1961]). This same rule would not apply to a mere witch hunt, and there is reason to believe that in the future, the courts may recognize the paramount right of the student (*People* v. *Overton*, 51 Misc. 2d 140, 273 N.Y.S. 2d 143 [1966]; *Moore* v. *Student Affairs Comm. of Troy State Univ.*, 284 F. Supp. 725 [M.D. Ala. 1968]).

11. This would probably include a right of notice, a right to have counsel present, to present witnesses, to cross-examine, to have records kept, to receive a copy of the findings and to receive appellate consideration upon request (Van Alstyne, op. cit., p. 538). *See* also Arthur H. Sherry, "Governance of the University: Rules, Rights and Responsibilities," *California Law Review, 54* (March 1966), pp. 23–39.

12. David Riesman and Christopher Jencks, "The Viability of the American College," in Nevitt Sanford, ed., *The American College* (New York: John Wiley, 1962), p. 78.

13. These beneficial effects had been confined primarily to members of the middle class. Children of the upper class really had no need for such assurance, although their parents were willing to allow the best schools (with the most prestige) to polish their scions in upper-class manners. The lower class until recently was unable to gain admission to the universities, although exceptions were occasionally made in favor of those young people who were considered good risks to acquire the middle-class "virtues." Cf. Riesman, loc. cit.

14. *See*, for example, Michael Lerner, "Respectable Bigotry," *The American Scholar, 38* (Autumn,

1969), pp. 606–617. Paradoxically his account of an actual experience with a policeman is a case that seems to disprove his theory of class conflict, because the officer reverses roles with the college student and defends the liberal middle-class position.

15. *New Republic*, December 7, 1968, p. 11.

16. For a detailed discussion of this situation *see* Lewis S. Feuer, *The Conflict of Generations* (New York: Basic Books, Inc., 1969), pp. 30–35, in which the author rejects the class conflict theory in favor of a sense of generational consciousness.

17. Herbert L. Packer, *The Limits of the Criminal Sanction* (Stanford: Stanford University Press, 1968), p. 10.

18. This is the advice offered by certain "experts" to police administrators:

It is essential that police personnel be assigned to maintain a continuous observation of campus activities. The identity and background of student organizers should be known since it may well provide a clue as to the action which can be anticipated. Rallies and meetings should be attended and published material carefully studied. If possible, contacts with responsible students should be established to provide a continuing source of information regarding campus response to the agitators (Raymond M. Momboisse, *Riots, Revolts and Insurrections*

[Springfield: Charles C. Thomas, 1967], pp. 321–322).

And from the campus comes this plaintive cry in response. Neil Rosenthal, former University of Denver student body president, complained to a college audience shortly after the largest drug raid on any campus:

We've done a lousy job of getting it together . . . plain clothes policemen don't look like 35-year-old men any more. The police look like us, dress like us and rap like us (*Stony Brook Statesman*, Feb. 11, 1970, p 2).

19. *Crisis at Columbia: Report of the Fact-Finding Commission on Columbia Disturbances* (New York: Vintage Books, 1968), p. 157.

20. *New York Times*, February 18, 1969, p. 25.

21. *New York Times*, October 28, 1969, p. 18.

22. Frank J. Donner, "The Injunction on Campus," *The Nation*, 208 (June 9, 1969), p. 719. It bears mention that the American Council of Education has distributed a pamphlet to college presidents which "amounts to tactical guidelines about where, and how to use court injunctions on campus." *See* Paul Lauter and Archibald W. Alexander, "ACE: Defender of the Educational Faith," in *The Antioch Review*, 29 (Fall 1969), p. 299.

The Police and the Urban Ghetto

JEROME H. SKOLNICK

Any inquiry into the role of police in contributing to or preventing civil disorders within the urban ghettos of the United States must begin with a clear recognition of how bad the situation is. The best single description of the dilemma of the policeman in the urban ghetto comes neither from a police official nor a social scientist. It comes instead from the pen of an eloquent black writer, James Baldwin. Baldwin vividly expresses the isolation of the ghetto policeman, as follows: (1)

The only way to police a ghetto is to be oppressive. None of the police commissioner's men, even with

SOURCE: Research Contributions of the American Bar Foundation, No. 3 (Chicago: American Bar Foundation, 1968), pp. 3–28.

the best will in the world, have any way of understanding the lives led by the people: they swagger about in twos and threes patrolling. Their very presence is an insult, and it would be, even if they spent their entire day feeding gum drops to children. They represent the force of the white world, and that world's criminal profit and ease, to keep the black man corralled up here, in his place. The badge, the gun in the holster, and the swinging club, make vivid what will happen should his rebellion become overt. . . .

It is hard, on the other hand, to blame the policeman, blank, good-natured, thoughtless, and insuperably innocent, for being such a perfect representative of the people he serves. He, too, believes in good intentions and is astounded and offended when they are not taken for the deed. He has never, himself, done anything for which to be hated, which of us has? And yet he is facing, daily and nightly, the people who would gladly see him dead, and he knows it. There is no way for him not to know it: There are few things under heaven more unnerving than the silent accumulating contempt and hatred of a people. He moves through Harlem, therefore, like an occupying soldier in a bitterly hostile country; which is precisely what, and where he is, and is the reason he walks in twos and threes.

Assuming this description to be essentially correct, and I believe on the basis of my observations that it is, what are its consequences? Unless we straightforwardly remark upon these consequences we may, out of politeness and circumspection, fail to perceive reality, grim as it may be. A realistic description is essential for understanding the situation and for attempting to alter it.

Racial Prejudice

One aspect of this reality is the racial prejudice of police. There is no training manual in the United States which presents the idea that Negroes should be treated differently in the criminal process from whites, nor that black men and women exhibit greater criminal tendencies than white men and women. Virtually all police departments explicitly subscribe to the principle of the equality of white and black people and the equal treatment that each ought to be accorded by law enforcement officials. Yet anyone who has spent any time observing police, with any degree of depth, would have to agree that as a group the police are highly antagonistic to Negroes. William Westley, who studied police in a midwestern city near Chicago, commented in 1951:

> For the police the Negro epitomizes the slum dweller and, in addition, he is culturally and biologically inherently criminal. Individual policemen sometimes deviate sharply from this general definition, but no white policeman with whom the author has had contact failed to mock the Negro, to use some type of stereotyped categorization, and to refer to interaction with the Negro in an exaggerated dialect when the occasion arose.

Westley's characterization was true for the police I studied on both the East and West Coasts. In my tenure with the West Coast police department I learned all the usual derisive terms referring to Negroes and a great many others I had never heard before. In fact, the chief issued a directive stating as a matter of policy: "The following words and other similar derogatory words shall not be used by members and employees in the

course of their official duties or at any other time." The chief's statement recorded a litany of racial prejudice— "boy, spade, jig, nigger, blue, smoke, coon, spook, head hunter, jungle bunny, boogie, stark, burr head, cat, black boy, black, shine, ape, spick, mau mau."

While such language is never to be condoned, it is a mistake, from the point of view of understanding police-Negro relations, simply to respond with indignation, without analyzing the use of such derogation in context. First, a disposition to stereotype is an integral part of the policemen's world. They are called upon in many areas of their work to make "hunch" judgments based on loose correlations. For example, the concept of *modus operandi* is nothing more than a technique for drawing probable relations between one criminal pattern and another. In effect, it is a stereotype, perhaps right more often than wrong, which may not be claiming much. Similarly, ethnic stereotypes, like the *modus operandi* of criminals, become part of the armory of investigation.

Second, if as Baldwin suggests, the police are viewed in the ghetto as an army of occupation, it is also true that in good part the policeman's attitude toward his work is reminiscent of that of the combat soldier. For the policeman out on the street, his life is one of constant "combat." Like the combat soldier, the policeman's perception of the world around him strains toward dualities—people are good/bad, safe/unsafe, we/they. For the white policeman patrolling an urban ghetto "they" are black.

Moreover, like the dogface, the policeman is irritated by minor organizational rules, legal technicalities, and embellished descriptions. He is neither a coiner nor a user of euphemisms. To the average cop, Joe DiMaggio was *not* an athlete of "Italian extraction." Rather, he was a "hell of a good wop centerfielder," no offense intended. It is hard to conclude that no offense is intended when a black man is termed a "nigger," rather than a member of a "minority group," but there is a sense in which such terms are not quite as bigoted as they sound.

Additionally, as one observes police, one notices their employment of two predominant models of discourse. One of these models, which might be termed "office language" or "working language," is frequently profane, loud, and good-humored. Transported into the cold light of print the words might have a shocking effect upon delicate sensibilities. But such discourse would ring familiar to a steelworker or longshoreman, a ballplayer or a soldier. Likewise, such language may not appear contextually inappropriate to the working policeman on the street.

Off the street, police frequently resort to an alternative model—"officialese"—out of fear that "working language" might spill out and offend higher officialdom. An outstanding example of police officialese is the substitution of the word "altercation" for "fight," as in "the two men were having an altercation." So the policeman is often not a graceful or moderate speaker or writer, and his inability or perhaps unwillingness to conceal true feelings gets him into trouble.

This is not to declare that police as a group are not racially prejudiced. Certainly they are. Yet the term "racial prejudice" implies something exceptional about the policeman's attitude toward the Negro, it suggests that the policeman's antipathy toward Negroes is different from the run-of-the-mill white community attitude. From the policeman's point of view, an accusation of racial prejudice tends to make a scapegoat of him, when as a rule he is probably no more prejudiced than his fellow citizens who lead lives isolated from Negroes. Those California citizens who voted "yes" in 1964 on a proposition to repeal the state law against discrimination in housing, and Milwaukee citizens who have opposed an anti-discrimination ordinance illustrate the general prejudice of the white community which the policeman so faithfully represents. Nevertheless, while a sociologist can perhaps explain away some of the racial prejudice of police by relating it to broader patterns of racial and ethnic stereotyping, to the black man the explanation is of no consequence—it is the action that counts.

Racial Discrimination

The sociologist can explain the attitude of the police in terms of prevailing informal norms in the communities in which the typical white policeman resides. But there is another set of norms to which the policeman is also held responsible. There is a critical distinction between the policeman and the ordinary citizen. The policeman is a law enforcement official and the norms of his organization as well as the norms of the larger society hold him to a higher standard of conduct than that prevailing for the ordinary private citizen.

The American dilemma described so well by Gunnar Myrdal is apparent in police work as it is everywhere else. There is an ideal, mentioned earlier, that the norm of racial equality shall prevail in law enforcement. The issue then is, how do the informal norms of prejudice influence the policeman in carrying out his work?

The answer is, it depends. The behavior of the policeman toward the black man is likely to vary with the policeman's assignment within the department. Thus, hostility toward black men is apt to be revealed especially on the street and especially in situations that invite stereotyping. Suppose police are on the lookout for a robbery assailant and have nothing to go on but a vague description of a Negro male. Under these circumstances, innocent Negro males will easily be assimilated to the policeman's stereotype of the subject. Thus, in a high-crime area a disproportionate number of black men will be stopped, not necessarily out of racial prejudice, but rather because black men in a high-crime area will tend to fit the description of the suspect.

The innocent black man who is stopped by a policeman will resent having been detained. This resentment may manifest itself in language or gestures challenging the authority of the policeman. When that happens, the policeman may assert his authority in a brusk, rude, sometimes demeaning and sometimes physically challenging fashion. From the point of view of the black man, he has been needlessly detained, solely because of his color, because he is by social circumstances required to live in a high-crime area, and because police are either bigoted, have difficulty distinguishing between one black man and another, or both.

The policeman's view, by contrast, is simply that he is doing his job, that the black man whom he has stopped is uncooperative, more than that he is insolent, that he deserves an insult, perhaps a crack in the head as well. The latter event is relatively infrequent—what most black men mean by police brutality is either insult or presumed insult. Street inquiries in the urban ghetto are the occasions most likely to provoke insult and indignation. Accordingly, "stop and frisk" laws that encourage a higher frequency of more direct contact—including a demeaning touching of the body—will serve to heighten ghetto tensions and increase the probability of violence.

In detective work, by contrast, where contacts do not take place on the street, where the policeman does not feel as threatened, where he generally has more information about the people with whom he is dealing, and where the outcome is likely to be something that will benefit his professional record—these are the conditions that tend to moderate hostile interactions between police and citizens. When the policeman really has probable cause for an arrest, when he is dealing with a suspect, he is more likely to proceed with procedural regularity. When he operates on the basis of mere *suspicion*, he is more likely to vent his *prejudices*.

Different Standards for Black and White

Every study of police activities in the North as well as in the South has commented on the different standards that police employ in the urban ghetto. For example, certain kinds of assaults may be treated differently depending upon whether the combatants are black or white. This is especially true of those involving husbands and wives. The employment of different standards creates problems for both the police and for the inhabitants of the urban ghetto. For example, the following item appeared in the *Chicago Daily Defender* (a Negro newspaper) on September 23, 1967.

A number of outsiders are lamenting the growing daring of gangs.

Four victims of Devils Disciples activity called this office over the weekend; said that they were harassed, robbed and trailed to their homes by almost a dozen Disciples. One of the young ladies said that as they emerged from a 63rd Street night club, about twenty of the gang members surrounded the car they entered, forcing them to dash out of the vehicle and run into the middle of the street where they waved down a passing squad car.

The two officers, one of the complainants said, told them to go home and although the gang members were standing right in the street, they did nothing to them. Since the car they were going home in had left the scene once the hoodlums had relaxed their grip, and the gang members had rifled their purses and taken their money, the four young women were forced to walk over ten blocks to their homes. One, who is the mother of several small children, said the Devils Disciples in their neighborhood roam the streets in packs and rather than trying to keep them in order, the police seem to condone their activities. She asked that her name be withheld because of possible reprisals against her youngsters. "People can't walk in the streets freely because these irresponsible gang members do not care whom they kill. Everyone around the area is afraid of them," she declared. From all reports, this 63rd Street area remains "Sin Corner."

This newspaper item suggests the dilemma of both the policeman and the black resident of the ghetto. The policeman is fearful of engaging in interactions that might provoke widespread violence. Street gangs are extremely difficult for ghetto police to deal with, because any stopping of a gang member may lead to a fight with others, which might provoke a larger incident. Thus, it is on the one hand understandable that police should be reluctant to engage in such encounters. On the other hand, this reluctance has the unintended effect of increasing the danger of ghetto living for the black man or woman who is leading a reasonably law-abiding existence. Accordingly, the police come to be seen not as protectors of those who need assistance against the depredations of gang activity but rather as those who fail in their essential task of maintaining public order.

Thus, the police are mistrusted in the ghetto, partly because they sometimes engage in actions or, more frequently, use language that is offensive to black people; partly because they are often seen by black people as failing in their fundamental responsibilities; and partly because they represent a hostile force keeping black people in their place.

Finally, the situation feeds upon itself. To the extent that police are bigoted and manifest prejudices in the daily performance of their duties, to the extent that they employ different standards, to the extent that they insult black people living in the ghetto, they receive the hostility and hatred of the black man in the ghetto. This hostility and hatred, in turn, reinforces the policeman's bigotry, the policeman's hatred, the policeman's fear, and the social isolation of the policeman from those black citizens with whom he must come in daily contact. The situation does not seem to be improving at all. Indeed in every way it seems to be becoming worse as underlying social conditions such as unemployment further frustrate the black man in the ghetto. Thus, as social conditions prod the black man into increasingly hostile responses, the police are on the receiving end and are themselves tempted to respond with renewed hostility.

Recommendations

Given this dismal portrait, is there anything we can do? In the remainder of this paper, I·intend to comment upon certain areas where I think improvements can be made. I do not intend to deal here with underlying social conditions, but solely with recommendations relating to criminal law and its administration, a sufficient topic. This omission, however, should not be interpreted as a failure to recognize that we need radical social changes within our communities. Especially we need to concentrate on the attitude and response of our *white* population, since it is fundamentally the white community's bigotry and narrow conception of self-interest, especially in the areas of employment and housing, that lead to quite under-standable hostility in the black communities of America.

First, I think that the most important intellectual contribution that can be made by the Commission would be to sponsor an investigation of police training in relation to actual police work. One must see this problem in historical context. Reports about the American police, especially for the period of the 1930's, reveal practices so appalling as to pose no intellectual issue for civilized men. It was no accident that a writer who summarized the 1931 Wickersham Commission report entitled his book "Our Lawless Police."

In the old fashioned police department, riddled with political appointees and working hand in hand with the rackets, a police reformer was not mainly concerned with the niceties of constitutional rights. As the citizenry faced the arbitrary use of "club, blackjack and gun," the problem of police reform was to reduce gross brutality, traditionally associated with corruption.

In response to this challenge, such men as O. W. Wilson and the late Chief Parker of Los Angeles infused into police work a new kind of professionalism, based upon a paramilitary model. The goals of the police were efficiency, integrity, and widespread law enforcement. In the abstract, such goals appear unquestionably sound. In practice, however, this sort of military technological orientation toward the police role was accompanied both by a failure to recognize the human dimension of police work and by an insufficient appreciation of legal values in a free society.

Police Professionalism: Legality

We find the late Chief Parker defining police as "that executive civil force of the state to which is entrusted the duty of maintaining order and of enforcing regulations for the prevention and detection of crime."(2) Later on in this book he says: "Police feel deployment is not a social agency activity. In deploying to suppress crime, we are interested in maintaining order."(3)

Criminal law, however, especially in a democratic polity, contains two parts. One part of the criminal law is concerned with the maintenance of order. Another part of the criminal law regulates the conduct of state officials who are charged with processing citizens suspected, accused, or found guilty of crime. Here we find such issues as the law of search, the law of arrest,

the elements and degree of proof, the right to counsel, the nature of a lawful accusation of crime, and the fairness of trial. The procedures of the criminal law, in contrast to the substantive criminal law, stress the protection of individual liberties within a system of social order.

This partition of criminal law suggests that the common juxtaposition of "law and order" is an oversimplification in which the idea of order tends to swallow up the idea of due process of law and the achievement of order. "Law" and "order" are frequently found to be in opposition precisely because the idea of law implies a rational restraint on the rules and procedures that may be used to achieve public order. Public order under a rule of law, therefore, subordinates the ideal of conformity to the ideal of legality.

In their salutary attempt to raise the standards of police conduct, leading police officials increasingly have been advocating a conception of police professionalism based upon a narrow view of the criminal law. They see the criminal law merely as an instrument for achieving public order, and therefore they conceive of the development of police professionalism in terms of enhancing managerial efficiency and organizational interest. A sociologist is not surprised at such a development: under the rule of law, it is not up to the agency of enforcement to generate the limitations that govern its actions. Moreover, administrators of all types understandably try to conceal the knowledge of their operations so that they may regulate themselves.

The police in a democratic polity are not merely bureaucrats. They are also legal officials, men who belong to an institution charged not only with the maintenance of public order but also with strengthening the ideas of constitutional restraints upon the arbitrary exercise of official conduct. If the professionalism of police is ever to resolve some of the strains between order and legality, this professionalism must be based upon a deeper set of values than currently prevails in so-called professional police literature. The problem of police in a democratic society is not merely a matter of obtaining new police cars or more sophisticated equipment, or communication systems, or of recruiting men who have to their credit more years of education. What is necessary is a significant alteration in the philosophy of police, so that police "professionalization" rests upon the values of a democratic legal polity, rather than merely on the notion of technical proficiency to serve the public order of the state.

No thoughtful person can believe that it will be

easy to effect such a transformation. In an article estimating the prospects for the rule of law in the Soviet Union, Leonard Schapiro has written: "It is perhaps difficult for dictators to get accustomed to the idea that the main purpose of law is, in fact, to make their task more difficult."(4) In the same article, Schapiro reports the case of two professors who advocated that certain principles of "bourgeois" law and criminal procedure (what we mean by constitutional protections of individual rights) be adopted, arguing that observance of legal norms must prevail over expediency in government legislation and administration. The professors were officially criticized by the Soviet government for misinterpreting "the role of legal science and the solution of the practical tasks of government," a criticism not too different from the sort often leveled by professional police administrators in the United States against professors who emphasize the importance of the rule of law as against merely the maintenance of public order.

If the police are ever to develop a conception of legal as opposed to managerial professionalism, two conditions must be met: First, the police must accustom themselves to the seemingly paradoxical yet fundamental idea of the rule of law, namely, that the observance of legal restraints may indeed make their task more difficult. That's how it is in a free society.

Second, the civic community must support compliance with the rule of law by rewarding police for observing constitutional guarantees, instead of looking to the police merely as an institution responsible for controlling criminality. In practice, regrettably, the reverse has been true. I will have something to say later about how I think the federal government can help to develop a more legally oriented concept of police professionalism.

Police Professionalism: Community

Legality alone is not sufficient to bridge the ever widening gulf between police and the minority groups in our society. Emphasis upon legality will help—it will cut down on unreasonable police interrogations, detentions, friskings, and other invasions of privacy to which black people in our urban areas are particularly subjected. In addition, however, we must work out ways to change the conceptions of the police role. (Police are, in fact, performing social agency activities, whether they like it or not.) Nor is it irrelevant, either, for police to understand why a certain group tends toward crime. The police are legal officials enjoying

considerable discretion, and they can use this discretion in constructive, rather than destructive, ways. One of the most heralded innovations was the development of police-community relations programs within police departments. I should like to describe in some detail, first, the police-community relations program in San Francisco as I was able to observe it, with the considerable help of my students (notably Miss Katherine Jacobs and Mr. Johannes Feest).

The San Francisco Police Department, until five years ago, devoted most of its energy to apprehending criminals. In May, 1962, Police Chief Thomas Cahill, at the recommendation of such civic groups as the National Association for the Advancement of Colored People and the National Conference of Christians and Jews, established a community relations bureau. It was designed to create a better understanding and closer relationship between the police department and the community and to promote greater public cooperation with the police department.

Implicit in the creation of this unit was a recognition that changing social needs required a more expansive concept of police work. The idea was that police work was no longer simply a matter of apprehension, that police work also should include the prevention of crime. More explicitly, the police-community relations idea gave organizational meaning to the notion that police prevent crime not only by the threat of deterrence but also by a sympathetic understanding of the problems of people residing in high-crime areas. Crime was not, in this view, simply an act of perverted will but was a phenomenon arising out of frustrations and degradations felt by disadvantaged people; thus, the police would help to reduce crime by reducing despair—by acting as a social service agency to ameliorate some of the difficulties encountered by minority group persons.

The history of the San Francisco Police Community Relations Unit reflects a struggle between two opposing interpretations of the role of the policeman and of his relationship to the community. Because the duties of the police affected the entire community, the polarity of these interpretations created two strongly opposing factions, each dedicated to the victory of its own perspective on police response to problems of law and order. Each faction successfully developed a secure power base whose function was to undermine the validity of the position of the opposing side. The success of the Police Community Relations Unit depended upon the sympathy of the chief of police. It was his burden to mediate between the supporters of the PCR Unit and the supporters of the more traditional conceptions of law enforcement. In reviewing the history of the unit, the role of the chief appears critical. When he supported the unit, and its conception, the unit was able to function successfully. When, with time, his enthusiasm for the unit waned, the influence of the unit diminished until it could no longer perform as it once had.

Several important well-established civic groups were involved in the formation of the PCR Unit. The suggestion of such a unit, and the need for it, was not a new idea. Observers interviewed all seemed to suggest that Chief Cahill was sincerely interested in developing a high-caliber police force and in sustaining its reputation. If PCR units were to be the new thing in police work, then the San Francisco chief of police was determined that his force should not be lacking in this latest development. In addition, the chief of police was under considerable political pressure to do something about minority group relations. Before the unit was established, an outspoken leader from the Hunters Point ghetto went to see the mayor about problems of police brutality and harassment. She suggested the introduction of a PCR unit. Staunchly lined up behind her was the NAACP leader, Terry Francois, and the *San Francisco Examiner* editorial staff. In addition, leading reporters of the *San Francisco Chronicle* supported such a unit. The assistant managing editor of the *San Francisco Examiner* claimed that an editorial campaign launched by that newspaper was responsible for the establishment of the unit. He said, "We originally brought out the fact that the relationship between the minority groups and the Police Department had deteriorated and would worsen if no special department was set up." He also suggested that the establishment of such a unit was not controversial with the public, and in fact received considerable support, but he added that the Police Department itself was in opposition to the new unit because it thought that these problems should be handled through precinct captains. We found it difficult to ascertain just which policemen were in opposition, but all persons interviewed—including rank-and-file policemen—suggested that the overwhelming majority of police were against the program. We did not require elegant sampling procedures—everybody, on both sides, agreed.

Police Culture and Police Resentment

For anyone familiar with the culture of police, police resentment of a PCR unit was understandable.

First, the establishment of a new unit specialized in dealing with the problems of minorities constituted an acknowledgment that the Police Department had been unsuccessful in handling these problems. No governmental agency is easily responsive to an innovation based upon a charge of failure by a portion of the community. At the time, however, in 1962, the general political climate was receptive to innovations in the area of race relations. The Kennedy Administration was in power, new victories were being made by the Negro community in the area of civil rights, and in general, the San Francisco political climate was receptive to innovation even if the overwhelming majority of the police were not. Thus, despite the objections of the police force, the unit was established in May, 1962, with Lieutenant Dante Andreotti as commanding officer and Officer David Roche as his assistant.

Although the first battle of new against old was won, the subsequent history of the unit revealed that the two opposing sides, rather than giving in, rallied increasing support—the San Francisco Police Department Community Relations Unit was both a microcosm and a barometer of what was to follow in race relations throughout the country: As the politics of the country became more polarized in the next five years, so too did the politics surrounding the unit.

In the beginning, Lieutenant Andreotti was given considerable support. For instance, he was flown to Michigan to study at the Community Relations Institute there, was the object of supportive newspaper publicity, and received public praise by the chief of police. Although the unit was the smallest in the Police Department, it grew to 13 men, all of whom considered themselves to be specialists in the field of community relations. What community relations meant, in fact, was quite ambiguous. To various officers in the unit it meant different things. To two officers working with drug addicts, alcoholics, male and female prostitutes, and homosexuals, it meant informing them of their rights. It also included talking to them for hours in a Central City Economic Opportunity Office and trying to get them jobs. To another, the program meant bringing the Negro into "focus." To others it meant spending time with the youth of the area, in groups such as Citizens Alert and Youth for Service, trying to sound out the problems of those dwelling in the Hunters Point area.

The initial problem of the unit persisted: How to maintain its identity as a police organization and at the same time to win the confidence of the minority group population—which, as indicated, included not only Negroes, but also prostitutes, homosexuals, and hippies, each an identifiable minority group ordinarily considered a police problem.

By January, 1964, the success of the PCR Unit in winning the confidence of minority groups was so great that four members of the unit were invited to work out of the Office of Economic Opportunity offices in four poverty pockets. In the spring of 1967, there were two men in the Hunters Point OEO office, one in Chinatown, two in Central City, one in the West End addition, one in the Mission district; the remaining six men worked out of the Central Unit in the Hall of Justice. Of these six, two were former college athletes who devoted a good deal of time to organizing sports teams in poverty areas, enlisting the aid of civic-minded businessmen to donate sports equipment. Two of the six spoke Spanish, and remained in the office to assist other officers having difficulty with people from Mexican backgrounds. The remaining two officers in the Central Unit consisted of Andreotti and a veteran sergeant, who handled records and file keeping.

As the duties and responsibilities of the men in the PCR Unit increased, so too did the hostility of the rest of the police force. The following incident, related by Andreotti illustrates this: One man, assigned to the homosexual community, took his wife to the Annual Homosexual Ball, a costume party that is the highlight of the homosexual social season. With the officer and his wife present, the party proceeded peacefully. At a point in the proceedings a sergeant from the local precinct walked in the door and insisted upon searching the toilets. The PCR officer objected to this procedure but was outranked by the sergeant. The sergeant asserted his own jurisdiction. The PCR officer called Andreotti at home, who hurried over to the party and in turn, overruled the local sergeant. It was this sort of conflict, coupled with the avowed sympathy of the PCR officer toward the minority group, that was one of the major factors accounting for the hostility of the other police.

Another gripe against the PCR Unit stemmed from the fact that its men worked in plain clothes, even though they were not of detective rank. The hostility that minority group communities felt toward police was so great that for a uniformed officer to enter a new community and try to make contacts with its citizens, such as Negro juveniles in Hunters Point, would have been out of the question. On the other hand, police outside the PCR Unit were un-

willing to accept the idea that their uniforms elicited as much hostility as they did. They saw the unwillingness on the part of PCR members to wear uniforms as either disrespect for their fellow policemen, or a special attempt to show that they were "better" than other members of the force, or part of some sinister Communist plot to disparage the uniform.

The PCR Unit suffered also from another stigma, that of deviation from standard police practices. The role of the PCR man was often described as a "social work" role by other police. For many members of the police force, as was demonstrated at the most recent Annual PCR Institute, "social worker = socialist = communist." At a session of the 8th Annual National Conference of Christians and Jews Institute, one of the captains present referred to the PCR Unit as the "Commie Relations Unit," a term that I understood from other informants to be the usual derisive one used by most San Francisco police when referring to the PCR Unit. One must attend one of these institutes with operating police and see the open hostility to believe it.

Police resentment may be, however, attributed to a more fundamental concern. It is not the simple notion that "social work = socialism = communism"—that is, a symbol—but rather that the idea of social work activities for police undercuts the basic conception of the policeman's role. Police like to see themselves as strong, aggressive, masculine hunters protecting the weak. They are the good guys who beat up the bad guys who threaten the littler people.

But the social worker role requires that police reconceptualize their identities. They must be understanding as well as tough, sensitive as well as courageous. As one man put it to me at the recent conference, "If I had wanted to be a social worker, I would have gone to social work school. I wanted to be a cop and you sociologists can't come around and tell me about being a social worker. I'm a cop, that's all I want to be and that's all I'm going to be." Of course, this issue, like most controversial issues, has become polarized. There are the apprehenders, and there are those who believe in prevention, but little emphasis or research has been given to the idea that both conceptions may be able to exist usefully and simultaneously.

Probably the greatest barrier to acceptance by the rest of the Police Department of the PCR Unit was the informal complaint procedure that the PCR Unit developed. Because it was responsive to the concerns of minority-group members, in fact, the PCR

Unit became an informal complaint bureau, not only for complaints directed against the police, but also for complaints directed against other public agencies such as the Fire Department, the Welfare Department, and the schools. In effect, by becoming successful and gaining the confidence of the minority group community, the San Francisco PCR Unit became the informal "ombudsman" of the City of San Francisco.

This service of the PCR Unit created the most interdepartmental antagonism and distrust. The police outside the unit tended to regard the PCR Unit as an internal security force. This notion, coupled with the fact that PCR men had so little contact with the rest of the force, caused the PCR Unit to be regarded as a suspicious, aloof, mysterious and probably subversive branch of the Police Department. Andreotti himself estimates that fully 90 per cent of the San Francisco police force was hostile to the unit.

As hostility within the Police Department grew, there were increasing pressures upon Chief Cahill to disband the unit. The most significant, perhaps, came when in the beginning of December, 1966, a committee of the Grand Jury of San Francisco recommended that the Central PCR Unit be broken up and its men assigned to do the same work in uniform under the district captains. The chairman of the grand jury was a labor union leader who had been trying to organize the police into a union and who was quite conservative politically. This appeared to be a triumph for the San Francisco Police Officers' Association, an organization representing the police rank and file that is, to put it mildly, conservative.

Chief Cahill, however, promised that this development would not take place. Yet, by the end of December, the chief had announced details of a new plan: Each district captain was to select two men from his station to work in close connection with the Central Unit to carry the work of the unit to the local stations. Significantly, however, these men were to be responsible to their captains and not to Lieutenant Andreotti. The significance of this procedure was clear: if the captain was unsympathetic to minorities and to the concept of community relations, he would prevail over Andreotti.

At the time, voices of dissent arose immediately from Andreotti's "constituency," which by this time was the minority group community. Meetings were held by local church and neighborhood organizations, which had become firm allies of the unit. Chief Cahill called an immediate meeting at which he attempted to justify his decision. He claimed that his decision was triggered by a meeting of 150 young men from all over the city after the Hunters Point riots, and that these young men had asked to be able to meet the captains of their districts. His goal, claimed Chief Cahill, was to establish community relations all over the city. In a speech, he said, "The Unit itself, operating to perfection, is not the ultimate objective. It is the man on the street, who day in and day out is meeting with the citizens, which we have to reach. And you are not, and neither are we, going to reach him, unless we involve the captains, the sergeants, and reach these men." Cahill promised further that, once the men were selected, there would be some training.

As Cahill took this position, his personal relations with Andreotti deteriorated. The situation became increasingly untenable for both. The lieutenant had, in effect, developed a political constituency of his own, and although he could not openly challenge the chief, he had so much political support that the chief had to be wary of publicly appearing to condemn him. At the same time, Andreotti constituted a threat to the authority of the chief, and conservative pressures within the department were growing more powerful. Andreotti was finally eased out of the department, was given a farewell party attended by the mayor, and was vigorously praised when he left for a job in the Justice Department. But his separation was such that he would never be able to return to the San Francisco Police Department without losing his pension rights. In effect, Andreotti—now employed by the Department of Justice—is barred from the San Francisco Police Department, although there are frequent rumors that someday soon he will be appointed chief of police.

Cahill, like most administrators, was between many cross-pressures. He was under fire from the majority of his men to put the elusive, "minority-coddling" PCR Unit out of existence. He was also under pressure from an increasingly restless minority population to continue with PCR work. If the PCR Unit had not obtained the support of such influential organizations as the National Conference of Christians and Jews, the NAACP, several members of the board of Supervisors, the *San Francisco Examiner*, and such large companies as Standard Oil, the Pacific Telephone Company, Sears Roebuck, and other local groups, it is quite possible that its program could have been quietly and slowly phased out. As it was, there was a ruckus.

What finally led to the demise of the San Francisco PCR Unit and Andreotti's exit? Probably more important than the clash of personalities was a change in political climate, which in turn altered and shaped the outlook of both Cahill and Andreotti. Each was playing a special and sensitive role within the department, and these roles were affected differently by emergent political influences. The most significant change in mood was signaled in California by the election of Ronald Reagan as governor. Reagan's election demonstrated the rise to power of a conservative political philosophy, dominated not so much by large business interests (although he received support from that quarter) as by indignation against violations of conventional middle-class morality. Reagan's support came from those opposed to precisely the sort of people—the poor, hippies, urban Negroes, homosexuals—whose interests the PCR Unit was intended to represent.

But the mood was not limited to California alone. In Washington the Johnson Administration became increasingly dependent upon "backlash" sentiment for political support in Vietnam and became increasingly receptive to the "crime in the streets" theme that had been used by his 1964 opponent, and publicly decried at that time by "liberal" supporters of the President. Furthermore, with greater involvement in the Vietnam war and with the escalation of urban violence, there was an increasing polarization of sentiment on both sides and a hardening of attitudes.

Cahill, who had been a "consensus" police chief in a pluralist, liberal city, was pushed increasingly into a more conservative position partly by the general political atmosphere, and more specifically by explicit demands of his men, coupled with his identification and sympathies with them. When riots broke out in September, 1966, he viewed them almost as a personal affront, because he felt he had demonstrated more sympathy to the plight of the Negro than most other police chiefs in America.

Andreotti was subject to even more intensive cross-pressures. The head of a police community relations unit steps immediately into a polarized world. If he is to remain on congenial terms with his colleagues, he cannot represent the interest of the minorities. On the other side, if he is to gain the confidence of the minority groups, he is required to break down the castelike lines that separate the police and the policed in our urban ghettoes. Thus, for Andreotti to have performed his job properly, that is, to have represented the needs of minority communities to the

majority community, he had to develop a new perspective in the world, and to accomplish this personal development is a task of heroic proportions for a middle-class white policeman. Although Andreotti could have defined his job as a public relations enterprise and remained on good terms with the police department, after seeing the social condition of urban American Negroes, he chose to represent their interests. He gradually became, in effect, a black man living in a white skin. As such, he came to share black frustration and despair, became more and more militant, and increasingly offensive to his fellow policemen. When he left San Francisco there was a testimonial dinner for him—well attended by minority group people—but the chief, the deputy chief, and the captains of the San Francisco police department were conspicuously absent.

So much for the story of the San Francisco Police Community Relations Unit. I have tried to tell it briefly and to make essential analytical points. There is a real question, however, as to what we can learn from the difficulties faced by San Francisco in the attempt to introduce a PCR unit. First, it seems to me that we can distinguish three types of police community relations approaches that have been recently tried in this country. They would seem to be as follows:

1. The public relations approach, exemplified by the late Chief Parker. This approach emphasizes relations with the press and contacts with "responsible" citizens including "responsible" minority group leaders. It does not seek police contact on a person-to-person basis with the grass roots of the minority group population. In my opinion, this approach, for a variety of proven reasons, must fail.

2. The second approach is exemplified by Andreotti and his Unit. It consists of a special unit which advertises itself as being friendly to minority-group peoples, in contrast to the rest of the department. It gives whatever help can be given to minority group peoples and adopts a social work approach. The chief problem with this sort of unit is that by implication it derogates the rest of the department. And this feature in turn, may increasingly alienate support from other police. Andreotti's unit was successful insofar as it improved relations between the PCR Unit and minority groups. It did not succeed, however, in bringing around the remainder of the police department toward the more sympathetic view that the Unit itself had developed.

3. The third approach is the "variation" suggested by Chief Cahill. The problem with this has to do more with the special training of men and the complicated area of rank and responsiblity. If captains who are unsympathetic to the PCR approach are in charge of men who are nominally doing PCR work, these men cannot do a PCR job of the type that Andreotti's men were doing. It is too easy for this approach to regress to the "public-relations" conception of police-community relations. Even a well-intentioned precinct captain may have to succumb to the pressures generated by the men under him. The difficult and basic issue is how to reduce the racial antagonisms of the rank-and-file policeman.

I know of no easy answers—or even difficult answers that are sure to work—but I would suggest the following. First, for each major police department there should be a centralized PCR unit, headed by a man like Andreotti. Certainly it is possible to find, in other police departments, men with the capacity to develop their sense of dedication and genuine feelings of empathy for minority group peoples. It is important, however, that the head of a PCR unit hold high rank so that the men in his unit can count on him to get them out of the conflicts they will inevitably run into with other high-ranking officers. Second, it would be a good idea to rotate general duty police through the PCR unit while at the same time maintaining a strong continuing cadre in the central PCR unit. The PCR unit would thus serve as a training agency for men to be fed into other units. The difficulty with this approach is that there are relatively few police who are really interested in PCR work, so there is a risk that men assigned to a PCR unit against their will would emerge even less sympathetic to minority group peoples than they already are. Nobody really knows the answer to this problem. It may be necessary to experiment by establishing different types of PCR work over a period of two or three years in order to learn what would be the most favorable organizational structure for a PCR unit.

The Solidarity and Isolation of Police

I have already suggested how strong the sense of police isolation and solidarity is throughout police departments in the United States. Indeed, if any one finding can be said to characterize all of the recent studies of police, it is this fact of social isolation, not only from black people in the ghetto, but also from the white citizenry as well. This isolation is accompanied by a police culture which, in general, tends to be characterized by a high degree of suspiciousness of outsiders. In my own contacts with police, I have found them to be at their most understanding and at their most flexible in private conversation when I was part of their working team. By contrast, in public situations, I have found police to be almost incredibly inflexible and defensive. (Perhaps this defensiveness can be attributed to the paramilitary character of police organization. It may be difficult, if not impossible, for a man who comes from a military, rigorous, and demanding organization to develop the sort of sympathies required by the human problems of our American cities.)

In a salutary attempt to increase the sensitivity and flexibility, as well as the learning and efficiency of police, several centers of police training are being developed. I recently spoke with a group of police specialists at the City University of New York where an attempt is being made to develop an educational program that goes beyond the training developed by the academy. Another center has been formed at Michigan State University. I think, however, that these worthwhile endeavors may be too narrowly constricted in their clientele.

The problem put bluntly is, how do we break down the defensiveness characteristic of police culture? Institutions composed primarily of police students may foster the least desirable features of police culture. If such institutions are not already doing so, it seems to me that they should change their emphasis from police service to public service. This may initially appear to be a radical idea—that the same institution would train police and social workers and other public service personnel. But the idea is neither radical nor difficult to implement. There is already a shortage of educational institutions in all public service areas, and those that exist invariably tend to be overtly insular. Nothing could be more forward-looking than the establishment of institutions which are composed, say, half of police, half of social workers. Each group would be offered the opportunity of broadening its horizons and its conceptions of the world.

It has been a long and well-established tradition of higher education that students learn probably as much from each other as they do from their professors. All major universities make every effort to recruit a student body that is as diverse as possible. Therefore, it is as important to provide a student body that will be a source of intellectual stimulation as it is to provide a faculty of high standing.

Now I am not suggesting that all police have a broad liberal education, although this is a goal we should ultimately aim toward. I am suggesting, however, that it would be relatively simple for newly developing institutions to broaden their mandate so as to encompass a more diverse student body. It may be argued, however, that these schools should not be compared with colleges as much as with professional schools, and that in particular the model for the school of criminal justice should be the law school. That analogy, however, is attenuated at too many points in the traditions and structure of the policing and lawyering occupations. Law as a profession has come to make increasing educational demands upon its students, with a B.A. degree now almost routinely required by major law schools. If the mandate of these schools is to develop a professional program comparable to that of the law school, it must rest upon a base of education comparable to that of the law school. Unfortunately, that broad base does not presently exist.

The problem may be analyzed in terms of shorter- and longer-run needs. It will be useful, in the long run, to generate several high-level training institutions for police, especially in view of the higher managerial functions police leaders are increasingly required to perform. But for the average policeman who requires more education, we must develop institutions that will afford a greater degree of breadth than our present police training academies or department-affiliated training programs presently appear to offer.

Neighborhood Service Centers

The Commission asked me to comment upon the paper that Professor James Q. Wilson of Harvard University has submitted to it. As always I find Professor Wilson's writing lively, thoughtful, thought-provoking, and constructive. I should like to address my comments specifically to the two suggestions in his paper that I have doubts about. One concerns his conceptions of neighborhood service centers; the other, his conception of grievance machinery.

Wilson's idea of providing needed social services through "neighborhood service centers" (staffed by civilians and police officers, and handling requests for information and service) is creative and useful. Yet I would disagree with offering it the mandate that Wilson envisions. As he sees it, the neighborhood service center would be performing two functions—first, to provide services to residents of the area, and second, to provide strategic intelligence for the prevention and control of civil disorder. If neighborhood centers were set up as Wilson suggests, there would be considerable danger that mixing the two functions would generate even greater hostility toward police and civil authority.

From the point of view of the ghetto resident, the police are already not very trustworthy. The typical ghetto resident has repeatedly been given promises by white authorities, especially prior to elections, of reforms that will be made. With much accuracy, ghetto residents describe these promises as "fat-mouthing." And to promise social service but deliver police surveillance would be fat-mouthing and worse. If a neighborhood service center is advertised as a place that provides social services for residents but is discovered to be a place that was also providing strategic intelligence, the police, no matter how well intentioned, would be liable to a charge of sham and hypocrisy. And such discovery would be certain to come as soon as the police began to use people they were helping in order to elicit information about the mood of the community. The police already have strategic intelligence outposts in ghetto communities —police precincts. It would be far more honest, it seems to me, to establish in the police precinct a separate division for neighborhood social services, and to recognize that in many ways it would operate in conflict with the strategic intelligence function. If a new form of organization is to be set up, called a "Neighborhood Service Center," then a wholly new philosophy must go along with it. It should not be used as an outpost for strategic intelligence.

Grievance Machinery

Let us turn to a second subject discussed by Wilson, namely, grievance machinery. Recall that a main issue for the San Francisco Police Community Relations Unit was dissatisfaction with internally run disciplinary procedures of the Police Department. As a result, the PCR Unit began itself to function as a grievance taker. This stance further alienated the rest of the Police Department. Yet the experience of the PCR Unit suggests the importance of an effective grievance procedure in any urban community. The difficult issue is whether such grievance machinery should be internally or externally controlled.

Wilson writes, "The most effective means to

prevent police misconduct, in the opinion of the President's Commission as well as most observers of police practice, is through effective internal police administrative procedures." That statement is somewhat misleading. It is true that the President's Commission recommended internal police administrative procedures; but it is not necessarily true that the most effective means to prevent police misconduct is through internal procedures. It is politic to say what Wilson says, but he necessarily has little evidence because no systematically investigated alternative has been attempted. We must face up to the fact that the main deterrent to external controls on police misconduct was not derived from experience but from effective political pressure impeding the possibility of an alternative form of control of police misconduct.

For instance, it does not seem unlikely that an ombudsman for all public services could provide an even more effective means of controlling police misconduct. All we know at present is that the police do not want to have their conduct reviewed by an outside agency, and that they have the political "clout" to maintain their organizational independence. A specialized unit within the police department is not a satisfactory alternative. The only "police complaint bureau" that I know of that was acceptable to the minority peoples it dealt with was the San Francisco PCR Unit. This was in part due to its superior relations with the minority community and in part its willingness to buck the ideology of police solidarity that pervades all police departments. This willingness can be traced to a separate organizational structure which could develop its own counter-ideology. That is, because the PCR Unit developed an identity of its own, separate from the remainder of the department, it was able to maintain a more detached view of police conduct and misconduct, perhaps sometimes leaning over backward in sympathy with its minority-group constituents. The issue, however, is not whether the San Francisco PCR Unit worked fairly, but whether, given the solidarity of police culture and the real tensions in our cities, a police-run complaint bureau can maintain or even hope to persuade others of its objectivity. Thus, I entertain little hope that the establishment of a complaint bureau in the police department will lead to the kind of fair and active investigation that Wilson contemplates.

In contrast to Wilson, I would consider it a major failure if this Commission did not come out for the *principle of external review*, not only for police, but for all public service agencies. We know enough about bureaucratic processes to predict that within bureaucracies people in the same organization will tend to be self-protective. Furthermore, the grievance of the individual living in the urban ghetto is not necessarily directed only toward police but toward other public service agencies as well. In addition, it seems to me that it would be grossly unfair to the police to single them out as the sole object of an external review procedure. One of the most constructive projects the Commission could engage in would be to appoint a distinguished committee, composed of lawyers and others who could contribute specialized knowledge, to draft a model grievance organization for America's cities. It would also seem to me important that such a committee stress the adoption of such grievance machinery throughout the United States. We have already recognized in the administration of criminal justice that justice must be dispensed with a minimum of variation. Just as wide variation in the dispensation of criminal justice is felt to be fundamentally unfair, so too will variation in the opportunity to vent grievance.

Police and Substantive Criminal Law

As the President's Commission on Law Enforcement and Administration of Justice notes, most cases in the criminal courts involve violations of moral norms or instances of annoying behavior, rather than acts of dangerous crime. What is the significance of this fact for police-minority group relations in the ghetto? The attempt to enforce conventional morality through the criminal law produces two closely related consequences. One consequence is a more threatening environment for the policeman. When society attempts to control large areas of moral misbehavior through criminal law, then the potential criminal population increases. Concomitantly, there is increased contact by the populace with policing officials charged with reducing criminality. Thus, the attempt to control morality through criminal law has to make the policeman's job more difficult. It has to increase the "production quotas" for police. As a representative of the FBI stated to the President's Commission on Law Enforcement and Administration of Justice:(5)

The criminal code of any jurisdiction tends to make a crime of everything that people are against, without regard to enforceability, changing social concepts, etc. . . . The result is that the criminal code becomes society's trash bin. The police have to rummage around in this material and are expected to prevent everything that is unlawful. They cannot do so because many of the things prohibited are simply beyond enforcement, both because of human inability to enforce the law and because, as in the case of prohibition, society legislates one way and acts another way. If we would restrict our definition of criminal offenses in many areas, we would get the criminal codes back to the point where they prohibit specific, carefully defined, and serious conduct, and the police could then concentrate on enforcing the law in that context and would not waste its officers by trying to enforce the unenforceable, as is done now.

It is no accident, for example, that the riots in Detroit were started when the police attempted to enforce the laws against "blind pigs." In some communities, people prefer to keep later hours than in other communities. In ghetto communities where people do not have the housing facilities that they have in middle-class communities, such activities as drinking and gambling often take place in public or semipublic areas. For instance, when I was working with a vice squad, we raided a Friday night poker game in a hotel in the ghetto. We received a tip from an informant, a warrant was duly drawn out, and five white police plus one white professor pretending to be a policeman, kicked in a hotel room door and discovered six black men, most of whom were gainfully employed, playing poker. From all I could gather these men were doing nothing other than what I and some of my professorial colleagues may do with some regularity—play Friday night poker. But they were subject to the indignity of having the door of their rented room kicked in, of being searched, of being transported to police headquarters and booked, and finally of being prosecuted and found guilty. This sort of demeaning experience need never have taken place if there were not laws on the books which attempted to enforce conventional morality. In fact, these laws tend to enforce conventional morality among the poor, while allowing the rich to go along relatively freely in their own vices, harmless or otherwise.

Second, when the attempt is made to enforce conventional morality through law, there is also a growth of social organizations for satisfying and creating illicit demands. Although it does not intend

to do so, in fact, what the criminal law does is to provide the economic underpinnings for the development of a criminal underworld. The forbidding of an activity offers a "protective tariff" to those engaged in the sale of illicit goods and services, thereby increasing the profits of their activities.

Moreover, the attempt to enforce conventional morality frequently leads to the corruption of police. In one of the cities that I studied, graft and corruption were openly acknowledged by the police, especially in connection with gambling rackets such as numbers and bookmaking. Involvement of police in rackets is widely understood in the ghetto communities and necessarily reveals the police to be hypocrites. It is extremely difficult for any police to escape this stigma, even if they are honest. In the eastern community I studied, there were honest police, but, as one policeman said to me, "You have to decide whether you're going to be an honest cop or a realistic cop." The attempt to enforce conventional morality presents the policeman with this choice, and when he becomes a dishonest cop—there are more than we would like to acknowledge, since we must recognize that in every community where there is organized gambling, there are dishonest cops—he is undermining the moral authority of the criminal law and is creating even greater hostilities among our minority group peoples.

Even when the police are honest, however, as in the western community that I studied, their honesty relates mainly to the police organization which they serve. That is, they may not be taking graft from gamblers, but they will use every means they can—including ignoring constitutionally protected rights—to fulfill production quotas that are set for them by efficiency-oriented police chiefs. Thus, I feel that this area of criminal law requires radical revision and requires strong leadership both at national and local levels in order to advance the necessary changes.

Leadership

I cannot close without writing a few words about what I consider to be a dramatic failure of leadership on the part of the federal government in both the areas of police community relations and the needed revisions in our substantive criminal laws. Let me suggest what I mean by indirection. According to the *New York Times* of September 15, 1967, when President Johnson addressed the Convention of the International Association of Chiefs of Police, the chiefs applauded loudest when the President said "Much can explain, but nothing can justify the riots of 1967." The President could have said, by contrast, "Although nothing can justify the riots of 1967, there is much that can explain them." I am virtually certain that if the President had used that sort of phraseology there would not have been loud applause.

Police chiefs are above all practical men sensitive to political cues. In my opinion, the President's speech indicated to chiefs of police that their job was to go out and "get those guys." That was what they wanted to hear but not what they needed to hear.

REFERENCES

1. James Baldwin, *Nobody Knows My Name* (New York: Dell, 1962), pp. 65–67.
2. O. W. Wilson, *Parker on Police* (Springfield, Ill.: Thomas, 1956), p. 20.
3. Ibid., p. 161.
4. Leonard Schapiro, "Prospects for the Rule of Law," *Problems of Communism*, *14* (March–April 1965), pp. 2–7.
5. The President's Commission on Law Enforcement and Administration of Justice, *Task Force Report: The Courts* (Washington, D.C.: U.S. Government Printing Office, 1967), p. 107.

North City Congress Police-Community Relations Program

ARTHUR NIEDERHOFFER AND ALEXANDER B. SMITH

Background of the Program

A forerunner of today's generalized antipoverty agency, the Philadelphia Council for Community Advancement (PCCA) serviced the depressed areas and minority groups in Philadelphia during the early 1960s. Encouraged by a grant from the Ford Foundation, the PCCA met with Temple University Faculty to develop a program for North Philadelphia, a critically depressed area in which the Philadelphia black population was heavily concentrated. Representatives of social agencies, churches, and neighborhood groups were brought together to discuss mutual problems; police-community relations was one of the foremost. As a result of these meetings, North City Congress was established in 1964 and funded by PCCA. At that time there were three major interests: (1) legal aid to the community, (2) housing and

SOURCE: Arthur Niederhoffer and Alexander B. Smith, *New Directions in Police-Community Relations*, New York: Holt, Rinehart and Winston, 1974, pp. 52–64.

physical environment, and (3) community organization. There was no formal program directed to the problem of police-community relations.

After the riots of August 1964 in the North Philadelphia area, the North City Congress (NCC) entered into negotiations with police commissioner Howard R. Leary. The NCC wanted to form an organization of citizens to represent the community in discussions with police on important issues and to serve as a clearing house for the processing of complaints that arose from neighborhood problems and police-community tensions. The NCC goal was to create a neighborhood organization with enough political power to influence the police. A civilian-dominated police review board had been established for just this purpose, but unfortunately the black community lacked confidence in it.

Commissioner Leary, who, from all reports, cooperated fully with the NCC, was more interested in developing an institute to educate and train policemen in the field of community relations than in encouraging a neighborhood agency of protest over which he would have little control. Alvin Echols, executive director of NCC, and Steven Turner of NCC designed a compromise plan for a police-community project. After some brief recommendations by the police department as to procedures, number of participants, and hours, the plan was accepted as a workable system by both the police and NCC. It had two divisions: (1) a training program for both police and community people, and (2) a demonstration and community organization program. This involved the formation of community committees, subcommittees, and area committees, to educate the community and provide liaison with police operations.

This proposal was submitted by NCC together with a letter of endorsement from Commissioner Leary to the Office of Juvenile Delinquency (OJD) in 1966. The OJD approved the project and offered a financial grant on the condition that a competent person be brought into the program as director. In compliance with this requirement, Mr. Alton Lemon, a social worker, who formerly had been executive director of other community relations programs in Pennsylvania, became the director of the NCC Police-Community Relations Project.

As evidence of Commissioner Leary's cooperative spirit, he asked that NCC conduct orientation sessions for all police superior officers in the general field of human relations and in the specific operation of the expected project. Thirty to forty officers attended the evening sessions of two hours each conducted by NCC.

It is significant that NCC wanted to involve agencies, such as CORE and NAACP, in the project, but Commissioner Leary vetoed this move and suggested that every effort should be made to keep the project between the police and the people of the community. NCC accepted his recommendation. Finally, Commissioner Leary made several statements in favor of the program, visited several group meetings, and kept the level of commitment high. During the life of the project, Leary went to New York City as commissioner and was replaced for a short time by Commissioner Bell, who was succeeded in turn by Commissioner Frank Rizzo, whose philosophy of police work was quite different from that of his predecessors.

The community relations program revolved in large measure around group sessions between the police and members of the community. An important innovation proved to be the prior training and orientation given to the participants before they entered the group session. In this connection, a police institute was established to train the police, consisting of two eight-hour seminars attended by sixteen members of the force under the direction of two black discussion leaders. These leaders were college graduates with backgrounds in community work or education. Although this police institute reached about 1,200 policemen of a total of 6,700, only 250 attended the ultimate intergroup sessions with the community representatives.

In January 1967 the NCC extended its police-community program to high schools and junior high schools. The NCC took over classes for two sessions of training without police participation. Later, one session was held with policemen present in the class. Finally, a fourth period of the class was devoted to a summary of what had been learned. A similar program was directed to gang members, and these sessions were held at public recreation centers.

Results of the Program

Following is an outline of the outcome of the North City Congress program:

1. All those interviewed by the authors agreed that there was an improved relation between the North Philadelphia community and the police department. They indicated that one of the signs of the improved relation was the absence of riots since the inception of the program.

2. In the police department:
    a. A community relations bureau was established under the direction of Chief Inspector Harry Fox, who was assigned responsibility for police participation in the NCC program. This bureau had three sections: community relations, civil disobedience, and public information.
    b. A human relations squad was developed to take immediate jurisdiction where dangerous racial tension occurs. As a result of the combined influence of the NCC project and the National Riot Commission's recommendations, all members of the Philadelphia department were trained in community relations.
    c. Operation Handshake introduced each newly assigned policeman to the neighborhood and community agencies before he went on patrol.

3. The NCC:
    a. Cooperated with other communities and held joint meetings to discuss police-community problems.

b. Expanded training programs in the high schools and junior high schools.

4. The community of North Philadelphia:

a. Began to understand police procedures and became more sophisticated in its relations with the police.

b. Was able, as a result of the increased awareness of the limits of police power and responsibility, to channel its efforts into more constructive enterprises, which brought legitimate pressure on proper governmental agencies. The police department was no longer the target of complaints relating to garbage disposal, boarding up closed houses, and landlord-tenant problems. This, in itself, tended to improve police-community relations.

Evaluation of the Program

True to their Quaker origins, the people of Philadelphia have long taken a special interest in public affairs. "A long period of citizen dissatisfaction with existing avenues for redress of grievances against policemen . . ."(1) led to the formation of the Philadelphia Police Review Board in October 1958. Never a success and impeded by court action, it finally was terminated by order of the Philadelphia Court of Common Pleas in 1967. The complaint in that case was instructive because it revealed dramatically how a strong professionalized police force responded to the threat of external review by the community. It is important to understand that while subscribing strongly to the ideology contained in the following excerpt, the Philadelphia Police Department nevertheless maintained that it was fully capable of creating its own police-community relations program. The following were the allegations made by the Fraternal Order of Police in Philadelphia in justification of its suit requesting the dissolution of the Philadelphia Board:

The complaint against the review board charged a waste of time and effort, a shortage of police personnel, an impairment of recruiting and efficiency of police and an increase of crime since the Board's creation. It averred that the Police Commissioner could have determined more efficiently than the Board the cases heard by the Board: that the Board, sitting in a judicial rather than in an advisory capacity, infringed on the legal

rights of policemen, lowered their morale, and hindered law enforcement.(2)

This represented the police backlash to a special kind of police-community relations program. The swift police response raised serious questions about the possible results of police-community relations programs. Can a police-community relations program be too successful? When a police department sees a community responding so well, and beginning to invade the territorial preserves of the police, will that department with a natural bureaucratic defensiveness respond with a backlash? Will it seem to fulfill the spirit of the police-community relations program, but actually resist it? For example, many black communities called for better protection by the police as part of the community relations program. The Philadelphia force, on several occasions, responded so fiercely to this demand, with tactical patrol forces, special squads, and highway patrol, that while it seemed to give more protection, it created a reign of terror for the average lower-class citizens.

Prior to the NCC project the Philadelphia police department's police-community relations unit had been a notable failure. A team of experts evaluated the unit and submitted the following negative report.

The mission of the Police-Community Relations Unit appears to be poorly understood—or misunderstood—both in the department and certainly in significant sections of the city. To do an effective job, it may well be necessary for the Unit to devote a significant part of its time to stimulating change within the Police Department itself. In addition, to be effective the Unit will probably find it increasingly necessary to involve itself in community and neighborhood matters, to organize itself in such a manner as effectively to engage the portions of the populations which have traditionally been "hard-to-reach."

While it is true that many portions of the population are aware of the existence of the Unit and applaud the work of the Unit, other portions of the population either do not know of the Unit or are suspicious and skeptical about the potential usefulness of the Unit. While most middle-class Negroes appear to know of the existence of the Unit, they also have an almost universal skepticism about its effectiveness. At the same time, subcultural enclaves which should most directly be engaged by the Unit do not even know of its existence. For a variety of reasons, it appears, the Police-Community Relations Unit has been unwilling or unable to establish even the beginnings of a relationship with these enclaves.(3)

To paraphrase this report, the police-community relations unit was inadequate, its mission was misunderstood, both in and outside the department; and, finally, it missed completely the very target population for which it was organized. There is also the danger that a police-community relations unit, such as the one in Philadelphia,

> . . . can become a meaningless superstructure, an empty gesture, a placebo, if the police out on the beat are barging around the community like misguided engines of destruction. . . .(4)

Out of this background, in order to provide channels of communication between the police and the black community, the North City Congress Police-Community Relations Program came into existence. The merits of this new program were evident:

1. It was well conceived and planned.
2. It was focused on the community, on youth groups, and the police.
3. The directors were successful in winning the cooperation of the community, youth groups, and the police.
4. There was interpersonal training for each of the target groups.
5. The plan was developmental and longitudinal; it worked in stages, utilizing both group processes at the microlevel, and going into schools, agencies, and the wider community, at the macrolevel, with the ultimate aim of building community responsibility and power.
6. The plan was fortunate in the superior quality of its administrators.

At the early planning stage, the question was raised of whether or not to involve CORE or the NAACP. Because of the strong objections of Commissioner Leary, the decision was taken not to invite these two agencies. There will always remain an unanswered question of the possible loss of power to the program caused by the exclusion of these national organizations. On the other hand, if they were included, it would almost be an inevitable development for the control of the program, to shift from the local community organization to the larger and stronger

agencies. The very wide contact that the North City Congress had established with the black community in Philadelphia gave them an advantage over other group-centered projects in the choice of citizen participants. Even here there was a preponderance of middle-class black people.

As with most programs of this kind, there were uncontrollable variables. A crucial factor was the attitude of the police commissioner. In this case the program was fortunate at its inception in finding a welcome response from Howard Leary, who was then Police Commissioner of Philadelphia. He gave enthusiastic and substantial cooperation to the program, and this was, undoubtedly, an important reason for its success. Previously, he invited Charlotte Epstein, a cultural anthropologist, to give regular lectures in minority group relations to the members of his department. Dr. Epstein is the author of a handbook on intergroup relations for police officers that is still widely used in police training programs.(5)

Subsequently, in 1966, Commissioner Leary became head of the New York City police department. His office passed first to Commissioner Bell, whose tenure was short and uneventful, and finally to Commissioner Frank L. Rizzo, a career policeman, who belonged "to the 'traditional' rather than the 'progressive' branch of the police spectrum."(6) From the moment of his appointment Commissioner Rizzo was a controversial figure and received extensive coverage in the mass media. The black community held mass meetings and threatened boycotts of schools and white merchants unless Commissioner Rizzo were replaced.(7) Norval Reece, the executive director of the Americans for Democratic Action (Philadelphia Branch), called upon Mayor Tate to appoint a new commissioner. Reece charged:

> Rizzo is "hostile" to the expression of civil rights and civil liberties. In such times of tensions and bitterness, Reece said, the city "cannot afford a police commissioner whose actions contribute to that tension and bitterness."(8)

Nevertheless, Commissioner Rizzo was praised by other segments of the community for his abiding interest in community relations:

> In Philadelphia, Chief of Police Frank L. Rizzo has given his department a face lifting. He has

conducted police-community relations seminars for police sergeants at Temple University. The department's community relations center has doubled in size. While other cities burned following the assassination of Martin Luther King, Rizzo sent four of his special "minister-policemen" into the street to preach nonviolence and calm. He forbade Philadelphia cops to fire unless fired upon. He had the force mobilize more than 200 clergymen and Negro leaders to cool the community. Philadelphia did not explode.

"I'm convinced Rizzo is trying desperately hard to be a good police commissioner," says Clarence Farmer, executive director of the city's Commission on Human Relations. "He bends over backward to support community relations."(9)

Based upon the voluminous material in the Philadelphia newspapers, and upon the reactions of the vast majority of the social agencies servicing the black communities in Philadelphia, it appeared that minority relations with the police were rapidly deteriorating.(10) Paradoxically, Philadelphia remained one of the few large cities in the country that was free from disastrous racial disturbances and riots. No one was in a position to ascribe this pragmatic test of peace in the community to the efforts of either the Commissioner or the NCC project. Apparently, something positive happened here that was missing in other cities.

There is no doubt that the flamboyant commissioner was politically astute enough to build upon his police image to run successfully for mayor of Philadelphia. In that position he has become one of the major political powers in the country. Even presidential candidates woo Mayor Rizzo to obtain his endorsement.

The North City Congress program was distinguished for an interesting innovation of training participants for group interaction sessions. The directors of this program felt that the training helped to make the group sessions successful. But one may well ask whether there can really be effective training for group confrontation. The question of prior training for group sessions really involves one of the subtle areas of group dynamics. Robert F. Bales of Harvard University has done the pioneer work in his observation of phase movement in task-oriented groups. He showed that there is a pattern in which these groups move through periods that he has called *orientation, evaluation,* and *control*.(11) In therapy groups, however, there is no similar patterning.(12)

The confrontation between police and members of the lower-class black community in group sessions resembles a therapy group more than a task-oriented group. If there is no patterning, and no tendency to establish equilibrium, and each session is dissimilar, what is the relevance of the training session?(13)

Training sessions between policemen and black discussion leaders raised the same questions that were discussed at the group sessions that came later. Would it not be true, then, that such training sessions might be harmful to the ultimate purpose of the group interaction? They could create psychological sets, latent resistances, inhibitions to communicating, and stronger negative stereotypes among the trainees than in a naive population.

The training sessions were valuable for raising for discussion important *intra*police department problems that would probably not emerge at the *inter*group sessions. For example, one of the sensitive areas of controversy that came up several times at training sessions for police was the experience of off-duty black policemen dressed in civilian clothes, who were stopped and questioned as potentially suspicious characters by white policemen on patrol. The black police officers complained that they were treated rudely, contemptuously, and that even after identifying themselves as policemen, they were not accorded the apology and respect to which they were entitled. As observers of the training sessions, we left with the feeling that many of the white policemen were rethinking their behavior and their perspectives.

As far as the youth phase of the group encounters was concerned, it seemed that training sessions for high school students, leading up to one encounter with the police, revealed a misplaced emphasis. It is hardly likely that the effects of one confrontation would be significant in changing attitudes.

The latent consequences of a wide-ranging community relations program have never been fully explored. In effect, this program was a vote of no confidence by the community in the Philadelphia Civilian Review Board. Was this community relations program the spark that gave the Philadelphia police department enough motivation and power to bring successful suit to terminate the Board? Would the Fraternal Order of Police, representing the department, have been brave enough to oppose the Board if it felt that such opposition would arouse widespread resentment against it in the black community? Does the greater understanding and awareness on the part of the black community create the background for better relations with the police, or does it result in the opposite? In other words, if the community finds out that what was only rumor of mistreatment or malfeasance is actually true in fact, do they become friends or enemies of the police? Does a strong police-community relations program, moving to a point where it makes suggestions, criticisms, and even demands on the police department, improve performance of duty? Or does the department, thrown on the defensive, cover itself traditionally, and best, by "following the book"? Book operations usually tend to be rougher and less sympathetic toward black people.

There are overt dangers that may block the realization of the police-community relations goals. There is a possibility that police departments will tend to use police-community relations programs as means rather than ends. They can be used as propaganda devices, as instruments of pressure in gaining concessions for the police from the body politic.

The most ominous outcome arising from a community relations program, powerful enough to threaten change in police mores, is the probability of a police department backlash against the black community. A well-documented technique available to police—slow down or speed up of activity—can do irreparable damage to the hopes of police-community relations program. It may be, therefore, that when a community agency such as NCC sponsors a community relations program, it should, in self-defense, aim at a moderate degree of success and not look for a revolutionary transformation.

A community-based program, naturally seeking to develop indigenous leadership, can be excused for failing to seek advice from police experts. Nevertheless, the agency will lose a great deal of the benefit that comes from knowing the police department from the inside. One of the complaints from the NCC project was that radio cars did not respond on time or with courtesy when they finally arrived. The project leaders were without a definite idea of how to proceed to correct this condition. This lack of orientation on the part of the public is common, according to Wilson:

> Police protection is an *exceptional* service, which exists to prevent things from happening. It is largely invisible, and the average citizen comes into contact with it only in the exceptional case. He has no way of telling whether he is getting good service or not, except in the (rare) case when he experiences it—and perhaps not even then. He has no way of knowing if he is being treated, either as

victim or suspect, differently from others. If his call for help is ignored or the response delayed, is it because the police are lazy or because all their cars are tied up on something more important? If the police fail to catch the burglar, is it because they are incompetent or because the burglar has left no clue?(14)

A police expert could have suggested many ways to handle the specific situation confronting this community: a campaign of phone calls to precincts, as well as to headquarters, with a demand for the names and shield numbers of the recipients of the calls; visits to station houses requesting the prompt dispatch of radio cars, asking for identification, if necessary; a campaign of letter writing; and complaints made to the proper agency about the specific police officers who respond improperly.

A police-community relations program may lose its thrust when the police department uses alternative means to enhance its general community relations. Eventually, the original program may be entirely superseded by new police procedures and organizations. This outcome, however, may not be the mark of failure, in that the department's overall performance will be improved. And this is, after all, the ultimate objective of any police-community relations program.

REFERENCES

1. President's Commission on Law Enforcement and Administration of Justice, *Field Surveys IV: The Police and the Community*, 2 (Washington, D.C.: U.S. Government Printing Office, 1966), p. 213.

2. Transcript, Philadelphia Court of Common Pleas No. 9, June Term, 1965, No. 6330, p. 3.

3. President's Commission, *Field Surveys IV*, p. 286.

4. A. C. Germann, *The Problem of Police-Community Relations: A Report Prepared for the Task Force on Law and Law Enforcement* (Washington, D.C.: National Commission on the Causes and Prevention of Violence, 1968), pp. 35–36.

5. Charlotte Epstein, *Intergroup Relations for Police Officers* (Baltimore: Williams & Wilkins, 1962).

6. Michelle Osborn, *Report on Conference on Police Power in a Free Society* (Philadelphia: Community Relations Division of the American Friends Service Committee, 1968), p. 4.

7. *Philadelphia Inquirer*, 20 November 1967.

8. *Sunday Bulletin* (Philadelphia), Section 1, 19 November 1967.

9. *Guardian* (New York City), 5 October 1968, p. 3.

10. Osborn, *Police Power*, pp. 19 to end.

11. Robert F. Bales, *Interaction Process Analysis* (Reading, Mass: Addison-Wesley, 1950).

12. C. A. Talland, "Task and Interaction Process: Some Characteristics of Therapy Group Discussion," *Journal of Abnormal and Social Psychology, 50* (1955), pp. 105–109; and Alexander B. Smith, Alexander Bassin, and Abraham Froehlich, "Inter-

group Process and Equilibrium in a Therapy Group of Adult Offenders," *Journal of Social Psychology, 56* (1962), pp. 141–47.

13. Ibid.

14. James Q. Wilson, *Varieties of Police Behavior* (Cambridge, Mass.: Harvard University Press, 1968), p. 235.

The Sociology and the Social Reform of the American Police: 1950—1973

LAWRENCE W. SHERMAN

The sociology of the American police, like the sociology of many institutions, has been closely linked to its social reform. The histories of each can be, and have been, discussed separately.(1) But since developments in one have resulted from developments in the other, it is more meaningful to discuss them together, even if the discussion must be brief.

To define our terms, the "sociology of the police" means research done by academics (not necessarily sociologists), with the central purpose of advancing knowledge rather than changing social policy. Thus, many national commission reports are excluded (though academic research sponsored by the commissions is included). "Social reform of the police" means all those events, proposals, and programs (except academic research) which tried to, or did, effect change in the American police. In this broad conception, social reformers of the police include newspaper editors, participants in race riots, and police administrators. Indeed the social reform of the American police after 1950 differs from most previous reform in that there were social reformers *inside* police departments as well as outside.

While discussion of police sociology can be fairly specific, discussion of police reform requires out-

rageous generalizations. As of 1965, there were 40,000 law enforcement agencies in the U.S.: 50 federal, 200 state, and 39,750 county, city, town and village agencies.(2) A five-man Alabama sheriff's department and New York's 30,000-man force are hardly comparable, yet they are both "the police." Though we shall restrict this discussion to municipal police departments of 200 or more officers, there are such great regional and community differences in the extent and kinds of police reform that such trends as "professionalization" can only be identified with great qualification. As the ABA Police Standards note:

> Given the common lag between proposals for change and their implementation, the police field is in the rather awkward situation today of having some police agencies aspiring to effect changes that are being substantially modified or abandoned by those agencies that have already adopted them.(3)

Thus, keeping the problem of lag in mind, trends in police reform will refer to the vanguard of national opinion: in the press, in police professional publications, and among the most innovative police administrators.

Chronology

1950–1959

The year 1950 was an important one for both police sociology and social reform. William Westley, a University of Chicago graduate student, was in Gary,

SOURCE: This article was presented as a paper at the Second Nuffield Seminar on the Sociology of the Police, University of Bristol [England], in April 1973.

Indiana beginning the first in-depth analysis of an American police organization. And in Berkeley, Professor O. W. Wilson was publishing the first edition of *Police Administration*, which was to become the source of much police change as the bible of "professionalism." Based on the scientific management principles of Frederick Winslow Taylor,(4) Wilson's book stressed efficiency, hierarchy, and bureaucratic regularity as the key to police reform. Yet, at the same time, Westley was finding that a complex informal organization governed such things as illegal police violence.(5) Police sociology and social reform were clearly not talking to each other.

Westley's study went unpublished for 20 years, while Wilson's became required reading for most police promotion exams. And while academics ignored the police for the rest of the decade (except for the massive ABA arrest study in three Midwestern states, done in 1955–56 and not fully published until 1965),(6) the Wilson-inspired trend in police reform was to abolish footbeats and motorize patrols, close local station houses, and centralize both radio dispatching and command decision-making. Los Angeles, Cincinnati and Oakland were leaders in this trend, while Boston, Chicago and other cities had little reform at all.

1960–1966

Pressures for reform, however, soon hit many old style police departments. Between 1960 and 1963, Chicago, Boston, Denver, Syracuse, Buffalo, New York, Indianapolis, Burlington, and other cities, experienced police scandals of corruption and burglary, all of which received nationwide publicity.(7) A typical, though not universal result of a scandal was the appointment of a reform police chief to do things "by the book," and the only book then available was O. W. Wilson's. The newly vitalized International Association of Chiefs of Police sent field survey teams to many scandalized departments, recommending reforms along the, by now, familiar lines of classic organization theory.

Meanwhile, academics ignored the scandals and busied themselves with the juvenile delinquency control projects of the Ford Foundation and the Kennedy Administration. These projects inevitably led to the police as a research topic, and two hypotheses were developed: first, that police apprehension of juveniles may stimulate more crime than such actions control, and second, that criminal apprehension is a selective process dependent primarily on situational factors in the police-juvenile encounter.(8) While the first hypothesis (labelling theory) has not been tested much further with regard to the police, the second hypothesis was called into question with Banton's emphasis on community factors (in his 1962 Scottish-American comparative research)(9) and Skolnick's emphasis on organizational factors (in his 1963 case study of the Oakland Police)(10) in determining the outcomes of police encounters.

More research on that second issue—police encounters—was stimulated by events in police reform. In the summers of 1964 and 1965, New York and Los Angeles, respectively, experienced major racial disorders. The police (or police brutalities) were alleged to have precipitated the riots. And in 1965, President Johnson established a national commission to examine crime and crime control, in response to massive reported crime increases. Thus, it is not surprising that in 1965 two major comparative studies on the urban police began: the Harvard study of eight medium-sized communities led by J. Q. Wilson,(11) and the University of Michigan study of three big cities led by Reiss (done for the U.S. Crime Commission).(12) Both these studies continued into 1966, the busiest year ever for police research. Bayley and Mendelsohn did a study of Denver, focusing on police relations with minority groups.(13) Bordua was editing six scholarly essays on the police,(14) Skolnick's book was published,(15) and Niederhoffer's case study of the New York Police was in preparation.(16)

Police reform activity, however, was as intense as police research. The Supreme Court had, allegedly, "handcuffed" the police by defining more precisely the rights of citizens regarding arrest, detention, search, and interrogation. A reform mayor in New York had created a civilian-dominated board for reviewing citizen complaints against the police and lost it through a referendum skillfully manipulated by a highly politicized Patrolmen's Benevolent Association. The national attention given to the New York civilian review battle sparked similar controversies in other cities, and police brutality became a national issue.

1967–1969

By 1967, enough police sociology had been published, and enough national concern about the police had been generated for the sociology and the social reform of the police to converge. While there were some policemen who felt that the revelations of police deviance in the work of Skolnick and Reiss were unethical violations of trust, more important were the thoughtful police reactions to the criticism of professionalism in the academic studies, particularly the Michigan study.(17) In the backdrop of the worst race riots yet (Detroit and Newark 1967), the Crime Commission,(18) and a year later the Riot Commission,(19) echoed the attack on professionalism: it had sacrificed the humanity and community relations skill of the old-style beat-cop.

In 1968, the riots after the assassination of Dr. Martin Luther King and during the Chicago Democratic convention kept the police in the center of controversy. In response, there emerged a new program for police reform: community control. Best articulated by Waskow (an academic social reformer),(20) the community control idea was to abolish the large law enforcement bureaucracies which dispensed "consensus law" in highly varied local communities, and establish locally recruited and governed peace-keeping units in their stead. But again, police sociology spoke to social reform. The 1968 publication of J. Q. Wilson's *Varieties of Police Behavior*,(21) while clarifying the differences in patrol styles between police agencies and some political reasons for the differences, concluded that community control was not a workable idea. Instead, Wilson suggested that administrative decentralization of power within existing police agencies could increase police responsiveness to the desires of local communities.(22)

Although community control was never a viable possibility, J. Q. Wilson's administrative decentralization provided an alternative means of reform that addressed the same issue as community control: community responsiveness. Combined with the Crime Commission's recommendation for team policing (which would operationally unite various police specialties—patrol, investigation, traffic—in a small local area)(23) and the growth of "human relations" organization theory in police thinking,(24) administrative decentralization became the social reform program for departments that had tried and failed with O. W. Wilson's bureaucratic centralization. Less "progressive" departments, of course, had just discovered *Police Administration* and were abandoning their old-style administrative decentralization.

The 1968 Omnibus Crime Control and Safe Streets Act established the Federal Law Enforcement Assistance Administration (LEAA) to give $1 billion per year in aid to local criminal justice systems. Much money was spent on scholarship aid to send policemen to college, and police science programs grew rapidly in state-operated colleges and junior colleges. Required reading often included the recent police sociology, so its link to police reform became even stronger. LEAA funds also enabled police departments to experiment with new ideas in training and organization, ideas that had been influenced at least somewhat by the sociological literature.

1970–1973

By 1970, the LEAA projects were starting to get off the ground, and the Ford Foundation established a $30 million Police Foundation to concentrate on police improvement on a more limited scale than LEAA's massive mandate. Both funding units began with a comprehensive strategy of making many reforms at once in a police department, rather than creating piecemeal demonstration projects. The implications of such a strategy for organizational change are not yet clear, though the strategy's controversial nature became obvious immediately. While the evaluations conducted for LEAA projects were too goal-specific to tell much about organizational change, the Police Foundation's social science consultants in Dallas, Cincinnati, and Kansas City will pay particular attention to that issue as those projects evolve.

The Police Foundation projects, perhaps more than any other social reforms of the police, have made particular use of the police sociological literature. Bittner's observation that the police receive less respect *inside* their station house than out(25) was one of several sources of the increased involvement of lower levels of police departments, especially patrolmen, in planning Police Foundation experiments. Reiss' analysis of patrol as a *reactive*, rather than *proactive* form of organization(26) ("dial-a-cop") led to an increased awareness of what the police actually do, and to Foundation-sponsored experiments in developing proactive styles of policing.(27)

But, as police sociology and social reform have converged, sociology has become as applied as social reform is now theoretical. Very little "pure" research is now being done to answer purely sociological questions about policing as an occupation, as a complex organization, as a social control mechanism, or as a law-making mechanism. The sociological focus on the police, like that on most service organizations, in our neo-welfare state, is that of a social problem, and to the extent that sociologists hope to *correct* the police, it may hinder their ability to *understand* the police sociologically. But before considering this issue fur-

Table 1.   Chronology of Major Events*

Sociology		Social Reform	
1950	Westley in Gary.	1950	*Police Administration* published.
1955–56	ABA Midwest Arrest Study.	1955–56	Wilsonian professionalism spreads to progressive departments.
1960–65	Juvenile Delinquency Studies.	1960–63	Major police scandals.
1962	Banton comparative study.	1964–65	N.Y. and L.A. race riots.
1963	Skolnick Oakland Study.	1966	*Miranda* v. *Arizona* N.Y.C. Civilian Review Board Fight.
1965–66	Wilson and Reiss Comparative Studies: Bordua's 6 essays, *Justice Without Trial* appears; Bayley and Mendelsohn in Denver.	1967	Worst urban race riots; U.S. Crime Commission report appears.
1967	*Behind the Shield* appears.	1968	U.S. Riot Commission report; King and Chicago Convention riots.
1968	*Varieties of Police Behavior* appears.	1969	LEAA established; Chevigny's *Police Power* appears.
1970	*Functions of Police* appears.	1970	U.S. Violence Commission report appears; Police Foundation established.
1971	*Police and the Public* appears.	1971	Police college programs and minority recruitment grows; Knapp Commission hearings begin.
1972	Police Foundation organizational change research begins.	1972	Police Foundation and LEAA "major cities" programs under way.

*In the interests of brevity, important events on both sides have been omitted.

ther, we should summarize sociology's substantive contribution to police reform and the questions police reformers are now asking of applied sociologists.

Sociological Conclusions and Police Response

With extreme simplification and omission of many important points, we can identify 10 major conclusions of recent police sociology (roughly in chronological order) and the response of police administrators to them:

1. *The police occupation is isolated from the general community, with great internal solidarity and secrecy* (Westley, Niederhoffer, others). When not interpreting this as a criticism, police administrators have made their departments more "open" in a public relations sense, with station house receptions, citizen ride-alongs, etc.

2. *The patrolman, due to his extraordinary discretion, is the most powerful criminal justice official* (LaFave, J. Q. Wilson). Some police administrators have tried to control police discretion through a proliferation of rules, while others have sought to train officers to use discretion more wisely.

3. *The effect of police action on many lawbreakers, particularly young ones, is to amplify the seriousness and frequency of their deviance* (Piliavin and Briar, others). This conclusion was largely dis-

missed as liberal nonsense, but is now being followed in such new programs as "alternatives to arrest" and diversion of offenders from criminal justice to welfare programs.

4. *Varieties of police behavior depend upon specific situational, organizational, and community factors* (a synthesis of Reiss, Skolnick, J. Q. Wilson and Banton). This comparative analysis has been put to little use by locally oriented police reformers.

5. *Police recruits are neither more "authoritarian" nor more deviant in any other respect than people of similar socio-economic backgrounds who do not become policemen, but they may become so through occupational socialization* (Niederhoffer, Bayley and Mendelsohn). This observation was originally used to rebut police critics, and has recently become the basis of peer-group pressure programs to reduce police violence in the Oakland and Kansas City police departments.

6. *The vast majority of police man-hours are expended in activity having little to do with law enforcement, but much to do with social service and peace-keeping* (Reiss, Wilson). While common knowledge to policemen, this conclusion demolished an organizational myth and brought discussion of what the police do into the open. One result has been a movement to divide patrol functions into two separate forces, one for social service and one for crime,(28) notably in Miami.

7. *Police organization is primarily reactive to citizen requests for service* (Reiss). This conclusion has been much discussed in relation to patrol, but its full implications for detectives and the overall police strategy towards crime have yet to be realized by most police reformers. Indeed, a proactive police role in a democratic society could provoke a very intense controversy, as it already has in such issues as wiretapping and "stop and frisk."

8. *Police subcultures often contain general values and practices which deviate widely from legal and organizational rules* (Skolnick, Reiss, and Wilson). This point has also been made by non-police social reformers, who demand stricter external account-ability for the police. The police internal response has been a general increase in the existence and activities of internal investigation units.

9. *Policemen work within a non-democratic organizational context which is antithetical to the democratic values they are supposed to protect in society* (Chwast,(29) Reiss, Bittner). While there has been no outright move to abandon the paramilitary structure of police organization, like in the liberalized "New Army" there have been many efforts to increase supervisors' sensitivity to human relations within police organizations. (The English police call this "man-management"). Team policing and participative management by objectives are two examples.

10. *Community control won't work, but administrative decentralization and de-bureaucratization can increase responsiveness to community desires* (Wilson, Reiss). In addition to numerous team policing experiments,(30) major decentralization programs are presently under way in New York, Dallas, and Los Angeles.

Social Reform Concerns and Police Questions

Our chronology observed that the convergence of police sociology and social reform did not occur until the mid-1960s. Yet the focal concerns for police social reform have been in continual change, both before and after its convergence with sociology. From 1950–1960 the focal concern was inefficiency; from 1960–65 corruption; 1965–70 racial discrimination; and from 1970 on organizational change and, again, corruption (though more so in the East than elsewhere). The aforementioned 10 major sociological conclusions were largely developed within the focus on police racial discrimination. While many of the conclusions are applicable to the new focal concerns, they are not

sufficient, and more police sociology—both pure and applied—will be sought by police reformers.

Specifically, police reformers may well ask of sociologists:

How can the police control crime better?

How can police-community relations be improved?

How can police corruption be minimized?

How can police organizations be changed to answer each of the above questions?

Sociology As Intelligence for Social Change

The question sociologists must now ask themselves is whether they *can*, and whether they *should*, try to answer the police reformers' questions. The blind faith that science can solve any problem, based on such physical science successes as the space program, may not be justified in the realm of human problems. While sociologists may be better equipped than anyone else to deal with the police reformers' questions, they would do both themselves and society a disservice by pretending that all the answers can be found. The fact is that they *cannot* be found, at least not in the same sense that answers to physical science questions have been found.(31)

Moreover, a conception of the sociologist's task for police reform as purely pragmatic—the discovery of the most "effective" solutions—denies the fundamental role of values in social change. One view of social action is that it is essentially, and not just incidentally, a discussion of values.(32) And for that discussion, sociologists are no better equipped than anyone else.(33)

Nonetheless, social science does perform "willingly or not, an intelligence function in the political process," as Black points out. And for sociologists to ignore the police reformers' questions would be, to my values, as wrong as answering them in a purely pragmatic way. There need be no dilemma so long as sociologists carefully distinguish fact and value, policy and science. Even though values may unknowingly influence scientific statements, this need not erase their distinction from value statements; scientific statements can be tested, value statements cannot.(34).

Thus, if a sociologist personally agrees with the values implied by the police reformers' questions, he can attempt to deal with them—to the limited extent of social science's ability—in a fashion that points out what is fact, what is value. And as a participant in a political process, there is no reason why he should not make the case for his own values.(35)

Directions for Pure and Applied Research

The ability of sociologists to deal with the scientific aspects of the police reformers' questions depends not only on their applied research, but also on the pure research that supports it. We have noted that major "pure" research on the American police (that which attempts to understand it as a social institution) has virtually stopped. The present sociology of the police is almost entirely "applied." It seeks to evaluate the effectiveness of alternative courses of action in reaching certain goals. But as Black has argued, applied sociology in the realm of law has rather little to apply.

Such criticism is not as serious as it seems when one considers the value of applied science in developing pure science. The view that the quality of applied science depends solely upon the quality of pure science(36) ignores the mutually beneficial nature of the two. Applied police sociology, blundering along in its ignorance, may provide important questions and data for a general theory of policing.

Even so, the present dearth of pure research on the police is cause for concern. If pure and applied research are to benefit from each other, both should be ongoing activities. Further, there is no intellectual reason why the same sociologists cannot engage in both activities (though there may be practical difficulties).

Since the applied police sociologists necessarily study one place at one brief period in history, the pure police sociologists should concentrate on comparative and historical methods. They should examine the stability or change over time, and in different cultural settings, of such phenomena as proactive/reactive methods, recruitment patterns and salaries relative to the general population, the centralization of police control, police relationships to criminal organization and organized crime, patterns of leadership succession, the use of discretion in arrests, corruption, brutality, and so on. The list of topics is endless, and the selection of each will, no doubt, be guided by the values of the researcher. But to the extent that pure research can formulate any general theories of policing, applied sociology will have that much more to apply. To the extent that pure research can improve the research methods of social science

—e.g. Reiss' systematic observation design for analyzing police encounters(37)—applied sociologists will have better tools for their work.

Applied police sociologists, for their part, must depart from the previous emphasis on patrol in order to deal with the police reformers' questions. Police tactics and crime should not just be an issue of alternative (uniformed or plain-clothes, saturation or mobile) patrol tactics, but of criminal investigation organization as well. Community relations must be viewed in the entire range of police activity—C.I.D., traffic, vice, narcotics, as well as patrol. Corruption should not just be a question of recruitment or training, but of organizational controls in general and internal investigation procedures in particular. And the concern for organizational change must take the broadest view possible, including the effects of corruption controls on morale, the way in which new community relations are viewed by line officers, the effects of experiments on internal job status and promotion possibilities, and the interrelated effects of simultaneous changes in different aspects of the organization. A broad view should also include the mapping of the informal network throughout the organization. This may seem esoteric, but its importance to organizational change was demonstrated by both O. W. Wilson in Chicago and Patrick Murphy in New York.

In sum, the recommendation here is that pure research should develop more specific foci for its general theories, and that applied research should adopt a broader view of the local problems it studies. If this paper has a moral, then it is that research for the sake of knowledge and research for the sake of action should complement, not contradict, each other. More specifically, the evidence presented here suggests that the common distinction between sociology *of* and *for* the police is false; in the long run, they both have the same functions.

REFERENCES

1. Maureen Cain critically assesses recent Anglo-American police sociology in *Society and the Policeman's Role* (London, 1973), pp. 13–25. Recent American police reform is discussed in the American Bar Association's *Standards Relating to the Urban Police Function* (New York: Institute of Judicial Administration, 1972), pp. 27–30.

2. President's Commission on Law Enforcement and the Administration of Justice, *Task Force Report: The Police* (Washington, D.C., U.S. Government Printing Office, 1967), p. 7.

3. American Bar Association Standards, p. 29.

4. F. W. Taylor, *Scientific Management* (1947).

5. W. A. Westley, *Violence and the Police* (1970).

6. W. LaFave, *Arrest* (1965).

7. R. L. Smith, *The Tarnished Badge* (1965).

8. *See*, in particular, I. Piliavin, and S. Briar, "Police Encounters with Juveniles," *Amer. Journal of Sociology*, *70* (1965), pp. 206–214.

9. M. Banton, *The Policeman in the Community* (London, 1964).

10. J. Skolnick, *Justice Without Trial* (1966).

11. J. Q. Wilson, *Varieties of Police Behavior* (1968).

12. D. J. Black and A. J. Reiss, Jr., "Patterns of Behavior in Police and Citizen Transactions," President's Commission on Law Enforcement, etc., *Studies in Crime and Law Enforcement in Major Metropolitan Areas*, Vol. 2, Field Surveys III (Washington, D.C.: U.S. Government Printing Office, 1967).

13. D. Bayley and H. Mendelsohn, *Minorities and the Police* (1968).

14. D. J. Bordua, ed., *The Police* (1967).

15. Skolnick, op. cit.

16. A. Niederhoffer, *Behind the Shield* (1967).

17. M. Furstenburg, Paper to the American Political Science Association, September 1972 Convention.

18. President's Commission, *Task Force Report: The Police*.

19. National Advisory Commission on Civil Disorders, *Report* (Washington, D.C.: U.S. Government Printing Office, 1967).

20. A. J. Waskow, "Community Control of the Police," *Transaction* (December 1969).

21. Wilson, op. cit.

22. For an interesting and sensible compromise between community control and administrative decentralization, *see* Danzig, "An Alternative, Decentralized System of Criminal Justice," a paper presented to the Association of the Bar of the City of New York, September 1970.

23. *Task Force Report: The Police*, p. 53.

24. A particularly popular book for police management courses has been D. McGregor, *The Human Side of Enterprise* (1960).

25. E. Bittner, *The Functions of the Police in Modern Society* (Bethesda: National Institute of Mental Health, 1970).

26. A. J. Reiss, Jr., *The Police and the Public* (1971).

27. *See Experiments in Police Improvement* (Washington, D.C.: The Police Foundation, 1972), p. 30.

28. *See* Furstenburg, op. cit., for a critical assessment of the separation of functions ideas.

29. J. Chwast, "Value Conflicts in Law Enforcement," *Crime and Delinquency, 11* (1965), p. 151.

30. L. W. Sherman et al., *Team Policing* (Washington, D.C.: The Police Foundation, 1973).

31. *See* F. Knight, "Fact Value in Social Science," *Freedom and Reform* (1947).

32. Ibid.

33. *See* Donald Black's provocative essay, "The Boundaries of Legal Sociology," *Yale Law Journal, 81*, 6 (June 1972).

34. Ibid.

35. For example, F. H. McClintock notes that even if science found capital punishment to control crime more "effectively," his value of human life would be the basis of his argument against it.

36. Black, op. cit.

37. Reiss, op. cit. *See* also his "Systematic Observation of Natural Social Phenomena," in H. L. Costner, ed., *Sociological Methodology* (1971).

7 | Police and the Legal System

Our founding fathers with great relief had overcome a foreign oppressor. Consequently, they were most diligent in avoiding a repressive domestic police system that might replicate that enterprise. They rejected the concept of a national police force, reposing their confidence in the individual states to establish appropriate police and peace-keeping systems. The original conceptualizations of our founding fathers have come down to us almost intact. And the legal system in America has been the principal instrument in the control of the police.

Police power and authority is derived from law. So much residual power, however, has been granted to the police in achieving their formal statutory responsibilities that they have carved out a large, amorphous, *de facto* area of informal power and authority. And the courts have sustained this control. Thus, searches incidental to a lawful arrest, stopping and questioning of suspicious persons, the use of informants, infiltration of radical organizations, monitoring of telephone conversations under specific circumstances, and seizure of evidence—which may include body fluids—have been recognized by the courts as acceptable police activities. Furthermore, the police have been granted exceptional legal powers, far greater than those permitted to any other occupational segment of society. In the performance of police duty, an officer may use firearms, run traffic lights, commandeer vehicles, clear streets of civilians, and, under specific circumstances, enter premises without warrants.

When coupled with the cynicism that is an attribute of the police world view, these powers granted by law and judicial authority convince many police officers that they are not merely servants of the law, but are in fact masters of the law. From this premise some police officers develop the rather peculiar philosophy that they can in good conscience exploit the legal mantle of their authority for their own purposes.

It is from this background that we are more easily able to understand police innovation in attempting to evade the legalistic strictures which are imposed by appellate courts in the attempt to regulate police field conduct. This is especially apparent in the areas we have mentioned, such as search and seizure and "stop and frisk." Understanding this feature of police culture teaches us that institutional restraints such as the United States Supreme Court can never be more than partially successful. Experienced policemen and detectives, especially in those instances where they sense they enjoy community and political support, are incredibly resourceful in perfecting strategies of evasion and seemingly nominal compliance with appellate court requirements. We are convinced that most of the law enforcement personnel who fall into the patterns we have described are the hard-working, competent, backbone of police organizations and are neither vicious nor corrupt. They fervently believe that their methods are not really evasions or violations but are their own intelligent, resourceful adaptations in furtherance of police goals of achieving law, order, and justice in a threatened democratic system.

Liberty and Justice: *Fair Play and Fair Trial*

LEO PFEFFER

From Magna Carta to Bill of Rights

The First Amendment . . . concerns laws that government in our democracy may not make: laws respecting an establishment of religion or prohibiting its free exercise, or abridging freedom of speech or of the press or of the right of the people peaceably to assemble and to petition for a redress of grievances. The other Amendments in the Bill of Rights deal mainly with laying down the rules of fair play in accordance with which laws that may constitutionally be made shall be enforced. Lawyers, as we have seen, call the rights secured by the First Amendment "substantive," those secured by the other Amendments "procedural."

Mention of procedures and methods of enforcing laws gives rise to images of lawyers quibbling over technicalities, throwing rules of pleading and evidence at each other—rules generally unintelligible to the non-lawyer—and apparently doing everything to avoid coming to grips with the simple question to be decided: Is the accused guilty or innocent of the crime with which he is charged? Particularly when the accused is charged with an especially heinous crime, such as committing a violent sex offense against a child or being a Communist, is there likely to be popular impatience with procedural technicalities.

The popular image is false, and the popular impatience lacks understanding. Neither appreciates the tremendous stake all Americans have in making sure that the accused rapist or Communist receives the full protection of all procedural requirements. It was such impatience with technicalities and procedures that for centuries justified the use of torture to exact a speedy confession from an accused person who everyone well knew was guilty—so why waste time on long-drawn-out trials? Justice Frankfurter has sagely

noted that the "history of liberty has largely been the history of observance of procedural safeguards."

Nor is the story of how these procedural safeguards developed a dull, uninteresting chronicle. On the contrary, it is one of the most fascinating chapters in human history. The temptation is great to recount it in detail here, but to accord it even minimal justice would require a volume at least as large as this book, whose purpose, after all, is to portray the contemporary scene. We must therefore content ourselves here with little more than a bare mention of the highlights of the struggle.

That part of the story which concerns procedural safeguards is generally considered to have begun at Runnymede on the Thames in 1215, when the rebellious barons and clergy of England, under the leadership of Stephen Langton, Archbishop of Canterbury, exacted the Magna Carta—the Great Charter— from King John. But the story goes back long before that. The Mosaic code imposed a number of procedural safeguards, such as public trial and the right of confrontation. Some of these were even more stringent than those imposed under our present constitutional system; Moses required at least two eyewitnesses for conviction in any capital case; our Constitution imposes this requirement only in trials for treason.

The Romans too enjoyed certain procedural safeguards now included among the liberties of Americans. According to the Acts of the Apostles, Porcius Festus, Roman procurator of Judea, deemed it "unreasonable to send a prisoner and not withal to signify the crimes laid against him." "It is not," Festus reported, "the manner of the Romans to deliver any man to die, before that he which is accused have the accusers face to face, and have license to answer for himself concerning the crime laid against him."

Thus, when King John consented to the thirty-ninth article of the Magna Carta—that "No freeman shall be taken, or imprisoned, outlawed, or exiled, or in any way harmed, nor will we go upon or send upon him, save by the lawful judgment of his peers or by the law of the land"—he was establishing no new precedent. This article itself was apparently taken from an earlier Continental source and reflected usages well established in England when the Great Charter was given.

SOURCE: *The Liberties of an American* (Boston: Beacon Press, 1963). Reprinted by permission of the Beacon Press, copyright © 1956, 1963 by the Beacon Press.

The importance of the Charter in the history of the struggle for civil liberties is not primarily intrinsic. The Charter had its greatness thrust upon it; it was not born great. Indeed it was to some extent a reactionary instrument. Its purpose was to insure feudal rights and protect baronial privileges against royal encroachment. Little in the seventy articles protected the vast majority of Englishmen, the villeins and the tenants. The intended beneficiaries of Article 39 and Article 40 ("To none will we sell, to none deny or delay right or justice") were not the common people but the noblemen.

Even to the limited extent that it sought to regulate governmental relations the Charter was largely ineffectual. No sooner had the barons returned to their castles than John repudiated it as having been obtained under duress. Pope Innocent III, with whom John had made his peace, sided with John as against the Pope's own appointee Langton, and released John from its observance. The committee of barons set up to insure the king's adherence to the Charter never had an opportunity to function, since civil war broke out again shortly after the Charter was granted.

To infer, nevertheless, that the Charter was a completely reactionary document and without intrinsic significance in the struggle for democratic liberties would be unfair and inaccurate. It did, for the first time in England, give written, constitutional form to libertarian advances that had been achieved. It recognized the rightful existence of representatives of those protected, with authority to insure observance of the guarantees. It constituted an acknowledgment by a divinely appointed monarch that he could be required to judge not according to his own will but according to "the law of the land." Repudiated by John, the Charter was reissued after his death in the name of his young son—although with some of its libertarian provisions conspicuously omitted. In 1354 its protection, limited as it may have been, was extended by statute to every man "of what estate or condition that he be," a statute that first used the modern equivalent for "law of the land" in assuring that no man should be harmed in any way except by "due process of law."

But the real importance of the Charter is extrinsic to it. Its greatness was ascribed to it by succeeding generations, and therein lies its real significance. For the Charter, whether as the result of bad historical research, romanticism, wishful thinking, or any other reason, in time came to be looked upon as truly the Charter of liberties of free Englishmen. Through the centuries Englishmen in trouble with the authorities invoked the Charter as guarantor of rights—such as trial by jury and habeas corpus—whose relationship with it was, if not fanciful, then certainly remote and tenuous. English public opinion was quick to rally around any claim for liberty made in the name of the Charter. By the time Madison and his colleagues added the Bill of Rights to the American Constitution, the Charter had acquired a gloss of centuries that made of it a world of liberties which the barons at Runnymede never dreamed of, and which would have shocked and terrified them if they had.

The one figure most responsible for this development was Sir Edward Coke, one of England's greatest jurists, whose writing and thinking were known to every American lawyer of the eighteenth century and profoundly influenced American constitutional development. As Chief Justice of the Common Pleas, Coke became the champion of Parliament against James I and Charles I, attacking the royal prerogative and setting the precedent for judicial supremacy in the United States by declaring that royal decrees contrary to law were null and void. His arguments and reasoning were based upon history as he saw it and upon historical documents such as the Magna Carta as he interpreted them. Although neither his history nor his historical interpretations were entirely accurate, his reasoning was brilliant and his arguments impressive—in no small measure because they harmonized so well with the growing libertarian spirit of seventeenth-century England and with the democratic libertarianism of eighteenth-century America. Coke's *Institutes*, published in 1628, contained a commentary upon the Magna Carta in which he showed to the satisfaction of the American colonists the identity in meaning between the Charter's "law of the land" and the prevalent "due process of law" and that the purpose of these provisions was to protect the citizen from governmental oppression. Coke it was also who, in the same year, was probably chief draftsman of the Petition of Right, sent by Parliament to Charles I, which reaffirmed the principle of habeas corpus by asserting that no person might be imprisoned without cause shown, and declared that martial law might not be employed in time of peace.

The only other figure we can mention in this brief chronicle is the radical Puritan pamphleteer, John Lilburne—"Freeborn John"—as obnoxious a character as one is likely to come across in history. (How much civilization owes to obnoxious characters!) It was Lilburne who contributed much to the abolition in 1641 of the Star Chamber, that secret tribunal of judges, clergy, lawyers, and laymen that for a century and a half acted as the Crown's instrument for tyranny and oppression. The Star Chamber's proceedings were totally devoid of the procedural safeguards that later became the liberties of Américans. One who incurred the displeasure of the Crown could be arrested in secret and tried in secret. He had no right to be informed of the charges leveled against him nor to face or examine his accusers. He could be tortured to exact a confession. If by any chance the jury should acquit him, the members of the jury could themselves be fined and imprisoned. If he was convicted, his nose could be slit, his ears cut off, his tongue drilled, and his cheeks branded. Whipping, pillory, and staggering fines were imposed. The Star Chamber could (and did) impose any penalty short of death.

Lilburne's troubles began in 1637, when he was barely twenty. Accused of importing unlicensed Puritan books from Holland, he was brought before the Star Chamber and ordered to take the usual inquisitorial oath. This he refused to do, claiming the right not to incriminate himself. For this he was sentenced to be publicly whipped and placed in the pillory. While this was going on he exhorted his hearers to resist the tyranny of the bishops and threw among them copies of the condemned books. The Star Chamber ordered him gagged and placed in solitary confinement, and immediately decreed that persons thereafter sentenced to whipping or pillory be searched before the sentence was carried out.

The Long Parliament, which abolished the Star Chamber, voted Lilburne £300 reparation (little of which was ever paid), declaring that his punishment had been "illegal and most unjust, against the liberty of the subject, and the law of the land and Magna Carta." But Lilburne—of whom it was said that "if the world was emptied of all but John Lilburne, Lilburne would quarrel with John and John with Lilburne"—soon found himself at odds with Oliver Cromwell and his Puritan Commonwealth. A left-wing Puritan himself, he nevertheless protested the illegal court that condemned Charles I to death. For this he was tried for treason and, though acquitted, later banished. Returning to England, he was again tried and, though again acquitted, placed in confinement as a dangerous character. Indeed, most of his adult life was spent shuttling between the prison walls and the courtroom chamber. But throughout his many trials, he continually and loudly asserted his procedural rights (such as the privilege against self-incrimination, the right to be informed of the crime charged against him, assistance of counsel, and public trial) and by doing so helped secure them for succeeding generations of Englishmen and Americans.

The long but ultimately successful struggle for procedural safeguards in criminal proceedings was an integral part of the long and ultimately successful struggle for constitutional democracy. These procedural safeguards rest upon two underlying assumptions of democracy, the integrity of the individual and government by law rather than men.

When Sir Walter Raleigh was tried for treason in 1603 he claimed that he was entitled to acquittal unless two eyewitnesses testified against him. To this one of the judges replied: "... many horse stealers may escape if they may not be condemned without witnesses." Both before that time and since then, every assertion by an accused of the benefits of a procedural safeguard not established by ancient precedent—from the assertion of the right not to be tortured into confessing, to an accused Communist's claim of the right to confront secret informers—has been met with the same objection: that, if it is granted, many guilty persons may escape. The fact that, notwithstanding this objection, procedural safeguards have developed and have become part of our legal system manifests the deliberate judgment of the people that the integrity of the individual in a democracy is so valuable that it is more important that he be accorded a fair trial than that every culprit be punished.

It is clear that observance of the procedural safeguards designed to insure a fair trial assumes the supremacy of laws over the arbitrary will of men. Under the Anglo-American legal system a criminal case is entitled *"The King* v. *Jones,"* or *"State* v. *Jones"*; and it is prosecuted in exactly that way—a contest between the government and the individual. But, with all its power, the government, whether king or state, must abide by the rules of the game. When Edward Coke contested the claimed right of James I to remove from the law courts and to judge for himself whatever cases he wished, the king replied that, if Coke was correct, then the king was "under the law, which was treason to affirm." But Coke stood his ground and replied that the king "ought not be under men but under God and the law." The inclusion in the Bill of Rights of the procedural safeguards deemed necessary to insure fair play for accused Americans constituted a recognition that in our democracy the state, like the king, is not above the law.

Due Process—Federal and State

By the time the colonies declared their independence of the king, the struggle for fair play in criminal trials had long been won in England. Indeed, one grievance against the king listed in the Declaration of Independence was that he had deprived the colonists of a number of important elements of fair play in criminal cases, such as trial by jury and trial at the place of commission of the charged offense. The concept of fair trial had been slow in developing and had come about by the gradual and erratic accretions of seemingly unrelated procedural safeguards. When, therefore, the Constitution and the Bill of Rights were framed here, the framers included specifically the more important components of fair trial that had by that time become established as liberties of Englishmen and Americans. These were:

1. Privilege of habeas corpus (Constitution, Art. I, sec. 9)
2. No bills of attainder (Art. I, sec. 9, 10)
3. No ex post facto laws (Art. I, sec. 9, 10)
4. Trial by jury (Art. III, sec. 2; Amendment 6)
5. No unreasonable searches and seizures (Amend. 4)
6. Right to indictment by grand jury and to be informed of crime charged (Amend. 5, 6)
7. No double jeopardy (Amend. 5)
8. No compulsory self-incrimination (Amend. 5)
9. Speedy and public trial at place of crime (Amend. 6)
10. Confrontation of witnesses (Amend. 6)
11. Compulsory process for defense witnesses (Amend. 6)
12. Right to counsel (Amend. 6)
13. Reasonable bail (Amend. 8)
14. No cruel and unusual punishments (Amend. 8)

These, of course, are not all the components of fair play in criminal proceedings. For example, while Amendment 6 guarantees trial by an "impartial jury," there is no specific guarantee that the *judge* be impartial. Nor is there any express abolition of the judge's power, which had survived to Freeborn John's day, of fining a jury for bringing in a verdict with which he disagreed. Nor is there anything expressly prohibiting a State from rushing an accused to trial immediately after indictment without affording him a reasonable time in which to prepare his defense. These unmentioned procedural safeguards are surely important elements of a fair trial.

To provide for unmentioned established safeguards and perhaps for those not yet established, Madison and his colleagues who drafted this Bill of Rights included an omnibus guarantee. No person, the Fifth Amendment states, shall "be deprived of life, liberty or property without due process of law." The phrase "due process of law" is much broader than its

Magna Carta ancestor "law of the land," which guaranteed only that no person should be proceeded against except for violation of an existing law. "Due process of law" includes this but goes much further; it guarantees that, when a person is proceeded against for violation of a law, the government will act fairly and will accord him all the procedural safeguards comprising fair play and within the concept of ordered liberty. The short phrase "due process of law" thus leaves unlimited room for the evolution and expansion of the Anglo-American concept of fair play.

Before the Civil War the requirements of fair play were applicable only to the Federal government. The only exception was the ban on bills of attainder and ex post facto laws, which Article I, Section 10, of the Constitution made applicable to the States as well as to Congress. The Fourteenth Amendment, enacted after the Civil War to secure the rights of Americans against infringement by the States, incorporated the "due process" clause but did not expressly declare that the specific procedural safeguards set forth in the Bill of Rights should be applicable to the States. As we have seen, Justices Black and Douglas believed that this was the purpose of the Amendment, but the majority of the Supreme Court has never accepted this view. The position of the Court is that the "due process" clause of the Fourteenth Amendment requires the States to accord defendants only such procedural safeguards as are at the particular time considered essential components of ordered liberty or fair play.

In most cases this interpretation will not result in any practical difference between State and Federal procedures. Thus, a "third degree" confession is barred to the States as outside the limits of fair play, and barred to the Federal government by the express ban on compulsory self-incrimination. On the other hand, there are many instances where permissible State procedures may differ from those in the Federal courts.

Since the Federal government is also subject to the "due process" clause, which in the Fifth Amendment means all that it means in the Fourteenth, the net result is that the States have substantially more leeway than the Federal government in the conduct of criminal proceedings, and correspondingly an accused American's procedural liberties are less comprehensive in the State courts than in the Federal courts. To a substantial degree the practical difference is lessened by the fact that most State constitutions themselves contain many of the specific guarantees of the Bill of Rights, and the State courts generally interpret these in the same way that the Supreme Court interprets those in the Bill of Rights.

Before considering the specific procedural safeguards constituting fair trial, one fact should be noted. With minor exceptions, these developed in the criminal law and relate to criminal trials. A serious and as yet largely unanswered question is to what extent they are applicable to noncriminal matters between the government and the individual. One often hears, in defense of the denial of many of these safeguards (e.g., confrontation, right of cross-examination) in Congressional investigations, that investigations, by legislative committees are not criminal proceedings and that procedural safeguards are therefore irrelevant. The same is said in respect to the dismissal of government employees on security grounds, and the deportation of aliens.

Two comments are appropriate here. In the first place, it rests upon an extremely legalistic if not fictional distinction. A person discharged as a security risk by the government or uprooted from his family and home of many years and deported to a foreign land suffers consequences far more serious than ensue from many criminal proceedings. In the second place, and more important, the contention recognizes only the procedural trees and is completely oblivious to the democratic forest. It is only because of historical accident that the procedural safeguards developed in criminal proceedings; there is nothing inherent in criminal proceedings that makes procedural safeguards relevant only there. Procedural safeguards evolved in criminal proceedings as part—and only part—of the development of constitutional democracy out of despotism and tyranny. Democracy differs from despotism in that in the former the government deals fairly with the people in all its relations with them—not in a selected few. A government that adheres to fair play only part of the time is only a part-time democracy.

"Stop and Frisk"

ROY WILKINS

One of the ranking sub-disturbances of Negro citizens that keep race relations simmering is the race's uphill fight for the fair administration of justice.

This always hot phase surfaced recently in the tension-loaded community of Watts in Los Angeles where a Negro autoist was killed by a policeman. It showed again in New Jersey where threats of a Negro counteraction and possible physical clashes led to an injunction against a rally of the Ku Klux Klan.

But a more ominous stirring of the Negro's disenchantment in this area is contained in the approval by the American Law Institute of a version of the "stop and frisk" procedure. Policemen, under this authority, will be able to halt and search any person whom the officer on the spot considers to be suspicious.

Thoughtful and learned members of the bar in the private organization want to include this section in their proposed model code for the guidance of state and municipal legislators and police administrators. Under it, a policeman who "does not have reasonable cause to believe that a felony or misdemeanor has been committed" may stop a person for as long as 20 minutes and search him.

This authority, where incorporated into state law, will subject any Negro to detention and search on the mere whim or the racial feeling of any police officer under any circumstances, for Negroes bear the brunt of this form of police action.

Already the tension between the Negro communities of the nation and elements in the police forces is strained by precisely this practice, now indulged in by some policemen without the sanction of legal or of even official departmental authority.

A Negro in a section of the city where he is not often seen may be stopped. A Negro driving a car which police officers may doubt is his lawful possession (or one within his means) may be questioned. Two or more

SOURCE: *New York Post*, May 28, 1966.

Negroes in conversation on a street or in a corridor or store or park may be deemed to be suspicious.

This suggested procedure in reality encourages the establishment of a police state because it gives a police officer the sole right (no matter what happens later) to halt, question and search any individual whom he (not the law) considers to be "suspicious."

For many years some police forces—notably that in Los Angeles—have been stopping Negroes for no reason except a notion in the mind of a policeman. Indeed, much of the bitter and continuing criticism of the Los Angeles regime of Chief William H. Parker is based upon this practice.

Now, Negro citizens recognize and agree that lawbreakers, black and white, must be apprehended and punished. Law and order must be upheld. We cannot have lynch-like reprisal murders. But in the present state of racial affairs, no Negro, even the most conservative, can look without apprehension upon a proposal to permit a policeman to monitor his comings and goings.

The United States Supreme Court declared in *Henry* v. *United States*, "Under our system suspicion is not enough for an officer to lay hands upon a citizen." Vigorous dissent on the proposed code was voiced by Judge George Edwards out of his rich experience as a former police commissioner in Detroit.

The administration of justice is one of the four key topics to be considered by the White House conference "To Fulfill These Rights," June 12. It is not likely that the delegates, seeking accelerated, peaceful and therefore equitable progress toward the exercise and enjoyment of civil rights, will be unconcerned with the "stop and frisk" proposal.

Terry *v.* Ohio, 392 U.S. 1 (1968)

NO. 67.—OCTOBER TERM, 1967.

John W. Terry, Petitioner, v. *State of Ohio.*	*On Writ of Certiorari to the Supreme Court of Ohio.*

[JUNE 10, 1968.]

Mr. Chief Justice WARREN delivered the opinion of the Court.

This case presents serious questions concerning the role of the Fourth Amendment in the confrontation on the street between the citizen and the policeman investigating suspicious circumstances.

Petitioner Terry was convicted of carrying a concealed weapon and sentenced to the statutorily prescribed term of one to three years in the penitentiary. Following the denial of a pretrial motion to suppress, the prosecution introduced in evidence two revolvers and a number of bullets seized from Terry and a codefendant, Richard Chilton, by Cleveland Police Detective Martin McFadden. At the hearing on the motion to suppress this evidence, Officer McFadden testified that while he was patrolling in plain clothes in downtown Cleveland at approximately 2:30 in the afternoon of October 31, 1963, his attention was attracted by two men, Chilton and Terry, standing on the corner of Huron Road and Euclid Avenue. He had never seen the two men before, and he was unable to say precisely what first drew his eye to them. However, he testified that he had been a policeman for 39 years and a detective for 35 and that he had been assigned to patrol this vicinity of downtown Cleveland for shoplifters and pickpockets for 30 years. He explained that he had developed routine habits of observation over the years and that he would "stand and watch people or walk and watch people at many intervals of the day." He added: "Now, in this case when I looked over they didn't look right to me at the time."

His interest aroused, Officer McFadden took up a post of observation in the entrance to a store 300 to 400 feet away from the two men. "I get more purpose to watch them when I seen their movements," he testified. He saw one of the men leave the other one and walk southwest on Huron Road, past some stores. The man paused for a moment and looked in a store window, then walked on a short distance, turned around and walked back toward the corner, pausing once again to look in the same store window. He rejoined his companion at the corner, and the two conferred briefly. Then the second man went through the same series of motions, strolling down Huron Road, looking in the same window, walking on a short distance, turning back, peering in the store window again, and returning to confer with the first man at the corner. The two men repeated this ritual alternately between five and six times apiece—in all, roughly a dozen trips. At one point, while the two were standing together on the corner, a third man approached them and engaged them briefly in conversation. This man then left the two others and walked west on Euclid Avenue. Chilton and Terry resumed their measured pacing, peering, and conferring. After this had gone on for 10 to 12 minutes, the two men walked off together, heading west on Euclid Avenue, following the path taken earlier by the third man.

By this time Officer McFadden had become thoroughly suspicious. He testified that after observing their elaborately casual and oft-repeated reconnaissance of the store window on Huron Road, he suspected the two men of "casing a job, a stick-up," and that he considered it his duty as a police officer to investigate further. He added that he feared "they may have a gun." Thus, Officer McFadden followed Chilton and Terry and saw them stop in front of Zucker's store to talk to the same man who had conferred with them earlier on the street corner. Deciding that the situation was ripe for direct action, Officer McFadden approached the three men, identified himself as a police officer and asked for their names. At this point his knowledge was confined to what he had observed. He was not acquainted with any of the three men by name or by sight, and he had received no information concerning them from any other source. When the men "mumbled something" in response to his inquiries, Officer McFadden grabbed petitioner Terry, spun him around so that they were facing the other two, with Terry between McFadden and the others, and patted down the outside of his clothing. In the left breast pocket of Terry's overcoat Officer McFadden felt a pistol. He reached inside the overcoat pocket, but was unable to remove the gun. At this point, keeping Terry between himself and the others, the officer ordered all three men to enter Zucker's store. As they went in, he removed Terry's overcoat completely, retrieved a .38 caliber revolver from the pocket and ordered all three men to face the wall with their hands raised. Officer McFadden proceeded to pat down the outer clothing of

Chilton and the third man, Katz. He discovered another revolver in the outer pocket of Chilton's overcoat, but no weapons were found on Katz. The officer testified that he only patted the men down to see whether they had weapons, and that he did not put his hands beneath the outer garments of either Terry or Chilton until he felt their guns. So far as appears from the record, he never placed his hands beneath Katz's outer garments. Officer McFadden seized Chilton's gun, asked the proprietor of the store to call a police wagon, and took all three men to the station, where Chilton and Terry were formally charged with carrying concealed weapons.

On the motion to suppress the guns the prosecution took the position that they had been seized following a search incident to a lawful arrest. The trial court rejected this theory, stating that it "would be stretching the facts beyond reasonable comprehension" to find that Officer McFadden had had probable cause to arrest the men before he patted them down for weapons. However, the court denied the defendant's motion on the ground that Officer McFadden, on the basis of his experience, "had reasonable cause to believe . . . that the defendants were conducting themselves suspiciously, and some interrogation should be made of their action." Purely for his own protection, the court held, the officer had the right to pat down the outer clothing of these men, whom he had reasonable cause to believe might be armed. The court distinguished between an investigatory "stop" and an arrest, and between a "frisk" of the outer clothing for weapons and a full-blown search for evidence of crime. The frisk, it held, was essential to the proper performance of the officer's investigatory duties, for without it "the answer to the police officer may be a bullet, and a loaded pistol discovered during the frisk is admissible."

After the court denied their motion to suppress, Chilton and Terry waived jury trial and pleaded not guilty. The court adjudged them guilty, and the Court of Appeals for the Eighth Judicial District, Cuyahoga County, affirmed. *State* v. *Terry*, 5 Ohio App. 2d 122, 214 N. E. 2d 114 (1966). The Supreme Court of Ohio dismissed petitioner's appeal on the ground that no "substantial constitutional question" was involved. We granted certiorari, 387 U.S. 929 (1967), to determine whether the admission of the revolvers in evidence violated petitioner's rights under the Fourth Amendment, made applicable to the States by the Fourteenth. *Mapp* v. *Ohio*, 367 U.S. 643 (1961). We affirm the conviction.

* * *

We must now examine the conduct of Officer McFadden in this case to determine whether his search and seizure of petitioner were reasonable, both at their inception and as conducted. He had observed Terry, together with Chilton and another man, acting in a manner he took to be preface to a "stick-up." We think on the facts and circumstances Officer McFadden detailed before the trial judge a reasonably prudent man would have been warranted in believing petitioner was armed and thus presented a threat to the officer's safety while he was investigating his suspicious behavior. The actions of Terry and Chilton were consistent with McFadden's hypothesis that these men were contemplating a daylight robbery—which, it is reasonable to assume, would be likely to involve the use of weapons—and nothing in their conduct from the time he first noticed them until the time he confronted them and identified himself as a police officer gave him sufficient reason to negate that hypothesis. Although the trio had departed the original scene, there was nothing to indicate abandonment of an intent to commit a robbery at some point. Thus, when Officer McFadden approached the three men gathered before the display window at Zucker's store he had observed enough to make it quite reasonable to fear that they were armed; and nothing in their response to his hailing them, identifying himself as a police officer, and asking their names served to dispel that reasonable belief. We cannot say his decision at that point to seize Terry and pat his clothing for weapons was the product of a volatile or inventive imagination, or was undertaken simply as an act of harassment; the record evidences the tempered act of a policeman who in the course of an investigation had to make a quick decision as to how to protect himself and others from possible danger, and took limited steps to do so.

The manner in which the seizure and search were conducted is, of course, as vital a part of the inquiry as whether they were warranted at all. The Fourth Amendment proceeds as much by limitations upon the scope of governmental action as by imposing preconditions upon its initiation. Compare *Katz* v. *United States*, 389 U.S. 347, 354–356 (1967). The entire deterrent purpose of the rule excluding evidence seized in violation of the Fourth Amendment rests on the assumption that "limitations upon the fruit to be gathered tend to limit the quest itself." *United States* v. *Poller*, 43 F. 2d 911, 914 (C. A. 2d Cir. 1930); see, *e.g.*, *Linkletter* v. *Walker*, 381 U.S. 618, 629–635 (1965);

Mapp v. *Ohio*, 367 U.S. 643 (1961); *Elkins* v. *United States*, 364 U.S. 206, 216–221 (1960). Thus, evidence may not be introduced if it was discovered by means of a seizure and search which were not reasonably related in scope to the justification for their initiation. *Warden* v. *Hayden*, 387 U.S. 294, 310 (1967) (Mr. Justice Fortas, concurring).

We need not develop at length in this case, however, the limitations which the Fourth Amendment places upon a protective seizure and search for weapons. These limitations will have to be developed in the concrete factual circumstances of individual cases. See *Sibron* v. *New York*, *post*, p. 40, decided today. Suffice it to note that such a search, unlike a search without a warrant incident to a lawful arrest, is not justified by any need to prevent the disappearance or destruction of evidence of crime. See *Preston* v. *United States*, 376 U.S. 364, 367 (1964). The sole justification of the search in the present situation is the protection of the police officer and others nearby, and it must therefore be confined in scope to an intrusion reasonably designed to discover guns, knives, clubs, or other hidden instruments for the assault of the police officer.

The scope of the search in this case presents no serious problem in light of these standards. Officer McFadden patted down the outer clothing of petitioner and his two companions. He did not place his hands in their pockets or under the outer surface of their garments until he had felt weapons, and then he merely reached for and removed the guns. He never did invade Katz's person beyond the outer surfaces of his clothes, since he discovered nothing in his pat down which might have been a weapon. Officer McFadden confined his search strictly to what was minimally necessary to learn whether the men were armed and to disarm them once he discovered the weapons. He did not conduct a general exploratory search for whatever evidence of criminal activity he might find.

We conclude that the revolver seized from Terry was properly admitted in evidence against him. At the time he seized petitioner and searched him for weapons, Officer McFadden had reasonable grounds to believe that petitioner was armed and dangerous, and it was necessary for the protection of himself and others to take swift measures to discover the true facts and neutralize the threat of harm if it materialized. The policeman carefully restricted his search to what was appropriate to the discovery of the particular items which he sought. Each case of this sort will, of course, have to be decided on its own facts. *We merely hold today that where a police officer observes unusual conduct which leads him reasonably to conclude in light of his experience that criminal activity may be afoot and that the persons with whom he is dealing may be armed and presently dangerous; where in the course of investigating this behavior he identifies himself as a policeman and makes reasonable inquiries; and where nothing in the initial stages of the encounter serves to dispel his reasonable fear for his own or others' safety, he is entitled for the protection of himself and others in the area to conduct a carefully limited search of the outer clothing of such persons in an attempt to discover weapons which might be used to assault him. Such a search is a reasonable search under the Fourth Amendment, and any weapons seized may properly be introduced in evidence against the person from whom they were taken.*

(Affirmed.)

Mr. Justice DOUGLAS dissenting.

I agree that petitioner was "seized" within the meaning of the Fourth Amendment. I also agree that frisking petitioner and his companions for guns was a "search." But it is a mystery how that "search" and that "seizure" can be constitutional by Fourth Amendment standards, unless there was "probable cause" to believe that (1) a crime had been committed or (2) a crime was in the process of being committed or (3) a crime was about to be committed.

The opinion of the Court disclaims the existence of "probable cause." If loitering were an issue and that was the offense charged, there would be "probable cause" shown. But the crime here is carrying concealed weapons; and there is no basis for concluding that the officer had "probable cause" for believing that crime was being committed. Had a warrant been sought, a magistrate would, therefore, have been unauthorized to issue one, for he can act only if there is a showing of "probable cause." We hold today that the police have greater authority to make a "seizure" and conduct a "search" than a judge has to authorize such action. We have said precisely the opposite over and over again.

In other words, police officers, up to today have been permitted to effect arrests or searches without warrants only when the facts within their personal knowledge would satisfy the constitutional standard of probable cause. At the time of their "seizure" without a warrant they must possess facts concerning the person arrested that would have satisfied a magistrate that "probable cause" was indeed present. The term "probable cause" rings a bell of certainty that is not

sounded by phrases such as "reasonable suspicion." Moreover, the meaning of "probable cause" is deeply imbedded in our constitutional history. As we stated in *Henry* v. *United States*, 361 U.S. 98, 100–102:

> The requirement of probable cause has roots that are deep in our history. The general warrant, in which the name of the person to be arrested was left blank, and the writs of assistance, against which James Otis inveighed, both perpetuated the oppressive practice of allowing the police to arrest and search on suspicion. Police control took the place of judicial control, since no showing of "probable cause" before a magistrate was required. . . .
>
> That philosophy [rebelling against these practices] later was reflected in the Fourth Amendment. And as the early American decisions both before and immediately after its adoption show, common rumor or report, suspicion, or even "strong reason to suspect" was not adequate to support a warrant for arrest. And that principle has survived to this day.

* * *

> It is important, we think, that this requirement [of probable cause] be strictly enforced, for the standard set by the Constitution protects both the officer and the citizen. If the officer acts with probable cause, he is protected even though it turns out that the citizen is innocent. . . . And while a search without a warrant is, within limits, permissible if incident to a lawful arrest, if an arrest without a warrant is to support an incidental search, it must be made with probable cause . . . . This immunity of officers cannot fairly be enlarged without jeopardizing the privacy or security of the citizen.

The infringement on personal liberty of any "seizure" of a person can only be "reasonable" under the Fourth Amendment if we require the police to possess "probable cause" before they seize him. Only that line draws a meaningful distinction between an officer's mere inkling and the presence of facts within the officer's personal knowledge which would convince a reasonable man that the person seized has committed, is committing, or is about to commit a particular crime. "In dealing with probable cause, . . . as the very name implies, we deal with probabilities. These are not technical; they are the factual and practical considerations of every-day life on which reasonable and prudent men, not legal technicians, act." *Brinegar* v. *United States*, 338 U.S. 160, 175.

To give the police greater power than a magistrate is to take a long step down the totalitarian path. Perhaps such a step is desirable to cope with modern forms of lawlessness. But if it is taken, it should be the deliberate choice of the people through a constitutional amendment. Until the Fourth Amendment, which is closely allied with the Fifth, is rewritten, the person and the effects of the individual are beyond the reach of all government agencies until there are reasonable grounds to believe (probable cause) that a criminal venture has been launched or is about to be launched.

There have been powerful hydraulic pressures throughout our history that bear heavily on the Court to water down constitutional guarantees and give the police the upper hand. That hydraulic pressure has probably never been greater than it is today.

Yet if the individual is no longer to be sovereign, *if the police can pick him up whenever they do not like the cut of his gib, if they can "seize" and "search" him in their discretion, we enter a new regime. The decision to enter it should be made only after a full debate by the people of this country.*

United States *v.* Robinson, 414 U.S. 218 (1973)

Mr. Justice REHNQUIST delivered the opinion of the Court.

On April 23, 1968, at approximately 11 o'clock p.m., Officer Richard Jenks, a 15-year veteran of the District of Columbia Metropolitan Police Department, observed the respondent driving a 1965 Cadillac near the intersection of 8th and C Streets, Southeast, in the District of Columbia. Jenks, as a result of previous investigation following a check of respondent's operator's permit four days earlier, determined there was reason to believe that respondent was operating a motor vehicle after the revocation of his operator's permit. This is an offense defined by statute in the District of Columbia which carries a mandatory minimum jail term, a mandatory minimum fine, or both. 40 D.C. Code § 302(d).

Jenks signaled respondent to stop the automobile, which respondent did, and all three of the occupants emerged from the car. At that point Jenks informed respondent that he was under arrest for "operating after revocation and obtaining a permit by misrepresentation." It was assumed by the majority of the Court of Appeals, and is conceded by the respondent

here, that Jenks had probable cause to arrest respondent, and that he effected a full custody arrest.

* * *

In accordance with procedures prescribed in Police Department instructions, Jenks then began to search respondent. He explained at a subsequent hearing that he was "face to face" with the respondent, and "placed [his] hands on [the respondent], my right hand to his left breast like this (demonstrating) and proceeded to pat him down thus (with the right hand)." During this patdown, Jenks felt an object in the left breast pocket of the heavy coat respondent was wearing, but testified that he "couldn't tell what it was" and also that he "couldn't actually tell the size of it." Jenks then reached into the pocket and pulled out the object, which turned out to be a "crumpled up cigarette package." Jenks testified that at this point he still did not know what was in the package:

> "As I felt the package I could feel objects in the package but I couldn't tell what they were. . . . I knew they weren't cigarettes."

The officer then opened the cigarette pack and found 14 gelatin capsules of white powder which he thought to be, and which later analysis proved to be, heroin. Jenks then continued his search of respondent to completion, feeling around his waist and trouser legs, and examining the remaining pockets. The heroin seized from the respondent was admitted into evidence at the trial which resulted in his conviction in the District Court.

The opinion for the plurality judges of the Court of Appeals, written by Judge Wright, the concurring opinion of Chief Judge Bazelon, and the opinion for the dissenting judges, written by Judge Wilkey, gave careful and comprehensive treatment to the authority of a police officer to search the person of one who has been validly arrested and taken into custody. We conclude that the search conducted by Jenks in this case did not offend the limits imposed by the Fourth Amendment, and we therefore reverse the judgment of the Court of Appeals.

I

It is well settled that a search incident to a lawful arrest is a traditional exception to the warrant requirement of the Fourth Amendment. This general exception has historically been formulated into two distinct propositions. The first is that a search may be made of the *person* of the arrestee by virtue of the lawful arrest. The second is that a search may be made of the area within the control of the arrestee.

Examination of this Court's decisions in the area show that these two propositions have been treated quite differently. The validity of the search of a person incident to a lawful arrest has been regarded as settled from its first enunciation and has remained virtually unchallenged until the present case. The validity of the second proposition, while likewise conceded in principle, has been subject to differing interpretations as to the extent of the area which may be searched.

Because the rule requiring exclusion of evidence obtained in violation of the Fourth Amendment was first enunciated in *Weeks* v. *United States*, 232 U.S. 383 (1914), it is understandable that virtually all of this Court's search and seizure law has been developed since that time. In *Weeks*, the Court made clear its recognition of the validity of a search incident to a lawful arrest:

What then is the present case? Before answering that inquiry specifically, it may be well by a process of exclusion to state what it is not. It is not an assertion of the right of the government, always recognized under English and American law, to search the person of the accused when legally

arrested to discover and seize the fruits or evidences of crime. This right has been uniformly maintained in many cases. 1 Bishop on Criminal Procedure, § 211; Wharton, Criminal Plead, and Practice, 8th ed., § 60; *Dillion* v. *O'Brien and Davis*, 16 Cox C. C. 245." 232 U.S., at 392.

Agnello v. *United States*, 269 U.S. 20 (1925), decided 11 years after *Weeks*, repeats the categorical recognition of the validity of a search incident to lawful arrest:

The right without a search warrant contemporaneously to search persons lawfully arrested while committing crime and to search the place where the arrest is made in order to find and seize things connected with the crime as well as weapons and other things to effect an escape from custody, is not to be doubted." *Id.*, at 30.

Throughout the series of cases in which the Court has addressed the second proposition relating to a search incident to a lawful arrest—the permissible area beyond the person of the arrestee which such a search may cover—no doubt has been expressed as to the unqualified authority of the arresting authority to search the person of the arrestee. *E.g., Carroll* v. *United States*, 267 U.S. 132 (1925); *Marron* v. *United States*, 275 U.S. 192 (1927); *Go-Bart Co.* v. *United States*, 282 U.S. 344 (1931); *United States* v. *Lefkowitz*, 285 U.S. 452 (1932); *Harris* v. *United States*, 331 U.S. 145 (1947); *Trupiano* v. *United States*, 334 U.S. 699 (1948); *United States* v. *Rabinowitz*, 339 U.S. 56 (1950); *Preston* v. *United States*, 376 U.S. 364 (1964); *Chimel* v. *California*, 395 U.S. 752 (1969). In *Chimel*, where the Court overruled *Rabinowitz* and *Harris* as to the area of permissible search incident to a lawful arrest, full recognition was again given to the authority to search the person of the arrestee:

"When an arrest is made, it is reasonable for the arresting officer to search the person arrested in order to remove any weapons that the latter might seek to use in order to resist arrest or effect his escape. Otherwise, the officer's safety might well be endangered, and the arrest itself frustrated. In addition, it is entirely reasonable for the arresting officer to search for and seize any evidence on the arrestee's person in order to prevent its concealment or destruction." 395 U.S., at 762–763.

* * *

II

In its decision of this case, the majority of the Court of Appeals decided that even after a police officer lawfully places a suspect under arrest for the purpose of taking him into custody, he may not ordinarily proceed to fully search the prisoner. He must instead conduct a limited frisk of the outer clothing and remove such weapons that he may, as a result of that limited frisk, reasonably believe the suspect has in his possession. While recognizing that *Terry* v. *Ohio*, 392 U.S. 1 (1968), dealt with a permissible "frisk" incident to an investigative stop based on less than probable cause to arrest, the Court of Appeals felt that the principles of that case should be carried over to this probable cause arrest for driving while one's license is revoked. Since there would be no further evidence of such a crime to be obtained in a search of the arrestee, the Court held that only a search for weapons could be justified.

Terry v. *Ohio, supra*, did not involve an arrest for probable cause, and it make quite clear that the "protective frisk" for weapons which it approved might be conducted without probable cause. 392 U.S., at 21–22, 24–25. The Court's opinion explicitly recognized that there is a "distinction in purpose, character, and extent between a search incident to an arrest and a limited search for weapons":

> "The former, although justified in part by the acknowledged necessity to protect the arresting officer from assault with a concealed weapon, *Preston* v. *United States*, 376 U.S. 364, 367 (1964), is also justified on other grounds, *ibid.*, and can therefore involve a relatively extensive exploration of the person. A search for weapons in the absence of probable cause to arrest, however, must, like any other search, be strictly circumscribed by the exigencies which justify its initiation. *Warden* v. *Hayden*, 387 U.S. 294, 310 (1967) (Mr. Justice Fortas, concurring). Thus it must be limited to that which is necessary for the discovery of weapons which might be used to harm the officer or others nearby, and may realistically be characterized as something less than a 'full' search even though it remains a serious intrusion.
>
> ". . . An arrest is a wholly different type of intrusion upon the individual freedom from a limited search for weapons, and the interests each is designed to serve are likewise quite different. An arrest is the initial stage of a criminal prosecution.

It is intended to vindicate society's interest in having its laws obeyed, and it is inevitably accompanied by future interference with the individual's freedom of movement, whether or not trial or conviction ultimately follows. The protective search for weapons, on the other hand, constitutes a brief, though far from inconsiderable, intrusion upon the sanctity of the person." 392 U.S., at 25–26 (footnote omitted).

Terry, therefore, affords no basis to carry over to a probable cause arrest the limitations this Court placed on a stop-and-frisk search permissible without probable cause.

* * *

The justification or reason for the authority to search incident to a lawful arrest rests quite as much on the need to disarm the suspect in order to take him into custody as it does on the need to preserve evidence on his person for later use at trial. *Agnello* v. *United States, supra; Abel* v. *United States*, 362 U.S. 217 (1960). The standards traditionally governing a search incident to lawful arrest are not, therefore, commuted to the stricter *Terry* standards by the absence of probable fruits or further evidence of the particular crime for which the arrest is made.

Nor are we inclined, on the basis of what seems to us to be a rather speculative judgment, to qualify the breadth of the general authority to search incident to a lawful custodial arrest on an assumption that persons arrested for the offense of driving while their license has been revoked are less likely to be possessed of dangerous weapons than are those arrested for other crimes. It is scarcely open to doubt that the danger to an officer is far greater in the case of the extended exposure which follows the taking of a suspect into custody and transporting him to the police station than in the case of the relatively fleeting contact resulting from the typical *Terry*-type stop. This is an adequate basis for treating all custodial arrests alike for purposes of search justification.

But quite apart from these distinctions, our more fundamental disagreement with the Court of Appeals arises from its suggestion that there must be litigated in each case the issue of whether or not there was present one of the reasons supporting the authority for a search of the person incident to a lawful arrest. We do not think the long line of authorities of this Court dating back to *Weeks*, nor what we can glean from the history of practice in this country and in England, requires such a case by case adjudication. A police officer's determination as to how and where to search the person of a suspect whom he has arrested is necessarily a quick *ad hoc* judgment which the Fourth Amendment does not require to be broken down in each instance into an analysis of each step in the search. The authority to search the person incident to a lawful custodial arrest, while based upon the need to disarm and to discover evidence, does not depend on what a court may later decide was the probability in a particular arrest situation that weapons or evidence would in fact be found upon the person of the suspect. A custodial arrest of a suspect based on probable cause is a reasonable intrusion under the Fourth Amendment; that intrusion being lawful, a search incident to the arrest requires no additional justification. It is the fact of the lawful arrest which establishes the authority to search, and we hold that in the case of a lawful custodial arrest a full search of the person is not only an exception to the warrant requirement of the Fourth Amendment, but is also a "reasonable" search under that Amendment.

IV

The search of respondent's person conducted by Officer Jenks in this case and the seizure from him of the heroin, were permissible under established Fourth Amendment law. While thorough, the search partook of none of the extreme or patently abusive characteristics which were held to violate the Due Process Clause of the Fourteenth Amendment in *Rochin* v. *California*, 342 U.S. 165 (1952). Since it is the fact of custodial arrest which gives rise to the authority to search, it is of no moment that Jenks did not indicate any subjective fear of the respondent or that he did not himself suspect that respondent was armed. Having in the course of a lawful search come upon the crumpled package of cigarettes, he was entitled to inspect it; and when his inspection revealed the heroin capsules, he was entitled to seize them as "fruits, instrumentalities, or contraband" probative of criminal conduct. *Harris* v. *United States, supra*, 331 U.S., at 154–155; *Warden* v. *Hayden*, 387 U.S. 294, 299, 307 (1967); *Adams* v. *Williams, supra*, 407 U.S., at 149. The judgment of the Court of Appeals holding otherwise is *Reversed.*

The New Supreme Court and the Police:

The Illusion of Change

RUTH G. WEINTRAUB AND HARRIET POLLACK

SOURCE: This article was expressly written for inclusion in this book.

Of all the decisions made by the U.S. Supreme Court since World War II none have been more controversial and more widely discussed than its criminal procedure decisions. *Brown* v. *Board of Education*(1) resulted in 10 years of organized massive resistance to school desegregation in the South. The school prayer(2) decisions were so unpopular that an attempt to overrule them by Constitutional Amendment received considerable support. Neither of these decisions, however, has been as roundly and widely condemned as *Miranda* v. *Arizona*(3) and other Supreme Court criminal procedure decisions.

Court protection of civil liberties is seldom popular with the public at large, since such protection frequently results in the restriction of majorities for the benefit of unpopular or unpleasant minorities, but in defending accused persons the Warren Court had the additional misfortune of acting precisely at a time when crime, especially street crime, was rising sharply throughout our cities. The result has been a widespread feeling that the two phenomena are linked: that the Warren Court's "permissiveness" and "coddling of criminals" has resulted in ever-worsening crime statistics.

Such a charge is grossly unfair. Sociologists point out that crime rates have risen all over the world; that crime is linked to urbanization and demographic patterns totally independent of the legal system; and that such failures of the American criminal justice system as are relevant to a rising evidence of crime (e.g., inappropriate plea bargaining, bail jumping, the inability of police to prevent street crime) have nothing to do with the decisions of the U.S. Supreme Court. Even more to the point, however, analysis of the questioned decisions shows that the so-called "permissiveness" of the Warren Court is a myth. The Warren Court did not add a single right to those already enjoyed by some accused persons. (What it did do was extend to the poor and ignorant those rights previously effectively enjoyed only by the well-to-do and well educated.) In the area of searches and seizures, moreover, (especially where the crime involved was violent or potentially violent) the Court actually *lowered* the standards for police action—made it *easier* for the police to arrest and search than had previously been the case. A study of these decisions makes it obvious that the reason for this conservative trend in an otherwise liberal court is that the Court, like the public, was concerned over the rising crime rate and was fearful of hampering the police.

The ambivalance of the U.S. Supreme Court toward questionable police procedures is illustrated by a study of two sets of cases: the "Stop-and-Frisk" cases(4) that came before the Warren Court and *Cupp* v. *Murphy*,(5) *Schneckloth* v. *Bustamonte*,(6) and *U.S.* v. *Robinson*,(7) which were decided by the Burger Court. All these cases involved procedural irregularities either in the detention of an accused person or in the search of his person or property. All the defendants were *in fact* guilty, and all had been convicted in the lower courts. The issue in each case, in legal terms, was whether the search or seizure that had produced the evidence was procedurally sufficiently correct to enable the conviction to stand.(8)

The earlier cases—*Terry* v. *Ohio, Peters* v. *N.Y.*, and *Sibron* v. *N.Y.*—concerned the legality of searches and seizures conducted by the police allegedly with less than "probable cause," the usual legal basis for arrests and searches. The later cases—*Cupp* v. *Murphy*, *Schneckloth* v. *Bustamonte*, and *U.S.* v. *Robinson*—had a variety of procedural defects. In *Cupp*, the police conducted a search of Cupp's person without having arrested him although they apparently had grounds to do so. In *Schneckloth*, the police conducted a search without grounds for either arrest or search, relying on the "consent" of the accused, a consent that was later challenged. In *Robinson*, a search was made incident to a valid arrest, but of such intensiveness as might be held to be unreasonable. In all cases, the Court faced a painful dilemma: whether to sanction lawlessness by the police by permitting illegally seized evidence to be used at the trial,(9) or in Cardozo's phrase, to permit the criminal to go free because the constable had blundered. In deciding them the Warren Court showed a consistent pattern (albeit with some misgivings) of support for the police. The Burger Court has reinforced that pattern, with its misgivings confined to dissents by three of the holdovers from the Warren Court. Both courts have clearly opted, wherever possible, to transform *de facto* guilt into *de jure* guilt even at some risk to civil liberties.

The Warren Court: Terry, Peters, Sibron

The *Terry*, *Peters* and *Sibron* cases, which were decided by the U.S. Supreme Court in June 1968, involved the admissibility of evidence seized pursuant to an arrest and search on less-than-probable cause. The question before the Court was whether such searches and seizures violated the due-process clause of the Fourteenth Amendment by violating the Fourth Amendment, which prohibits "unreasonable" searches and seizures. In the two New York cases, *Peters* and *Sibron*, the police had acted under authority granted by the so-called New York State Stop-and-Frisk Law,(10) which provided that:

"1. A police officer may stop any person abroad in a public place whom he reasonably suspects is committing, has committed, or is about to commit a felony or any of the crimes specified in section five hundred fifty-two of this chapter, and may demand of him his name, address, and an explanation of his actions.

"2. When a police officer has stopped a person for questioning pursuant to this section and reasonably suspects he is in danger of life or limb, he may search such person for a dangerous weapon. If the police officer finds such weapon or any other thing the possession of which may constitute a crime, he may take and keep it until the completion of the questioning, at which time he shall either return it, if lawfully possessed, or arrest such person."

In the Ohio case, *Terry*, the police acted under the aegis of time-honored practice, without benefit of formal statutory authorization.

Sibron v. *New York*. A New York City patrolman on his beat observed, over a period of eight hours, a man (Sibron) engaged in lengthy conversations with known drug addicts. Relying on his professional expertise, the patrolman suspected that the man might be a drug pusher. He followed Sibron into a restaurant and asked him to step outside. Once on the street, the patrolman said to him, "You know what I am looking for." When Sibron reached into his pocket, the patrolman, fearing that he was reaching for a weapon, reached in there also and pulled out a foil-wrapped package containing heroin. Sibron was arrested and charged with possession of narcotics. At the trial, his attorney moved to suppress the evidence on the ground that it was illegally seized, since the patrolman had not had probable cause to arrest or search Sibron. When the motion to suppress was denied, Sibron was convicted. The conviction was sustained by the New York State appellate courts as a proper action by the policeman under the Stop and Frisk Law.(11)

Peters v. *New York.* Lasky, an off-duty New York City policeman of 18 years' experience, heard a noise at the front door of his apartment. Peering through the peephole, he observed two men tiptoeing around the hallway in a suspicious manner. He telephoned for the police, put on his clothing, and, on finding the two men still acting in the same manner, entered the hallway, slamming the door behind him. At the noise, the two men fled using the staircase rather than the elevator. Lasky gave chase with gun drawn. He caught Peters on the stair landing, collared him, and patted him down for a weapon. He felt something hard in Peters' pocket which he thought might be a knife. He reached in and found a set of burglar's tools. When the police arrived, Peters was arrested and charged with possession of burglar's tools. At the trial, his attorney moved to suppress the evidence as having been illegally seized without probable cause. The prosecutor contended, however, that Lasky had acted under authority of the Stop-and-Frisk Law. The court admitted the evidence. Peters was convicted, and his conviction was upheld by the appellate courts.

Terry v. *Ohio.* A Cleveland policeman observed two men repeatedly walking back and forth in front of a store and pausing to peer into the window. They stopped to speak to a third man and followed him up the street about ten minutes later. The officer, relying on his professional judgment, decided that they might be "casing" the store for a possible robbery. He followed the suspects and found them conversing with a third man. He asked their names and patted Terry down, finding a pistol. A superficial search revealed that Terry's companion was also armed; the third man apparently was not armed and was not searched

further. Terry was charged with carrying a concealed weapon. His attorney moved to suppress the evidence on the ground that the policeman had no probable cause to search. The court denied the motion, holding that on-the-street investigations were traditionally permissible on standards of less-than-probable cause. The appellate court confirmed Terry's conviction.

Fourth Amendment Problems Raised by on-the-Street Encounters

At the time of its passage in 1964, the New York Stop and Frisk Law raised a storm of controversy; proponents argued that it was a limited and necessary response to the rise in criminal activity, and opponents charged that it was a regressive and unconstitutional invasion of privacy. The wording of the law was clearly designed to modify the traditional requirements for arrest and search—probable cause (regardless of whether the police action was taken with or without a warrant). Probable cause has no specific meaning, but has been defined by the courts as constituting more than mere suspicion, but less than beyond a reasonable doubt. In using the term "reasonable suspicion," the legislature acted to make it easier for police to stop and question suspects abroad in public places. The constitutionality of the law was immediately questioned as violating the Fourth Amendment prohibition of unreasonable searches and seizures. The U.S. Supreme Court has held illegal searches and seizures to be unreasonable and, since the *Mapp* decision in 1961, has barred the use of illegally seized evidence in state courts. If, therefore, the "reasonable suspicion" standard of the new statute could be shown to be "unreasonable" in that it eroded excessively the protection against police action that the Constitution affords to individuals, convictions obtained after arrests and searches made pursuant to this law would be invalid. Aware of the constitutional pitfalls inherent in the law, the Combined Council of Law Enforcement Officials(12) was instrumental in the New York City Police Department's adoption of a set of stringent administrative guidelines that limited greatly the possible scope of the law. For example, an officer might stop only those who he was "reasonably suspicious" had committed one of the listed offenses; he might use reasonable force if necessary, but only that of his body (nightsticks and weapons being impermissible); he might act only in a public place, not including theater or hotel lobbies; he might not compel answers to his questions; and the suspect's refusal to answer might not become the basis for an arrest;(13) searches might be made for weapons, for the officer's protection only, not as a pretext for obtaining evidence. Thus the Stop and Frisk Law became, officially at least, a rather narrowly limited relaxation of the standards for arrest and search.

Thus the basic question before the Court in *Terry, Peters,* and *Sibron* was: Does the Fourth Amendment permit any relaxation of the probable-cause standard? To ask this question is to pose a series of subsidiary questions. Is a stop valid on grounds of less than probable cause? Is a stop an arrest?

There is considerable legal ground for the belief that persons may be detained for questioning under circumstances that would not warrant an arrest and that such questioning is considered to be a detention different from the detention exercised in an arrest. In common law, watchmen could detain suspicious persons until morning without arresting them. Private persons could also question suspicious persons on grounds of less-than-probable cause in the belief that a crime had been committed or was about to be committed. The legality of detentions that are not arrests has been shaped by cases brought as suits for false arrest or by contentions by defendants that their detention was unlawful. Judge Fuld, while dissenting from the majority opinion in *People* v. *Rivera,* acknowledged:(14)

I have no doubt that the police, in the proper performance of their duties, have a responsibility to investigate suspicious activities and that one permissible form of investigation is the temporary stopping and questioning of individuals so engaged.

As a practical matter, the discretionary power of the police to stop suspicious persons for questioning is so well established by usage as to be completely taken for granted. The U.S. Supreme Court, as of 1968, had not ruled conclusively on the permissibility of an informal detention. The court had held that an illegal arrest *per se* violates the Fourth Amendment(15) but had never determined whether a stop on less-than-probable cause in a public place is an illegal arrest.

Is a search for weapons permissible on grounds of less-than-probable cause? Is there a difference between a search and a frisk? The legality of the frisk is entirely dependent on the legality of the preceding stop or

arrest, since it is clear that an unauthorized search for evidence to justify a subsequent arrest is absolutely impermissible. Assuming for the moment that the police have the power to stop on reasonable suspicion, do they also have the power to search on such grounds? Such a search is most easily justified as a necessary protection for the policeman. The Uniform Arrest Law authorizes searches for dangerous weapons of persons who are stopped on reasonable suspicion. One of the grounds for search incident to a formal arrest is protection of the arresting officer. Again, as a practical matter, the frisk is an everyday occurrence, and the police are unlikely to accept a ruling that gives them power to detain a suspect but denies them power to disarm him. The police agree with Judge Bergan's reasoning on *Rivera:* (16)

The answer to the question propounded by the policeman may be a bullet; in any case the exposure to danger could be very great. We think the frisk is a reasonable and constitutionally permissible precaution to minimize the danger.

Assuming the validity of the stop and frisk for weapons, may nonweapons that are found be used against the defendant?

This problem is closely related to the admissibility of evidence seized in a search based on probable cause, either with or without a warrant. The extent to which the police may seize and use evidence not related either to objects named in the warrant or to the crime they are investigating is not entirely clear. It would appear, however, that seizure of such contraband as narcotics or burglar tools probably would be permitted. In *Harris* v. *U.S.,*(17) the Court upheld a search by FBI agents with a valid search warrant, who, while looking for canceled checks, found draft board cards that Harris had no legal right to possess. Although this was a 5–4 decision and is considered an extreme case, the thinking of the Court up to 1968 on the problem of the admissibility of evidence showed an inclination to liberalize the rules. In *Warden* v. *Hayden,*(18) decided May 29, 1967, the Court admitted as evidence clothing seized during a search of the suspect's home and allegedly used in a robbery. For the first time, the Court permitted the seizure of "mere evidence" as contrasted to contraband or the instrumentalities or fruits of a crime. While *Sibron* and *Peters* did not present problems of "mere evidence," they did present a problem of whether a search that is begun for weapons should be permitted to result in other types of evidence.

The Stop-and-Frisk Decisions

The Court thus found itself in a position where the legal precedents permitted it to rule either way on the validity of detentions, searches, and seizures under the Stop and Frisk Law. The decisions were based, therefore, on considerations other than *stare decisis*. What these considerations were is perhaps suggested by an analysis of the opinions themselves.

1. The Court, first of all, accepted the reasoning of the New York State Court of Appeals that recognized the appropriateness of lower standards for police action involving lesser invasions of personal security. Four justices (Brennan, Fortas, Stewart, and Marshall) joined in Warren's opinion, which held that on-the-street stops for questioning and a brief patting down for weapons are definitely invasions of privacy even if called by names other than arrest and search, but nevertheless are not such serious invasions of privacy as the more formal arrest and search. For such less serious incursions on the right to be let alone, the standard for legitimate police action may also be lower, i.e., reasonable suspicion rather than probable cause. White, Harlan, and Black wrote separate concurrences that did not affect acceptance of the basic doctrine of lower standards for less serious detentions and searches. Thus eight justices accepted the flexible-standards rationale.

2. The Court recognized the limitations on the exclusionary rule. Much of the criticism of the original Stop and Frisk law was predicated on the assumption that to approve stop-and-frisk, the Court of necessity would be backing away from *Mapp* v. *Ohio*. The Court took this occasion to recognize the realities of police action:(19)

> Street encounters between citizens and police officers are incredibly rich in diversity. . . . Encounters are initiated by the police for a wide variety of purposes some of which are wholly unrelated to a desire to prosecute for crime. Doubtless some "field interrogation" conduct violates the Fourth Amendment. But a stern refusal by this Court to condone such activity does not render it responsive to the exclusionary rule. . . . It is powerless to deter invasions of constitutionally guaranteed rights where the police either have no interest in prosecuting or are willing to forego successful prosecution in the interest of serving some other goal.

The Court thus recognized that even if the exclusionary rule were to be applied with utmost rigidity to every stop and search made by the police, it would have limited value only as a deterrent to illegal police action.(20) There are many reasons why this is so. The most important of these, perhaps, is that often when a policeman detains a minor offender, he is not so much interested in arresting him as in obtaining him as an informant. Once the evidence is found, it matters little to the suspect that the search was illegal: the path of least resistance is to purchase freedom by supplying the police with information on more important criminals. Supporting the stop-and-frisk rationale therefore was not a repudiation of *Mapp* v. *Ohio*, since *Mapp* was at best only a partial deterrent.

3. Terry's conviction was upheld 8–1 (Douglas dissenting), Peters' was upheld 9–0, and Sibron's conviction was set aside 8–1 (Black dissenting). In *Terry*, all justices but Douglas agreed that under the flexible-standards rationale, Terry's observed actions had given the policeman sufficient grounds to make an on-the-street investigatory stop and the precautionary search incident thereto. In *Peters*, all nine justices agreed that Officer Lasky was legally correct in collaring and questioning the defendant, and a majority of the Court felt that Lasky had not only reasonable suspicion but probable cause for his action. Indeed, Justice Douglas, the dissenter in *Terry*, concurred in the result in *Peters* specifically on that ground. Warren, for the Court, went so far as to say, "It is difficult to conceive of stronger grounds for an arrest, short of actual eyewitness observation of criminal activity."(21) Justice Harlan, however, while concurring in the result, differed flatly from the Warren view of the events: "I do not think that Officer Lasky had anything close to probable cause to arrest Peters before he recovered the burglar's tools."(22) To Harlan, this was a stop on reasonable suspicion, not probable cause. In *Sibron*, all justices but Black agreed that the policeman had not had even reasonable suspicion to stop Sibron and therefore the subsequent search was illegal. To sum up, the Court in each case reviewed the action of the accused as judged by an experienced policeman in the light of his experience and decided whether the policeman had (a) no grounds, (b) reasonable suspicion, or (c) probable cause to justify an investigatory stop and superficial search.

Two inconsistencies are evident in these decisions: (a) The facts in *Peters* were viewed by the majority as clearly presenting probable cause, while to Justice

Harlan they just as clearly did not; (*b*) the Court's evaluation of the policeman's judgment in *Sibron* is one that is somewhat hard to justify on intellectual grounds, at least to those with practical knowledge of police operations. Why is it reasonable for a policeman to deduce criminal intent on the part of two men peering in a store window, but unreasonable for him to deduce criminal intent on the part of one who maintains continuous lengthy contact with known drug addicts? Does it really tax credulity to assume that a conversation with known addicts that lasts eight hours is related to drugs? Does it tax probability to infer an intent to sell rather than buy from such lengthy negotiations? Most books on the subject of police enforcement of narcotics laws would consider the officer's view of the situation quite reasonable. Certainly few policemen would agree with Harlan's judgment that:

> For eight continuous hours. . . . Officer Martin apparently observed not a single suspicious action and heard not a single suspicious word on the part of Sibron himself or any person with whom he associated.

To the working policeman, Sibron's actions were highly suspicious.(23)

Is there an explanation other than the reasonableness or unreasonableness of Officer Martin's conclusions as to why the Court was willing to accept the police view in *Peters* and *Terry* but not in *Sibron*? Justice Harlan may have given a clue when he said:(24)

> In *Terry*, the police officer judged that his suspect was about to commit a violent crime and that he had to assert himself in order to prevent it. . . . While no hard-and-fast rule can be drawn, I would suggest that one important factor, missing here, that should be taken into account in determining whether there are reasonable grounds for a forcible intrusion is whether there is any need for immediate action.

Certainly it is very reasonable to argue that police action is more urgent in preventing a burglary or armed robbery than in preventing a drug sale. The difficulty with this approach is that the legality of the stop or search then turns not so much on what the policeman is known to have done as on what the accused is alleged to have done or is planning to do—for the nub of the difficulty is that until the evidence is legally admissible it is only an allegation. This brings us around to the question of whether the Court can ignore the nature of

the evidence when its admissibility is in question. One can argue in response that the nature of the evidence is irrelevant, that it is the nature of the crime that is the deciding factor determining how much leeway the police have. This may be true—but it is the questioned evidence that links the accused to the crime, and if Harlan's rationale is the implied Court rationale, then the Court in effect is saying that the standards for the enforcement of the law will vary with the seriousness of the crime the accused is alleged to have committed or planned to commit; thus police action unacceptable against a suspected gambler would be acceptable against a suspected kidnapper.

It is, of course, difficult to say how much acceptance Harlan's rationale would be accorded by other members of the Court. Justice Douglas surely would take exception. There are, however, certain bits of evidence embodied in recent decisions that suggest a tendency to accept the idea that the production of *de facto* evidence of the accused's guilt of a crime of potential violence will give the police more leeway than they would have were the crime or the questioned evidence different.

The Court has grown increasingly permissive of police action designed to secure reliable, objective, independent evidence of the accused's guilt. In *McCray* v. *Illinois*,(25) the Court relaxed the standard for the admissibility of evidence obtained by a police search resulting from an unidentified informer's tip. Because the resulting evidence was reliable, the Court ignored the dubiousness of the source of the original information leading to the search. In *Warden* v. *Hayden*,(26) the Court permitted the robber's clothing ("mere evidence"), as opposed to the usual fruits of a crime, instrumentalities of a crime, or contraband, to be admitted against the accused. In a whole series of cases beginning with *Breithaupt* v. *Abram*(27) and culminating with *U.S.* v. *Wade*(28) the Court permitted nontestimonial evidence derived from the accused ranging from blood samples to the sound of the accused's voice to be used against the defendant even though allegedly self-incriminatory, therefore violative of the Fifth Amendment. The Court in May 1969 went so far as to suggest that with judicial permission, fingerprints obtained through a dragnet investigation might be admissible.(29) The cases of *Berger* v. *New York*(30) and *Katz* v. *U.S.*,(31) even though decided for the accused in each case, nevertheless have, through clarification and relaxation of standards, made it possible for previously inadmissible information obtained through wiretapping or electronic eavesdropping to be used in court. In all these cases, the Court has made the job of the police easier and actually has substantially extended their powers, while correspondingly diminishing the rights of the accused.

But wasn't this tendency on the part of the Court contradicted and counterbalanced by the *Miranda*(32) decision?

Miranda was the culmination of a whole series of cases relating to confessions and the right to counsel that are widely thought to have severely restricted the powers of the police. While *Miranda* involved a violent crime (rape) and only mildly offensive police conduct, the Court nevertheless did not permit the evidence (Miranda's confession) to be admitted. This may seem to contradict the rationale suggested above (that the Court in a case involving a violent crime will admit evidence of even dubious legality where the defendant is *de facto* guilty). On closer examination of the *Miranda* decision, however, the apparent contradiction fades. In the first place, the Court did little more in *Miranda* than make effective for the poor and ignorant those rights that had always existed for the well-to-do and knowledgeable, and in reality the decision seems to have had relatively little impact on the way the police do operate and on the effectiveness of their performance.(33) More to the point, however, is that *Miranda* and all other cases where the admissibility of self-incriminating statements is in question differ in a very important respect from *Terry, Warden, Breithaupt*, et al.: self-incriminating statements, no matter how seemingly voluntary, are of questionable reliability by their very nature; and they are certainly less reliable as evidence of guilt than a gun, a fingerprint, or a blood sample. Miranda's confession, for example, even though it was elicited after only two hours of questioning and with no evidence of coercion on the part of the police, contained words that did not sound like his own. Terry's gun was *res ipsa loquitur*; not so Miranda's confession or possibly any confession. Statements made under the influence of extreme emotional tension, drink, or drugs are certainly open to question, even if completely voluntary. Thus, the accused is not as clearly *de facto* guilty in a case built on self-incriminating statements as in one built on independent objective evidence. Even so, it is worth noting that, coincidentally or not, the records of *Miranda* and its companion cases (*Vignera* v. *New York* and *Westover* v. *U.S.*) indicate that in each case the police had sufficient independent evidence to convict the accused, and the confessions in question were, therefore, virtually superfluous. This meant, in practical terms, that

even if the Court reversed the original convictions, the defendants would in all probability be convicted in a new trial anyway, and the public would suffer no danger through the release of dangerous criminals. Thus, the situation in *Miranda* and others differed on two counts from *Terry* et al.: (1) the questioned evidence was not unimpeachably reliable, and (2) even an exclusion of the evidence would probably not have freed the defendant.

The inconsistency of *Sibron*, however, remains to be explained. Why should the Court have accepted the judgment of two working policemen and rejected that of the third? Again the answer seems to lie in the nature of the offense and its effect on police conduct. It is in the area of enforcing morals legislation (gambling, drug, and sex laws) that the greatest abuses of police practice occur. Because these "crimes without victims" are so difficult for the police to cope with, they are driven to illegal searches and seizures to obtain evidence. The most serious problem presented by *Sibron* was that if the Court permitted the introduction of the heroin seized while the policeman was searching for a weapon, it would open the door to thousands of searches for drugs, gambling slips, etc., which would be justified as searches for weapons.(34) Thus, the effect of *Sibron* was to preserve, for the moment at least, the exclusionary rule in relation to gambling and drug offenses that are brought to court. The Court, in balancing the equities between curbing the police (to the extent that the exclusionary rule curbs them) and convicting the *de facto* (but possibly not *de jure*) guilty, was unwilling to give the police additional leeway in this area.

The Burger Court: Cupp, Schneckloth, and Robinson

After the stop-and-frisk cases, the U.S. Supreme Court made very few decisions in the area of procedurally defective searches and seizures for five years. In 1973, however, three decisions—*Cupp, Schneckloth*, and *Robinson*—were handed down that essentially continued the line of reasoning of *Terry* and *Peters* and went slightly further in lowering procedural standards. The more conservative bias of the Burger Court, moreover, was made evident by the *Robinson* decision, which seemed to eliminate the distinctions the Warren Court was willing to recognize in *Sibron*. Although all three cases were decided in favor of the police, there were, however, more dissenters than in *Terry* and *Peters* (*Cupp* 7–2, Douglas and Brennan dissenting in part; *Schneckloth* and *Robinson* 6–3,(35) Douglas, Brennan, and Marshall dissenting).

Cupp v. *Murphy.* The estranged wife of one Daniel Murphy died of strangulation in her home in Portland, Oregon. Abrasions and lacerations were found on her throat, and there was no sign of forced entry or robbery. Upon receiving word of the murder, Murphy telephoned the Portland police and voluntarily came into the station house for questioning. At the station house, he was met by an attorney he had retained. The police noticed a dark spot they suspected might be blood on Murphy's finger and asked if they could take a sample of scrapings from his fingernails. Murphy refused, whereupon under protest and without a warrant, the police took samples that turned out to contain bits of blood, skin, and fabric from the victim's nightgown. The evidence was introduced at the trial and resulted in Murphy's conviction.

On appeal, Murphy claimed that the evidence was inadmissible as the product of an illegal search since he had not been arrested nor had the police obtained a warrant at the time of the search. When the state courts denied Murphy's appeal, he applied for federal *habeas corpus* relief, which was granted by the Court of Appeals for the 9th Circuit. The Court of Appeals assumed the police had had probable cause to search or arrest, but in the absence of a formal arrest or other exigent circumstances, the search was unconstitutional. The U.S. Supreme Court granted *certiorari* for a hearing on the constitutional question. The decision of the Court of Appeals was reversed, Justices Douglas and Brennan dissenting in part.

Schneckloth v. *Bustamonte.* While on routine patrol at 2:40 a.m., a California police officer, James Rand, stopped a car that was operating with a burned-out headlight and license plate light. Six men were in the car, including Joe Alcala, Robert Bustamonte, and Joe Gonzalez (the driver), in the front seat. Only Alcala had identification, and Gonzalez could not produce a driver's license. The six occupants then left the car at the request of the police officer. Two additional police officers arrived, and Alcala (who had explained that the car belonged to his brother) was asked by Officer Rand if he could search the car. No one had yet been threatened with arrest, and Rand offered uncontradicted testimony that the situation at that time "was all very congenial." Alcala said, "Sure, go ahead," and even helped by opening the trunk and glove compartment. Under the left rear seat the police found three checks previously stolen from a car wash.

Bustamonte was brought to trial on a charge of possessing a check with intent to defraud. He moved to suppress the evidence on the ground that the search was unconstitutional, having been conducted without a prior arrest or search warrant or probable cause. The trial judge denied the motion to suppress on the ground that consent is one of the specifically established exceptions to the requirements of both a warrant and probable cause. Bustamone was convicted and after being denied relief by the California appellate courts asked for a federal writ of *habeas corpus.* His request was denied at the district court level but granted by the Court of Appeals for the 9th Circuit.

The Court of Appeals held that in a case involving the waiving of constitutional rights, the burden of proof is on the government to show not only that consent was uncoerced but that it had been *intelligently* given, that is, with the understanding that it could be freely and effectively withheld. Consent could not be deduced solely from the absence of coercion and verbal expression of assent. Since no evidence was introduced that Alcala knew he could refuse consent, consent could therefore not be assumed to have been given.

The U.S. Supreme Court granted *certiorari*, and the decision of the Court of Appeals was reversed (Douglas, Brennan, and Marshall dissenting).

U.S. v. *Robinson.* On April 23, 1968, at 11:00 p.m., Officer Richard Jenks, a 15-year veteran of the District of Columbia Metropolitan Police Department, observed one Willie Robinson, Jr., driving a 1965 Cadillac in the southeast area of the District. Robinson was known to Jenks, who, as a result of a previous investigation four days earlier, had reason to believe Robinson was operating the vehicle after revocation of his operator's license. Jenks signaled Robinson to stop, which he did. On the officer's instructions, the three occupants of the car left the vehicle. Jenks then ascertained that Robinson was in fact driving with a revoked permit and arrested him. (In the District of Columbia driving with a revoked permit is a statutory offense that carries a mandatory minimum jail term, fine, or both. D.C. police department regulations also provide that in the case of some traffic offenses, including driving with a revoked permit, the officer shall make a summary arrest and take the violator, in custody, to the station house.) Both litigants in the case conceded that Jenks had had probable cause to arrest and at this point had effected a full-custody arrest. In accordance with prescribed police department procedures, Jenks then searched Robinson. He felt an object in the left breast pocket of the heavy coat Robinson was wearing, reached in, and pulled out a crumpled cigarette package. Jenks testified:

> As I felt the package I could feel objects in the package but I couldn't tell what they were . . . I knew they weren't cigarettes.

The officer then opened the cigarette package and found 14 capsules of a white powder, which subsequent analysis proved to be heroin. The heroin was admitted into evidence at the trial.

Robinson was convicted in U.S. District Court for the District of Columbia of the possession and facilitation of concealment of heroin. The court of appeals reversed the conviction on the ground that the heroin had been obtained as a result of a search that violated the Fourth Amendment. The U.S. Supreme Court reversed the court of appeals (Marshall, Douglas, and Brennan dissenting).

The Decisions

An analysis of the decisions in *Cupp, Schneckloth*, and *Robinson* makes it clear that the Burger Court is following and extending many of the rationales developed by the Warren Court in relation to procedurally defective searches and seizures.

1. The Burger Court, like the Warren Court, continues to rely on police expertise as justification for a valid arrest, i.e., both Courts have in effect held that if a trained, experienced policeman testifies that he had cause to take action against a suspect, not only his good faith but also his professional competence is to be assumed in the absence of proof to the contrary. The Court was willing to accept police judgment as to the meaning of Terry's attention to the store, Peters' actions in the hallway of the apartment house, the nature of the stain on Murphy's finger, and the likelihood of Robinson's driving with a revoked permit. Other interpretations were possible, of course: Terry could have been a casual stroller, Peters an ordinary visitor to the apartment house, and Cupp simply a man with dirty hands; but neither Court had difficulty with this proposition. In these four cases at any rate, no significant challenge to the propriety of the detentions based on these police judgments was expressed by any justice.

2. The willingness of both Courts to concede the validity of the arrests or detentions in these cases is especially significant because the Burger Court, like the Warren Court, leaned heavily toward basing its judgment of the validity of subsequent searches almost entirely on the validity of the preceding arrest. To put the matter somewhat differently, neither Court was inclined to limit the power of the police to assume such control *as the police deemed to be necessary* over a suspect once a valid arrest or detention had been effected. In *Terry* and *Peters*, of course, since a full-scale arrest had not been effected, only a frisk for weapons was permitted; but once the weapon was found, the suspect was arrested and a full-scale search ensued. (Had no weapon been found, there would of course have been no arrest, no search, and no suspect.) At any rate, the action taken by the police on the spot was upheld.

In *Robinson*, validity of the arrest having been conceded, the majority upheld the right of the police to conduct a complete search not merely for weapons, but for contraband, fruits of a crime, and evidence. The minority, in an attempt to apply the stop-and-frisk rationale to a full-scale arrest, protested vigorously that it was unreasonable for Jenks to look for more than weapons on Robinson, since the traffic offense Robinson was charged with did not warrant a more extensive search. The majority, distinguishing a stop from a full-scale arrest based on probable cause, held that where the police have total custody they must have total control. What if the cigarette package enabled Robinson to commit suicide or to pass contraband to another prisoner? Even the argument of the dissenters that Jenks should simply have taken custody of the cigarette package without looking inside and "checked it" in the station house was rejected, presumably on grounds of police administrative convenience.

Again in *Cupp* the fact that the police had probable cause to arrest, *even though they had not exercised it*, was sufficient for seven justices to uphold a search of Murphy's person. Indeed, the decision might well have been unanimous had the determination of probable cause been made more definitively in the lower courts. The arguments of the two dissenters (Douglas and Brennan) were based primarily on the lack of judicial determination of the existence of probable cause rather than on the impropriety of a search antecedent to the actual arrest.

3. The contrasting fates of Sibron and Robinson illustrate the only significant area of divergence between the Warren and Burger courts. Both men were

convicted of drug offenses on the basis of heroin discovered—in Sibron's case after a stop-and-frisk search
for weapons and in Robinson's case after his arrest for a
traffic offense. The problem in these cases (for civil
libertarians at any rate) is the danger of legitimatizing
widespread and unjustifiable police searches for drugs
(especially of blacks and Hispanics) by using an arrest
for a minor offense as a pretext for conducting what
would otherwise be an illegal search. Reversal of
Sibron's conviction was a deviation from the main
corpus of the Warren Court's search-and-seizure decisions, apparently in reaction to this danger. The Burger
Court, however, has not seen fit to address itself to the
problem. It is possible that the facts of *Robinson* did
not lend themselves to a decision limiting the discretion
of the police; but the total absence of clues, hints, or
dicta suggesting that the police exercise their powers
prudently in this area seems to indicate an unwillingness on the part of the Burger Court even to recognize
the potential danger of intrusive police conduct in
obtaining drug law convictions.

Conclusion

What then is the significance of these six cases
relating to searches and seizures of dubious legality?

In the first place, in this type of case it is clear that
in balancing the equities between the rights of suspected persons and the need for security in the community, the U.S. Supreme Court consistently and
increasingly in close cases has opted for security for the
community rather than liberty for the suspect. It
should be noted however, that these are close cases,
that the police improprieties are not flagrant, and that
procedural standards even under the Burger Court are
quite high. If the Court's message to the police is simply
that they will not be hampered in reasonable, restrained efforts to produce reliable, nontestimonial
evidence of guilt of real crimes, then it would appear
possible to hope that the liberty-versus-security dilemma may be satisfactorily contained.

There are certain aspects of these decisions which
are troubling, however, precisely because they may
convey a different message to the police—a message
that searches and seizures that are basically unfair and
unwarranted will be upheld if they are masked by a thin
pretense of legality. The absence of awareness by the
majority in the *Robinson* case of the real danger of the
police using minor offenses of all sorts as pretexts for
illegal searches, particularly of members of groups they
don't like—blacks, Hispanics, hippies, vagrants, homo-

sexuals, insolent youngsters, and the like—is perhaps a
danger signal. Surely the Court could have addressed
itself more fully to the justification for opening rather
than simply "checking" Robinson's cigarette package;
to how customary full-custody arrests are for offenses
like Robinson's; to the limits of a search if only a
summons is given, and so forth. The Court sloughed off
the dissenters' protest that general rules are not
enough, and that a case-by-case approach is necessary;
but surely if a particular search is unreasonable, even if
technically within the rules, it should be considered on
its own merits. The rules set down in Robinson seem
sound enough—but as applied to this case they leave
some nagging doubts.

Not only *Robinson* but *Schneckloth* raises unresolved questions.(36) In some respects, *Schneckloth*
seems the easiest of the six cases. After all, Alcala *did*
consent to the search—or did he? Again the general rule
is sound enough, but the end result creates a situation
that does not quite ring true. How many persons alone
on a dark road with three armed policemen would say
anything but, "Sure, go ahead," when the policeman
said, "Mind if I look in your car?" Surely it is the
exceptional individual who would be secure enough
and well informed enough to say no. How realistic is it
to assume that the men named Gonzalez, Alcala and
Bustamonte, driving a shabby car, had a real choice?
Admittedly the facts of the case are difficult. As a
practical matter it is hard (and maybe impossible) to
enforce a rule that the police must inform a suspect
that he can refuse consent; but a recognition by the
majority of the inherent lack of credibility of this
particular situation would have made clearer the
Court's intent in upholding the power of the police.
Indeed, the singular insensitivity of the Burger Court
majority opinions to the civil liberties problems involved may be the primary target of the dissenters'
opinions. It is difficult to fault the holdings of the
Court, because they are technically correct; and the
purely legal arguments of the dissenters are not overly
persuasive. But these dissents are perhaps an appeal to
what Holmes called "the brooding spirit" of the law. If
justice is not only to be done, but to be seen to be done,
then the underlying intent of a decision, not simply the
decision itself, must be made explicit—and it is in this
area that the majority decisions are deficient.

To the surprise of much of the public which saw
the Warren Court as permissive, the Burger Court has
not markedly changed the substance of the criminal-
procedure decisions made by the Warren Court.
Despite its conservatism in this area, the Warren Court

nevertheless maintained a reasonable level of protection for the suspect. In the Burger Court, however, there have been small movements lowering this level, the significance of which remains to be seen.* The implementation of the ideal of ordered liberty is still elusive.

*The pessimism of the civil libertarians would

appear to be justified. On January 26, 1976, in U.S. *v.* Watson, the Court not only upheld a warrantless arrest where the police had time to obtain a warrant, but elected not to do so, and further held that the subsequent search incident to that arrest was based on the *uncoerced consent* of the suspect.

REFERENCES

1. 347 U.S. 483 (1954).
2. Engel v. Vitale 370 U.S. 421 (1962); School District v. Schempp 347 U.S. 203 (1963).
3. 374 U.S. 436 (1966).
4. Terry v. Ohio, 392 U.S. 1 (1968); Sibron v. New York (No. 63), 392 U.S. 40 (1968); Peters v. New York (No. 74), 392 U.S. 40 (1968). For an extended discussion of these cases see Wayne R. LaFave, "Street Encounters and the Constitution: Terry, Sibron, Peters and Beyond," *Michigan Law Review,* 67 (November 1968), p. 39.
5. 412 U.S. 291 (1973).
6. 412 U.S. 218 (1973).
7. 414 U.S. 218 (1963).
8. At the risk of stating the obvious, it should be noted that only legal *(de jure)* guilt is punishable under the American legal system. Legal guilt is guilt that has been established by certain delineated procedures relating to the various steps from accusation to sentence (e.g., arrest, arraignment, indictment, trial). When these procedures have been followed, the accused is said to have received due process of law. If they have not been followed, then be he ever so guilty in fact *(de facto),* he cannot be legally punished because he has not received due process of law.
9. In Mapp v. Ohio 367 U.S. 643 (1961) the U.S. Supreme Court applied the exclusionary rule to the state courts, i.e., illegally seized evidence was not permitted to be used at the trial. This rule had been in effect in federal courts since Weeks v. U.S. 232, U.S. 383 (1914). The rationale behind the exclusionary rule is the hope that the police will be deterred from making illegal searches and seizures if the fruits of such action cannot be used to secure convictions.
10. Section 180—a Code of Criminal Procedure (now Section 140.50 of the Criminal Procedure Law).
11. The Sibron case had a trial record so woefully inadequate as to lead Brooklyn District Attorney Aaron Koota to confess error before the U.S. Supreme Court and ask that the case be dismissed. The Court refused and decided the case on the basis of the arguments made before the New York Court of Appeals. Actually, at the trial, no stop-and-frisk argu-

ment was raised. The arresting officer (Martin) claimed probable cause. The defense was able to establish, however, that Martin had been unable to overhear Sibron's conversation. When Sibron admitted to incriminating conversation with his companions, the trial judge then ruled that the search was legal, apparently forgetting that Martin had not heard the incriminating conversation. The district attorney's office, faced with this trial error, salvaged the case on appeal by raising the stop-and-frisk issue. The judgment of the trial court was affirmed by the Appellate Division and by the New York State Court of Appeals without majority opinion. Judge Van Voorhis wrote a dissenting opinion, and Judge Fuld noted his dissent for reasons stated in his dissenting opinion in Peters v. New York, decided the same day as a companion case.
12. An organization formed in 1962 representing both police officials and prosecuting authorities that sponsored the Stop and Frisk Law.
13. However, in 1967 under the New Penal Code of New York State, Section 240.35, Subdivision 6, Loitering, the police may arrest a person under certain circumstances for merely refusing to answer the policeman's questions. This authority is independent of the Stop and Frisk Law.
14. People v. Rivera, 14 N.Y. 2d 441, 201 N.E. 2d 32 (1964).
15. Henry v. U.S., 361 U.S., 98 (1959).
16. People v. Rivera at 446.
17. 331 U.S. 145 (1947).
18. Warden, Maryland Penitentiary v. Hayden, 387 U.S. 294 (1967).
19. Terry v. Ohio at 13–14.
20. Even in important cases, where prosecution rather than information is the controlling consideration, the finding of contraband, for example, inevitably shifts the balance of forces against the suspect. Courts tend to rationalize the legality of police behavior when the results in terms of evidence prove the police to have been correct in their original suspicions. The norms of police organization also put pressure on the police to confiscate such harmful objects as narcotics or weapons, so that even if prose-

cution fails, the policeman feels that at least he has protected the community to the extent of removing dangerous commodities from circulation. Noteworthy is the increase in "dropsie" evidence since the Mapp decision. In all these instances, the penalty to the policeman for an illegal search is minimal—usually only the loss of a conviction—and certain positive goals have been achieved. *See* Jerome H. Skolnick, *Justice Without Trial* (New York: Wiley, 1966), chapter 10.

21. Peters v. New York at 66.

22. Peters v. New York at 74.

23. *See* a discussion of the entire problem of police judgment in relation to on-the-street encounters in Jerome H. Skolnick, *Justice Without Trial* (New York: Wiley, 1966), pp. 215–19.

24. Sibron v. New York at 73.

25. McCray v. Illinois, 386 U.S. 300 (1967).

26. Warden, Maryland Penitentiary v. Hayden, 387 U.S. 294 (1967).

27. Breithaupt v. Abram, 352 U.S. 432 (1957).

28. U.S. v. Wade, 388 U.S. 218 (1967).

29. Davis v. Mississippi, 89 S. Ct. 1394 (1969).

30. Berger v. New York, 388 U.S. 41 (1967).

31. Katz v. U.S., 389 U.S. 347 (1967).

32. Miranda v. Arizona (No. 759), 384 U.S. 436 (1966).

33. *See* James Vorenberg and James Q. Wilson, "Is the Court Handcuffing the Cops?" *New York Times Magazine* (May 11, 1969); Richard Ayres, "Confessions and the Courts." *Yale Magazine* (Alumni Publication, December 1968), p. 18.

34. *See* Jerome Skolnick, *Justice Without Trial* (New York: Wiley, 1966). Also, James Q. Wilson, *Varieties of Police Behavior* (Cambridge University Press, 1968) for a description of some of the realities of police operations.

35. University of Pittsburgh Law Review 655, Spring 1974.

36. Another case which raises civil libertarian hackles though technically defensible is *Cardwell* v. *Lewis* 94 S. Ct. 2464 (1974). In *Cardwell*, the subject Lewis was called into police headquarters for questioning in regard to a murder, some months after the commission of the crime and the initiation of the police investigation. When he appeared at 10 a.m. the police already had a warrant for his arrest, although Lewis was not arrested until 5 p.m. When he was arrested, Lewis was searched and his car keys and parking receipt for his car taken from him. The police then removed his car from the nearby commercial lot where it was parked, towed it to a police lot, and the next day took exterior paint scrapings and a tire mold. The evidence produced proved that Lewis's car was used in the murder.

It was conceded that the police had probable cause to seize and search the car. They did not, however, have a warrant, and the car was too remote physically from Lewis to be seizable incident to his arrest. The majority justified the search on the grounds that the Fourth Amendment protects the right of privacy, and Lewis had no right of privacy in the *exterior* of his car when it was parked in a public place. Further, since the police could have conducted the search on the spot, the removal of the car to the police lot was irrelevant. The dissenters brushed aside the privacy argument because for them the search was preceded by an illegal seizure. In the absence of a warrant, the police had no right to tow away the car.

Once again, the majority may be technically correct. A policeman with probable cause probably does not need a warrant to conduct this type of search of the exterior of a car in a public place, and perhaps it is substantively unimportant where the search was conducted. Yet, the record shows that the police could easily have obtained a warrant for the car prior to seizing it but failed to do so. It is the willingness of the Court to sanction without a qualm administrative shortcuts (or sloppiness) that are potentially very dangerous that makes the decision so unpalatable.

DOUBLE STANDARD—"There is a law for the poor and a law for the rest of us"—and, says the author, a judge, that means inequities in housing, employment and the ability to defend oneself in court.

Drawing by JAMES FLORA

The Policeman: *Must He Be a Second-Class Citizen*
with Regard to His First Amendment Rights?

I. Introduction

Today the policeman, as a public employee, stands in an uncertain position in relation to the exer-

SOURCE: *New York University Law Review*, 46 (May 1971), pp. 536–59.

cise of his fundamental rights of free speech and association. The traditional view that a public employee holds his position as a privilege subject to the conditions established by his employer, the state,(1) has been eroded.(2) Constitutional rights may be limited as a condition of public employment only where the restrictions are narrowly drawn, specific and directly related to a vital state interest.(3) Despite this new standard, however, the first amendment rights(4) of public employees have not as yet been clearly defined. With regard to policemen this problem is even more troublesome since their rights must be defined in relation to their arguably unique, paramilitary function.(5) Nevertheless, the difficulties in defining policemen's rights should not relegate their fundamental freedoms to a level of second-class citizenship.(6)

Although there is an extremely strong public interest in the preservation of efficiency and effectiveness within the police department,(7) this interest does not justify broad restrictions on the first amendment rights of a policeman as a public servant in a society which values free and open discussion and affiliation.(8) Faced with these two competing principles, courts have recently begun to determine the circumstances under which the first amendment rights of public employees may be limited by their governmental employer.(9) Most decisions in this area, however, have not defined in general terms the limitations which may be placed upon a public employee's first amendment rights, but have instead relied upon the particular facts of each case.(10) The purpose of this Note is to examine the role and structure of the modern police department and to determine how both the first amendment freedoms of policemen and the efficient functioning of the police department may be harmoniously preserved.

II. The Police Department as a Paramilitary Organization

Before reaching the question of the extent of permissible restrictions on the first amendment rights of policemen, it is advisable to examine the paramilitary nature of the police department. The argument that the first amendment freedoms of a policeman may be limited to a greater extent than those of other public employees stems from the fact that the police force is peculiarly dependent on strict and rigid discipline.(11) In *Muller* v. *Conlisk*,(12) the court noted that the need for internal discipline or any other characteristic which distinguishes policemen from other public servants would affect the balance which must be attained between the individual's right to exercise his first amendment freedoms and the government's interest in efficient and effective public service.(13)

The policeman is charged with the duty to protect life and property, prevent crime, detect and arrest offenders, preserve the public peace and enforce the laws, ordinances and administrative code provisions over which the department has jurisdiction.(14) No other public service is entrusted with as

vital a public trust as the enforcement of law and the preservation of order. Moreover, the police department, like the military, is one of the few types of employment entrusted with the legitimate use of lethal force.

Also, the police department structurally resembles a military organization. A police department has a hierarchy of command and jurisdictional division which by its very nature depends on discipline and obedience in order to perform police services.(15) In New York City, for example, there are twelve ranks of descending order, each of which is assigned limited and carefully enumerated powers and duties.(16) The stress laid on the responsibility of command and the importance of discipline denotes a structure and priority system very much like that found in the military.(17) It has been observed that a large proportion of policemen have had prior military experience when they join the police department and are suited to a system which stresses obedience to orders within a chain of command.(18) Just as the members of the military see themselves as a separate entity apart from civilians, so too, it is desirable for some purposes that policemen identify with their department.(19)

The Uniform Code of Military Justice prohibits numerous types of speech ordinarily enjoyed by civilians under the protection of the first amendment.(20) One article forbids soldiers from expressing "contemptuous words against the President" and other high government officials and bodies.(21) The prosecution of a soldier under this article for off-duty participation in an anti-Vietnam war demonstration in which he carried signs critical of governmental personnel and policy has been held not to violate any constitutional guarantee under the first amendment.(22) Moreover, the right to participate in picketing or other public demonstrations has been denied to soldiers when they should be present for duty, when they are in uniform, when they are on military reservations or in foreign countries, or when such activities breach law and order or may reasonably be expected to result in violence.(23) Despite these limitations the first amendment has been held to apply to members of the military.(24) The strong government interest in military discipline, however, has clearly stripped it of much of its effectiveness.

The government has an analogously strong interest in preserving efficiency and harmony in the police department by means of a paramilitary structure. Viewed from this perspective, the limitations which may be placed upon the first amendment rights of policemen should fall somewhere between those of other civilian public employees and those of the military. It is the purpose of the rest of this Note to attempt to define what those rights are and what they should be.

III. Critical Speech by Policemen

When the breadth of permissible restrictions on a policeman's first amendment rights is in issue in a case involving speech criticizing either his own department and superiors or more distantly removed governmental policies and personages, the balancing test set forth by the Supreme Court in *Pickering* v. *Board of Education*(25) should determine the outcome.(26) In *Pickering*, the Court, while dealing specifically with the issue of whether a teacher's public statements concerning a proposed local school board could be sanctioned by dismissal, addressed itself directly to the nature of the public employee's first amendment rights of free speech. The Court held that, absent a finding that the employee's statements were knowingly false or made with a reckless disregard of whether or not they were false, the school board could not discharge a public employee unless its interests as an employer in promoting efficient and effective services outweighed the interest of protecting the public employee's right to speak freely.(27) By employing a balancing test weighing these countervailing interests, *Pickering* unequivocally rejected the proposition that a public employee could be denied his first amendment rights by any regulation imposed by his employer.(28) However, the Court also refused to attempt formulation of a general standard by which all such cases might be decided because of the enormous variety of fact situations in which such an issue might be raised.(29)

Instead, the Court spelled out a number of matters of legitimate public interest against which it would be appropriate to balance the need for guaranteeing the public employee his first amendment rights. In reversing the board of education's dismissal of Pickering, the Court noted that his speech did not involve any injury to superior-subordinate relationships(30) or the necessary harmony among co-workers.(31) The Court also pointed out that there had been no issue of a breach of confidentiality which might otherwise furnish a permissible ground for dismissal.(32) Leaving unsettled any requirement that a public servant exhaust departmental grievance procedures before speaking out,(33) the Court went on to consider the possible harmful effect of Pickering's statements on the operation of the schools(34)

and on the performance of his daily duties in the classroom.(35) Furthermore, the Court felt that although the statements might have been entirely baseless, this fact was only an indication of the teacher's unfitness and not a separate ground for discharge.(36) Under *Pickering*, therefore, the government's right to restrict a public employee's speech will be upheld only where the former's interest as an employer outweighs the need to protect the individual's rights.(37)

In two recent cases, *Brukiewa* v. *Police Commissioner*(38) and *In re Gioglio*,(39) state courts have reversed disciplinary action taken against policemen who publicly criticized their departments in contravention of departmental rules. In each case, since the statements were not made with "actual malice," the telling factor was that the court could detect no appreciable effect on either the performance of the individual or the efficiency of departmental operations.(40) In a third case, *Meehan* v. *Macy*,(41) the Court of Appeals for the District of Columbia originally held, without pointing to any harmful effects on the police department, that the first amendment did not protect a police officer who sharply criticized by way of a defamatory poem the policies of the Governor of Panama under whom he served.(42) The court felt that this "conduct unbecoming a Police Officer"(43) was sufficient grounds for a dismissal. Subsequently, the same court, sitting en banc, vacated its opinion and remanded with orders that the case be reconsidered in light of the *Pickering* holding and rationale.(44)

In the most recent notable case, *Muller* v. *Conlisk*,(45) the Court of Appeals for the Seventh Circuit held that the regulation(46) which furnished a basis for disciplinary action against a policeman was unconstitutionally overbroad(47) and therefore, the court reinstated the policeman without analyzing the facts of the case by means of the *Pickering* approach. The court based its holding on the well-established doctrine that regulations which touch upon the exercise of first amendment freedoms must be narrowly and specifically drawn.(48) Reasonable restrictions of first amendment rights will be allowed but only where they are composed so as not to impinge upon those first amendment activities which may not be proscribed in light of a well-defined state interest.(49) This state interest must be directly related to the activity restricted, and the means employed by the state must specifically pertain to the activity to be curtailed.(50) Despite the court's reliance in *Muller* on the issue of overbreadth, it did indicate that the particular demands of the police department should be considered and might ultimately determine whether the policeman's speech could be limited.(51)

In examining the particular state interests to be weighed against a policeman's right of free speech, it must be remembered that the police department is a public service which relies upon a military structure.(52) The importance of maintaining discipline among policemen, therefore, is arguably much greater than in the case of public employees such as teachers or social workers. Furthermore, where cooperation and team work are very important, as they are in police work,(53) the conceivable impact of a statement upon the harmonious relationships of coworkers may have to be viewed with special consideration. Perhaps the strongest argument for the necessity of discipline and harmony in the ranks is the very nature of the role of the policeman. The police department, like the military, must perform duties which are singularly vital and dangerous, *i.e.*, the protection of life and property while enforcing the law. To some extent at least, therefore, a system within which there is great emphasis on efficient response to orders and little room for independent action must be maintained.

The second factor to be fed into the *Pickering* balance is any failure by a policeman to comply with established grievance procedures. Although the *Pickering* Court noted that it was not faced with a failure to utilize such procedures,(54) it would appear harsh to dismiss a policeman who failed to utilize available departmental grievance channels before making his criticism public since such a rule would penalize him for not bringing forth his complaint in a forum which may very likely be unsympathetic to his views. In many situations a policeman may be asked to bring his case before a departmental tribunal having close associations with the very target of his criticism. Fear of censure and the realization of the strong interest of police officials in existing policies and structures would severely restrict the possibility of any effective voicing of a critical or unpopular opinion. In *Meehan* v. *Macy*, where one of the charges upon which the state based its dismissal of a policeman was failure to comply with grievance procedures as ordered, the court refused to uphold the discharge on that basis and dismissed the charge.(55) Although the court eventually upheld the discharge, it did not base the decision on the policeman's disregard for the prescribed procedure, thus indicating that a policeman's failure to utilize the established grievance

procedure should not be dispositive of his first amendment rights.(56)

A third legitimate state interest, which might justify the restriction of a policeman's critical speech, is the requirement of loyalty or confidentiality in certain positions. The *Pickering* Court did not attempt to define the positions or types of information which create confidential relationships.(57) Nevertheless, the Court did indicate that such a relationship might be based on either the need to keep certain information within the confines of public employment or on the need to protect the confidences established between superiors and subordinates from being exposed to public criticism.(58) In a case where a policeman's first amendment right of speech may be restricted by an allegation of confidentiality, there should be a showing either that the relationship between the two parties was necessarily so close that criticism could not be tolerated without effectively destroying the essential mutual trust or that the critical speech released information which was of such a character as to require that access to it be limited to certain governmental officials.(59) However, in any case where the need for confidentiality exists, it should provide a basis for restricting the policeman's speech regardless of the veracity of his statements.(60) For example, a policeman who worked as an assistant to a chief inspector might be expected not to criticize his superior publicly if the subordinate's position were of such a nature that he was trusted and relied upon not to speak out publicly. In such situations, however, the nature of the confidential relationship should be well defined and the policeman's freedom of speech should not be restricted more broadly than necessary.(61)

Furthermore, where the speech indicates unfitness, such unfitness might furnish a separate ground for discharge. First, the baselessness of the statement may be evidence of the policeman's unfitness.(62) However, since every statement which is not entirely true might allow for an allegation of unfitness because of the speaker's lack of reliability, honesty and trustworthiness, such an allegation should be viewed skeptically by the courts.(63) In a case where the reliability of a policeman is really put in question because of his statement's lack of foundation, the statement should still be "merely . . . evidence of the [employee's] general competence, or lack thereof, and not an independent basis for dismissal."(64) Secondly, the content of the statement, or the qualities of the speaker evidenced therein, might well indicate a lack of fitness to perform one's duties as a policeman. In any such case, however, the burden should rest on the police department to show that the policeman is unfit not only by his statements but also by the effects of such statements or by other evidence bearing upon the policeman's ability to perform his duties. To base a discharge solely on a statement of the policeman without showing any undesirable effects of his speech might arguably be proscribed by the first amendment guarantee of free speech.(65) Moreover, where a policeman is alleged to be unfit the basis for such a charge should be clearly articulated and precisely defined.(66)

An illustration might be appropriate. A policeman who voices an opinion that blacks are racially inferior to whites could conceivably be charged with unfitness since his publicly expressed views are at odds with his responsibility of enforcing the law objectively and without prejudice. In enforcing the law, the policeman often makes decisions which are not subject to review by higher authority;(67) even within a paramilitary structure some informality is unavoidable.(68) The policeman's role as enforcer of the law thus becomes an extremely sensitive one since his daily decisions define the law, as it will be enforced, for the public.(69) Neutrality and freedom from bias are essential qualities for good policework.(70) Nevertheless, in order to protect the speaker, something more than the statement alone should indicate an inability to enforce the law fairly. If the policeman is truly unfit for his position, it should not be too difficult to substantiate the fact by evidence other than his own statements. Moreover, such a statement might not be protected under the *Pickering* balance test since the effect of such a statement on black coworkers might conceivably undermine the state's interest in smooth and effective police service.

With the exception of unfitness to perform one's duties, the mere finding of the existence of any of the above factors would not in itself be grounds for disciplinary action according to *Pickering*. The state interest in efficient police operations must be balanced against the need to protect the individual policeman in the exercise of his right of free speech. Although the *Pickering* rule is oriented towards the effect of the speech on the performance of the individual as a public servant and the operation of the public service,(71) it is unwise to concentrate only upon the harmful effect of a statement without balancing it against the corresponding need to protect

speech. The *Pickering* Court may well have placed too much stress on the entire issue of the disruptive effects of critical speech.(72) If *Pickering* really sets up a balancing test, the mere showing that speech has caused some disruption should not dispose of the issue; an evaluation of the need to protect the speech involved as well as of the extent of the disruption must be made.

It is therefore necessary to examine the factors which may contribute to the protection of a policeman's right of free speech. Besides the general consideration that this is a Nation based upon free and open debate and association,(73) there are several matters peculiarly significant to speech by policemen which should be taken into account when the need to protect their speech is evaluated.

First, the public has a strong interest in hearing a policeman's statements concerning his department. Where the speech is directed at matters closely related to his job, the policeman speaks as an expert with what is probably the best information available. Moreover, most issues of police policy and operations are matters of public concern. If these policies or operations are in need of change or investigation, the policeman's opinion is extremely relevant for the public's consideration.(74) Since the first amendment seeks to benefit the hearers rather than license the speaker,(75) the interest of the public in hearing what the policeman has to say would militate strongly in favor of protecting a policeman who speaks out on a matter of public concern which is closely related to his job.

The need for a constant dialogue between the police and the members of the community in which they work is another factor in favor of greater protection for the free speech rights of policemen. Today police-community relations have suffered greatly because of a feeling of alienation on the part of the community and a lack of trust in the policeman.(76) There is a vital need to involve the community in matters of police policy and operations; some have even suggested the local control of police forces in major urban areas.(77) In light of this fact and the general lack of intercourse between the community and the police, any unnecessary limitations upon the right of policemen to speak out may deprive the community of an important source of information and can only lead to further alienation.

Finally, where a policeman's speech is directed at matters other than the department itself, the interests involved in protecting his speech are similar to those associated with the speech of an ordinary citizen. *Pickering* seems to imply that the fact that the statements are not directed at a person with whom the speaker deals on a daily basis would tend to weigh in favor of protecting the speech.(78) Any disruption of superior-subordinate relations or harmony among coworkers which results from such speech may reasonably be presumed to be caused by the unpopularity of the viewpoint expressed. Since dissident and minority speech adds to the richness of political debate,(79) such speech by a policeman should be highly valued. This is especially important in a public service such as the police department where because most members share common backgrounds and attitudes(80) there is a great danger of repression of atypical views. This type of repression is analogous to that envisioned by Justice Black in *United Public Workers* v. *Mitchell*(81) with regard to the effect of partisan activity by superiors on the political activity of subordinate employees.(82) Although *Pickering's* concentration on the harmful effects of a public employee's speech may imply that the existence of this type of subtle but potent repression of dissident expression was not fully appreciated by the Court, that case may also be read to provide in its balancing test for those situations in which the right to entertain and voice unpopular opinions is so precious to our ideals of free speech that it outweighs any disruptive effect. The reaction of those sharing views prevalent among police superiors and the ranks should not be allowed to chill the rights of dissidents.

IV. Partisan Political Activity by Policemen

A. *Individual Activity*

The right of governmental employees to engage in political activity has been traditionally governed by the theory that a public employee takes his job subject to the reasonable conditions which his employer imposes upon the privilege of employment.(83) Although the Hatch Act(84) and its sweeping restrictions on the political activity of public employees was upheld by the Supreme Court in *United Public Workers* v. *Mitchell*,(85) there has been a very definite move away from permitting broad restrictions on the political activity of public employees.(86)

A significant new approach to the question of whether the state may proscribe the public employee's political activity is embodied in two California cases: *Bagley* v. *Washington Township Hospital District*(87) and *Fort* v. *Civil Service Commission*.(88) In reversing the discharges in both cases the California Supreme Court held that a state could not restrict political activity on a broad basis but rather could only regulate the conduct of public employees in order to prevent a specific evil.(89) Thus, while the political affiliation and partisanship of some public employees may threaten the integrity of the public service,(90) there is no reason to permit broadly drawn restrictions which deprive persons of their rights without cause.(91)

It has been suggested that political activity by public employees in policymaking positions might lawfully be curtailed because of the chilling effect of such activity on the first amendment rights of their subordinates.(92) On the other hand, individual political activity by the large majority of public employees whose positions do not involve the power to coerce subordinates should not be subject to such regulations.(93) The significant state interest in an impartial and efficient police force makes it highly desirable that political activity by members of the police force conform to such a standard. Moreover, the hierarchical structure of the police department would seem to make such a delineation between policymakers and other rank and file policemen both possible and practical.(94)

Existing police regulations, however, may go further than the above standard in limiting the individual political activity of policemen. For example, a New York City Police Department regulation forbids policemen, regardless of rank, from belonging to a political club or actively partaking "in the nomination or election of candidates for public office."(95) According to the policymaker rank and file standard, superior officers in the police department might legitimately be forbidden from belonging to a political party, taking part in primary or election campaigns, or contributing money to political funds.(96) Such activities on the part of policemen entrusted with making departmental policy might weaken the integrity of the police force by introducing political patronage and partisanship into those positions. Furthermore, the political activity of such officials might have a coercive or chilling effect on their subordinates in the department. However, independent contributions to a favored cause, mere membership in a political party or partaking in the organizational activity of our electoral processes by lower ranking policemen clearly would not present these dangers and should, therefore, not be restricted by the state.

Nevertheless, certain activities on the part of any policeman would constitute an abuse of the power entrusted to him and ought to be barred by the state. If a policeman's authority is used to punish or reward the political activity of another citizen, or to aid or impede a political party's activities,(97) such action should not be protected by the first amendment. Since such conduct would damage the integrity of our political process and the police department as a public service by unlawfully interfering with the exercise of the first amendment rights of other persons, it should be unequivocally proscribed.

Other political activity by policemen may also be offensive, irrespective of the policymaker rank and file standard. Because of the closeness of the police to the daily political processes and their frequent and conspicuous contact with the public, certain types of activity may constitute an abuse of a policeman's position of public trust and be detrimental to the efficient operation of his department.(98) The wearing of political symbols(99) while in uniform or the displaying of bumper stickers on departmental vehicles are typical examples of these abuses.(100) Although the first amendment freedom of speech is not limited to verbal modes of expression but also applies to nonverbal communication,(101) such activity clearly could and should be forbidden, since no public employee has the right to engage in activity otherwise protected by the first amendment where it interferes with the performance of his duties.(102)

When a policeman is in uniform as an objective enforcer of the law, his involvement in such forms of political expression could create antagonism between the police and public. It is vital that the police department be trusted by the public and not subject to doubt regarding potential partisanship. Moreover, a policeman who is in uniform and armed with lethal weaponry may have a coercive or threatening effect upon the views of members of the public if he is espousing a political view or preference. Not only fairness in substance but also fairness in appearance must be demanded. In addition, since there are alternative means of expressing the same message which do not impair police services, i.e., off-duty wearing of such symbols or verbal speech on these issues,(103) it does not seem overly restrictive to proscribe this type of on-duty symbolic speech. Thus, reasonable and narrowly drawn limitations upon the political activity of individual policemen applied in nondiscriminatory fashion should contribute to the elimination of the evils of partisanship in police departments without depriving the individual police-man of any significant aspect of his first amendment right of political activity.

B. Group Activity

In addition to individual political activity, group political activity by police organizations has recently raised some new problems. Organizations of patrolmen originally set up to serve as social organizations or labor unions have become conscious of their political potential and have provided the basis for the policeman's move into areas of municipal politics and social policy.(104) This organized political power has to date been exerted in three areas outside the realm of material benefits for policemen: First, groups have campaigned through their members to defeat proposals for civilian boards of review over police activity;(105) second, organizations have campaigned for or against certain candidates for political office;(106) and third, associations have acted as lobbies in the State and local legislatures with regard to certain policies and programs.(107)

Although there does not appear to be any legitimate basis upon which organized activity by patrolmen concerning ballot measures and lobbying efforts may be regulated, partisan political activity is arguably distinguishable.(108) Organized partisan activism by patrolmen poses a danger that policemen may become a force capable of controlling the city governments which should in fact control them.(109) The nature of the problem is the potential damage to the political and electoral processes which might result from a coalition of the members of a large, organized, paramilitary group with one or more political parties. For this reason it may be advisable for the state to forbid or limit political expenditures and contributions of organizations of patrolmen in connection with partisan state or municipal elections. Such a regulation would eliminate the possibility of holding an election in an atmosphere of coercion created by the active support of a political party by an organization whose members are skilled in the use of lethal force. In drafting such a law, the State legislature could prohibit any contribution or expenditure in connection with any partisan election at the local or state level(110) by a police organization without affecting the policeman's right to individually contribute to favored causes. Alternatively, it could limit such spending by police organizations to that amount voluntarily contributed for such purposes by its members.(111)

There is ample precedent for governmental regulation of partisan political activity by patrolmen's organizations. Labor unions are prohibited from making a "contribution of expenditure in connection with" federal elections,(112) and this restriction has been upheld by the Supreme Court.(113) It has been observed that in the context of political activity there may be good reason to distinguish the nature and power of the speaker for purposes of the first amendment.(114) Since an entity with large aggregate resources presents different dangers, it is arguable that its rights should be more restricted than those of the individual.(115) While it is not suggested that individual members of a union should be restricted from contributing money to partisan political campaigns, the collective power and resources of a union may provide the basis for regulation in order to prevent "subversion of the integrity of the electoral process"(116) and "to sustain the active, alert responsibility of the individual citizen in a democracy for the wise conduct of government."(117)

V. The Right of Association for Policemen

In examining the first amendment rights of policemen, the question of whether a policeman may engage in political activity through affiliation with or membership in organizations which advocate a particular political or social ideology must be considered. Certain organizations may desire social or political results which are totally inconsistent with the role of a policeman.(118) Conduct in furtherance of such goals may well indicate that the policeman presents a danger to the operation and administration of the police department against which the government should be able to guard.

The extent to which the government may limit the freedom of association of public employees has been the subject of several Supreme Court decisions. In *Adler* v. *Board of Education*(119) the Court upheld the constitutionality of a New York statute(120) which prohibited state agencies from employing past or present members of the Communist Party.(121) The basis for the Court's holding was that public employees had no right to work for the state unless they submitted to the conditions which the employer had placed upon their employment.(122) In *Keyishian* v. *Board of Regents*,(123) however, the Court repudiated that theory by declaring unconstitutional the same statute which the *Adler* case had upheld.(124) In *Elfbrandt* v. *Russell*,(125) the Supreme Court held that a law which discrim-

inates with regard to public employment on the basis of membership in an organization, without requiring either a showing of active participation or specific intent to further the illegal ends of the organization, "rests upon the doctrine of 'guilt by association' which has no place" in our constitutional system.(126) Therefore, statutes touching upon the freedom of association must be narrowly drawn so as to define and punish only specific conduct which constitutes a "clear and present danger" to a strong governmental interest.(127) Mere affiliation is not enough to be the basis for an exclusion from public employment; rather, disloyalty on the part of the individual, shown by proof of specific intent or active participation to further the illegitimate ends of the organization, must be demonstrated.(128)

In *United States* v. *Robel*, the Court found a statute which had made it unlawful for members of the Communist Party to be employed in areas involving national defense to be unconstitutionally overbroad.(129) Thus, even the fact that an employee was to be engaged in a function as sensitive as national defense has been deemed to be insufficient to support a statute which employs broader means than are necessary to accomplish its ends.(130) Indeed, in *Stapp* v. *Resor*,(131) a United States district court held that the mere association of a member of the armed forces with the Communist Party did not furnish a basis for other than an honorable discharge where there was no evidence that it interfered with his military duties.(132) It would seem that in light of these cases the state may only refuse to employ or discharge those persons whose intent to further the unlawful or subversive aims of organizations poses a threat to the state or makes them unfit for public employment.

Undoubtedly, there are strong reasons for weeding out those individuals whose political commitments make them unsuitable for employment in a police force. First, the police are entrusted with the legitimate use of force.(133) Second, the nature of the policeman's duties in maintaining order and enforcing the law makes police work an area of great public trust.(134) Nevertheless, in light of the applicable decisions,(135) it does not appear that even knowing association with an organization can form a foundation for discharge from the police department. Despite the sensitivity of police work, a danger to the government would only be present when the individual policeman specifically intended or acted to further the illegitimate ends or means of the organization to which he belonged. Even the unique character of the police department does not allow for restrictions of a person's rights of association beyond those justified by the unfitness of the policeman(136) or a vital and well-recognized state interest.(137) Where such a situation exists all restrictions must be precisely drawn within the holding of *Elfbrandt*.

An examination of typical police regulations regarding membership in organizations by policemen, however, does not reveal this to be the case. The types of affiliation barred by police regulations are often only vaguely outlined by departmental regulations.(138) Restrictions are sometimes phrased in terms that exclude membership in all organizations which would interfere with or prevent the performance of police duties.(139) They may also be more specific, barring "knowing association" with groups fostering oppression of or prejudice against racial or religious groups.(140) A regulation like the former, if construed as to bar membership only where the policeman is shown to be unfit to perform his duties, would raise no problem since it is clear that unfit personnel have no right to remain in government service. The latter type of restriction might also be defensible if it were construed to exclude unfit policemen since the state has a strong interest in maintaining a police department free of racial tension and prejudice. However, in either instance more than mere membership would be required to prove unfitness under the *Elfbrandt* rule.

Where regulations touching upon the exercise of first amendment rights are drawn broadly there are three problems. First, as previously discussed, they may be unconstitutional.(141) Secondly, because of difficulties in applying such regulations, they may not be enforced.(142) Thirdly, such regulations may be applied discriminatorily. Regarding the last problem, a significant danger may arise if some associations are tacitly approved,(143) while others of equal or less danger to efficient police service are prohibited because they are offensive to police administrators or the rank and file of the department. Since the personnel of police departments are drawn largely from similar backgrounds and certain prejudices are commonly shared and predominate throughout most

urban police departments,(144) nonconformity is ordinarily viewed with little tolerance.(145) This attitude toward unorthodox or unpopular views and affiliation may well lead to serious repression of minority views.(146)

It should be noted that even narrowly drawn regulations do not necessarily safeguard the rights of the unorthodox policemen. The policeman seeking to exercise his first amendment right of association may be faced with retaliatory dismissals and disciplinary action based upon broad general charges such as insubordination(147) or upon the selective enforcement of certain rules normally not enforced against other policemen. In such cases, although the policeman is clearly being sanctioned for engaging in activities offensive to the common attitudes of police officials, he may not be given the opportunity to raise the issue of his first amendment rights.(148)

VI. Conclusion

In a legal system which is based upon the concept of a free and open dialogue for the achievement of political and social changes desired by the people, restrictions upon the ability of a class of persons to partake in that exchange should be tolerated only if justified by an equally strong countervailing interest. The considerable interest of the government as an employer in providing public services which are efficient and fairly administered has been deemed sufficient to require that the need to preserve individual rights be weighed against it. Although in the case of policemen the state's interest as an employer may be stronger than with any other civil servant because of overriding importance of policemen's duties, the unique nature and structure of the police department should not cause a wholesale forfeiture of their first amendment rights. Hopefully, in the future, policemen will be allowed to participate in the free exchange of ideas envisioned by the first amendment to the greatest degree possible and will be restricted only where the interest in effective, efficient and objective police services demands it.

REFERENCES

1. *See*, e.g., McAulliffe v. Mayor of New Bedford, 155 Mass. 216, 220, 29 N.E. 517–18 (1892), where Justice Holmes spoke in terms of the nonexistence of a right to public employment:

The petitioner may have a constitutional right to talk politics, but he has no constitutional right to be a policeman. There are few employments for hire in which the servant does not agree to suspend his constitutional right of free speech as well as of idleness by the implied terms of his contract. The servant cannot complain, as he takes the employment on the terms which are offered him. On the same principle the city may impose any reasonable condition upon holding offices within its control.

A long line of cases followed in which courts held that public employees forfeited their first amendment rights by accepting their positions. See, e.g., People ex rel. Clifford v. Scannell, 74 App. Div. 406, 77 N.Y.S. 704 (1st Dep't 1902), aff'd per curiam, 173 N.Y. 606, 66 N.E. 1114 (1903); Commonwealth ex rel. Rotan v. Hasskarl, 21 Pa. Dist. 119 (Phila. C.P. 1912). In Duffy v. Cooke, 239 Pa. 427, 86 A. 1076 (1913), the court held that city employees could be discharged for violating a statute prohibiting political expression since the city could expect the most loyal service from its employees. The condition of abstention from certain political activity was said to be part of the service for which the employee was paid. Id. at 441, 86 A. at 1081.

2. In recent years this theory has been rejected. See, e.g., Pickering v. Board of Educ., 391 U.S. 563 (1968); Keyishian v. Board of Regents, 385 U.S. 589 (1967); Meehan v. Macy, 392 F.2d 822 (D.C. Cir. 1968), vacated upon rehearing, 425 F.2d 472 (1969) (per curiam). In Meehan the court, remarking that the "constitutional climate of today is different from that of 1892 when Justice Holmes struck off his oft-quoted phrase," specifically refused to apply Holmes' reasoning in McAuliffe. 392 F.2d at 832.

3. See, e.g., Keyishian v. Board of Regents, 385 U.S. 589 (1967); Wieman v. Updegraff, 344 U.S. 183 (1952); Muller v. Conlisk, 429 F.2d 901 (7th Cir. 1970); Bagley v. Washington Township Hosp. Dist., 65 Cal. 2d 499, 421 P.2d 409, 55 Cal. Rptr. 401 (1966).

4. While the first amendment expressly limits the power of the Federal Government, the due process clause of the fourteenth amendment has been held to incorporate the first amendment guarantees so that these rights are now protected against actions by State governments as well. Gitlow v. New York, 268 U.S. 652 (1925).

5. See text accompanying notes 11–19 infra.

6. The Supreme Court has stated that policemen should not be "relegated to a watered down version of constitutional rights." Garrity v. New Jersey, 385 U.S. 493, 500 (1967).

7. In society's day to day efforts to protect its citizens from suffering, fear and property loss produced by crime . . . the policemen occupies the front line. It is he who directly confronts criminal situations, and it is to him that the public looks for personal safety. The freedom of Americans to walk their streets and be secure in their homes . . . depends to a great extent on their policemen.
President's Comm'n on Law Enforcement and Administration of Justice, The Challenge of Crime in a Free Society 92 (1967).

8. This principle has been accepted regarding the first amendment rights of public employees. See, e.g., Pickering v. Board of Educ., 391 U.S. 563 (1968) (teacher); Keyishian v. Board of Regents, 385 U.S. 589 (1967) (teacher); Muller v. Conlisk, 429 F.2d 901 (7th Cir. 1970) (policeman); Bagley v. Washington Township Hosp. Dist., 65 Cal. 2d 499, 421 P.2d 409, 55 Cal. Rptr. 401 (1966) (nurse's aide).

9. See cases cited in note 8 supra.

10. See, e.g., Pickering v. Board of Educ., 391 U.S. 563, 569 (1968), where the Court refused to lay down a rule generally applicable to the formulation of a fixed standard but rather discussed a list of general guidelines "along which an analysis of the controlling interests should run." See text accompanying notes 29–37 infra.

11. Muller v. Conlisk, 429 F.2d 901, 904 (7th Cir. 1970). The court noted that defendant's brief attempted to distinguish Pickering v. Board of Educ., 391 U.S. 563 (1968), by pointing out that policemen are different from teachers in that there is a need for a paramilitary structure and rigid internal discipline to guarantee effective police service. 429 F.2d at 904.

12. 429 F.2d 901 (7th Cir. 1970).

13. Id. at 904. See Brukiewa v. Police Comm'r, 257 Md. 36, 263 A.2d 210 (1970); In re Gioglio, 104 N.J. Super. 88, 248 A.2d 570 (Middlesex County Ct. 1968).

14. See, e.g., New York City Police Department Rules and Procedures ch. 1, ¶ 1.0 [hereinafter N.Y.C. Police Rules].

15. Id. ch. 1. This chapter outlines the chain of command, assignment of duties and responsibilities and the jurisdictional division of the department.

16. Id. ¶ ¶ 16.0–.5.

17. See id. ¶ ¶ 14.0–.3.

18. S. Asch. Police Authority and the Rights of the Individual 33 (1967).

19. 10 Nat'l Comm'n on the Causes and Prevention of Violence, Law and Order Reconsidered 300 (staff study report 1969). While it may be true that the "we-they" identity of the police has some undesirable aspects, such as creating hostility between the police and the community, the nature of the policeman's job requires that a group identity be preserved to some extent in order to guarantee that the police force will be respected as an effective and objective law enforcement agency by the community. Id.

20. The articles of the Uniform Code of Military Justice [hereinafter UCMJ] which limit the freedom of speech of members of the military are: art. 88, which prohibits the use of contemptuous language "against the President, the Vice President, Congress, the Secretary of Defense...." and other Government officials, 10 U.S.C. § 888 (1964); art. 89, which prohibits disrespectful behavior toward a superior, id. § 889; art. 91, which forbids the use of contemptuous language against noncommissioned officers, id. § 891; art. 117, which bars the use of "provoking or reproachful words" against other persons under the jurisdiction of the code, id. § 917; and arts. 133 and 134, which broadly and generally proscribe "conduct unbecoming an officer and a gentleman," id. §§ 933, 934.

21. UCMJ art. 88, 10 U.S.C. § 888 (1964).

22. United States v. Howe, 17 U.S.C.M.A. 165, 37 C.M.R. 429 (1967).

23. U.S. Army Reg., No. 600–20, ¶ 46 (Jan. 31, 1967).

24. *See*, e.g., United States v. Howe, 17 U.S.C.M.A. 165, 37 C.M.R. 429 (1967); United States v. Wysong, 9 U.S.C.M.A. 249, 26 C.M.R. 29 (1958); United States v. Noriega, 7 U.S.C.M.A. 196, 21 C.M.R. 322 (1956); United States v. Voorhees, 4 U.S.C.M.A. 509, 16 C.M.R. 83 (1954). Commentators have also recognized that the first amendment applies to soldiers. *See* Quinn, The United States Court of Military Appeals and Individual Rights in the Military Service, 35 Notre Dame Law, 491 (1960); Warren, The Bill of Rights and the Military, 37 N.Y.U.L. Rev. 181 (1961).

25. 391 U.S. 563 (1968).

26. *See*, e.g., Muller v. Conlisk, 429 F.2d 901, 903 (7th Cir. 1970).

27. 391 U.S. at 572–74. The Court in *Pickering* did not afford public employees threatened with the sanction of discharge the same protection that it had afforded the speech of the general citizenry in New York Times Co. v. Sullivan, 376 U.S. 254 (1964). In *New York Times* the Court ruled that in civil libel cases liability for statements critical of public officials attached only upon a showing that the statement was "made with 'actual malice,' that is, with knowledge that it was false or with reckless disregard of whether it was false or not." 376 U.S. at 279–80. This standard of protection was later also applied in a case of criminal libel. Garrison v. Louisiana, 379 U.S. 64 (1964). *Pickering*, however, qualified the application of the *New York Times* rule by first weighing the respective interests of the state against those of the citizen's freedom of speech. 391 U.S. at 568–73.

28. 391 U.S. at 568.

29. Id. at 569.

30. Id. at 570.

31. Id.

32. Id. at 570 n.3.

33. "There is ... no occasion furnished by this case for consideration of the extent to which teachers can be required by narrowly drawn grievance procedures to submit complaints ... to their superiors for action thereon prior to bringing the complaints before the public." Id. at 572 n.4.

34. Id. at 573.

35. Id.

36. We also note that this case does not present a situation in which a teacher's public statements are so without foundation as to call into question his fitness to perform his duties in the classroom. In such a case, of course, the statements would merely be evidence of the teacher's general competence, or lack thereof, and not an independent basis for dismissal.

Id. at 573 n.5. It is arguable not only that the fact that a statement was baseless but also that the content of the statement might indicate an unfitness to be a public employee. *See* text accompanying notes 55–59 infra.

37. In any case where the interest of the government in preserving efficient and effective public services does not outweigh the need to protect the individual's speech, the only remaining issue is whether the *New York Times* rule protects the speech, i.e., whether the statements were made with actual malice. 391 U.S. at 574.

The balancing test, adopted by the Court in *Pickering* to take account of the state's interest in maintaining a public service free from disruption, with discipline and harmony among coworkers, has been criticized as overly stressing the effect of one's speech. Id. at 582–84 (White, J., dissenting in part). *See* Note, The First Amendment and Public Employees: *Times* Marches On, 57 Geo. L.J. 134, 150–56 (1968). The author criticizes the *Pickering* Court's "overwhelming emphasis upon effectiveness" of the speech and the implication that "only ineffective speech is constitutionally protected." Id. at 155. Such a result-oriented approach to first amendment questions is not unusual since the traditional "clear and present danger" test is also based on the effect of one's speech yet it is a well-established principle of constitutional law. *See* Dennis v. United States, 341 U.S. 494 (1951); Abrams v. United States, 250 U.S. 616 (1919) (dissenting opinion); Schenck v. United States, 249 U.S. 47 (1919).

38. 257 Md. 36, 263 A.2d 210 (1970).

39. 104 N.J. Super. 88, 248 A.2d 570 (Middlesex County Ct. 1968).

40. 257 Md. at 52–57, 263 A.2d at 218–20; 104 N.J. Super. at 98–99, 248 A.2d at 575–76.

41. 392 F.2d 822 (D.C. Cir. 1968).

42. Id. at 834.

43. Id. at 828.

44. 425 F.2d 472 (D.C. Cir. 1969).

45. 429 F.2d 901 (7th Cir. 1970).

46. The rule governing the speech of policemen on matters of police business prohibited policemen from "engaging in any activity, conversation, deliberation, or discussion which is derogatory to the Department or any member or policy of the Department." Id. at 902.

47. Id. at 903–04.

[I]t is clear that the First Amendment would reach and protect some speech by policemen which could be considered "derogatory to the department." Rule 31 on its face prohibits all such speech, even private conversation, and is for that reason unavoidably overbroad in violation of the First Amendment as it applies to the states through the Fourteenth Amendment.

Id. at 904.

48. The court in *Muller* stated that "because First Amendment freedoms need breathing space to survive, government may regulate only with narrow specificity." Id. at 903, citing Cantwell v. Connecticut, 310 U.S. 296, 311 (1940).

49. *See*, e.g., Keyishian v. Board of Regents, 385 U.S. 589 (1967); Elfbrandt v. Russell, 384 U.S. 11 (1966); NAACP v. Button, 371 U.S. 415 (1963); Talley v. California, 362 U.S. 60 (1960); Whitney v. California, 274 U.S. 357 (1927).

50. *See* cases cited in note 49 supra. There are two different approaches to the issue of overbreadth. Under the narrower view a statute may be judged overly broad on the basis of its application to the specific case. If its application to the facts of the instant case infringes upon constitutionally protected activity the statute is unconstitutional. *See*, e.g., Whitney v. California, 274 U.S. 357 (1927). According to the newer approach, on the other hand, a statute may be judged to be void because it has been drafted so as to touch to some extent upon legitimate expression or association regardless of its application to the facts of the case. *See*, e.g., Talley v. California, 362 U.S. 60 (1960). It is primarily the latter approach which is of concern in the area of policemen's first amendment rights.

51. 429 F.2d at 904.

52. *See* text accompanying notes 14–19 supra.

53. President's Comm'n On Law Enforcement and Administration of Justice, Task Force Report: The Police 53 (1967). The nature of the police work and the need for using the full resources available indicate that not only is there a need for cooperative work among those in the same division of the department but also between detective and uniformed divisions. A lack of coordination and team-

work means a waste of resources or a duplication of effort. Id.

54. *See* text accompanying note 33 supra.

55. 392 F.2d 822, 838 (D.C. Cir. 1968), vacated upon rehearing, 425 F.2d 472 (1969). While in this case the court was not dealing with what might literally be described as a formal grievance procedure, the policeman was ordered to gain permission to publish comments and so in effect had to bring his grievances before his superiors before making them public. Id. at 838.

56. *See* Watts v. Seward School Bd., 391 U.S. 592 (1968) (per curiam). The Court was faced with a case in which the discharge of two teachers was based on a failure to comply with grievance procedures within their school boards. It remanded the case for reconsideration in light of *Pickering*. Id. Apparently the Court did not feel that the fact that the teachers did not follow the prescribed grievance procedures was sufficient to warrant upholding the discharge.

57. *See* text accompanying note 32 supra.

58. 391 U.S. at 570 n.3.

It is possible to conceive of some positions in public employment in which the need for confidentiality is so great that even completely correct public statements might furnish a permissible ground for dismissal. Likewise, positions in public employment in which the relationship between superior and subordinate is of such a personal and intimate nature that certain forms of public criticism of the superior by the subordinate would seriously undermine the effectiveness of the working relationship between them can also be imagined.

Id.

59. The Freedom of Information Act places restrictions on what matters of information a government agency may keep from the public. 5 U.S.C. § 552 (Supp. V, 1970). While that statute has no immediate application to the police department, its listing of nine exemptions from the government agency's duty to disclose information upon request to the public includes exemptions for investigatory files compiled for law enforcement purposes, id. § 552(b)(7), and an exemption for privileged or confidential matters given to the agency by others under an implied promise of secrecy, id. § 552(b)(4). Moreover, the Act exempts personnel rules and practices, id. § 552(b)(2), and also matters relating to personnel or medical files or the like containing intimate details, the revelation of which would be an invasion of privacy, id. § 552(b)(6). *See* generally Note, Freedom of Information: The Statute & The Regulations, 56 Geo. L.J. 18 (1967). Such standards as those provided by the Freedom of Information Act are not ultimately helpful in formulating a definition of confidentiality. It is probably useful only in suggest-

ing some areas which might be treated as such so long as the public employee is informed of this duty of confidentiality.

60. Pickering v. Board of Educ., 391 U.S. 563, 570 n.3 (1968). *See* Meehan v. Macy, 392 F.2d 822 (D.C. Cir. 1968), where the court justified the dismissal of a police officer on the basis of a finding that he had breached a duty of confidentiality which he owed the Governor of Panama whose policies he had criticized. It does not appear that the policeman was told of his duty of loyalty nor what subjects were to be treated as confidential. Rather, the court broadly used the concept of breach of confidentiality in justifying the dismissal. Subsequently, the court, sitting en banc, remanded the case for retrial in light of *Pickering.* 425 F.2d 472 (D.C. Cir. 1969) (per curiam).

61. But *see* N.Y.C. Police Rules, Supra note 14, ch. 2, ¶ 6.0. Under this broad regulation all matters of official business of the police department are to be treated as confidential and can only be spoken about under limited conditions.

> The policeman shall not talk for publication nor be interviewed nor make public speeches or statements on police business. He shall not give information about the official business of the department to any one except:
>
> a. Under due process of law
> b. With permission of the Police Commissioner
> c. As authorized by these Rules and Procedures
> d. A representative of the press . . . shall be advised of current news if the ends of justice are not defeated. . . .

Id. Other narrow exceptions are made regarding information about arrests, current news and information requested by the City Department of Personnel if the commanding officer feels such information is necessary. Id. No exception seems to permit the policeman to speak out on matters of police policy or operations. Id.

62. *See* text accompanying note 36 supra.

63. *See* Note, The First Amendment and Public Employees: *Times* Marches On, 57 Geo. L.J. 134, 152–53 (1968).

64. Pickering v. Board of Educ., 391 U.S. 563, 573 n.5 (1968).

65. Id. *Pickering* does not elaborate on what is meant by saying that the teacher's statements would merely be evidence of his general competence or incompetence and not an independent basis for discharge. However, if a statement itself formed the sole basis for a discharge there would be a serious problem whether this could be allowed in light of the first amendment guarantee of free speech. In the area of labor relations, Congress has balanced an employer's right of free speech against an employee's

right not to be coerced in the exercise of his rights under § 7 of the National Labor Relations Act, 29 U.S.C. § 157 (1964), by providing that:

> The expressing of any views, argument or opinion or the dissemination thereof, whether in written, printed, graphic or visual form, shall not constitute . . . an unfair labor practice under any of the provisions of this Act, if such expression contains no threat of reprisal, or force or promise of benefit.

Id. § 8(c), 29 U.S.C. § 158(c) (1964).

66. Realistically, it would be impossible to discuss every quality which a capable policeman should possess. In general, however, they can be defined in terms of three well-organized categories of duties: first, peace keeping; second, providing assistance and services for the public; and third, combatting crime by enforcing the law. *See* 10 Nat'l Comm'n on the Causes and Prevention of Violence, Law and Order Reconsidered 306 (staff study report 1969). *See* generally J. Wilson, Varieties of Police Behavior (1968) [hereinafter Wilson, Police Behavior]; O. Wilson, Municipal Police Administration (1961).

67. 3 Nat'l Comm'n on the Causes and Prevention of Violence, The Politics of Protest 202 (staff study report 1969) [hereinafter The Politics of Protest].

68. Id. *See* generally Wilson, Police Behavior, supra note 66. Even within rigid hierarchies of command, the policeman often works independently where his ad hoc decisions may determine police policy.

69. *See*, e.g., W. LaFave, Arrest: The Decision to Take a Suspect into Custody (1965).

70. *See*, e.g., The Politics of Protest, supra note 67, at 183–201. This discussion concludes that racial prejudices and hostility toward students and other young people is a major cause of the recent escalation of police-protester violence. See 10 Nat'l Comm'n on the Causes and Prevention of Violence, Law and Order Reconsidered 301 (staff study report 1969).

72. *See* text accompanying notes 30–36 supra.

73. *See*, e.g., New York Times Co. v. Sullivan, 376 U.S. 254, 270 (1964), quoting Whitney v. California, 274 U.S. 357, 375–76 (1927) (Brandeis & Holmes, J.J., concurring):

> Those who won our independence believed . . . that public discussion is a political duty; and that this should be a fundamental principle of the American government. . . . Believing in the power of reason as applied through public discussion, they eschewed silence coerced by law—the argument of force in its worst form. Recognizing the occasional tyrannies of governing majorities, they amended the Constitution so that free speech and assembly should be guaranteed.

74. The opinion of a policeman on matters of

police service would be just as valuable to the public as a teacher's opinion on a matter concerning the school system. In *Pickering* the Court said:

> Teachers are, as a class, the members of a community most likely to have informed opinions as to how funds allotted to the operation of the schools should be spent. Accordingly, it is essential that they be able to speak out freely on such questions without fear of retaliatory dismissal.

391 U.S. at 572.

75. A. Meikeljohn, Political Freedom 20–26 (1960). "What is essential is not that everyone shall speak, but that everything worth saying shall be said." Id. at 20.

76. *See* 10 Nat'l Comm'n on the Causes and Prevention of Violence, Law and Order Reconsidered 298–304 (staff study report 1969).

77. The Politics of Protest, supra note 67, at 217.

78. 391 U.S. at 569–70.

79. *See* note 75 supra.

80. Asch. supra note 18, at 35.

81. 330 U.S. 75 (1947).

82. Id. at 113–14 (Black, J., dissenting in part).

83. *See* note 1 supra.

84. Act of August 2, 1939, ch. 410, 53 Stat. 1147 (as amended and codified in scattered sections of 5, 18 U.S.C.). The Hatch Act prohibits "person(s) employed in the executive branch of the Federal Government" from actively partaking "in the political management or in the political campaigns." 5 U.S.C. § 118(i)(a) (1964).

85. 330 U.S. 75 (1947).

86. *See* text accompanying notes 2–3 supra.

87. 65 Cal. 2d 499, 421 P.2d 409, 55 Cal. Rptr. 401 (1966).

88. 61 Cal. 2d 331, 392 P.2d 385, 38 Cal. Rptr. 625 (1964).

89. 65 Cal. 2d at 507–08, 421 P.2d at 415–16, 55 Cal. Rptr. at 407–08; 61 Cal. 2d at 337–38, 392 P.2d at 389, 38 Cal. Rptr. at 629. In *Fort*, the court said:

> The principles set forth in the recent decisions do not admit of wholesale restrictions on political activities merely because the persons affected are public employees, particularly when it is considered that there are millions of such persons. It must appear that restrictions imposed by a government entity are not broader than are required to preserve the efficiency and integrity of its public service.

61 Cal. 2d at 337–38, 392 P.2d at 389, 38 Cal. Rptr. at 629. The same reasoning was used by Justice Douglas in his dissent in United Public Workers v. Mitchell, 330 U.S. 75, 115 (1947).

See id. at 111 (Black, J., dissenting in part), where Justice Black focused not only on the deprivation of the right of the individual but also the damage done to the public at large by removing many citizens from the scene of political activity:

> Legislation which muzzles several million citizens threatens popular government, not only because it injures the individuals muzzled, but also because of its harmful effect on the body politic in depriving it of the political participation and interest of such a large segment of our citizens.

90. *See* United Public Workers v. Mitchell, 330 U.S. 75, 115 (1947) (Douglas, J., dissenting). Justice Douglas sees partisan political activity on the part of higher ranking officials as threatening to the efficiency and integrity of government service:

> [T]hose who give continuity to administration, those who contribute the basic skill and efficiency to the daily work of government, and those on whom the new as well as the old administration is dependent for smooth functioning ... are the core of the civil service. If they are beneficiaries of political patronage ... serious results might follow.... Public confidence in the objectivity and integrity of the civil service system might be so weakened as to jeopardize the effectiveness of administrative government. Or it might founder on the rocks of incompetency, if every change in political fortunes turned out the incumbents, broke the continuity of administration, and thus interfered with the development of expert management.... Or if the incumbents were political adventurers or party workers, partisanship might color or corrupt the processes of the administration of law....

Id. at 121–22.

91. Id. at 120. Douglas distinguishes those in policymaking positions from the "industrial workers" whose job in no way affects policy and whose political activity does not pose any threat to the efficiency or integrity of the government service in which they work. Id.

92. Note, The First Amendment and Public Employees—An Emerging Constitutional Right to be a Policeman?, 37 Geo. Wash. L. Rev. 409, 421 (1968).

93. *See* id.

94. Those persons in the police department whose rank confers upon them executive duties, the power to issue orders and broad administrative authority, or the duty to advise the Police Commissioner, are clearly involved in the making of policy for the department. These ranks have the power and authority to act on a department-wide basis and so their duties are not defined in terms of supervision or administration of assigned precincts. See generally N.Y.C. Police Rules, supra note 14, ch. 1, ¶ ¶ 2.0–15.0. The following ranks are positions of depart-

ment-wide command: Police Commissioner, id. ¶ 2.0; Chief of Planning, id. ¶ 3.0; Deputy Commissioners, id. ¶ ¶ 5.0–11.0; Chief Inspector, id. ¶ 12.0; Chief of Detectives, id.; Chief of Staff, id ¶ 13.0. All of the above ranks and deputy chief inspectors and inspectors of divisions may issue orders pursuant to ¶ 15.0. Captains in the police department may be assigned to act in higher capacities; otherwise, captains act as commanders of precinct units, squads, bureaus or offices which the Police Commissioner feels are important enough to warrant the assignment of a captain. Id. ¶ 16.1. Since captains may be detailed to act in higher ranks, it seems reasonable that they should be treated as members of the administration and not as members of the rank and file and, therefore, be subject to the same restrictions as those ranks listed above. The duties and responsibilities of lieutenants, sergeants, patrolmen and policewomen, on the other hand, while they may involve some administration, are much more limited. Therefore, there is no significant relationship between policy-making and those who serve in the lower ranks. Id. ¶ ¶ 16.2–.4.

Taking the New York City Police Department as an example, therefore, those persons serving in the rank of police captain or above should be distinguished from those below captain for purposes of restricting political activity. Of course, there may be variations among the several police departments in terms of the duties and responsibilities of certain ranks; nevertheless, these general guidelines should provide a workable standard for distinguishing between administrators and the rank and file among policemen.

95. N.Y.C. Police Rules, supra note 14, ch. 2, ¶ 8.0.

96. In New York State, for example, it is a misdemeanor for any police commissioner, officer or any member of a police force within the State to "contribute any money, directly or indirectly to . . . or [become] a member of any political club . . . or committee." N.Y. Elections Law § 426 (McKinney Supp. 1970). Applied to those members of the force in ranks of captain or above, this statute would serve a very useful purpose. See note 94 supra. Read literally, however, it seems needlessly restrictive of the rights of lower ranking policemen and may arguably be unconstitutionally overbroad. See text accompanying notes 48–50 supra.

97. N.Y. Elections Law § 426 (McKinney 1970) provides in part that it is a misdemeanor for any police commissioner, officer or policeman to use or attempt to use "his official power or authority . . . directly or indirectly, in aid of or against any political party . . . or society, or to control, affect,

influence, reward or punish, the political adherence . . . action . . . or opinion of any citizen. . . ." It also subjects any person who "appoints, promotes, transfers, retires or punishes an officer or member of a police force, or asks for or aids in" such misconduct "because of the party adherence or affiliation of such officer or member" or "for or on request . . . of any political party . . . or society, or of any officer . . . or representative official or otherwise of any political party . . . or society" to conviction for a misdemeanor. Id.

98. The Politics of Protest, supra note 67, at 213.

99. For the purposes of this Note there is no need to distinguish between such symbols as campaign buttons, i.e., expressions of a party preference, and more amorphous symbols, such as peace buttons or even American flags, which may well connote the same sort of political bias and present the same problems to the policeman's ability to exercise his freedom of speech.

100. The Politics of Protest, supra note 67, at 213.

101. See, e.g., Tinker v. Des Moines Independent Community School Dist., 393 U.S. 503 (1969); Brown v. Louisiana, 383 U.S. 131 (1966); Stromberg v. California, 283 U.S. 359 (1931). In Kaufman, The Medium, The Message and the First Amendment, 45 N.Y.U.L. Rev. 761, 778–79 (1970), the author discusses the cases cited in this footnote and other nonverbal speech in relation to the first amendment.

102. The Court in *Pickering* indicated that their holding might have been different had there been a showing or reason to presume that the teacher's statements had "impeded the teacher's proper performance of his daily duties. . . ." 391 U.S. at 572. See London v. Florida, 313 F. Supp. 59 (N.D. Fla. 1970), where the court held that the state as an employer could discipline, by transfer, a social worker whose activities in the community interfered with his effectiveness in performing his duties.

See N.Y.C. Police Rules, supra note 14, ch. 2, ¶ 8.0. This rule, which forbids expressions of political or partisan views which concern "the immediate discharge of his [the policeman's] duties," is legitimate if it is meant to prohibit expression of political views while a policeman is on duty. The permissible target of the rule would include not only oral expression but also button wearing or placing bumper stickers on police department vehicles.

103. See text accompanying notes 78–82 supra.

104. The Politics of Protest, supra note 67, at 208–13.

105. Id. at 208–09.

106. Id. at 210–11.

107. Id. at 212–13.

108. It does not seem reasonable to argue that the political activity of groups of patrolmen concerned with nonpartisan ballot measures or proposals as to departmental policy should be restricted beyond limitations which apply to individual on-duty activity. The policeman or police group has a strong interest in such matters and likewise the public has a right to hear what those persons have to say. It is important not to limit discussion beyond necessity in a society based on the concept of a free interchange of ideas. See text accompanying notes 73–77 supra. Furthermore, whether this sort of activity is carried on by organized groups or not, there is no danger of subversion of the electoral process as there is where the group activity is directed at partisan political matters.

109. See The Politics of Protest, supra note 67, at 212–13.

110. See, e.g., Taft-Hartley Act § 304, 18 U.S.C. § 610 (1964), which provides in part that "it is unlawful . . . for any corporation whatever, or any labor organization to make a contribution or expenditure in connection with any election at which Presidential and Vice-Presidential electors or a Senator or Representative in, or a Delegate or Resident Commissioner to Congress are to be voted for. . . ."

111. This type of regulation would be more in line with the present construction of the Taft-Hartley Act § 304, 18 U.S.C. § 610 (1964); see note 104 supra. This statute has been held to be inapplicable to direct contributions or expenditures from that part of membership dues voluntarily paid and explicitly declared by the individual members of a labor organization to be intended for political purposes. United States v. Teamsters Local 688, 47 L.R.R.M. 2005 (D. Mo. 1960).

112. Taft-Hartley Act § 304, 18 U.S.C. § 610 (1964).

113. United States v. UAW, 352 U.S. 567 (1957). Although the Court avoided the first amendment question, id. at 592, it has not to date found the statute unconstitutional. But see id. at 593–98 (Douglas, J., dissenting).

114. Ruark, Labor's Political Spending and Free Speech, 53 Nw. U.L. Rev. 61, 73–75 (1957). The author points out that even assuming that corporations and labor unions are entitled to the protection of the first amendment the potentially massive expenditures on the part of these large entities may be a consideration to be weighed in determining the constitutionality of restrictions on political spending. Id. at 73–74.

115. There are three traditional reasons which apply to police organizations for limiting the partisan political activity of an organization to a greater extent

than that of its individual members. First, police organizations usually have greater amounts of money available to them than any individual policeman. Second, the contributions of a police group, if publicized, have the effect of an official endorsement which may have a significant effect on the formation of public opinion. Third, if a police organization is entitled to spend funds for political purposes as it wishes, or as the majority of its members decide, there is a danger of the repression and denial of the rights of minority members who do not wish to contribute to causes with which they do not sympathize. This final point is discussed in the context of labor organizations in Ruark, supra note 114, at 70–72, 77.

116. United States v. UAW, 352 U.S. 567, 569 (1957).

117. Id.

118. While it is difficult to formulate a definition of what kinds of association this activity encompasses, it seems that not only the Communist Party but also groups such as the Ku Klux Klan, the Minutemen, the John Birch Society and the Black Panthers might be included.

119. 342 U.S. 485 (1952).

120. The Feinberg Law, N.Y. Laws ch. 360, § 3 (1949), as amended, N.Y. Laws ch. 681, § 1 (1953). This law was declared unconstitutional in Keyishian v. Board of Regents, 385 U.S. 589 (1967); see text accompanying notes 123–24 infra.

121. The Feinberg Law incorporated by reference the following language of Civil Service Law § 12-a, N.Y. Laws ch. 564 (1940), which provided that: "Any person who becomes a member of any . . . group of persons which teaches . . . that the government of the United States . . . shall be overthrown by force or violence, or by any unlawful means [shall be] dismissed or declared ineligible" from any public employment.

122. It is clear that [public employees] have the right . . . to assemble, speak, think and believe as they will. It is equally clear that they have no right to work for the State. . . . They may work . . . upon the reasonable terms laid down. . . . [Or] they are at liberty to retain their beliefs and associations and go elsewhere. . . .
342 U.S. at 492. See text accompanying note 1 supra.

123. 385 U.S. 589 (1967).

124. The constitutional doctrine which has emerged since Adler has rejected its major premise. "That premise was that public employment . . . may be conditioned upon the surrender of constitutional rights which could be abridged by direct government action." Id. 15 605.

125. 384 U.S. 11 (1966).

126. Id. at 19.

127. Id. at 18.

128. *See* text accompanying note 126 supra.

129. 389 U.S. 258, 266 (1967).

130. *See* text accompanying notes 48–50 supra.

131. 314 F. Supp. 475 (S.D.N.Y. 1970).

132. Id. at 479.

133. The Politics of Protest, supra note 67, at 213. The report considers the fact that the "police have a practical monopoly on the legal use of force" as the primary basis for the traditional concern over politicization within the police department. Id.

134. *See* text accompanying notes 14–15 supra.

135. *See* text accompanying notes 125–32 supra.

136. *See* Murphy, "Academic Freedom—An Emerging Constitutional Right," 28 Law & Contemp. Prob. 447, 465–66 (1953), where after discussing a number of loyalty oath cases and the issue of subversive associations, the author concludes that the key issue in deciding whether such activities are grounds for dismissal is the relevance of the activities to the employee's fitness to perform the duties of his position.

137. *See* Israel, Elfbrandt v. Russell: The Demise of the Oath?, 1966 Sup. Ct. Rev. 193, 219, where the author outlines the significant state interests commonly advanced to justify disqualification of individuals from public employment on the basis of membership in "subversive" organizations. The interests of the state are: (1) the elimination of the potential for sabotage, spying or other activities directly harmful to security; (2) the elimination of persons likely to be unfit or untrustworthy; (3) the elimination of persons undeserving of public employment by reason of their hostility to the basic tenets of the Government.

138. *See* Asch, supra note 18, at 33–34.

139. *See* e.g., N.Y.C. Police Rules, supra note 14, ch. 2, ¶11.0. This type of regulation may well be constitutionally overbroad in that it does not clearly define those associations which are prohibited. The policeman seeking to comply with such a mandate would have a difficult time determining which associations would be forbidden. *See* text accompanying notes 48–50 supra.

140. *See*, e.g., N.Y.C. Police Rules, supra note 14, ch. 2, ¶14.0. This regulation might well be subject to challenge if it were constructed to sanction mere membership and did not conform to the standard laid down in *Elfbrandt*. *See* text accompanying notes 120–22 supra.

141. *See* text accompanying notes 48–50, 124–30 supra.

142. *See* Asch, supra note 18, at 33. In Nassau County, New York policemen are not permitted to join any group that is either subversive or political. Even apart from the issue of the unconstitutional overbreadth of the rule, pragmatically such a rule may result in nonenforcement since it is impossible to determine what types of association are proscribed. Id.

143. Id. In Boston, New York City and Chicago, membership in the John Birch Society is permitted and never questioned by police officials although arguments could be made concerning the desirability of employing such persons. On the other hand, membership in black solidarity groups has not always met with such silent assent. Id. See note 147 infra.

144. *See*, e.g., A. Niederhoffer, Behind the Shield: The Police in Urban Society (1967); J. Skolnick, Justice Without Trial (1966); Levy, Cops in the Ghetto: A Problem of the Police System, Am. Behavioral Scientist, Mar.-Apr. 1968, at 31–34. Various studies reveal a high degree of prejudice towards blacks. Levy, supra at 31–34.

145. *See* Politics of Protest, supra note 67, at 194–97.

146. *See* text accompanying notes 75–76 supra.

147. One example of this type of abuse has been reported in which a black policeman has been subtly persecuted for his beliefs and associations. Since becoming one of the organizers of the Afro-American Patrolmen's League in Chicago, he has been suspended from his job five times. Prior to this incident he had been awarded more than 50 citations for outstanding police work. He may even be dismissed on pending charges of insubordination. While a formal dismissal proceeding may not provide the opportunity to raise an issue of first amendment rights, the effect is the same as if he were being discharged for his association with an unpopular group. *See* Time, Nov. 23, 1970, at 13.

148. Since he is not being discharged for any improper exercise of his first amendment right but rather on the basis of other charges, a policeman in such a situation may find it difficult to raise the issue and then to prove that the discharge was a restriction of his right of association. During dismissal proceedings the department would most likely present evidence of misconduct or unfitness based on incidents unrelated to the policeman's affiliations or political conduct which, whether they are true or not, could be difficult to rebut. The policeman would therefore have to defend his case on the basis of the charges against him; thus, he might not be able to raise the first amendment as a defense to the disciplinary sanction.

Confessions and the Court

RICHARD AYRES

Crime and the courts have become major political issues in the United States for the first time since the 1930s. Not since then have politicians been so clamorously united in their determination to "do something" about the "wave of crime" said to be sweeping the country; and probably never before have the courts—and in particular the United States Supreme Court—been held responsible for creating the problem in the first place.

Critics of the recent criminal law decisions of the Supreme Court—including members of Congress and Presidential candidates—have argued again and again that the Court has altered the balance in criminal cases to favor lawbreakers against the police. However, despite the concern, there have been few serious attempts to determine what impact the Court's decisions in the past decade have actually had on the administration of criminal justice. Have the Courts *actually* been guilty of limiting the effectiveness of the police?

During the summer of 1966, I participated along with nine other law students in a study of the impact on the New Haven police department of one of the more controversial of these decisions, *Miranda* v. *Arizona*.

The *Miranda* decision, which requires a policeman to advise a suspect of his constitutional rights before any interrogation, provoked heavy criticism from law enforcement officials and some judges and legal commentators. These critics said it would reduce significantly the capacity of the police to control crime. They believed that most suspects, if told of their rights, would either remain silent or call a lawyer who would immediately advise them to remain silent; and that, as a result, the police would be unable to obtain statements from suspects and would be substantially handicapped in enforcing the law. Our findings in New Haven, a city with a rather typical police department and crime pattern, controverted these contentions completely.

SOURCE: *Yale Alumni Magazine* (December, 1968).

To learn how *Miranda* affected interrogations, we stationed observers in New Haven's police headquarters 24 hours a day, seven days a week, for an 11-week period. With the cooperation of the police, the observers were able to witness personally all the interrogations conducted during this period. We also interviewed all participants in the criminal process—detectives, lawyers, prosecutors, and suspects. (To test whether our presence in the police station affected the detectives' behavior towards suspects, we also interviewed some 40 suspects who had been interrogated during the months immediately preceding and following our study. Their descriptions of the interrogation process tallied remarkably well with the descriptions given by our observers.)

It is important to realize that the *Miranda* decision, like many of the controversial Supreme Court decisions, is primarily concerned with the *procedure* the police must follow in investigating crime, rather than with the underlying rights of the suspect. Basically, *Miranda* attempts to insure that a person suspected of a crime will be fully aware of his legal rights before he decides whether to answer questions in an interrogation. Before questioning, the decision says, the policeman must inform the suspect: (1) that anything he says may be used against him; (2) that he has the right to remain silent under questioning; (3) that "he has the right to consult with a lawyer and to have the lawyer with him during interrogation"; and (4) that if he is indigent, "a lawyer will be appointed to represent him."

To assure that the police will inform the suspect and will respect his rights if he chooses to assert them, the opinion requires that "If the individual indicates in any manner, at any time prior to or during questioning, that he wishes to remain silent, the interrogation must cease." Furthermore, it provides a penalty if the policeman fails to abide by these rules—any information obtained cannot be admitted into evidence against the suspect in a trial.

Despite these rules, the *Miranda* decision had virtually no effect on police investigation in New Haven. One major reason is that interrogations are simply not very important in police work. After each of the interrogations we observed, we discussed with the detective the information he had obtained, and asked what other information he had in addition to that which developed through interrogation. We also asked him whether *he* thought that the interrogation had been necessary in the case. The answers to these questions showed that interrogation played a minor role in gathering evidence for the typical criminal case. In only a tiny minority of the cases did the detective say that the interrogation was necessary to gain enough information for a conviction. And our independent assessment, based upon the detectives' answers to our other questions, generally agreed.

The reason for this seeming anomaly is simple. The police in New Haven, like those in most cities, seldom make an arrest unless they already have substantial evidence in hand. Most crimes for which arrests are made are actually committed in the presence of witnesses or a policeman, and the testimony of either is usually sufficient to insure conviction without any "confession."

For most crimes in which there is no witness—crimes such as burglary—the police seldom arrest anyone, because once the perpetrator has fled there is virtually no way to discover his identity. The police cannot simply interrogate everyone found in the neighborhood. Nor can the police discover burglars and the like through the kind of scientific sleuthing portrayed so often on television. In the first place, the manpower resources necessary for serious scientific crime solution are far beyond anything now available (or foreseeable) for the New Haven police or any other American police department. The analysis of finger-prints from a single burglary, for example, might well take an entire day of work by a laboratory technician. Given the value of the property stolen in an average burglary, it is doubtful whether such an investment of time would even be economically justifiable.

Furthermore, the kind of clues which would be amenable to scientific analysis are found in only a small minority of cases. Fingerprints, to use the common example again, are rarely left in a condition which offers any hope that laboratory analysis will produce identification. Few materials will take a good set of fingerprints, and most fingerprints found are smudged or mixed hopelessly with those of innocent people. It is therefore hardly a surprise that we saw only one case in which fingerprints were used to identify a burglar.

In brief, the police can seldom arrest someone for a crime unless there is a witness who can identify the criminal. If the police have this sort of evidence, they do not need to interrogate the suspect, and, on the whole, if they do not have this kind of evidence, they cannot make an arrest.

Interrogations may, however, serve other purposes than producing evidence for use against a suspect. The police told us they sometimes interrogate a suspect to learn the names of accomplices to a crime, or to gather general intelligence about criminal activity in the city. But we saw only a few cases in which the efforts of the police to learn about accomplices might have been curtailed by their desire not to trespass against *Miranda.*

As to the gathering of intelligence about criminal activity, we could only speculate because we never saw interrogation used for this purpose. However, the only reason forcing a policeman to give the *Miranda* warnings is that otherwise the information he gathers will not be admitted into evidence at a trial. Since the policeman uses the general information he collects to increase his chances of preventing crimes and making arrests, rather than to convict a particular suspect, there seems no reason why he need give the *Miranda* warnings if he merely wishes to obtain general intelligence.

But what of the interrogations we saw conducted? Did *Miranda* hinder the police in these interrogations? At least in New Haven, the answer to this question is a strong "no."

In the first place, the police simply did not comply with the decision in many cases. Despite the presence of our observers, the detectives gave all the warnings required by *Miranda* to only 20 percent of the suspects we saw questioned. Most of the suspects were told of their right to silence, but few of their right to counsel. Some of the failure to give the warnings may have been because the decision was still new when we were in the stationhouse; the detectives' performance did improve as the summer progressed.

When the warnings were given, the detectives invented a number of ways to nullify their effect. Most detectives hedged somewhat. Some changed the warnings slightly: "Whatever you say may be used *for* or against you in a court of law." Often detectives incorporated some inconsistent qualifying remarks in their statement, such as "You don't have to say a word, but you ought to get everything cleared up," or "You don't have to say anything, of course, but can you explain how. . ."

Even when detectives informed suspects of their rights without undercutting devices, the advice was often defused by implying that the suspect had better not exercise his rights, or by delivering the statement in a formalized, bureaucratic tone to indicate that the remarks were simply a routine, meaningless legalism. Instinctively, perhaps, detectives tended to create a sense of unreality about the *Miranda* warnings by bringing the flow of conversation to a halt with the statement, ". . . and now I am going to inform you of your rights." Afterwards, they would solemnly intone: "Now you have been warned of your rights," then immediately shift into a conversational tone to ask, "Now would you like to tell me what happened?" By and large the detectives regarded advising the suspect of his rights as an artificial imposition on the natural flow of interrogation.

In the few cases in which a suspect showed an interest in finding a lawyer and did not already know one, the police usually managed to head him off simply by not helping him locate someone. Sometimes they refused to advise the suspect whether he should have a lawyer with him during questioning, but more often they merely offered him the telephone book without comment, and that was enough to deter him from calling a lawyer.

Nor did the detectives abide by *Miranda's* injunction that questioning must cease if the suspect indicates he does not want to continue. From the suspect's point of view, this aspect of *Miranda* is probably more important than the warnings, yet on the whole the detectives did not even feel constrained to inform him that they would stop if requested. Most of the suspects were too passive to try to end the questioning on their own. But the majority of those few who did try were coaxed into talking anyway.

In general, the detectives' compliance with this aspect of the *Miranda* requirements was closely related to the seriousness of the crime and the amount of evidence available prior to questioning. Whenever detectives were dealing with a less serious crime or had sufficient evidence to insure the suspect's conviction, they were likely to allow him to end the questioning at his wish. But they were unlikely to let him terminate questioning when they thought additional information would help wrap up a conviction for a serious crime.

The compliance with this part of the *Miranda* decision did not increase during the summer as the detectives became more familiar with the new ruling. This finding contrasts sharply with our discovery that warnings of rights were given more often as the summer progressed, perhaps because the detectives began to realize subconsciously that suspects could be advised of their rights with no effect on the subsequent interrogation.

The refusal of the police to abide by the *Miranda*

rules cannot be attributed to the effects of the warnings upon the suspects, for the suspects hardly ever reacted to the words of the policemen, even when the warnings were fully given. Whatever the critics of *Miranda* had expected, the suspects did not refuse to talk, nor did they call in lawyers to help them.

We ran a number of statistical tests to determine whether people who received warnings were less likely to talk than those who did not. By any measure of a "successful" interrogation we could devise, the police were as successful with those who received warnings as with those who did not. In our estimation, warnings were a factor in reducing the success of interrogation *in any way at all* in only about 10 percent of the cases that we evaluated.

This conclusion is hardly surprising in view of our impression of the process of interrogation. In the first place, although most of the interrogations we saw were not intimidating, they were engineered to discourage any initiative on the part of the suspect. Most of the suspects apparently could not grasp the significance of the warnings. They seemed unable really to understand that the object of the policeman's questions was to gather evidence in order to put them in jail.

Furthermore, most suspects seemed to feel compelled by the circumstances to say something, and the police were usually successful in getting them to talk until they contradicted themselves. At that point the detectives could almost always induce the suspect to make some kind of incriminating statement.

Finally, a number of suspects seemed to think they could escape blame by talking to the police. For example, suspects in assault cases would often describe the fight while blaming some other participant for starting it. In most cases, the suspect succeeded only in supplying enough information to assure his own conviction.

Virtually none of the suspects called lawyers to help them, despite their undisputed legal right to. We are therefore quite confident that, contrary to early predictions, *Miranda* did not bring droves of lawyers to the stationhouse to "interfere" with the interrogation process.

Since practically no lawyers appeared at the stationhouse, we had to interview a number of them in the city in order to learn what they *would have* advised if they *had* been called to the stationhouse. These interviews turned up several further surprises for the critics of the *Miranda* decision. Most of the lawyers felt that their presence in the stationhouse would not have altered the outcome of a later trial. The police usually had overwhelming evidence of guilt when an arrest was made, the lawyers said, and thus the suspects generally had little choice but to plead guilty.

A client could, of course, plead not guilty regardless of the evidence against him, but in New Haven, as elsewhere, the defendant who goes to trial and loses—particularly with a foolish or outlandish defense—risks a far more severe sentence than one who pleads guilty. A lawyer could change none of these circumstances, and so defendants would continue to plead guilty, lawyer or no lawyer.

Contrary to our expectations, the lawyers did not even unanimously feel that they would counsel a suspect to say nothing to the police. Most said that upon arrival at the stationhouse they would tell their client to "say nothing while I size up the situation." And most said they would normally advise a client against making a statement at the time of arrest. However, more than two-thirds said that in many instances they would advise the suspect to answer questions. Depending on the suspect's age, the crime he was charged with, the circumstances of the offense, and the strength of the evidence in the hands of the police, they felt that cooperation with the authorities might help a client. In short, it appears that Mr. Justice Jackson, who once wrote, "Any lawyer worth his salt will tell the suspect in no uncertain terms to make no statement to the police under any circumstances," was incorrect; a good lawyer would look to the overall best interests of his client and counsel him accordingly.

The one significant effect of the *Miranda* decision which we did find was psychological: the decision disturbed the police greatly. Most of them saw *Miranda*, along with other Supreme Court decisions in the past ten years, as a slap in the face.

Some of them seemed to think the Court was trying to take the enjoyment from their work. They told us that the "battle of wits" between detective and suspect is the most interesting and exciting part of a detective's job. As one detective put it, "I particularly like sparring with suspects. It is a great challenge. Getting a suspect to talk gives one a sense of real accomplishment." These men complained that the Court's decisions have destroyed much of the pleasure in interrogation. According to one, "Interrogating used to be fun, but now with all these court rules there's not much point in it anymore. They are now *interviews*, not interrogations."

But most detectives reacted with more hostility to the *Miranda* decision. Their feelings seemed to spring from a basic distrust of courts and lawyers. New Haven detectives see their job as a thankless one already, and they believe courts and lawyers are making it even more

difficult. To a man, they believe that crime is becoming a more serious problem and that morality is declining, and they see themselves as the embattled "thin blue line" protecting society from its own follies. They cannot understand why the Supreme Court impedes them in doing their job as they think best. The only explanation imaginable to many detectives is that the Justices do not understand the crime problem ("Let one of the judges' daughters get raped or mugged and then see what they do"), or that the Justices are either Communists or Communist-sympathizers.

Our data and impressions from New Haven converge to a single conclusion: Despite the dark predictions by critics, the impact of the *Miranda* decision has apparently been negligible. This is true for two reasons. First, interrogations are simply not very important in solving crimes. Second, the *Miranda* rules, even when applied (as they often are not) affect interrogations only slightly because the police can still question suspects virtually at will.

How, then, shall we assess *Miranda*, and how does our assessment bear on the current furor over the criminal procedure decisions of the Supreme Court? I think our study shows, on the one hand, that too much energy has been wasted claiming the Court has "swung the balance in favor of the criminal." On the other hand, it also illustrates the Court's powerlessness to protect the rights of citizens in the face of determined opposition from other institutions, such as the police.

The stated objectives of the *Miranda* decision were to assure that suspects were informed of their legal rights and that they would be allowed to exercise them if they chose to. Yet the only penalty the Court could impose for violations of its rules was that information gathered illegally could not be admitted into evidence at a trial. But as we learned in New Haven, this penalty seldom has any operational meaning, because the police usually have ample evidence to convict without a confession.

Then why did the Court promulgate the *Miranda* rules? I think the police have perceived the meaning of *Miranda* accurately. The decision was a last-ditch effort by the Court to control the conduct of the police. It reflects the Court's dismay at the inability or lack of desire of other social institutions to oversee the police. The Court has had ample evidence in the cases which have come before it over the last 35 years that policemen are often all too willing to engage in manifestly unfair behavior.

Numerous studies, beginning with the massive Wickersham Commission Report of the early 1930s, have documented police practices which no citizen would feel were fair if they were applied to him. Yet there has been little sign that state legislatures, city governments, or police departments themselves are willing to take effective action to assure that all citizens are treated fairly and equally by policemen.

Decisions such as *Miranda* also reflect the paucity of devices which the court has to "police the police." Unlike a local police chief, the Supreme Court cannot fire or fine an officer who refuses to abide by the law of the land. The only weapon—a pitifully weak one—is to deprive him of one of the objects of his labors if he refuses to implement the law as he was sworn to. This is a roundabout, undesirable, and ineffective method of disciplining police forces.

The *Miranda* decision should provoke neither strong attack nor strong defense, but rather a strong and effective commitment to overhauling our police forces so that the Court will not feel the need for future *Mirandas*.

Does Punishment Deter Crime?

GORDON TULLOCK

Traditionally there have been three arguments for the punishment of criminals. The first of these is that punishment is morally required or, another way of putting the same thing, that it is necessary for the community to feel morally satisfied. I will not discuss this further. The two remaining explanations are that punishment deters crime and that it may rehabilitate the criminal. The rehabilitation argument was little used before about 1800, presumably because the punishments in vogue up to that time had little prospect of producing any positive effect upon the moral character of the criminal.(1)

But with the turn to imprisonment as the principal form of punishment—a movement which occurred in the latter part of the 18th and early part of the 19th century—the idea that the prison might "rehabilitate" the prisoner became more common. The word "penitentiary" was coined with the intent of describing a place where the prisoner has the time and the opportunity to repent of his sins and resolve to follow a more socially approved course of action after his release. The idea that prisons would rehabilitate the criminal and that this was their primary purpose gradually replaced the concept of deterrence as the principal publicly announced justification for the punishment system. I should like to defer discussing my views as to why this occurred until the latter part of this article, but here I should like to point out that, whatever the motive or the reason for this change, it certainly was not the result of careful scientific investigation.

So far as I have been able to discover, there were no efforts to test the deterrent effect of punishment scientifically until about 1950. At that time, several studies were made investigating the question whether the death penalty deterred murder more effectively than life imprisonment. These studies showed that it did not, but they were extremely primitive statistically. This is not to criticize the scholars who made them. Computers were not then readily available, the modern statistical techniques based on the computer had not yet been fully developed, and, last but by no means least, the scholars who undertook the work were not very good statisticians. Under the circumstances, we cannot blame them for the inadequacies of their work, but neither should we give much weight to their findings.

Moreover, even if it were the case that the death penalty did not deter murder, it would not automatically follow that deterrence does not work in general. The argument is frequently made that life imprisonment is actually a more severe punishment than the death penalty and it might turn out to be true—at least in the eyes of potential murderers. If this were the case, then one would anticipate that life imprisonment would have a greater deterrent effect than would

SOURCE 103–111   *The Public Interest, 36* (Summer 1974), pp.

execution. But in any event, the findings obtained in these early studies were largely the result of their very primitive statistical techniques.

Statistically testing deterrence is not easy because the prospect of punishment obviously is not the *only* thing that affects the frequency with which crimes are committed. The crime rate varies with the degree of urbanization, the demographic composition of the population, the distribution of wealth, and many other circumstances. Some statistical technique is necessary to take care of these factors—and such techniques are now available. Using multiple regression (or, in a few cases, a complicated variant on the Chi-Square test), it is possible to put figures on each of these variables into the same equation and to see how much they influence the dependent variable which, in this case, is the rate of a specific crime. Although there are difficulties, this procedure will give a set of numbers called coefficients that are measures of the effect of *each* of the purported causative factors on the rate of commission of the given crime. If punishment deters crime, it will show up in these figures as a coefficient that is both significant and negative. A number of other things in the equation may also show up as affecting the crime rate, but the purpose of this article is to discuss only whether *punishment* does or does not deter crime.

One of the basic problems with any kind of statistical research in the field of criminology is the appallingly poor quality of the data. Any study will have a great deal of what the statistician calls "random noise" in it. Most of the studies mentioned below use the FBI's *Uniform Crime Reports* statistics, and almost all of the authors have made comments about how bad these statistics are. I am happy to say that the Law Enforcement Assistance Administration has begun a project aimed at a sharp improvement in crime statistics, and hence we can anticipate that such research will be a great deal easier in the future. All of the studies I will report are based on the earlier and poorer statistics, but in about a year or so there should be a new generation of studies drawing upon the much better data that will be available at that time.

The recent studies in deterrence come partly from economists and partly from sociologists. As an economist myself, I may be pardoned for starting with the economic studies, but I should say that, due to the long delay that intervenes between research and publication, it is not at all obvious which discipline actually had priority.

Most economists who give serious thought to the problem of crime immediately come to the conclusion that punishment will indeed deter crime. The reason is perfectly simple: Demand curves slope downward. If you increase the cost of something, less will be consumed. Thus, if you increase the cost of committing a crime, there will be fewer crimes. The elasticity of the demand curve, of course, might be low, in which case the effect might be small; but there should be at least *some* effect.

Economists, of course, would not deny that there are other factors that affect the total number of crimes. Unemployment, for example, quite regularly raises the amount of crime and, at least under modern conditions, changes in the age composition of the population seem to be closely tied to changes in the crime rate. The punishment variable, however, has the unique characteristic of being fairly easy to change by government action. Thus, if it does have an effect, we should take advantage of that fact.

The 19th-century utilitarians had drawn this conclusion, and when economists in the 1950's and early 1960's began turning their attention to the problem of deterrence, this rather simple application of economic theory was one of the first things that occurred to them.(2) The first econometric test of this theoretical deduction from economics was performed by one of Gary Becker's graduate students, Arleen Smigel Leibowitz, in her Master's thesis.(3) The basic design of this research project was reasonably sophisticated, although, as can be seen below, it has been improved upon since then. Leibowitz used as her basic data the crime rate and the punishment for a number of different crimes in each state in the United States. She took into account both the severity of punishment (i.e., the average prison sentence) and the probability that punishment will actually be imposed (i.e., the percentage of crimes whose perpetrators are caught and sent to prison). A number of essentially sociological factors that might affect the crime rate were also included in her multiple regressions. Leibowitz's findings revealed an unambiguous deterrence effect on each of the crimes studied—that is, when other factors were held constant, the states which had a higher level of punishment showed fewer crimes. Such crimes as rape and murder were deterred by punishment just as well as (indeed, perhaps better than) burglary and robbery.

Another of Becker's students, Isaac Ehrlich, in his doctoral dissertation went over much the same ground as Leibowitz but with a much more sophisticated and careful statistical methodology. The results, which are available in full text in his dissertation and in a somewhat abridged form in an article,(4) once again indicate that punishment does deter crime.

Further work along the same general lines was carried out by Llad Phillips, Harold L. Votey, Jr., and John Howell. In general, these scholars used the same basic data and analytical methods as Leibowitz and Ehrlich, and confirmed their findings. More recently, this group of scholars has used the same data and similar methods in an effort to produce more detailed and specific results.(5) These studies, which are of great interest in themselves, are relevant to our present purpose only in that, as a sort of by-product, they contain further confirmation of the basic finding that punishment does deter crime. Further, Phillips has run a time-series test using national data in his multiple regression to supplement the cross-sectional tests on state data.(6) It also produced similar results. Last along this particular line, Morgan Reynolds in his doctoral dissertation has treated the same basic research design en route to some new results in another area.(7)

In addition to these studies using essentially the same data on crime and punishment in the 50 states, there are two important studies using different data. Michael Block compared the crime rates for Los Angeles police districts with the likelihood in each of these districts that offenders would be caught and sent to prison, and found a clear deterrence effect.(8) And R. A. Carr-Hill and N. H. Stern carried out a study using data drawn from England and Wales and, once again, determined that punishment does deter crime.(9)

Joseph Magaddino and Gregory Krohm, using California county data, have begun work which, from the results shown by their first regressions, apparently will lead to the same conclusion.(10) David Sjoquist and Phillips, Votey, and Donald Maxwell investigated somewhat different problems, but their statistical outcomes provide further support for the deterrence theory.(11)

Finally, some students under my direction attempted to make a cost-benefit analysis of certain property crimes, primarily burglary, from the standpoint of the criminal—that is, they looked into the question of whether crime does pay. The data were particularly bad in this area, as the reader can well imagine, but they supported the conclusion that most people who took up the profession of burglary had made a sensible career choice. They did not make very much from burglary, but they were not very high-quality laborers and would have done as badly (or

worse) if they had elected honest employment.(12) This is not of direct relevance to the deterrence hypothesis, but it does seem to indicate that at least some criminals make fairly rational decisions with respect to their careers, and hence that raising the price of crime would presumably reduce the frequency with which it is committed.

Recently this point of view has been questioned by a short study by Michael Sesnowitz.(13) (The article was commented upon by Krohm and a reply was made by Sesnowitz(14)) Following an approach rather similar to that used by my students, Sesnowitz found that burglary did not pay in Pennsylvania. Basically, the difference between Sesnowitz's results and those which I would have expected comes from the fact that there are no data on the amount of time served by burglars in Pennsylvania who are sentenced to jail rather than prison. Sesnowitz assumed that the average jail sentence was the same as the average prison sentence for burglary (43 months). But since it is illegal in Pennsylvania for anyone to spend more than 23 months in jail (as opposed to prison), it is most unlikely that this is so; and if adjustments for this discrepancy are made, the results wind up rather similar to those obtained by my students. Incidentally, Pennsylvania apparently does have an exceptionally high punishment level for burglars—and, correspondingly, an exceptionally low rate of burglaries, just as the deterrence hypothesis would predict.

So much for the economists; let us now turn to the sociologists. All the economists I have cited began their studies under the impression that punishment *would* deter crime. All the sociologists I am about to cite began under the impression that it *would not* and, indeed, took up their statistical tools with the intent of confirming what was then the conventional wisdom in their field—that crime cannot be deterred by punishment. When they found out they were wrong, they quite honestly published their results, although they found it rather difficult to get their work accepted in the more conventional sociological journals.

The first of these sociologists was Jack Gibbs, who published a study in the *Social Science Quarterly* which indicated that punishment did indeed deter crime.(15) His statistical methods were basically rather different from those used by the economists—indeed, speaking as an economist, I would say they were more primitive; but the fact that the same conclusion comes from two different statistical techniques is further confirmation of its validity. The publication of this paper set off a spate of other papers by Louis Gray and David Martin,

Frank Bean and Robert Cushing, and Charles Tittle.(16) All of these scholars took up their cudgels with the intention of demonstrating that Gibbs was wrong, and all ended up agreeing with him. In the process, they greatly expanded and improved upon his work. Moreover, they continued using statistical tools that were somewhat different from those that had been employed by the economists; hence, their work can be taken as an independent confirmation of the economists' approach.

The sociologists were very much interested in a problem that had also concerned the economists, but not so vitally. This is the question whether the severity of the sentence or the likelihood that it will be imposed is more important in deterring crime. In my opinion, this is not a very important question. Suppose a potential criminal has a choice between two punishment systems: One gives each person who commits burglary a one-in-100 chance of serving one year in prison;(17) in the other there is a one-in-1,000 chance of serving 10 years. It is not obvious to me that burglars would be very differently affected by these two punishment systems, although in one case there is a heavy sentence with a low probability of conviction, and in the other a lighter sentence with a higher probability of conviction.

I would suggest that the appropriate technique is simply to divide the average sentence by the frequency with which it is imposed, and to use that as the deterrent measure. Most of the sociologists and a good many of the economists mentioned above have attempted to determine which of these two variables is more important. Leaving aside my theoretical objections, I do not think the statistics are accurate enough for the results obtained from these tests to be of much value. Be that as it may, more often than not the researchers have found that the frequency with which the punishment is applied is of greater importance than its severity.

The first studies in this field, the ones I criticized at the beginning of my survey of the empirical literature, dealt with the death penalty. Recently Ehrlich has returned to this problem and, by using a much more sophisticated method, has demonstrated a very sizeable deterrence payoff to the death penalty for murder.(18) His figures indicate that each execution prevents between 8 and 20 murders. Unfortunately, the data available for this study were not what one would hope for, so not as much reliance can be put upon his results as one normally would give to work by such a sophisticated econometrician. Earlier, and using a quite different set of statistics and a different method, I arranged to have a graduate student do a preliminary study of the same issue; his results showed that each execution prevented two murders. Here again, however, the data were bad and the methods were suitable only for a preliminary exploration.(19)

It should be emphasized that the question of whether the death penalty deters murder is a different one from the question of whether we wish to have the death penalty. One widespread minor crime is failing to return to the parking meter and put in a coin when the time expires. I take it that we could reduce the frequency with which this crime is committed by boiling all offenders in oil. I take it, also, that no one would favor this method of deterrence. *Thus, the fact that we can deter a crime by a particular punishment is not a sufficient argument for use of that punishment.*

In discussing the concept of deterrence, I find that a great many people seem to feel that, although it would no doubt work with respect to burglary and other property crimes, it is unlikely to have much effect on crimes of impulse, such as rape and many murders. They reason that people who are about to kill their wives in a rage are totally incapable of making any calculations at all. But this is far from obvious. The prisoners in Nazi concentration camps must frequently have been in a state of well-justified rage against some of their guards; yet this almost never led to their using violence against the guards, because punishment—which, if they were lucky, would be instant death, but was more likely to be death by torture—was so obvious and so certain. Even in highly emotional situations, we retain some ability to reason, albeit presumably not so well as normally.

It would take much greater provocation to lead a man to kill his wife if he knew that, as in England in the 1930's, committing murder meant a two-out-of-three chance of meeting the public executioner within about two months than if—as is currently true in South Africa—there were only a one-in-100 chance of being executed after about a year's delay.(20)

Another example can be drawn from the American South. Before about 1950, there was a great deal of violence among blacks, particularly on Saturday nights. The local authorities took the view that this was an inherent matter of black character, and hence were reluctant to punish it severely. It has been pointed out that the reluctance of the police to punish such "black" traits was probably the principal reason for their existence. A black who slashed another black's face with a razor on Saturday night would probably merely be reproved by the police and, at most, would get a short term in jail. A white who did the same thing to another white would probably get several years in prison. The difference between the statistical frequency with which blacks and whites performed this kind of act is thus explicable in terms of the deterrence effect of punishment as it was then administered.

It should be noted that thus far I have said nothing whatsoever about how well-informed criminals or potential criminals are as to the punishments for each crime in each state. For punishment to have a deterrent effect, potential criminals must have at least some information about its likely severity and frequency. Presumably, the effect of variations in punishment would be greater if criminals were well-informed than if they were not. In practice, of course, potential criminals are not very well-informed about these things, but they do have some information.

Reports of crimes and punishments are a major part of most newspapers. It is true that most intellectuals tend to skip over this part of the newspaper, but the average person is more likely to read it than some things that appeal to intellectuals. And an individual who is on the verge of committing a crime or has already taken up a career of crime is apt to be much more interested in crime stories than is the average man. He should have, therefore, a rough idea of the severity of punishments and of the probability that they will be imposed. This information should affect the likelihood that he will choose to commit a given crime.

Nevertheless, the information that he will have is likely to be quite rough. Undoubtedly, if we could somehow arrange for people to have accurate information on these matters, we would get much better coefficients on our multiple regression equations for the deterrence effect of punishment. But since governments have a motive to lie—i.e., to pretend that punishment is more likely and more severe than it actually is—it is unlikely that we can do much about improving this information. Still, the empirical evidence is clear. Even granting the fact that most potential criminals have only a rough idea as to the frequency and severity of punishment, multiple regression studies show that increasing the frequency or severity of the punishment does reduce the likelihood that a given crime will be committed.

Finally, I should like to turn to the issue of why "rehabilitation" became the dominant rationale of our punishment system in the latter part of the 19th century and has remained so up to the present, in spite of the absence of any scientific support. The reasons, in my opinion, have to do with the fallacy, so common in the social sciences, that "all good things go together." If we have the choice between preventing crime by training the criminal to be good—i.e., rehabilitating him—or deterring crime by imposing unpleasantness on criminals, the former is the one we would *like* to choose.

The Reverend Sydney Smith, a follower of the deterrence theory, said a prison should be "a place of punishment, from which men recoil with horror—a place of real suffering painful to the memory, terrible to the imagination . . . a place of sorrow and wailing, which should be entered with horror and quitted with earnest resolution never to return to such misery . . ."(21) This is an exaggeration. Our prisons do not have to be that bad; the deprivation of liberty in itself may be a sufficiently effective punishment. But in any case, deterrence necessarily involves the deliberate infliction of harm.

If, on the other hand, we can think of the prison as a kind of educational institution that rehabilitates criminals, we do not have to consciously think of ourselves as injuring people. It is clearly more appealing to think of solving the criminal problem by means that are themselves not particularly unpleasant than to think of solving it by methods that *are* unpleasant. But in this case we do not have the choice between a pleasant and an unpleasant method of dealing with crime. We have an unpleasant method—deterrence—that works, and a pleasant method—rehabilitation—that (at least so far) never has worked. Under the circumstances, we have to opt either for the deterrence method or for a higher crime rate.

REFERENCES

1. Of course, they might prevent him from committing the crime by making it physically impossible. Cutting off both hands of a forger and hanging them about his neck probably had no effect on his desire to commit forgery, but certainly made it very hard to do.

2. *See* Gary Becker, "Crime and Punishment: An Economic Approach," *Journal of Political Economy*,

76 (March/April 1968), pp. 169–217. *See*, also, Gordon Tullock. "The Welfare Costs of Tariffs, Monopolies, and Theft," *Western Economic Journal, 5* (June 1967), pp. 224–32; and "An Economic Approach to Crime," *Social Science Quarterly, 50* (June 1969), pp. 59–71.

3. Arleen Smigel Leibowitz, "Does Crime Pay: An Economic Analysis" (Master's thesis, Columbia University, 1965).

4. Isaac Ehrlich, "Participation in Illegitimate Activities: An Economic Analysis" Ph.D. dissertation, Columbia University, 1970); and "Participation in Illegitimate Activities: A Theoretical and Empirical Investigation," *Journal of Political Economy, 81* (May/June 1973), pp. 521–65.

5. Harold L. Votey, Jr., and Llad Phillips, *Economic Crimes: Their Generation, Deterrence, and Control* (Springfield, Va.: U.S. Clearinghouse for Federal Scientific and Technical Information, 1969); Harold L. Votey and Llad Phillips, "The Law Enforcement Production Function," *Journal of Legal Studies, 1* (June 1972); Llad Phillips and Harold L. Votey, Jr., "An Economic Analysis of the Deterrent Effect of Law Enforcement on Criminal Activity," *Journal of Criminal Law, Criminology, and Police Science, 63* (September 1972); and Llad Phillips and Harold L. Votey, Jr., "The Control of Criminal Activity: An Economic Analysis," in *Handbook of Criminology*, ed. by Daniel Glaser (Chicago: Rand McNally & Co., forthcoming).

6. Llad Phillips, "Crime Control: The Case for Deterrence," in *The Economics of Crime and Punishment*, ed. by Simon Rottenberg (Washington, D.C.: American Enterprise Institute for Public Policy Research, 1973), pp. 65–84.

7. Morgan Reynolds, "Crimes for Profit: The Economics of Theft" (Ph.d. dissertation, University of Wisconsin, 1971).

8. Michael Block, "An Econometric Approach to Theft" (Stanford University, mimeographed paper).

9. R. A. Carr-Hill and N. H. Stern, *An Econometric Model of the Supply and Control of Recorded Offenses in England and Wales*, rev. (University of Sussex: School of Social Science, 1972).

10. Joseph P. Magaddino and Gregory C. Krohm (untitled paper, in progress).

11. *See* David L. Sjoquist, "Property Crime and Economic Behavior: Some Empirical Results," *American Economic Review, 83*, 3 (1973); and Llad Phillips, Harold L. Votey, Jr., and Donald Maxwell, "Crime, Youth, and the Labor Market," *Journal of Political Economy, 80* (May/June 1972).

12. William E. Cobb, "Theft and the Two Hypotheses," in *The Economics of Crime and Punishment*, ed. by Simon Rottenberg (Washington, D.C.: The American Enterprise Institute for Public Policy Research, 1973), pp. 19–30; Gregory C. Krohm, "The Pecuniary Incentives of Property Crime," idem, pp. 31–34; and J. P. Gunning, Jr., "How Profitable is Burglary," idem, pp. 35–38.

13. *See* Michael Sesnowitz, "The Returns to Burglary," *Western Economic Journal, 10* (December 1972), pp. 177–81.

14. Gregory C. Krohm, "An Alternative View of the Returns to Burglary," *Western Economic Journal, 11* (September 1973), pp. 364–7; and Michael Sesnowitz, "The Returns to Burglary: An Alternative to the Alternative," idem, pp. 368–70.

15. Jack Gibbs, "Crime, Punishment, and Deterrence," *Southwestern Social Science Quarterly, 48* (March 1968), pp. 515–30.

16. Louis N. Gray and J. David Martin, "Punishment and Deterrence: Another Analysis of Gibbs' Data," *Social Science Quarterly, 50* (September 1969), pp. 389–95; Frank D. Bean and Robert C. Cushing, "Criminal Homicide, Punishment, and Deterrence: Methodological and Substantive Reconsiderations," *Social Science Quarterly, 52* (September 1971), pp. 277–89; and Charles R. Tittle, "Crime Rates and Legal Sanctions," *Social Problems, 16* (Spring 1969), pp. 409–23.

17. This is actually somewhat higher than the risk that burglars now face in most parts of the United States.

18. Isaac Ehrlich, "The Deterrent Effect of Capital Punishment: A Question of Life and Death." This is to be published in the *American Economic Review*.

19. Since I cannot possibly claim to have read everything that has ever been written on the subject, I have been conducting part of my research in this area by asking people who hear my speeches or read my papers to tell me if they know of any other articles or books in which the effectiveness of deterrence has been tested in a reasonably scientific manner. I have never received a positive response to this question, but I repeat it here.

20. These figures are for blacks killing blacks, not for blacks killing whites, or, for that matter, whites killing whites.

21. Sydney Smith, *On the Management of Prisons* (London: Warde Locke and Company, 1822), pp. 226 and 232.

8 | Critiques of the Police

Like other institutions the police system produces much that is socially valuable, but it inevitably reveals the blemishes of human failings. Investigative commissions have documented malfeasance, negligence, and corruption in law enforcement. Obviously the police have no monopoly on the negative characteristics of a flawed humanity.

On the other hand, it would be difficult to find another group in our society so prepared and willing to sacrifice its own well being and even its life, if necessary, in the service of others. And to the public there is no sight so comforting as a police officer in uniform patrolling his beat, guarding a school crossing, directing traffic, or responding to emergencies.

Given the symbolic power of the police role in America, many of the critiques of the police reflect the internal psychological state and political ideology of the observer. Although there is much fundamental data about which there should be universal agreement, police behavior is subjected to a variety of interpretations of reality. The police office in uniform generates an emotionally charged response which often reveals as much about the observer as about the object being observed.

It seems that the political context tends to dominate in most assessments of the police just as labeling theory does in its application to deviance. As a general proposition, therefore, we can assert that when an observer can be fairly identified as of a "liberal-radical" political persuasion, his critiques of the police will tend to stress the negative qualities of police behavior. Similarly, when his counterpart on the politically "conservative" level of the spectrum offers his evaluation of the police, it is likely to be defined in favorable terms.

The first article in this section, by Walter B. Miller, analyzes the ideological components of critiques of the police. The selections that follow provide clear examples of "objective" observers who demonstrate some of the angles of vision that are possible in the assessment of police behavior. The police establishments must recognize that by virtue of their status and function in society, their actions will precipitate strong criticism. They must guard against extreme or vindictive responses. In the past, police reactions to criticism have been generally to deny the truth of the allegation and to attack the motives or character of the critic. This sort of extreme response not only tends to alienate potential allies of the police, but also can be used by their critics as further evidence of police excesses. As the police have improved their professional credentials, educational backgrounds, and political sophistication, the time has come for police spokesmen to present systematic, carefully reasoned responses to the inevitable critiques. Only in this fashion will they achieve trust and credibility, the sustaining force of democratic institutions.

Ideology and Criminal Justice Policy:

Some Current Issues

WALTER B. MILLER

There is currently in the United States a wide-spread impression that our country is experiencing a major transitional phase—a period in which long-established social arrangements and the moral and conceptual notions that undergird them are undergoing substantial change. Optimists see this process as a transition from one relatively effective social order to another; pessimists see it as a one-way passage to catastrophe.

It is hard to judge the validity of these conceptions. Few generations have been free from the conviction that the nation was in the throes of "the crisis of our times," and such perceptions have not always corresponded with judgments of later historians.(1)

Since criminal behavior, ways of thinking about crime, and methods of dealing with crime make up an intrinsic component of any social order, the notion of à transitional phase also affects the perceptions and actions of both criminals and criminal justice system personnel. As soon as one considers crime as one facet of a larger set of social and historical shifts, however, a paradox emerges. One gets an impression both of striking and substantial change, and striking and substantial stability.

This paradox seems to apply equally to crime and to societal response to crime. On the one hand, patterns of contemporary criminal behavior reflect substantial shifts—*e.g.*, a massive increase in drug use and drug-related crimes, a new dimension of political motivation affecting many adult prisoners. On the other hand, an impression of changelessness and stability is evident in the relatively unchanging nature of youth crime and periodic attention to youth gang violence.(2)

A similar paradox affects those responsible for making and implementing criminal justice policy. On the one hand, we seem to be in the midst of a radical shift in conceptualizing and coping with crime, indicated by a host of current slogans such as decentralization, deinstitutionalization, victimology and others. On the other hand, there is a surprising sameness in the basic issues which these slogans reflect—issues such as free will versus determinism, individual rights versus state's rights, concentration versus diffusion of power. Do these concerns represent progressive movement or merely contemporary replays of ancient dramas?

Intriguing as it might be to explore these issues with respect to the behavior of both those who engage in crime and those who attempt to deal with it, I shall treat only the latter. The terms "criminologist" or "criminal justice personnel" will be used here to refer to those persons who maintain some consistent responsibility for dealing with criminals and their behavior.

One may seek to escape this paradox by employing the concept of "ideology." Ideology is also a central element in the complex patterns of change and stability, and a key to their understanding. A useful point of departure may be found in a quotation from Myrdal's *An American Dilemma:*

> The place of the individual scientist along the scale of radicalism-conservatism has always had strong influences on both the selection of research problems and the conclusions drawn from research. In a sense, it is the master scale of biases in social science.(3)

It is this master scale, and its influence on the field of criminal justice, which will be my major concern here.

The term "ideology" may be used in many ways.(4) It will be used here only to refer to a set of general and abstract beliefs or assumptions about the correct or proper state of things, particularly with

SOURCE: *The Journal of Criminal Law and Criminology*, Copyright © 1973 by Northwestern University School of Law.

respect to the moral order and political arrangements, which serve to shape one's positions on specific issues. Several aspects of ideology as used in this sense should be noted. First, ideological assumptions are generally pre-conscious rather than explicit, and serve, under most circumstances, as unexamined presumptions underlying positions taken openly. Second, ideological assumptions bear a strong emotional charge. This charge is not always evident, but it can readily be activated by appropriate stimuli, in particular by direct challenge. During the process of formation, ideological premises for particular individuals are influenced by a variety of informational inputs, but once established they become relatively impervious to change, since they serve to receive or reject new evidence in terms of a self-contained and self-reinforcing system.

The major contention of this presentation is that ideology and its consequences exert a powerful influence on the policies and procedures of those who conduct the enterprise of criminal justice, and that the degree and kinds of influence go largely unrecognized. Ideology is the permanent hidden agenda of criminal justice.

The discussion has two major aims. First, assuming that the generally implicit ideological basis of criminal justice commands strong, emotional, partisan allegiance, I shall attempt to state explicitly the major assumptions of relevant divergent ideological positions in as neutral or as nonpartisan a fashion as possible. Second, some of the consequences of such ideologies for the processes of planning, program, and policy in criminal justice will be examined.

I shall use a simple conceptual device for indicating ideological positions—a one-dimensional scale that runs from five on the right to zero in the middle to five on the left. Various ideological positions under consideration will be referred to this scale, using the terms "left" and "right" in an attempt to achieve neutrality. Although not all eleven possible distinctions will be made in every analysis, five scale distinctions on each side seem to be the minimum needed for present purposes. Later discussions will in some instances attribute considerable importance to differences as small as one scale degree.

The substance of ideologically divergent positions with respect to selected issues of current concern will be presented in three ways. Positions will be formulated first as "crusading issues"—shorthand catchwords or rallying cries that furnish the basic impetus for action or change in the criminal justice field. Such catch phrases are derived from a deeper and more abstract set of propositions as to desired states or outcomes. These will be designated "general assumptions." Third, differentiated positions will be delineated for all points along the full range of the scale—extreme right to extreme left—for three major policy issues.(5)

Ideological Positions

Right: Crusading Issues

Crusading issues of the right differ somewhat from those of the left; they generally do not carry as explicit a message of movement toward new forms, but imply instead that things should be reconstituted or restored. However, the component of the message that says, "Things should be different from the way they are now," comes through just as clearly as in the crusading issues of the left. Current crusading issues of the right with respect to crime and how to deal with it include the following:

1. *Excessive leniency toward lawbreakers.* This is a traditional complaint of the right, accentuated at present by the publicity given to reform programs in corrections and policing, as well as to judicial activity at various levels.

2. *Favoring the welfare and rights of lawbreakers over the welfare and rights of their victims, of law enforcement officials, and the law abiding citizen.* This persisting concern is currently activated by attention to prisoners' rights, rehabilitation programs, attacks on police officers by militants, and in particular by a series of well-publicized Supreme Court decisions aimed to enhance the application of due process.

3. *Erosion of discipline and of respect for constituted authority.* This ancient concern is currently manifested in connection with the general behavior of youth, educational policies, treatment of student dissidents by college officials, attitudes and behavior toward law-enforcement, particularly the police.

4. *The cost of crime.* Less likely to arouse the degree of passion evoked by other crusading issues, resentment over what is seen as the enormous and increasing cost of crime and dealing with criminals—a cost borne directly by the hard working and law abiding citizen—nevertheless remains active and persistent.

5. *Excessive permissiveness.* Related to excessive leniency, erosion of discipline, and the abdication of

responsibility by authorities, this trend is seen as a fundamental defect in the contemporary social order, affecting many diverse areas such as sexual morality, discipline in the schools, educational philosophies, child-rearing, judicial handling of offenders, and media presentation of sexual materials.

Right: General Assumptions

These crusading issues, along with others of similar import, are not merely ritualized slogans, but reflect instead a more abstract set of assumptions about the nature of criminal behavior, the causes of criminality, responsibility for crime, appropriate ameliorative measures, and, on a broader level, the nature of man and of a proper kind of society. These general assumptions provide the basic charter for the ideological stance of the right as a whole, and a basis for distinguishing among the several subtypes along the points of the ideological scale. Major general assumptions of the right might be phrased as follows:

1. The individual is directly responsible for his own behavior. He is not a passive pawn of external forces, but possesses the capacity to make choices between right and wrong—choices which he makes with an awareness of their consequences.

2. A central requirement of a healthy and well functioning society is a strong moral order which is explicit, well-defined, and widely adhered to. Preferably the tenets of this system of morality should be derived from and grounded in the basic precepts of a major religious tradition. Threats to this moral order are threats to the very existence of the society. Within the moral order, two clusters are of particular importance:

    a. Tenets which sustain the family unit involve morally-derived restrictions on sexual behavior, and obligations of parents to maintain consistent responsibility to their children and to one another.

    b. Tenets which pertain to valued personal qualities include: taking personal responsibility for one's behavior and its consequences; conducting one's affairs with the maximum degree of self-reliance and independence, and the minimum of dependency and reliance on others, particularly public agencies; loyalty, particularly to one's country; achieving one's ends through hard work, responsibility to others, and self-discipline.

3. Of paramount importance is the security of the major arenas of one's customary activity—particularly those locations where the conduct of family life occurs. A fundamental personal and family right is safety from crime, violence, and attack, including the right of citizens to take necessary measures to secure their own safety, and the right to bear arms, particularly in cases where official agencies may appear ineffective in doing so.

4. Adherence to the legitimate directives of constituted authority is a primary means for achieving the goals of morality, correct individual behavior, security, and other valued life conditions. Authority in the service of social and institutional rules should be exercised fairly but firmly, and failure or refusal to accept or respect legitimate authority should be dealt with decisively and unequivocally.

5. A major device for ordering human relations in a large and heterogeneous society is that of maintaining distinctions among major categories of persons on the basis of differences in age, sex, and so on, with differences in religion, national background, race, and social position of particular importance. While individuals in each of the general categories should be granted the rights and privileges appropriate thereto, social order in many circumstances is greatly facilitated by maintaining both conceptual and spatial separation among the categories.

Left: Crusading Issues

Crusading issues of the left generally reflect marked dissatisfaction with characteristics of the current social order, and carry an insistent message about the desired nature and direction of social reform. Current issues of relevance to criminal justice include:

1. *Overcriminalization.* This reflects a conviction that a substantial number of offenses delineated under current law are wrongly or inappropriately included, and applies particularly to offenses such as gambling, prostitution, drug use, abortion, pornography, and homosexuality.

2. *Labelling and Stigmatization.* This issue is based on a conception that problems of crime are aggravated or even created by the ways in which actual or potential offenders are regarded and treated by persons in authority. To the degree a person is labelled as "criminal," "delinquent," or "deviant," will he be likely to so act.

3. *Overinstitutionalization.* This reflects a dissatisfaction over prevalent methods of dealing with suspected or convicted offenders whereby they are

physically confined in large institutional facilities. Castigated as "warehousing," this practice is seen as having a wide range of detrimental consequences, many of which are implied by the ancient phrase "schools for crime." Signalled by a renewed interest in "incarceration," prison reform has become a major social cause of the left.

4. *Overcentralization.* This issue reflects dissatisfaction with the degree of centralized authority existing in organizations which deal with crime—including police departments, correctional systems, and crime-related services at all government levels. Terms which carry the thrust of the proposed remedy are local control, decentralization, community control, a new populism, and citizen power.

5. *Discriminatory Bias.* A particularly blameworthy feature of the present system lies in the widespread practice of conceiving and reacting to large categories of persons under class labels based on characteristics such as racial background, age, sex, income level, sexual practices, and involvement in criminality. Key terms here are racism, sexism, minority oppression and brutality.

Left: General Assumptions

As in the case of the rightist positions, these crusading issues are surface manifestations of a set of more basic and general assumptions, which might be stated as follows:

1. Primary responsibility for criminal behavior lies in conditions of the social order rather than in the character of the individual. Crime is to a greater extent a product of external social pressures than of internally generated individual motives, and is more appropriately regarded as a symptom of social dysfunction than as a phenomenon in its own right. The correct objective of ameliorative efforts, therefore, lies in the attempt to alter the social conditions that engender crime rather than to rehabilitate the individual.

2. The system of behavioral regulation maintained in America is based on a type of social and political order that is deficient in meeting the fundamental needs of the majority of its citizens. This social order, and the official system of behavioral regulation that it includes, incorporates an obsolete morality not applicable to the conditions of a rapidly changing technological society, and disproportionately geared to sustain the special interests of restricted

groups, but which still commands strong support among working class and lower middle class sectors of the population.

3. A fundamental defect in the political and social organization of the United States and in those components of the criminal justice enterprise that are part of this system is an inequitable and unjust distribution of power, privilege, and resources—particularly of power. This inequity pervades the entire system, but appears in its more pronounced forms in the excessive centralization of governmental functions and consequent powerlessness of the governed, the military-like, hierarchical authority systems found in police and correctional organization, and policies of systematic exclusion from positions of power and privilege for those who lack certain preferred social characteristics. The prime objective of reform must be to redistribute the decision-making power of the criminal justice enterprise rather than to alter the behavior of actual or potential offenders.

4. A further defect of the official system is its propensity to make distinctions among individuals based on major categories or classes within society such as age, sex, race, social class, criminal or noncriminal. Healthy societal adaptation for both the offender and the ordinary citizen depends on maintaining the minimum separation—conceptually and physically—between the community at large and those designated as "different" or "deviant." Reform efforts must be directed to bring this about.

5. Consistent with the capacity of external societal forces to engender crime, personnel of official agencies play a predominantly active role, and offenders a predominantly reactive role, in situations where the two come in contact. Official agents of behavioral regulation possess the capacity to induce or enhance criminal behavior by the manner in which they deal with those who have or may have engaged in crime. These agents may define offenders as basically criminal, expose them to stigmatization, degrade them on the basis of social characteristics, and subject them to rigid and arbitrary control.

6. The sector of the total range of human behavior currently included under the system of criminal sanctions is excessively broad, including many forms of behavior (for example, marijuana use, gambling, homosexuality) which do not violate the new morality and forms which would be more effectively and humanely dealt with outside the official system of criminal processing. Legal codes should be redrafted

to remove many of the behavioral forms now proscribed, and to limit the discretionary prerogatives of local authorities over apprehension and disposition of violators.

An Ideological Spectrum:
Differentiated Positions of Left and Right

The foregoing ideologically-relevant propositions are formulated as general assumptions common to all those designated as "left" or "right." The present section will expand and differentiate these generalized propositions by distributing them along the ideological scale proposed earlier. Charts I, II, and III (see Appendix) present thirty differentiated positions with respect to three major issues of relevance to criminal justice policy. Statements concerning each issue are assigned ten positions along scales running from right five through left five. The three issues are: conceptions as to the causes of crime and the locus of responsibility for criminality; conceptions of proper methods of dealing with offenders; conceptions of proper operating policies of criminal justice agencies. Not included in these tables is a theoretically possible "centrist" position.

Several features of the charts in the Appendix should be noted. Statements representing ideologically-influenced positions on the scale are formulated in a highly condensed and simplified manner, lacking the subtleties, qualifications, and supporting arguments which characterize the actual stances of most people. The basic model is that of an "ideal type" analysis which presents a series of simplified propositions formulated to bear a logical relationship to one another and to underlying abstract principles, rather than to reflect accurately the actual positions of real people.(6) Few readers will feel entirely comfortable with any of the statements exactly as phrased here; most will feel instead that given statements might reflect the general gist of their position, but with important qualifications, or that one can subscribe to selected parts of statements at several different points along the scale. On the other hand, few readers will fail to find some statements with which they disagree completely; it is most unlikely, for example, that one could support with equal enthusiasm the major tenets attributed here to positions at left four and right four.

In "placing" oneself with respect to the scaled positions outlined here, one should look for those statements with which one feels least uncomfortable rather than expecting to find formulations which correspond in all respects to his viewpoint. The process of ascertaining discrepancies between actual positions and those represented here as "pure" examples of rightist or leftist ideology serves one of the purposes of ideal-typical analysis; few are ideological purists, but this type of analysis makes it possible to identify positions which correspond more or less closely to ideological orthodoxy. Those whose positions are closer to the extremes will feel least comfortable with statements attributed to the opposing side of the spectrum; those closer to "centrist" positions will tend to find orientations congenial to their own at a larger number of scale positions, possibly including positions on both sides of the spectrum.

To say that the statements show some logical relationship to one another and to underlying principles is not to say that they are logically consistent; in fact, several obvious inconsistencies appear in the charts. For example, right five maintains that criminals are unwitting puppets of a radical conspiracy and, at the same time, holds that they are responsible for their own behavior. Left four calls for maximum access to information concerning the inner workings of criminal justice agencies and, at the same time, advocates minimum access by employers, personnel departments and others to criminal records of individuals. If one fails to find in internal consistency the "logical" basis for these propositions, where do the logical relationships lie?

Although some degree of logical inconsistency is likely in almost any developed set of propositions about human behavior, the consistency in the above propositions lies largely in the degree to which the interests of particular classes of persons are supported, defended, and justified. The inconsistencies often lie either in the means advocated to achieve such ends or in the rationales used to defend or exculpate favored interests and condemn opposing ones. In the above examples, if one assumes that a basic interest of left four is maximum protection of and support for actual or putative offenders, then these ends are served in the one instance by maximum access to information which might reveal errors, inequities or violations in their treatment by criminal justice officials, and in the other by denying to potential employers and others access to information that might jeopardize their welfare. Similarly, in attempting to reconcile the apparent contradiction in assertions that offenders are pawns of radical conspiracy and also that they are directly responsible for their behavior, a rightist could argue that offenders are indeed responsible for their behavior, and that they make a deliberate personal choice to follow the crime-engendering appeals of the radicals.

While statements at different scale positions frequently present differing orientations to the same sub-issue (e.g., scope of criminal law, appropriate degree of restraint of offenders, extent to which "rehabilitation" should be an objective), not all of the statements on each major issue treat all of the included sub-issues. The positioned statements are defective with respect to "dimensionality," the possibility of full scalability across all issues. Each of the included sub-issues represents an independently scalable dimension. The "cause" issue incorporates approximately 14 distinguishable dimensions or sub-issues, the "offender" issue 15, and the "agencies" issue 18. To include a separate statement for each dimension at each scale position for all three issues would require a minimum of 470 statements—an impractical number for a presentation at this level. Selection of sub-issues and their assignment to given positions were guided by an attempt both to produce internally-coherent statements and to cover a fairly broad range of sub-issues.

One often finds convergences at the extremes of a distribution of ideological positions. Several instances can be found in the charts; for example, both right five and left five attribute criminality to deliberate or systematic efforts or policies of highly-organized interest groups, although of differing identities (radicals, the ruling class). If quantifiable weights can be assigned to the scalable dimensions of the chart, two major types of distribution are included—"opposition" and "convergence" distributions. "Opposition" distributions occur where the maximum weight or magnitude is found at one extreme of the scale and the minimum at the other, with intermediate positions showing intermediate values. Examples may be found in the sub-issues "degree of coercive power to be exercised by official agencies"; (left five espouses the minimum degree, right five the maximum, with others occupying intermediate positions), and "degree of personal culpability of offenders" (right five maximum, left five minimum, others in between). Policy disputes involving this type of distribution tend to be most difficult to resolve.

In "convergence" distributions similarities or partial similarities are found in the positions of those at opposing ends of the spectrum. One instance is found in attitudes toward rehabilitation of offenders—an objective strongly opposed by partisans at both left four and right four, although for different reasons. A rather complex but crucial instance is found in the statements concerning "localized" versus "centralized" authority. Both left four and right four call for increased local autonomy, whereas the more "moderate" of both left and right favor continued or increased federal authority and support for criminal justice programs and operations. The apparent convergence of the extremes is, however, complicated by a number of factors. One relates to which branch of government exercises authority; another relates to the particular policy area at issue. Those at left four are not adverse to strong federal initiatives to improve social-service delivery capacity of local welfare agencies. Those at right four, while decrying the iron grip of federal bureaucrats over local affairs, are not adverse to strong federal initiatives to improve technological capacity of local police forces. The more extreme leftists seek greatly increased local autonomy for citizen control over police and correctional operations, but welcome strong federal power in formulating and enforcing uniform civil rights measures. The more extreme rightists adamantly oppose the use of centralized power to enforce "mixing" of racial and other social categories or to compel uniform operations of local police, courts and corrections, but welcome strong federal power in the development and maintenance of military forces, or a strong federal investigatory branch with the power to probe corruption and collusion in local programs, particularly those of left-oriented agencies.

The unifying principle behind these apparent contradictions is the same as that noted for intraposition inconsistencies; ideologically-derived objectives are supported despite possible discrepancies involving the means to achieve them or the identity of sources of support. An additional dimension of considerable importance is also involved—that of time. Ideological positions of left and right are delineated on the basis of a given point in time earlier designated as "current." But specific stances of the left and right can change rapidly in response to changing circumstances, or they can even reverse themselves. Moreover, some of the "crusading issues" currently fashionable will become passé in the near future.

The "decentralization" issue again provides a good example. Whether one favors more or less power for "centralized" or federal agencies depends on the current ideological complexion of the several federal departments or branches. Viewed very broadly, in the early 1930's the left looked to the executive branch as a prime source of support for policies they favored, and the right to the judicial and legislative; in the 1960's the left viewed both the executive and judicial as allies, the legislature as a potential source of opposition, and sought more power for the High Court and the Presidency. At present the right views the executive as supportive, and the left looks to the legislature as an ally in an attempt to curb the power of the presidency. Reflecting these shifts have been changes in attitudes of the left and right toward "local control." While traditionally a crusading issue of the right (state's rights), the banner for community control was taken up in the 1960's by the left as an effective method of bypassing entrenched political power at the local level—primarily with respect to civil rights. Recently the trend has begun to reverse because of a resurgence of the right's traditional "anti-big-government" stance and an increasing resort to local control by community groups pursuing rightist causes (e.g., exclusion of blacks from white schools).

Further detailed analyses of convergences and divergences, consistencies and contradictions, past, present and future fashions of both these issues and others could be developed. It might be useful at this point, however, to briefly consider a more fundamental level—the basic philosophical underpinnings of the two sides—and to compress the variety and complexity of their varied positions into a single and simple governing principle.

For the right, the paramount value is order—an ordered society based on a pervasive and binding morality—and the paramount danger is disorder—social, moral and political. For the left, the paramount value is justice—a just society based on a fair and equitable distribution of power, wealth, prestige, and privilege—and the paramount evil is injustice—the concentration of valued social resources in the hands of a privileged minority.

Few Americans would quarrel with either of these values since both are intrinsic aspects of our national ideals. Stripped of the passion of ideological conflict, the issue between the two sides could be viewed as a disagreement over the relative priority of two valuable conditions: whether *order with justice*, or *justice with order* should be the guiding principle of the criminal justice enterprise.

These are ancient philosophical issues, and their many aspects have been argued in detail for centuries. Can both order and justice be maximized in a large, heterogeneous, pluralistic society? Can either objective be granted priority under all circumstances? If not, under what circumstances should which objective be seen as paramount? It might appear that these issues are today just as susceptible to rational discussion as they have been in the past; but this is not so, because the climate militates against such discussion. Why this is so will be considered shortly—after a brief discussion of the ideologies of the formal agencies of criminal justice.

Ideological Complexion of Criminal Justice Agencies

The ideological positions of four major professional fields will be discussed—academic criminology, the police, the judiciary, and corrections. Rather than complex analysis or careful delineation, tentative impressions will be offered. Each system will be characterized on a very gross level, but it is important to bear in mind the possibility that there is as much ideological variability within each of the several systems as there is among them. Of particular importance within these systems are differences in age level, social class and educational level, and rank.

Academic Criminologists. This group is included not out of any presumption about the importance of the role they play, but rather because academic criminology provides the platform from which the present analysis is presented. Probably the most important point to make here is that the day-to-day ideological environment of the average academic criminologist, viewed within the context of the total society, is highly artificial; it reflects the perspectives of a deviant and unrepresentative minority. Academic criminology, reflecting academic social science in general, is substantially oriented toward the left, while the bulk of American people are oriented toward the right.(7) Furthermore, the members of the large liberal academic majority do proportionately more writing and speechmaking than those of the small conservative minority, so that their impact on the ideological climate exceeds even their large numbers. If the proportion of right-oriented persons in academic criminology comes close to being just the reverse of that in the general population, then this marked ideological divergence certainly has implications for those situations in which academicians come in contact with the public, particularly where they interact with representatives of other criminal justice branches. It also has an important impact on their own perceptions of the ideological positions of the public and other criminal justice professionals.

Police. The bulk of police officers have working-class backgrounds, and the contemporary working class is substantially rightist. Archie Bunker is a caricature, but the reality he exaggerates is a significant one. Rightist ideology in one of its purest versions may be found in the solemn speeches of Officer Joe Friday to temporarily discouraged young police officers or disgruntled citizens. Among police departments, differences in ideological complexion are found in different regions (for example, West Coast departments generally have higher proportions of college-trained personnel), different sized communities, and departments with different personnel policies. Within departments, age differences may be important (some younger officers are less rightist), as well as differences in rank and function (some departments have more liberally-oriented chiefs or research and planning personnel). The majority of working police professionals, however, subscribe to the ideological premises here designated as "rightist."

Judiciary. The legal and judicial field is probably characterized by greater ideological diversity than either the police or corrections. One reason is that leftist positions are more common among those with college degrees than among those with less education. Since college education is a prerequisite to formal legal training, lawyers are more likely to have been exposed to the leftward orientation characteristic of most academic faculties, particularly those of the larger and more prestigious universities.(8) Judges show enormous variation in ideological predilections, probably covering the full range from right five to left four. Variation is related to factors such as the law school attended, size of jurisdiction, social status of jurists and their clientele, region, level of the court. While public attention is often directed to the actions of highly moralistic, hard line judges at right four and five positions, such jurists are probably becoming less common.

Ideological orientations of the legal profession have recently been subject to public attention, partic-

ularly in connection with two developments. First, the Supreme Court has in the recent past been associated with a series of decisions that reflect basic tenets of the left. Included have been such issues as increased protection for the rights of suspected and accused persons, inadmissibility of illegally-obtained evidence, minimization of distinctions based on race, reduction of discretionary powers of law-enforcement personnel, and reduction of judicial discretion in juvenile proceedings.(9) These decisions and others were perceived by the right as posing a critical threat to an established balance of power and prerogatives between law-enforcement personnel and offenders, seriously endangering the law-enforcement process and the security of the public.

The second development is the emergence during the past ten years of a group of young left-oriented lawyers whose influence is probably disproportionate to their small numbers. Able, dedicated, active on a variety of fronts, many representing low-income or black clients, their activities became best known in connection with Federal Anti-Poverty programs. Many of these lawyers have assumed positions along the ideological scale as far left as the left three and left four positions.

Despite these well-publicized manifestations of leftward orientations in some sectors of the legal profession, it is unlikely that a substantial proportion of the profession consistently espouses the tenets of the left, particularly those of left three and beyond. The more liberal judges are generally found in federal and higher-level state courts, but conservative views are still common among jurists of the lower level courts, where the great bulk of day-to-day legal business is transacted. Moreover, as part of the ideological shifts noted earlier, the Burger court is regarded by the right with considerably less antipathy than the Warren court.(10)

Corrections. Corrections, the current hot spot of the criminal justice field, probably contains a mixture of ideological positions, with the bulk of correctional personnel ranged along the right. The average lower-echelon corrections employee has a working-class background similar to that of the average patrolman, and thus manifests the rightist orientation characteristic of that class. As in the case of police, age may be an important basis for differentiation, with older officials more likely to assume right-oriented positions. Among other bases are size of the institution and age level of the bulk of inmates. Juvenile corrections tends to have a higher likelihood of left-oriented staff, both at administrative and lower-echelon levels.

Prison reform is currently one of the most intense crusading issues of the left. While most reform efforts are exerted by persons not officially part of the correctional system, there has been some influx of left three and four persons into the official system itself, particularly among younger staff in juvenile correction facilities.

Consequences of Ideology

If, as is here contended, many of those involved in the tasks of planning and executing the major policies and procedures of our criminal justice system are subject to the influence of pervasive ideological assumptions about the nature of crime and methods of dealing with it—assumptions which are largely implicit and unexamined—the question then arises: what are the consequences of this phenomenon?

While both the crusading issues and graded ideological positions presented earlier were phrased to convey the tone of urgent imperatives, the assumptions from which they arise were phrased in relatively neutral terms as a set of general propositions about the nature, causes, and processes of coping with crime. So phrased and so regarded, these assumptions are susceptible to rational consideration. Their strengths and weaknesses can be debated, evidence can be employed to test the degree of validity each may possess, contradictions among them can be considered, and attempts made to explain or reconcile differences among them. Formulated and used in this manner, the question arises: why are they characterized here as "ideological"?

The scale of ideology presented comprises a single major parameter—substantive variation along a left-right scale with respect to a set of issues germane to crime and the criminal justice process. But there is an additional important parameter which must also be considered: that of intensity—the degree of emotional charge which attaches to the assumptions. It is the capacity of these positions to evoke the most passionate kinds of reactions and to become infused with deeply felt, quasi-religious significance that constitutes the crucial element in the difference between testable assumptions and ideological tenets. This dimension has the power to transform plausibility into ironclad certainty, conditional belief into ardent conviction, the reasoned advocate into the implacable zealot. Rather than being looked upon as useful and conditional hypotheses, these assumptions, for many, take the form of the sacred and inviolable dogma of the one true faith, the questioning of which is heresy, and the opposing of which is profoundly evil.

This phenomenon—ideological intensification—appears increasingly to exert a powerful impact on the entire field. Leslie Wilkins has recorded his opinion that the criminal justice enterprise is becoming progressively more scientific and secularized;(11) an opposite, or at least concurrent, trend is here suggested—that it is becoming progressively more ideologized. The consequences are many. Seven will be discussed briefly: Polarization, Reverse Projection, Ideologized Selectivity, Informational Constriction, Catastrophism, and Distortion of Opposing Positions.

Polarization. Polarization is perhaps the most obvious consequence of ideological intensification. The more heavily a belief takes on the character of sacred dogma, the more necessary it becomes to view the proponents of opposing positions as devils and scoundrels, and their views as dangerous and immoral. Cast in this framework of the sacred and the profane, of virtuous heroes and despicable villains, the degree of accommodation and compromise that seems essential to the complex enterprise of criminal justice planning becomes, at best, enormously complicated, and at worst, quite impossible.

Reverse Projection. This is a process whereby a person who occupies a position at a given point along the ideological scale perceives those who occupy any point closer to the center than his own as being on the opposite side of the scale. Three aspects of this phenomenon, which appears in its most pronounced form at the extremes of the scale, should be noted. First, if one grants the logical possibility that there can exist a "centrist" position—not a position which maintains no assumptions, but one whose assumptions are "mixed," "balanced," or not readily characterizable—then this position is perceived as "rightist" by those on the left, and "leftist" by those on the right.

A second aspect concerns the intensity of antagonism often shown by those occupying immediately adjacent positions along the ideological scale. Perhaps the most familiar current manifestation of this is found in the bitter mutual denunciations of those classified here as occupying the positions of left four and left five. Those at left four are often taken by those at left five as far more dangerous and evil than those seen as patent fascists at right four and five. Left fours stand accused as dupes of the right, selling out to or being co-opted by the establishment, and blunting the thrust of social activism by cowardly vacillation and compromise.

A third aspect of reverse projection is that one tends to make the most sensitive intrascale distinctions closest to the point that one occupies. Thus, someone at right four might be extremely sensitive to differences between his position and that of an absolute dictatorship advocate at right five, and at the same time cast left four and five into an undifferentiated class of commies, communist dupes and radicals, quite oblivious to the distinctions that loom so large to those who occupy these positions.

Ideologized Selectivity. The range of issues, problems, areas of endeavor, and arenas of activity relevant to the criminal justice enterprise is enormous. Given the vastness of the field relative to the availability of resources, decisions must be made as to task priorities and resource allocation. Ideology plays a paramount but largely unrecognized role in this process, to the detriment of other ways of determining priorities. Ideologized selectivity exerts a constant influence in determining which problem areas are granted greatest significance, which projects are supported, what kinds of information are gathered and how research results are analyzed and interpreted. Divergent resource allocation policies of major federal agencies can be viewed as directly related to the dominant ideological orientation of the agency.

Only one example of ideologized selectivity will be cited here. The increasing use of drugs, soft and hard, and an attendant range of drug-related crime problems is certainly a major contemporary development. The importance of this problem is reflected in the attention devoted to it by academic criminologists. One major reason for this intensive attention is that explanations for the spread of drug use fit the ideological assumptions shared by most academicians (drug use is an understandable product of alienation resulting from the failure of the system to provide adequate meaning and quality to life). Also one major ameliorative proposal, the liberalization of drug laws, accords directly with a crusading issue of the left—decriminalization.

Another contemporary phenomenon, quite possibly of similar magnitude, centers on the apparent disproportionate numbers of low-status urban blacks arrested for violent and predatory crimes, brought to court and sent to prison. While not entirely ignored by academic criminologists, the relatively low amount of attention devoted to this phenomenon stands in sharp contrast to the intensive efforts evident in the field of drugs. Important aspects of the problem of black crime do not fit the ideological assumptions of the majority of academic criminologists. Insofar as the issue is studied, the problem is generally stated in terms of oppressive, unjust and discriminatory behavior by society and its law-enforcement agents—a formulation that accords with that tenet of the left which assumes the capacity of officials to engender crime by their actions, and the parallel assumption that major responsibility for crime lies in conditions of the social order. Approaches to the problem that involve the careful collection of information relative to such characteristics of the population itself as racial and social status run counter to ideological tenets that call for the minimization of such distinctions both conceptually and in practice, and thus are left largely unattended.

Informational Constriction. An attitude which is quite prevalent in many quarters of the criminal justice enterprise today involves a depreciation of the value of research in general, and research on causes of crime in particular. Several reasons are commonly given, including the notion that money spent on research has a low payoff relative to that spent for action, that past research has yielded little of real value for present problems, and that research on causes of crime in particular is of little value since the low degree of consensus among various competing schools and theorists provides little in the way of unified conclusions or concrete guidance. Quite independent of the validity of such reasons, the anti-research stance can be seen as a logical consequence of ideological intensification.

For the ideologically committed at both ends of the scale, new information appears both useless and dangerous. It is useless because the basic answers, particularly with respect to causes, are already given, in their true and final form, by the ideology; it is dangerous because evidence provided by new research has the potential of calling into question ideologically established truths.

In line with this orientation, the present enterprise, that of examining the influence of ideology on criminal justice policy and programs, must be regarded with distaste by the ideologically intense—not only because it represents information of relevance to ideological doctrine, but also because the very nature of the analysis implies that ideological truth is relative.

Catastrophism. Ideological partisans at both extremes of the scale are intensely committed to particular programs or policies they wish to see effected, and recurrently issue dire warnings of terrible catastrophes that will certainly ensue unless their proposals are adopted (Right: Unless the police are promptly given full power to curb criminality and unless rampant permissiveness toward criminals is halted, the country will surely be faced with an unprecedented wave of crime and violence; Left: Unless society promptly decides to provide the resources necessary to eliminate poverty, discrimination, injustice and exploitation, the country will surely be faced with a holocaust of violence worse than ever before). Such predictions are used as tactics in a general strategy for enlisting support for partisan causes: "Unless you turn to us and our program. . . ." That the great bulk of catastrophes so ominously predicted do not materialize does not deter catastrophism, since partisans can generally claim that it was the response to their warnings that forestalled the catastrophe. Catastrophism can thus serve to inhibit adaptation to real crises by casting into question the credibility of accurate prophets along with the inaccurate.

Magnification of Prevalence. Ideological intensification produces a characteristic effect on perceptions of the empirical prevalence of phenomena related to areas of ideological concern. In general, targets of ideological condemnation are represented as far more prevalent than carefully collected evidence would indicate. Examples are estimates by rightists of the numbers of black militants, radical conspirators, and welfare cheaters, and by leftists of the numbers of brutal policemen, sadistic prison personnel, and totally legitimate welfare recipients.

Distortion of the Opposition. To facilitate a demonstration of the invalidity of tenets on the opposite side of the ideological scale it is necessary for partisans to formulate the actual positions of the opposition in such a way as to make them most susceptible to refutation. Opposition positions are phrased to appear maximally illogical, irrational, insupportable, simplistic, internally contradictory, and

if possible, contemptible or ludicrous. Such distortion impedes the capacity to adequately comprehend and represent positions or points of view which may be complex and extensively developed—a capacity that can be of great value when confronting policy differences based on ideological divergencies.

Implications

What are the implications of this analysis for those who face the demanding tasks of criminal justice action and planning? It might first appear that the prescription would follow simply and directly from the diagnosis. If the processes of formulating and implementing policy with respect to crime problems are heavily infused with ideological doctrine, and if this produces a variety of disadvantageous consequences, the moral would appear to be clear: work to reverse the trend of increased ideological intensification, bring out into the open the hidden ideological agenda of the criminal justice enterprise, and make it possible to release the energy now consumed in partisan conflict for a more direct and effective engagement with the problem field itself.

But such a prescription is both overly optimistic and overly simple. It cannot be doubted that the United States in the latter 20th century is faced with the necessity of confronting and adapting to a set of substantially modified circumstances, rooted primarily in technological developments with complex and ramified sociological consequences. It does not appear too far-fetched to propose that major kinds of necessary social adaptation in the United States can occur only through the medium of ardently ideological social movements—and that the costs of such a process must be borne in order to achieve the benefits it ultimately will confer. If this conception is correct, then ideological intensification, with all its dangers and drawbacks, must be seen as a necessary component of effective social adaptation, and the ideologists must be seen as playing a necessary role in the process of social change.

Even if one grants, however, that ideology will remain an inherent element of the policy-making process, and that while enhancing drive, dedication and commitment it also engenders rigidity, intolerance and distortion—one might still ask whether it is possible to limit the detrimental consequences of ideology without impairing its strengths. Such an objective is not easy, but steps can be taken in this direction. One such step entails an effort to increase one's capacity to discriminate between those types of information which are more heavily invested with ideological content and those which are less so. This involves the traditional distinction between "fact" and "value" statements.(12) The present delineation of selected ideological stances of the left and right provides one basis for estimating the degree to which statements forwarded as established conclusions are based on ideological doctrine rather than empirically supportable evidence. When assertions are made about what measures best serve the purposes of securing order, justice, and the public welfare, one should ask "How do we know this?" If statements appear to reflect in greater or lesser degree the inter-related patterns of premises, assumptions and pre-scriptions here characterized as "ideological," one should accommodate one's reactions accordingly.

Another step is to attempt to grant the appropriate degree of validity to positions on the other side of the scale from one's own. If ideological commitment plays an important part in the process of developing effective policy, one must bear in mind that both left and right have important parts to play. The left provides the cutting edge of innovation, the capacity to isolate and identify those aspects of existing systems which are least adaptive, and the imagination and vision to devise new modes and new instrumentalities for accommodating emergent conditions. The right has the capacity to sense those elements of the established order that have strength, value, or continuing usefulness, to serve as a brake on over-rapid alteration of existing modes of adaptation, and to use what is valid in the past as a guide to the future. Through the dynamic clash between the two forces, new and valid adaptations may emerge.

None of us can free himself from the influence of ideological predilections, nor are we certain that it would be desirable to do so. But the purposes of effective policy and practice are not served when we are unable to recognize in opposing positions the degree of legitimacy, validity, and humane intent they may possess. It does not seem unreasonable to ask of those engaged in the demanding task of formulating and implementing criminal justice policy that they accord to differing positions that measure of respect and consideration that the true idealogue can never grant.

REFERENCES

1. A few examples of perceptions that "our times" are witnessing radical or unprecedented changes are found in selected excerpts from statements published in 1874, 1930, and 1939, respectively.

Society has grave charges to answer in regard to its influence on the present and rising generation. . . . The social conditions of the present age are such as to favor the development of insanity. The habits inculcated by . . . growing wealth . . . among individuals of one class and the stinging poverty . . . of another . . . nurture dispositions which might . . . under more equitable distributions . . . have died out. Have we not seen [youth] emerging from the restraints of school, scoffing at the opinions of the world, flouting everything but their own conceit . . . ?

Dickson, "The Science and Practice of Medicine in Relation to Mind, and the Jurisprudence of Insanity," (1874), quoted in M. Altschule, *Roots of Modern Psychiatry* (1957), pp. 122 and 133.

In our nineteenth century polity, the home was a chief reliance . . . discipline was recognized as a reality . . . the pressure of the neighborhood . . . was strong . . . in the urban industrial society of today there is a radical change. . . . This complete change in the background of social control involves much that may be easily attributed to the ineffectiveness of criminal justice. . . .

Pound, "Criminal Justice in America" (1930), quoted in F. Tannenbaum, *Crime and the Community* (1938), p. 29.

Men's ways of ordering their common lives have broken down so disastrously as to make hope precarious. So headlong and pervasive is change today that . . . historical parallels are decreasingly relevant . . . because so many of the variables in the situation have altered radically. . . . Professor James T. Shotwell recently characterized "the anarchy we are living in today" as "the most dangerous since the fall of Rome."

R. Lynd, *Knowledge for What* (1939), pp. 2 and 11.

2. An analysis involving long-term trends in youth gang violence and periodically recurrent representations of such violence as a new phenomenon engendered by contemporary conditions is included in Miller, "American Youth Gangs: Past and Present," in A. Blumberg, *Current Perspectives on Criminal Behavior* (1974), pp. 210–239.

3. G. Myrdal, An American Dilemma: *The Negro Problem and Modern Democracy* (1944), p. 1038. Myrdal's citation of the "radicalism-conservatism"

scale is part of an extended discussion of sources of bias in works on race relations, appearing as Appendix 2, "A Methodological Note on Facts and Valuations in Social Science," pp. 1035–64. His entire discussion is germane to issues treated in this article.

4. A classic treatment of ideology is K. Mannheim, *Ideology and Utopia* (1936). *See* ch. II.1 "Definition of Concepts." *See* also G. Myrdal, *supra* note 3, at 1035–64. There is an extensive literature, much of it sociological, dealing with ideology as it relates to a wide range of political and social phenomena, but the specific relation between ideology and criminal justice has received relatively little direct attention. Among more recent general discussions are E. Shils, *The Intellectuals and the Powers* (1972); Orlans, "The Political Uses of Social Research," *Annals of the American Academy of Political and Social Science*, 393 (1971), p. 28; Kelman, "I.Q., Race, and Public Debate," *Hastings Center Rep.*, 2 (1972), p. 8. Treatments more specific to crime and criminal justice appear in L. Radzinowicz, *Ideology and Crime* (1966); Andanaes, "Punishment and the Problem of General Prevention," *International Annals of Criminology*, 8 (1969), p. 285; Blumberg, "The Adversary System," in C. Bersani, *Crime and Delinquency* (1970), p. 435; Glaser, "Criminology and Public Policy," *American Sociologist*, 6 (1971), p. 30.

5. The substance of ideologically-relevant statements formulated here as crusading issues, general assumptions, or differentiated positions was derived from examination and analysis of a wide range of materials appearing in diverse forms in diverse sources. Materials were selected primarily on the basis of two criteria: that they bear on issues of current relevance to criminal justice policy, and that they represent one possible stance with respect to issues characterized by markedly divergent stances. With few exceptions, the statements as formulated here do not represent direct quotes, but have been generalized, abstracted or paraphrased from one or more sets of statements by one or more representatives of positions along the ideological scale. A substantial portion of the statements thus derived were taken from books, articles, speeches, and media reporting of statements by the following: Robert Welch, writer; John Schmitz, legislator; Gerald L. K. Smith, writer; Meyer Kahane, clergyman; Edward Banfield, political scientist; William Loeb, publisher; George Wallace, government; Julius Hoffman, jurist; L. Patrick Gray III, lawyer; William Rehnquist, jurist; William Buckley, writer; Spiro Agnew, government; Robert M. McKiernan, police; Howard J. Phillips, government; Lewis F. Powell Jr., jurist; Andrew Hacker, political scientist; Kevin Phillips, writer; Victor Reisel, labor; Albert Shanker, educator; Fred P. Graham, lawyer/writer; Warren Burger, jurist; James Q. Wilson, political scientist; Hubert H. Humphrey,

legislator; James Reston, writer; Jacob Javits, legislator; Ramsey Clark, lawyer; Tom Wicker, writer; Earl Warren, jurist; James F. Ahearn, police; Henry Steele Commager, historian; Alan Dershowitz, lawyer; Julian Bond, legislator; Herbert J. Gans, sociologist; Ross K. Baker, political scientist; Russell Baker, writer; William Kunstler, lawyer; Benjamin Spock, physician; Noam Chomsky, anthropologist; Richard Cloward, sociologist; Herman Schwartz, lawyer; Richard Korn, sociologist; Michael Harrington, writer; Richard Quinney, sociologist; Frank Reissman, sociologist; Tom Hayden, writer; Eldridge Cleaver, writer; H. Bruce Franklin, professor; Abbie Hoffman, writer; Phillip Berrigan, clergyman; Jerry Rubin, writer. Among a range of non-academic reports, pamphlets, and periodicals which served as sources for statements by these and other persons were: *John Birch Society Reprint Series; Ergo: The Rational Voice of Libertarianism; New Solidarity: National Caucus of Labor Committees; Hastings Center Report; S.D.S. New Left Notes; Guardian; Ramparts; National Review; Nation; New Republic; New York Review; Commentary; Fortune; Time; Life; Newsweek; New York Times; New York Times Magazine; Washington Post; Manchester Union Leader.* It should be noted that the substance of materials appearing in published sources represents the publicly-taken positions of the individuals involved. The relation between public positions and "actual" or private positions can be very complex, ranging from "close" to "distant" along a "degree of correspondence" axis, and with variation involving changes over time, differences according to the subissue involved, nature of audience addressed, and other factors.

6. The classic application of ideal-type method is that of Max Weber. *See*, e.g., the discussion of Weber's method and typology of authority and coordination in A. Henderson and T. Parsons, *Max Weber: The Theory of Social and Economic Organization* (1974), pp. 98 and 347. In the field of criminology, MacIver applies ideal-type analysis to discussions of social causality in general and crime causality in particular. R. MacIver, *Social Causation*, (1942), p. 174. Neither of these applications directly parallels present usage, but underlying principles are similar.

7. Several recent studies provide indirect evidence of differences between academics and the general public in the likelihood that one will characterize his ideological position as "right" or "left." Of 60,000 professors surveyed by the Carnegie Commission, approximately 70% characterized themselves as "left" or "liberal," and fewer than 25% as "conservative" or "middle-of-the-road." A survey of social science professors by Everett Ladd and Seymour Lipset showed that approximately 70% voted against the "conservative" presidential candidate in 1972, compared with approximately 75% against four years

before. These studies were reported in Hacker, "On Original Sin and Conservatives," *New York Times*, Feb. 25, 1973, §6 (Magazine) at 13. Henry Turner and Carl Hetrick's survey of a systematic sample of members of the American Political Science Association showed that approximately 75% characterized themselves as Democrats (among academics "Democratic" almost invariably means "liberal," whereas it generally means "conservative" in blue collar populations), a percentage which had remained stable for ten years. Those designating themselves as "Republicans" had declined to about 10% at the time of the survey. Turner and Hetrick's survey also showed that the Democratic majority was significantly more active in publication and political activity than the non-Democratic minority. H. Turner and C. Hetrick, "Political Activities and Party Affiliations of American Political Scientists" (paper delivered at the 1971 Meetings of the American Political Science Association).

By comparison, a Gallup survey conducted in 1972 found that 71% of a systematically-selected sample of voters designated themselves as "conservative" (41%) or "Middle-of-the-road" (30%), with 24% characterizing themselves as "liberal." A survey by Daniel Yankelovich during the same period found that 75% of the voters surveyed viewed themselves as "conservative" (37%) or "moderate" (38%), and 17% as "liberal" (15%) or "radical" (2%). *See* Rosenthal, "McGovern is Radical or Liberal to Many in Polls," *New York Times*, Aug. 27, 1972, at 34, col. 3. An earlier poll by Yankelovich of American college students, seen by many as among the most liberal of large population categories, showed that approximately 70% reported themselves as holding "mainstream" positions, and that among the remainder, conservatives outnumbered left-wing radicals by two-to-one. D. Yankelovich, *The Changing Values on Campus: Political and Personal Attitudes of Today's College Students* (1972).

8. Hacker states that ". . . the higher one climbs on the prestige ladder [of American colleges and universities] the less likely are conservatives to be found on the faculty." Hacker, *supra* note 7, at 71.

9. Issues involved here fall into two general clusters: those affecting the rights and resources available to law-enforcement officials relative to those available to persons suspected, accused, or convicted of crimes; those relating to the conceptual or physical separation or combining of major population categories. Stands of the right and left with respect to the first cluster have been delineated in several places (right crusading issue 2; left general assumptions 3, 5; right policies respecting offenders 3, 4, respecting agencies 3, 4; left policies respecting offenders 3, 4, respecting agencies 3, 4). Major decisions of the

United States Supreme Court during the 1960's which appear to accord with ideological stances of the left and to run counter to those of the right include: Mapp v. Ohio, 367 U.S. 643 (1961), which reduced resources available to law-enforcement officials and increased resources available to the accused by extending limitations on the admissibility of illegally-obtained evidence; Escobedo v. Illinois, 378 U.S. 478 (1964), and Miranda v. Arizona, 384 U.S. 436 (1966), which reduced the power of law-enforcement officials to proceed with criminal processing without providing suspects with knowledge of and recourse to legal rights and resources; *In re* Gault, 387 U.S. 1 (1967), which reduced the power of judges to make dispositions in juvenile proceedings and increased the legal rights and resources of defendants; Katz v. United States, 389 U.S. 347 (1967), which reduced prerogatives of law-enforcement officials with respect to the gathering of evidence by increasing protection of suspects against intrusions of privacy; Gilbert v. California, 388 U.S. 263 (1967), and United States v. Wade, 388 U.S. 218 (1967), which decreased the freedom of law enforcement officials to seek identification of suspects, and increased the legal rights and resources available to suspects.

With respect to the second cluster, separation of population categories, stands of the right are delineated under general assumption 5, sources of crime 4, policies respecting criminal justice agencies 4, and of the left under crusading issue 5 and general assumption 4. The landmark decision here was Brown v. Board of Education, 347 U.S. 483 (1954), which held that racially segregated public education was *per se* discriminatory. While preceding the above-cited decisions by about a decade, *Brown* set a precedent for later court actions which provided support for the diminution of categorical segregation, as favored by the left, and reduced support for the maintenance of such separation, as espoused by the right.

10. It has been widely held that the Burger Court, reflecting the influence of right-oriented Nixon appointees such as Justices Rehnquist and Powell, would evince marked support for rightist ideological premises, stopping or reversing many of the initiatives of the Warren Court in areas such as equal protection and due process. This viewpoint is articulated by Fred. P. Graham, who writes, "Mr. Nixon's two new justices are strikingly like his first two appointments in conservative judicial outlook, and . . . this cohesion is likely to produce a marked swing to the right—particularly on criminal law issues. . . ." Graham, "Profile of the 'Nixon Court' Now Discernible," *New York Times*, May 24, 1972, p. 28, col. 3. *See* also Graham, "Supreme Court, in Recent Term, Began Swing to Right That Was Sought

by Nixon," *New York Times*, July 2, 1972, p. 16, col. 1; "Nixon Appointees May Shift Court on Obscenity and Business," *New York Times*, October 2, 1972, p. 16, col. 4. However, Gerald Gunther, in a careful review of the 1971 term of the Burger Court, characterizes the Court essentially as holding the line rather than moving in new directions of its own. Gunther writes, "There was no drastic rush to the right. The changes were marginal. . . . The new Court . . . has shown no inclination to overturn clear, carefully explained precedent." Gunther, "The Supreme Court 1971 Term, Foreword: In Search of Evolving Doctrine on a Changing Court: A Model for Newer Equal Protection," *Harvard Law Review, 86* (1972), pp. 1, 2–3. Cf. Goldberg, "Supreme Court Review 1972, Foreword—The Burger Court 1971 Term: One Step Forward, Two Steps Backward?" *Journal of Criminal Law, Criminology, and Police Science, 63*

(1972), p. 463. Although the court has shown an inclination to limit and specify some of the broader decisions of the Warren Court (e.g., limiting rights to counsel at line-ups as dealt with in *Gilbert* and *Wade*, see Graham, July 2, 1972, *supra*), there does not appear at the time of writing any pronounced tendency to reverse major thrusts of Warren Court decisions relevant to presently-considered ideological issues, but rather to curb or limit momentum in these directions.

11. Wilkins, "Crime in the World of 1990," *Futures, 4* (1970), p. 203.

12. The classic formulations of the distinction between "factual" and "evaluative" content of statements about human behavior are those of Max Weber. *See*, e.g., A. Henderson and T. Parsons, *supra* note 6, at 8 *passim*. *See* also G. Myrdal, *supra* note 3.

Appendix

CHART I
Sources of Crime: Locus of Responsibility

Left

Right

5. Behavior designated as "crime" by the ruling classes is an inevitable product of a fundamentally corrupt and unjust society. True crime is the behavior of those who perpetuate, control, and profit from an exploitative and brutalizing system. The behavior of those commonly regarded as "criminals" by establishment circles in fact represents heroic defiance and rebellion against the arbitrary and self-serving rules of an immoral social order. These persons thus bear no responsibility for what the state defines as crime; they are forced into such actions as justifiable responses to deliberate policies of oppression, discrimination, and exploitation.

5. Crime and violence are a direct product of a massive conspiracy by highly-organized and well-financed radical forces seeking deliberately to overthrow the society. Their basic method is an intensive and unrelenting attack on the fundamental moral values of the society, and their vehicle is that sector of the populace sufficiently low in intelligence, moral virtue, self-control, and judgment as to serve readily as their puppets by constantly engaging in those violent and predatory crimes best calculated to destroy the social order. Instigators of the conspiracy are most often members of racial or ethnic groups that owe allegiance to and are supported by hostile foreign powers.

4. Those who engage in the more common forms of theft and other forms of "street crime" are essentially forced into such behavior by a destructive set of social conditions caused by a grossly inequitable distribution of wealth, power, and privilege. These people are actually victims, rather than perpetrators of criminality; they are victimized by discrimination, segregation, denial of opportunity, denial of justice and equal rights. Their behavior is thus a

4. The bulk of serious crime is committed by members of certain ethnic and social class categories characterized by defective self-control, self-indulgence, limited time-horizons, and undeveloped moral conscience. The criminal propensities of these classes, which appear repeatedly in successive generations, are nurtured and encouraged by the enormous reluctance of authorities to apply the degree of firm, swift, and decisive

Chart I—*Continued*

perfectly understandable and justified reaction to the malign social forces that bring it about. Forms of crime perpetrated by the wealthy and powerful —extensive corruption, taking of massive profits through illicit collusion, outright fraud and embezzlement—along with a pervasive pattern of marginally legal exploitative practices—have far graver social consequences than the relatively minor offenses of the so-called "common" criminal. Yet these forms of crime are virtually ignored and their perpetrators excused or assigned mild penalties, while the great bulk of law-enforcement effort and attention is directed to the hapless victims of the system.

3. Public officials and agencies with responsibility for crime and criminals must share with damaging social conditions major blame for criminality. By allocating pitifully inadequate resources to criminal justice agencies the government virtually assures that they will be manned by poorly qualified, punitive, moralistic personnel who are granted vast amounts of arbitrary coercive power. These persons use this power to stigmatize, degrade and brutalize those who come under their jurisdiction, thus permitting them few options other than continued criminality. Society also manifests enormous reluctance to allocate the resources necessary to ameliorate the root social causes of crime— poverty, urban deterioration, blocked educational and job opportunities—and further enhances crime by maintaining widespread systems of segregation—separating race from race, the poor from the affluent, the deviant from the conventional and the criminal from the law-abiding.

2. Although the root causes of crime lie in the disabling consequences of social, economic, and educational deprivation concentrated primarily among the disadvantaged in low-income communities, criminal behavior is in fact widely prevalent among all sectors of the society, with many affluent people committing crimes such as shoplifting, drunkenness, forgery, embezzlement, and the like. The fact that most of those subject to arrest and imprisonment have low-income or minority backgrounds is a direct consequence of an inequitable and discriminatory application of the criminal justice process—whereby the offenses of the more affluent are ignored, suppressed, or treated outside of a criminal framework, while those of the poor are actively prosecuted. A very substantial portion

punishment which could serve effectively to curb crime. Since criminality is so basic to such persons, social service programs can scarcely hope to affect their behavior, but their low capacity for discrimination makes them unusually susceptible to the appeals of leftists who goad them to commit crimes in order to undermine the society.

3. The root cause of crime is a massive erosion of the fundamental moral values which traditionally have served to deter criminality, and a concomitant flouting of the established authority which has traditionally served to constrain it. The most extreme manifestations of this phenomenon are found among the most crime-prone sectors of the society —the young, minorities, and the poor. Among these groups and elsewhere there have arisen special sets of alternative values or "counter-cultures" which actually provide direct support for the violation of the legal and moral norms of law-abiding society. A major role in the alarming increase in crime and violence is played by certain elitist groups of left-oriented media writers, educators, jurists, lawyers, and others who contribute directly to criminality by publicizing, disseminating, and supporting these crime-engendering values.

2. A climate of growing permissiveness and stress on immediate personal gratification are progressively undermining the basic deterrents to criminal behavior—self-discipline, responsibility, and a well-developed moral conscience. The prevalent tendency by liberals to attribute blame for criminality to "the system" and its inequities serves directly to aggravate criminality by providing the criminal with a fallacious rationalization which enables him to excuse his criminal behavior, further eroding self-discipline and moral conscience.

Chart I—*Continued*

of the crime dealt with by officials must in fact be attributed to the nature of the criminal statutes themselves. A wide range of commonly pursued forms of behavior such as use of drugs, gambling, sexual deviance—are defined and handled as "crime," when in fact they should be seen as "victimless" and subject to private discretion. Further, a substantial portion of these and other forms of illegal behavior actually reflect illness—physical or emotional disturbance rather than criminality.

1. Crime is largely a product of social ills such as poverty, unemployment, poor quality education, and unequal opportunities. While those who commit crimes out of financial need or frustration with their life conditions deserve understanding and compassion, those who continue to commit crimes in the absence of adequate justification should in some degree be held accountable for their behavior; very often they are sick or disturbed persons who need help rather than punishment. Officials dealing with crime are often well-meaning, but they sometimes act unjustly or repressively out of an excessively narrow focus on specific objectives of law-enforcement. Such behavior in turn reflects frustration with the failure of society to provide them adequate resources to perform their tasks for which they are responsible, as it also fails to provide the resources needed to ameliorate the community conditions which breed crime.

1. The behavior of persons who habitually violate the law is caused by defective upbringing in the home, parental neglect, inadequate religious and moral training, poor neighborhood environment, and lack of adequate role-models. These conditions result in a lack of proper respect for the law and insufficient attention to the basic moral principles which deter criminality. The federal government also contributes by failing to provide local agencies of prevention and law-enforcement with sufficient resources to perform adequately the many tasks required to reduce or control crime.

CHART II
Modes of Dealing with Crime:
Policies with Respect to Offenders

Left

5. Since the bulk of acts defined as "crime" by the ruling classes simply represent behavior which threatens an invalid and immoral social system, those who engage in such acts can in no sense be regarded as culpable, or "criminal." There is thus no legitimate basis for any claim of official jurisdiction over, let alone any right to restrain, so-called offenders. Persons engaging in acts which help to hasten the inevitable collapse of a decadent system should have full and unrestrained freedom to continue such acts, and to be provided the maximum support and backing of all progressive elements. The vast bulk of those now incarcerated must be considered as political prisoners, unjustly deprived of freedom by a corrupt regime, and freed at once.

Right

5. Habitual criminals, criminal types, and those who incite them should bear the full brunt of social retribution, and be prevented by the most forceful means possible from further endangering society. Murderers, rapists, arsonists, armed robbers, subversives and the like should be promptly and expeditiously put to death. The more vicious and unregenerate of these criminals should be publicly executed as an example to others. To prevent future crimes, those classes of persons who persistently manifest a high propensity for criminality should be prevented from reproducing, through sterilization or other means. Those who persist in crimes calculated to undermine the social order should be completely and permanently removed from the society, preferably by deportation.

Chart II—*Continued*

4. All but a very small proportion of those who come under the jurisdiction of criminal justice agencies pose no real danger to society, and are entitled to full and unconditional freedom in the community at all stages of the criminal justice process. The state must insure that those accused of crimes, incarcerated, or in any way under legal jurisdiction be granted their full civil rights as citizens, and should make available to them at little or no cost the full range of legal and other resources necessary to protect them against the arbitrary exercise of coercive power. Criminal justice processing as currently conducted is essentially brutalizing—particularly institutional incarceration, which seriously aggravates criminality, and which should be entirely abolished. "Rehabilitation" under institutional auspices is a complete illusion; it has not worked, never will work, and must be abandoned as a policy objective. Accused persons, prisoners, and members of the general public subject to the arbitrary and punitive policies of police and other officials must be provided full rights and resources to protect their interests—including citizen control of police operations, full access to legal resources, fully developed grievance mechanisms, and the like.

3. Since contacts with criminal justice officials—particularly police and corrections personnel—increase the likelihood that persons will engage in crime, a major objective must be to divert the maximum number of persons away from criminal justice agencies and into service programs in the community—the proper arena for helping offenders. There should be maximum use of probation as an alternative to incarceration, and parole as an alternative to extended incarceration. However, both services must be drastically overhauled, and transformed from ineffective watchdog operations manned by low-quality personnel to genuine and effective human services. Institutionalization should be the alternative of last resort, and used only for those proven to be highly dangerous, or for whom services cannot be provided outside of an institutional context. Those confined must be afforded the same civil rights as all citizens, including full access to legal resources and to officially-compiled information, fully-operational grievance mechanisms, right of petition and appeal from official decisions. Every attempt must be made to minimize the separation between institution and

4. Dangerous or habitual criminals should be subject to genuine punishment of maximum severity, including capital punishment where called for, and extended prison terms (including life imprisonment) with air-tight guarantees that these be fully served. Probation and parole defeat the purposes of public protection and should be eliminated. Potential and less-habituated criminals might well be deterred from future crime by highly visible public punishment such as flogging, the stocks, and possibly physical marking or mutilation. To speak of "rights" of persons who have chosen deliberately to forfeit them by engaging in crime is a travesty, and malefactors should receive the punishment they deserve without interference by leftists working to obstruct the processes of justice. "Rehabilitation" as a policy objective is simply a weakly disguised method of pampering criminals, and has no place whatever in a proper system of criminal justice. Fully adequate facilities for detection, apprehension, and effective restraint of criminals should be granted those police and other criminal justice personnel who realize that their principal mission is swift and unequivocal retribution against wrongdoers and their permanent removal from society to secure the full protection of the law-abiding.

3. Rampant permissiveness and widespread coddling of criminals defeat the purposes of crime control and must be stopped. Those who persist in the commission of serious crime and whose behavior endangers the public safety should be dealt with firmly, decisively and forcefully. A policy of strict punishment is necessary not only because it is deserved by offenders but also because it serves effectively to deter potential criminals among the general public. A major effort must be directed toward increasing the rights and resources of officials who cope with crime, and decreasing the rights and resources—legal, statutory, and financial—of those who use them to evade or avoid deserved punishment. Predetention measures such as bail, suspended sentences and probation should be used only when it is certain that giving freedom to actual or putative criminals will not jeopardize public safety, and parole should be employed sparingly and with great caution only in those cases where true rehabilitation seems assured. The major objective both of incarceration and rehabilitation efforts must be the protection of law-abiding society, not the welfare of the offender.

Chart II—*Continued*

community by providing frequent leaves, work-release furloughs,' full visitation rights, full access to citizens' groups. Full rights and the guarantee of due process must be provided for all those accused of crimes—particularly juveniles, minorities, and the underprivileged.

2. Since the behavior of most of those who commit crimes is symptomatic of social or psychological forces over which they have little control, ameliorative efforts must be conducted within the framework of a comprehensive strategy of services which combines individually-oriented clinical services and beneficial social programs. Such services should be offered in whatever context they can most effectively be rendered, although the community is generally preferable to the institution. However, institutional programs organized around the concept of the therapeutic community can be most effective in helping certain kinds of persons, such as drug users, for whom external constraints can be a useful part of the rehabilitative process. Rehabilitation rather than punishment must be the major objective in dealing with offenders. Treatment in the community—in group homes, halfway houses, court clinics, on probation or parole—must incorporate the maximum range of services, including vocational training and placement, psychological testing and counselling, and other services which presently are either unavailable or woefully inadequate in most communities. Where imprisonment is indicated, sentences should be as short as possible, and inmates should be accorded the rights and respect due all human beings.

2. Lawbreakers should be subject to fair but firm penalties based primarily on the protection of society, but taking into account as well the future of the offender. Successful rehabilitation is an important objective since a reformed criminal no longer presents a threat to society. Rehabilitation should center on the moral re-education of the offender, and instill in him the respect for authority and basic moral values which are the best safeguards against continued crime. These aims can be furthered by prison programs which demand hard work and strict discipline, for these serve to promote good work habits and strengthen moral fiber. Sentences should be sufficiently long as to both adequately penalize the offender and insure sufficient time for effective rehabilitation. Probation and parole should not be granted indiscriminately, but reserved for carefully selected offenders, both to protect society and because it is difficult to achieve the degree of close and careful supervision necessary to successful rehabilitation outside the confines of the institution.

1. Effective methods for dealing with actual or putative offenders require well-developed and sophisticated methods for discriminating among varying categories of persons, and gearing treatment to the differential needs of the several types thus discriminated. A major goal is to insure that those most likely to benefit from psychological counseling and other therapeutic methods will receive the kinds of treatment they need, rather than wasting therapeutic resources on that relatively small group of offenders whose behavior is essentially beyond reform, and are poor candidates for rehabilitation. All those under the jurisdiction of criminal justice agencies should be treated equitably and humanely. Police in particular should treat their clients with fairness and respect—

1. An essential component of any effective method for dealing with violators is a capability for making careful and sensitive discriminations among various categories of offenders, and tailoring appropriate dispositional measures to different types of offenders. In particular, the capacity to differentiate between those with a good potential for reform and those with a poor potential will ensure that the more dangerous kinds of criminals are effectively restrained. Probationers and parolees should be subject to close and careful supervision both to make sure that their activities contribute to their rehabilitation and that the community is protected from repeat violations by those under official jurisdiction. Time spent in prison should be used to teach inmates useful skills so that they may re-

Chart II—*Continued*

especially members of minority groups and the disadvantaged. Careful consideration should be given before sentencing offenders to extended prison terms to make sure that other alternatives are not possible. Similarly, probation and parole should be used in those cases where these statutes appear likely to facilitate rehabilitation without endangering public safety. Prisoners should not be denied contact with the outside world, but should have rights to correspondence, visiting privileges, and access to printed and electronic media. They should also be provided with facilities for constructive use of leisure time, and program activities aimed to enhance the likelihood of rehabilitation.

enter society as well-trained and productive individuals.

CHART III
Modes of Dealing with Crime:
Policies with Respect to
Criminal Justice Agencies

Left	*Right*
5. The whole apparatus of so-called "law-enforcement" is in fact simply the domestic military apparatus used by the ruling classes to maintain themselves in power, and to inflict harassment, confinement, injury or death on those who protest injustice by challenging the arbitrary regulations devised by the militarists and monopolists to protect their interests. To talk of "reforming" such a system is farcical; the only conceivable method of eliminating the intolerable injustices inherent in this kind of society is the total and forceful overthrow of the entire system, including its so-called "law-enforcement" arm. All acts which serve this end, including elimination of members of the oppressor police force, serve to hasten the inevitable collapse of the system and the victory of progressive forces.	5. Maximum possible resources must be provided those law-enforcement officials who realize that their basic mission is the protection of society and maintenance of security for the law-abiding citizen. In addition to substantial increases in manpower, law-enforcement personnel must be provided with the most modern, efficient and lethal weaponry available, and the technological capacity (communications, computerization, electronic surveillance, aerial pursuit capability) to deliver maximum force and facilities possible to points of need—the detection, pursuit, and arrest of criminals, and in particular the control of terrorism and violence conducted or incited by radical forces.
4. The entire American system of criminal justice must be radically reformed. Unless there is a drastic reduction in the amount of power now at the disposal of official agencies—particularly the police and corrections, a police state is inevitable. In particular, unchecked power currently possessed by poorly qualified, politically reactionary officials to deal with accused and suspected persons as they see fit must be curtailed; their behavior brutalizes and radicalizes the clients of the system. To these officials, "dangerous" usually means	4. The critical crime situation requires massive increases in the size of police forces and their technological capacity to curb crime—particularly in the use of force against criminals and radical elements. It is imperative that police command full freedom to use all available resources, legal and technical, without interference from leftist elements seeking to tie their hands and render them impotent. The power of the courts to undermine the basis of police operations by denying them fundamental legal powers must be curbed. The

Chart III—*Continued*

"politically unacceptable." Increasing concentration of power in entrenched bureaucracies must be checked, and the people given maximum rights to local control of their own lives, including the right to self protection through associations such as citizens councils and security patrols to counter police harassment and brutality and to monitor the operations of local prisons. Means must be found to eliminate the extensive corruption which pervades the system—exemplified by venal criminality within police departments and the unholy alliance between organized crime, corrupt politicians, and those who are supposedly enforcing the laws. Most of the criminal offenses now on the books should be eliminated, retaining only a few truly dangerous crimes such as forceful rape, since most of the offenses which consume law-enforcement energies have no real victims, and should be left to private conscience. However, statutes related to illegality by business interests, bureaucrats, corporations and the like should be expanded, and enforcement efforts greatly increased. Virtually all prisons should be closed at once, and the few persons requiring institutional restraint should be accommodated in small facilities in local communities.

3. The more efficiency gained by law enforcement agencies through improvements in technology, communications, management, and so on, the greater the likelihood of harassment, intimidation, and discrimination directed against the poor and minorities. Improvements in police services can be achieved only through fundamental and extensive changes in the character of personnel, not through more hardware and technology. This should be achieved by abandoning antiquated selection and recruitment policies which are designed to obtain secure employment for low-quality personnel and which systematically discriminate against the minorities and culturally disadvantaged. Lateral entry, culture-free qualification tests, and other means must be used to loosen the iron grip of civil-service selection and tenure systems. The outmoded military model with its rigid hierarchical distinctions found among the police and other agencies should be eliminated, and a democratic organizational model put in its place. The police must see their proper function as service to the community rather than in narrow terms of law

nation's capacity for incarcerating criminals—particularly through maximum security facilities—must be greatly expanded, and prison security strengthened. The "prison reform" movement rests on a mindless focus on the welfare of convicted felons and a blind disregard for the welfare of law-abiding citizens. Particularly pernicious is the movement now underway to unload thousands of dangerous criminals directly into our communities under the guise of "community corrections" (halfway houses, group homes, etc.). The local citizenry must unite and forcefully block this effort to flood our homes and playgrounds with criminals, dope addicts, and subversives. Increasing concentration of power in the hands of centralized government must be stopped, and basic rights returned to the local community—including the right to exclude dangerous and undesirable elements, and the right to bear arms freely in defense of home and family. Strict curbs must be imposed on the freedom of the media to disseminate materials aimed to undermine morality and encourage crime.

3. Law enforcement agencies must be provided all the resources necessary to deal promptly and decisively with crime and violence. Failure to so act encourages further law breaking both by those who are subject to permissive and inefficient handling and by those who become aware thereby how little risk they run of being caught and penalized for serious crimes. The rights of the police to stringently and effectively enforce the law must be protected from misguided legalistic interference—particularly the constant practice of many judges of granting freedom to genuine criminals laboriously apprehended by the police, often on the basis of picayune procedural details related to "due process" or other legalistic devices for impeding justice. The scope of the criminal law must be expanded rather than reduced; there is no such thing as "victimless" crime; the welfare of all law-abiding people and the moral basis of society itself are victimized by crimes such as pornography, prostitution, homosexuality and drug use, and offenders must be vigorously pursued, prosecuted, and penalized. Attempts to prevent crime

Chart III—*Continued*

enforcement. As part of their community responsibility, law enforcement agencies should stringently limit access to information concerning offenders, especially younger ones, and much of such information should be destroyed. There must be maximum public access to the inner operations of police, courts and prisons by insuring full flow of information to the media, full accountability to and visitation rights by citizens and citizen groups, and full public disclosure of operational policies and operations. The major burden of corrections should be removed from the institutions, which are crime-breeding and dehumanizing, and placed directly in the communities, to which all offenders must at some point return.

2. A basic need of the criminal justice system is an extensive upgrading of the quality of personnel. This must be done by recruiting better qualified people—preferably with college training, in all branches and at all levels, and by mounting effective in-service training programs. Higher quality and better trained personnel are of particular importance in the case of the police, and training must place more stress on human relations studies such as psychology and sociology, and relatively less stress on purely technical aspects of police work. Quality must be maintained by the development and application of performance standards against which all personnel must be periodically measured, and which should provide the basis for promotion. Sentencing procedures must be standardized, rationalized, and geared to specific and explicit rehabilitative objectives rather than being left to the often arbitrary and capricious whims of particular judges. Corrections as well as other criminal justice agencies must be made more humane and equitable, and the rights of prisoners as individuals should be respected. Attempts should be made to reduce the degree of separation of prison inmates from the outside world. Changes in both legislation and law enforcement policies must be directed to reducing the disparities in arrest rates between richer and poorer offenders, so that commensurately fewer of the poor and underprivileged and more of the better off, are sought out, convicted, and imprisoned. Promising programs of humane reform must not be abandoned simply because they fail to show immediate measurable results, but should receive continued or increased federal support.

by pouring massive amounts of tax dollars into slum communities are worse than useless, since such people can absorb limitless welfare "benefits" with no appreciable effect on their criminal propensities. Communities must resist attempts to open up their streets and homes to hardened criminals through halfway houses and other forms of "community corrections."

2. There should be substantial increases in the numbers and visibility of police, particularly in and around schools, places of business, and areas of family activity. Although a few bad apples may appear from time to time, the bulk of our police are conscientious and upstanding men who deserve the continued respect and support of the community, and who should be granted ample resources to do the job to which they are assigned. Some of the proposed prison reforms may be commendable, but the burden to the taxpayer must never be lost sight of: most of the reforms suggested or already in practice are of dubious benefit or yield benefits clearly not commensurate with their costs. More efforts should be directed to prevention of crime; in particular, programs of moral re-education in the schools and communities, and the institution of safeguards against the influence of those in the schools, media and elsewhere who promote criminality by challenging and rejecting the established moral values which serve to forestall illegal and immoral conduct.

Chart III—Continued

1. There must be better coordination of existing criminal justice facilities and functions so as to better focus available services on the whole individual, rather than treating him through disparate and compartmentalized efforts. This must entail better liaison among police, courts and corrections and greatly improved lines of communication, to the end of enabling each to attain better appreciation, understanding and knowledge of the operational problems of the others. Coordination and liaison must also increase between the criminal justice agencies and the general welfare services of the community, which have much to contribute both in the way of prevention of crime and rehabilitation of criminals. Local politicians often frustrate the purposes of reform by consuming resources in patronage, graft, and the financial support of entrenched local interests, so the federal government must take the lead in financing and overseeing criminal justice reform efforts. Federal resources and standards should be utilized to substantially increase the level and quality of social service resources available to criminal justice enterprises, promulgate standardized and rationalized modes of operation in local communities, and bring administrative coherence to the host of uncoordinated efforts now in progress.

1. The operations of the police should be made more efficient, in part through increased use of modern managerial principles and information processing techniques. Police protection should focus more directly on the local community, and efforts should be made to restore the degree of personal moral integrity and intimate knowledge of the local community which many older policemen had but many younger ones lack. Prison reform is important, but innovations should be instituted gradually and with great caution, and the old should not be discarded until the new is fully proven to be adequate. There should be much better coordination among law enforcement agencies, to reduce inefficiency, wasteful overlap, and duplication of services. The federal government must assume a major role in providing the leadership and financial resources necessary to effective law-enforcement and crime control.

When the Cops Were Not "Handcuffed"

YALE KAMISAR

Are we losing the war against crime? Is the public getting a fair break? Has the pendulum swung too far to the left? Do the victims of crime have some rights, too? Are the courts handcuffing the police?

If there were a hit parade for newspaper and magazine articles, speeches and panel discussions, these questions would rank high on the list. Not only are they being raised with increasing frequency, but they are being debated with growing fury.

Last year, probably the most famous police chief in the United States, William H. Parker of Los Angeles, protested that American police work has been "tragically weakened" through a progressive "judicial takeover." These are strong words, but Boston District Attorney Garrett Byrne, then president of the National Association of District Attorneys, easily topped the chief with the cry that the Supreme Court is "destroying the nation." (Despite this rant, Mr. Byrne has since been appointed to the President's newly established National Crime Commission, which has been assigned the task of making a

SOURCE: New York Times Magazine, November 7, 1965, p. 34; © 1965 by The New York Times Company. Reprinted by permission.

systematic study of the entire spectrum of the problems of crime.)

This year, Michael J. Murphy, former Police Commissioner of New York, is the leading contender for anti-Supreme Court honors, Mr. Murphy's pet line is: "We [the police] are forced to fight by Marquis of Queensberry rules while the criminals are permitted to gouge and bite."

Not infrequently, one who dares to defend the Court, or simply to explain what the Court is doing and why, is asked which side he is on: the side of law and order—or the side of the robber, the dope peddler and the rapist. Any defense of the Court is an attack on the police. And any attack on the police (to quote Mayor Sam Yorty of Los Angeles, and he is not alone) is an "attack on our American system," perhaps even part of "a world-wide campaign by Communists, Communist dupes and sympathizers."

Today, the course of the Court is clear. Once concerned with property rights much more than with human liberty, it is now, as Anthony Lewis wrote several years ago, "the keeper, not of the nation's property, but of its conscience." If that role constitutes lending aid and comfort to the criminal element, then the Court is guilty.

As Judge Walter Schaefer of the Illinois Supreme Court pointed out in his famous Holmes Lecture of a decade ago, however, many of those safeguards of criminal procedure which we now take for granted came surprisingly late. Whether a state had to appoint counsel for an indigent defendant was a question which did not confront the Court until 1932, and it held then that counsel had to be provided only when the defendant was facing a possible death sentence. Whether the state could convict a defendant on the basis of a coerced confession was an issue first presented to the Court in 1936, and all the Court was asked to do then was ban confessions extracted by brutal beatings.

What was it like in 1910 and 1920 and 1930 when the effectuation and implementation of criminal procedural safeguards were pretty much left to the states themselves? What was it like in the days when, as Dean Erwin Griswold of the Harvard Law School recently pointed out, "some things that were rather clearly there" (in the Constitution) had not yet "been given the attention and effect which they should have if our Constitution is to be a truly meaningful document"? Or, if you prefer, what was it like

in the "good old days" before the Supreme Court began to mess up things?

In 1910, Curtis Lindley, president of the California Bar Association, declared the need for an "adjustment" in our criminal procedures "to meet the expanding social necessity." "Many of the difficulties," he continued, "are due to an exaggerated respect for the individual. . . ." He proposed (1) that a suspect be interrogated by a magistrate and, if he refused to answer the inquiries, that the state be permitted to comment on this fact at the trial; and (2) that the requirement of a unanimous verdict of guilty be reduced to three-fourths, "except possibly in cases where infliction of the death penalty is involved." This, he pointed out, would still "give the defendant three-fourths of the show."

The following year, 1911, in a hard-hitting Atlantic Monthly article entitled "Coddling the Criminal," New York prosecutor Charles Nott charged that "the appalling amount of crime in the United States compared with other civilized countries is due to the fact that it is generally known that the punishment for crime in America is uncertain and far from severe." Where lay the fault? According to Nott, the two law-enforcement obstacles which had to be cleared were the protection against double jeopardy and the privilege against self-incrimination.

Eight years later, Hugo Pam, president of the Institute of Criminal Law and Criminology, also addressed himself to the "crime problem," one which had been greatly aggravated by "the advent of the automobile." As he viewed the situation in 1919, "the boldness of the crimes and the apparent helplessness of the law have embittered the public to the extent that any advance in treatment of criminals save punishment is looked upon with disfavor." Law-enforcement officials, he noted, "have repeatedly charged that in the main these serious crimes have been committed by people on probation or parole." It followed, of course, that there was a strong movement afoot to curtail or completely repeal these provisions.

The following year, 1920, and again in 1922, Edwin W. Sims, the first head of the newly established Chicago Crime Commission, added his voice to the insistent demands "for action" that would reduce crime. He had the figures: "During 1919 there were more murders in Chicago (with a population of three million) than in the entire British Isles (with a population of 40 million)." Moreover, the prosecution had obtained only 44 convictions as against 336 murders. The situation called for strong words and Mr. Sims was equal to the occasion:

"We have kept on providing criminals with flowers, libraries, athletics, hot and cold running water, and probation and parole. The tender solicitude for the welfare of criminals publicly expressed by social workers conveys to 10,000 criminals plying their vocation in Chicago the mistaken impression that the community is more interested in them than it is in their victims. . . .

"There has been too much mollycoddling of the criminal population. . . . It is time for plain speaking. Murderers are turned loose. They have no fear of the police. They sneer at the law. It is not a time for promises. It is a time for action. The turning point has come. Decency wins or anarchy triumphs. There is no middle course."

If Edwin Sims were still in fine voice today, he would be much in demand. At home and on the road, he would probably outdraw even Messrs. Byrne, Murphy and Parker. About all Sims would have to do would be to strike "social workers," insert "Supreme Court," and maybe add a paragraph or two about recent Supreme Court decisions. But his era, I repeat, was 1920.

The nineteen-twenties were troubled times. In speaking of the need for a National Crime Commission, The New Republic of Aug. 26, 1925, declared: "It is no exaggeration to assert that the administration of criminal justice has broken down in the United States and that in this respect American state governments are failing to perform the most primitive and most essential function which society imposes on government." At about the same time, the great criminologist Edwin H. Sutherland reported: "Capital punishment has been restored in four states since the war, and in many places there is a strenuous demand for the whipping post. . . . Crime commissions are recommending increased severity and certainty of punishment."

By 1933, the public had become so alarmed at an apparent increase in professional criminality that a U.S. Senate investigating committee, headed by Royal S. Copeland of New York, scoured the country for information which could lead to a national legislative solution.

The Detroit hearings brought out that the murder rate in the United States was nine times higher than in England and in Wales, "where they have basically the same Anglo-Saxon institutions," and even twice as high as Italy's, "the home of the Mafia, the 'Black Hand.' " In New York, a witness solemnly declared that "the crime situation in this country is so serious that it approaches a major crisis in our history, a crisis which will determine whether the nation is to belong to normal citizens or whether it is to be surrendered completely to gangster rule."

In Chicago, drawing upon his 20 years of experience as a lawyer, prosecutor and municipal judge, a witness concluded that "there is entirely too much worry, consideration and too many safeguards about the criminal's constitutional rights." He recommended for the Senate committee's consideration Illinois's new "reputation vagrancy law, which provides that all persons who are reputed to habitually violate the criminal laws and who are reputed to carry concealed weapons are vagrants." "Under this law," he reported, "we have harassed and convicted . . . numerous mad dogs of the West Side." (The following year, the Illinois Supreme Court struck down the law as unconstitutional.)

Senator Copeland told assembled witnesses of his desire for "a frank expression of opinion, no matter how critical you may be of existing institutions." Most of the witnesses were equal to the challenge.

A Maj. Homer Shockley urged that "constitutional and statutory guarantees, applicable to the average citizen, be suspended by special court procedure for the person who is known to be an habitual criminal . . . or who habitually consorts with criminals, to the end that the burden of proof of innocence of any fairly well substantiated charge be squarely placed on the accused; that he be tried without the benefit of a jury; and that, if convicted, all of his property and wealth be confiscated except such portion as the accused can prove were honestly gained by honest effort." The presumption of innocence is "fair enough" for the normal person, but not "for the dirty rat whom everybody knows to be an incurably habitual crook."

(Lest the major be peremptorily dismissed as a nonlegally trained commentator, it should be noted that two years earlier the dean of a Middle Western law school was reported to have advocated the establishment of a commission empowered to convict persons as "public enemies" and fix terms of their removal from society without convicting them for any specific offense, as historically required.)

Citing Toronto, where whippings were said to have broken a wave of jewelry-store stick-ups, another witness at the 1933 hearings, New York Police Commissioner Edward Mulrooney, came out for 30 or 40 lashes to be applied at the time a criminal entered prison, others every six months thereafter.

Lewis E. Lawes, the famous warden of Sing Sing prison, exclaimed: "Strip our hysterical reaction in the present emergency and what have you? A confession that our agencies are not keeping step with crime, are falling short of their mark. Yesterday it was robbery, today it is kidnapping, tomorrow it will be something else. With every new crime racket will come a new hysteria." After delivering these refreshingly sober remarks, Warden Lawes proceeded to disregard his own advice:

"I think I am a liberal, but at the same time, in case of war I would fight for the country, and this is war. I believe if they do not have some form of martial law against this particular group [racketeers and kidnappers] that there will come in . . . lynch law and from lynch law they will have the martial law. . . . It seems to me that this is a war to be stamped out quickly and could be stopped in 60 days if all the authorities get together honestly and let the public know exactly what they are doing. . . . If I were Mussolini I could do it in 30 days."

Even renowned defense attorney Sam Liebowitz, honored "to be called upon to speak from the viewpoint of the criminal lawyer," seemed to get into the swing of things. He proposed a "national vagrancy law," whereby if a well-dressed crook "cannot give a good account of himself" to a police officer who spots him on the street or in his Cadillac "you take him into the station house and question him, and then take him before a judge. The judge says, 'Prove you are earning an honest living.'

"No honest man need rebel against a thing like that," contended the great criminal lawyer. "If you are earning an honest dollar, you can show what you are doing. . . . It is the crook that sets up the cry of the Constitution, and the protection of the Constitution, when he is in trouble."

Detroit prosecutor Harry Toy agreed that "a national vagrancy act—we call it a public-enemy act—is a wonderful thing." Mr. Liebowitz had assumed that a national vagrancy act would require an amendment to the privilege against self-incrimination, but the Detroit prosecutor insisted that such an act "could be framed under the present Federal Constitution as it now stands." (His own state's "public-enemy" law was held unconstitutional by the Michigan Supreme Court a few months later. The following year New Jersey made it a felony, punishable by 20 years' imprisonment, to be a "gangster"; the U.S. Supreme Court struck the law down in 1939 on the grounds of vagueness and uncertainty.)

Chicago Municipal Court Judge Thomas Green plumped for an amendment to the Fourth Amendment permitting searches of persons "reputed" to be criminals and to be carrying firearms. The reason the framers of the Constitution stressed personal liberty, he explained, was that "there were no gangsters" then. "I think personal liberty is a wonderful thing," he hastened to add, "but today the man who takes advantage of personal liberty is the gangster, the gunman, the kidnapper."

Virtually every procedural safeguard caught heavy fire in the Senate hearings. One witness called "the right to the 'shield of silence' " (the privilege against self-incrimination) "the greatest stumbling block to justice and incentive to crime in all common-law countries." Another maintained that "the present provisions against self-incrimination were intended to protect the citizen against the medieval methods of torture, and they have become obsolete in modern life."

A report of the International Association of Chiefs of Police listed as "contributing factors to our serious crime problem . . . the resort to injunctions, writs of habeas corpus, changes of venue, etc., all with a view of embarrassing and retarding the administration of justice." The "founders of the Republic," it was argued, "never intended that habeas corpus and bail should be granted to a thug or serious thief."

Judge William Skillman of Detroit Criminal Court, known as "the one-man grand jury," maintained that permitting the state to appeal an acquittal "would do much to insure to society, represented by the state, a fair break in the trial of a lawsuit" because "the so-called 'former jeopardy clause' . . . has many times been used as a shield by a weak or timid or even a venal judge." Capt. A. B. Moore of the New York State Police proposed that an "expert adviser" or legally trained "technician" sit with and retire to the jury room with the jury "to advise them [on] those technicalities that had been implanted in their minds by a very clever attorney."

So much for the teens and twenties and thirties, the so-called golden era when the U.S. Supreme Court kept "hands off" local law enforcement.

When Chief Parker warns us in our time that "the police ... are limited like the Yalu River boundary, and the result of it is that they are losing the war just like we lost the war in Korea," I wonder: When, if ever, weren't we supposedly losing the war against crime? When, if ever, weren't law enforcement personnel impatient with the checks and balances of our system? When, if ever, didn't they feel unduly "limited"? When, if ever, will they realize that our citizens are free *because* the police are "limited"?

When an official of the National District Attorneys Association insists in our time: "This country can no longer afford a 'civil-rights binge' that so restricts law-enforcement agencies that they become ineffective and organized crime flourishes," I wonder: When, if ever, in the opinion of law-enforcement personnel, could this country afford a "civil-rights binge"? When, if ever, wasn't there a "crime crisis"? When, if ever, weren't there proclamations of great emergencies and announcements of disbelief in the capacities of ordinary institutions and regular procedures to cope with them?

When Chicago's famous police chief, O. W. Wilson, stumps the country, pointing to the favorable crime picture in England, and other nations "unhampered" by restrictive court decisions, and exclaiming that "crime is overwhelming our society" (at the very time he is accepting credit in Chicago for a 20 per cent drop in crimes against the person), I am reminded of a story, apocryphal no doubt, about a certain aging promiscuous actress. When asked what she would do if she could live her life all over again she is said to have replied: "The same thing—with different people."

I venture to say that today too many law-enforcement spokesmen are doing "the same thing—with different people." They are using different crime statistics and they are concentrating on a different target—the Supreme Court rather than the state courts, parole boards, social workers and "shyster lawyers"—but they are reacting the same way they reacted in past generations.

They are reconciling the delusion of our omnipotence with the experience of limited power to cope with the "crime crisis" by explaining failure in terms of betrayal. To borrow a phrase from Dean Acheson, they are letting a "mood of irritated frustration with complexity" find expression in "scapegoating."

Secretaries and ex-Secretaries of State know almost as much about scapegoating as Supreme Court justices. If the task of containing or controlling "change" in Africa or Asia is beyond our capabilities, to many people it means simply, or at least used to mean simply, that the State Department is full of incompetents or Communists or both. Here, as elsewhere, if things seem to be going wrong, but there is no simple and satisfactory reason why, it is tempting to think that "the way to stop the mischief is to root out the witches."

Crime is a baffling, complex, frustrating, defiant problem. And as James Reston once pointed out in explaining Barry Goldwater's appeal to millions of Americans: "The more complicated life becomes, the more people are attracted to simple solutions; the more irrational the world seems, the more they long for rational answers; and the more diverse everything is, the more they want it all reduced to identity."

As the Wickersham Report of 1931 disclosed, the prevailing "interrogation methods" of the nineteen-twenties and thirties included the application of the rubber hose to the back or the pit of the stomach, kicks in the shins and blows struck with a telephone book on the side of the victim's head.

These techniques did not stem the tide of crime. Nor did the use of illegally seized evidence, which most state courts permitted as late as the nineteen-forties and fifties. Nor, while they lasted, did the "public-enemy" laws, or the many criminal registration ordinances stimulated by the Copeland hearings.

If history does anything, it supports David Acheson, who, when U.S. Attorney for the District of Columbia (the jurisdiction which has borne the brunt of "restrictive" court rules), dismissed the suggestion that "the crime rate will go away if we give back to law-enforcement agencies 'power taken from them by Federal court decisions'" with the assurance that "the war against crime does not lie on this front. Prosecution procedure has, at most, only the most remote causal connection with crime. Changes in court decisions and prosecution procedure would have about the same effect on the crime rate as an aspirin would have on a tumor of the brain."

Unfortunately this speech was not given the publicity it deserved. Nor were the refreshingly cool, thoughtful remarks of the new Deputy Attorney General, Ramsey Clark, who last August pointed out:

"Court rules do not cause crime. People do not commit crime because they know they cannot be questioned by police before presentment, or even because they feel they will not be convicted. We as a people commit crimes because we are capable of committing crimes. We choose to commit crimes. . . . In the long run, only the elimination of the causes of crime can make a significant and lasting difference in the incidence of crime.

"But the reduction of the causes of crime is a slow and arduous process and the need to protect persons and property is immediate. The present need for greater protection . . . can be filled not by . . . court rulings affirming convictions based on confessions secured after hours of questioning, or evidence seized in searches made without warrants. The immediate need can be filled by more and better police protection."

Chief Parker has expressed the hope that in searching for answers to our crime problem the new National Crime Commission "not overlook the influencing factor of the judicial revolution." The greater danger is that too much attention will be paid to this "revolution."

Critics of the courts are well represented, but not a single criminologist or sociologist or psychologist sits on the 19-man commission. These are conspicuous omissions for a group asked "to be daring and creative and revolutionary" in its recommendations. These are incredible omissions for those of us who share the views of the Deputy Attorney General that "the first, the most pervasive and the most difficult" front in the war on crime "is the battle against the causes of crime: poverty, ignorance, unequal opportunity, social tension, moral erosion."

By a strange coincidence, the very day the President announced the formation of the Crime Commission, the F.B.I. released new figures on the crime rate —soaring as usual—and J. Edgar Hoover took a sideswipe at "restrictive court decisions affecting police prevention and enforcement activity." And at their very first meeting, last September, the commission members were told by Mr. Hoover that recent court decisions had "too often severely and unfairly shackled the police officer."

Probably the most eminently qualified member of the President's Commission is Columbia Law School's Herbert Wechsler, the director of the American Law Institute and chief draftsman of the recently completed Model Penal Code, a monumental work which has already had a tremendous impact throughout the nation. The commission would have gotten off to a more auspicious start if, instead of listening to a criticism of recent court decisions, its members had read (or reread) what Mr. Wechsler, then a young, obscure assistant law professor, once said of other crime conferences in another era of "crisis" (those called by the U.S. Attorney General and a number of states, including New York, in 1934–36):

"The most satisfactory method of crime prevention is the solution of the basic problems of government—the production and distribution of external goods, education and recreation. . . . That the problems of social reform present dilemmas of their own, I do not pretend to deny. I argue only that one can say for social reform as a means to the end of improved crime control what can also be said for better personnel but cannot be said for drastic tightening of the processes of the criminal law—that even if the end should not be achieved, the means is desirable for its own sake."

From Professor to Patrolman:

A Fresh Perspective on the Police

GEORGE L. KIRKHAM

Persons such as myself—members of the academic community—have traditionally been quick to find fault with the police. From isolated incidents reported in the various news media we have fashioned for ourselves a stereotyped image of the police officer which conveniently conforms to our notions of what he is. We see the brutal cop, the racist cop, the grafting cop, the discourteous cop. What we do not see, however, is the image of thousands of dedicated men and women struggling against almost impossible odds to preserve our society and everything in it which we cherish.

For some years, first as a student and later as a professor of criminology, I found myself troubled by the fact that most of us who have written books and articles about the police have never served as policemen. I began to be increasingly bothered by the attitude of many of my students who were former policemen. Time and again they would respond to my frequently critical lectures on the police with the argument that I could not possibly understand what a police officer has to endure in modern society until I had been one myself. Under the weight of this frustration, and my personal conviction that knowledge has an applied as well as a theoretical dimension, I decided to take up this challenge. I would become a policeman myself as a means of establishing once and for all the accuracy of what we criminologists had been saying about the police for so long.

My announced intention to become a uniformed patrolman was at first met with fairly widespread disbelief on the part of family, friends, and colleagues alike. At 31, with a family and an established career as a criminologist, I was surely an unlikely candidate for the position of police recruit. The very idea, it was suggested to me, was outrageous and absurd. I

SOURCE: *Journal of Police Science and Administration*, *2* (June 1974), pp. 127–137.

was told that no police administrator in his right mind would allow a representative of the academic world to enter his organization. It has never been done and could not be done.

Fortunately, many of my students who either had been or were then policemen sounded a far more optimistic and enthusiastic note. Police administrators and officers alike, they said, would welcome the opportunity to expose members of the academic community to the problems of their occupation. If one of us was really willing to see and feel the policeman's world from behind a badge and blue uniform, instead of from the safe and comfortable vantage point of a classroom or university office, police officers themselves would do everything in their power to make the opportunity available. Despite these assurances from my policeman-students, I remained skeptical about my chances of being allowed to do such an unorthodox thing.

This skepticism was, however, soon to be overcome. One of my better criminology students at the time was a young police officer on educational leave from the Jacksonville, Florida, Sheriff's Office. Upon learning of my desire to become a police officer in order to better understand the problems of the police, he urged me to contact Sheriff Dale Carson and Undersheriff D. K. Brown of his department with my proposal. I had earlier heard other police officers describe the consolidated 800-man force of Jacksonville-Duval County as one of the most progressive departments in the country. I learned that Sheriff Carson and Undersheriff Brown, two former FBI agents, had won considerable respect in the law enforcement profession as enlightened and innovative administrators.

The size and composition of Jacksonville, as well as its nearness to my university and home, made it appear to be an ideal location for what I wished to do. Numbering just over one-half million residents, Jacksonville impressed me as being the kind of large and rapidly growing American city which inevitably experiences the major social problems of our time: crime and delinquency, racial unrest, poverty and mental illness. A seaport and industrial center, Jacksonville offered a diversity of urban, suburban, and even rural populations in its vast land area. I took particular note of the fact that it contained a fairly typical inner-city slum section and black ghetto, both of which were in the process of being transformed through a massive program of urban redevelopment. This latter feature was especially important to me insofar as I wanted to experience personally the stresses and strains of today's city policeman. It is, after all, he who has traditionally been the subject of such intense interest and criticism on the part of social scientists such as myself.

Much to my surprise, both Sheriff Carson and Undersheriff Brown were not only supportive of my proposal but enthusiastic as well. I made it clear to them at the onset that I did not wish to function as an observer or reserve officer. I wanted to become a sworn and full-time member of their department for a period of between four and six months. I further stated that I hoped to spend most of this period working as a uniformed patrolman in those inner-city beats most characterized by violence, poverty, social unrest and high crime rates. They agreed to this, with the understanding that I would first have to meet the same requirements as any other police candidate. It would be necessary, for example, to submit to a thorough character investigation, a physical examination, and to meet the same requirements as any other police candidate, including the training standards required of all Florida police officers. Since I was to be unpaid, I would be exempted, however, from departmental civil service requirements. Both Carson and Brown set about overcoming various administrative and insurance problems which had to be dealt with in advance of my becoming a police officer. Suppose, for example, I should be injured or killed in the line of duty, or should injure or kill someone else; what of the department and city's liability? These and other issues were gradually resolved with considerable effort on their part. The only stipulation set forth by both administrators was one with which I strongly agreed: for the sake of morale and confidence in the department, every officer must know in advance exactly who I was and what I was doing. Other than being in the unusual position of a "patrolman-professor," I would be indistinguishable from other officers in every respect, from the standard-issue .38 Smith and Wesson revolver I would carry to the badge and uniform I would wear.

The biggest and final obstacle which I faced was the necessity that I comply fully with a 1967 Florida Police Standards law, which requires that every police officer and deputy sheriff in the state complete a minimum of 280 hours of law enforcement training prior to being sworn in and assigned to regular duty. Since I had a full-time university job nearly 200 miles from Jacksonville, this meant that I would be unable to attend the regular Sheriff's Academy. I would have to attend a certified academy in my own area, something which I arranged to do with Sheriff Carson's sponsorship.

For four months, for four hours each evening, and five nights a week, I attended the Tallahassee Area Police Academy, along with 35 younger classmates. As a balding intellectual, I stood out at first as an oddity in the class of young men destined to become local law enforcement officers. With the passage of time, however, they came to accept me, and I them. We joked, drank coffee, and struggled through various examinations and lessons together. At first known only as "the professor," the men later nicknamed me "Doc," over my good-natured protests.

As the days stretched into weeks and the weeks into months, I took lengthy notes on interviewing witnesses at crime scenes, investigated imaginary traffic accidents, and lifted fingerprints. Some nights I went home after hours of physical defense training, designed for my uniformly younger and stronger peers, with tired muscles, bruises, and the feeling that I should have my head examined for undertaking such a rugged project.

As someone who had never fired a handgun, I quickly grew accustomed to the noise of 35 revolvers firing at the cardboard silhouettes which we transformed into real assailants at the sound of the range whistle. I learned how to make car stops properly, approach a front door or a darkened building, question suspects, and a thousand other things that every modern police officer must know. After what seemed an eternity, graduation from the academy finally came, and with it what was to become the most difficult but rewarding educational experience of my life: I became a policeman.

I will never forget standing in front of the Jacksonville police station on that first day. I felt incredibly awkward and conspicuous in the new blue uniform and creaking leather. Whatever confidence in my ability to "do the job" I had gained during the academy seemed to evaporate as I stood there watching other blue figures hurrying in the evening rain toward assembly. After some minutes, I summoned the courage to walk into the station and into my new career as a core city patrolman.

That first day seems long ago now. As I write this, I have completed over 100 tours of duty as a patrolman. Although still a rookie officer, so much happened in the short space of six months that I will never again be either the same man or the same scientist who stood in front of the station on that first day. While it is hard even to begin to describe in a brief article the many changes which have occurred within me during this time, I would like to share with fellow policemen and colleagues in the academic community a few of what I regard as the more important of my "street lessons."

I had always personally been of the opinion that police officers greatly exaggerate the amount of verbal disrespect and physical abuse to which they are subjected in the line of duty. During my first few hours as a street officer, I lived blissfully in a magic bubble which was soon to burst. As a college professor, I had grown accustomed to being treated with respect and deference by those I encountered. I somehow naively assumed that this same quality of respect would carry over into my new role as a policeman. I was, after all, a representative of the law, identifiable to all by the badge and uniform I wore as someone dedicated to the protection of society. Surely that fact would entitle me to a measure of respect and cooperation—or so I thought. I quickly found that my badge and uniform, rather than serving to shield me from such things as disrespect and violence, only acted as a magnet which drew me toward many individuals who hated what I represented.

I had discounted on my first evening the warning of a veteran sergeant who, after hearing that I was about to begin work as a patrolman, shook his head and cautioned, "You'd better watch yourself out there, Professor! It gets pretty rough sometimes!" I was soon to find out what he meant.

Several hours into my first evening on the streets, my partner and I were dispatched to a bar in the downtown area to handle a disturbance complaint. Inside, we encountered a large and boisterous drunk who was arguing with the bartender and loudly refusing to leave. As someone with considerable experience as a correctional counselor and mental health worker, I hastened to take charge of the situation. "Excuse me, sir," I smiled pleasantly at the

drunk, "but I wonder if I could ask you to step outside and talk with me for just a minute?" The man stared at me through bloodshot eyes in disbelief for a second, raising one hand to scratch the stubble of several days growth of beard. Then suddenly, without warning, it happened. He swung at me, luckily missing my face and striking me on the right shoulder. I couldn't believe it. What on earth had I done to provoke such a reaction? Before I could recover from my startled condition, he swung again—this time tearing my whistle chain from a shoulder epaulet. After a brief struggle, we had the still shouting, cursing man locked in the back of our cruiser. I stood there, breathing heavily with my hair in my eyes as I surveyed the damage to my new uniform and looked in bewilderment at my partner, who only smiled and clapped me affectionately on the back.

Something was very wrong, I remember thinking to myself in the front seat as we headed for the jail. I had used the same kind of gentle, rapport-building approach with countless offenders in prison and probation settings. It had always worked so well there. What was so different about being a policeman? In the days and weeks which followed, I was to learn the answer to this question the hard way. As a university professor, I had always sought to convey to students the idea that it is a mistake to exercise authority, to make decisions for other people, or rely upon orders and commands to accomplish something. As a police officer myself, I was forced time and again to do just that. For the first time in my life, I encountered individuals who interpreted kindness as weakness, as an invitation to disrespect or violence. I encountered men, women, and children who, in fear, desperation, or excitement looked to the person behind my blue uniform and shield for guidance, control and direction. As someone who had always condemned the exercise of authority, the acceptance of myself as an unavoidable symbol of authority came as a bitter lesson.

I found that there was a world of difference between encountering individuals, as I had, in mental health or correctional settings, and facing them as the patrolman must: when they are violent, hysterical, desperate. When I put the uniform of a police officer on, I lost the luxury of sitting in an air-conditioned office with my pipe and books, calmly discussing with a rapist or armed robber the past problems which had led him into trouble with the law. Such offenders had seemed so innocent, so harmless in the sterile setting of prison. The often terrible crimes which they had committed were long since past, reduced like their victims to so many printed words on a page.

Now, as a police officer, I began to encounter the offender for the first time as a very real menace to my personal safety and the security of our society. The felon was no longer a harmless figure sitting in blue denims across my prison desk, a "victim" of society, to be treated with compassion and leniency. He became an armed robber fleeing from the scene of a crime; a crazed maniac threatening his family with a gun; someone who might become my killer crouched behind the wheel of a car on a dark street.

Like crime itself, fear quickly ceased to be an impersonal and abstract thing. It became something which I regularly experienced. It was a tightness in my stomach as I approached a warehouse where something had tripped a silent alarm. I could taste it as a dryness in my mouth as we raced with blue lights and siren toward the site of a "Signal Zero" (armed and dangerous) call. For the first time in my life, I came to know—as every policeman knows—the true meaning of fear. Through shift after shift it stalked me, making my palms cold and sweaty and pumping the adrenalin through my veins.

I recall particularly a dramatic lesson in the meaning of fear which took place shortly after I joined the force. My partner and I were on routine patrol one Saturday evening in a deteriorated area of cheap bars and pool halls when we observed a young black male double-parked in the middle of the street. I pulled alongside and asked him in a civil manner to either park or drive on, whereupon he began loudly cursing us and shouting that we couldn't make him go anywhere. An angry crowd began to gather as we got out of our patrol car and approached the man, who was by this time shouting that we were harassing him and calling to bystanders for assistance.

As a criminology professor, some months earlier I would have urged that the police officer who was now myself simply leave the car double-parked and move on rather than risk an incident. As a policeman, however, I had come to realize that an officer can never back down from his responsibility to enforce the law. Whatever the risk to himself, every police officer understands that his ability to back up the lawful authority which he represents is the only thing which stands between civilization and the jungle of lawlessness.

The man continued to curse us and adamantly refused to move his car. As we placed him under arrest and attempted to move him to our cruiser, an unidentified male and female rushed from the crowd, which was steadily enlarging, and sought to free him. In the ensuing struggle, a hysterical female unsnapped and tried to grab my service revolver, and the now-angry mob began to converge on us.

Suddenly, I was no longer an "ivory-tower" scholar watching typical police "overreaction" to a street incident; I was part of it, fighting to remain alive and uninjured. I remember the sickening sensation of cold terror which filled my insides as I struggled to reach our car radio. I simultaneously put out a distress call and pressed the hidden electric release button on our shotgun rack as my partner sought to maintain his grip on the prisoner and hold the crowd at bay with his revolver.

How harshly I would have judged the officer who now grabbed the shotgun only a few months before. I rounded the rear of our cruiser with the weapon and shouted at the mob to move back. The memory flashed through my mind that I had always argued that policemen should not be allowed to carry shotguns because of their "offensive" character and the potential damage to community relations as a result of their display. How readily as a criminology professor I would have condemned the officer—now myself, trembling with fear and menacing an unarmed assembly with a shotgun. The new circumstances in which I now found myself had suddenly changed my perspective. The tables were turned on me. Now it was *my* life and safety that were in jeopardy; it was *my* pregnant wife who in a few seconds might be a widow, and *my* child who might never see his father again. I was no longer sitting comfortably in my study with a morning cup of coffee reading an impersonal newspaper account of some patrolman who had been seriously injured or killed trying to uphold the law.

For all the things that were to happen to me as a rookie patrolman, this particular incident represented a major turning point in my perspective as a professor of criminology. It marked the beginning of what was to become the most profoundly important of all my street lessons—a depressing and at times personally crushing awareness that the toughest adversary a street cop must confront each day is not the armed robber or enraged mob, not the addict, the burglar or the mugger. Rather it is, ironically, the very law which he must struggle against increasingly difficult odds to enforce. It is the smugness and complacency of courts and legislatures, which spin out a hopelessly entangling web of procedural restraints upon men who are charged with the awesome responsibility of protecting our society. This was a bitter discovery, one which the liberal scientist within me had long refused to accept.

I remember feeling a sense of imminent justice as I wrote "resisting arrest with violence" on the booking forms of the couple who had sought to free the prisoner in the previously described double-parking case incident. True, we had narrowly escaped injury in our attempts to enforce the law, but I derived some comfort from the expectation that persons like that would soon learn in court the meaning of attacking a police officer—or so I naively thought! Peering over my shoulder at the arrest reports, my partner shook his head. "Hell, Doc. They'll get off. Just wait and see!" The next evening I recognized the same couple standing on a street corner, laughing and jeering at us, confident in the experience-based belief that the felony charge of resisting arrest with violence would soon be bargained down to a bare misdemeanor. I will never forget the feeling of bitterness and despair which filled me a few days later when I learned that both of our assailants had been allowed to plead guilty to "breach of peace." "Breach of peace!" I raged in disbelief to my partner. Only a lucky grasp had prevented me from being shot with my own service revolver; now our assailants were being let off with a mild slap on the wrist, a charge which contained the implicit legal view that what had happened to us that night was no more serious in the eyes of the courts than spitting on the sidewalk or uttering a public obscenity.

As a policeman myself, I learned that there is something terribly wrong in the relationship between our police and those who make and administer the law. As a university professor, I had hailed the spate of restrictive Supreme Court decisions which had been levied on the police in recent years. *Mapp! Escobedo! Miranda!* All were victories for individual liberty, steps essential to prevent abuses of power in American police officers. It never crossed my mind that such decisions might represent personal triumphs for law violators, and that they might diminish the ability of the police to protect society.

Like the average judge, juror, or legislator, who seldom views the law as anything more than an abstract phenomenon, I was really unconcerned in my life as a university professor with the practical consequences of piling an even larger burden of restrictive legislation upon the American police. Until I

put on the uniform myself and stepped into the role, I could not realize the profoundly negative consequences of such action upon both the policeman and the society he strives to protect.

As a policeman myself, I had to struggle on a daily basis through a maze of incredibly and incomprehensibly complex restrictions on how the game of enforcing the law is to be played. And a game I discovered it was indeed, with the odds stacked heavily against the police and society and decidedly in favor of the criminal. I well remember one evening drawing my "*Miranda* warning" card from my wallet and reading it slowly and carefully to a known narcotics pusher whom we had just arrested with a large quantity of heroin in his possession, fearful that a recitation of it from memory might cause me to omit some word or syllable which might later be transformed by a skilled attorney into a violation of the suspect's "rights." "Lay it on me, baby!" he said as he convulsed with laughter halfway through my reading of his rights. Still amused with the degrading spectacle of forcing me to read a statement which I knew by heart from previous arrests, he joined in a word for word recall of his "rights" as I methodically read them off to him. Experiences such as this, which I encountered time and again, led me to the inescapable conclusion that we often allow the law to be turned into a mockery of justice, a tool to be used against society by law violators who are its enemies.

Like every police officer today, I was often overcome with a sense of being forced to walk through a legal minefield in my attempts to protect the community, being distracted from my primary mission on calls by the haunting fear that I might be violating some obscure element of an offender's rights. One night my partner and I responded to a call of several suspects sniping with firearms from an apartment building. As two other units covered the rear and sides of the building, my partner and I approached the front door with guns drawn. One suspect appeared at the door, started to step out, then abruptly jumped back into the apartment. As I ran after him and put my hand on the doorknob, a virtual blast of legal considerations hit my mind; it was dark and I had not actually *seen* a gun in his hands. Should I enter? What if there were no visible weapons in the room or on the suspects? Dare we search the rest of the house? I submit that it is patently absurd—cruel, even monstrous—for a police officer, palms sweating at the prospect of being shot down in such a situation, to have to deal with such considerations. Yet, as we entered the house, I could imagine myself having to provide to superiors and a defense attorney a detailed recollection of our every move, with the virtual certainty that a single wrong move would quickly cast us in the role of law violators.

Given the drift of legislation and the decisions of the Supreme Court under Chief Justice Warren during the decade 1960–70, it is little wonder to me that police officers often despair of their mission, and shirk enforcement responsibilities. I recall a rather typical illustration of the pessimism which assails every policeman today. My partner and I pulled up abruptly one evening on a "junkie" who stood trem-. bling for a fix at curbside. As he watched us approach, he quickly, and in our plain view, removed several objects from a bag he was holding and furtively dropped them behind him on the ground. We quickly discovered that the objects in question were pieces of a narcotics kit, and we placed the individual under arrest. On the way to jail my partner sighed heavily and suggested with an air of resignation, "Well, we didn't find any drugs. Hell, Doc, not much point in charging him with possession of narcotics paraphernalia. They (the courts) won't do anything. Let's just destroy the kit and book him on P.I. (public intoxication)."

Today's police officer is inexorably pushed toward viewing the entire judicial process as his enemy. He senses that it represents a great and impenetrable barrier which stands between him and his goal of protecting society. It is not that he values individual liberty any less than those who make and administer our system of laws, but as one who must live with the law in action, he simply cannot understand why the preservation of our democracy should require crippling the efficiency of law enforcement.

As someone who has always been greatly concerned with the rights of offenders, I have begun to consider for the first time the rights of police officers and the law-abiding public they serve. It is wrong that the safety and security of both should be menaced by the instrumentality of the law. As a policeman myself, I have many times felt that this is precisely so. As with other patrolmen, I have grown weary of trying to do my job in the face of frustrating—sometimes impossible—legal restrictions, while thugs and hoodlums consistently twist the law to their own advantage. Each time I put on my uniform and step into the streets, I have the distinct feeling that my personal safety is diminished and my task as a law enforcement officer is made more difficult by our

society's great solicitude for the law violator's rights, and its ostensible indifference to mine. As an educated man, I find myself unable to answer the questions of fellow police officers as to why our society manifests so little concern for their physical safety.

The policeman's inner conviction that the law often menaces his very life was brought home to me recently on a very personal level. One night my patrol car was hailed by a passing motorist. As I approached the darkened driver's side of the man's car, he began to shout hysterically and sob: "I've just killed a man. I've got a gun!" My first concern *should* have been for my personal safety and that of anyone else in the area. Instead, like so many police officers who have been killed or injured because of hesitation, the first thing to rush into my mind was a jumble of legalistic considerations: "A confession? Rights . . . no, wait, it's a spontaneous confession. Okay, admissible!" If I had been shot to death because of the split-second delay caused by anxiety over following procedural technicalities, where would the moral responsibility for my death lie? Clearly, a measure of it would reside with a society which consciously jeopardizes the safety of its police officers by requiring them to function within a maze of unwarranted legal considerations.

As a corrections worker, and as someone raised in a comfortable middle-class home, I had always been insulated from the kind of human misery and tragedy which become part of the policeman's everyday life. Now, however, the often terrible sights, sounds, and smells of my job began to haunt me hours after I had taken off the blue uniform and badge. Some nights I would lie in bed unable to sleep, trying desperately to forget the things I had seen during a particular tour of duty: the rat-infested shacks that served as homes to those less fortunate than I; a teen-age boy dying in my arms after being struck by a car; small children, clad in rags, with stomachs bloated from hunger, playing in urine-spattered halls; the victim of a robbery, senselessly beaten and murdered.

In my new role as a police officer, I found that the victims of crime ceased to be impersonal statistics. As a corrections worker and criminology professor, I had never given much thought to those who are victimized by criminals in our society. Now the sight of so many lives ruthlessly damaged and destroyed by the perpetrators of crime left me preoccupied with the question of society's responsibility to protect the men, women and children who are victimized daily.

Of all the tragic victims of crime I have seen during my first six months as a police officer, one case stands out above all. There was an elderly man who lived with his dog in my apartment building downtown. He was a retired bus driver and his wife was long since deceased. As time went by, I became friends with the old man and his dog. I could usually count on finding both of them standing at the corner as I was on my way to work. I would engage in casual conversation with the old man, and sometimes he and his dog would walk several blocks toward the station with me. They were both as predictable as a clock: each evening around 7 o'clock, the old man would walk to the same small restaurant several blocks away, where he would eat his evening meal while the dog waited dutifully outside. One evening my partner and I received a call to a street shooting near my apartment building. My heart sank as we pulled up. I saw the old man's mutt in a crowd of people gathered on the sidewalk. The old man was lying on his back in a large pool of blood, half trying to brace himself on an elbow. He clutched a bullet wound in his chest and gasped to me that three young men had stopped him and demanded his money. After taking his wallet and seeing how little he had, they shot him and left him on the street. As a police officer, I became enraged, as I was to become enraged time and again, at the cruelty and senselessness of acts such as this—at the arrogance of the brazen thugs who prey with impunity on innocent citizens, confident in the belief that the likelihood of their being brought to justice and punished has steadily diminished in recent years.

The same kinds of daily stresses which affected my fellow officers soon began to take their toll on me. I became sick and tired of being reviled and attacked by criminals who could usually find a most sympathetic audience in judges and jurors eager to understand their side of things and provide them with "another chance." I grew tired of living under the ax of news media and community pressure groups, eager to seize upon the slightest mistake made by me or by a fellow police officer. As a criminology professor, I had always enjoyed the luxury of having great amounts of time in which to make difficult decisions. As a police officer, however, I found myself forced to make the most critical choices in a time frame of seconds, rather than days: to shoot or not to shoot, to arrest or not to arrest, to give chase or let go— always with the nagging certainty that others, those with great amounts of time in which to analyze and think, stood ready to judge and condemn me for whatever action I might take or fail to take. I found myself not only forced to live a life consisting of seconds and adrenalin, but also forced to deal with human problems which were infinitely more difficult than anything I had ever confronted in a correctional or mental health setting. Family fights, mental illness, potentially explosive crowd situations, dangerous individuals—I found myself progressively awed by the complexity of tasks faced by men whose work I once thought was fairly simple and straightforward. Indeed, I would like to take the average clinical psychologist or psychiatrist and invite him to function for just a day in the world of the policeman, to confront people whose problems are both serious and in need of immediate solution. I would invite him to walk, as I have, into a smoke-filled pool room where five or six angry men are swinging cues at one another. I would like the prison counselor and parole officer to see their client—not calm and composed in an office setting, but as the street cop sees him: beating his small child with a heavy belt buckle, or kicking his pregnant wife. I wish that they, and every judge and juror in our country, could see the ravages of crime as the cop on the beat does—innocent people cut, shot, beaten, raped, robbed, and murdered. It would give him, I feel certain, a different perspective on crime and criminals, just as it did to me.

For all the human misery and suffering which police officers must witness in their work, I found myself amazed at the incredible humanity and compassion which seems to characterize most of them. My own stereotypes of the brutal, sadistic cop were time and again shattered by the sight of humanitarian kindness on the part of the thin blue line: a young patrolman giving mouth-to-mouth resuscitation to a filthy derelict; a grizzled old veteran embarrassed when I discovered the bags of jelly beans which he carried in the trunk of his car for impoverished ghetto kids, to whom he was the closest thing to an Easter Bunny they would ever know; an officer giving money out of his own pocket to a hungry and stranded family he would probably never see again; and another one taking the trouble to drop by on his own time in order to give worried parents information about their problem son or daughter.

As a police officer, I found myself repeatedly surprised at the ability of my fellow patrolmen to withstand the enormous daily pressures of their work: long hours, frustration, danger, and anxiety— all seemingly taken in stride as just part of the business of being a cop. I eventually went through the humbling discovery that I, like the men in blue with whom I worked, was simply a human being with definite limits to the amount of stress I could endure in a given period of time.

I recall, in particular, one evening when this point was dramatized to me. My tour of duty had been a long, hard one—one that had ended with a high-speed chase of a stolen car in which we narrowly escaped serious injury when another vehicle pulled in front of our patrol car. As we checked off duty, I was vaguely aware of feeling tired and tense. My partner and I were headed for a restaurant and a bite of breakfast when we both heard the unmistakable sound of breaking glass coming from a church, and we spotted two long-haired, teenaged boys running from the area. We confronted them and I asked one for identification, displaying my own police identification. He sneered at me, cursed, turned, and started to walk away. The next thing I knew I had grabbed the youth by his shirt and spun him around, shouting, "I'm talking to you, punk!" I felt my partner's arm on my shoulder and heard his reassuring voice behind me, "Take it easy, Doc!" I released my grip on the adolescent and stood silently for several seconds, unable to accept the inescapable reality that I had "lost my cool." My mind flashed back to a lecture during which I had told my students, "Any man who is not able to maintain absolute control of his emotions at all times has no business being a police officer." I was at the time of this incident director of a human relations project designed to teach policemen "emotional control" skills. Now here I was, an "emotional control" expert, being told by a patrolman to "calm down!"

As someone who had always regarded policemen as a "paranoid" lot, I discovered that, in the daily round of violence which became a part of my life, chronic suspiciousness is something which a good cop cultivates in the interest of being able to go home to his family after each tour of duty. As with so many other officers, my daily exposure to street crime soon had me carrying an off-duty weapon virtually everywhere I went. I began to become watchful of who and what was around me. Things began to acquire a new meaning: an open door, someone loitering on a dark corner, a rear license plate covered with dirt. According to my family, friends, and colleagues, my personality slowly began to change as my career as a policeman progressed. Once quick to drop critical barbs about policemen to intellectual friends, I now became extremely sensitive about such remarks—and

several times became engaged in heated arguments over them.

As a police officer myself, I found that society demands too much of its policemen. Not only are they expected to enforce the law, they must also be curbside psychiatrists, marriage counselors, social workers—even ministers and doctors. I found that a good street officer combines in his daily work splinters of each one of these complex professions, and many more. It is unreasonable, of course, to ask so much of the men in blue; nevertheless, there is no one else to whom a person can turn for help in the kind of crises and problems with which policemen must deal. No one else wants to counsel a family with problems at 3 a.m. on Sunday morning! No one else wants to enter a darkened building after a burglar! No one else wants to stare poverty, mental illness, and human tragedy in the face, day after day, or to pick up the pieces of shattered lives.

As a policeman, I have often asked myself "Why does a man become a cop? What makes him stay with it?" Surely it is not the disrespect, or the legal restrictions which make the job increasingly rough, or the long hours and low pay, or the risk of being killed or injured trying to protect people who often do not seem to care. The only answer I can offer to this question is the one based upon my own limited experience as a policeman. As I came home from work and took off the badge and blue uniform I experienced a sense of satisfaction over a contribution to society—something that I have never known in any other job. Somehow that feeling seemed to make everything worthwhile, despite the disrespect, the danger, and the boredom so often associated with police responsibility.

For all too long, America's colleges and universities have conveyed to young men and women the subtle message that there is, somehow, something wrong with "being a cop." It's time for that to stop! And that point was forcibly brought home to me one evening not long ago. I had just completed a day shift and had to rush back to the university with no chance to change out of uniform for a late afternoon class. As I rushed into my office to pick up my lecture notes, my secretary's jaw dropped at the sight of the uniform. "Why, Dr. Kirkham, you're not going to class looking like *that*, are you?" I felt momentarily embarrassed. And then I was struck by the realization that I would not feel the need to apologize if I appeared before my students with long hair or a beard. After all, free love advocates and revolutionaries do not apologize for their group memberships, so why should someone whose appearance symbolizes a commitment to serve and protect society? "Why not?" I replied with a slight smile. "I'm proud to be a cop!" I picked up my notes and went on to class.

Let me conclude by saying that I hope that other educators might take the trouble to observe firsthand some of the policeman's problems before being so quick to condemn and pass judgment on him. We are all familiar with the old expression which urges us to refrain from judging the worth of another man's actions until we have walked at least a mile in his shoes. To be sure, I have not walked that mile as a rookie patrolman, but at least I have tried the shoes on, and I have taken a few difficult steps in them. Those few steps, however, have given me a profoundly new understanding and appreciation of our police. They left me with the humbling realization that possession of even a top-flight college degree does not give a person a corner on knowledge, or place him in the lofty position where he cannot take lessons from those with considerably less education.

Police Brutality—Answers to Key Questions

ALBERT J. REISS JR.

For three years, there has been through the courts and the streets a dreary procession of citizens with broken heads and bruised bodies against few of whom was violence needed to effect an arrest. Many of them had done nothing to deserve an arrest. In a majority of such cases, no complaint was made. If the victim complains, his charge is generally dismissed. The police are practically above the law.

This statement was published in 1903, and its author was the Hon. Frank Moss, a former police commissioner of New York City. Clearly, today's charges of police brutality and mistreatment of citizens have a precedent in American history—but never before has the issue of police brutality assumed the public urgency it has today. In Newark, in Detroit, in Watts, in Harlem, and, in fact, in practically every city that has had a civil disturbance, "deep hostility between police and ghetto" was, reports the Kerner Commission, "a primary cause of the riots."

Whether or not the police accept the words "police brutality," the public now wants some plain answers to some plain questions. How widespread is

SOURCE: *Trans-action*, 5 (1968). Copyright © 1968 by *Trans-action* Magazine, St. Louis, Missouri.

police mistreatment of citizens? Is it on the increase? Why do policemen mistreat citizens? Do the police mistreat Negroes more than whites?

To find some answers, 36 people working for the Center of Research on Social Organization observed police-citizen encounters in the cities of Boston, Chicago, and Washington, D.C. For seven days a week, for seven weeks during the summer of 1966, these observers, with police permission, sat in patrol cars and monitored booking and lockup procedures in high-crime precincts.

Obtaining information about police mistreatment of citizens is no simple matter. National and state civil-rights commissions receive hundreds of complaints charging mistreatment, but proving these allegations is difficult. The few local civilian review boards, such as the one in Philadelphia, have not produced any significant volume of complaints leading to the dismissal or disciplining of policemen for alleged brutality. Generally, police chiefs are silent on the matter, or answer charges of brutality with vague statements that they will investigate any complaints brought to their attention. Rank-and-file policemen are usually more outspoken: They often insinuate that charges of brutality are part of a conspiracy against them, and against law and order.

The Meaning of Brutality

What citizens mean by police brutality covers the full range of police practices. These practices, contrary to the impression of many civil-rights activists, are not newly devised to deal with Negroes in our urban ghettos. They are ways in which the police have traditionally behaved in dealing with certain citizens, particularly those in the lower classes. The most common of these practices are:

1. The use of profane and abusive language
2. Commands to move on or get home
3. Stopping and questioning people on the street or searching them and their cars
4. Threats to use force if not obeyed
5. Prodding with a nightstick or approaching with a pistol
6. The actual use of physical force or violence itself

Citizens and the police do not always agree on what constitutes proper police practice. What is "proper," or what is "brutal," it need hardly be pointed out, is more a matter of judgment about what someone did than a description of what police do. What is important is not the practice itself but what it means to the citizen. What citizens object to and call "police brutality" is really the judgment that they have not been treated with the full rights and dignity among citizens in a democratic society. Any practice that degrades their status, that restricts their freedom, that annoys or harasses them, or that uses physical force is frequently seen as unnecessary and unwarranted. More often than not, they are probably right.

Many police practices serve only to degrade the citizen's sense of himself and his status. This is particularly true with regard to the way police use language. Most citizens who have contact with the police object less to their use of four-letter words than to *how* the policeman talks to them. Particularly objectionable is the habit policemen have of "talking down" to citizens, of calling them names that deprecate them in their own eyes and those of others. More than one Negro citizen has complained: "They talk down to me as if I had no name—like 'boy' or 'man' or whatever, or they call me 'Jack' or by my first name. They don't show me no respect."

Members of minority groups and those seen as nonconformists, for whatever reason, are the most likely targets of status degradation. Someone who has been drinking may be told he is a "bum" or a "shitty wino." A woman walking alone may be called a "whore." And a man who doesn't happen to meet a policeman's standard of how one should look or dress

may be met with the remark, "What's the matter, you a queer?" A white migrant from the South may be called a "hill-billy" or "shitkicker"; a Puerto Rican, a "pork chop"; a young boy, a "punk kid." When the policeman does not use words of status degradation, his manner may be degrading. Citizens want to be treated as people, not as "nonpersons" who are talked about as if they were not present.

That many Negroes believe that the police have degraded their status is clear from surveys in Watts, Newark, and Detroit. One out of every five Negroes in our center's post-riot survey in Detroit reports that the police have "talked down to him." More than one in ten says a policeman has "called me a bad name."

To be treated as "suspicious" is not only degrading, but is also a form of harassment and a restriction on the right to move freely. The harassing tactics of the police—dispersing social street-gatherings, the indiscriminate stopping of Negroes on foot or in cars, and commands to move on or go home—are particularly common in ghetto areas.

Young people are the most likely targets of harassing orders to disperse or move on. Particularly in summer, ghetto youths are likely to spend lots of time in public places. Given the inadequacy of their housing and the absence of community facilities, the street corner is often their social center. As the police cruise the busy streets of the ghetto, they frequently shout at groups of teenagers to "get going" or "get home." Our observations of police practices show that *white as well as Negro youths* are often harassed in this way.

Frequently the policeman may leave the car and threaten or force youths to move on. For example, one summer evening as the scout car cruised a busy street of a white slum, the patrolman observed three white boys and a girl on a corner. When told to move on, they mumbled and grumbled in undertones, angering the police by their failure to comply. As they slowly moved off, the officers pushed them along the street. Suddenly one of the white patrolmen took a lighted cigarette from a 15-year-old boy and stuck it in his face, pushing him forward as he did so. When the youngsters did move on, one policeman remarked to the observer that the girl was "nothing but a whore." Such tactics can only intensify resentment toward the police.

Police harassment is not confined to youth. One in every four adult Negroes in Detroit claims he has been stopped and questioned by the police without good reason. The same proportion claim they have been stopped in their cars. One in five says he has been searched unnecessarily; and one in six says that his car was searched for no good reason. The members of an interracial couple, particularly a Negro man accompanying a white woman, are perhaps the most vulnerable to harassment.

What citizens regard as police brutality many policemen consider necessary for law enforcement. While degrading epithets and abusive language may no longer be considered proper by either police commanders or citizens, they often disagree about other practices related to law enforcement. For example, although many citizens see "stop and question" or "stop and frisk" procedures as harassment, police commanders usually regard them merely as "aggressive prevention" to curb crime.

Physical Force—or Self Defense?

The nub of the police-brutality issue seems to lie in police use of physical force. By law, the police have the right to use such force if necessary to make an arrest, to keep the peace, or to maintain public order. But just how much force is necessary or proper?

This was the crucial problem we attempted to answer by placing observers in the patrol cars and in the precincts. Our 36 observers, divided equally among Chicago, Boston, and Washington, were responsible for reporting the details of all situations where police used physical force against a citizen. To ensure the observation of a large number of encounters, two high-crime police precincts were monitored in Boston and Chicago; four in Washington. At least one precinct was composed of primarily Negro residents, another primarily of whites. Where possible, we also tried to select precincts with considerable variation in social-class composition. Given the criterion of a high-crime rate, however, people of low socio-economic status predominated in most of the areas surveyed.

The law fails to provide simple rules about what —and how much—force that policemen can properly use. The American Bar Foundation's study *Arrest*, by Wayne La Fave, put the matter rather well, stating that the courts of all states would undoubtedly agree that in making an arrest a policeman should use only that amount of force he reasonably believes necessary. But La Fave also pointed out that there is no agreement on the question of when it is better to let the suspect escape than to employ "deadly" force.

Even in those states where the use of deadly force is limited by law, the kinds of physical force a policeman may use are not clearly defined. No kind of force is categorically denied a policeman, since he is always permitted to use deadly force in self-defense.

This right to protect himself often leads the policeman to argue self-defense whenever he uses force. We found that many policemen, whether or not the facts justify it, regularly follow their use of force with the charge that the citizen was assaulting a policeman or resisting arrest. Our observers also found that some policemen even carry pistols and knives that they have confiscated while searching citizens; they carry them so they may be placed at a scene should it be necessary to establish a case of self-defense.

Of course, not all cases of force involve the use of *unnecessary* force. Each instance of force reported by our observers was examined and judged to be either necessary or unnecessary. Cases involving simple restraint—holding a man by the arm—were deliberately excluded from consideration, even though a policeman's right to do so can, in many instances, be challenged. In judging when police force is "unwarranted," "unreasonable," or "undue," we rather deliberately selected only those cases in which a policeman struck the citizen with his hands, fist, feet, or body, or where he used a weapon of some kind, such as a nightstick or a pistol. In these cases, had the policeman been found to have used physical force improperly, he could have been arrested on complaint and, like any other citizen, charged with a simple or aggravated assault. A physical assault on a citizen was judged to be "improper" or "unnecessary" only if force was used in one or more of the following ways:

1. If a policeman physically assaulted a citizen and then failed to make an arrest; proper use involves an arrest.
2. If the citizen being arrested did not, by word or deed, resist the policeman; force should be used only if it is necessary to make the arrest.
3. If the policeman, even though there was resistance to the arrest, could easily have restrained the citizen in other ways.
4. If a large number of policemen were present and could have assisted in subduing the citizen in the station, in lockup, and in the interrogation rooms.

5. If an offender was handcuffed and made no attempt to flee or offer violent resistance.
6. If the citizen resisted arrest, but the use of force continued even after the citizen was subdued.

In the seven-week period, we found 37 cases in which force was used improperly. In all, 44 citizens had been assaulted. In 15 of these cases, no one was arrested. Of these, 8 had offered no verbal or physical resistance whatsoever, while 7 had.

An arrest was made in 22 of the cases. In 13, force was exercised in the station house when at least four other policemen were present. In two cases, there was no verbal or physical resistance to the arrest, but force was still applied. In two other cases, the police applied force to a handcuffed offender in a field setting. And in five situations, the offender did resist arrest, but the policeman continued to use force even after he had been subdued.

Just how serious was the improper use of force in these 44 cases? Naturally there were differences in degree of injury. In about one-half of the cases, the citizen appeared little more than physically bruised; in three cases, the amount of force was so great that the citizen had to be hospitalized. Despite the fact that cases can easily be selected for their dramatic rather than their representative quality, I want to present a few to give a sense of what the observers saw and reported as undue use of force.

Observing on Patrol

In the following two cases the citizens offered no physical or verbal resistance, and the two white policemen made no arrest. It is the only instance in which the observers saw the same two policemen using force improperly more than once.

The police precinct in which these incidents occurred is typical of those found in some of our larger cities, where the patrolmen move routinely from gold coast to slum. There are little islands of the rich and poor, of old Americans and new, of recent migrants and old settlers. One moves from high-rise areas of middle- and upper-income whites through an area of the really old Americans—Indians—to an enclave of the recently arrived. The recently arrived are primarily those the policemen call "hillbillies" (migrants from Kentucky and Tennessee) and "pork chops," (Puerto Ricans). There are ethnic islands of Germans and Swedes. Although there is a small area where Negroes live, it is principally a precinct of whites. The police in the district are, with one exception, white.

On a Friday in the middle of July, the observer arrived for the 4 to 12 midnight watch. The beat car that had been randomly chosen carried two white patrolmen—one with 14 years of experience in the precinct, the other with three.

The watch began rather routinely as the policemen cruised the district. Their first radio dispatch came at about 5:30 P.M. They were told to investigate two drunks in a cemetery. On arriving they found two white men "sleeping one off." Without questioning the men, the older policeman began to search one of them, ripping his shirt and hitting him in the groin with a nightstick. The younger policeman, as he searched the second, ripped away the seat of his trousers, exposing his buttocks. The policemen then prodded the men toward the cemetery fence and forced them to climb it, laughing at the plight of the drunk with the exposed buttocks. As the drunks went over the fence, one policeman shouted, "I ought to run you fuckers in!" The other remarked to the observer, "Those assholes won't be back; a bunch of shitty winos."

Not long after they returned to their car, the policemen stopped a woman who had made a left turn improperly. She was treated very politely, and the younger policeman, who wrote the ticket, later commented to the observer, "Nice lady." At 7:30 they were dispatched to check a suspicious auto. After a quick check, the car was marked abandoned.

Shortly after a 30-minute break for a 7:30 "lunch," the two policemen received a dispatch to take a burglary report. Arriving at a slum walkup, the police entered a room where an obviously drunk white man in his late 40s insisted that someone had entered and stolen his food and liquor. He kept insisting that it had been taken and that he had been forced to borrow money to buy beer. The younger policeman, who took the report, kept harassing the man, alternating between mocking and badgering him with rhetorical questions. "You say your name is Half-A-Wit [for Hathaway]? Do you sleep with niggers? How did you vote on the bond issue? Are you sure that's all that's missing? Are you a virgin yet?" The man responded to all of this with the seeming vagueness and joviality of the intoxicated, expressing gratitude for the policemen's help as they left. The older policeman remarked to the observer as they left, "Ain't drunks funny?"

For the next hour little happened, but as the two were moving across the precinct shortly after 10 P.M., a white man and a woman in their 50's flagged them down. Since they were obviously "substantial" middle-class citizens of the district, the policemen listened to their complaints that a Negro man was causing trouble inside the public-transport station from which they had just emerged. The woman said that he had sworn at her. The older policeman remarked, "What's a nigger doing up here? He should be down on Franklin Road!"

With that, they ran into the station and grabbed the Negro man who was inside. Without questioning him, they shoved him into a phone booth and began beating him with their fists and a flashlight. They also hit him in the groin. Then they dragged him out and kept him on his knees. He pleaded that he had just been released from a mental hospital that day and, begging not to be hit again, asked them to let him return to the hospital. One policeman said: "Don't you like us, nigger? I like to beat niggers and rip out their eyes." They took him outside to their patrol car. Then they decided to put him on a bus, telling him that he was returning to the hospital; they deliberately put him on a bus going in the opposite direction. Just before the Negro boarded the bus, he said, "You police just like to shoot and beat people." The first policeman replied, "Get moving, nigger, or I'll shoot you." The man was crying and bleeding as he was put on the bus. Leaving the scene, the younger policeman commented, "He won't be back."

For the rest of the evening, the two policemen kept looking for drunks and harassing any they found. They concluded the evening by being dispatched to an address where, they were told, a man was being held for the police. No one answered their knock. They left.

The station house has long been suspected of harboring questionable police practices. Interrogation-room procedures have been attacked, particularly because of the methods the police have used to get confessions. The drama of the confession in the interrogation room has been complete with bright lights and physical torture. Whether or not such practices have ever existed on the scale suggested by popular accounts, confessions in recent years, even by accounts of offenders, have rarely been accompanied by such high drama. But recently the interrogation room has come under fire again for its failure to protect the constitutional rights of the suspect to remain silent and to have legal counsel.

Backstage at the Station

The police station, however, is more than just a series of cubicles called interrogation rooms. There are other rooms and usually a lockup as well. Many of these are also hidden from public view. It is not surprising, then, that one-third of all the observations of the undue use of force occurred within the station.

In any station there normally are several policemen present who should be able to deal with almost any situation requiring force that arises. In many of the situations that were observed, as many as seven and eight policemen were present, most of whom simply stood by and watched force being used. The custom among policemen, it appeared, is that you intervene only if a fellow policeman needs help, or if you have been personally offended or affronted by those involved.

Force is used unnecessarily at many different points and places in the station. The citizen who is not cooperative during the booking process may be pushed or shoved, have his handcuffs twisted with a nightstick, have his foot stomped, or be pulled by the hair. All of these practices were reported by policemen as ways of obtaining "cooperation." But it was clear that the booking could have been completed without any of this harassment.

The lockup was the scene of some of the most severe applications of force. Two of the three cases requiring hospitalization came about when an offender was "worked over" in the lockup. To be sure, the arrested are not always cooperative when they get in the lockup, and force may be necessary to place them in a cell. But the amount of force observed hardly seemed necessary.

One evening an observer was present in the lockup when two white policemen came in with a white man. The suspect had been handcuffed and brought to the station because he had proved obstreperous after being arrested for a traffic violation. Apparently he had been drinking. While waiting in the lockup, the man began to urinate on the floor. In response, the policemen began to beat the man. They jumped him, knocked him down, and beat his head against the concrete floor. He required emergency treatment at a nearby hospital.

At times a policeman may be involved in a kind of escalation of force. Using force appropriately for an arrest in the field seemingly sets the stage for its later use, improperly, in the station. The following case illustrates how such a situation may develop:

Within a large city's high-crime rate precinct, occupied mostly by Negroes, the police responded to an "officer in trouble" call. It is difficult to imagine a call that brings a more immediate response, so a large number of police cars immediately converged at an intersection of a busy public street where a bus had been stopped. Near the bus, a white policeman was holding two young Negroes at gun point. The policeman reported that he had responded to a summons from the white bus-driver complaining that the boys had refused to pay their fares and had used obscene language. The policeman also reported that the boys swore at him, and one swung at him while the other drew a screwdriver and started toward him. At that point, he said, he drew his pistol.

The policemen placed one of the offenders in handcuffs and began to transport both of them to the station. While driving to the station, the driver of one car noted that the other policeman, transporting the other boy, was struggling with him. The first policeman stopped and entered the other patrol car. The observer reported that he kept hitting the boy who was handcuffed until the boy appeared completely subdued. The boy kept saying, "You don't have any right to beat me. I don't care if you kill me."

After the policemen got the offenders to the station, although the boys no longer resisted them, the police began to beat them while they were handcuffed in an interrogation room. One of the boys hollered: "You can't beat me like this! I'm only a kid, and my hands are tied." Later one of the policemen commented to the observer: "On the street you can't beat them. But when you get to the station, you can instill some respect in them."

Cases where the offender resists an arrest provide perhaps the most difficulty in judging the legitimacy of the force applied. An encounter that began as a dispatch to a disturbance at a private residence was one case about which there could be honest differences in judgment. On arrival, the policemen—one white, the other Negro—met a white woman who claimed that her husband, who was in the back yard and drunk, had beaten her. She asked the policemen

to "take him in." The observer reported that the police found the man in the house. When they attempted to take him, he resisted by placing his hands between the door jamb. Both policemen grabbed him. The Negro policeman said, "We're going to have trouble, so let's finish it right here." He grabbed the offender and knocked him down. Both policemen then wrestled with the man, handcuffed him, and took him to the station. As they did so, one of the policemen remarked, "These sons of bitches want to fight, so you have to break them quick."

A Minimal Picture?

The reader, as well as most police administrators, may be skeptical about reports that policemen used force in the presence of observers. Indeed, one police administrator, indignant over reports of undue use of force in his department, seemed more concerned that the policemen had permitted themselves to be observed behaving improperly than he was about their improper behavior. When demanding to know the names of the policemen who had used force improperly so he could discharge them—a demand we could not meet, since we were bound to protect our sources of information—he remarked, "Any officer who is stupid enough to behave that way in the presence of outsiders deserves to be fired."

There were and are a number of reasons why our observers were able to see policemen behaving improperly. We entered each department with the full cooperation of the top administrators. So far as the men in the line were concerned, our chief interest was in how citizens behave toward the police, a main object of our study. Many policemen, given their strong feelings against citizens, fail to see that their own behavior is equally open to observation. Furthermore, our observers are trained to fit into a role of trust—one that is genuine, since most observers are actually sympathetic to the plight of the policeman, if not to his behavior.

Finally, and this is a fact all too easily forgotten, people cannot change their behavior in the presence of others as easily as many think. This is particularly true when people become deeply involved in certain situations. The policeman not only comes to "trust" the observer in the law-enforcement situation—regarding him as a source of additional help if necessary—but, when he becomes involved in a dispute with a citizen, he easily forgets that an observer is present. Partly because he does not know what else to do, in such situations the policeman behaves "normally." But should one cling to the notion that most policemen modify their behavior in the presence of outsiders, one is left with the uncomfortable conclusion that our cases represent a minimal picture of actual misbehavior.

Superficially it might seem that the use of an excessive amount of force against citizens is low. In only 37 of 3826 encounters observed did the police use undue force. Of the 4604 white citizens in these encounters, 27 experienced an excessive amount of force—a rate of 5.9 for every 1000 citizens involved. The comparable rate for 5960 Negroes, of whom 17 experienced an excessive amount of force, is 2.8. Thus, whether one considers these rates high or low, the fact is that the *rate of excessive force for all white citizens in encounters with the police is twice that for Negro citizens.*

A rate depends, however, upon selecting a population that is logically the target of force. What we have just given is a rate for *all* citizens involved in encounters with the police. But many of these citizens are not logical targets of force. Many, for example, simply call the police to complain about crimes against themselves or their property. And others are merely witnesses to crimes.

The more logical target population consists of citizens whom the police allege to be offenders—a population of suspects. In our study, there were 643 white suspects, 27 of whom experienced undue use of force. This yields an abuse rate of 41.9 per 1000 white suspects. The comparable rate for 751 Negro suspects, of whom 17 experienced undue use of force, is 22.6 per 1000. If one accepts these rates as reasonably reliable estimates of the undue force against suspects, then there should be little doubt that in major metropolitan areas the sort of behavior commonly called "police brutality" is far from rare.

Popular impression casts police brutality as a racial matter—white police mistreating Negro citizens. The fact is that white suspects are more liable to being treated improperly by the police than Negro suspects are. This, however, should not be confused with the chances a citizen takes of being mistreated. In two of the cities we studied, Negroes are a minority. The chances, then, that any Negro has of being treated improperly are, perhaps, more nearly comparable to those for whites. If the rates are comparable,

then one might say that the application of force unnecessarily by the police operates without respect to the race of an offender.

Many people believe that the race of the policeman must affect his use of force, particularly since many white policemen express prejudice against Negroes. Our own work shows that in the police precincts made up largely of Negro citizens, over three-fourths of the policemen express prejudice against Negroes. Only 1 percent express sympathetic attitudes. But as sociologists and social psychologists have often shown, prejudice and attitudes do not necessarily carry over into discriminatory actions.

Our findings show that there is little difference between the rate of force used by white and by Negro policemen. Of the 54 policemen observed using too much force, 45 were white and 9 were Negro. For every 100 white policemen, 8.7 will use force; for every 100 Negro policemen, 9.8 will. What this really means, though, is that about one in every 10 policemen in high-crime rate areas of cities sometimes uses force unnecessarily.

Yet, one may ask, doesn't prejudice enter into the use of force? Didn't some of the policemen who were observed utter prejudiced statements toward Negroes and other minority-group members? Of course they did. But the question of whether it was their prejudice or some other factor that motivated them to mistreat Negroes is not so easily answered.

Still, even though our figures show that a white suspect is more liable to encounter violence, one may ask whether white policemen victimize Negroes more than whites. We found, for the most part, that they do not. Policemen, both Negro and white, are most likely to exercise force against members of their *own* race: 67 percent of the citizens victimized by white policemen were white; 71 percent of the citizens victimized by Negro policemen were Negro.

To interpret these statistics correctly, however, one should take into account the differences in opportunity policemen have to use force against members of their own and other races. Negro policemen, in the three cities we studied, were far *less* likely to police white citizens than white policemen were to police Negroes. Negro policemen usually policed other Negroes, while white policed both whites and Negroes about equally. In total numbers, then, more white policemen than Negro policemen used force against Negroes. But this is explained by the fact that whites make up 85 percent of the police force, and more than 50 percent of all policemen policing Negroes.

Though no precise estimates are possible, the facts just given suggest that white policemen, even though they are prejudiced toward Negroes, do not discriminate against Negroes in the excessive use of force. The use of force by the police is more readily explained by police culture than it is by the policeman's race. Indeed, in the few cases where we observed a Negro policeman using unnecessary force against white citizens, there was no evidence that he did so because of his race.

The disparity between our findings and the public's sense that Negroes are the main victims of police brutality can easily be resolved if one asks how the public becomes aware of the police misusing force.

The Victims and the Turf

Fifty years ago, the immigrants to our cities—Eastern and Southern Europeans such as the Poles and the Italians—complained about police brutality. Today the new immigrants to our cities—mostly Negroes from the rural South—raise their voices through the civil-rights movement, through black-nationalist and other race-conscious organizations. There is no comparable voice for white citizens since, except for the Puerto Ricans, they now lack the nationality organizations that were once formed to promote and protect the interests of their immigrant forbears.

Although policemen do not seem to select their victims according to race, two facts stand out. All victims were offenders, and all were from the lower class. Concentrating as we did on high-crime rate areas of cities, we do not have a representative sample of residents in any city. Nonetheless, we observed a sizable minority of middle- and upper-status citizens, some of whom were offenders. But since no middle- or upper-class offender, white or Negro, was the victim of an excessive amount of force it appears that the lower class bears the brunt of victimization by the police.

The most likely victim of excessive force is a lower-class man of either race. No white woman and only two Negro women were victimized. The difference between the risk assumed by white and by Negro women can be accounted for by the fact that far more Negro women are processed as suspects or offenders.

Whether or not a policeman uses force unnecessarily depends upon the social setting in which the encounter takes place. Of the 37 instances of excessive force 37 percent took place in police-controlled settings such as the patrol car or the precinct station. Public places, usually streets, accounted for 41 percent, and 16 percent took place in a private residence. The remaining 6 percent occurred in commercial settings. This is not of course a random sample of settings where the police encounter suspects.

What is most obvious, and most disturbing, is that the police are very likely to use force in settings that they control. Although only 18 percent of all situations involving suspects ever ended up at the station house, 32 percent of all situations where an excessive amount of force was used took place in the police station.

No one who accepts the fact that the police sometimes use an excessive amount of force should be surprised by our finding that they often select their own turf. What should be apparent to the nation's police administrators, however, is that these settings are under their command and control. Controlling the police in the field, where the policeman is away from direct supervision, is understandably difficult. But the station house is the police administrator's domain. The fact that one in three instances of excessive force took place in settings that can be directly controlled should cause concern among police officials.

The presence of citizens who might serve as witnesses against a policeman should deter him from undue use of force. Indeed, procedures for the review of police conduct are based on the presumption that one can get this kind of testimony. Otherwise, one is left simply with a citizen complaint and contrary testimony by the policeman—a situation in which it is very difficult to prove the citizen's allegation.

In most situations involving the use of excessive force, there were witnesses. In our 37 cases, there were bystanders present three-fourths of the time. But in only one situation did the group present sympathize with the citizen and threaten to report the policeman. A complaint was filed on that incident—the only one of the 37 observed instances of undue force in which a formal complaint was filed.

All in all, the situations where excessive force was used were devoid of bystanders who did not have a stake in being "against" the offender. Generally, they were fellow policemen, or fellow offenders whose truthfulness could be easily challenged. When a policeman uses undue force, then, he usually does not risk a complaint against himself or testimony from witnesses who favor the complainant against the policeman. This, as much as anything, probably accounts for the low rate of formal complaints against policemen who use force unnecessarily.

A striking fact is that in more than one-half of all instances of undue coercion, at least one other policeman was present who did not participate in the use of force. This shows that, for the most part, the police do not restrain their fellow policemen. On the contrary, there were times when their very presence encouraged the use of force. One man brought into the lockup for threatening a policeman with a pistol was so severely beaten by this policeman that he required hospitalization. During the beating, some fellow policemen propped the man up, while others shouted encouragement. Though the official police code does not legitimate this practice, police culture does.

Victims—Defiant or Deviant

Now, are there characteristics of the offender or his behavior that precipitate the use of excessive force by the police? Superficially, yes. Almost one-half of the cases involved open defiance of police authority (39 percent) or resisting arrest (9 percent). Open defiance of police authority, however, is what the policeman defines as *his* authority, not necessarily "official" authority. Indeed in 40 percent of the cases that the police considered open defiance, the policeman never executed an arrest—a somewhat surprising fact for those who assume that policemen generally "cover" improper use of force with a "bona-fide" arrest and a charge of resisting arrest.

But it is still of interest to know what a policeman *sees* as defiance. Often he seems threatened by a simple refusal to acquiesce to his own authority. A policeman beat a handcuffed offender because, when told to sit, the offender did not sit down. One Negro woman was soundly slapped for her refusal to approach the police car and identify herself.

Important as a threat to his authority may appear to the policeman, there were many more of these instances in which the policeman did *not* respond with the use of force. The important issue seems to be whether the policeman manages to assert his authority despite the threat to it. I suspect that policemen are more likely to respond with excessive force when they define the situation as one in which there remains a question as to who is "in charge."

Similarly, some evidence indicates that harassment of deviants plays a role in the undue use of force. Incidents involving drunks made up 27 percent of all incidents of improper use of force; an additional 5 percent involved homosexuals or narcotics users. Since deviants generally remain silent victims to avoid public exposure of their deviance, they are particularly susceptible to the use of excessive force.

It is clear, though, that the police encounter many situations involving deviants where no force is used. Generally they respond to them routinely. What is surprising, then, is that the police do not mistreat deviants more than they do. The explanation may lie in the kind of relationships the police have with deviants. Many are valuable to the police because they serve as informers. To mistreat them severely would be to cut off a major source of police intelligence. At the same time, deviants are easily controlled by harassment.

Clearly, we have seen that police mistreatment of citizens exists. Is it, however, on the increase?

Citizen complaints against the police are common, and allegations that the police use force improperly are frequent. There is evidence that physical brutality exists today. But there is also evidence, from the history of our cities, that the police have long engaged in the use of unnecessary physical force. No one can say with confidence whether there is more or less of it today than there was at the turn of the century.

What we lack is evidence that would permit us to calculate comparative rates of police misuse of force for different periods of American history. Only recently have we begun to count and report the volume of complaints against the police. And the research reported in this article represents the only attempt to estimate the amount of police mistreatment by actual observation of what the police do to citizens.

Lack of Information

Police chiefs are notoriously reluctant to disclose information that would allow us to assess the nature and volume of complaints against the police. Only a few departments have begun to report something about citizen complaints. And these give us very little information.

Consider, for example, the 1966 Annual Report released by the New Orleans Police Department. It tells us that there were 208 cases of "alleged police misconduct on which action was taken." It fails to tell us whether there were any allegations that are *not* included among these cases. Are these all the allegations that came to the attention of the department? Or are they only those the department chose to review as "police disciplinary matters"? Of the 208 cases the department considered "disciplinary matters," the report tells us that no disciplinary action was taken in 106 cases. There were 11 cases that resulted in 14 dismissals; 56 cases that resulted in 72 suspensions, fines, or loss of days; and 35 cases involving 52 written or verbal "reprimands" or "cautionings."

The failure of the report to tell us the charge against the policeman is a significant omission. We cannot tell how many of these allegations involved improper use of force, how many involved verbal abuse or harassment, how many involved police felonies or misdemeanors, and so on. In such reports, the defensive posture of the nation's police departments is all too apparent. Although the 1966 report of the New Orleans Police Department tells us much about what the police allege were the felonies and misdemeanors by citizens of New Orleans, it tells us nothing about what citizens allege was misconduct by the police!

Many responsible people believe that the use of physical brutality by the police is on the wane. They point to the fact that, at least outside the South, there are more reports of other forms of police mistreatment of citizens than reports of undue physical coercion. They also suggest that third-degree interrogations and curbstone justice with the nightstick are less common. It does not seem unreasonable, then, to assume that police practices that degrade a citizen's status or that harass him and restrict his freedom are more common than police misuse of force. But that may have always been so.

Whether or not the policeman's "sense of justice" and his use of unnecessary force have changed remains an open question. Forms may change while practices go on. To move misuse from the street to the station house, or from the interrogation room to the lockup, changes the place but not the practice itself.

Our ignorance of just what goes on between police and citizens poses one of the central issues in policing today: How can we make the police accountable to the citizenry in a democratic society and yet not hamstring them in their legitimate pursuit of law and order? There are no simple answers.

Police departments are organizations that process people. All people-processing organizations face certain common problems. But the police administrator faces a problem in controlling practice with clients that is not found in most other organizations. The problem is that police contact with citizens occurs in the community, where direct supervision is not possible. Assuming our unwillingness to spend resources for almost one-to-one supervision, the problem for the police commander is to make policemen behave properly when they are not under direct supervision. He also faces the problem of making them behave properly in the station house as well.

Historically, we have found but one way—apart from supervision—that deals with this problem. That solution is professionalization of workers. Perhaps only through the professionalization of the police can we hope to solve the problem of police malpractice.

But lest anyone optimistically assume that professionalization will eliminate police malpractice altogether, we should keep in mind that problems of malpractice also occur regularly in both law and medicine.

"Viva La Policia"

DAVID DURK

I'm here because I'm a policeman and it's just very hard to say it, but these have been a very lonely five years for Frank Serpico, Paul Delise and me. I've had a lot of time to think about what being a cop means. So that's why I'd like to take a few minutes and tell you what being a cop means to me. Then maybe you can understand better some of the things I have said.

At the very beginning, the most important fact to understand is that I had and have *no special knowledge* of police corruption. We knew nothing about the PEP Squad that Waverly Logan didn't know. We knew nothing about the divisions that wasn't known and testified to by Officer Philips, that wasn't known to every man and officer in those divisions. We knew nothing about the police traffic in narcotics that wasn't known and testified to here by Paul Curran of the State Investigations Commission. We knew these things because we were involved in law enforcement in New York City. And anyone else who says he didn't know, had to be blind either by choice or by incompetence.

The facts have been there waiting to be exposed. This commission, to its enormous credit, has exposed them in a period of six months. We simply could not believe, as we do not believe today, that those with authority and responsibility in the area—whether the district attorneys, the police commanders, or those in power in City Hall—couldn't also have exposed them in six months, or at least six years: that is, if they wanted to do it.

Let me be explicit. I am not saying that all those who ignored the corruption were themselves corrupt. Whether or not they were is almost immaterial in any case. The fact is that the corruption was ignored. The fact is that when we reported the corruption to Com-

missioner Fraiman, he refused to act upon his responsibility. The fact is that almost wherever we turned in the police department, wherever we turned in the city administration, and almost wherever we went in the rest of the city, we were met not with cooperation, not with appreciation, not with an eagerness to seek out the truth, but with suspicion and hostility, and laziness and inattention, and with our fear that any moment our efforts might be betrayed.

There has been testimony that Frank Serpico didn't want to testify. Some of it has been critical in tone. Frank Serpico was willing to help. He was begging. All he wanted was support, and what did he get? Commissioner Walsh said yesterday that his plan was to "leave Frank on his own." Walsh was telling Frank, "You do it alone."

These are very tough things to believe if you're a cop. Because to me being a cop means believing in the rule of law. It means believing in a system of government that makes fair and just rules, and then enforces them.

Being a cop also means serving, helping others. If it's not too corny, to be a cop is to help an old lady walk the streets safely; to help a 12-year-old girl reach her next birthday without being gang-raped; to help a storekeeper make a living without keeping a shotgun under his cash register; to help a boy grow up without needles in his arm.

And therefore to me being a cop is not a job but a way to live a life. Some people say that cops live with the worst side of humanity—in the middle of all the lying and cheating, the violence and hate—and I suppose that in some sense is true. But being a cop also means being engaged with life. It means that our concern for others is not abstract, that we don't just write a letter to the *Times* or give ten dollars to the United Fund once a year; it means that we put something on the line from the moment we hit the street every morning of every day of our lives. In this sense police corruption is not about money at all, because there is no amount of money that can pay a cop to risk his life 365 days a year. Being a cop is a vocation, or it is nothing at all.

And that is what I saw being destroyed by the corruption of the New York City Police Department —destroyed for me, and for thousands of others like

SOURCE: This is the concluding statement of Sergeant David Durk at the Knapp Commission Hearing in New York City, December 17, 1971.

me. We wanted to believe in the rule of law; we wanted to believe in a system of responsibility; but those in high places everywhere—in the department, in the DA's offices, and in City Hall—were determined not to enforce the law but to turn their heads away when law and justice were being sold on every street corner.

We wanted to serve others, but the department was a home for the drug dealers and thieves; the force that was supposed to be protecting people was selling poison to their children. . . .

And there could be no life, no real life for me or anyone else on that force, when everyday we had to face the facts of our own terrible corruption. I saw that happening to men all around me—men who could have been good officers, men of decent impulse and even of ideals; but men who were without decent leadership, men who were told in a hundred ways every day: go along. Forget about the law. Don't make waves. Shut up. So they did shut up, they did go along, they did learn the unwritten code of the department. They went along, and they lost something very precious. They weren't cops any more. They were a long way toward not being men any more.

And all the time I saw the other victims too— especially the children. Children of 14 and 15 and 16, wasted by heroin, turned into street corner thugs and whores, ready to mug their own mother for the price of a fix. That was the price of going along, the real price of police corruption; not free meals or broken regulations, but broken dreams and dying neighborhoods and a whole generation of children being lost. That was what I had joined the department to stop.

So that was why I went to the *New York Times.* Because attention had to be paid. And in a last desperate hope that if the facts were known, someone must respond.

And now it is up to you. I speak to you now as nothing more and nothing less than a cop: a cop who has lived on this force, and who is *staying* on this force, and therefore as a cop who needs your help. My fellow policemen and I: we didn't appoint you; you don't report to us; but all the same there are some things that, as policemen, we must have from you.

First, we need you to fix responsibility for the rottenness that was allowed to fester. It must be fixed both inside and outside the department.

Inside the department, responsibility has to be fixed against those top commanders who allowed or helped the situation to develop. Responsibility has to be fixed because no patrolman will believe that he should care about corruption if his superiors can get away with not caring. Responsibility also has to be fixed because commanders themselves have to be told, again and again, and not only by the police commissioner, that the entire state of the department is up to them. And most of all, responsibility has to be fixed because it is the first step toward recovering our simple but necessary conviction that right will be rewarded and wrongdoing punished.

Responsibility must also be fixed outside the department—on all the men and agencies that have helped bring us to our present pass, against all those who could have exposed this corruption, but never did. Like it or not, the policeman is convinced that he lives and works in the middle of a corrupt society; that everyone else is getting theirs, and why shouldn't he; and that if anyone really cared about corruption, something would have been done about it a long time ago. We are not animals. We are not stupid, and we know very well, we policemen, that corruption does not begin with a few patrolmen, and that responsibility for corruption does not end with one aide to the mayor or one investigations commissioner. The issue, for all of today's testimony, is not just Jay Kriegel or Arnold Fraiman. We know that there are many people beyond the police department who share in the corruption and its rewards. So your report has to tell us about the district attorneys and the courts and the bar, and the mayor and the governor—about what they have failed to do, and how great a measure of responsibility they also bear. Otherwise, if you suggest, or allow others to suggest, that the responsibility belongs only to the police— then for the patrolman on the beat and in the radio car, this commission will be just another part of the swindle. That is a harsh statement, and an impolite and a brutal statement. It also is a statement of the truth.

Second, you have to speak as the conscience of this city—speak for all those without a voice, all those who are not here to be heard today, although they know the price of police corruption more intimately than anyone here: the people of the ghetto, and all the other victims, those broken in mind and spirit and hope. Perhaps more than any other people in this city, they depend on the police and the law, to protect not just their pocketbooks but their very lives, and the lives and welfare of their children. Tow truck operators can write off bribes on their income tax; the expense account executive can afford a prostitute; but no one can pay a mother for the pain of seeing her children hooked on heroin.

This commission, for what I am sure are good reasons, has not invited testimony from the communities of suffering in New York City. But this commission must remind the force, as it must tell the rest of the city, that there are human lives at stake, that when police protect the narcotics traffic, then we are participating in the destruction of a generation of children. It is this terrible crime for which you are fixing the responsibility, and it is this terrible crime against which you must speak with the full outrage of the community's conscience.

Third, as a corollary, you must help to give us a sense of priorities, to remind us that corruption, like sin, has its gradations and classifications. Of course, all corruption is bad. But we cannot fall into the trap of pretending that all corruption is *equally* bad. There is a difference between accepting free meals and selling narcotics. If we are unable to make that distinction, then we are saying to the police that the life of a child in the South Bronx is of the same moral value as a cup of coffee. That cannot be true, for this society or for its police force. So you must show us the difference.

Finally, in your deliberations, you must speak for the policemen of this city—for the best that is in them, for what most of them wanted to be, for what most of them will be if we try.

Once I arrested a landlord's agent who offered to pay me if I would lock up a tenant who was organizing other tenants, and as I put the cuffs on the agent and led him away, a crowd of people assembled and started yelling, "Viva la policia!"

Of course, it was not just me, or even the police, that they were cheering. They were cheering because they had glimpsed, in that one arrest, the possibility of a system of justice that could work to protect them too. They were cheering because if that agent could get arrested, then that meant they had rights, they were citizens, and maybe one day life would really be different for their children.

For me, that moment was what police work is all about. But there have been far too few moments like it, and far too many times when I looked into the faces of the city and saw not hope and trust, but resentment and hate and fear. Far too many of my fellow officers have seen only hate; far too many of them have seen their dreams of service and justice frustrated and abandoned by a corrupt system, and superiors and politicians who just didn't care enough.

It took five years of Frank Serpico's life, and five years of mine, to help bring this commission about. It has taken the lives and dedication of thousands of others to preserve as much of a police force as we have. It has taken months of effort by all of you to help show this city the truth. What I ask of you now is to help make us clean again; to help give us some leadership we can look to; to make it possible for all the men on the force to walk at ease with their better nature and with their fellow citizens—and perhaps one day, on a warm summer night, to hear again the shout of "Viva la policia."

9 | The Future of Law Enforcement

We have stressed that the police and police institutions are largely a product of the historical past. It would be naive and a serious mistake, however, to think of police institutions as prisoners of the past, static and unchanging. As the forces which shape a society emerge and seek primacy and power, the police must respond to this changing environment.

Perhaps one of the most powerful forces effecting change in police organizations is that of the process of police unionization, which the police establishment has resisted determinedly for decades. Even the most powerful industrial corporations have succumbed to labor organization. The transfer and sharing of power that unionization entails is a revolutionary force in police administration. It will create new relations across the board with a potential for democratization of this quasi-military organization.

Another dimension which has much promise, but the impact of which is as yet not clear, is the introduction of equality for women in an essentially male occupation. One of the unresolved problems here is whether the integration of women in police forces is going to be a sustained, sincere effort, or another instance of token compliance with our concept of equality and justice for all.

The effect of higher education for many police officers will not be evident for many years to come. The emergence of a college-educated cadre does introduce an element of uncertainty. They will be the internal critics, the contenders for power, and the connecting link to the academic community. A certain degree of resentment within the police system on the part of those who have been unable or unwilling to pursue higher education may be a disruptive force for polarization. Yet for all the portents of change as a result of higher education, the traditional police culture may prove to be strong enough to absorb and coopt the "new breed." In all probability our society's technology will not produce some magical, innovative crime-fighting apparatus. Instead, assuming present trends and developments, computer technology and information retrieval will have the greatest impact on law enforcement.

The future political and economic development of the United States will determine in large measure the future direction of law enforcement. Given the inevitable cyclical fluctuations which are inherent in our economic system, the political implications and prospects which may result are not clear at this time. If a long period of economic stagnation persists, the police may be the ultimate instrument to control discontented and hostile forces that will emerge as a consequence of widespread economic dislocation and its concomitant unemployment. Political demagogues may seize upon the general unrest to arouse the explicit fears of crime in an effort to mobilize popular sentiments, thus enabling them to exploit the police and police institutions for their own purposes. This may place the police in a dangerous situation in which they become pawns in a larger political struggle over which they have little control. Whatever the outcome, one of the crucial elements will be the police system.

The FBI and American Law Enforcement:

A Future View

CLARENCE M. KELLEY

It has unfortunately become commonplace to observe that crime and its consequences constitute a national menace and challenge of huge proportions and deep implications for us all. Nonetheless, the evidence for this assessment is overwhelming.

As a society and as individuals, we all pay a heavy price for the lawlessness and violence that plague this nation—and the price steadily mounts. The fact and fear of crime strike hard at a vast and increasing number of our citizenry to whom predatory and violent lawbreakers constitute a constant threat to life, property, and freedom. Any number of studies, surveys, and public opinion polls have amply documented the tragic degree to which crime virtually tyrannizes great segments of this populace.

Criminal activity in America today occurs in such diversity and on such a sweeping scale that it is indeed difficult to even estimate its full extent. Although anything approaching a complete picture of our total crime problem can only be surmised, data compiled nationally under the FBI's Uniform Crime Reporting Program provide the most statistically complete view available of crime's impact on the United States.

Based on information furnished to the FBI by law enforcement agencies throughout the country, there was an estimated total of 8,638,400 serious crimes (murder, forcible rape, robbery, aggravated assault, burglary, larceny-theft, and auto theft) recorded during 1973, of which 869,500 were violent crimes. Property valued at over 2.5 billion dollars was stolen as a result of 382,680 robberies, 923,600 auto thefts, 2,540,900 burglaries, and 4,304,400 larcenies. During that year, approximately 15 of every 100 law enforcement officers were assaulted in the line of

This article was written expressly for inclusion in this book by the Director of the FBI.

duty, and 127 local, county, and state officers were slain due to felonious criminal action.

As some indication of the growth of crime in recent years, it is interesting to note that while our population increased by only 5 percent during the period 1968 through 1973, the volume of crime in America, as measured by the aforementioned serious offenses, rose 30 percent over this brief span of years, and the crime rate increased by 24 percent.

Although lawlessness has obviously grown to alarming proportions in America, the basic challenge it poses is far from new to our society and has, over the years, resulted in considerable concern and attention. A tremendous amount of research has been conducted in an effort to define and understand this enormously complex problem and to seek ways of coping with it. Within the last decade alone, a President's Commission on Law Enforcement and Administration of Justice, and, later, a National Advisory Commission on Criminal Justice Standards and Goals undertook massive and expert studies relating to our crime problem. Other important studies too numerous to mention have added to our fund of knowledge in this area. As a result of such efforts and concern, the years have brought innumerable anticrime strategies and programs which have met with varying degrees of implementation and success. Yet, overall, crime continues to flourish and to challenge us anew.

While there are demonstrably no panaceas that will rid society of crime and the conditions that breed and contribute to it, we can do much to reduce crime by improving and strengthening our administration of justice. A good deal of our crime problem, for example, rests with the repeat offender. It has long been known that much of our crime is committed by a relatively small number of individuals who are recidivists. In fact, there is strong evidence that as many as two-thirds of all offenses are committed by recidivists—individuals who have previously been arrested for and convicted of crimes. More realistic treatment of these hardcore offenders by our criminal justice system would undoubtedly go a long way toward reducing crime. It must be recognized that unrealistic treatment of criminals, particularly those of a hardened nature, in respect to bail procedures, plea bargaining, use of concurrent sentences, and in the administration of parole and probation, aggravates our crime problem immeasurably.

By virtue of its function in the administration of justice, law enforcement affords a positive, direct response to the growth of crime. Although this single element of our criminal justice system cannot alone carry the burden of crime reduction, our nation's success in dealing with lawlessness and violence will to a significant degree depend upon the professionalism and dedication of its law enforcement community. Any meaningful assessment of American law enforcement's ability to meet this challenge of the future must consider the role—past, present, and future—of the Federal Bureau of Investigation.

In point of time, one need go back no further than May 10, 1924, when a 29-year-old attorney, John Edgar Hoover, was placed in charge of the United States Department of Justice's Bureau of Investigation—later to be known as the Federal Bureau of Investigation or, to most Americans, as simply the FBI. Some organizational housecleaning was in order, and young Mr. Hoover was more than equal to the task. In 1933, Supreme Court Justice Harlan Fiske Stone, who, as attorney general, had been responsible for the appointment, described Hoover's success in the following fashion:

> He removed from the Bureau every man as to whose character there was any ground for suspicion. He refused to yield to any kind of political pressure; he appointed to the Bureau men of intelligence and education, and strove to build up morale such as should control such an organization. He withdrew it wholly from extra-legal activities and made it an efficient organization for investigation of criminal offenses against the United States.[1]

In brief, the man who was to head the FBI for nearly 48 years quickly set the bureau straight and embarked upon a remarkable career that was to have profound and far-reaching effects on not only the FBI but on the entire development and practice of American law enforcement.

During the passage of years, the FBI experienced substantial growth in size, responsibilities, and importance. The FBI did not map out its jurisdictional growth. This development was essentially the product of certain emerging law enforcement needs of a national character on the part of modern America—a nation of traditionally localized police powers but growing national demands of a criminal and security nature. An investigative agency with the interstate jurisdiction and resources of the FBI best answered these needs.

Misconceptions regarding the fundamental nature of the FBI and the extent of its authority continue to persist. There is a concern among some that the FBI may be moving in the direction of a repressive police/intelligence agency of virtually boundless and unchecked power. The facts are otherwise.

The FBI is not a national police force nor does there appear any likelihood that it will become one. During his long tenure as director of the FBI, Mr. Hoover steadfastly opposed any moves to cast the bureau in this role. He believed, and with good reason, that it would be a grave and very possibly dangerous mistake to invest the FBI with such sweeping police power. Under our democratic system of government, policing is best handled and controlled at the local level. In harmony with this concept, the FBI has traditionally done all in its power to strengthen and assist law enforcement at all levels of government. This attitude will not change.

Unquestionably, the FBI—no less than any other law enforcement agency—must be safeguarded from misuse. To preclude the FBI of the future from ever becoming an instrument of repression, appropriate limitations and checks on the bureau's jurisdiction and activities must continue to exist.

In addition to the very powerful constraints of law, FBI operations and policies are subject to the approval of the attorney general and review by various congressional committees. One such committee, which was recently created and has the wholehearted support of the bureau in its task, is the Senate Subcommittee on FBI Oversight. The bureau's investigations are also subject to court review. In addition, vigilant news media and, ultimately, the public that the FBI seeks to serve act to guard against potential abuses of authority and power.

Beyond these very necessary and proper external safeguards, there operate within the organization itself other strong assurances of propriety in the form of deeply ingrained traditions of integrity and dedicated public service. There has been no diminution of these high ideals of conduct and service nor of the quality of FBI personnel who continue to be inspired and guided by them.

The FBI today stands as the principal investigative arm of the United States Department of Justice. The scope of its jurisdiction and activities has derived from congressional enactments and the constitutional powers and responsibilities of the President. More specifically, the FBI has extensive responsibilities for internal security, criminal and civil investigations. In addition, the bureau provides a number of essential services in support of our entire law enforcement community.

To carry out these extensive investigative responsibilities and services, the modern FBI employs more than 19,000 men and women, maintains 59 field offices strategically located in major cities throughout the United States and in San Juan, Puerto Rico, and operates a number of liaison posts in various foreign countries.

Although this brief discussion does not permit any detailed treatment of important FBI investigative areas, two fields of deep consequence to the future of American law enforcement in meeting our crime problem merit particular comment.

One is the organized crime field. For a number of years the FBI has stressed the investigation of major cases in this field. In alliance with local, state, and other federal law enforcement agencies, the bureau has achieved notable successes in this area. In fiscal year 1974 alone, FBI organized crime investigations resulted in 1,367 convictions, including syndicate functionaries in New York City, Philadelphia, Cleveland, and in New England. Recoveries and confiscations in organized crime cases exceeded 3.4 million dollars. Extremely important in this nation's war on organized crime has been the criminal intelligence information developed by the FBI and disseminated to other agencies. The dissemination of such information to these agencies yielded the following impressive results during fiscal year 1974: Nearly 3,300 organized crime arrests were made; some 35 million dollars' worth of narcotics, about 2 million dollars' worth of cash, property, weapons, and gambling paraphernalia, and more than 3 million dollars' worth of counterfeit bills were confiscated; and nearly 15.5 million dollars' worth of property was confiscated or assessed tax liens in connection with gambling cases.

Despite the striking successes achieved by attacking organized crime along these lines of prosecution, intelligence gathering and dissemination of information to appropriate federal, state, and local agencies having jurisdiction, crime cartels continue to sap billions of tax-free dollars from our economy through illicit gambling operations, narcotics, vice, loansharking, fraud, and the infiltration and exploitation of legitimate business. The major part played by the organized underworld in our total crime problem will continue to call for the concerted efforts of our entire law enforcement community.

Another area of criminal activity that has been afforded priority attention by the FBI involves so-called "white-collar" crimes which include complicated financial manipulations and computer frauds. These offenses, usually committed by individuals occupying responsible positions in private business, labor, and government, are often perpetrated with considerable finesse. Coping with such crime demands a high degree of investigative skill. The FBI has undertaken an intensive training effort to provide greater expertise in these investigative areas. In addition to bureau personnel, other representatives of our criminal justice system have profited by this advanced and urgently needed training.

The FBI takes a great deal of pride in the many essential support services it provides American law enforcement at all levels of government. The contributions which these services have made toward the advancement of police professionalism have been impressive, to say the least. Progress in these service areas promises even greater support in the years ahead.

Since its establishment in 1924, the FBI's identification division has rendered indispensable support to American law enforcement by acting as this nation's central repository and clearinghouse for fingerprint data and by performing other identification services. During fiscal year 1974, fingerprint receipts totaled 5,518,387, of which 2,768,663 were criminal in nature. Also during this period, 37,804 cases were received for latent fingerprint identification. As a major move toward increasing the efficiency of its identification services, the division undertook a research project which led to the development of a prototype automated fingerprint reader system, called "FINDER," which reads and records fingerprints through the use of computerized optical scanning equipment. With the beginning of 1975, several advanced models of these readers were in the process of construction. Upon completion, these production-model readers will serve as the nucleus of a computerized system.

Certainly one of the fastest-growing and most useful technical services of benefit to law enforcement is that provided by the FBI National Crime

Information Center, or NCIC. At the beginning of 1975, more than 6,600 criminal justice agencies in the United States, the District of Columbia, the Commonwealth of Puerto Rico, and Canada had the capability through telecommunications devices in their possession of being serviced by the center's computerized index of documented data relating to crime and criminals. At this time, the NCIC computer contained more than 5.5 million active records. Indicative of the degree to which it is being used, NCIC transactions on one day during 1974 totaled 210,053—an average of 2.43 transactions every second. Without exaggeration, it may be said that NCIC constitutes one of the most potent crime-fighting weapons in the arsenal of law enforcement. There is little doubt that NCIC will prove even more potent in the years ahead as our criminal justice system struggles to deal with increasingly sophisticated and fast-moving crime.

The facilities of the FBI laboratory provide yet another area of vital service to progressive law enforcement. Of the 557,454 examinations conducted by this laboratory during fiscal year 1974, 25 percent were made for agencies other than the FBI. Through research and study, personnel of the laboratory are constantly increasing the value of this support by developing new and improved methods of scientific crime detection. In addition to these continuing endeavors and others designed to increase the laboratory's effectiveness, a new program of assistance to state and local forensic science laboratories was initiated during fiscal year 1974.

It would be most difficult to overly emphasize the key function that training plays in improving the effectiveness of law enforcement. The FBI's long involvement in law enforcement training has been extensive and highly productive. In recent years, this involvement has been substantially enlarged. FBI training activities carried out at the new FBI academy at Quantico, Virginia, and at the regional and local level address a wide range of law enforcement needs. In connection with its field training program, the FBI offered upon request during fiscal year 1974 instruction in over 11,000 law enforcement schools attended by more than 343,000 criminal justice personnel. Also during that fiscal period, the FBI conducted a wide variety of training programs at the field level

and at the FBI academy concerning such critical subjects as kidnappings and hostage situations, crisis intervention, and executive development. In addition, nearly 1,000 career supervisory and command personnel from all levels of law enforcement were graduated from the prestigious FBI National Academy.

A review of FBI training over the past several years reflects a remarkable responsiveness to the changing and critical needs of the law enforcement community. Every effort is being made to insure that this degree of responsiveness will characterize FBI training activities in the future.

Yet another service of continuing value to law enforcement and other elements of our criminal justice system is the FBI Uniform Crime Reporting Program which compiles and publishes a broad range of crime data.

These invaluable service functions comprise only a part of the cooperative relationship that has traditionally existed between the FBI and other law enforcement agencies and has, over the years, been responsible for much of the effectiveness achieved in the fight against crime. By fostering this spirit within the administration of justice system, an even greater alliance against crime may be attained.

In assessing the capabilities of American law enforcement today, a great amount of assurance for the future may be drawn from its past advancement as a profession. The progress has in recent years been swift and is reflected in the dedication, competence, and high ideals that distinguish professional law enforcement today.

Over the decades, the FBI has by action and example done all in its power to promote these qualities of professionalism throughout the ranks of law enforcement. If nothing else, the FBI story chronicles a steady pursuit of professional excellence —an excellence of spirit as well as skill—and the rewards of this pursuit have been freely shared with others in the profession.

In the years ahead, as in years past, this determined pursuit of professional excellence is certain to pay rich dividends to the FBI, the administration of justice system, and a nation struggling to control crime.

REFERENCES

(1) Alpheus Thomas Mason, *Harlan Fiske Stone, Pillar of the Law* (New York: The Viking Press, 1956), p. 152.

Law Enforcement:

A Look into the Future

A. C. GERMANN

Our peoples face the perils of population explosion, energy shortages, maldistribution of food, pollution of air and water, proliferation of lethal weaponry, inadequate health services, and monetary inflation. None of these perils are, today, domestic; all are global. Almost all can be solved by the application of science and technology and by a concerted international community.

But there is one peril that requires more than the application of science and technology and more than concerted action and that is the peril of excessive social control. To meet this peril—and the problems surrounding it, such as unresponsive leadership, violations of basic human rights, the expansion of control and enforcement institutions to a degree that may threaten traditional democratic processes—we must rethink the goals and priorities of law enforcement, and we must redirect our efforts in order to make it humane and effective.

We seem to be prisoners of our cliches and the thinking of 25 and 50 years ago. Our police and their predecessors seem wholly unable to emancipate themselves from thinking about weaponry and repression as the key social control solution. We carry the stereotypes of the past and are unable to disabuse ourselves of them. We have only to read police literature to realize the extent to which our police establishment has been unable to adjust to the realities of the present and future.

Look at the articles, editorials, and advertisements. Almost all give tacit acceptance and approval to the traditional repressive processes, continue the myopic trust in technology, and assume that the people will continue to support the present ineffective posture and program.

This article was written expressly for inclusion in this book.

Somehow we must face up to our failures, rather than continue to disguise them with modern glitter. Some 8,600,000 index offenses were reported in 1973, in the Uniform Crime Reports, with a 21 percent clearance rate. National crime surveys, sponsored by our government, continue consistently to indicate that crime is two to five times higher than reported. If but three times higher, we have over 25,000,000 index offenses for 1973, and a true clearance rate of 7 percent. In such a case, about 93 percent of the offenses—some 24,000,000—are unaffected by the actions or nonactions of the police! I am inclined to believe that our police are really dealing with the unlucky, or the inept, or the mentally retarded antisocial offender who represents that 7 percent identified and charged. Thus we have been, are, and will be almost totally ineffective in controlling antisocial behavior by police intervention, no matter how many times we double our forces, no matter how many computers we purchase, no matter how lethal our firepower, no matter how paramilitary our agencies, and no matter how contrived our public relations. Yet we go on, replicating the useless efforts of the past.

We must, somehow, it seems to me, abate our traditional trust in force and cease our worship at its altar. We must increase our regard for our fellow citizen, our ideals of service to humanity, and repudiate all tyrannical and unjust social forms wherever found on this planet—and that includes a challenge of our own social control when it becomes obvious that human rights are being violated by any of our institutions.

Our Bill of Rights, dating from 1789, contains the ideal of equal justice under law. But this ideal has been ignored, or circumvented, or violated continuously—and we all know it! Who would deny that there are indeed separate justices for youth, for minorities, for women, for nonconformists, and more obviously, for the rich and poor?

At one time in our society, the young saw police as all-good, all-wise, and all-powerful; and later, adult acceptance of the legitimacy of police flowed from that youthful idealization. Positive feelings in formative years can have lasting consequences, as we all know.

Now, as children grow up and see police in more critical and less enthusiastic fashion, such youthful lack of respect may create latent feelings difficult to change. If such childhood feelings are negative, the child will see the police, not as benign and protective, but as dangerous and arrogant, models not to be emulated, but to be rejected. This may have important and lasting consequences as the years go by, and such disillusioned young people grow up with ineradicably antagonistic mental sets relative to police, their work, and their worth. And such is now happening, wherever the police are less than humane.

I think that it is no wonder that intelligent, motivated, and humanistic people are discouraged from affiliation with police. Or, if affiliated, it is no wonder that they become frustrated and depart the service. Or, if they remain, it is no wonder that they are considered oddballs by police traditionalists and are consigned to innocuous positions.

I suspect, looking to the future, that one or the other of two diametrically opposed scenarios is likely to come to pass. Each one is sketched out here to its extreme. At the moment we are limping along with a hodgepodge of both. If given the choice, I would opt for an amalgam of the efficiency of the first with the humanism of the second: an omnipotent twenty-first century genie directed and controlled by a wise, just, and loving people. For me, the maximum disaster would be an amalgam of the efficiency and repressive potential of the first: an omnipotent twenty-first century genie directing and controlling a supine, frightened, Orwellian slave-labor camp that believes it is free and willingly suffers the loss of liberty.

The Repressive Scenario

Crime in all categories—street, organized, and white-collar—continues to increase in amount and repulsiveness. Citizens become more panicked and angry. The police, more frustrated than ever, ask for more manpower, facilities, and equipment, and suggest to the public that the "war on crime" be intensified. They convince a frightened citizenry that all "handcuffs" should be taken off the police and that discretion should be given for more data bank utilization, for more surveillance capability, for greater

authority to search and bug and wiretap, for authority to hold subjects in preventive detention, and for greater latitude in dealing with nonconforming minorities and dissidents of any type. The police double and triple their secret-service budgets, utilizing many more informants of all ages and life-styles.

The police agencies increase their ranks, tripling and quadrupling their forces; they build hundreds of fortress-stations in every metropolitan area, adding software and hardware of all types and using ever more space-age electronic capacity for data banks, surveillance equipment, and communications. In addition to the currently stockpiled weaponry, massive additions of combat-proven armaments accrue. To the array of saps, batons, magnum handguns, rifles, riot guns, chemical sprays, armored tanks, and helicopter gun ships are added a variety of gases, grenades, flame-throwers, shields, screens, armor, and security barriers for all facilities. "Green Beret" militarism becomes the order of the day.

Police assume, unilaterally, all decision-making authority for social control in the nation; and they apply immediate massive force in any situation where police are not awarded instant obedience, deference, and compliance. The International Association of Chiefs of Police and the FBI and the police associations continue to question the absence of stronger laws, the leniency of the courts, and the failure of prisons to maintain long-term custody. All babies, at birth, have radioactive social security numbers embedded in the soles of their feet by means of high-pressure air injection, such numbers easily read by readout plates, so that police can make instant identifications, surreptitiously if they so desire. All citizens are photographed and fingerprinted regularly, and they carry up-to-date identification at all times or face immediate arrest and penalty. All members of the nonconforming minority are subject to continuous harassment. Any person who is particularly suspect is subject to implantation of electronic locater devices for continuous surveillance.

In times of any special unrest, dissident groups are subject to neutralization—by infiltration of their organizations by informers or undercover agents, by contrived arrests via incitation to illegal acts by agents provocateurs, and, if necessary, by elimination of their leadership by any means possible.

The police continue their close affinity to conservative, ultraconservative and extreme right-wing movements and philosophies. No radical changes are made in police organization or traditional procedures. Sensitive and humanistic members of the police establishment are even more ostracized; incoming recruits are even more intensively screened to eliminate socially sensitive probationers and those who would question traditional police procedures; and the criminal justice system, as a whole, is purged of liberal and humane careerists.

The 800 college-degree programs in criminal justice are becoming more highly developed as adjuncts to the local police academy, with safe traditionalists remaining in control of faculty, curriculum, and student progress.

The police establishment continues to foster nonquestioning support from the conforming majority by frightening it even further with the spectre of criminal/dissident takeover, by confusing it even more with 1930's-type public education programs, and by continuing the police/media myth that the handsome white supercop, occasionally accompanied by a token minority assistant, aided by technology and weaponry, making unilateral determination of all means used, will subdue and convict the unkempt, dark, and ugly supercriminal. Slowly but surely, executive, legislative, and corporate power is manipulated or coerced into supporting police budgets second only to military—with intelligence dossiers and coordinated data-bank exchanges of personal information making docility and cooperation a mandatory condition of continuance in office. Slowly but surely, the alienation of nonconforming minorities— youths, pacifists, humanists, liberals, radicals, progressives, feminists, blacks, Chicanos, Native Americans, civil libertarians, consumer advocates, environmentalists, life-style experimentalists, eccentrics, one-world advocates, religious sectarians, academicians, artists, and other independent thinkers— becomes complete. And the police, coldly efficient, with the most reactionary traditionalists in total control, become as hated as was the German Gestapo (and probably more so, for the Gestapo never had the use of space-age science and technology). And slowly but surely the dream of a free society in the United States, a society linked to all other freedom-loving societies, fades, and the world is left with only dictatorships—variously disguised—with the military and the police serving rich and powerful individuals and corporations. And slowly but surely, the charge that police are but the hired guns of the "haves" is documented and proved again and again by daily evidence,

as police "crack-downs" concentrate, as usual, on those unfortunates most readily available.

What, then, is the other extreme? Scenario two calls for a large-scale change in attitude and practice, indeed!

The Humanistic Scenario

Crime in all categories—street, organized, and white-collar—continues to increase in amount and repulsiveness. Citizens become more panicked and angry. The police, rapidly moving away from past militaristic configurations, engage in serious heart-to-heart communication with the entire community. Many hundreds of police chiefs and subordinate commanders are retired, replaced, or reeducated. Many thousands of social science graduates are now productively serving their fellow citizens as professional police officers. The accent is changed; the former unilateral social control *by* police has disappeared; in its place has come collective responsibility for social control and community control *of* police. Policing is now a profession with equal status and economic reward along with law, medicine, and teaching. The former accent on repression and "crushing" is replaced by an emphasis on serving and "helping." The police agency is totally transformed. The police academies of the nation are almost completely phased out, and education for police service is now the responsibility of universities. Top ranks of police agencies contain many women, minorities, intellectuals, and representatives of every segment of American society. These leaders, open to the world, see the problems of social control and human rights as global matters. The need for planetary concern is stressed, and these leaders understand that both problems and solutions are interdependent, as are the citizens of the world. Police leaders are candid in admitting that the policing of past years has been largely wasteful of effort, resources, and emphasis. The de-emphasis of force, the re-emphasis of personal moral responsibility and development of concerned neighborhoods, and the continuous example of concern for one's brother citizen mark the new police attitude. Everywhere, now, the policeman is a warm, trusted, and approachable friend to *all* people in the community. The police readily accept the role of ombudsman of the weak, ignorant, confused, frustrated, unemployed, cold, sick, hungry, lonely, and hopeless. The police at all levels of government see themselves as examples for youth, as teachers of the community, and as helpful members of the human family; and the community responds in kind, no longer viewing the police as merely heavily armed mercenaries or as cold and indifferent bureaucrats, but rather, it sees them as concerned and capable friends.

The changes are immense: a nation which had been supporting, without question, an almost *carte-blanche* police authority and its ever-enlarging lethal potential, radically alters its goals and programs. The seemingly invincible indifference of the police to public opinion alters quickly as people and their representatives opt for a collective responsibility to the planetary family of man, rather than perpetuating individual competition and narrow self-interest. The people-oriented police, convinced that a police establishment divorced from militaristic postures and right-wing identification is more representative of a humane democracy, now assist enthusiastically in the largest alteration of social control methods since the Peelian reforms of 1829.

Criminal law, at all levels of government, is reformed and limited in scope. Simplified and clarified laws and more just penalties receive overwhelming public understanding and support; and the people are edified in knowing that their police have led the fight for such reforms.

Existing laws are expanded and new laws are enacted to shield the people from racial and sex discrimination, pollution and misuse of public resources, manufacture and sale of defective products, deceptive advertising and packaging, fraudulent housing and insurance schemes, and other "white-collar" crimes. Units are established in all police agencies to investigate private or governmental invasions of civil liberties, and others are formed to deal with consumer protection and the implementation of gun control laws. The police lead the effort to strengthen the Bill of Rights by amending the First Amendment to the Constitution to add the right of privacy to the right of assembly and by amending the Second Amendment to define the limits of the government's right to bear arms against its citizens. In addition, such leadership is effective in securing new laws to protect citizens from private or governmental misuse of electronic surveillance or data bank information. Such police leadership gives notice to the entire world that our law enforcement is, indeed, the enemy of all forms of tyranny.

Other existing laws are revoked and behavior decriminalized in the area of "morals offenses," such as drunkenness, vagrancy, gambling, prostitution, obscenity, pornography, drug use, fornication, adultery, bigamy, incest, and homosexuality as relates to consenting adults.

Police are demilitarized in appearance, equipment, and methods; domestic warfare by police is emphatically rejected.

The police of the United States now set a planetary example of humanistic professional law enforcement. As part of its program of international cooperation, it works with police of other nations in implementing a planetary registry, so that the passport becomes a world-wide means of identification, credit, and assistance.

Our police put priority emphasis, now, on developing neighborhood and community organizations, and new police units are found in every city with the function of assisting people to know each other and to cooperate collectively. During the changeover period our police establish the tradition of inviting all segments of the public, from all enclaves, to assume the responsibility of making decisions about police goals, methods, and priorities. Police secrecy (except for data bank security and ongoing current investigations) is a thing of the past, all agency facilities and operations are open to public scrutiny, and all equipment and weaponry are a matter of bilateral police-community agreement. Ombudsmen and criminal justice review commissions work cooperatively with all citizens to eliminate corruption and injustice, and they receive enthusiastic cooperation from law enforcement.

The people and the police give primary attention to the reduction of violent antisocial behavior, working with prosecutors, courts, and corrections to neutralize the person who threatens or causes physical harm to his fellow citizen. The people and the police assist in the community-based treatment and rehabilitation of nonviolent offenders, aiding their successful reentry into the community family.

The reform of criminal law results in much less police intervention, the participation of the public in policing results in much more swift and certain conviction of arrestees, and the limitation of incarceration only to violent offenders results in highly reduced prison populations.

Our police, educated and humanistic, are not inclined to harass nonconforming minorities, and they relate more easily to a wide variety of life-styles. Our police, educated and humanistic, are not angered by citizens who gather to protest tyranny or injustice. As a matter of fact, our police, educated and humanistic, encourage community organization for collective action; they encourage citizen concern for civil rights and civil liberties; and they encourage the struggle to make the American dream of liberty and justice for all both a national and a planetary objective. Thus, the second scenario is a drastic departure from the current reality.

A Final Word

Which scenario will come to pass? Hard-nosed police traditionalists, and their Archie-Bunker-type supporters, are very much a part of the national landscape. Out of ignorance or misguided zeal they contribute to the possible development of the repressive scenario.

But just as real, no matter how outnumbered, are the humanistic police professionals, with their academic soul-brothers and like-minded citizens. By motivated example they make the humanistic scenario a future possibility.

Whichever scenario is developed will carry the mark of the other, for it is unlikely that any human institution can be as pure as its motivating ideal; but the nation will see the distinct emergence of either a more repressive or a more humanistic law enforcement than exists in the present hodgepodge.

The total answer really lies outside the police precinct or university classroom and depends upon the hearts of our general citizenry and their representatives. Will they continue to support the terribly wasteful and almost totally ineffective mode of social control? If so, the repressive scenario will bloom ever more healthily. Will they finally say "Enough is enough" and demand a radical change of goals, methods, priorities, and posture? If so, the humanistic scenario can become more than the idle chatter of idealists.

I wish I could suggest that the 800 college and university criminal justice programs are a force potent enough to humanize and reorient American policing, but I can't. Although some programs work intensively to raise the consciousness of their students, far too many are captives of the current police establishment and serve only to perpetuate the crude cliches of the present criminal justice nonsystem.

I wish I could suggest that the billions of dollars expended by the Law Enforcement Assistance Administration—LEAA—will result in substantial positive change in American policing, but I can't. Too many of those dollars are buying only a slicked-up, gadget-oriented, firepower-worshipping remake of what we already have; too many dollars go toward installing a police-industrial complex and further misleading our nation with a continuation of the myth that computers and firepower will bring order and tranquility to our people.

I wish I could suggest that recent national scandals involving the Presidency, the FBI, the CIA, the Attorney General, the Pentagon, and domestic surveillance have alerted our people and their representatives to the probability of hundreds of mini-Watergates throughout the land and to the need for extensive scrutiny and monumental change of our military and social-control mechanisms; but I can't. The sordid, sleazy, unconstitutional and arrogantly pragmatic practices recently exposed are not really new or surprising to any sensitive person who has worked within the criminal justice nonsystem for any length of time, and they will continue to occur until radical change of attitude and practice is a nationwide reality.

When I look into the future of law enforcement I am frightened and, at the same time, hopeful. I am frightened because the humanists are so badly outnumbered within the criminal justice establishment. I am hopeful because it is very obvious that we have come to the end of an era: we either surrender to the most repressive elements in the institution and go the way of the police state, or we damn well get it together and humanize criminal justice by making substantial changes. There is no other way!

Now is the time for humanistic academics and humanistic police chiefs to lead the way. Even though our students and citizens are anxious, they are ever receptive to the idea of humane and progressive change, particularly when espoused by intelligent and compassionate professors and by intelligent and compassionate criminal justice leaders. The nation is waiting. Speak out! Lead! The classroom is waiting. Speak out! Lead! The criminal justice agency is waiting. Speak out! Lead! The local community is waiting. Speak out! Lead! The future of law enforcement can be a matter of great pride instead of horrible embarrassment! Speak out! Lead! NOW!

Police Organizations:

The Challenges and Dilemmas of Change

JACK A. MARK

Organisms and organizations must adapt and change in order to survive. The characteristic order of the day is change. The milieu in which police organizations function and the vast external and generated internal forces that impact on and forge changes in the role and in the activities of the police reflect that order. The tempo of change is speeding up, but its beat and rhythms are quite uneven. Exacerbating the perplexities and complexities of police organizational change is that it is occurring in a sea of uncertainty—in a society uncertain of its own direction, under economic stress and dislocation, with a considerable degree of dissensus, with individuals under severe tensions dys- or malfunctioning under the pressure cooker, groups in conflict, volatile pockets of racial polarization, people in fear of crime, easy accessibility to and rampant use of firearms, and, in the wings, the ever-lurking threat of nuclear holocaust.

Compounding the difficulties and dilemmas of comprehensive police change in the United States are the extreme fragmentation of its policing system, the proliferation of local and county jurisdictions, and the concrete realities of metropolitan regions that transcend state lines and function as entities more viable than each of their separate parts, their viability, however, substantially diminished by the different laws of the states overlapped. Then again, there is the clinging to, the reluctance to let go of the "home-rule" concept of policing by too many small communities, each feeling that it is imperative to have and to exercise exclusive control over its own police department, even if only a few members comprise the total force. Add the desire of numerous political machines and elected public officials to go beyond acceptable policy formulation to dominating and to bending the administration of police departments to

SOURCE: This article was written expressly for inclusion in this book.

suit their own purposes, even if it entails dictating and meddling into the most routine of daily operations. The perspective of police agencies as military-like organizations and the viewpoint of treating their personnel accordingly still hold sway over police practices, if not in the recent literature on policing. This predominant outlook embraces the doctrine of close supervision of subordinates and increased manpower to meet the problems in police administration and ineffectiveness in operations that surface. Despite the lack of confirming evidence as to the doctrine's applicability, disenchantment with it grows slowly but not sufficiently to date to have made significant inroads on a broad enough scale into the operant behavior of police organizations.

Police Consolidation and Regionalization

Policing in the United States will not emerge as a respectable profession until there is a decided swing away from the staggering disproportion of small police agencies whose governance is molded and straitjacketed by the longtime revered but no longer viable and, therefore, certainly questionable tradition of "home rule." Insistence upon perpetuating the tradition as it applies to policing at the level of the tiniest of local hamlets carries the tradition to the point of severely depriving too many communities of essential police services and to the edge, if not to the state, of fiscal squandering and irresponsibility.

Many in and out of law enforcement rightly fear the spectre of one gigantic national police force for a nation of 215 million people, in a country that stretches some three thousand miles across the mainland at its waist, sandwiched as it is between the Atlantic and Pacific Oceans, and whose jurisdiction now takes it several thousand miles more across the Pacific and whose northern boundaries reach above the Arctic Circle and whose southern extremities dip into the semi-tropics. One can easily conjecture about the dangers of one force of 500,000 police and some 35,000 civilians and the susceptibility of such a huge police bureaucracy to unscrupulous manipulation. It is not difficult to envision self-anointed as well as charismatic leaders who could throttle and destroy democracy in pursuit of illicit gain or personal aggrandizement. The national wounds of recent history are still raw and the lessons compelling; moreover, the variances in state constitutions, statutes and case law, the states' rights embedded in the Constitution of the United States, the vast differences in the concentration of ethnic groups and cultures, the dispersion of commerce and industry, topography, climate, natural barriers extant, minerals, nutritional resources, land use, educational prospects, scales and styles of living —all stagger the mind at the complexities of establishing a national police agency and inveigh against it.

Maintaining the fragmentation of our policing system anywhere near its current state, however, is to continue to fault it grievously in the reverse direction, a luxury the nation's communities can ill afford. The severe fragmentation constitutes a major obstacle to effective policing standards and vitiates law enforcement accountability. It pyramids law enforcement costs without commensurate return in the delivery of services. The pervasiveness of the fragmentation has a chilling effect on the development of genuine career patterns in policing and contributes to the frustration of ambitious and potentially upward mobile personnel by constricting the avenues to promotion. Currently, with advancement confined for the most part to one police agency, a relatively young age and little seniority of one's superiors, there is a dim outlook on the chances for promotability, particularly so in small or modest-size organizations, and especially so when the growth of an agency is relatively stagnant. Sooner than later, the organizational leadership tends toward parochial views, personnel attitudes become ingrown, and an organizational hardening of the arteries sets in. Severely curtailed, if not denied the police organization, are the invigorating aspects stemming from a reasonably open vertical and horizontal career movement that fosters both a testing of new command and different peer-to-peer relationships against the old, and a continuing infusion of new perspectives and new ideas.

It is some forty-five years since the National Commission on Law Observance and Enforcement (Wickersham Commission) criticized the dearth of coordination between law enforcement agencies, attributing considerable blame for this situation to a fractionalized policing system that lacked cohesive direction of its forces and tolerated poor performance, hampering seriously the efforts against crime:

The multitude of police forces in any State and the varying standards of organization and service have contributed immeasurably to the general low grade of police performance in this country. The independence which police forces display toward each other and the absence of any central force which requires either a uniform or a minimum standard of service leave the way open for the profitable operation of criminals in an area where protection is often ineffectual at best, generally only partial, and too frequently wholly absent.(1)

In 1960, almost three decades after the Wickersham Commission's observations, Professor Misner still found justification to say, "Despite gross changes in other facets of our society, the basic organizational structure of law enforcement has remained relatively unchanged since the turn of the century." Two years later, Chapman pointed to the great void in standards applicable to organizational structure and in the gauging of effectiveness and accountability for the 40,000 police jurisdictions with about 300,000 sworn personnel. The agencies, according to Chapman, included some of the best in the world and others that were undergoing marked, progressive change. Nevertheless, he added these shortcomings:

Included also are a considerable number of agencies that have failed to show any sign of renaissance and seem bypassed by constructive impulses that have brought development and progress to the first two groups. These last police forces constitute a burden on the entire machinery of justice and are detrimental to the process of achieving a professional police service held in esteem by the citizens of the nation.(2)

In the intervening thirteen years, the de-Balkanization of the American policing system has moved at a glacial pace, despite the comprehensive treatment given the fragmentation problem by the President's Commission on Law Enforcement and Administration of Justice. The Commission's Task Force Report, *The Police*, thoroughly covered the then current state of police coordination and consolidation, including the arguments advanced for and against the unification of police agencies, the legal obstacles and other hurdles to be overcome, and the suggested remedial approaches. It described working and proposed models for institutionalized and less formalized cooperative arrangements for sharing resources and policing responsibilities and reported on achievements, accomplished or in progress, in county-wide law enforcement, metropolitan policing, regionalization, jurisdictional extension, contract policing, agency amalgamation, territorial annexation, and variations on the theme.(3)

Norrgard chronicled, detailed, and updated the movement in a monograph specifically addressed to the subject.(4) The National Advisory Commission on Criminal Justice Standards and Goals cited the following observations in the 1970 Report on State-Local Relations in the Criminal Justice System, issued by the Advisory Commission on Intergovernmental Relations:

> Small local police departments, particularly those of 10 or less men, are unable to provide a wide range of patrol and investigative services to local citizens. Moreover, the existence of these small agencies may work a hardship on nearby jurisdictions. Small police departments which do not have adequate full-time patrol and preliminary investigative services may require the aid of larger agencies in many facets of their police work.(5)

Notwithstanding the extensive fragmentation still about, the National Advisory Commission approached the problem guardedly. Noting the ineffectiveness of small police departments, the Commission called for state legislation that would enable local governments to "take the necessary steps to provide police services through mutual agreements or joint participation with other police or other criminal justice agencies," should such arrangements improve efficiency. It urged, however, that state legislatures reaffirm policing as "primarily a local responsibility and refrain from making any agreements mandatory." It cautiously recommended that police agencies with "fewer than 10 sworn officers should combine with one or more agencies to improve efficiency...," a standard that would affect less than ten percent of the nation's police departments.(6)

One can appreciate the National Advisory Commission's sensitivity to challenging "home rule"; however, its hesitation to press vigorously for consolidation and regionalization was a costly missed opportunity to catalyze drastic restructuring of our splintered policing system. The headway required for strategically planning the needed change has been irrevocably shortened; moreover, whatever headway still remains is seriously threatened by the stringent

fiscal situation that may stampede legislatures and local governments into ill-conceived blunderbuss approaches violative of community as well as service-personnel needs.

It appears to this observer that as of some yesterdays back, serious commitments should have been made and intensive planning undertaken to create within the United States a policing system comprised of some 250 to 300 municipal, county or multi-county, and regional police departments, noninclusive of Federal, state police and special-purpose law enforcement agencies. The suggested ceiling of 300 police agencies should permit keeping intact the major municipal and county police departments, advance policing of the metropolitan and suburban areas, and ensure comprehensive services to the counties and relatively undeveloped large rural areas having fragmented, sporadic, poor policing coverage.

The consolidations would ease the setting and monitoring of desirable national policing standards, improve service cost effectiveness, open up career opportunities, reduce undesirable political and parochial influences, foster cooperative relationships on a much wider area basis, enable institutionalized in-service training, increase administrative responsibilities and service options, and provide for accountability, but retain agency accessibility.

The proposed restructuring, with no need to break up the major city and county departments, would bring about a policing system whose agencies average, let's say by 1985, some 1850 or some 2150 sworn personnel, dependent upon the number of separate agencies created. The police system's reorganization should stimulate a professional orientation and make needed change, as required by future circumstances, less difficult. The possibilities of Federal and state incentives and resources, financial or in other forms, for maintaining and raising standards, would brighten.

Any such bold restructuring requires strategic planning and comprehensive preparation for change, with a timetable for implementation, not in piddling, but in substantial steps. The British experience suggests a model for police consolidation that may be profitably studied, without need to consider the model definitive. Critchley reports the progress in British police amalgamation:

> ... The problems of crime and road traffic, however, would not wait; and on May 18th,

1966, the Home Secretary announced a nation-wide programme of amalgamations, to be enforced if necessary by compulsion, the effect of which would be to reduce the number of separate forces in England and Wales from 117 to forty-nine. Their strength would range from about 700 to nearly 7,000, the majority being in the range of 1,000 to 2,500.

This programme was tackled vigorously, and by the end of 1967 two-thirds of it had been accomplished; the whole programme was in operation in 1969. Predictable misgivings were expressed in some quarters about the effect which such wholesale slaughter of small forces would have on local influences over the police, and on the men's morale. But at the end of it all the Home Office was well satisfied: 'Benefits in the shape of improved efficiency, greater flexibility and increased resources are widely acknowledged by those involved, including many who were firmly opposed to the amalgamation proposals,' ...(7) (8)

The montage of arguments for police consolidation and regionalization far outweighs the arguments against; moreover, the objections to such restructuring can be more than adequately met by creative plans for community involvement, scientific and imaginative deployment of manpower, team and community policing, electronics and modern communications equipment, departmental substations or precincts in relatively populous or large areas (as, for example, the organization of the Nassau County Police Department), comprehensive public relations, and the like. The arguments for consolidation and regionalization can, at best, be overcome only partially. The constraints upon the fiscal resources of most communities no longer permit each of them the luxury of an independent police service. Space, differences in race, religion, ethnicity, income level and cultural values no longer comprise an impenetrable moat between the blight of inner cities and the heretofore conceived pastoralness of suburbia; or for that matter of the hinterlands. Just about all places are more accessible to the criminal. Violence and crime grow and their incidence, though much more frequent in particular areas of the cities, acknowledges no municipal boundaries, nor does the fear induced. Witness the widespread dispersion of firearms and other dangerous weapons, the illicit possession of handguns,(9) the recent crime data reports. (10)

Economic dislocation, class and group conflict, racial confrontation, drug contagion and alcoholism, and mental depression and disorders are sharply increasing the calls upon police services. Major disasters, chemical plant and fuel storage fires, large-scale combustion accidents, lethal atmosphere inversion, nuclear accidents, and perhaps in the not-too-distant future, nuclear blackmail have wrought and will occasion increasing demands for police protection.

As to the magnitude of the disaster risk, Mesarovic and Pestel project a very frightening scenario of the probabilities of radiological hazard or accident owing to nuclear mishaps or to human malevolence. They forecast that within the next one hundred years "all primary energy will be nuclear," some 3,000 "nuclear parks" averaging eight fast-breeder reactors each dispersed on earth. To reach the level of 24,000 operating breeder reactors will require building "in each and every year, between now and then, four reactors per week," without allowing for the "life-span" of nuclear reactors, which is estimated at about thirty years. Eventually, it will necessitate building "two reactors per day simply to replace those that have worn out." The 24,000 breeder reactors will require 15 million kilograms of plutonium-239, "the core material of the Hiroshima bomb," to be processed and transported annually. Plutonium-239 can be safely shipped or transported without "significant radiological hazards," if not inhaled or otherwise ingested.(11)

As to the consequences of mishap or purposive mishandling we'll let Mesarovic and Pestel fill in the details:

... But if it is inhaled, ten micrograms of plutonium-239 is likely to cause fatal lung cancer. A ball of plutonium the size of a grapefruit contains enough poison to kill nearly all the people living today. Moreover, plutonium-239 has a radioactive life of more than 24,000 years. Obviously, with so much plutonium on hand, there will be a tremendous problem of safeguarding the nuclear parks—not one or two, but 3,000 of them. And what about their location, national sovereignty, and jurisdiction? Can one country allow inadequate protection in a neighboring country, when the slightest mishap could poison adjacent lands and populations for thousands and thousands of years? And who is to decide what constitutes adequate protection, especially in the case of social turmoil, civil war, war between nations, or even only when a national leader comes down with a case of bad nerves? The lives of millions could easily be beholden to a single reckless and daring individual.(12)

The comprehensive knowledge and complex social skills required of the police today and more so in the future mandates continuing education in the physical and social sciences, the expansion of interactive skills, heightened social sensitivity, the mastering of new technologies and keeping abreast of legal changes and developments. The demands for standards, productivity and efficiency, critical performance, accountability, and a professionalized police service no longer accord viability to the small police department. This observer submits that a planned, scheduled, and vigorous progression toward the restructuring suggested, radical as it may seem, is essential, critical, and in both the practitioner and public interest; that such progression should be far less causative of dislocations in police services and in police personnel than would permitting police fragmentation to prevail until the only recourse is a crisis-impelled, massive, uncharted disruption of the policing system at the brink of its default.

Traditional Responses to Police Ineffectiveness: Incompatiblity with Professionalization

The traditional and inseparable answers to meeting charges of police failures and ineffectiveness have been "increase personnel" and "tighten up supervision." They seemed to be adequate, noncontroversial responses that would readily gain both administrative and rank-and-file approval. The community too could look forward to increased protection by the enlargement of the police force and to better personnel performance because the supervisors were about to ride herd over, suspend, or get rid of the police subordinates who neither could nor would carry out their tasks and assignments properly. Additional complaints of police ineffectiveness would be countered by more proposals for putting on still more police personnel and for impressing exacting supervision. Although fiscal constraints would temper the level of response to demands for more police manpower, the budgetary situation was rarely invoked to deny completely persistent political, community, or departmental clamor for added personnel.

Unfortunately, sound assessments of the relationships between increased police personnel and goals accomplishment were few; moreover, too frequently did situations occur where particular police objectives or goals were not clearly delineated, much less in writing, creating a dearth of reference points against which to measure the efficacy of added police manpower. The promised tightening of supervision often did not take place. Where police administration did intensify supervision, it frequently took the form of oppressive monitoring practices that manifested more of bureaupathology(13) than of enlightened supervision, reflecting no or scant appreciation of the short and long-term costs in subordinate commitment, work satisfaction, morale, and growth of the consequent impact on the quality of services rendered to the public, and of the corrosive effect on police-community grass-roots relationships. Supervisory practices were wont to degenerate either into sporadic cosmetic applications of discipline, more for show than for substance, or, in a climate of pervasive suspicion, to evolve into a paranoic display of punitive discipline, neither outcome helpful or conducive to a constructive public purpose.

It is highly questionable in the first place whether the institutionalization of a policy of intense, over-the-shoulder supervision is an effective police organizational response to meeting the policing needs of the communities. It seems logical to assume, moreover, that this style of supervision is counterproductive to furthering true professionalization. Much more likely than not, intense, close supervision stunts required growth at the echelon levels that directly and primarily deliver police services, retards if not extinguishes the willingness of subordinates to assume greater responsibility, and blunts measures to develop valid and reliable productivity standards and professional accountability.

If the concept of accountability is to have essence rather than to constitute bureaucratic jargon, to signify responsibility for carrying out some task or delegated assignment at a desired level of performance, then the persons to be held accountable must have the proper organizational climate, clear policy focus, essential resources, latitude within the bureaucracy and reasonable preparation for meeting the responsibility assigned. Unless such conditions characterize the police organization's environment and those who evaluate performance take into account the "fixed constraints" that confine the breadth of available options and limit individual and group performance, accountability is at its worst more like the sword of Damocles ready to sever the head of the unfortunate accountable one when things go wrong, and at its best but a meaningless buzzword.

If the police practitioner, particularly one who directly delivers police services, is encouraged and permitted within the framework of unambiguous, written departmental policies, guidelines to enlarge his functional role, to expand his service activities, and to exercise discretion with greater latitude, then there is set in motion an environment to nurture professionalization. The public acceptance of police discretion, however, is crucial to professional growth. The public served must see the need for police discretion and acknowledge the competency of the practitioner to use discretion constructively and in the public interest. It is largely by the level of public acknowledgement of the police practitioner's competency to exercise discretion for the public good that one may sense the real impact of and progress toward true professionalization. Without such accordance, no matter how skillful, how trained the practitioner, how internalized the discipline, how developed and shared the relevant body of knowledge, claims to professionalism, even when based upon some valid criteria, lack essence and reality and ring hollow.

Susan O. White's commentary is apropos. Holding no ultimate objection to the thesis of police professionalization, White sees several questions left answered unsatisfactorily in its application to the police: What are acceptable criteria for positive behavior? What mode of control identifies professionalization? What role perceptions characterize professionalization and to what extent do they influence behavior?(14)

Observing the rather meagre challenging to date of the assumption of efficacy implicit in police professionalization and the lack of "clear evidence of better performance" offered by reformers, White comments:

> . . . There are no clear criteria for what would count as better performance of police tasks; and second, we know very little about the behaviors that professionalization has produced or will produce. In other words, no one is presently in a position to accept or reject the professionalization solution. The variety of normative standpoints from which perceptions of the police role stem are not defensible by the simple assertion of professionalism; if neutral competence is to be the claim, the relevant behaviors must still be specified to enable one to judge their neutrality and their competence. Otherwise,

the 'better performance of police tasks' will become an unexamined label rather than a description whose validity might be tested against appropriate criteria. It is true, of course, that a specification of behaviors will not itself produce the appropriate criteria, but neither will such criteria evolve from a vacuum. We cannot make adequate policy judgments in the absence of information about the real world possibilities of behavior modification.(15)

One may rightly raise the point that the adoption or achievement of "the internalized discipline of a professional practitioner" is too vacuous a prescription for it to be useful or to have meaning. Moreover, follow up with a set of interrelated questions as to who would set and approve the parameters and guidelines that spell out police professionalization. Would the prevailing input come from local, state, county, or nationally elected officials, the communities, and at what level; from special commissions set up by the governors of the states, the pertinent academic disciplines, the courts—and at what level; from the National Advisory Commission on Police Standards and Goals, or from a comparable body or task force constituted especially to flesh out the professional police credo? Or would it fall to the International Association of Chiefs of Police, local, regional, or state police leadership, or police unions and rank-and-file associations to draw the overriding professional code?

Whatever the input of the authoritative commissioners and groups, or individuals helping set the governing professional standards, the undertaking should encourage substantial rule making by law enforcement agencies.(16)

Police Internal Organizational Restructuring—Flattening the Pyramid of Command: A Must for Professionalization

One dilemma of consequence facing police administration as it moves into the final quarter of the twentieth century is that of determining how to shape the internal structure of organization best to meet the swelling demand for police services, set priorities, and yet respond to the changing roles, perspectives, and needs of its personnel. The crux of the dilemma is that if police organizations in the ensuing years are to epitomize responsible professionalization, it will call for extensive flattening of the pyramid of command by drastically shortening unnecessarily elongated chains of command. The organizational surgery and restructuring would sharply reduce the ostensible controls, so manifest in the lines of authority drawn between the boxes on organizational charts, which are so dear to the traditionalists and chartists. Such restructuring would require turning police organizations just short of about face on traditional concepts of control and command. Sharply etching the dilemma is the charged atmosphere of tightening fiscal constraints, narrowing resource options, and considerable and growing disenchantment with, suspicion, and some outright distrust of government, amid demands for a taut rein on public-service employees, calls for productivity standards and accomplishments, and for accountability.

How, then, does police administration institute what is obviously a very diminished hierarchy of command, flaunting change against established doctrine and accepted principles, contradictory as they are, and yet gear operations to the more and more complex tasks ahead? Dare one attempt such radical restructuring of hierarchical ordering in the face of more militant union membership, without and within the public service, and police associations acting, in fact, as unions as they press demands for improved wage scales, salaries, working conditions and rights, fringe benefits, and pensions through collective bargaining, lobbying, and media campaigns? This question becomes particularly troublesome when rank-and-file pressures may take the form of letter-of-the-law enforcement against target groups, work slow-downs and stoppages, and "blue flu"? Need one risk a drastic revision of the police command structure in an uncertain environment of extensive change, intense challenging of long-held values, and the toppling of some cherished traditions? One could conjecture, perhaps, that stressful conditions in the communities—sharply escalating, even runaway costs for essential commodities and services, the extended period of high unemployment, numerous pockets of dissatisfaction and frustration in urban centers and spread through suburban areas, ethnic animosities, and racial polarization—conditions over which the police essentially have no or very little control but that add, nevertheless, difficulties and complexities to the police function, would render such a proposed restructuring inappropriate.

At closer inspection neither is the dilemma for police organization to resolve as difficult as posed nor is a decision to reduce the pyramid of command as radical as implied; moreover, some progressive police agencies have been moving in the direction of job enlargement at the level where the patrol services are delivered, and encouraging decision-making by lower-echelon supervisors by concomitantly expanding their authority. The use of team policing, for example, has brought about greater flexibility in the deployment of police patrols and pushed downward greater decision authority upon the first- and second-line supervisors, commensurate with the added responsibilities assumed. The greater participation by members of the team in developing patrol objectives and in planning and mapping out manpower assignments accordingly, the integration of specialists, as needed, in the team effort, the authority delegated for on-the-spot decisions within the framework of overall departmental policy, the clearing of red tape for obtaining support resources, and the ready availability to the team of essential data and updated information—each and every measure extends downward the decision-making process. The more realistic assessment of effectiveness by gauging input/output ratios with the pace and degree of accomplishing stipulated goals, the encouragement of suggestions from members of the patrol team and the formal recognition of deserving performance, the incentives for continuing self-evaluation of individual and team efforts—all of the foregoing comprise a moving away from the you-can't-expect-much-from-a-subordinate syndrome toward an organizational philosophy that senses the far richer potential for organizational effectiveness stemming from individual interest and involvement in task design and performance, assumption of responsibility, work satisfaction, recognition, growth, and accountability.

Police agencies show an increasing use of specializations that require a spectrum of sophisticated or distinctive skills and extended periods of preparation, experience, or formal education of their practitioners. Specialization enables its practitioner to focus consummate talents, knowledge, skills and experience upon highly differentiated tasks on particularly involved or complex functions that the non-specialist rarely handles capably or effectively. The trend to specialization in selective areas of the police function reflects incremental phases in the shifting away from rigid command relationships.

The specialist's experience most likely involves exposure to others performing like tasks or coping with comparable problems in other agencies, and not necessarily to individuals or organizations in law enforcement. The specialist probably has been subjected to the rigors of a discipline or of a professional area of study—law, accounting, business administration, chemistry, communications, engineering, operations research, psychology, sociology, statistics, urban planning—to name just some, each field with its own constructs, body of knowledge, parameters, prerequisites for certification, professional demands and obligations. The specialist reinforces his (her) professional orientation and affiliation by (1) keeping up with the literature in the field, (2) joining professional societies, (3) taking courses and attaining higher degrees, (4) attending conferences and seminars and the like, and (5) achieving success and recognition in the discipline or specialization.

In a sense, the specialist develops ambivalent feelings and conflicting loyalties toward the department and specialization. Often the mandates of a profession and the dictates of departmental policies and of one's superiors are antagonistic and occasion hard, agonizing decisions for the specialist. Recognition and acceptance by superiors of the specialist's expertise diminish the potential of departmental conflict and advance the organizational purpose, although a role reversal occurs in superior-subordinate relationships in respect to the specialization.

The development of intra- and extradepartmental task forces to combat special crime problems that manifest themselves locally, but whose operations and resources are controlled across municipal, county, and state lines—gambling, narcotics, trafficking in stolen goods and contraband, other illegal conspiracies and activities of organized crime—has been weakening the traditional rigidities of police command. The need to share, readily to exchange pertinent criminal intelligence across unit, divisional, and departmental lines under the agreed-upon procedures and with proper safeguards, makes it that much more difficult for any unit commander to hoard or to stint the release of needed information. The commander who does hold back in such circumstances, whether for arbitrary control, position aggrandizement, or other self interests, or orders his (her) subordinates to do so, risks resistance from if not outright conflict with subordinates, their wrath, and charges for impeding the criminal investigation or for obstructing justice.

The growing emphasis on commander accountability coupled with the disenchantment with line-item budgeting as a meaningful management instrument places a greater onus upon the commander or head of a unit to justify its administration and operations. The acceptance by a number of police agencies of the concept, if not the actual practice of program performance budgeting and variations of planned program performance systems requires the heads of budgeted units to develop or to conform to performance standards, gauge goal or program accomplishment with acceptable, valid, and reliable units of measurement, plan ahead, and under the more sophisticated budgeting instruments and practices, develop alternative optimal programs. In a sense the commander has more options in planning but much less freedom from accountability.

To meet the more closely defined responsibilities of command, to survive the pinpointing of accountability, the superior-in-charge and each lower-level supervisor in the descending order will have to depend far less on imperious order giving and insistence upon the prerogatives of command and far more on gaining a very high level of subordinate cooperation and coordination. Notwithstanding the advanced technology of electronic communications that can readily summon or dispatch a police officer or vehicular patrol unit within seconds and by sophisticated tracking and time-recording instrumentation monitor the response movements, police officers deliver the bulk of police services not in the physical presence of a superior, but working alone or with a peer. The quality of service rendered and a continuing commitment to a desirable level of performance depend, then, far more on the individual or team of officers providing the service, than they do on numerous layers of intensive supervision that distort the delegation of authority, weaken responsibility, and smother the lower-echelon police officer in a swaddling, bureaucratic environment.

Police Appointments and Promotions: Discrimination and Reverse Discrimination

The legal and ethical responsibility to recruit competent police personnel and to do so in a manner that as far as is humanly possible eradicates bias and prejudice from the total recruitment and personnel function is not a standard or maxim with which one does or should take issue. Nor is it debatable that civil service commissions and police agencies should be in the forefront of critical examination into the validity and consistency of current personnel testing and screening instruments and processes. In fact, theirs is a professional obligation to subject the eligibility requirements and other parameters drawn for police appointment and promotion to continuing objective inquiry; moreover, should the personnel commissions and police administrators find the requisite qualifications unsound or wanting, it would be their professional mandate and in the public interest to move for the elimination or refinement of the qualifications.

The police service, however, cannot be looked upon as employment of last resort for the marginally employable. There is an incongruity between holding out the policing service as requiring personnel capable of a professional orientation that demands essential intellectual abilities to acquire and to master the knowledge and complex skills frequently called upon, a high order of emotional maturity, above average physical stamina, skills of coordination and good health and then using the service as a readily accessible governmental agency for hiring those with questionable qualifications or for pacifying those unsuccessful in finding other jobs.

The spate of recent controversial and conflicting court decisions that intend to rectify past inequities in public service or police employment by setting up appointment and promotional quotas and separate listings based upon racial and ethnic distinctions raises the ugly spectre of legalized reverse discrimination. The court holdings seem more like arbitrary exercises of judicial power rendering quicksandy solutions to and makeshift intrusions upon the civil service and comparable selective processes for public employment and are highly suspect of violating the spirit and language of the 14th Amendment and the intent and prescriptions of derivative civil rights legislation. The legal and moral answers to discriminatory practices and unequal treatment of those seeking public service appointment and promotion do not lie in bestowing judicial blessings and sanctification to pockets of and Gantt charts for reverse discrimination, in and of themselves disruptive of morale and violative of legislative intent. Rather, the answers find themselves in rational, fair, unambiguous employment standards, continually tested, assessed, and refined for both validity and reliability, and in unrelenting vigilance against and in the rooting out of discriminatory practices with vigorous prosecution of those who do discriminate. The fields of employment, public and private, as do applicants for admission to the universities and professional schools, among others, eagerly await the day when the U.S. Supreme Court squarely and definitively meets the quota issue by a landmark decision that brings relief and reason to the current chaotic state.

Challenge and Dilemma Ahead: The Optimal Use and Retention of Qualified Personnel

Police organizations of the future face a momentous challenge in attempting optimal use of their personnel talents. It calls for a comprehensive strategy for change. For example, the recommendation of the National Advisory Commission on Criminal Justice Standards and Goals proposes that by 1982 all entrants into the ranks of sworn police personnel have earned baccalaureate degrees.(17) What this means in numbers of college graduates embarking on sworn duty in 1982, if this proposed standard of the National Advisory Commission is but approximated, can be estimated from current manpower logistics:

> ... With a projected average annual increase of 3.5 percent in sworn personnel, there will be some 127,228 sworn personnel serving in 1982, for every 100,000 serving in 1975. If we take a rounded base of 400,000 sworn personnel serving in 1975, we can project close to 509,000 serving in 1982. If one adds at least a 4.0 percent average annual turnover in police ranks owing to superannuation, voluntary retirements, deaths and disabilities in service, resignations, and dismissals, one can estimate that a minimum of 7.5 percent, or some 38,175 of the sworn personnel at the start of the year in 1982, will be newcomers to the police ranks.(18)

With some 38,000 or more college graduates annually joining police departments by 1982 and in increasing numbers thereafter, unless drastic cutbacks in personnel and unlikely severe extensions in the years in service necessary to qualify for pensions take place (which may reduce somewhat the projections, but not seriously affect the trend), the onus for holding on to good manpower and using it effectively will fall heavily upon administrative shoulders.(19) The departments that will not be able to expand the delivery of basic police services into an interesting, challenging, and creative function will bear a costly administrative burden and toll in frustrated personnel, job induced psychosomatic illness, wasted supervisory effort and in-service training costs, excessive resignations, non-constructive disciplinary actions, dismissals, and ineffective performance. The usual profile of police resignations reflects that they take place preponderantly in the first few years of service and includes among those withdrawing for sundry reasons personnel with excellent potential who find little job satisfaction and opportunity in the police service and seek brighter prospects elsewhere, often in another branch or agency in law enforcement.

To attract and to retain the best of personnel by planned, continuing, creative programming that is at the same time, under the constraints of available resources, also responsive to the realistic needs for policing services in the communities is a most critical challenge and dilemma facing police organizations in a world of intensive change. The professional commitment required tomorrow can only sketchily be conveyed today; nevertheless, it is to the pioneers of yesteryear with faint but positive perceptions who provided, in effect, an early warning system of the need for change that much is owed.

REFERENCES

(1) National Commission on Law Observance and Enforcement, *Report on the Police* (Washington, D.C.: U.S. Government Printing Office, 1931), p. 125.

(2) The President's Commission on Law Enforcement and Administration of Justice, *Task Force Report: The Police* (Washington, D.C.: U.S. Government Printing Office, 1967), p. 62, citing Samuel G. Chapman, *The Police Heritage in England and America: A Developmental Survey* (East Lansing, Michigan: Michigan State University Institute for Community Development and Services, 1962), p. 30.

(3) *Ibid.*, particularly Chap. 4, pp. 68–117.

(4) David L. Norrgard, *Regional Law Enforcement: A Study of Intergovernmental Cooperation and Coordination* (Chicago: Public Administration Service, 1969).

(5) National Advisory Commission on Criminal Justice Standards and Goals, *Police* (Washington, D.C.: U.S. Government Printing Office, 1973), p. 110.

(6) *Ibid.*, p. 110.

(7) T. A. Critchley, *A History of Police in England and Wales*, second edition (Montclair, New Jersey: Patterson Smith, 1972), pp. 315–316.

(8) For a historical treatment of the British police from 1829 to 1969, with comprehensive statistics as to the size and number of police forces and a detailed account of their staffing and deployment problems through the years, see J.P. Martin and Gail Wilson, *The Police: A Study in Manpower* (London: Heinemann Educational Books Ltd., 1969).

(9) U.S. Department of Justice, Law Enforcement Assistance Administration, National Criminal Justice Information and Statistics Service, *Criminal Victimization in the United States: 1973 Advance Report*, Volume 1 (Washington, D.C.: U.S. Government Printing Office, 1975).

(10) The U.S. Bureau of the Census has, during the past two years, conducted several National Crime Panel Surveys for the Law Enforcement Assistance Administration. Census undertakes personal interviewing of a representative sampling of the residents, households, and businesses in a community to gauge the volume and rate of criminal victimization. The survey findings indicate a volume of crime in particular violent and non-violent categories that ranges from two to five times that reported to the police. The figures are not reconcilable with the annual Uniform Crime Reports, which the Federal Bureau of Investigation compiles from periodic submissions by the police. Differences in population addressed, unit count, and numerical base for computing particular criminal victimization rates, among other dissimilarities, render the crime data incomparable. For a critique of the method used to survey criminal victimization, its strongpoints and deficiencies, see U.S. Department of Justice, Law Enforcement Assistance Administration, National Criminal Justice Information and Statistics Service, *Criminal Victimization Surveys in 13 American Cities* (Washington, D.C.: U.S. Government Printing Office, 1975), pp. iii–vii, 1–5.

(11) Mihajlo Mesarovic and Eduard Pestel, *Mankind at the Turning Point:* The Second Report to the Club of Rome (New York: E. P. Dutton & Co., Inc., 1974), p. 132.

(12) *Ibid.*, pp. 134–135.

(13) Victor Thompson, *Modern Organization* (New York: Alfred L. Knopf, 1961), *et passim*, particularly Chapters 7 & 8, pp. 138–177.

(14) Susan O. White, "A Perspective on Police Professionalization," in *The Police Community*, Jack Goldsmith and Sharon S. Goldsmith, editors (Pacific Palisades, California: Palisades Publishers, 1974), pp. 41–42.

(15) *Ibid.*, pp. 39–40.

(16) Gerald M. Caplan, "The Case for Rule-

making by Law Enforcement Agencies," *Law and Contemporary Problems*, Vol. XXXVI, No. 4 (Autumn 1971), 500–514.

(17) See Standard 15.1 of the National Advisory Commission on Criminal Justice Standards and Goals, *op. cit.*, p. 369.

(18) Jack A. Mark, "You Too Can Be 'El

Exigente'—the Demanding One—When Checking into Criminal Justice Degree Programs," *The Police Chief*, Vol. XLII, No. 8 (August 1975), 53.

(19) Calvin J. Swank, "The Police in 1980," *The Journal of Police Science and Administration*, Vol. 3, No. 3 (September 1975), 298.

The Changing Role of Policewomen

THERESA M. MELCHIONNE

There is no doubt that a major re-evaluation of the policewoman's place in law enforcement is taking place in America today. The recent assignment of women police officers to street patrol on an interchangeable basis with patrolmen provides a significant cue to a developing trend toward widening the role of policewomen so as to encompass all aspects of the police function. Cities such as Miami, Washington, D.C., Indianapolis, Peoria and New York have helped set the course, and, in view of a recent change in the civil rights law, there is every reason to believe that this trend will gather momentum.

As the integration of women police moves forward, discussions re differential capacities, on the basis of sex, are inevitable. For example, the assignment of women to patrol has focussed attention on an important question: Can a woman perform as well as a man when placed in a patrol situation?

There is very little objective information available on this subject either in police literature or in official police reports. Hard data is only now beginning to emerge as a consequence of experimental studies (recently conducted) in both Washington, D.C., and New York City. Notwithstanding the lack of validated information, however, the issue tends to be controversial in police circles and to evoke diverse opinion, even among policewomen. This is not surprising, when one considers how much police work is

SOURCE: *The Police Journal*, 47 (October 1974), pp. 340–58.

bound by tradition and precedent. In a nation such as ours, where police administrators have directed their operations on the premise that policing is a "man's" job, assigning policewomen to street patrol, interchangeably with policemen, can indeed be a debatable policing concept. Still, the question it has raised is too important to be resolved by mere opinion. Inherent in the question are valid concerns for the public-at-large, the police administrator, and for policemen as well as for policewomen.

The Public

The public, understandably, is primarily interested in the quality of the police services provided for the citizen. From the public's point of view, the issue of policewomen street patrol quickly boils down to this: Is police protection improved in any way? Will the quality of police services be enhanced somehow through the use of women in policing the streets? Or will it remain the same? Or will it be significantly impaired in any way?

In making an assessment, many elements will have to be considered because the tasks that police perform while on street patrol are far more diverse and complex than is generally supposed. These tasks involve a host of emergency, community service and peace-keeping functions, as well as activities relating to the prevention of serious crime and the apprehension and prosecution of criminals. Caring for neglected children; aiding the aged, the mentally ill, the sick and the injured, mediating disputes between husbands and wives, landlords and tenants, merchants and their customers; regulating traffic; investigating accidents; dispersing disorderly crowds; handling complaints of unruly youth, of congregating boisterous groups, or the presence of "undesirables"; protecting the rights of citizens to free speech and assembly—these are all routine patrol tasks. And since it is estimated that they occupy some 90 percent of a patrol officer's time, the public will be interested to know: Are there any significant differences between men and women officers in the performance of these functions? Moreover, in the congested areas of our large cities, we know that street patrol is often performed under conditions of stress and conflict; it is in these areas where the crime rate is high, where social cleavages run deep, where there is racial strife, and where the police officer must deal with citizens who are frequently hostile.

Realistically, then, any appraisal of policewomen street patrol must be studied in a variety of urban settings. In both the New York City and Washington, D.C., studies, this has been the case, and it is significant to note that the initial public response has been favorable. Citizens appear to find police service by policewomen and policemen equally acceptable.

It is hoped that from these field experiences it may be possible also to determine what special qualities women bring to policing. For example, there is some evidence that policemen, in asserting their masculinity, sometimes provoke violence in commonplace street encounters between policemen and citizens and consequently exacerbate conflict, rather than resolve it. Does the presence of a woman in patrol teams help avert challenges to the policeman, threatening his self-respect and manhood—and thus serve to defuse the potential for violence in such street situations? Stated in another way, does the presence of a woman help de-emphasize the use of physical encounters to resolve difficulties? Do women tend to be less aggressive in their intervention style? Do women induce greater public co-operation in obtaining crime information because, by nature, they are more compassionate and empathetic? Do women tend to lessen the use of bad language or threats by the public? Or, on the other hand, does the presence of large numbers of women police on the patrol force make the policeman's job more difficult, thereby increasing the personal risk factor for him? Can women be trained to handle violent or potentially violent situations satisfactorily? Obviously, these and many other aspects of policewomen street patrol need to be objectively assessed in as scientific a manner as possible. The Washington, D.C., and New York City studies have attempted to accomplish just this.

The findings, although limited by virtue of the restricted scope of the experiments with respect to time span and numbers of women participating, nevertheless should be both enlightening and helpful to the public in making some rational conclusions with respect to the merits of this current policing concept.

The Police Administrator

From the point of view of the police administrator, there are very practical considerations in giving policewomen already on the force the same patrol responsibilities as policemen. In doing so, additional personnel is made available for assignment to the police function with highest public "visibility"—and at no extra expense to the police budget! Admittedly, the numbers involved will be small and intensive re-training of the policewomen will be necessary, but it still makes good sense, administratively and politically, where a police agency is understaffed and where the police administrator must respond to a public hue and cry with respect to crime on the streets. Furthermore, many police administrators continue to encounter little success in attracting male recruits from minority communities, although there seems to be no shortage of female applicants from these areas. Giving policewomen the same patrol responsibilities as policemen may be one way to help overcome under-representation of minorities on the police force, as well as provide some remedy for other problems with respect to manpower shortages. This is not to say that police administrators have any less responsibility to institute and maintain dynamic recruitment programs that attract qualified male candidates in sufficient numbers: but it does suggest that police administrators need to re-evaluate women's potentialities in law enforcement.

Of course, we can anticipate that making women officers occupationally equal to their male colleagues will generate some sticky adjustment problems for many members of the force, which, in turn, may provoke some nettlesome issues for the police administrator. For one thing, it has been found that a goodly number of women officers, particularly those on the force for some time, are reluctant to relinquish their traditional specialist role; they voice serious scepticism about the value of the street experience in providing policewomen a milieu for making their optimal contribution to police work. There is no question that for most of them patrol constitutes an entirely new "job," since most were detailed to their specialist assignments immediately following recruit training; to be plummeted now to the level of novice amid seasoned male patrol officers (who may be years junior in job-seniority and age), can indeed be a trial.

On the other side of the coin, adjustment may be even more trying for an appreciable number of male officers in overcoming their stereotyped attitude toward women. Perhaps a few may seek to work with women officers with the idea of developing a sexual relationship, but male officers, by and large, resist being paired with women, contending that a woman's limitations in physical strength and stamina pose an added job hazard. In their view, the potential for physical resistance is constantly present in patrol assignments; ergo, a woman officer cannot be logically substituted for a male partner, nor can a female team provide an adequate "back up" for a male team. Sundry statistics are offered in defence of this premise: 90 percent of all violent crimes (according to Federal Crime Reports) are committed by males; 70 percent of all assaults sustained while in the performance of duty by the state police of one jurisdiction (Michigan) were perpetrated by assailants 5 feet 9 inches or taller, etc. From such data, some infer that there is the possibility that female officers would be required to use a firearm more frequently in effecting an arrest for self-defence than male officers. And sometimes the issue of "propriety" is raised, in that, because of the ratio of male to female arrests, women officers would be searching male prisoners in a great majority of cases.

At this point, let me state that the preliminary reports of both the Washington and New York studies—as well as the final report of the Washington experience that has just been published—provide little objective substantiation for such fears. And although it is found that male officers generally persist in their negative attitude toward women, at least one report notes some very enthusiastic responses by patrolmen when women officers working with men perform competently in dangerous situations. Moreover, all reports indicate that younger officers (and black officers) are more receptive of women officers than are older officers. For the police administrator, these findings are significant: they provide him with meaningful cues for effectively dealing with preconceived notions and with the deeply rooted bias against women that appears to be so much a part of the police culture.

The answer, of course, lies in the intensive reorientation, proper motivation and relevant training for *all* members of the force, male and female— buttressed by strong leadership and direction on the part of the field commanders—and by a little time! As they acquire more and more field experience, female officers on patrol will, with time, develop a sense of self-confidence and know-how that will encourage them to assume the initiative, to "take charge" in field situations and to do so with the skill and competence that will gradually dissipate the resistance of the men, earn their respect, and, ultimately, their acceptance. Moreover, as new recruits (male and female) entering the police service are indoctrinated in this new policing concept, they will, at this level of police experience, come to accept each other as fellow workers; when finally assigned to field duty, the male recruit is then less likely to be hostile or resistive to the concept of male-female patrol teams; with time, these "young bloods" will represent a larger and larger percentage of the force—and of the "new order." Finally, with time, patrol will come to be seen by both male and female officers for what it is, essentially a service function—rather than the prevalent "cops and robbers," "vigor and brawn" myth. Once the latter misconception is effectively scotched, a female patrol partner will be less of a threat to the male officer's ego and sense of manhood.

"Favoritism" is another issue that is sure to surface with respect to women officers on patrol. Any evidence of special treatment, such as excusing women from selected patrol tasks, will not only exacerbate the male officer's resentment, but, in the long run, will deprive women of the wide range of street experiences needed to develop skill, know-how, and effectiveness in patrol. Furthermore, such protective practices only tend to perpetuate the image of "weakness" of female officers. Intuitive police administrators, such as Chief Jerry W. Wilson of Washington, D.C., have taken a very firm stand on this issue, directing that all women officers assigned to patrol be assigned in the same manner as patrolmen and be required to perform the same tasks as their male counterparts. By implication this policy highlights the role of field supervisors in facilitating the full acceptance of policewomen as patrol officers. A double standard on the basis of sex, in any form, will not promote acceptance. For example, one report found that supervisors feel extremely awkward disciplining policewomen, and that they are reluctant to order women to do the kind of things they would order a man to do, once women complain. A policy such as

Chief Wilson's obviously dictates a single standard as to treatment and expectations: it also helps the police administrator place the responsibility for the successful integration of women police into patrol operations where it should be—on the field commanders.

Police administrators must anticipate having to deal with still another issue—that of jealous wives, or for that matter, jealous husbands. In at least two jurisdictions, wives have openly protested having women officers assigned to patrol cars with men. Also, interviews conducted as part of a special study reveal that almost 50 percent of the married patrolmen stated they believed that their wives would be strongly opposed to their having a woman patrol partner. Although such statements may more accurately reflect the personal bias of the patrolmen than of their spouses, police administrators realize that this issue can pose serious family problems for individual officers, and most provide some reasonable flexibility for accommodating these men. Possible domestic or disciplinary problems are no justification, however, for restricting assignment to patrol to one sex; as noted by the Equal Employment Opportunity Commission, "It is clearly unjust to limit employment opportunities of a class of people because of the projected improprieties of a few." But police administrators now recognize the necessity for adequate, advance publicity when integrating women into the patrol force, so that the public will be thoroughly informed as to the administrative and legal rationale underlying this new policing policy; otherwise, opposing pressure tactics initiated by the patrolmen through their representative organizations, their wives or others, may generate considerable confusion in the mind of the public.

The Policewoman

Now let us take a hard look at the policewoman's point of view. From a historical perspective, there can be no question that assigning women to street patrol, on an equal basis and interchangeably with men, marks the beginning of a new era for women in police work. It represents a significant widening of what has been the conventional role of policewomen in this country. That role was largely limited to police protective and preventive functions as they pertain to women, teenage females, pre-teen youngsters (male and female) and infants, and, in a few of the large cities, to a modicum of narcotics and morals laws

enforcement. True, since World War II there has been a strong trend in most jurisdictions to integrate women into more areas of law enforcement—criminal and vice investigations, criminalistics, radio dispatching—and policewomen with professional degrees are serving in some urban centers as legal advisors, laboratory analysts, police administrators, instructors in police academies, and community relations experts. Nevertheless, for the overwhelming majority of policewomen, patrol could be the real breakthrough to the full integration of women into all branches of police service. Patrol after all, is the "backbone" of police work and a basic experience required of all male police officers, even of those who qualify for assignment to specialized units. And once incorporated into this mainstream of police operations—and confronted with the whole gamut of police problems and responsibilities at the street level—the policewomen's role could no longer be seen as that of an adjunct specialist with limited purpose.

However, in all candor, I must repeat what I have already stated: not all policewomen view this development with enthusiasm or approval. There are those who are convinced that women will experience a diminution of status when they shift from the specialist to the generalist role. They know that the male officer's strong, negative attitudes about women on patrol are shared by the supervisory and administrative ranks and they fear that this prejudice could prove to be a subtle barrier to productive performance by policewomen on patrol and preclude any objective appraisal of their true potentialities. Moreover, the advocates of a specialist role for policewomen are persuaded that it is as specialists that women have secured a place for themselves in law enforcement. For example, nationwide, more policewomen are assigned to the handling of juveniles than to any aspect of police work. Since the public regards police work with juveniles as having social value, this role is seen as giving women status and as securing their position in the police hierarchy. Those with this point of view also maintain that whenever women police have been given the opportunity to contribute their natural aptitudes and skills—as women—to other sectors of police work, they have generally succeeded in expanding their use in these areas. The New York City experience is illustrative: increasing numbers of policewomen have been assigned to the vice squads, to criminal investigations relating to narcotics, rape, pickpocket and confidence games, and to investigations of missing persons.

On the other hand, those policewomen who herald the advent of street patrol for the promise it holds for full integration of women into police work are equally convinced of the futility of the specialist role for the future of policewomen. In their view, as specialists women have played only a peripheral role in law enforcement; and as specialists, they will continue to be subject to rigid chauvinistic definitions of their "proper" place in police work. For example, policewomen in substantial numbers are still being used for secretarial and clerical duties even by the more "enlightened" administrators, and despite the current emphasis on the need to "professionalize" police, this practice is rationalized on the basis of "sensitivity of the post," "security," or "confidentiality of records." New York City, for one, had some twenty percent of its female force detailed to such functions throughout the tenure of several recent police commissioners.

Moreover, it is generally known that male officers, in the main, do not share the public's esteem for the policewoman's juvenile tasks; in fact, the policewoman's juvenile functions are not perceived to be "real" police work, but rather a form of "social work"—and pejorative references to the juvenile section as the "diaper detail" are not uncommon.

Policewomen who favor a generalist approach are also convinced that one result of making a distinction between the role of male and female officers on the basis of sex has been to more or less isolate policewomen from the mainstream of police operations. Another has been to keep the number of policewomen in this country unbelievably small by opening the door to the establishment of quotas. In 1971, for example, there were approximately 3,700 policewomen in the United States; although this figure represented an increase of over 50 percent in five years' time—which is indeed a heartening development—nevertheless, in 1971 policewomen represented no more than 1.5 percent of all full-time law enforcement officers in the nation. By and large, this ratio seems to hold for individual jurisdictions as well. Even New York City, which for many years now has had the largest policewoman corps in the country, only very recently enlarged its female force to over 700 strong; still, impressive as this number may appear to be, it represents little more than 2 percent of the total police force of that huge metropolis. From a policewoman's point of view, there can be no question that quotas operate as discriminatory barriers; they restrict a woman's access to police

work; they impede expansion of the policewoman's role; they limit opportunities for career and development.

You may ask, "How does the policewoman-generalist react to the negative attitudes of male officers to women on patrol?" Her sentiments are probably succinctly stated in the cynical phrase: "So what's new?" Past experience has conditioned her to anticipate that the old bugaboo of her limitations in physical strength and endurance will be raised whenever she seeks an expansion of her police role and will be consistently cited as a liability to her overall usefulness in police work. This, despite the fact that policewomen have demonstrated time and again that they generally have the resourcefulness and ingenuity to handle effectively even very hazardous criminal investigations, such as narcotics traffic, vice and morals violations, racketeering, extortion, etc. As to the specific issue of street patrol, the policewoman generalist is quick to point out that police agencies have yet to objectively validate what strength level is job-related; moreover, should the difference in the comparative strength between the sexes prove to be a legitimate concern, the generalist is convinced that appropriate training measures can be devised to compensate for them—such as on-the-job training by seasoned field training officers and physical training geared to the realities of patrol situations.

But when all is said and done, the generalist has few illusions about winning the whole-hearted support of male officers in widening the policewoman's role so as to encompass patrol. If history has taught policewomen anything, it has demonstrated that any significant advance women have made in police work has been precipitated by forces outside the police establishment. A close look at the events that have generated the current trend toward integrating women into patrol will confirm this observation. I shall detail these events, but before doing so, I should like to present a very brief overview of three highlights in the history of New York City's policewomen that illustrate this point.

Some Historical Highlights

Women were first introduced in the New York City police department as a consequence of a national movement for moral reform that crystallized in this country around the end of the 19th century, spearheaded by several organized women's groups such as the Women's Prison Association of New York, American Female Guardian Society, and the National Women's Christian Temperance Union, which actively concerned themselves with the plight of female prisoners temporarily lodged in police stations pending court arraignment, and vigorously campaigned for separate detention quarters for women and for the appointment of police matrons to care for them. Earlier in the century, in 1845, a similar movement, largely inspired by the American Female Moral Reform Society, had succeeded in introducing prison matrons in the New York City jails. But when the later reformers attempted to extend this innovation to the Police Department, their campaign encountered an avalanche of ridicule and opposition, largely led by the police hierarchy itself and supported by such interest groups as the Doormen's Association and The Men's Prison Association. The latter sanctimoniously rationalized its opposition on the basis that a "decent, sober, respectable woman" would be "contaminated and demoralized by her contact with such depraved creatures" as female alcoholic prisoners. Today a like protective solicitude is proffered by some opposed to the integration of women into patrol on the basis that they fear female officers may be assaulted, if not raped.

It should be noted that the police of New York City, before the turn of the century, were charged with the care of homeless persons as well as prisoners, since no other facilities such as municipal lodging houses existed. The enormity of the problem can be gleaned from the fact that in 1887 there were 14,000 women prisoners detained at the precinct station houses and 42,000 women lodgers received overnight shelter. The facilities provided were far from adequate, even for the standards of that era: there was no way of effectively separating male and female prisoners in the cell blocks, nor for segregating young female offenders; and all were supervised by a male turnkey. The lodgers—generally dirty, and often diseased—crowded the underground precinct cells like cattle. Two children were born in the station houses to women detained there that year; sometime later a 15-year-old girl, under custody, was the victim of an assault.

The reformers finally succeeded in having women appointed as police matrons in New York City in October, 1891—but only after a relentless, undaunted campaign of more than ten years' duration. Cities like Boston, Providence, Jersey City, Philadelphia, Baltimore, St. Louis and Milwaukee had accepted the reform at least seven years earlier.

It was Los Angeles that hired the first woman with full police powers. That was in 1910. At that time the New York City police matrons still had no such powers, their duties being limited to the search and care of arrested females; they did seek to have their role expanded so as to include work with problem youth, but their proposal was totally ignored by the police hierarchy.

Ultimately, women with police powers and responsible for preventive work with youth were brought into the New York City police force. Once again, forces outside the police establishment took the initiative to bring it about.

The stage was set with the advent of World War I and the consequent social ferment generated by the war preparedness movement and by a feverish woman suffrage campaign. An important catalyst was the young, reform, fusion Mayor, John Purroy Mitchel, who, in recognition of the patriotic efforts of the City's women, created the Mayor's Committee of Women on National Defense, to which he appointed leaders in the fields of woman suffrage, social work, labor, industry, education and journalism, as well as many of the social elite. It was this Committee that concerned itself with the community problems created by the mass concentration of armed personnel (New York City was now a major port of embarkation) and with the noticeable increase of waywardness among the young, in particular "the girl who goes wrong because of the lure of the khaki." It was this Committee that moved to have established within the police force, on a temporary, war emergency basis, policewomen who could function in a protective capacity with respect to delinquent and wayward youth.

The Commissioner of Police demurred, but in this instance his resistance was not too forceful or too long, perhaps because the advocates for the proposal maintained direct access to the office of the Mayor. Eager to assume the functions of the proposed policewoman position were the police matrons; however, they were rebuffed by the members of the Mayor's Committee, who, conceiving the policewoman role as social-work oriented, considered the police matron's background and experience unsuitable.

Policewomen were appointed at first on a limited, experimental basis, but very rapidly their numbers increased. Once the war ended, these policewomen moved to have their positions made permanent via state legislation. But the police matrons countered by demanding legislation that would widen their role so as to encompass the policewomen's functions.

The legislators accommodated both groups by giving each full police powers and each a separate "police" designation. As a result, the police force now had two groups of women with identical authority and powers, but with distinct titles. The consequent rivalry, the competition for status between these two groups stymied the progress of women police in the New York City jurisdiction for many years. The dilemma was finally resolved in 1937, once again by an "outside" force: another reform, fusion mayor (La Guardia) merged the two titles of women police into one.

I might say in passing that the period between the advent of World War I and the mid-20s witnessed a remarkably rapid growth of the policewoman "movement" throughout the nation. Events following mobilization gave impetus to the movement, as did the active interest and support of many important national women groups and prestigious civic and social hygiene associations, such as the League of Women Voters, the Federation of Women's Clubs, the American Social Hygiene Association, the National Young Women's Christian Association, and the National Women's Christian Temperance Union. By the end of the war, about 220 cities had policewomen in their employ.

This was also the era that established a solid footing for the preventive-protective service concept of the policewoman's role in this country. The fact that many of the early policewomen had social service backgrounds, were often graduate social workers, was no doubt an influencing factor in bringing this social viewpoint into police work, focussing as it did on the social protection of women and children and on securing social treatment calculated to reform the delinquent. The International Association of Policewomen was formed by these early policewomen, not only to give them a national forum for propagandizing the need for policewomen, but also for making their definition of the policewoman's role a national standard and for advocating uniform, high standards with respect to the qualifications and training of women police. It was a momentous triumph for them when, in 1922, the International Association of Chiefs of Police, in an official statement, acknowledged that policewomen were essential to police work and recommended the very definition of role and standards re qualifications and training that the Policewomen's Association espoused.

There was one more significant recommendation. That is, that police departments establish a woman's unit, to function under the direct supervision of the Chief of Police, and to be officered by a woman "with rank." Many cities, including New York City, did form a Bureau of Policewomen, but supervised in most cases by an experienced female officer, since "rank" was otherwise unavailable. Some jurisdictions, such as Washington, D.C., and Portland, Oregon, ultimately provided policewomen a very narrow avenue for career development by permitting them to compete among themselves for a handful of promotive ranks within the Bureau.

It was this formula for career advancement that was generally proffered whenever agitation for promotional opportunities for policewomen threatened to become a public issue. From the point of view of the police hierarchy, the formula provided a neat resolution to several thorny problems with respect to policewomen promotion: it posed no threat to the male force, obviating as it did any competition with policewomen (who generally had higher educational qualifications); it precluded women as supervisors of men by restricting their authority and assignment to this separate, segregated unit. And to further reinforce sex differentiation in the supervisory ranks, many police chiefs insisted on distinct titles and salary scales for women superiors. However, from the policewoman's point of view, the opportunities for career advancement under this formula were so circumscribed as to constitute mere "window dressing."

In the main, New York City's policewomen doggedly resisted this resolution of the promotion issue. For several decades, they struggled to have the Department's existing career opportunity structure opened to women, employing a variety of tactics and strategies to pressure the levels into instituting the change. These efforts were consistently fruitless in the face of adamant, intransigent opposition by the male members of the force and their representative organizations.

Ironically, New York City holds something of a record in this country in appointing women to the very high office of Deputy Police Commissioner; beginning way back in 1918, three women have held that important post, in one case for almost a decade. But promotion for the female police troops—well, that was "something else"!

In their abortive campaigns to attain this objective, the policewomen now and then sparked a twinge of conscience among the decision-makers in both police executive and legislative circles. Various arrangements for the "formula" were then advanced as "appropriate" alternative solutions—with the superiors' title, in every instance, carefully structured so as to limit its supervisory authority to women. Because these proposed compromises emanated from the "establishment," they tended to produce considerable divisiveness among the policewomen, some of whom favored acceptance on the premise that "half a loaf was better than none," while the majority generally concluded that the career opportunity offered was so limited as to be meaningless. And so the promotion issue remained in limbo, and the struggle to attain it continued.

In the interim, the only other avenue for recognition open to the policewomen of New York City was by way of assignment to the Detective Division where three grades of advancement were possible, with the first (top) grade carrying a salary scale equal to that of Lieutenant rank. In 1952, the leadership of the Policewomen's Endowment Association won a spectacular increase in the policewomen's quota of detective ratings (yes, these quotas were established on the basis of sex) and the numbers of women assigned to special units of the Detective Division from then on continued to increase. Moreover, in 1963, for the first time in the history of the Department, detective ratings were allocated to members of the Bureau of Policewomen who performed outstanding work in the investigation of various criminal practices victimizing women. For New York City's policewomen, these were indeed significant achievements—but certainly no substitutes for career advancement via promotional opportunity.

Ultimately, that opportunity was accorded the policewoman—not by the police hierarchy—but, again, by an "outside" force: this time, a court of law. In June, 1963, in a final affirming decree, the New York State Court of Appeals upheld a suit instituted by a policewoman two years earlier for the right of women to take the examination for Sergeant.

From this historical judicial ruling have flowed some momentous administrative changes: today, New York City's police officers—male and female—compete in unisex promotional examinations, from which a single promotion list is promulgated and eligibles are appointed in descending order, regardless of sex; superiors (male and female) are assigned interchangeably to field commands and exercise supervisory authority over all police subordinates, regardless of sex (there are currently 16 female sergeants,

five female lieutenants, one female captain, one female deputy inspector on the force); moreover, the basic position classifications, "patrolman" and "policewoman," have been merged into the unisex title, "police officer." There are no longer any height requirements for candidates for the police service; all candidates (male and female) now compete in the same written examination, qualify in identical physical fitness and agility tests, meet identical medical requirements, and are appointed from a single eligibles' list. Basic training, conducted by a staff of instructors (male and female) of various police ranks, provides a unisex curriculum to "integrated" classes of recruits, who upon graduation are assigned to field commands, regardless of sex, and there they perform patrol on foot, in radio motor patrol cars, or on scooters. The Policewomen's Section has been abolished and female police officers formerly assigned thereto have been integrated into precinct commands throughout the City (women are also being trained in the Mounted Division). The personnel of one Manhattan precinct (the 13th) perhaps best illustrates the current trend: women constitute 10 percent of the patrol force and 20 percent of the supervising staff—and are represented in all ranks from Sergeant to Captain.

In short, New York City's policewomen appear to be on the threshold of full integration into all aspects of police operations. The long, circuitous, bumpy route they have travelled to arrive at this point is by no means an experience unique to the New York scene. To a greater or lesser degree, it has been the common lot of policewomen throughout the nation.

Current Happenings

There are some compelling reasons for concluding that the various interacting forces of social change that have confronted America in the past decade are at the root of the current trend among police toward eliminating discriminatory barriers on the basis of sex, and of the consequent widening of the policewoman's role so as to encompass patrol and all other aspects of police work.

We all remember the turbulence and civil disorders that scarred our cities and college campuses when political strife took to the streets. Although the Civil Rights movement had come of age and dominated the social scene and the American conscience, nevertheless our complex, urbanized society was slow to implement the changes demanded by groups who had previously been denied power and status, such as blacks, youth, women and the poor, and who were now highly vocal and assertive of their rights.

As violence and crime, urban riots, charges of harassment and brutality in the ghetto and of inequities in the criminal justice system increased public concern throughout the nation, President Johnson responded by forming The President's Commission on Law Enforcement and Administration of Justice to undertake a most comprehensive study of the crime problem and of the related complex problems of civil disorder and community conflict—and of the criminal justice system's capacity to cope with them. The police, of course, were centrally involved. And so when the Commission, a prestigious corps of experts in a broad range of professions—police administration, criminology, sociology, law—submitted its Report in 1967, police administrators could not cavalierly dismiss the recommendations it contained, or skirt the issues raised. Among the recommendations was the following with respect to women police:

> Qualified women should be utilized in such important staff service units as planning and research, training, intelligence, inspection, public information, community relations, and as legal advisors ... and communications ... (and) should also serve regularly in patrol, vice and investigative divisions ... (and) as more and more qualified women enter the service, they could assume administrative responsibilities.

We also witnessed the Women's Liberation Movement gather feverish momentum during this period. By March, 1972, the United States Senate had approved the Equal Rights Amendment to the Constitution (which prohibits denial of equal rights on the basis of sex) and forwarded same to the States for ratification. At the same time (also March 1972), Title VII of the Civil Rights Act of 1964 was amended and its provisions made applicable to the public, as well as private employers.

The latter is the "happening" that has particular significance with respect to the issue of policewomen patrol and the status of policewomen in general. The law not only prohibits any discrimination on the basis of sex, but it further provides that where women are *not* to be hired or assigned on the same basis as men, the agency would be required to prove that sex is a "bona fide occupational qualification"—that is, that

there be shown to be significant differences between men and women in terms of job performance.

For the police establishment, this amended legislation made for a new ball game: police agencies could now anticipate legal challenges to the status quo.

Indeed, in several jurisdictions, women have already instituted proceedings under both this statute and under the 14th Amendment, charging sex discrimination in hiring standards, or in promotion practices. Moreover, because of the scarcity of documented research on the policewoman's occupation, police administrators realized that the legislation could also pose them some problems where advocates of a wider role for women police alleged sex discrimination with respect to assignment. One of the prime objectives of the two independent studies conducted by the Police Foundation in Washington, D.C. and in New York City was to develop some hard data with respect to policewoman patrol performance, and thus provide the respective police agencies a basis for objective analysis and evaluation.

A number of other cities are also experimenting with policewomen patrol, but the findings of the New York and Washington, D.C. studies are of special interest to police administrators since these studies have been conducted under professional auspices. Their conclusions are apt to have considerable impact on the personnel and administrative policies of police agencies throughout the country.

In the meantime, the new provisions of Title VII of the Civil Rights Act continue to make their mark in the various sectors of law enforcement. For the first time in history, women are being hired as Agents by the Federal Bureau of Investigation, as U.S. Marshals, as members of the Secret Service, as military police and as State Troopers in New York State. The list continues to grow.

The Equal Employment Opportunity Commission's guidelines on employment policy constitute another important "happening"—another force for the elimination of discriminatory barriers on the basis of sex. Under these federal guidelines, employers—public or private—must demonstrate that any requirement for employment or promotion is specifically related to some objective measure of job performance—i.e., must be job-related and demonstrably non-discriminatory. Police departments, for example, have traditionally made height requirements a job qualification, and, although not intentionally discriminatory, the standards set serve to eliminate disproportionately more women than men. Since these requirements have never been shown to be job-related, there is now considerable debate as to whether, in fact, such requirements are discriminatory as job qualifications. The matter has been the subject of litigation in two jurisdictions, but the issue is still unclarified and continues to be debatable. As I have already noted, height requirements are no longer a job qualification for police service in New York City.

Some Important Findings

The results of the Washington study, as recently reported by the Police Foundation, indicate that in that year-long experiment there was no significant difference in job performance of male and female officers on patrol. Moreover, during the study, there were no reported incidents that questioned the ability of women to satisfactorily handle patrol assignments. The report concluded that it was appropriate to assign women to patrol duty on the same basis as men.

The study did discover, however, some difference in performance between male and female patrol officers and this was noted very early in the experiment. For example, the study's preliminary findings, published when the newly hired policewomen contingent involved in the experiment had had only four months' average experience on patrol, made the following interesting observations:

> . . . The number of felony arrests made by new policewomen was about the same as those made by comparison men but the new policewoman was more likely to have made no felony arrests. The new policewoman made fewer misdemeanor arrests and gave fewer moving violations . . .
> . . . Reassigned women made felony and misdemeanor arrests at about the same rate as the comparison men, but they gave fewer moving traffic violations . . .
> . . . Observers found that male-female teams are less likely than male-male teams to initiate traffic or non-traffic incidents, such as questioning suspicious persons, stopping vehicles for traffic problems, spot checks for stolen autos, and business or bank checks.
> Observers found that new women were more likely than comparison men to be given instructions by their partner, and they are less likely to "take charge" at an incident in which their partner is present.
> . . . So far, policewomen and comparison men have been involved in few situations involving violence or potential violence. There appears to

be no difference in the performance of new women and comparison men in these few situations . . .

The New York study is considerably less comprehensive than the Washington, D.C. experiment, especially in terms of the numbers of women officers participating. Nevertheless, the tentative conclusions suggested in its preliminary findings, as well as the particulars noted therein with respect to the difference in performance between male and female patrol officers, tend to reinforce the general findings of the Washington study:

> In most areas reported, . . . there seems to be little difference in the productivity of patrolmen and women. This includes number of arrests, parking summonses, attendance at community meetings, etc. In some areas, however, differences are more striking:
> 1. Patrolmen tend to give more summonses for moving violations and do more taxi auto checks than do policewomen.
> . . . Policewomen spend more time in anti-crime patrol than do patrolmen.
> . . . The figures on mean calls for service per active day in command indicate that policewomen in radio cars are as productive as patrolmen.

Police Work—1984

When we scan the profound changes now under way in the role and status of women police in this country, our thoughts understandably project to the future. Can we glean from these current "happenings" what lies ahead, especially in such critical areas as the composition of the force, and the role of women police? In short, what about Police Work—1984?

Let's consider first of all, will police agencies become overpopulated with female law enforcement officers? This is the opinion of those who oppose the new policy of appointing qualified applicants to the police service without regard to sex. They maintain that women tend to score better than men in written examinations, and thus are likely to be overrepresented on any eligibles' list, and, ultimately, on the force.

There is no question that giving women equal access to the police service and to opportunity for career development will substantially expand the numbers of female police officers in this country.

Women, after all, have become an integral part of the work force; in 1968, nearly half the women in this country between the ages of 18 and 65 were working, and their numbers are apt to grow as the cross currents of inflation, Women's Liberation and an ever-rising standard of living make their impact on our society. Once in the job market, women—like men—seek employment on the basis of the potential for gratification in job satisfaction, monetary reward and working conditions.

In these terms, police work has more than average appeal. Salaries, especially in the large urban communities and their wealthier suburbs, have risen so sharply as to compare most favorably with private industry (in fact police entrance pay often out-distances that in social work or education, which require higher educational qualifications); moreover, almost every police agency now guarantees its personnel—male and female—the same salary scale, a circumstance yet to be realized in private industry. There are other considerations as well: job security; handsome pension provisions, often with retirement after 20 years' service; sick leave; health insurance and death benefits; generous maternity leaves; the opportunity for interesting, varied work, dealing with people from all walks of life, very often in a service capacity; finally, ample and attractive promotion opportunities. (A Sergeant in New York City can earn almost $20,000 a year.)

These are attractions enough. Certainly enough for the women who applied to take New York City's December, 1973 examination for police officer. Of the 53,515 who took the examination, fully 27 percent were women.

On the other hand, many women are likely to reject police work because of other features: the around-the-clock work schedule, including weekends and holidays; the personal risk factor due to dangers inherent in the job; the exposure to the more sordid, seamy side of life; the semi-military pattern of operations and discipline. I think that these factors are sufficiently important to many women so as to militate against the likelihood of females "over-populating" the police force. While predicting the size of the 1984 female police population is something of a risky business because of unknown variables (an economic recession, for example, may suddenly lure unusually large numbers of male college graduates to the job security of a police career, as happened in New York City in 1939–1943), nevertheless, I hazard to guess that in 1984 females will still be a minority

of the police force—although a substantial minority—perhaps between 10 and 15 percent.

Will women be integrated into all aspects of police work and be used interchangeably with men, especially in patrol?

There is no doubt that some police chiefs will resist altering their present administrative policies with respect to women police until challenged to do so via litigation. However, in the main, Title VII of the Civil Rights Act is likely to make recruitment, training and assignment to field commands, without regard to sex, a basic administrative practice in most police jurisdictions. But as this occurs and as the immediate prospect of more and more women entering the service increases, resistance on the part of the male rank-and-file will no doubt be forcefully vocalized by their powerful representative organizations and we may see in the immediate future some very sophisticated pressure tactics and political leverage exercised by these groups in an effort to mold public opinion and alter executive policy. Thus, the pattern of policewoman patrol in the immediate future will depend, in each jurisdiction, upon the Chief's personal commitment to the underlying philosophy, principles and spirit of Title VII of the Civil Rights Act. Some will follow Chief Jerry Wilson's lead and mandate a single standard for personnel with respect to assignment, treatment and expectations, without regard to sex. Others, sensitive to the mores and traditions of the police culture, are likely to hedge a bit on the principles of the law and allow field commanders discretion in their use of female officers, on the premise that such discretion will be exercised to further the cause of efficient police service. Where this occurs, we may once again see policewomen used as specialists—this time, within the patrol function, and their tasks generally limited to selected patrol activities such as handling family arguments; work with juveniles; performing community relations duties; aiding the sick, the aged, the lost and the stranded; dealing with female complainants; handling neglected or abandoned children; questioning a rape victim; or performing clerical work. In brief, particular service aspects of patrol may be assigned to female officers, and this specialized use of women rationalized on the basis that it "emphasizes" their natural aptitudes. Where individual female officers challenge such an arrangement, then, in view of the law, an "accommodation" is likely to be made.

It should be apparent, however, that as their numbers continue to grow, women officers will acquire political "muscle" and leverage of their own. For one thing, their number will be represented in the very police organizations that are now opposed to their equal access to police service; if women can avoid divisiveness among themselves as to the scope of their role, there will come the time when the female officer corps could be the "swing" vote to a new leadership slate and a new policy within these police organizations. Furthermore, their "natural aptitudes" in the performance of the service aspects of patrol are bound to garner for women officers the respect and regard—and support—of the public. This was the case when they specialized in protective-preventive services to women and children; now, with women officers in far greater numbers and functioning at the neighborhood level, their "natural aptitudes" for rendering service will attain even greater public visibility.

What about 1984? We should see women close indeed to full equality and total integration into the police service.

Higher Education and the Police

WILLIAM J. MATHIAS

Higher education generally has held a revered place of honor in American society since Harvard opened its doors in 1636. In the more than three centuries since that time, higher education has had its highs and lows with a considerable number of its accomplishments contributing significantly to the progress and development of American society. The early contributions were generally in the arts and humanities. Then, as the industrial revolution began in the United States, higher education responded with institutes of technology which assisted in developing our manufacturing capacity. When the agricultural crises struck in the nineteenth century, schools of agriculture responded by providing ways of preventing soil erosion and increasing yields per acre. In the twentieth century, research facilities in higher education have provided many solutions to medical health problems, lengthening our average life span and even developing a system of "spare parts" for our bodies.

The general trend seems to be moving from the primary concerns of ancient times, the humanities, to material things, agriculture and mechanics, to human matters, medicine, and, today, human behavior. As one can see from this oversimplified view of the evolution of American higher education, the involvement in direct human problems basically is a twentieth-century phenomenon.

There are a number of reasons as to why attention has not been turned to this area of concern until this time. One explanation has been the natural progression of knowledge, which has been substantially affected by the fact that human problems of health, mental health, and crime are very difficult problems with which to deal. Police departments are operating today substantially on the principles set forth by Sir Robert Peel in 1829. The only *major* advances until the late 1960s have been the use of radios and automobiles. The situation in the courts is perhaps worse. Two of the most notable changes that have been made in this sector have been "the removal of wigs from judges and the introduction of ball-point pens to replace quill pens." Corrections also has seen little change. The printed program of the organizational meeting of what is now the American Correctional Association, in Cincinnati in 1870, looks like a mirror image of a current conference on corrections. Only the names of the speakers would have to be changed. Even though this component of the criminal justice system identified many of the key issues over a century ago, they have made precious little progress in *solving* any of these problems.

A startling contrast is a comparison of the pace of development in aeronautics with that of criminal justice. In the space of about 70 years, since the first

SOURCE: This article was written expressly for inclusion in this book.

flight at Kitty Hawk, North Carolina, in 1905, a flight shorter than the length of a Boeing 747, man has visited the moon and returned.

Some will say that these illustrations are oversimplifications of reality, and they are. However, the points to be noted are:

1. Higher education has traditionally been the one institution to which society has turned for assistance in the solution of its major problems.
2. The involvement of higher education in the field of human problem solution is in its infancy.
3. The involvement of higher education with criminal justice to any significant degree is a post-1960 phenomenon.

It is most appropriate for the criminal justice system to turn to higher education for assistance in meeting its needs, because the university may well be the only institution in American society with a range of resources as broad as the complex problem of crime.

Recent Focus on Criminal Justice Education

There are a number of reasons for the attention that has been given to criminal justice higher education in the United States in the last decade or so. The U.S. Supreme Court has handed down more landmark decisions in criminal cases since the Second World War than in all of previous history. The increasing affluence of the country has meant that more consumer goods have been available for theft, and television has raised the expectations of many people who traditionally have not had access to these consumer goods, but were not so aware of their economic deprivation before the age of television. The civil rights movement laid bare some of the inadequacies in all components of the criminal justice system. The idea of universal education beyond the secondary level came into vogue, and criminal justice practitioners began saying, "We want our share of the action." These same practitioners began moving toward professionalism by supporting state statutes on minimum standards and other reforms. The various forms of the news media now bring the daily operations of the criminal justice system, especially the police, into American homes; television, in dramatic style, highlights murder, rape, and robbery in "living color." The President's Commission on Law

Enforcement and the Administration of Justice in 1967 recommended that "the ultimate aim of all police departments should be that all personnel with general enforcement powers have baccalaureate degrees."(1) Charles Saunders acknowledges the desirability of this goal, but points out that education is a long-range approach to this goal.(2) All of these factors have interacted in complex ways to cause a greatly increased demand for criminal justice education, and every reader probably can add to this list other factors which have contributed to the explosive growth from approximately 50 degree programs in the criminal justice field in 1960 to more than 500 by the mid-1970s.(3) Two pieces of federal legislation materially contributed to the development of academic programs in criminal justice. The Law Enforcement Assistance Act of 1965 provided some "seed-money" grants to encourage the initiation of programs. A greater thrust came three years later, when Congress passed the Omnibus Crime Control and Safe Streets Act of 1968, which provided scholarship monies for students in criminal justice academic programs through the *Law Enforcement Education Program* (LEEP).(4) The original appropriation of some $6 million for this program had been increased to about $40 million by the mid-1970s.

The Early Beginnings of Criminal Justice Education

The first recorded involvement of formal higher education in criminal justice was the first National Conference on Criminal Law and Criminology hosted by the law school faculty of Northwestern University in Chicago. Academicians and practitioners from the criminal justice system, convening for the first time in a joint meeting, passed three resolutions which:

1. Established the American Institute of Criminal Law and Criminology.
2. Initiated in 1910 the publication of the *Journal of the American Institute of Criminal Law and Criminology.*
3. Made possible the translation of major books on criminology authored by foreign scholars. Nine of these volumes were published under the general title, *Modern Criminal Science Series.* This series included the following: Hans Gross, *Criminal Psychology;* Bernaldo de Quiros, *Modern Theories of Criminology;* Enrico Ferri, *Criminal Sociology;* Raymond Soleilles, *The Individualization of Punish-*

ment; Cesare Lombroso, *Crime, Its Causes and Remedies*; Gabriel Tarde, *Penal Philosophy*; W. A. Bonger, *Criminality and Economic Conditions*; Raffaele Garofalo, *Criminology*; and Gustav Aschaffenburg, *Crime and Its Repression*. These books are considered the early classics of criminal justice education.

August Vollmer, town marshal of Berkeley, California, initiated a training program in 1908 which evolved into the Berkeley Police School. A year later, in 1909, Vollmer was appointed chief of the Berkeley Police Department and served in that capacity until 1932. During this period, he included University of California professors as instructors in his school to discuss the application of their disciplines to law enforcement.

In 1917, August Vollmer and Albert Schneider stated the following:

> A school for the special training of police officers is a requirement of the times. Those authorized and empowered to enforce the laws, rules and regulations which are intended for the better protection of the public should have some knowledge of the fundamental principles underlying human actions, especially those actions which are commonly designated as criminal or contrary to law and order.(5)

At about the same time on the east coast, Commissioner Arthur Woods of the New York Police Department initiated an academy in 1914 after Detroit began one in 1911. These early programs were designed to upgrade field-level police officers in their vocational skills. The New York effort became the prototype for the "state-of-the-art" approach, while the Berkeley concept was the forerunner of the "educational approach," i.e., the involvement of higher education.

By 1913, the Berkeley Police School offered a three-year program of formal classes, examinations and quality standards. Vollmer felt that even more instruction was necessary and, through his efforts, the University of California at Berkeley began offering courses in police administration during its summer session in 1916.

The training efforts of the New York Police Department in 1918 involved Columbia University. The University of California at Los Angeles offered a course for women police in the same year. The University of Washington offered courses for a short time

in the 1920s. In 1925, Northwestern University began offering a program under the leadership of Frank Kreml which developed into its present Traffic Institute. In the same year, Harvard University initiated its Bureau of Street Traffic Research. The University of Wisconsin developed some courses for police officers in 1927 which were administered through its extension division. The University of Chicago offered police administration courses starting in 1929. Also in that year, the University of Southern California began teaching courses in this field, followed a year later by San Jose State College. Of these programs, only San Jose State, Southern California, and the University of California at Berkeley survived the first year or two. The other institutions' programs were dropped after only a short period of time.

After Vollmer provided the impetus for starting the program at the University of California at Berkeley, leadership was next offered by O. W. Wilson, who was appointed as the first dean of the program. Wilson, during the 1930s, assumed the position of chief of police of Wichita, Kansas, and encouraged Wichita State University to offer a program in police administration.

In 1935, Michigan State University inaugurated a five-year baccalaureate degree in police administration. This program required at least two years of chemistry, physics, and mathematics, with little or no administration or organizational theory taught. One of the major features of the Michigan State program was a required internship of 18 months, a requirement reflecting the influence of the land-grant philosophy of the university. During the internship, students were paid $1 per day and lived in the Michigan State Police barracks, a very attractive arrangement in the Depression days of the 1930s. After graduation, those students who joined the Michigan State Police were paid the salary of an officer in his third year. This was the first known "salary-incentive" plan instituted by a police agency.

The Michigan State program was the first outside of the state of California which has existed continuously to this day. During these years, the program has seen many changes. There was a transition from the emphasis on the natural sciences to an emphasis on a liberal arts foundation. The major fields of study increased from one to three: law enforcement administration, security administration, and correctional administration. There were three subdivisions of the law enforcement area: police science, highway traffic administration, and delinquency prevention and control. The program was shortened to four years by reducing the internship to one quarter and, in 1967, making it optional. The terminology of the program was changed in the 1960s to criminal justice and graduate degrees were added: the Master of Science in the mid-fifties and the Ph.D. in the late 1960s.

In 1935, Indiana University established an Institute of Criminal Law and Criminology which evolved into the Department of Police Administration in 1949. The Bachelor of Arts degree with a certificate in police science was initiated in 1935 under the leadership of Dr. Edwin Sutherland.

Washington State University entered the field in 1941, under the leadership of V. A. Leonard, as the last program to be established prior to the entry of the United States into World War II. The global conflict caused a number of the colleges and universities in the field to suspend or to cut back operations until after the war.

At this point, 1941, the following institutions had established programs which have endured to the present: the University of California at Berkeley, the University of Southern California, California State University at San Jose (formerly San Jose State College), Michigan State University, Indiana University, Wichita State University, and Washington State University.

These programs were not designed to consider the comprehensive criminal justice system, and neither were there any national professional organizations yet concerned with the full range of criminal justice education. The dominant theme was fragmentation by function, locale, and police agency involvement. A beginning had been made, however, toward the criminal justice education system of today by the inroads that had been made in the traditional and provincial attitudes relative to the roles of the police and institutions of higher education.

Post World War II Developments

The years after the Second World War saw the field of criminal justice education begin slowly and then accelerate its growth to reach its present level of activity. In 1950, there were seven baccalaureate and 10 associate degree programs in five states.

One of the most significant efforts during this period was the establishment of a police science program at the City College of New York under the joint sponsorship of the Bernard Baruch School of Business and Public Administration and the New York City Police Department. The original program offered an Associate in Applied Science degree as well as an option within the baccalaureate program. A police science major under the Master of Public Administration degree was soon added. Jointly administered by the college and the police department, this program admitted only in-service law enforcement officers. The commanding officer of the police academy served as an assistant dean of the college, and a joint committee on curriculum and personnel operated with three members from the police department and three from the college.

The John Jay College of Criminal Justice evolved from this program as one of the units of the City University of New York (C.U.N.Y.) system. It now offers a broader range of undergraduate and graduate degrees and follows an "open-admissions" policy, as do other units in C.U.N.Y.

It was against the panorama of societal changes and pressures cited earlier that, by 1960, there were some 15 baccalaureate and 35 associate degree programs. The explosive growth of community colleges provided a ready-made vehicle for the expansion of academic programs at the associate degree level. This can be seen clearly in a comparison of the figures for 1960 (35 A.A. programs), 1964 (83), (6) and 1966 (133).(7) Because of the initial efforts in California and the early acceptance of academic programs by police agencies, the greatest growth has occurred in that state. Other states with large numbers of degree programs are Texas, New York, Florida, and Michigan (see Table 1, which shows the number of programs by degree level by state).(8)

Models of Criminal Justice Education

More and more junior colleges and universities expanded existing programs or developed new entities in police science and police administration. The several directions in which programs were moving was the keynote of this era, and meeting to define and identify roles and goals became an accepted part of the annual conference of the various associations at the state and national level.

Many of the programs which were begun between 1960 and 1965 reflected the ideas of parent programs, with minimal adaptation. Certain existing programs served more or less as models, depending upon the influence of key personnel who were involved in the planning and implementing process. Many of the two-year, and some four-year programs, became extensions of or substitutes for departmental training operations, while other programs denied their heritage as descendants of "police education" and found their development involved more closely with sociology, corrections, and other more "intellectually" acceptable titles. Little was done to define roles and goals of the many programs because of the vast expansion efforts in such a wide range of schools and geographic areas. Competition and striving for power positions "as having THE WORD in police education" seemed more prevalent than complementary or supplementary efforts toward a common goal. This competition seemed most noticeable between the "police association" based schools and the "academic group" programs.(9)

Two primary models of criminal justice educational programs have emerged. The first is the *technical model*, which is primarily concerned with the preparation of persons to enter directly into the criminal justice system without further training.(10) General characteristics of this type of program are: (1) practical, vocationally-oriented courses (e.g., police patrol, criminal investigation, and testifying in court); (2) hands-on instructional techniques; and (3) instructors who generally come from agency backgrounds, usually with no previous experience in higher education and often lacking the typical academic credentials (in some cases lacking even a baccalaureate degree) and academic interests considered requisite by most academic disciplines.

The second model is referred to as the *academic model*. The rationale for this model holds that universities, as the repositories of knowledge in society, have a special contribution to make in preparing personnel to enter the field of criminal justice or in upgrading persons presently employed.(11) If the assertion that a liberal arts education is the optimal preparation for citizenship in general is accepted, it is true many times over for those in society who enforce the behavioral standards established by law. Universities have for many centuries offered preparation for those entering the legal profession and, in the past century or so, for persons preparing for administrative positions. In the late 1800s, the behavioral sciences split off from philosophy and began the arduous task of seeking the determinants of human behavior. One might visualize criminal justice practitioners as applied behavioral scientists, thus gaining a measure of the importance of this particular area to criminal justice. The fields of science and technology virtually bypassed the criminal justice system until the mid-1960s. There is much to be gained from the direct transfer of technology as well as contributing new developments in target hardening and the scientific detection of crime. The academic model seeks to complement and supplement the technical information supplied by academies. This approach is analogous to the business administration model of educating accountants as generalists who can function in many different corporations with specialized orientation courses by the employing firm providing parallel information to that supplied by a police or corrections training academy for new police or corrections officers.

In the writer's judgment, the academic model allows the university to make its highest and best contribution to the preparation of criminal justice personnel as well as offering the approach that is the most cooperative with and complementary to existing academy training.

Nomenclature of Program Titles

Programs in the criminal justice field have operated under a variety of titles, such as police science, police administration, law enforcement, corrections, criminology, and the like. However, with the trend of moving toward the comprehensive systemwide approach, two titles are now the most prevalent: criminal justice and administration of justice. These titles are reflective of the evolution of this field at this time.

Problems of Criminal Justice Programs

Each academic discipline has encountered problems of growth as it has developed, and criminal justice has been no exception. Among these issues are the following:

1. The attempts by small colleges to imitate the university in the scope and number of its course offerings.

2. A proliferation of courses.

3. Inadequate staff resources to support extensive specialization.

4. Heavy teaching loads that can develop in academic departments (18 hours a week is not uncommon, and some have as many as 25 hours).

5. The number of different preparations for instructors (for example, one instructor taught 20 different courses, five each semester over a four-semester cycle).

6. The educational preparation of those selected

to teach courses: Is it adequate and compatible with the subject matter assigned?

7. In terms of organizational arrangements, the assignment of criminal justice education as a sub-ordinate unit of study in another major teaching program (e.g., a subunit of the political science or sociology department).

8. Inadequate library holdings: How many volumes should an undergraduate library contain in order to meet the minimal needs of criminal justice education?(12)

Graduate Education in Criminal Justice

The growth of programs at the graduate level roughly parallels the development of undergraduate programs. In 1967, there were only 14 graduate programs.(13) This figure increased to 18 in 1968–69, five doctoral programs and 13 at the master's level.(14) The number of master's programs skyrocketed to 121 for 1974–75, with 19 doctoral programs.(15) (See Table 1.)

These programs are typically criminal-justice-systems-oriented, and the greatest single employer of holders of doctorates are educational institutions. This is a start toward meeting the critical need for faculty with preparation in the field of criminal justice. The need for doctorates currently exceeds the supply. The number of degree programs in this field has far outstripped the production of Ph.D.'s available for faculty employment. From present indications, this need will exist for several more years.

There seems to be no significant correlation between the number of years that an institution has offered a program in this field and whether it offers a doctorate. Two of the oldest programs (University of Southern California and Michigan State University) offer doctorates, and two relative newcomers (John Jay College and Rutgers University) have programs in the planning stage.

National Criminal Justice Educational Consortium

A major effort in the graduate area is the National Criminal Justice Educational Consortium. In 1973, seven universities were funded by the Law Enforcement Assistance Administration of the U.S. Department of Justice. The goals of the consortium are as follows:

1. To develop and/or strengthen graduate—particularly Ph.D.—programs in criminal justice or related studies.

2. To develop and maintain an ongoing research capability at each of the member institutions, particularly in those areas related to the identification of criminal justice manpower needs and utilization and the education and training of criminal justice personnel (technology and scientific applications).

3. To provide a framework for cooperation and the exchange of knowledge between affiliated institutions.

4. To develop a model for a nationally oriented effort by universities to collect, exchange, and disseminate knowledge concerning subjects of interest among universities and criminal justice agencies.

5. To strengthen the planning and research capabilities of criminal justice agencies by increasing the number and improving the quality of professionally educated personnel available to them.

Members of the consortium are: Northeastern University, University of Maryland, Michigan State University, Eastern Kentucky University, University of Nebraska at Omaha, Arizona State University, and Portland State University.

Major activities to date of the consortium include: development and evaluation of curricula, development of work-study programs, faculty exchange programs, needs assessment of college-educated personnel, international comparative research, and dissemination of information.(16) This is the second major educational program of LEAA, the first being LEEP.

Professional Associations

The first professional association in the field of criminal justice education was the American Society of Criminology, founded in 1948. August Vollmer and O. W. Wilson were instrumental in its organization, and, by 1959, most degree programs in this field across the nation were represented within its membership. By 1963, many of the original members who were oriented to law enforcement became disenchanted with the organization's thrust toward the areas of crime causation and the treatment of criminals. In May 1963, a number of the police-oriented group came together for the retirement dinner for V. A. Leonard, Professor Emeritus of the police administration program at Washington State University in Pullman. As a result of discussions during this occasion, the International Association of Police Professors was begun. This organization changed its name to the Academy of Criminal Justice Sciences in 1970 to reflect its move to serve the full range of criminal justice educational programs.(17) Today, both the American Society of Criminology and the Academy of Criminal Justice Sciences are well established and serve mainly academic constituencies which overlap only partially.

Issues Facing Criminal Justice Education Today

As the criminal justice field continues to evolve, some issues that will have to be dealt with can be predicted; some cannot. The author offers the following issues for consideration:

1. Can criminal justice earn respectability from the various disciplines in the academic community? Is a national strategy advisable in working toward this goal? What role should the professional associations play relative to this matter?

2. Should criminal justice degree programs be accredited separately, as are law schools and nursing programs? What organization should conduct the accreditation, if it is established?

3. Will faculty in this field be expected to present the same credentials for initial employment as for most traditional disciplines, i.e., the Ph.D.? If so, should the terminal degree be in criminal justice or in a related field? How important will agency experience be for faculty members in the future? What criteria will be used for academic promotions? What role will criminal justice faculty members across the United States generally play in a broad-scale research effort relative to the problems of crime?

Table 1. Number of Criminal Justice Degree Programs Available in the United States and Outlying Areas (1974–75)

State	Associate	Baccalaureate	Master's	Doctorate	Number of Institutions	State	Associate	Baccalaureate	Master's	Doctorate	Number of Institutions
Alabama	12	13	8	0	18	Nevada	0	2	0	0	2
Alaska	1	0	0	0	1	New Hampshire	1	0	0	0	1
Arkansas	1	1	0	0	1	New Jersey	14	9	1	0	18
Arizona	7	12	2	0	9	New Mexico	4	6	2	0	3
California	92	24	18	5	76	New York	36	22	2	1	37
Colorado	4	2	0	0	3	North Carolina	9	7	0	0	11
Connecticut	14	3	3	0	9	North Dakota	1	0	0	0	1
Delaware	7	2	0	0	5	Ohio	20	11	5	0	20
District of Columbia	4	3	1	0	5	Oklahoma	8	5	1	0	9
Florida	56	15	4	1	33	Oregon	17	3	1	0	12
Georgia	19	8	2	0	17	Pennsylvania	30	22	8	2	22
Hawaii	4	1	0	0	4	Rhode Island	1	1	0	0	1
Idaho	6	5	0	0	3	South Carolina	8	1	0	0	7
Illinois	36	11	8	0	36	South Dakota	1	1	1	0	3
Indiana	12	12	6	0	16	Tennessee	5	5	2	0	7
Iowa	23	4	1	0	14	Texas	50	33	11	4	64
Kansas	17	6	7	0	8	Utah	3	2	1	0	3
Kentucky	10	9	4	1	7	Vermont	5	3	0	0	3
Louisiana	6	7	0	0	8	Virginia	22	8	1	0	18
Maine	7	1	0	0	4	Washington	25	15	3	0	20
Maryland	16	6	3	2	13	West Virginia	2	1	0	0	2
Massachusetts	19	7	3	0	21	Wisconsin	10	9	2	1	14
Michigan	36	22	3	1	27	Wyoming	2	0	0	0	3
Minnesota	12	9	1	0	14	Guam	1	4	1	0	1
Mississippi	5	3	1	0	7	Virgin Islands	—	—			—
Missouri	20	15	2	0	18	Total	729	376	121	19	664
Montana	5	2	1	1	4	Canada	6				
Nebraska	3	3	1	0	3						

SOURCE: Richard W. Kobetz, *Law Enforcement and Criminal Justice Education Directory, 1975–76,* (Gaithersburg, Md.: International Association of Chiefs of Police, 1975).

4. Will nontraditional degree programs flourish in the field to a greater extent than in other areas of study? Will the issue of credit for life experience bring the educational and the training communities closer together?

5. What is the future for enrollments in this field? What would be the consequence of the elimination of scholarship monies presently made available through LEEP?

6. Will the recommendation of the President's Commission on Law Enforcement and the Administration of Justice be accepted that all law enforcement officers with general arrest powers be required to have a baccalaureate degree?

7. What would be the impact upon degree programs if middle entry became a common personnel practice of police departments across the nation?

8. Can criminal justice educators build the necessary linkages with other academic disciplines to secure their most appropriate input into the battle against crime?

9. Will a faculty in the future plan a role of leadership in bringing about needed changes in the criminal justice system?

10. Should criminal justice be considered a new social science discipline, on the same level academically as political science and sociology?

11. Will LEAA appoint a professional criminal justice educator as the administrator of LEEP?(18)

REFERENCES

1. President's Commission on Law Enforcement and the Administration of Justice, *The Challenge of Crime in a Free Society* (Washington, D.C.: U.S. Government Printing Office, 1967), p. 109.

2. Charles B. Saunders *Upgrading the American Police* (Washington, D.C.: The Brookings Institution, 1970), p. 79.

3. This introductory section was taken from William J. Mathias, "Presidential Address," Academy of Criminal Justice Sciences, Reno, Nevada, March 6, 1974, unless otherwise noted.

4. Support for the thrust of this section of this chapter can also be found in Joseph J. Senna, "Criminal Justice Higher Education," *Crime and Delinquency*, 20, 4 (October 1974), pp. 389-97.

5. This quote is taken from an article in the *Journal of Criminal Law, Criminology and Police Science*, 7 (1917) and from Farris' thesis which is cited below.

6. Thompson S. Crockett, *First Annual Survey of Two Year Degree Programs in Law Enforcement*, St. Petersburg Junior College, St. Petersburg, Florida, October 1, 1965.

7. The 1960 and 1966 figures are taken from the Brandstatter citation below.

8. The historical background for this article was combined from two sources unless otherwise noted: Arthur F. Brandstatter, Director, School of Criminal Justice, Michigan State University, in an address to the Conference on Police Education sponsored by the Office of Law Enforcement Assistance, U.S. Department of Justice, June 8-9, 1967, at the University of Maryland, College Park, Maryland; and Edward A. Farris, "The Role of the Junior College in Police Education in California" (Master's thesis, University of California, Berkeley, September 1964).

9. This quotation is taken from the Farris citation above.

10. Jack McArthur, "California's Standardized Police Curriculum," *Journal of Criminal Law, Criminology and Police Science*, 57, 3 (September 1966), pp. 360-64.

11. A. C. Germann, "Education and Professional Law Enforcement," *Journal of Criminal Law, Criminology and Police Science*, 58, 4 (December 1967), p. 609.

12. This list of issues is taken from the Branstatter citation above.

13. *Police Science Programs in Universities, Colleges and Junior Colleges in the United States* (Washington, D.C.: International Association of Chiefs of Police, 1967).

14. *Law Enforcement Education Directory 1968–1969* (Washington, D.C.: International Association of Chiefs of Police, 1969).

15. Some general support for this section is found in Fred I. Klyman and Thomas A. Karman, "A Perspective for Graduate-Level Education in Criminal Justice," *Crime and Delinquency*, 20, 4 (October 1974), pp. 398–404.

16. "National Criminal Justice Educational Consortium," pamphlet published by the Law Enforcement Assistance Administration, U.S. Department of Justice, no date, and *LEAA Newsletter*, 4, 5 (November 1974).

17. This historical account of the development

of the American Society of Criminology and the Academy of Criminal Justice Sciences is taken from the Farris citation above.

18. Deborah H. Noxon, ed., *LEAA Newsletter*, 4, 4 (Washington, D.C.: U.S. Department of Justice, October 1974), p. 6. This citation applies only to no. 11; the remainder are presented by the author for your consideration.

The Impact of Police Unions:

Summary Report

HERVEY A. JURIS and PETER FEUILLE

The Scope and Method of the Study

Objectives

The object of this study was to learn something about the impact of police unions on police agencies; however, we found that to study impact we first had to examine the whole spectrum of labor-management relations. Specifically, we gathered data in six areas:

1. The nature of police employee organizations.

2. The structure, scope, and process of police labor relations, including the use of power by police unions.

3. The impact of police unions on the potential for professionalization of police service.

4. The impact of police unions on the chief's ability to manage the police department.

5. The impact of police unions on law enforcement policy formulation in the community.

6. The relationship between police unions and black officer organizations.

This project was supported by Grant No. NI-70-044, awarded by the National Institute of Law Enforcement and Criminal Justice, Law Enforcement Assistance Administration, U.S. Department of Justice [December 1973] under the Omnibus Crime Control and Safe Streets Act of 1968, as amended. Points of view or opinions stated in this document are those of the authors and do not necessarily represent the official position or policies of the U.S. Department of Justice.

Methodology

Our information was obtained primarily via a field study in 22 cities selected on the basis of information contained in questionnaires received from approximately 50 cities. During field visits (which were usually of four to five days duration), information was collected in interviews with the police chief or his representative(s), city labor relations representatives, police union leaders, and black officer organization leaders (where such an organization existed). In all, 137 interviews were conducted in the summer and fall of 1971.

In these field visits the authors used an issue-oriented data-gathering approach. That is, the field investigator, usually through archival research in local newspaper libraries, became familiar with particular police union-management issues which had arisen in each city in recent years. The investigator then pursued each party's relationship to these issues in subsequent interviews. This approach permitted the researchers maximum freedom to investigate the parties' actual conduct and impact on each other.

Before summarizing our findings, we apologize for the fact that the anonymity of the responses may inconvenience those who want to know *what* city was involved. Information of this type is only available if anonymity is provided and we have no intention of embarrassing any of our respondents. Second, please note that the research results in this report cannot and should not be generalized to cover all labor-management relations in the police service. Our study consists primarily of observations in 22 unionized cities, and it was never our intention to select a sample which might be representative of the several thousand police agencies in this country Finally, our data was collected in the summer and fall of 1971.

Fact situations may have changed, but we have based our report on the data collected then.

Police Employee Organizations

Police Organization Development

Enduring police employee organizations have existed in many cities since the turn of the century. Over the decades, these organizations have at various times provided welfare benefits for their members, lobbied for higher pay, and fulfilled certain social and fraternal needs. Police organizations in many cities affiliated with the organized labor movement after World War I; but the notoriety of the 1919 Boston police strike quickly ended these attempts at affiliation and, more importantly, had a chilling effect on police union organization efforts by organized labor for several decades.

Despite this chilling effect on labor union affiliation, policemen during the post-1919 period continued to form local associations many of which affiliated with larger state or national groups. By the 1960s the two largest of these national organizations were the International Conference of Police Associations and the Fraternal Order of Police. In addition, the American Federation of State, County, and Municipal Employees (AFL-CIO) and two other (police only) organizations had also been organizing police officers. By the time that police militancy emerged into full public attention late in the 1960s, most urban policemen were members of some kind of employee organization which was available to serve as a vehicle for the expression of increased police discontent.

Emergence of Police Militancy

We identify four factors which we feel have contributed to police employee dissatisfaction and three which contributed to the willingness of the police to engage in the use of militant tactics such as job actions.

The first factor contributing to police employee dissatisfaction is the increased public hostility toward the police in the 1960s. This is a broad label which includes such specific phenomena as the emergence of black and student militancy, U.S. Supreme Court decisions which were seen as restricting police discretion, the clamor for civilian complaint review boards, increased violence directed at the police, rising crime rates, and the frequent police employee perceptions of a lack of support for police actions among top police and city officials. Second, while the police faced increased public hostility, they also faced the problem of coping with increased public demands to solve the "crime problem," i.e., the call for "law and order." Thus, many of the same environmental factors which made the policeman's job more difficult also tended to increase the demands for more effective police work. Third, the more hostile and demanding environment increased the police workload and the perceived danger of the job, while at the same time most policemen felt that their economic rewards had not increased commensurately. Finally, employee dissatisfaction had been exacerbated by the existence of poor personnel practices within most police departments (no grievance procedures, no premium overtime pay or court time, etc.).

These four factors offer a possible explanation for the increase in police employee dissatisfaction in recent years, but three other factors are important in contributing to the overt expression of police militancy. First, the fact that the confrontation tactics of blacks, students, and groups of organized public and private employees have achieved both attention and results was not lost on the police. Second, today's urban police forces have a high proportion of young policemen who appear to be more willing to engage in overt action to achieve their goals than older officers. Third, the high degree of occupational cohesion among policemen contributes to a propensity for the police to be more aggressive in the pursuit of group goals than most other groups of city employees (with the exception of firemen).

While police militancy may emerge in many forms, the most visible widespread response has been the emergence of police employee organizational militancy, either through the formation of new aggressive organizations or through the transformation of relatively complacent existing associations into more active organizations.

Police Unions Today

Our research shows that national and state bodies do not play major roles in police labor relations at this time; police unionism is primarily a local phenomenon. This local emphasis is due primarily to the fact that the police industry is a local industry: labor is recruited locally, the product is delivered and consumed locally, and local taxes pay the bill. Because this reduces the collective bargaining arena to local city officials versus local union officials (although sometimes the state legislature may become involved), the role of a national organization is minimized—especially when compared to the industrial situation in the private sector—where the existence of multiplant companies and a national product market necessitates a leading role for the national union. The locus of collective bargaining may be one reason why the FOP and ICPA with their emphasis on local autonomy have been more successful in this field than AFSCME, NAGE,* and SEIU† where the emphasis is essentially on a strong national organization. Should the center of bargaining shift, so to would the center of organizational strength.

The Structure, Scope, and Process of Labor Relations

Labor Relations Structure

One of the chief characteristics of public sector and police labor relations is the fragmentation of managerial decision-making authority. In addition to posing multiple adversaries for the union (as we will see later, this fragmentation also offers multiple potential allies with whom police unions may coalesce), this fragmentation raises the question of who is the employer. Generally, labor relations is an executive function, though legislative approval of changes in budget items is almost always necessary. City councils tend to have stronger labor relations roles in weak-mayor and council-manager cities than in strong-mayor cities. The extent of police management involvement in union-city relations varies, but the basic thrust of such involvement is to protect managerial prerogatives.

Police unions also deal directly with police management over departmentally-controlled employment conditions. Local elected union leaders who are full-time policemen dominate union affairs, though hired attorneys may play leading roles as union representatives. State and national police union officials play very limited roles in union-management relations (unless they also happen to be local leaders). Police labor relations are very localized, with almost no multiemployer or multiunion negotiation units (though the unit of direct impact in a single city may extend far beyond the police department).

The Scope of Labor Relations

Our analysis suggests that police unions are not significantly different from other American trade unions in their desire to participate in the determination of a wide variety of direct economic and noneconomic conditions of employment. Police unions have devoted significantly greater resources toward securing "bread and butter" goals than law enforcement policy goals (though union efforts may have a decisive impact on policy issues). As in the private sector, police unions have attempted to participate in subjects which police management regards as solely within the sphere of managerial prerogatives and there are many issues in which police unions have attempted to establish a voice by means outside the institutionalized collective bargaining process.

The Labor Relations Process

Collective bargaining in the private sector is characterized by bilateralism (two parties participate in bargaining—the union(s) and the employer or employer association representative) within the existence of economic market constraints (employers can be priced out of the market and the workers will lose their jobs). Public sector bargaining is quite different. The fragmented management authority structure and political context in the public sector tend largely to eliminate the existence of private sector-type bilateral collective bargaining arrangements. We found that because of local government's fragmented authority structure, the lack of institutionalized collective bargaining procedures in several cities, and the necessity for many employment conditions to be changed via the legislative or electoral political processes, police unions cannot and do not use the institutionalized collective bargaining framework exclusively. Because police unions engage in lobbying, elective politics, referenda campaigns, and other political activities, it seems appropriate to include all such behavior under the label of "police labor relations."

While 18 of 22 of our sample cities have a formalized collective bargaining system through which most union-management contracts are channeled, many significant union-management interactions occur outside the *collective* bargaining system and we refer to this process as *multilateral* bargaining. Governmental multilateral bargaining includes exploiting the divided management authority structure through such processes as public and private lobbying, whereas community multilateral bargaining includes direct involvement or pressure from citizens or community groups in the union-management relationship, including union attempts to secure voter

*National Association of Government Employees.
†Service Employees International Union.

approval of union goals. Unions in cities which have no collective bargaining procedure use the traditional political interest group methods such as public and private lobbying, public relations efforts, and direct appeals to the voters for approval of benefit increases to obtain union goals. Five of the cities in our sample have had experience with the compulsory arbitration of negotiation impasses. We found that in these five cities compulsory arbitration has tended to reduce genuine good faith efforts to reach agreement on the arbitrable issues via the negotiation process.

The Dimensions of Police Union Bargaining Power

Bargaining power is the ability to move your opponent to your way of thinking, usually by showing him that the cost of agreement with your terms is less than the cost of disagreement. In the private sector the cost of disagreement is usually expressed in economic terms through a strike (union) or lockout (employer). In the same vein, since police labor-management relations take place in a political environment, the union's bargaining power consists primarily of the ability to inflict political costs or bestow political rewards. For analytical purposes we distinguish between contextual sources of union power and directly manipulatable sources of union power.

Contextual Sources of Power

The economic context of police bargaining includes four salient variables which may add to or detract from the strength of the union's bargaining position with management, particularly over money items. These are the supply-demand pressures in the local labor market, changes in the cost of living, orbits of coercive comparisons with other visible groups of employees (usually other police or high-wage groups), and the city's ability to pay. While the union can influence supply (through restrictions on hiring standards) or the city's ability to pay (through efforts on behalf of tax proposals) the union does face a relatively fixed economic context at any given point in time.

The statutory context governing police union-management interactions is extremely important. The existence of a statutory provision which requires a city to bargain collectively if a majority of the police desire to do so means that a city can no longer treat employee representatives as supplicants, but instead must negotiate with them as equals.

The political environment in which a police union operates contains three important dimensions which affect the union's power. The first is the balance of political power, or the manner in which the concentration or diffusion of political authority affects the union's ability to increase its bargaining power by allying with various political figures. Second, the emergence of "law and order" politics in the latter 1960s has affected police bargaining power by making it more costly for elected officials to oppose many union demands and thereby appear "anti-police." Third, the political concomitant of the city's ability to pay is the degree of the city's willingness to pay for police services. If city officials accord high priority to funding police services, this willingness is a source of union power. While not directly manipulatable, this latter can be influenced indirectly by union political activity.

The high degree of occupational cohesion in the police service is a source of union power, for it increases membership willingness to agree to and support a course of action.

At any particular point in time a police union must accept as given the quantitative and qualitative natures of the sources of power discussed above (though in the long run, the union can affect these variables). Union leaders, however, have some choice in the application of the sources of power identified below.

Directly Manipulatable Power

A police union's direct sources of power may include: a higher degree of negotiating expertise; the filing of court actions; lobbying (both public and private, with legislative and executive branch officials); electoral politicking (which includes bargaining publicity, issue electoral efforts, candidate electoral efforts, and other efforts designed to change the voters' opinion in favor of the union's goals); disruptive politicking (the ability to actually or convincingly threaten to disrupt the delivery of normal police services to the citizenry, usually through job actions); the ability to enter into long-run alliances with other unions or with politicians; the use of dispute resolution mechanisms (mediation, fact-finding, arbitration); and the use of the power of anticipated reactions (i.e., management's concern for the union's reaction if management pursues a particular course of action). These sources of power are very interrelated: for example, we found situations where one tactic was substituted for another (after an issue's electoral effort failed, the union obtained the desired goals by lobbying in the city council and the state legislature). We also found that the units of police union power are not independent of each other but are more accurately perceived as being arranged in a loose hierarchy. For example, the high level of occupational cohesion, the perceived essentiality of police services, and the police coercive license form the foundation for the exercise of other sources of power. The statutory context may provide the opportunity to engage in collective bargaining or use dispute resolution mechanisms. We found the unions' use of power to be shaped by such variables as the nature of the issue, the relevant political structure (the existing combination of *de jure* and *de facto* governmental decision-making authority), union leader preferences for various courses of action and perceptions of success, and the economic and political costs of using various sources of power. We did not attempt to quantify amounts of power because of the extreme difficulty of devising accurate comparative measures.

Union Impact on the Potential for Professionalization

We found a large variety of opinion among police executives and union leaders regarding the concepts of the police profession, the professional policeman, and the professional police department.

The Concept of Professionalization

The term *profession* refers to an abstract ideal model, which occupations strive to achieve because the attainment of professional status brings with it several rewards. Some of these rewards are monetary but more important, professional status involves a great deal of autonomy in the way in which the occupation carries out its work, i.e., knowledge is assumed to be so specialized that only members of the profession can deal authoritatively with problems in their jurisdiction.

The process of *professionalization* is the achievement of professional status—the extent to which an occupation has achieved the ideal state. We believe that the degree of professionalization can be measured by observing three scales: the extent to which

the locus of specialization is occupational as opposed to individual or organizational; the extent to which the occupation stresses the process by which ends are achieved as well as the ends themselves (and the extent to which the reward structure emphasizes process over product); and the extent to which there exists a body of intellectual knowledge which can be codified and transmitted abstractly. Applying these measures to the police service, we found that the police are still at the beginning of the professionalization process and that it is not clear whether professionalization is the most effective way to achieve the goals of a police agency.

Professionalization and the Police Service

We have defined professionalization as the process of achieving the ideal state of a profession. This is not the definition being used generally in the police service. Rather, we found two other definitions which serve as the object of professionalization efforts: the first is the *struggle for professional status*; the second is the desire for a *professionally led department*.

A professionally led department is one in which efficiency and managerial rationality are emphasized to the exclusion (or attempted exclusion) of politics. The struggle for professional status involves the quest for the trappings of professionalism; e.g., autonomy, professional authority, the power to determine the character and curriculum of the training process.

We found that many of the unions in our sample have systematically frustrated management's quest for professional status. The actions of these unions regarding advanced education, lateral transfer; development of a master patrolman classification, and changes in recruitment standards have been essentially negative and from management's point of view, clearly counterproductive. Police unions appear to see advanced education and master patrolman proposals as wedges to obtain more money for all their members, whereas management sees them as a way of rewarding individual achievement. We classify both of these under the quest for status rather than professionalization because in each case it has yet to be shown that the proposed move would, in fact, lead to increased professionalization. Lateral entry, on the other hand, would represent a move toward increased professionalization in that increased mobility would help to shift the locus of specialization from the organization to the occupation. Here, however, in most cases the unions and management have been opposed and where management was in favor, the union was opposed. The question separating management and the unions on changes in entry requirements is whether such changes should be viewed as *lowering* standards (union position) or introducing the concept of *flexible* standards so as to better meet the goals of the agency (management).

The potential impact of the police union movement may be greatest in achieving the professionalization of police supervisory and managerial personnel. To the extent that unionization will drive a wedge between patrolmen on the one hand and the sergeants, lieutenants, and captains on the other, and force a recognition of their differential responsibilities within the department, this realization may open the door to the type of specialization prerequisite to the professionalization of management in police agencies. However, we are not terribly optimistic in this regard, since the majority of the unions in our sample strongly preferred to have patrolmen and the superior officer ranks in the same bargaining unit and union.

The Impact on the Chief's Ability to Manage

The demands of police unions seem to be consistent with traditional trade union demands regarding wages, hours, and other conditions of work. For all their talk of professionalization, the police appear to be quite indistinguishable from steel workers or auto workers in their on-the-job concerns.

Money Items

Particularly in the area of wages the demands of police unions have been traditional—higher wages, time and a half pay for overtime, compensation for call-in, call-back, and standby, protection against abuse of court-time requirements. The major impact of these wage demands has been to force management to come to grips with the fact that the human resources of the department are not a free commodity but rather a scarce commodity, which in turn requires management to deal with the problem of allocating those scarce resources among competing ends.

Other police union monetary issues include higher pensions, earlier retirement, increased uniform and equipment allowances, increased pay differentials among the various ranks, and in some cases, an attack on police-fire pay parity where fire fighter pay parity is seen as limiting the ability of the police to secure greater benefits for themselves.

Hours and Working Conditions

Some unions have had a substantial impact on scheduling. In cities where management has tried to introduce a fourth shift during the high crime hours of 6 p.m. to 2 a.m. the typical union response has been one of strong resistance. Similarly, some unions have resisted the changing of other shift hours. In several cities unions have sought shorter work weeks. Union demands for paid lunch time, paid roll call time, paid court time, time and a half for overtime, pay for call-in, call-back, and standby, and payment of a night shift differential have all had an impact on management's ability to freely allocate manpower in the traditional manner.

Police unions in our sample have expressed the same kinds of protectionist concerns over working conditions issues as private sector unions. For example, most of the unions in our sample have opposed the civilianization of police department staff and support jobs (clerical, administrative, technical, traffic control) though few of these resistance efforts have been successful. Most policemen and police unions are vehemently opposed to one man police cars; in some cases, union opposition has been successful, while in other cities management has expanded the use of one man cars over union objections.

Seniority is seen by the men as a factor guaranteeing equal opportunity and a hedge against favoritism, and police unions generally have sought to make seniority an important variable in shift and job assignments and a more important factor in promotions. Management has successfully resisted most union efforts for strict seniority provisions but has increased the use of seniority when it did not unduly restrict management's ability to deploy manpower. Police unions have secured a measure of protection for their members against arbitrary transfers; pushed for broad moonlighting rights; resisted the introduction of a requirement to wear name tags on uniforms (in some cities); and objected (largely unsuccessfully) to stricter controls on the use of sick leave. Unions have also resisted departmental reorganization where they did not participate in the planning and implementation of the changes.

With regard to discipline, unions have pressed for

regularizing procedures, minimizing ad hoc decision-making on punishment, and eliminating certain kinds of punishment such as working days off and long suspensions with no right of appeal. Union pressure has tended to make hearing procedures more legalistic than previously and to insure greater attention to the civil rights of officers during investigations, hearings, and appeals.

In sum, police unions have narrowed management discretion, fostered the development of management by policy, and they have protected employees against arbitrary or inconsistent treatment. In a few cases, contractual provisions negotiated between the union and the city have caused serious managerial problems, but the primary union impact has been to force police management to focus greater attention to the needs and wants of policemen and to improve personnel practices within the police department.

Impact on the Formulation of Law Enforcement Policy

The question of what constitutes law enforcement policy is a difficult one. A department has many policies: on prostitution, on use of sick leave, on the number of times squad cars are washed each month. The first is clearly a law enforcement policy issue; the others are administrative policies. A more difficult plan arises when we attempt to classify policies regarding "manning." We discussed manning under the rubric "ability to manage," but the use of civilians, the number of men in a squad car and the number of cars on the street are also an important aspect of law enforcement policy. Conversely, the use of weapons is discussed under law enforcement policy but is also clearly related to the chief's ability to manage. A further complication is the fact that the unions have not so much raised policy issues directly as they have attacked specific issues which have policy implications. Civilian review is opposed because civilians cannot appreciate the street problems of an officer, but the underlying issue is less thoroughly discussed—who will control police behavior, who will make policy.

A final complication in discussing impact on law enforcement policy is the fact that recent court decisions have broadened the rights of public employees in the areas of free speech and participation in elective politics. Both of these developments serve to legitimize the participation of police officers in debates on law enforcement policy and legitimize

their participation in all aspects of the policy making process, thus encouraging the expansion of these kinds of activities.

Issues

We have grouped the objects of police union activity in this area under five issue headings. The five issues and the incidents associated with them are: how is the law to be enforced (calls for 100 percent enforcement of the law, electoral political activity for favored judicial candidates, prosecutors, and others with policy making powers in this area; and impact on entry standards, minority recruitment, and residency requirements); the functioning of the criminal justice system (court watching, the electoral political activity mentioned above); the use of force (number of weapons, type of weapons, conditions under which weapons will be used and review of conditions under which force was used); the involvement of civilians in the review of police actions and behavior (civilian review is an issue in 12 of the 22 cities); and the degree to which a police agency should facilitate identification of police officers where a complaint is filed (name tags, badge numbers painted on riot helmets, officer liability if asked to appear in a line up).

Impact

It is important to distinguish the direct impact of police unions from the indirect impact. On a direct impact level the unions' influence was spotty. The greatest direct impact was on the issue of civilian review where several unions were successful in thwarting implementation of proposed—or elimination of existing—review boards. Other successes were in the areas of lobbying for criminal statutes, electing "law and order" judges, prosecutors and mayors, hampering efforts at flexible standards to encourage minority recruitment, and influencing weapons policy and the use of civilians.

The indirect impact is a much more difficult area with which to deal. While direct impact is observable, in the long run the indirect impact—which is less subject to direct measure—is apt to be the more important implication of the police union movement involvement in policy formulation. One aspect of this is the extent to which the chief and other police officials have failed to take action because of anticipated reactions from the union. A second aspect of indirect impact is the fact that the public statements of police unions on policy issues and their endorsements in political campaigns have tended to contribute to racial polarization in several communities. Thus, while the unions may have valid reasons for opposition to civilian complaint review boards, gun guidelines, coroners' inquest procedures, or Model Cities programs, and while each officer accused of misfeasance or malfeasance deserves a vigorous defense, the fact is that these efforts are perceived as hostile signs in the black community.

The major impact of the union, then, may have come less from direct success in implementing change than it has come indirectly through creation of an environment of tension and through possible frustration of more aggressive behavior by elected officials anticipating the union's response. These specific issues are part of larger political questions: not civilian review but whether the police or civilians will make law enforcement policy; not weapons policy but the question of who determines the conditions under which fatal force will be allowed. The resolution of these issues will not be a function of collective bargaining unless the parties, especially management, make a conscious effort to bring these subjects into the bargaining process. In the absence of such conscious effort, they will remain political issues to be fought out in the political arena.

Black Officer Organizations

We found that black officer organizations exist in almost every city we visited which had more than 25 to 30 black policemen. We talked with organization representatives in eleven cities.

Development, Areas of Concern, Activities

Black police associations in some cities evolved from social and fraternal organizations into "racial rights" organizations and in others they were founded in recent years explicitly to seek satisfaction of racially-based grievances. In either case, the organizations centered their energies on two types of grievances—grievances arising out of the relationships between black officers and white officers and the role of the black officer in the department; and grievances arising out of the relationship between the police agency and the black community.

Complaints on intradepartmental relations included lack of promotional opportunities (vertical segregation), prohibition of blacks from holding cer-

tain jobs (horizontal segregation), blacks being disciplined unjustly, and prejudicial treatment of black officers by white officers. Specific community relations efforts included: recruiting efforts to increase the number of black candidates and classes to prepare candidates for the examination; protesting police mistreatment of prisoners; offering assistance to citizens in filing complaints against police officers; forming alliances with black activist groups in the city and sponsoring athletic, social, and recreational programs for black youth.

We found a wide range of militancy among black officer associations with the degree of militancy being a function of the perceived hostility of the department's managerial hierarchy (including the chief); the perceived hostility of the majority union; association leader preferences (for various courses of action); and the balance of political power within the association between the militant members and the more conservative ones.

Black-White Police Relations

Our evidence suggests that relations between black and white policemen are quite poor, and appear to have become publicly worse in recent years. Why? First, there are many more black policemen than there used to be, thus increasing the frequency of black-white police interaction. Second, most of these recent black entrants are young men whose racial abuse tolerance level is extremely low. Black policemen have become quite willing to fight back at instances of racial injustice, and this aggressiveness has made many white policemen fearful, distrustful, and antagonistic toward black officers.

These poor individual relations have carried over to the relations between the black associations and the white-dominated majority unions. Probably the most important reason for these poor interorganizational relations are union fears that the black associations may be attempting to usurp the unions' exclusive representation role. In addition, white policemen, including union leaders, appear to resent the black associations because these groups have emerged as the vehicles for black officer protest, much of which is directed at the whites.

Despite these fears, we found that in most cities the union fulfills the traditional role of bargaining for economic and noneconomic benefits and pushing traditional grievances (overtime, seniority, transfer, discipline, etc.) for all of its members, while the black officer association concerns itself with the racial grievances of its members and improving police-black community relations. Black policemen appear to be as appreciative as white policemen for union-achieved benefits, yet black interviewees said that white union officers could not properly represent the racial interests of black policemen, and hence the need for black officer associations.

Just as police unionism is primarily a locally-controlled phenomenon, so are black associations mostly local efforts. We encountered two regional and one national organizational amalgamation of local associations which hold occasional meetings to exchange information about their activities and to obtain publicity for their efforts. While originally we had concluded that because of personal differences, limited financial resources, and especially the localized nature of black association operations it might be some time before a national black organization became solidly established, we do note that the National Black Police Association, formed in 1972, has apparently bridged many of these difficulties and brought most of the local and regional associations together in a national organization dedicated to increasing the number and responsibility of black policemen.

Some Concluding Observations

It is our feeling that the major impact of the union has been the creation of a new system of governance in the police agency to which management will have to adapt itself. Adaptation involves two major adjustments. The first deals with the rationalization of the bargaining process and the second with the role of the chief.

Rationalizing the Bargaining Process

The diversity of managerial jurisdictions and the changing constitutional climate regarding free speech and political activity for public employees provide both a motive and an opportunity for police employee organizations to exploit the power potential inherent in the current labor relations process. However, the union incurs two costs in this process: its competition with management in several jurisdictions making bargaining a never-ending process and limiting the extent to which it can effect *quid pro quo* since issues are spread over so many different bargaining arenas. If management were willing to offer a commitment to jointly seek necessary legislative and charter changes necessitated by contractual agreements, and if management were willing to recognize a need to buy out the power advantages which the union was giving up by coming to a centralized bargaining table, some kind of rationalization might be achieved. Management can gauge the cost of buying out this power advantage by considering the advantages it gains, not only in power equalization, but also in the ability to exercise some measure of control over the size and shape of the total employment relations package.

The Role of the Chief

The "traditional" autocratic authority of the chief in personnel matters has been undermined, the victim not only of union pressure but also of the underlying changes in the environment, which give rise to the union—high turnover, a declining average age, the tight labor market of the 1960s and the other factors discussed above. The union's role has been to negotiate a new set of operating rules which move the system toward some new equilibrium positions: management by policy; protection of employees against arbitrary or inconsistent treatment; and the institutionalization of the mechanism of collective bargaining for continuing power based interactions.

This new system of governance not only entails shared decision-making power and review of management personnel decisions, it has also formally removed the sole responsibility for the formulation of personnel policy from the chief's hands to a central labor relations office. To maintain a firm hand the chief will have to play several important roles in the collective bargaining process. Most important he will have to insist on a seat in the policy council of the management bargaining team for himself or his representative. Second, he will have to emphasize the program and capital requirements of his budget so his entire resources are not absorbed in personnel expenses. He will have to advise on what *new* clauses he wants in the contract and which clauses he would like to see revised. He will need to review union proposals for their potential impact on the operation of the department and review management counter-proposals as well. In short, he must insist on an active role in the bargaining process in order to maintain his ability to manage in the "new order."

The Bargaining Process and Law Enforcement Policy

One of the major problems in policing today is "how to be responsive to the majority interest in the community while protecting the rights of minorities." It is in the context of this question that the law enforcement policy issues raised above have real meaning. In our discussion of these issues, or more correctly the manifestations of these issues, we saw how the union, regardless of motivation, was essentially a conservative, reactionary force. We discussed the implications of the impressions these union actions create among members of the minority community, especially minority perceptions of police attitudes toward them.

As we have emphasized, however, this behavior by police employee organizations would not cease if both unionism and collective bargaining were to be outlawed tomorrow. Rather, police employee organizations would continue to utilize the media, the courts, the legislative process, and electoral politics (both issue and candidate oriented) to achieve these same goals. In fact, the addition of collective bargaining to these other channels of communication and action serve to enhance, rather than restrict, the rights of minorities *over the long run*.

Some of the encouraging steps we perceive in the protection of minority rights are the rise of black officer associations; the fact that some racial grievances can be filed in an established grievance procedure (perhaps leading to final and binding arbitration); and the fact that regularized discipline procedures protect blacks and whites. As more minority group members become police officers, and as blacks gain increased political power in our major urban areas, these institutionalized procedures will gain even more significance. Thus, the machinery now being established and utilized for the purposes of the incumbent majority will continue to be utilized for the purposes of the future majority, even as the nature of that majority changes over time.

BIBLIOGRAPHY

Books, Monographs, Government Publications, Unpublished Materials

Alex, Nicholas. *Black in Blue.* New York: Appleton-Century-Crofts, Inc., 1969.

American Bar Association Project on Standards for Criminal Justice. *Standards Relating to the Urban Police Function.* American Bar Association, 1972.

Bakke, E. Wight. *Why Workers Join Unions.* New Haven, Conn.: Yale University, Labor and Management Center, Reprint No. 1, 1946.

Banfield, Edward. *Political Influence.* New York: Free Press, 1961.

Barbash, Jack. *American Unions: Structure, Government, and Politics.* New York: Random House, 1967.

Bennis, Warren and Slater, Phillip. *Temporary Society.* New York: Harper & Row Publishers, Inc., 1969.

Berney, Don. "Law and Order Politics: A History and Role Analysis of Police Officer Organizations." Ph.D. dissertation, University of Washington, 1971.

Bittner, Egon. *The Functions of the Police in Modern Society.* Washington, D.C.: U.S. Government Printing Office, November, 1970.

Bopp, William. *The Police Rebellion: A Quest for Blue Power.* Springfield, Ill.: Charles C. Thomas, Publisher, 1971.

Bordua, David J., ed. *The Police: Six Sociological Essays.* New York: John Wiley and Sons, 1967.

Burpo, John. *The Police Labor Movement.* Springfield, Ill.: Charles C Thomas, Publisher, 1972.

Chamberlain, Neil, and Cullen, Donald. *The Labor Sector.* 2nd ed. New York: McGraw Hill Book Co., Inc., 1971.

Chamberlain, Neil, and Kuhn, James. *Collective Bargaining.* 2nd ed. New York: McGraw-Hill Book Co., Inc., 1965.

Fuess, Claude M. *Calvin Coolidge: The Man From Vermont.* Boston: Little, Brown & Co., 1940.

Gifford, J. P. "The Political Relations of the Patrolmen's Benevolent Association in New York City." Ph.D. dissertation, Columbia University, 1970.

Graham, Fred P. *The Self-Inflicted Wound.* New York: The Macmillan Company, 1970.

Hall, Richard H. *Occupations and the Social Structure.* Englewood Cliffs, N.J.: Prentice-Hall, Inc., 1969.

International Association of Chiefs of Police. *Police Unions.* Washington, D.C.: IACP, 1958.

—— "Report of the Special Committee on Police Employee Organizations." Typescript, 1969.

Kienast, Philip. "Police and Fire Fighter Organizations." Working paper, Michigan State University, 1971.

Kleingartner, Archie. *Professionalism and Salaried Worker Organization.* Madison, Wis.: Industrial Relations Research Institute, University of Wisconsin, 1967.

Kochan, Thomas, "Internal Conflict and Multilateral Bargaining." Manuscript, University of Wisconsin, Industrial Relations Research Institute, 1972.

Labor Management Relations Service. *Public Employee Strikes: Causes and Effects,* No. 7. (No date.)

Mailer, Norman. *Miami and the Siege of Chicago.* New York: Signet Books, 1968.

Maslow, Abraham. *Motivation and Personality.* New York: Harper & Row Publishers, Inc., 1954.

Moskow, Michael; Loewenberg, Joe; and Koziara, Ed. *Collective Bargaining in Public Employment.* New York: Random House, Inc., 1970.

Niederhoffer, Arthur. *Behind the Shield: The Police in Urban Society.* Garden City, N.Y.: Doubleday & Co., Inc., 1967.

President's Commission on Law Enforcement and Administration of Justice. *The Challenge of Crime in a Free Society.* Washington, D.C.: U.S. Government Printing Office, 1967.

——. *Task Force Report: The Police.* Washington, D.C.: U.S. Government Printing Office, 1967.

"Public Education" in Seymour Wolfbein, ed. *Emerging Sectors of Collective Bargaining.* Braintree, Mass.: D. H. Mark, 1970.

Purcell, Theodore. *The Worker Speaks His Mind on Company and Union.* Cambridge, Mass.: Harvard University Press, 1953.

Rees, Albert. *The Economics of Trade Unions.* Chicago: University of Chicago Press, 1962.

Reiss, Albert. *Police and the Public.* New Haven: Yale University Press, 1971.

Rose, Arnold. *Union Solidarity: The Internal Cohesion of a Labor Union.* Minneapolis: University of Minnesota Press, 1952.

Saunders, Charles B., Jr. *Upgrading the American Police.* Washington, D.C.: Brookings Institution, 1970.

Sayles, Leonard, and Strauss, George. *The Local Union.* New York: Harper & Row Publishers, Inc., 1953.

Schweppe, Emma. *The Firemen's and Patrolmen's Unions in the City of New York.* New York: King's Crown Press, 1948.

Seidman, Joel, et al. *The Worker Views His Union.* Chicago: University of Chicago Press, 1958.

Skolnick, Jerome. *Justice Without Trial.* New York: John Wiley & Sons, Inc., 1966.

——. *The Politics of Protest.* New York: Simon and Schuster, 1969, Ballantine Book Edition (paper).

Slichter, Sumner; Livernash, Robert; and Healy, James. *The Impact of Collective Bargaining on Management.* Washington, D.C.: Brookings Institution, 1960.

Spero, Sterling. *Government as Employer.* New York: Remsen Press, 1948.

Stanley, David. *Managing Local Government Under Union Pressure.* Washington, D.C.: Brookings Institution, 1972.

Tannenbaum, Arnold, and Kahn, Robert. *Participation in Union Locals.* Evanston, Ill.: Row, Peterson and Co., 1958.

Truman, David B. *The Governmental Process.* New York: Alfred A. Knopf, Inc., 1964.

Vollmer, Howard M., and Mills, Donald L., eds. *Professionalization.* Englewood Cliffs, N.J.: Prentice-Hall, Inc., 1966.

Walton, Richard, and McKersie, Robert. *A Behavioral Theory of Labor Negotiations.* New York: McGraw-Hill Book Co., Inc. 1965.

Wellington, Harry, and Winter, Ralph. *The Unions and the Cities.* Washington, D.C.: Brookings Institution, 1971.

Westley, William A. "The Police: A Sociological Study of Law, Custom and Morality." Ph.D. dissertation, University of Chicago, 1951.

Wilson, James Q. *Varieties of Police Behavior.* New York: McGraw-Hill Book Co., Inc., 1968.

Wilson, O. W. *Police Administration.* 2nd ed. New York: McGraw-Hill Book Co., 1963.

Articles and Periodicals

Adams, I. S., and Rosenbaum, W. E. "The Relationship of Worker Productivity to Cognitive Dissonance About Inequities," *Journal of Applied Psychology, 46* (1962), pp. 161–64.

"American Youth: Its Outlook Is Changing the World," *Fortune, 79,* 1 (January 1969).

Andrews, I. R. "Wage Inequity and Job Performance: An Experimental Study," *Journal of Applied Psychology, 51* (1967), pp. 39–45.

Ashenfelter, Orley, and Pencavel, John. "American Trade Union Growth: 1900–1960," *Quarterly Journal of Economics, 83,* 3 (August 1969), pp. 434–48.

Burton, John F. "Local Government Bargaining and Management Structure," *Industrial Relations, 11,* 2 (May 1972), pp. 123–40.

Burton, John, and Krider, Charles. "The Role and Consequences of Strikes by Public Employees," *Yale Law Journal,* 69 (January 1970).

Cook, Alice. "Public Employee Bargaining in New York City," *Industrial Relations,* 9, 3 (May 1970), p. 267.

Dahl, Robert. "The Concept of Power," *Behavioral Science,* 2, 3 (July 1957), pp. 201–15.

———. "A Critique of the Ruling Elite Model," *The American Political Science Review,* 52, 2 (June 1958), pp. 463–469.

Duncan, Robert B. "The Climate for Change in Three Police Departments: Some Implications for Action," *Fourth National Symposium on Law Enforcement Science and Technology* (Washington, D.C., May 2, 1972).

Edelman, Murray. "Concepts of Power," *Proceedings of the 1958 Spring Meeting of the Industrial Relations Research Association.* Reprinted in *Labor Law Journal,* 9, 9 (September 1958), p. 627.

Eszterhas, Joseph. "Police Unions Are Reaching for More," *Cleveland Plain Dealer* (August 24, 1969).

"The First Amendment and Public Employees: *Times* Marches On," *Georgetown Law Review,* 57 (1969), p. 134.

Friedman, A., and Goodman, P., "Wage Inequity, Self-Qualifications, and Productivity." *Organizational Behavior and Human Performance,* 2 (1967), pp. 406–17.

Gerhart, Paul. "The Scope of Bargaining in Local Government Labor Negotiations," *Industrial Relations Research Association, Proceedings of the 1969 Spring Meeting, Labor Law Journal,* 20, 8 (August 1969), pp. 545–52.

Gilroy, Thomas P., and Sinicropi, Anthony V. "Impasse Resolution in Public Employment: A Current Assessment," *Industrial and Labor Relations Review,* 25, 4 (July 1972).

Greenwood, Ernest. "Attributes of a Profession," *Social Work,* 2, 3 (July 1957) pp. 45–55.

Groves, W. E., and Rossi, Peter. "Police Perceptions of a Hostile Ghetto," *American Behavioral Scientist,* 13, 5 and 6 (May–June, July–August, 1970).

Hildebrand, George. "The Public Sector," in Dunlop, John, and Chamberlain, Neil, eds. *Frontiers of Collective Bargaining.* New York: Harper & Row, Publishers, Inc., 1967, p. 152.

Juris, Hervey. "The Implications of Police Unionism," *Law and Society Review,* 6, 2 (November 1971), pp. 231–45.

———. "Police Personnel Problems, Police Unions, and Participatory Management," *Proceedings of the 22nd Annual Winter Meeting* (Industrial Relations Research Association, Madison, Wis., 1969), p. 318.

Juris, Hervey, and Hutchison, Kay. "The Legal Status of Municipal Police Employee Organizations," *Industrial and Labor Relations Review,* 23, 3 (April 1970), pp. 352–66.

Karson, Marc. "The Psychology of Trade Union Membership," *Mental Hygiene,* 41, 1 (January 1957).

Kelling, George, and Kliesmet, Robert. "Resistance to the Professionalization of the Police," *Police Chief* (May 1971), p. 35.

Krinsky, Edward. "Public Employment Fact-Finding in Fourteen States," *Labor Law Journal,* 17, 9 (September 1966), pp. 532–40.

Lawler, E. E., and O'Gara, P. W. "Effects of Inequity Produced by Underpayment on Work Output, Work Quality, and Attitudes Toward the Work," *Journal of Applied Psychology,* 51 (1967), pp. 403–10.

Levy, Burton. "Cops in the Ghetto: A Problem of the Police System," *American Behavioral Scientist* (March–April, 1968).

Long, Norton. "The City as Reservation," *Public Interest* (Fall 1971).

Lyons, Richard L. "The Boston Police Strike of 1919," *The New England Quarterly,* 20, 2 (June 1947).

McLennan, Kenneth, and Moskow, Michael H. "Multilateral Bargaining in the Public Sector," *Proceedings of the Twenty-First Annual Meeting* (Industrial Relations Research Association, Madison, Wis., 1969).

McNamara, John H. "Uncertainties in Police Work: The Relevance of Police Recruits' Backgrounds and Training," in Bordua, David J., ed. *The Police: Six Sociological Essays.* New York: John Wiley & Sons, Inc., 1967.

Mondello, Anthony. "The Federal Employee's Right to Speak," *Civil Service Journal* (January–March, 1970), pp. 16–21.

Oakland Police Officers Association. *Call Box,* 1, 4, 5 (April and May, 1972).

"Permissiveness is the *seed cancer to the destruction of our society,*" Fraternal Order of Police, Fort Pitt Lodge No. 1, *The Manchester Incident: A Report.* Pittsburgh, Pa., 1970.

Reichley, A. James. "The Way to Cool the Police Rebellion," *Fortune,* 78, 7 (December 1968), pp. 109–14.

Russell, Francis. "The Strike That Made a President," *American Heritage,* 14, 6 (October 1963).

San Francisco Police Officers Association. *Notebook* (January 1972).

Scott, W. Richard. "Reactions to Supervision in a Heteronomous Professional Organization,"

Administrative Science Quarterly, *20*, 1 (June 1965), pp. 65–81.

Sheehan, Robert. "Lest We Forget," *Police*, Part 1 (September–October, 1959) and Part 2 (November–December, 1959).

Simon, Herbert A. "Notes on the Observation and Measurement of Political Power," *The Journal of Politics*, *15*, 4 (November 1953), pp. 500–16.

Stern, James L. "The Wisconsin Public Employee Fact Finding Procedure," *Industrial and Labor Relations Review*, *20*, 1 (October 1966), pp. 3–29.

Stieber, Jack. "Collective Bargaining in the Public Sector," in Ulman, Lloyd, ed. *Challenges to Collective Bargaining*. Englewood Cliffs, N.J.: Prentice-Hall, Inc., 1967.

Weber, Arnold R. "Stability and Change in the Structure of Collective Bargaining," in Ulman, Lloyd, ed. *Challenges to Collective Bargaining*. Englewood Cliffs, N.J.: Prentice-Hall, Inc., 1967.

——. "Paradise Lost; or Whatever Happened to the Chicago Social Workers?" *Industrial and Labor Relations Review*, *22*, 3 (April 1969), p. 335.

White, Sheila. "Work Stoppages of Government Employees," *Monthly Labor Review*, *92*, 12 (December 1969), p. 30.

Selected Bibliography

Abernathy, M. Glenn. *Civil Liberties and the Constitution.* New York: Dodd, Mead, 1968.

Abraham, Henry J. *The Judicial Process: An Introductory Analysis of the Courts of the United States, England, and France.* 2nd ed. New York: Oxford University Press, 1968.

Abrahamsen, David. *Our Violent Society.* New York: Funk and Wagnalls, 1970.

Adams, Thomas F. *Law Enforcement: An Introduction to the Police Role in the Community.* Englewood Cliffs, N.J.: Prentice-Hall, Inc., 1968.

Adams, Thomas F. *Police Patrol Tactics and Techniques.* Englewood Cliffs, N.J.: Prentice-Hall, Inc., 1971.

Ahern, James F. *Police in Trouble.* New York: Hawthorne Books, 1971.

Albini, Joseph L. *The American Mafia: Genesis of a Legend.* New York: Appleton-Century-Crofts, 1972.

Alderson, J. C., and Stead, Philip John, eds. *The Police We Deserve.* London: Wolfe Publishing Ltd., 1973.

Alex, Nicholas. *Black in Blue.* New York: Appleton-Century-Crofts, 1969.

Allen, Francis A. *The Borderland of Criminal Justice: Essays on Law and Criminology.* Chicago: University of Chicago Press, 1964.

Allen, Richard C.; Ferster, Elyce Zenoff; and Rubin, Jesse G., eds. *Readings in Law and Psychiatry.* Baltimore: Johns Hopkins Press, 1968.

Alsop, Kenneth. *The Bootleggers and Their Era.* Garden City, N.Y.: Doubleday, 1962.

American Bar Association Project on Standards for Criminal Justice. *Standards Relating to the Urban Police Function.* Chicago: American Bar Association, 1973.

American Friends Service Committee. *Struggle for Justice.* New York: Hill and Wang, 1971.

Ardrey, Robert. *The Territorial Imperative.* New York: Atheneum, 1966.

Arendt, Hannah. *Eichmann in Jerusalem.* New York: Viking Press, 1963.

——. *On Revolution.* New York: Viking Press, 1963.

Arens, Richard. *Insanity Defense.* New York: Philosophical Library, 1974.

Arens, Richard, and Lasswell, Harold D. *In Defense of Public Order: The Emerging Field of Sanction Law.* New York: Columbia University Press, 1961.

Asbury, Herbert. *The Gangs of New York.* New York: Alfred A. Knopf, Inc., 1928.

Asch, Sidney H. *Police Authority and the Rights of the Individual.* New York: Arco Books, Inc., 1971.

Astor, Gerald. *The New York Cops.* New York: Scribners, 1971.

Aubert, Vilhelm. *The Hidden Society.* Totowa, N.J.: Bedminster Press, 1965.

Backer, Harold K. *Issues in Police Administration.* Metuchen, N.J.: Scarecrow Press, 1970.

Bacon, Selden D. "The Early Development of American Municipal Police: A Study of the Evolution of Formal Control in a Changing Society." Ph.D. dissertation, Yale University, New Haven, 1939.

Baker, Joseph. *The Law of Political Uniforms, Public Meetings and Private Armies.* London: H.J. Just, 1937.

Balbus, Isaac D. *The Dialectics of Legal Repression.* New York: Russell Sage Foundation, 1973.

Ball, John C., and Chambers, Carl C., eds. *The Epidemiology of Opiate Addiction in the United States.* Springfield, Ill.: Charles C. Thomas, 1971.

Bandura, Albert. *Principles of Behavior Modification.* New York: Holt, Rinehart and Winston, 1969.

Banton, Michael. *The Policeman in the Community.* New York: Basic Books, 1964.

Banton, Michael. *Police Community Relations.* London: William Collins Sons and Co. Ltd., 1973.

Barron, Milton L. *The Juvenile in Delinquent Society.* New York: Alfred A. Knopf, Inc., 1960.

Barth, Alan. *Law Enforcement Versus the Law.* New York: Collier Books, 1963.

Bayley, David H. *The Police and Political Development in India.* Princeton, N.J.: Princeton University Press, 1969.

Bayley, David H., and Mendelsohn, Harold. *Minorities and the Police.* New York: Free Press, 1969.

Becker, Harold K. *Law Enforcement: A Selected Bibliography.* Metuchen, N.J.: Scarecrow Press, 1968.

Becker, Howard S. *Outsiders: Studies in the Sociology of Deviance.* New York: Free Press, 1963.

Bedford, Sybille. *The Trial of Dr. Adams.* New York: Simon & Schuster, 1958.

Bell, Daniel. *The End of Ideology.* New York: The Macmillan Co., 1958.

Belli, Melvin. *Dallas Justice.* New York: David McKay, 1964.

Belson, William A. *The Public and the Police.* London: Harper & Row, 1975.

Bent, Alan Edward. *The Politics of Law Enforcement.* Lexington, Mass.: D.C. Heath and Company, 1974.

Berger, Monroe. *Equality by Statute: The Revolution in Civil Rights.* Rev. ed. Garden City, N.Y.: Doubleday, 1967.

Berger, Peter. *Invitation to Sociology: A Humanistic Perspective.* Garden City, N.Y.: Doubleday, 1963.

Berger, Peter, and Luckman, Thomas. *The Social Construction of Reality.* Garden City, N.Y.: Doubleday, 1966.

Berkley, George E. *The Democratic Policeman.* Boston: Beacon Press, 1969.

Bianchi, Hermanus. *Position and Subject Matter of Criminology: Inquiry Concerning Theoretical Criminology.* Amsterdam: North Holland, 1956.

Bird, Otto A. *The Idea of Justice.* New York: Praeger, 1967.

Bittner, Egon. *The Function of the Police in Modern Society.* Washington, D.C.: U.S. Government Printing Office, 1970.

Black, Algernon D. *The People and the Police.* New York: McGraw-Hill, 1968.

Black, Charles L., Jr. *Capital Punishment: The Inevitability of Caprice and Mistake.* New York: Dell Publishing, 1970.

Blake, James. *The Joint.* New York: Dell Publishing, 1970.

Bloch, Herbert A., and Geis, Gilbert. *Man, Crime and Society.* New York: Random House, 1970.

Bloch, Herbert A., and Niederhoffer, Arthur. *The Gang.* New York: Philosophical Library, 1958.

Block, Peter B., Anderson, Deborah. *Policewomen On Patrol.* Washington, D.C.: Police Foundation, 1974.

Blum, Richard H., ed. *Police Selection.* Springfield, Ill.: Charles C. Thomas, 1964.

Blumberg, Abraham S. "The Criminal Court: An Organizational Analysis." Ph.D. dissertation, New School for Social Research, 1965.

Blumberg, Abraham S. *Criminal Justice.* Chicago: Quadrangle Books, 1967.

Blumberg, Abraham S., ed. *Law and Order.* 2nd ed. New York: E.P. Dutton, 1973.

Blumberg, Abraham S., ed. *Perspectives on Criminal Behavior.* New York: Alfred A. Knopf, Inc., 1974.

Bonsignore, John J., et al. *Before the Law: An Introduction to the Legal Process.* Boston: Houghton-Mifflin Co., 1974.

Bopp, William J. *The Police Rebellion.* Springfield, Ill.: Charles C. Thomas, 1971.

Bordua, David J. *The Police: Six Sociological Essays.* New York: John Wiley and Sons, 1967.

Boskin, Joseph. *Urban Racial Violence in the Twentieth Century.* Beverly Hills: Glencoe Press, 1969.

Bouza, Anthony. *The Operation of a Police Intelligence Unit.* Unpublished M.A. Thesis. John Jay College of Criminal Justice, CUNY, 1968.

Brakel, Samuel J. *Judicare.* Chicago: American Bar Foundation, 1974.

Bramsted, Ernest J. *Dictatorship and Political Police.* London: Routledge and Kegan Paul, 1945.

Brandstatter, A.F., and Hyman, Allen A. *Fundamentals of Law Enforcement.* Beverly Hills, Calif.: Glencoe Press, 1971.

Brant, Irving. *The Bill of Rights: Its Origin and Meaning.* New York: Mentor Books, 1967.

Brecher, Edward M., et al. *Licit and Illicit Drugs.* Boston: Little, Brown & Co., 1972.

Bromberg, Walter. *Crime and the Mind.* New York: Funk and Wagnalls, 1968.

Brown, Claude. *Manchild in the Promised Land.* New York: The Macmillan Co., 1965.

Brown, Wenzell. *Women Who Died in the Chair.* New York: Collier Books, 1963.

Bryant, Clifton D., ed. *Deviant Behavior: Occupational and Organizational Bases.* Chicago: Rand McNally & Co., 1974.

Buisson, Henry. *La Police, Son Histoire*. Paris: Nouvelles Editions Latines, 1958.

Burpo, John H. *The Police Labor Movement: Problems and Perspectives*. Springfield, Ill.: Charles C. Thomas, 1971.

Caffi, Andrea. *A Critique of Violence*. New York: Bobbs-Merrill, 1970.

Cain, Maureen E. *Society and the Policeman's Role*. London: Routledge and Kegan Paul, 1973.

Cardozo, Benjamin. *The Nature of the Judicial Process*. New Haven: Yale University Press, 1931.

Carlin, Jerome E.; Howard, Jan; and Messinger, Sheldon L. *Civil Justice and the Poor: Issues for Sociological Research*. New York: Russell Sage Foundation, 1967.

Carmichael, Stokely, and Hamilton, Charles. *Black Power: The Politics of Liberation in America*. New York: Vintage Books, 1967.

Carney, Frank J.; Mattick, Hans W.; and Callaway, John D. *Action on the Streets: A Handbook for Inner City Youth Work*. New York: Association Press, 1969.

Casper, Jonathan D. *American Criminal Justice: The Defendant's Perspective*. Englewood Cliffs, N.J.: Prentice-Hall, Inc., 1972.

Chambliss, William J. *Crime and the Legal Process*. New York: McGraw-Hill, 1969.

Chambliss, William J., ed. *Criminal Law in Action*. Santa Barbara, Calif.: Hamilton Publishing Co., 1975.

Chambliss, William J., and Seidman, Robert B. *Law, Order, and Power*. Reading, Mass.: Addison-Wesley Publ., 1971.

Chapman, Brian. *Police State*. New York: Praeger, 1970.

Chapman, Samuel G. *The Police Heritage in England and America*. East Lansing, Mich.: Michigan State University Press, 1962.

Chevigny, Paul. *Cops and Rebels*. New York: Pantheon Books, 1972.

———. *Police Power: Police Abuses in New York City*. New York: Pantheon Books, 1969.

Cicourel, Aaron V. *The Social Organization of Juvenile Justice*. New York: John Wiley and Sons, 1968.

Cipes, Robert M. *The Crime War*. New York: New American Library, 1968.

Citizens Research and Investigation Committee and Tackwood, Louis E. *The Glass House Tapes*. New York: Avon Books, 1973.

Clark, Kenneth B. *Dark Ghetto*. New York: Harper & Row, 1965.

Clark, Ramsey. *Crime in America*. New York: Simon & Schuster, 1970.

Clegg, Reed K. *Probation and Parole*. Springfield, Ill.: Charles C Thomas, 1964.

Clinard, Marshall B. *Sociology of Deviant Behavior*. 4th ed. New York: Holt, Rinehart and Winston, 1968.

Clinard, Marshall B., and Abbott, Daniel J. *Crime in Developing Countries: A Comparative Perspective*. New York: John Wiley and Sons, 1973.

Clinard, Marshall B., and Quinney, Richard. *Criminal Behavior Systems*. 2nd ed. New York: Holt, Rinehart and Winston, 1973.

Cloward, Richard A., and Ohlin, Lloyd E. *Delinquency and Opportunity*. New York: Free Press, 1960.

Coffey, Alan; Eldefonso, Edward; and Hartinger, Walter. *Police-Community Relations*. Englewood Cliffs, N.J.: Prentice-Hall, Inc. 1971.

Cohen, Albert K. *Deviance and Control*. Englewood Cliffs, N.J.: Prentice-Hall, Inc., 1966.

Cohen, Robert, et al., eds. *Working with Police Agencies*. New York: Human Sciences Press, 1975.

Cole, George F. *Criminal Justice: Law and Politics*. Belmont, Calif.: Duxbury Press, 1972.

Cole, Hubert. *Fouche: The Unprincipled Patriot*. New York: The McCall Publishing Co., 1971.

Conklin, John E. *Robbery and the Criminal Justice System*. Philadelphia: J. B. Lippincott Co., 1972.

Conklin, John E., ed. *The Crime Establishment*. Englewood Cliffs, N.J.: Prentice-Hall, Inc., 1973.

Conklin, John E. *The Impact of Crime*. New York: The Macmillan Co., 1975.

Connors, Bernard. *Don't Embarrass the Bureau*. New York: Bobbs-Merrill Co., Inc., 1972.

Conot, Robert. *Rivers of Blood, Years of Darkness*. New York: Bantam Books, 1967.

Cook, Fred J. *The FBI Nobody Knows*. New York: The Macmillan Co., 1964.

———. *The Corrupted Land*. New York: The Macmillan Co., 1966.

———. *The Secret Rulers*. New York: Duell, Sloan and Pearce, 1966.

Cowan, Paul; Egleson, Nick; and Hentoff, Nat. *State Secrets: Police Surveillance in America*. New York: Holt, Rinehart and Winston, 1974.

Cramer, James. *The World's Police*. London: Cassell, 1964.

Cray, Ed. *The Big Blue Line*. New York: Coward-McCann, 1967.

Cray, Ed. *The Enemy in the Streets: Police Malpractice in America*. New York: Doubleday/Anchor Books, 1972.

Creamer, J. Shane. *The Law of Arrest, Search and Seizure*. 2nd ed. Philadelphia: W.B. Saunders Company, 1975.

Cressey, Donald R. *Theft of the Nation*. New York: Harper & Row, 1969.

Cressey, Donald R., and Ward, David A. *Delinquency, Crime, and Social Process*. New York: Harper & Row, 1969.

Critchley, Thomas A. *A History of Police in England and Wales*. 2nd ed. Montclair, N.J.: Patterson Smith, 1972.

Curran, James T.; Fowler, Austin; and Ward, Richard H., eds., with intro. *Police and Law Enforcement*. New York: AMS Press, Inc., 1973.

Curran, William J. *Law and Medicine*. Boston: Little, Brown & Co., 1960.

Dahl, Robert A. *Pluralist Democracy in the United States: Conflict and Consent*. Chicago: Rand McNally & Co., 1967.

Darrow, Clarence. *The Story of My Life*. New York: Scribners, 1934.

Dash, Samuel; Knowlton, Robert; and Schwartz, Richard. *The Eavesdroppers*. New Brunswick, N.J.: Rutgers University Press, 1959.

Deacon, Richard. *A History of the Russian Secret Police*. New York: Toplinger Publishing Co., Inc., 1972.

Decrow, Karen. *Sexist Justice*. New York: Vintage/Random House, 1975.

DeGrazia, Sebastian. *The Political Community: A Study of Anomie*. Chicago: University of Chicago Press, 1966.

Denisoff, R. Serge, ed. *The Sociology of Dissent*. New York: Harcourt, Brace, Jovanovich, Inc., 1974.

Denisoff, R. Serge, and McCaghy, Charles H. *Deviance, Conflict, and Criminality*. Chicago: Rand McNally & Co., 1973.

Dernfeld. Duane. *Street-wise Criminology*. Cambridge, Mass.: Schenkman Publishing Co., 1974.

DeRopp, Robert S. *Drugs and the Mind*. New York: Grove Press, 1961.

de Toledano, Ralph J. *Edgar Hoover: The Man and His Times*. New Rochelle, N.Y.: Arlington House, 1973.

Deutsch, Albert. *The Trouble with Cops*. New York: Crown Publishers, 1955.

Devlin, Patrick. *The Enforcement of Morals*. New York: Oxford University Press, 1965.

Donnelly, Richard; Goldstein, J.; and Schwartz, Richard D. *Criminal Law*. New York: Free Press, 1962.

Douglas, Jack D., ed. *Deviance and Respectability*. New York: Basic Books, 1970.

Dreyer, Peter. *The Future of Treason*. New York: Ballantine Books, 1973.

Durkheim, Emile. *The Rules of Sociological Method*. New York: Free Press, 1964.

Duster, Troy. *The Legislation of Morality: Drugs and Moral Judgment*. New York: Free Press, 1970.

Earle, Howard H. *Police-Community Relations: Crisis in Our Time*. 2nd ed. Springfield, Ill.: Charles C Thomas, 1970.

Easton, David. *The Political System*. New York: Alfred A. Knopf, Inc., 1953.

Eidelberg, Paul. *The Philosophy of the American Constitution: A Reinterpretation of the Intentions of the Founding Fathers*. New York: Free Press, 1968.

Eisenstein, James. *Politics and the Legal Process*. New York: Harper & Row, 1973.

Eisner, Victor. *The Delinquency Label*. New York: Random House, 1968.

Eldefonso, Edward. *Youth Problems and Law Enforcement*. Englewood Cliffs, N.J.: Prentice-Hall, Inc., 1972.

Elliott, J. F., and Sardeno, Thomas J. *Crime Control Team: An Experiment in Municipal Police Department Management and Operations*. Springfield, Ill.: Charles C Thomas, 1971.

Elton, G. R. *Policy and Police: The Enforcement of the Reformation in the Age of Cromwell*. London: Cambridge University Press, 1972.

Emerson, Robert M. *Judging Delinquents: Context and Process in Juvenile Court*. Chicago: Aldine, 1969.

Endleman, Shalom. *Violence in the Streets*. Chicago: Quadrangle Books, 1970.

Erikson, Kai T. *Wayward Puritans*. New York: John Wiley and Sons, 1966.

Ernst, Morris L., and Schwartz, Alan U. *Privacy: The Right to Be Let Alone*. New York: The Macmillan Co., 1962.

Falk, Richard A. *Legal Order in a Violent World*. Princeton, N.J.: Princeton University Press, 1968.

Faralicq, Rene. *The French Police from Within.* London: Cassell, 1933.

Feifer, George. *Justice in Moscow.* New York: Simon & Schuster, 1964.

Ferri, Enrico. *Criminal Sociology.* New York: Appleton, 1896.

Fiddle, Seymour. *Portraits from a Shooting Gallery.* New York: Harper & Row, 1967.

Filstead, William J., ed. *An Introduction to Deviance.* Chicago: Markham Publishing Co., 1972.

Fiammong, C. J. *The Police and the Underprotected Child.* Springfield, Ill.: Charles C. Thomas, 1970.

Fontana, Vincent J. *The Maltreated Child.* Springfield, Ill.: Charles C Thomas, 1964.

Ford, Gerald R., and Stiles, John R. *Portrait of the Assassin.* New York: Simon & Schuster, 1965.

Fosdick, Raymond B. *American Police Systems.* Montclair, N.J.: Patterson Smith, 1972.

Fosdick, Raymond B. *European Police Systems.* Montclair, N.J.: Patterson Smith, 1972.

Frank, Jerome. *Courts on Trial.* Princeton, N.J.: Princeton University Press, 1949.

Frankfurter, Felix. *The Case of Sacco and Vanzetti.* Boston: Little, Brown & Co., 1927.

Franklin, Charles. *The Third Degree.* London: Robert Hale and Co., 1970.

Freund, Paul A. *On Law and Justice.* Cambridge, Mass.: Harvard University Press, 1968.

Friedlander, C.P., and Mitchell, E. *The Police: Servants or Masters?* London: Hart-Dairs, 1974.

Friendly, Alfred, and Goldfarb, Ronald. *Crime and Publicity.* New York: Twentieth Century Fund, 1967.

Fuller, Lon L. *The Morality of Law.* New Haven, Conn.: Yale University Press, 1964.

Gammage, Allen Z., and Hemphill, Charles F. *Basic Criminal Law.* New York: McGraw-Hill, 1974.

Garbus, Martin. *Ready for the Defense.* New York: Avon Books, 1971.

Gardner, Erle Stanley. *Cops on Campus and Crime in the Streets.* New York: William Morrow, 1970.

Gardner, Thomas J. *Principles and Cases of the Law of Arrest, Search, and Seizure.* New York: McGraw-Hill, 1974.

Geis, Gilbert, ed. *White Collar Criminal.* New York: Atherton Press, 1968.

Gellhorn, Walter. *Ombudsmen and Others: Citizen Protectors in Nine Countries.* Cambridge, Mass.: Harvard University Press, 1966.

Germann, A.C.; Day, Frank D.; and Gallati, Robert R. J. *Introduction to Law Enforcement.* Springfield, Ill.: Charles C Thomas, 1962.

Gibbons, Don C. *Society, Crime, and Criminal Careers.* 2nd ed. Englewood Cliffs, N.J.: Prentice-Hall, Inc., 1973.

Gladwin, Irene. *The Sheriff: The Man and His Office.* London: Victor Gollancz Ltd., 1974.

Glaser, Daniel, ed. *Crime in the City.* New York: Harper & Row, 1970.

Glaser, Daniel, ed. *Handbook of Criminology.* Chicago: Rand McNally & Co., 1974.

Goffman, Erving. *Stigma.* Englewood Cliffs, N.J.: Prentice-Hall, Inc., 1963.

Goldfarb, Ronald. *Ransom.* New York: Harper & Row, 1965.

Goldfarb, Ronald. *Jails.* Garden City, N.Y.: Anchor Press/Doubleday, 1975.

Goldfarb, Ronald, and Singer, Linda R. *After Conviction.* New York: Simon & Schuster, 1973.

Goldsmith, Jack, and Goldsmith, Sharon S., eds. *The Police Community.* Pacific Palisades, Calif.: Palisades Publishers, 1974.

Goldstein, Abraham S. *The Insanity Defense.* New Haven, Conn.: Yale University Press, 1967.

Goldstein, Herman. *Police Corruption:* A Perspective on Its Nature and Control. Washington, D.C.: Police Foundation, 1975.

Goldstein, Joseph; Dershowitz, Alan M.; and Schwartz, Richard D. *Criminal Law: Theory and Process.* New York: Free Press, 1974.

Gooberman, Lawrence A. *Operation Intercept: The Multiple Consequences of Public Policy.* New York: Pergamon Press, Inc., 1974.

Goode, Erich. *Drugs in American Society.* New York: Alfred A. Knopf, Inc., 1972.

——. *The Marijuana Smokers.* New York: Basic Books, 1970.

Gourley, G. Douglas. *Effective Municipal Police Organization.* Beverly Hills, Calif.: Glencoe Press, 1971.

Graham, Hugh Davis, and Gurr, Ted Robert, eds. *Violence in America: Historical and Comparative Perspectives.* New York: Bantam Books, 1969.

Grant, Douglas. *The Thin Blue Line.* London: John Lang Ltd., 1973.

Greenwald, Harold. *The Call Girl.* New York: Ballantine Books, 1958.

Griffiths, Percival. *To Guard My People: The History of the Indian Police.* London: Ernest Benn Ltd., 1971.

Gross, Bertram, ed. *A Great Society?* New York: Basic Books, 1968.

Guenther, Anthony L., ed. *Criminal Behavior and Social Systems: Contributions of American*

Sociology. New York:' Rand McNally & Co., 1973.

Hahn, Harlan, ed. *Police in Urban Society.* Beverly Hills, Calif.: Sage Publications, 1971.

Hall, Jerome. *Theft, Law and Society.* 2nd ed. Indianapolis, Ind.: Bobbs-Merrill, 1952.

Halleck, Seymour L. *Psychiatry and the Dilemmas of Crime.* New York: Harper & Row, 1967.

Hamilton, Alastair. *The Appeal of Fascism.* New York: Discus/Avon, 1971.

Hansen, David A. and Culley, Thomas R. *The Police Leader.* Springfield, Ill.: Charles C Thomas, 1971.

Harris, Richard N. *The Police Academy: An Inside View.* New York: John Wiley and Sons, 1973.

Hart, H. L. A. *Law, Liberty and Morality.* Stanford, Calif.: Stanford University Press, 1963.

———. *Punishment and Responsibility: Essays in the Philosophy of Law.* New York: Oxford University Press, 1967.

Hart, J. M. *The British Police.* London: Allen and Unwin, 1951.

Hartjen, Clayton A. *Crime and Criminalization.* New York: Praeger, 1974.

Hartogs, Renatus, and Artzt, Eric, eds. *Violence: Causes and Solutions.* New York: Dell Publishing, 1970.

Haskell, Martin R., and Yablonsky, Lewis. *Juvenile Delinquency.* Chicago: Rand McNally College Publ. Co., 1974.

Heffernan, Esther. *Making It in Prison.* New York: John Wiley and Sons, Inc., 1972.

Henry, Andrew F., and Short, James F., Jr. *Suicide and Homicide.* New York: Free Press, 1964.

Herman, Robert D., ed. *Gambling.* New York: Harper & Row, 1967.

Hersey, John. *The Algiers Motel Incident.* New York: Alfred A. Knopf, Inc., 1968.

Hess, Henner. *Mafia and Mafiosi: The Structure of Power.* Lexington, Mass.: D. C. Heath and Co., 1973.

Hewitt, William and Newman, Charles L. *Police-Community Relations: An Anthology and a Bibliography.* Mineola, N.Y.: Foundation Press, 1970.

Hewitt, William H. *British Police Administration.* Springfield, Ill.: Charles C Thomas, 1965.

———. *A Bibliography of Police Administration, Public Safety and Criminology.* Springfield, Ill.: Charles C Thomas, 1967.

Hingley, Ronald. *The Russian Secret Police.* New York: Simon & Schuster, 1970.

Hirschi, Travis, and Selvin, Hanan C. *Delinquency Research: An Appraisal of Analytic Methods.* New York: Free Press, 1967.

Hoffman, Abbie. *Steal This Book.* New York: Grove Press, 1971.

Hofstadter, Richard. *The Paranoid Style in American Politics.* New York: Alfred A. Knopf, Inc., 1965.

Hood, Robert, and Sparks, Richard. *Key Issues in Criminology.* New York: McGraw-Hill, 1970.

Horgan, John J. *Criminal Investigation.* New York: McGraw-Hill, 1974.

Hormachea, C. R., and Hormachea, M. *Confrontation: Violence and the Police.* Boston: Holbrook Press (Allyn & Bacon), 1971.

Howard, John R. *The Cutting Edge.* Philadelphia: J. B. Lippincott Co., 1974.

Humphreys, Laud. *Tearoom Trade: Impersonal Sex in Public Places.* Chicago: Aldine, 1970.

Hunt, Morton. *The Mugging.* New York: Atheneum, 1972.

Ianni, Francis A. J. *Black Mafia: Ethnic Succession in Organized Crime.* New York: Simon & Schuster, 1974.

Iannone, Nathan F. *Supervision of Police Personnel.* Englewood Cliffs, N.J.: Prentice-Hall, Inc., 1970.

———. *Principles of Police Patrol.* New York: McGraw-Hill, 1975.

Inbau, Fred E., and Reid, John E. *Criminal Interrogation and Confessions.* Baltimore: Williams and Wilkins, 1962.

———, and Sowle, Claude R. *Criminal Justices: Cases and Comments.* Brooklyn: Foundation Press, 1964.

Inciardi, James A. *Careers in Crime.* Chicago: Rand McNally College Publ. Co., 1975.

Inciardi, James, and Chambers, Carl, eds. *Drugs and the Criminal Justice System.* London: Sage Publications, 1973.

Irwin, John. *The Felon.* Englewood Cliffs, N.J.: Prentice-Hall, Inc., 1970.

Jacobs, Paul. *Prelude to Riot.* New York: Random House, 1968.

Janowitz, Morris. *Social Control of Escalated Riots.* Chicago: University of Chicago Center for Policy Study, 1968.

Jeffrey, Sir Charles. *The Colonial Police.* London: M. Parrish, 1952.

Johnson, Richard M. *The Dynamics of Compliance: Supreme Court Decision-Making from a New Perspective.* Evanston, Ill.: Northwestern University Press, 1968.

Johnston, William. *Cruising.* New York: Random House, 1970.

Jones, Harry W., ed. *The Courts, The Public, and The Law Explosion.* Englewood Cliffs, N.J.: Prentice-Hall, Inc., 1965.

Jones, Harry W., ed. *Law and the Social Role of Science.* New York: Rockefeller University Press, 1967.

Josephson, Matthew. *The Robber Barons.* New York: Harcourt, Brace and World, 1962.

Judge, Anthony. *A Man Apart: The British Policeman and His Job.* London: Arthur Barker Ltd., 1972.

Kafka, Franz. *The Trial.* New York: Vintage Books, 1969.

Kamisar, Yale; Inbau, Fred; and Arnold, Thurman. *Criminal Justice in Our Time.* Charlottesville: University Press of Virginia, 1965.

Kaplan, John. *Marijuana: The New Prohibition.* Cleveland: World Publishing Co., 1970.

Kaplan, J., and Waltz, J. R. *The Trial of Jack Ruby.* New York: The Macmillan Co., 1965.

Karlen, Delmar. *Anglo-American Criminal Justice.* New York: Oxford University Press, 1967.

Kefauver, Estes. *Crime in America.* New York: Doubleday, 1951.

Kempton, Murray. *The Briar Patch.* New York: Dell Publishing, 1973.

Kennedy, Robert F., *The Pursuit of Justice.* New York: Harper & Row, 1964.

Kenny, John P., and Pursuit, Dan G. *Police Work with Juveniles.* 3rd ed. Springfield, Ill.: Charles C. Thomas, 1965.

Kephart, William M. *Racial Factors and Urban Law Enforcement.* Philadelphia: University of Pennsylvania Press, 1957.

Kinney, John P. *Police Administration.* Springfield, Ill.: Charles C. Thomas, 1972.

Kirchheimer, Otto. *Political Justice.* Princeton, N.J.: Princeton University Press, 1961.

Klockars, Carl B. *The Professional Fence.* New York: Free Press, 1974.

Klonoski, James R., and Mendelsohn, Robert I., eds. *The Politics of Local Justice.* Boston: Little, Brown & Co., 1970.

Klotter, John C. *Constitutional Law for Police.* Cincinnati: W. H. Anderson, 1970.

The Knapp Commission Report on Police Corruption. New York: George Braziller, 1973.

Knopf, T. *Youth Patrols.* Waltham, Mass.: Lemberg Center for the Study of Violence, 1969.

Kobitz, Robert W. *The Police Role and Juvenile Delinquency.* Gaithersburg, Md.: International Assoc. of Chiefs of Police, 1971.

Krausnick, Helmut, et al. *Anatomy of the SS State.* New York: Walker and Co., 1968.

Krisberg, Barry. *Crime and Privilege: Toward a New Criminology.* Englewood Cliffs, N.J.: Prentice-Hall, Inc., 1975.

Krislov, Samuel. *The Supreme Court and Political Freedom.* New York: Free Press, 1968.

Kulis, Joseph C.; Lorinskas, Robert A.; and Byrne, Rebecca. *Psychology and the Police.* Chicago: Police Academy, 1972.

La Fave, Wayne R. *Arrest: The Decision to Take a Suspect into Custody.* Boston, Little, Brown & Co., 1965.

Lambert, John R. *Crime, Police and Race Relations.* New York: Oxford University Press, 1970.

Lane, Roger. *Policing the City: Boston 1822–1882.* Cambridge, Mass.: Harvard University Press, 1967.

Lasswell, Harold D. *Politics: Who Gets What, When, How.* New York: McGraw-Hill, 1936.

Laurie, Peter. *Scotland Yard: A Study of the Metropolitan Police.* New York: Holt, Rinehart and Winston, 1970.

Lea, Henry Charles. *The Inquisition of the Middle Ages: Its Organization and Operation.* New York: The Citadel Press, 1954.

Lefcourt, Robert. *Law Against the People.* New York: Vintage Books, 1972.

Lemert, Edward M. *Human Deviance: Social Problems and Social Control.* Englewood Cliffs, N.J.: Prentice-Hall, Inc., 1967.

Leonard, V. A. *The Police Communications System.* Springfield, Ill.: Charles C. Thomas, 1970.

Leonard, V. A. *Police Crime Prevention.* Springfield, Ill.: Charles C. Thomas, 1971.

Leopold, Nathan F. *Life Plus 99 Years.* New York: Doubleday, 1958.

Letkemann, Peter. *Crime as Work.* Englewood Cliffs, N.J.: Prentice-Hall, Inc., 1973.

Levi, Primo. *Survival in Auschwitz.* New York: Collier Books, 1961.

Levy, Leonard W. *Against the Law: The Nixon Court and Criminal Justice.* New York: Harper & Row, 1974.

Levytsky, Boris. *The Uses of Terror: The Soviet Secret Police, 1917–1970.* New York: Coward, McCann, 1972.

Lieberman, Jethro K. *How the Government Breaks the Law.* Baltimore, Md.: Penguin Books, Inc., 1973.

Liebow, Elliot. *Tally's Corner.* Boston: Little, Brown & Co., 1967.

Lindesmith, Alfred R. *The Addict and the Law.* Bloomington, Ind.: Indiana University Press, 1965.

Lipset, Seymour M. *Political Man.* Garden City, N.Y.: Doubleday, 1960.

Lipsky, Michael, ed. *Law and Order: Police Encounters.* Chicago: Aldine, 1970.

Lofland, John. *Deviance and Identity.* Englewood Cliffs, N.J.: Prentice-Hall, Inc., 1969.

Lofton, John. *Justice and the Press.* Boston: Beacon Press, 1966.

A Look at Criminal Justice Research. Washington, D.C.: Law Enforcement Assistance Administration, 1971.

Lorenz, Konrad. *On Aggression.* Marjorie Wilson, trans. New York: Harcourt, Brace and World, 1966.

Lowenthal, Max. *The Federal Bureau of Investigation.* New York: Sloane Associates, 1950.

Luttwak, Edward. *Coup d'Etat.* New York: Alfred A. Knopf, Inc., 1969.

Maas, Peter. *Serpico.* New York: Viking Press, 1973.

———. *The Valachi Papers.* New York: G. P. Putnam's Sons, 1968.

Marshall, Geoffrey. *Police and Government.* London: Methuen, 1965.

Marshall, James. *Intention in Law and Society.* New York: Funk and Wagnalls, 1968.

Marshall, James. *Law and Psychology in Conflict.* New York: Doubleday, 1969.

Martin, J. P. and Wilson, Gail. *The Police: A Study in Manpower.* London: Heinemann, 1969.

Marx, Gary T. *Protest and Prejudice.* New York: Harper & Row, 1969.

Matza, David. *Delinquency and Drift.* New York: John Wiley and Sons, 1964.

Matza, David. *Becoming Deviant.* Englewood Cliffs, N.J.: Prentice-Hall, Inc., 1969.

McCague, James. *The Second Rebellion: The Story of the New York City Draft Riots of 1863.* New York: Dial Press, 1968.

McEachern, A. W. et al. *Criminal Justice System Simulation Study: Some Preliminary Projections.* Los Angeles: University of Southern California, Public Systems Research Institute, 1970.

McLean, Robert Joe, ed. *Education for Crime: Prevention and Control.* Springfield, Ill.: Charles C Thomas, 1975.

Medalie, Richard J. *From Escobedo to Miranda.* Washington, D.C.: Lerner Law Book, 1966.

Melstner, Michael. *Cruel and Unusual: The Supreme Court and Capital Punishment.* New York: William Morrow, 1974.

Menninger, Karl. *The Crime of Punishment.* New York: Viking Press, 1968.

Messick, Hank. *John Edgar Hoover.* New York: David McKay, 1972.

———. *Lansky.* New York: G. P. Putnam's Sons, 1971.

Michael, Jerome, and Adler, Mortimer. *Crime, Law and Social Science.* New York: Harcourt, Brace, 1933.

Michener, James A. *Kent State: What Happened and Why.* New York: Random House, 1971.

Miller, Arthur R. *The Assault on Privacy: Computers, Data Banks, and Dossiers.* Ann Arbor: University of Michigan Press, 1971.

Miller, Frank W. *Prosecution: The Decision to Charge a Suspect with a Crime.* Boston: Little, Brown & Co., 1969.

Mills, C. Wright. *The Power Elite.* New York: Oxford University Press, 1957.

Mills, James. *One Just Man.* New York: Simon & Schuster, 1974.

Mitford, Jessica. *Kind and Usual Punishment: The Prison Business.* New York: Alfred A. Knopf, Inc., 1973.

Mollenhoff, Clark. *Tentacles of Power: The Story of Jimmy Hoffa.* Cleveland: World Publishing Co., 1965.

Momboisse, Raymond M. *Community Relations and Riot Prevention.* Springfield, Ill.: Charles C. Thomas, 1970.

Morris, Norval, and Hawkins, Gordon. *The Honest Politician's Guide to Crime Control.* Chicago: University of Chicago Press, 1970.

Morris, Norval. *The Future of Imprisonment.* Chicago: University of Chicago Press, 1974.

Moynihan, Daniel P. *Violent Crime: The Challenge to Our Cities.* The Report of the National Commission on the Causes and Prevention of Violence. New York: George Braziller, 1970.

Myers, Gustavus. *History of the Great American Fortunes.* New York: Modern Library, 1936.

National Advisory Commission on Criminal Justice Standards and Goals. *Police*. Washington, D.C.: U.S. Government Printing Office, 1973.

Navasky, Victor S. *Kennedy Justice*. New York: Atheneum, 1971.

Nettler, Gwynn. *Explaining Crime*. New York: McGraw-Hill, 1974.

Neubauer, David W. *Criminal Justice in Middle America*. Morristown, N.J.: General Learning Corp., 1974.

Neumann, Franz. *Behemoth*. London: V. Gollancz, 1942.

Newman, Donald J. *Conviction: The Determination of Guilt or Innocence Without Trial*. Boston: Little, Brown & Co., 1966.

——. *Introduction to Criminal Justice*. New York: J. P. Lippincott Co., 1975.

New York State Special Commission. *Attica: The Official Report of the New York State Special Commission*. New York: Bantam Books, 1972.

Niederhoffer, Arthur. *Behind the Shield*. Garden City, N.Y.: Doubleday, 1967.

——. *A Study of Police Cynicism*. Ph.D. dissertation, New York University, 1963.

Niederhoffer, Arthur, and Smith, Alexander B. *New Directions in Police-Community Relations*. San Francisco: Rinehart Press, 1974.

Nimmer, Raymond T. *Diverson—The Search for Alternative Forms of Prosecution*. Chicago: Foundation Publications, 1974.

Norman, Charles, *The Genteel Murderer*. New York: Collier Books, 1962.

Nye, F. Ivan. *Family Relationships and Delinquent Behavior*. New York: John Wiley and Sons, 1958.

Oaks, Dallin H., and Lehman, Warren. *A Criminal Justice System and the Indigent: A Study of Chicago and Cook County*. Chicago: University of Chicago Press, 1968.

Packer, Herbert L. *The Limits of the Criminal Sanction*. Stanford: Stanford University Press, 1968.

Palmer, Stuart. *Prevention of Crime*. New York: Human Sciences Press, 1973.

Pasternack, S. A., ed. *Violence and Victims*. New York: Halsted Press, 1975.

Patrick, Clarence H. *The Police, Crime, and Society*. Springfield, Ill.: Charles C Thomas, 1971.

Payne, Howard C. *The Police State of Louis Napoleon Bonaparte, 1851–1860*. Seattle: University of Washington Press, 1966.

Pearlstein, Stanley. *Psychiatry, the Law and Mental Health*. Dobbs Ferry, N.Y.: Oceana Publications, Inc., 1967.

Perry, David C. *Police in the Metropolis*. Columbus, Ohio: Charles E. Merrill Publishing Co., 1975.

Phillips, William, and Shecter, Leonard. *On the Pad*. New York: G. P. Putnam's Sons, 1973.

Platt, Anthony. *The Child Savers*. Chicago: University of Chicago Press, 1969.

Platt, Anthony and Lynn Cooper. *Policing America*. Englewood Cliffs, N.J.: Prentice-Hall, Inc., 1974.

Police Practices. Law and Contemporary Problems. Chapel Hill, N.C.: Duke University, 1971. (No. 4), Vol. XXXVI.

Polier, Justine W. *The Rule of Law and the Role of Psychiatry*. Baltimore: Johns Hopkins Press, 1968.

Porterfield, Austin L. *Youth in Trouble*. Fort Worth: Leo Potishman Foundation, 1946.

Portune, Robert. *Changing Adolescent Attitudes Toward Police*. Cincinnati, Ohio: Anderson Publishing Co., 1971.

Prassel, Frank R. *Introduction to American Criminal Justice*. New York: Harper & Row, 1975.

Preiss, Jack J., and Ehrlich, Howard J. *An Examination of Role Theory: The Case of the State Police*. Lincoln, Neb.: University of Nebraska Press, 1966.

President's Commission on Law Enforcement and Administration of Justice. *Task Force Reports: The Police; the Courts; Corrections; Juvenile Delinquency and Youth Crime; Organized Crime; Science and Technology; Assessment of Crime; Narcotics and Drugs; Drunkenness*. Washington, D.C.: U.S. Government Printing Office, 1967.

Pringle, Patrick. *Hue and Cry: The Birth of the British Police*. London: Museum Press Ltd., 1955.

Pritchett, C. Herman. *The American Constitution*. 2nd ed. New York: McGraw-Hill, 1968.

Prouty, Col. L. Fletcher. *The Secret Team: The CIA and Its Allies in Control of the World*. New York: Ballantine Books, 1973.

Puttkammer, Ernest W. *Administration of Criminal Law*. Chicago: University of Chicago Press, 1963.

Quinney, Richard, ed. *Crime and Justice in Society*. Boston: Little Brown & Co., 1969.

——. *Criminal Justice in America*. Boston: Little, Brown & Co., 1974.

——. *Criminology: Analysis and Critique of Crime in America*. Boston: Little, Brown & Co., 1975.

Raab, Selwyn. *Justice in the Back Room.* New York: World Publishing Co., 1967.

Radzinowicz, Leon. *Ideology and Crime.* New York: Columbia University Press, 1966.

——. *A History of English Criminal Law and Its Administration from 1750.* Vols. 1–4. New York: Barnes and Noble, 1968.

Ransom, Harry Howe. *The Intelligence Establishment.* Cambridge, Mass.: Harvard University Press, 1970.

Rawls, John. *A Theory of Justice.* Cambridge, Mass.: Harvard University Press, 1972.

Ray, Isaac. *A Treatise on the Medical Jurisprudence of Insanity.* Winfred Overholser, ed. Cambridge, Mass.: Harvard University Press, 1962.

Reasons, Charles E. *The Criminologist: Crime and the Criminal.* Pacific Palisades, Calif.: Goodyear Publishing Co., Inc., 1974.

Reasons, Charles E., and Kuykendall, Jack L., eds. *Race, Crime, and Justice.* Pacific Palisades, Calif.: Goodyear Publishing Co., Inc., 1972.

Reid, Ed. *Mafia.* New York: New American Library, Inc., 1964.

Reith, Charles. *A New Study of Police History.* London: Oliver and Boyd, 1956.

——. *The Blind Eye of History.* Montclair, N.J.: Patterson Smith, 1975.

Reppetto, Thomas A. *Residential Crime.* Cambridge, Mass.: Ballinger Publishing Co., 1974.

Rhodes, Henry T. F. *Alphonse Bertillon.* London: George G. Harrap and Co., 1956.

Richardson, James. *A History of Police Protection in New York City, 1800–1870.* Ph.D. dissertation, New York University, 1967.

Richardson, James. *The New York Police: Colonial Times to 1901.* New York: Oxford University Press, 1970.

Richardson, James F. *Urban Police in the U.S.* New York: Kenniket Press, 1974.

Rock, Paul. *Deviant Behavior.* London: Hutchinson University Library, 1973.

Rolph, C. H., ed. *The Police and the Public.* London: Heinemann, 1962.

Rose, Arnold M. *Libel and Academic Freedom: A Lawsuit Against Political Extremists.* Minneapolis: University of Minnesota Press, 1968.

Rosenberg, Charles E. *The Trial of Assassin Guiteau: Psychiatry and Law in the Gilded Age.* Chicago: University of Chicago Press, 1968.

Rosenthal, Douglas E. *Lawyer and Client: Who's in Charge?* New York: Russell Sage Foundation, 1974.

Roszak, Theodore. *The Making of a Counterculture: Reflections on the Technocratic Society and Its Youthful Opposition.* Garden City, N.Y.: Doubleday, 1969.

Rovere, Richard H. *Senator Joe McCarthy.* New York: World Publishing Co., 1960.

Royal Commission on the Police. *Final Report.* Cmnd. 1728. London: Her Majesty's Stationery Office, 1962.

Rubington, Earl, and Weinberg, Martin S. *Deviance: The Interactionist Perspective.* 2nd ed. New York: The Macmillan Co., 1973.

Rubinstein, Jonathan. *City Police.* New York: Farrar, Straus and Giroux, 1973.

Rueschemeyer, Dietrich. *Lawyers and Their Society.* Lawrence, Mass.: Harvard University Press, 1973.

Rule, James B. *Private Lives and Public Surveillance.* New York: Schocken Books, 1974.

Rumbelow, Donald. *I Spy Blue.* London: The Macmillan Co., 1972.

Russell, Bertrand. *Power.* London: George Allen and Unwin Ltd., 1962.

Salerno, Ralph and Tompkins, Ralph. *The Crime Confederation.* Garden City, N.Y.: Doubleday, 1969.

Samaha, Joel. *Law and Order in Historical Perspective.* New York: Academic Press, 1974.

Saunders, Charles B., Jr. *Police Education and Training: Key to Better Law Enforcement.* Washington. D.C.: Brookings Institution, 1970.

——. *Upgrading the American Police.* Washington, D.C.: The Brookings Institution, 1970.

Schafer, Stephen. *The Political Criminal.* New York: Free Press, 1971.

——. *Theories in Criminology.* New York: Random House, 1969.

Scheff, Thomas J. *Labeling Madness.* Englewood Cliffs, N.J.: Prentice-Hall, Inc., 1975.

Schneir, Walter and Schneir, Marian. *Invitation to an Inquest.* New York: Doubleday, 1965.

Schur, Edwin M. *Crimes Without Victims.* Englewood Cliffs, N.J.: Prentice-Hall, Inc., 1965.

——. *Law and Society: A Sociological View.* New York: Random House, 1968.

——. *Radical Non-Intervention: Rethinking the Delinquency Problem.* Englewood Cliffs, N.J.: Prentice-Hall, Inc., 1973.

Schur, Edwin M., and Bedau, Hugo Adam. *Victimless Crimes.* Englewood Cliffs, N.J.: Spectrum Books, 1974.

Schwartz, Bernard. *The Law in America: A History.* New York: McGraw-Hill, 1974.

Schwartz, Louis B., and Goldstein, S. R. *Law Enforcement Handbook for Police.* St. Paul, Minn.: West Publishing Co., 1970.

Seligman, Ben B. *Permanent Poverty: An American Syndrome.* Chicago: Quadrangle Books, 1968.

Shaw, Clifford R. *The Jack Roller.* Chicago: University of Chicago Press, 1930.

Shaw, George Bernard. *The Crime of Imprisonment.* New York: The Citadel Press, 1961.

Sherman, Lawrence W., ed. *Police Corruption: A Sociological Perspective.* Garden City, N.Y.: Doubleday-Anchor Books, 1974.

Sherrill, Robert. *The Saturday Night Special.* New York: Penguin Books, Inc., 1975.

Shoolbred, Claude F. *The Administration of Criminal Justice in England and Wales.* New York: Pergamon Press, Inc., 1966.

Shostak, Arthur B.; Van Til, Jon; and Van Til, Sally Bould. *Privilege in America: An End to Inequality?* Englewood Cliffs, N.J.: Spectrum Books, 1973.

Silver, Isidore, ed. *The Crime Control Establishment.* Englewood Cliffs, N.J.: Prentice-Hall, Inc., 1974.

Simon, Rita. *The Jury and the Plea of Insanity.* Boston: Little, Brown & Co., 1966.

Simon, Rita, ed. *The Sociology of Law: Interdisciplinary Readings.* San Francisco: Chandler, 1968.

Sinclair, Upton. *The Jungle.* New York: Doubleday and Page, 1906.

Skolnick, Jerome H. *Justice Without Trial: Law Enforcement in Democratic Society.* New York: John Wiley and Sons, 1966.

Skolnick, Jerome H., and Gray, Thomas C. *Police in America.* Boston: Little, Brown & Co., 1975.

Smigel, Erwin O., and Ross, H. Laurence. *Crimes Against Bureaucracy.* New York: Van Nostrand Reinhold Company, 1970.

Smith, Alexander B., and Pollack, Harriet. *Crime and Justice in a Mass Society.* New York: Holt, Rinehart and Winston, 1972.

Smith, Bruce. *The New York Police Survey.* New York: Institute of Public Administration, 1952.

———. *Police Systems in the United States.* 2nd rev. ed. New York: Harper & Row, 1960.

Smith, Dwight. *The Mafia Mystique.* New York: Basic Books, 1975.

Smith, Edgar. *Brief Against Death.* New York: Alfred A. Knopf, Inc., 1968.

Smith, R. Harris. *OSS: The Secret History of America's First Central Intelligence Agency.* New York: Dell Publishing, 1972.

Smith, Ralph L. *The Tarnished Badge.* New York: Crowell, 1965.

Snibbe, John R. and Snibbe, Homa M., eds. *The Urban Policeman in Transition.* Springfield, Ill.: Charles C Thomas, 1973.

Solmes, Alwyn. *The English Policeman, 1871–1935.* London: George Allen and Unwin, 1935.

Sowle, Claude R., ed. *Police Power and Individual Freedom.* Chicago: Aldine, 1962.

Stark, Rodney. *Police Riots.* Belmont, Calif.: Wadsworth Publishing Co., Inc., 1972.

Stead, Philip John. *Vidocq: A Biography.* London: Staples Press, 1953.

———. *The Police of Paris.* London: Staples Press, 1957.

Steadman, Robert F., ed. *The Police and The Community.* Baltimore: Johns Hopkins University Press, 1972.

Steffens, Lincoln. *The Shame of the Cities.* New York: McClure Phillips, 1904.

———. *Autobiography.* New York: Harcourt, Brace and World, 1936.

Strecher, Victor G. *The Environment of Law Enforcement: A Community Relations Guide.* Englewood Cliffs, N.J.: Prentice-Hall, Inc., 1971.

Stuckey, Gilbert. *Evidence for the Law Enforcement Officer.* 2nd ed. New York: McGraw-Hill, 1974.

Sullivan, John L. *Introduction to Police Science.* New York: McGraw-Hill, 1966.

Sussman, Barry. *The Great Cover-Up.* New York: New American Library, 1974.

Sutherland, Edwin H. *White Collar Crime.* New York: Holt, Rinehart and Winston, 1949.

Sykes, Gresham. *Society of Captives.* Princeton, N.J.: Princeton University Press, 1958.

Sykes, Gresham, and Drobek, Thomas E. *Law and the Lawless.* New York: Random House, 1969.

Szasz, Thomas. *Law, Liberty and Psychiatry.* New York: The Macmilian Co., 1963.

———. *Psychiatric Justice.* New York: The Macmillan Co., 1965.

———. *Ceremonial Chemistry: The Ritual Persecution of Drug Addicts and Pushers.* Garden City, N.Y.: Anchor Press/Doubleday, 1974.

———. *Ideology and Insanity.* Garden City, N.Y.: Doubleday, 1970.

Tannenbaum, Frank. *Crime and the Community.* New York: Columbia University Press, 1938.

Tarde, Gabriel. *Penal Philosophy.* Boston: Little, Brown & Co., 1912.

Taylor, Ian; Walton, Paul; and Young, Jack. *The New Criminology.* London: Routledge and Kegan Paul Ltd., 1973.

Thompson, Craig. *The Police State.* New York: E. P. Dutton, 1950.

Thompson, Hunter S. *Hell's Angels.* New York: Random House, 1966.

Tiffany, Lawrence P.; McIntyre, Donald M., Jr.; and Rotenberg, David L. *Detection of Crime: Stopping and Questioning, Search and Seizure, Encouragement and Entrapment.* Boston: Little, Brown & Co., 1967.

Tobias, John J. *Urban Crime in Victorian England.* New York: Schocken Books, 1972.

Toch, Hans. *Violent Men: An Inquiry into the Psychology of Violence.* Chicago: Aldine, 1969.

Train, Arthur. *Courts, Criminals, and the Camorra.* New York: Scribners, 1911.

Trebach, Arnold S. *The Rationing of Justice.* New Brunswick, N.J.: Rutgers University Press, 1964.

Tullett, Toni. *Inside Interpol.* London: Frederick Muller Ltd., 1963.

Turk, Austin T. *Legal Sanctioning and Social Control.* Washington, D.C.: U.S. Government Printing Office, 1972.

Turkus, Burton, and Feder, Sid. *Murder, Inc.* New York: Farrar, Straus, 1951.

Turner, William. *The Police Establishment.* New York: G. P. Putnam's Sons, 1968.

Turner, William W. *Hoover's FBI: The Men and The Myth.* Los Angeles: Shelbourne Press, 1970.

Tyler, Gus. *Organized Crime in America.* Ann Arbor: University of Michigan Press, 1962.

Uviller, H. Richard. *The Processes of Criminal Justice: Investigation.* St. Paul, Minn.: West Publishing Co., 1974.

――――. *The Processes of Criminal Justice: Adjudication.* St. Paul, Minn.: West Publishing Co., 1975.

Valentine, Lewis J. *Night Stick.* New York: Dial Press, 1947.

Vollmer, August. *The Police and Modern Society.* Berkeley: University of California Press, 1936.

Vollmer, Howard M., and Mills, Donald L., eds. *Professionalization.* Englewood Cliffs, N.J.: Prentice-Hall, Inc., 1966.

Walker, Nigel. *Crime and Insanity in England: Vol. 1; The Historical Perspective.* Edinburgh: Edinburgh University Press, 1968.

Wallace, Samuel E. *Skid Row As a Way of Life.* Totowa, N.J.: Bedminster Press, 1965.

Wambaugh, Joseph. *The New Centurions.* Boston: Little, Brown & Co., 1970.

――――. *Blue Knight.* Boston: G. K. Hall, 1972.

――――. *Onion Field.* New York: Dell Publishing, 1974.

Watters, Pat, and Gillers, Stephen, eds. *Investigating the FBI.* New York: Doubleday, 1973.

Weistart, John C., ed. *Police Practices.* Dobbs Ferry, N.Y.: Oceana Publications, Inc., 1974.

Wertham, Frederick. *A Sign for Cain.* New York: The Macmillan Co., 1966.

Westley, William A. *The Police: A Sociological Study of Law, Custom and Morality.* Ph.D. dissertation, University of Chicago, 1951.

Weston, Paul B., and Willis, Kenneth M. *Law Enforcement and Criminal Justice.* Pacific Palisades, Calif.: Goodyear Publishing Co., Inc., 1972.

Wheeler, Stanton, ed. *On Record: Files and Dossiers in American Life.* New York: Russell Sage Foundation, 1969.

Whisenand, Paul M. *Police Supervision: Theory and Practice.* Englewood Cliffs, N.J.: Prentice-Hall, Inc., 1971.

Whisenand, Paul M., and Ferguson, R. Fred. *The Managing of Police Organizations.* Englewood Cliffs, N.J.: Prentice-Hall, Inc., 1973.

Whitaker, Ben. *The Police.* Middlesex, England: Penguin Books, Inc., 1964.

Whittemore, L. H. *Cop: A Closeup of Violence and Tragedy.* New York: Holt, Rinehart and Winston, 1969.

Whyte, William F. *Street Corner Society.* Chicago: University of Chicago Press, 1943.

Wicker, Tom. *A Time to Die.* New York: Quadrangle Books, 1975.

Wicks, Robert J. *Applied Psychology for Law Enforcement and Corrections Officers.* New York: McGraw-Hill, 1974.

Willett, T. C. *Criminal on the Road.* London: Tavistock, 1964.

Williams, Edward Bennett. *One Man's Freedom.* New York: Atheneum, 1962.

Wilson, James Q. *Explaining Crime.* New York: McGraw-Hill, 1975.

――――. *Varieties of Police Behavior: The Management*

of Law and Order in Eight Communities. New York: Atheneum, 1971.

Wilson, O. W. *Police Administration.* 2nd ed. New York: McGraw-Hill, 1963.

Wilson, O.W., and McLaren, Roy C. *Police Administration.* 3rd ed. New York: McGraw-Hill, 1972.

Winick, Charles, and Kinsie, Paul M. *The Lively Commerce: Prostitution in the United States.* Chicago: Quadrangle Books, 1971.

Wise, David, and Ross, Thomas. *The Invisible Government.* New York: Random House, 1964.

Wolfe, Bertram D. *Three Who Made a Revolution.* New York: Dell Publishing, 1964.

Wolfgang, Marvin E.; Figlio, Robert M.; and Sellin, Thorsten. *Delinquency in a Birth Cohort.* Chicago: University of Chicago Press, 1972.

Wright, R. Gene, and Marlo, John A. *The Police Officer and Criminal Justice.* New York: McGraw-Hill, 1970.

Yablonsky, Lewis. *Robopaths.* Baltimore: Penguin Books, Inc., 1972.

Zarr, Melvyn. *The Bill of Rights and the Police.* Dobbs Ferry, N.Y.: Oceana Publications, Inc., 1970.

Zeisel, Hans; Kalven, Harry, Jr.; and Buckholz, Bernard. *Delay in the Court.* Boston: Little, Brown & Co., 1959.

Index

The Boylston Press